Food Policy for Developing Countries

Food Policy for Developing Countries

The Role of Government in Global, National, and Local Food Systems

Per Pinstrup-Andersen and Derrill D. Watson II

Foreword by Søren E. Frandsen, Arie Kuyvenhoven, and Joachim von Braun

Cornell University Press
Ithaca and London

First published 2011 by Cornell University Press

Printed in the United States of America

Library of Congress Cataloging-in-Publication Data

Pinstrup-Andersen, Per.
    Food policy for developing countries : the role of government in
global, national, and local food systems / Per Pinstrup-Andersen
and Derrill D. Watson II ; foreword by Søren E. Frandsen, Arie
Kuyvenhoven, and Joachim von Braun.
        p. cm.
    Includes bibliographical references and index.
    ISBN 978-0-8014-4818-8 (cloth : alk. paper)
    1. Food supply—Government policy—Developing
countries. 2. Nutrition policy—Developing countries. 3. Food
security—Developing countries. I. Watson, Derrill D. II. Title.
    HD9018.D44P56 2011
    338.1'91724—dc22   2011017387

Figures and tables are reproduced with the permission of the following
    sources:
Elsevier: Figs. 2.1, 3.5, 5.1.
International Food Policy Research Institute, www.ifpri.org: Figs. 3.3,
    3.7, 5.2a, 5.2b, 7.8; Tables 5.1, 8.1.
World Health Organization: Fig. 3.2; Table 3.4.
Food and Agriculture Organization of the United Nations: Figs. 3.8, 4.2,
    7.2, 7.3, 7.4, 7.6, 7.7; Tables 3.3, 4.1, 6.1.
American Academy of Pediatrics: Fig. 3.4.
International Bank for Reconstruction and Development / The World
    Bank: Fig. 7.1; Tables 3.1, 5.2, 5.3, 5.4, 7.1, 9.2.
Waterfootprint: Fig. 8.1.
International Service for the Acquisition of Agri-Biotech Applications:
    Fig. 10.1.
Wiley and Sons: Table 2.1.
Jørgen Oleson: Table 8.2.
American Economic Association: Table 9.1.

Cornell University Press strives to use environmentally responsible
suppliers and materials to the fullest extent possible in the publishing
of its books. Such materials include vegetable-based, low-VOC inks
and acid-free papers that are recycled, totally chlorine-free, or partly
composed of nonwood fibers. For further information, visit our website
at www.cornellpress.cornell.edu.

Cloth printing   10 9 8 7 6 5 4 3 2 1

Contents

Figures

Tables

Foreword

Nearly 1 billion people around the world currently suffer from hunger and inadequate nutrition. Another billion are overweight or obese. Technological advances in agriculture have lifted hundreds of millions of people out of hunger, poverty, and hopelessness, but such progress has not been uniform. In addition to these perennial challenges, new issues face the food system as well, including climate change, dietary transition, natural resource degradation, water scarcity, ethical and environmental ramifications of genetically modified organisms, and globalization. These challenges call for an improved food policy analysis that can both address their multidimensional effects and improve public awareness of how food policies are made, as well as how such policies affect lives. The goal of this book is to provide an important tool for students, policymakers, and people who work throughout the food system, as well as consumers and concerned citizens, to understand food policies.

Realizing the necessity for improved training in food policy analysis, in 2005 World Food Prize laureate Per Pinstrup-Andersen envisioned a "social entrepreneurship" approach to teaching food policy analysis. Entrepreneurship education helps students become leaders, innovators, and creative problem solvers. In the face of apocalyptic stories, the sensationalization of problems in the food system, and the unhelpful advocacy of particular food lifestyles without due consideration of the consequences of such proposals for other actors in the food system, this new approach to understanding and teaching food policy analysis provides a forward vision. The social entrepreneurship approach is much more than plain common sense or an abstract theory; as shown throughout this book, it is capable of addressing the challenges to the food system, policymakers' needs, and public concerns.

To effectively communicate this new approach to food policy, we joined Per as collaborators to address the need for more effective training and policymaking. Together we organized an Advisory Task Force, consisting of seven individuals—including university faculty members, high-level policy advisers, and former policymakers—from the developing regions of the world:

- Kwadwo Asenso-Okyere, Professor Emeritus, Office of the Vice-Chancellor, University of Ghana, and Director, IFPRI East and Southern Africa Office, Addis Ababa, Ethiopia
- Bernard Bashaasha, Head, Department of Agricultural Economics, Makerere University, Uganda
- Sattar Mandal, Professor, Department of Agricultural Economics, Bangladesh Agricultural University, Bangladesh
- Eugenia Serova, Professor, Institute for Transition Economics, Moscow, Russia
- Fernando Vio, Director, Institute of Nutrition, University of Chile, Chile
- Zhong Tang, Professor, School of Agricultural Economics and Rural Development, Renmin University, Beijing, China
- Ricardo Uauy, Professor, School of Public Health and Nutrition, University of Chile, Chile, and Professor, London School of Hygiene and Tropical Medicine, University of London, United Kingdom

The efforts of this team culminated in the current textbook that covers the key aspects of global food system policies and the related series of case studies that describe real policymaking environments in detail.

Food Policy for Developing Countries: The Role of Government in Global, National, and Local Food Systems covers the many policies that affect food systems, from agricultural and climate change policies to nutrition, poverty, and trade policies, and political governance. The approach and this work then expand on, update, and complement the seminal 1983 text in this area, *Food Policy Analysis*, by C. Peter Timmer, Walter D. Falcon, and Scott R. Pearson (Baltimore, MD: World Bank/Johns Hopkins University Press). Not only the effects of policies are addressed, but attention is paid to the political and ethical reasons governments favor one policy over another. The principles and messages here apply to and provide a common framework to study a wide variety of circumstances.

This wide applicability is amply demonstrated by the case studies, which cover more than thirty-five countries and regions and were contributed to by more than one hundred researchers with real life and professional experience with the issues they address. Per and Fuzhi Cheng, then a postdoctoral research associate at Cornell University, edited the cases, with the benefit of advice from many outside experts, in a three-volume work published by Cornell University Press. All the cases in these volumes and new additional cases are archived and available via open access at http://cip.cornell.edu/gfs. The case studies have already been incorporated with great success in classrooms across south and east Asia, sub-Saharan Africa, the United States, and Europe.

Food Policy for Developing Countries was designed as a core text to be used in conjunction with the case studies primarily with advanced undergraduate and first-year graduate students from a wide variety of disciplines in mind. Earlier editions of the text have been used by students in nutrition, economics and agricultural economics, sociology, political science, plant and soil science, and business. It has proven effective in clearly communicating the principles of food policy analysis across a wide disciplinary spectrum. This means that no prior background is required to appreciate the points being made and that the work is readily accessible by a broad audience. The textbook is the worthy culmination of more than five years of labor by Per, the collaborators, the Advisory Task Force, the case study authors, and the external reviewers. Worthy of special mention is Derrill D. Watson II, Assistant Professor at American University of Nigeria, whose collaborations with Per resulted in work presented to the United Nations, Kuwait, Egypt, and Australia. Derrill joined the team in 2008 to help synthesize the vast bodies of research on the global food system's many facets into the coherent, comprehensive, and accessible book you hold in your hands.

Per's vision has proven to be prophetic. As the 2006–2008 food price crisis shows, as well as more recent developments and challenges in the global food markets, the lessons in this book on global food policy are needed now more than ever to help the world overcome the perennial problems of hunger, malnutrition, and poverty in a sustainable way that addresses our ever-changing food system and the new challenges it faces. We are excited to bring this book to your attention and believe it will serve you as a highly relevant text. It has been prepared and reviewed with care, conviction, and concern for our food systems, and the high caliber of its scholarship and writing make it the essential and definitive text on food policy.

SøREN E. FRANDSEN, Pro-Rector, Aarhus University, Denmark

ARIE KUYVENHOVEN, Professor Emeritus and former Director,
Wageningen School of Social Sciences, the Netherlands

JOACHIM VON BRAUN, Director, Center for Development
Research (ZEF), Bonn University, Germany

Preface

This book is about global, national, and local food systems and how they can be influenced by policies and programs. The first two chapters describe what food systems are and how food policy is made. Before going into detail about specific policies addressed at the various parts of the system, the book seeks to take account of the complexity of food systems and their interactions with other sectors of societies by casting the analyses in a cohesive multidisciplinary systems framework. Emphasis is on identifying policy options to guide food systems relevant for developing countries to better achieve societal goals such as reducing poverty, food insecurity, and malnutrition; improving health and economic growth; sustainably managing natural resources; and reducing adverse interactions with climate change.

The book is designed on the premise that a better understanding of food systems and how they may be improved through policy and program interventions will result in more effective and enlightened interventions. We believe that policymakers will more likely achieve their various stated goals and better meet the challenges and pressures they face when policy is founded on evidence drawn from a holistic understanding of food systems.

The book is tailored to strengthen university-level training to understand, analyze, advise, and make decisions about government policies. We believe the book can serve as an appropriate textbook in courses on food systems broadly defined to include human health and nutrition; food security, economics, and policy; food demand, production, and supply; domestic and international trade policies; and environmental policies and ethics. Using a political economy framework, the importance of stakeholder interests and pressures are highlighted in a complex systems analysis of food policy processes.

Although we are both economists, this book takes a multidisciplinary systematic approach to policy analysis. It is written with students and other readers from a range of disciplinary backgrounds in mind, though it can also be useful for lay audiences attempting to understand the complexity of the global food system and the challenges we face in it. Economic and other single-disciplinary concepts are explained when first introduced so that prior course work in economics or nutrition is not essential in order to understand the content of the book.

This book may be used as the sole text for a course on food policy or it may be used in combination with a set of case studies covering policy aspects of specific key components of the food system each within a specific context.[1] Together with the case studies, the book provides the teaching material for an approach we call "a social entrepreneurship approach to the teaching of food policy." This approach, which we believe is innovative and participatory, is described in the references cited in note 1 below where the cases may also be found. The approach is being used by several universities in south and east Asia, sub-Saharan Africa, Europe, and the United States, including Cornell University, where it has been used since 2006 to train undergraduate and graduate students from varied disciplines such as nutrition, international agriculture, agronomy, business, agricultural economics, sociology, and economics. Both student and instructor evaluations of the approach have been very positive.

We hope that this book will make a significant contribution to the understanding of what governments can do to guide the future food situation and the consequences of various policy actions. If our work results in a more enlightened set of policies that improve the lives of disadvantaged people and a more sustainable management of the earth's natural resources, our goal has been achieved.

PER PINSTRUP-ANDERSEN AND DERRILL D. WATSON II

Notes

1. Available in open access on http://cip.cornell.edu/gfs and in a three-volume book: Per Pinstrup-Andersen and Fuzhi Cheng, eds., *Case Studies in Food Policy for Developing Countries* (Ithaca, NY: Cornell University Press, 2009).

Acknowledgments

The preparation of the manuscript for this book benefitted from the support of many individuals. We are grateful for the advice and feedback to earlier drafts of the manuscript received from our collaborators (Søren E. Frandsen, Arie Kuyvenhoven, and Joachim von Braun) and the members of the Advisory Task Force (Kwadwo Asenso-Okyere, Bernard Bashaasha, Sattar Mandal, Eugenia Serova, Fernando Vio, Zhong Tang, Ricardo Uauy, and Funing Zhong).

We are grateful for the feedback received from faculty and students who used earlier drafts of the manuscript and/or the related case studies in courses held at several universities including: Alem Araya, Mekelle University, Ethiopia; Anoma Ariyawardana, University of Peradeniya, Sri Lanka; Subhasish Biswas, West Bengal University of Animal and Fishery Science, India; Bethany F. Econopouly, Patrick F. Byrne, and Marc A. Johnson, Colorado State University; Zhongxing Guo, College of Public Administration, Nanjing Agriculture University, China; Sheryl Hendricks, African Centre for Food Security, University of KwaZulu-Natal, South Africa; Zakir Hussain, University of Sargodha, Pakistan; Charles Jumbe, Bunda College, University of Malawi, Malawi; Shiv Kumar, National Centre for Agricultural Economics and Policy Research, India; Yu Leng, Antai College of Economics and Management, Shanghai Jiaotong University, China; Emily Levitt and Suresh Babu, American University and IFPRI; Reneth Mano, University of Zimbabwe, Zimbabwe; Gideon Obare, University of Hohenheim, Germany; Robert Paarlberg, Harvard University; Anthony Panin, CMMAE Program, University of Pretoria, South Africa; Beatrice Rogers, Tufts University; Basanta K. Sahu, Indian Institute of Foreign Trade (Deemed University), India; Le Ha Thanh, Hanoi National Economics University, Vietnam; and Henrik Zobbe, University of Copenhagen, Denmark.

The preparation of the manuscript benefitted greatly from the technical support by Mary-Catherine French, Colleen Boland, and Lynne Morgan. Comments and suggestions by an anonymous reviewer strengthened the manuscript.

Food Policy for Developing Countries

Chapter 1

Toward a Dynamic Global Food System

Introduction

In the more than three decades since the 1974 World Food Conference announced its goal of eradicating hunger and malnutrition, worries about global food problems have continued unabated. In some cases, these worries have been misplaced and resulted in misguided policies. In other cases, complacency has resulted in missed opportunities to resolve challenges. Reliable unbiased evidence is of critical importance to assist policymakers in arriving at the most appropriate decisions. The primary concern of the international community has been food security, a condition "when all people, at all times, have physical and economic access to sufficient, safe and nutritious food to meet their dietary needs and food preferences for an active and healthy life" (FAO 1996a). Decision makers, policy analysts, and concerned citizens have widely debated questions of how much food the world grows; whether production entails sustainable management of natural resources; and how that food is distributed at the global, regional, national, and household levels. These concerns have been prominent in bringing about concerted efforts and international commitments, such as the World Food Summit's Plan of Action (FAO 1996a), the Millennium Summit's Millennium Development Goals (United Nations 2000), and IFPRI's 2020 (IFPRI n.d.) Vision. The concerns have succeeded in increasing resource flows to agricultural development, improved food security, and better nutrition.

Increasing acknowledgment of other food problems has placed the discussion of the food system in a much broader context. These problems include human health concerns related to food safety and the growing incidence of nutrition-related illnesses, especially cardiovascular diseases; the commercialization and industrialization of food and agriculture; the penetration of new technologies with potentially positive or adverse economic and environmental impacts; the rise of transnational

corporations in international food markets; increasing concentration in food production, processing, and retail; the acceleration of instability and armed conflicts;
and ethical issues related to food. Among the environmental challenges affecting
the food system are climate change, the depletion of natural resources, salinization,
pesticide runoff, GMO concerns, and biodiversity problems associated with monocropping (Timmer 2009). Each of these problems crosses traditional disciplinary
borders, making the study of the food system itself a valuable and important en-
deavor. The chapters of this book address these topics.

The food problems now facing the world are both diverse and complex. Yet much
of the debate and evidence available to decision makers fail to take into account such
diversity and complexity and instead present simpleminded arguments to sensa-
tionalize the extent of existing food problems while making doomsday predictions
for the future. Short-term fluctuations in food production and resulting food price
spikes are often misinterpreted as long-term trends. In particular, much of the news
media interpreted the abrupt food price increases in the international market such
as those that occurred in 1974, 1996, 2007–2008, and 2010 to mean that the earth's
productive capacity was insufficient to feed current and future generations. Subsequent falls in real food prices demonstrated the fallacy of the interpretation, yet were
not widely reported.

Book titles such as *The End of Food* (Roberts 2008), *Food Wars* (Lang and Heasman 2004), *The Food Revolution* (Robbins 2001), *Stuffed and Starved* (Patel 2007),
and *Fearing Food* (Morris and Bate 1999) may catch the attention of the news media,
the public, and decision makers. However, the sense of fear and panic these titles
convey may lead to inappropriate action, misallocation of resources, and loss of
confidence in the evidence presented. Other recent books such as *The Omnivore's Dilemma* (Pollan 2006) and *In Defense of Food* (Pollan 2008) promote the consumption
of locally produced food; while books such as *Just Food* (McWilliams 2009) question
whether emphasis on locally produced food is an environmentally sound strategy;
and still others such as *Food Politics* (Nestle 2007) aim to illustrate the influence of
the food industry on food systems. A more comprehensive assessment of the challenges facing the global food system and of proposed solutions is provided by *Ending
Hunger in Our Lifetime* (Runge et al. 2003). These books and many more contribute
to the debate about the current and future food situation.

Goals and Purposes

In this book we attempt to capture the food system diversity and complexity and
the implications for action by situating questions in a food systems context, questions such as: What are the causes of existing food problems? How severe are these
problems and whom do they affect? Why do they persist? What are the links among
the various parts of the food systems? How can policy analysts determine which
solutions will be most effective in which context? What are the roles of government,
civil society, and the private sector in a *systems* conceptual framework? The focus of
the book is on identifying policy options available to governments, how such options affect the various stakeholder groups, and how they interact with the various

elements of the food systems. Thus, the concept of food systems used in this book covers several more narrowly defined concepts such as agricultural, environmental, health, and nutrition policies in an attempt to capture the interactions among these components of a food system.

We define a *food system,* in its most general sense, as the aggregate of all food-related activities and the environments (political, socioeconomic, and natural) within which these activities occur. This chapter discusses the evolution of the food systems concept, identifies its primary components, and briefly discusses some of the most influential factors expected to drive global, national, and local food systems over the next several decades.

The next chapter is similarly foundational, explaining that public food policies emerge from a complex interaction of stakeholder groups and different government agents. Thus stakeholder analysis and political economics are tools needed to understand how food policies are created, both their intended and unintended effects, and how to craft better policy.

Because the food system contains many feedback loops, it is not linear and has no unique beginning or end. It is frequently argued that a food system begins with the combination of resources such as land, water, labor, and capital for the purpose of food production, and ends when the food is consumed. However, the availability and efficiency of resources used (e.g., labor efficiency) and agent behavior are influenced by the outcomes of the food system (e.g., the extent to which nutritional needs are met). It could therefore be argued that the food system begins and ends with what we refer to as outcomes, particularly human health and nutrition.

We therefore organized the chapters to discuss first the principal purposes of the food system (chapters 3–5), followed by the means by which the world achieves these purposes (chapters 6–7), and the biophysical, institutional, and international environments within which food systems operate (chapters 8–10). Thus, we treat the health and nutrition aspects of the system in chapter 3, food security and demand in chapter 4, and poverty in chapter 5. We follow with a discussion of the market and exchange functions in chapter 6 and production and supply in chapter 7. We present natural resource management and climate change policies in chapter 8, governance and institutional issues in chapter 9, and globalization and international trade in chapter 10. Ethical considerations, which affect all parts of the food systems, conclude the book (chapter 11). Relevant policy issues and options are discussed in each chapter.

Toward a Global Food Systems Approach

Historically, commentators have considered the food system as a set of activities that produce food products and meet consumer demands. Phrases such as "from farm to fork" or "farm to table" are common. In this linear, one-dimensional model ("the input-output model"), the food supply chain is treated as a neutral, static tool. Though still useful for some purposes, the model's inability to address many of the current world's food problems signals the need for a new paradigm (Waltner-Toews and Lang 2000).

In an attempt to move toward such a paradigm, we propose a systems approach to the analysis of food and food policy. Within this system are biophysical, socioeconomic, demographic, and political subsystems that need to be identified and related to each other in complex, nonlinear ways. The food system may then be studied in a holistic manner utilizing methodologies from many disciplines including economics, nutrition and medicine, soil science, sociology, anthropology, political science, demography, environmental science, and geography.

All elements in the food system function together as collective units. The food system thus creates emergent properties greater than the sum of their parts (chapter 2). In this book, we visualize the food system as a dynamic, behavioral system affected by social and economic changes brought about by public policy and action by the private sector and civil society as well as forces such as globalization, urbanization, and technological advancement. Adding to these changes are persistent problems, including poverty, hunger, and malnutrition, climate change and other environmental concerns. Within this context, we identify policy opportunities to improve people's well-being.

Changes in food systems may be rapid or glacially slow. They are nearly always complex, involving uncertainty and unknown consequences. The interlinkages among the food system components create further feedback effects so that changes ripple throughout the system, possibly compounding and magnifying each other. This context of change, uncertainty, and complexity poses considerable research and policymaking challenges to understanding where, when, and how to change the global food system and its environments so as to produce greater equity, reduce hunger, and assure the sustainability of the food system and the freedom of its agents.

The Systems Approach

The *systems approach* is a method of analyzing organizations and interdependent relationships within a complex entity. Systems describe a set of linked elements and how they interact. Examples of elements in the global food system include individual farmers and groups of farmers, government organizations, market systems, food safety, technology, feeder roads, consumers (both at an individual and group level), soil fertility, and zoonotic diseases, to mention a few. These elements interact through various processes, such as purchases, deforestation, infection, metabolization, marginalization, and regulation. These processes alter elements' states, changing consumers from hungry to full, for example, or a local water source from potable to polluted. Time is therefore an essential dimension in systems analysis. Most systems are nested, with multiple subsystems that (potentially) interact to form a more complex whole.

Some of these processes happen passively, such as metabolization or infection. Most processes, however, occur deliberately at the instigation of human agents. *Agents* are decision makers, including producers, consumers, traders, policymakers, and others, who influence how the elements interact with each other. Humans are thus both agents and elements, affecting and effected by the food system. Many of the questions to be addressed in this book deal with how food systems influence those people who have little influence over it.

Because most of the processes are deliberate, they can be changed by human choice and action. Ensuring that these changes bring about the ends societies or stakeholder groups want requires knowledge and education at individual, societal, and government levels. We aim to strengthen such knowledge and education through this book.

When a system is open, it interacts with its outside environment through *inputs* that enter the system from the outside and *outputs* that leave the system. The environments here considered include the natural environment, as well as the social, political, community, and individual contexts in which food system processes occur. A permeable boundary separates the system and its environments.

The systems approach addresses complex problems that have multiple causes and multiple outcomes brought about by interactions among the interdependent elements within a system. In contrast to traditional forms of analysis that focus on individual pieces, the systems approach takes into account the whole system of inputs, interactions, outputs, feedback, and controls. Rather than trying to remove complexity, the systems approach embraces interconnectedness in order to identify "the critical factors that lead to particular outcomes or the interactions that govern a specific behavior of interest" (Ericksen 2007).

The concept of a food system elaborated in this book is best understood as a mixture of the conceptual frameworks in the disparate literatures, which are summarized in the following section, uniting different disciplinary perspectives (e.g., biophysical, social, economic, political, etc.; see Scoones 1999). This approach renounces the narrow separation of different disciplines that forms the basis of much of modern research. Its comprehensive nature means that the food system includes all activities, critical interactions, and factors influencing outcomes, as well as the environments within which they take place. In addition, the framework is generic enough to allow its universal application to widely different contexts. The same basic categories of food-related activities exist in any food system, as do the primary objectives of food systems, e.g., food security, freedom from poverty, and improved human health and nutrition. However, the conditions under which elements interact can differ, which affects whether or not these goals are equitably and universally achieved and what needs to be altered so that they can be.

Conceptual Framework

Applications of a systems approach abound in the literature but are nonetheless fragmented among a number of different scientific disciplines, such as nutritional and agricultural sciences, sociology, economics, and environmental studies. In most contexts, the term "food system" describes the elements and processes that produce food and nutrients for human consumption. For example, Sobal, Khan, and Bisogni (1998, 853) define the food system as "the set of operations and processes involved in transforming raw materials into foods and transforming nutrients into health outcomes." Whether regarded as linear processes (food chains) or more complex food webs where each element in the chain interacts with all the others, the relevant elements are only those directly involved in producing and consuming food.

There are several competing conceptualizations of how the food system functions within its ecological environment. An agroecosystem approach adds ecological concerns to a standard food web, accounting for feedbacks between food processes and environmental quality. The 1992 Rio Earth Summit Convention on Biological Diversity describes "the ecosystem approach" as "a strategy for the integrated management of land, water and living resources that promotes conservation and sustainable use in an equitable way" (Holling 2001; Carpenter et al. 2001). While the ecosystem approach ranks environmental sustainability as the first priority, with agriculture being one of the activities that influence the environment for good and ill, integrated natural resource management unites several approaches so that livelihoods, agriculture, and environmental quality each receive high priority.

Rural sociologists embedded political, economic, and social structures in the food system (Arce and Marsden 1993; Fine 1994; Dixon 1999; Lockie and Kitto 2000; Goodman 2002). The term "agro-food network" is frequently used to refer to this sociological view of the food system. Early research on agro-food networks incorporated farmers into agro-industrial commodity systems, taking into account policies, regulations, and economic factors (Ericksen 2007). Issues studied include increasing food market concentration (Wilkinson 2002) and globalization versus localization of food systems (Nygard and Storstad 1998; Hendrickson and Heffernan 2002a).

Figure 1.1 depicts the conceptual framework of a food system used in this book. Each chapter will highlight a specific subsystem from this figure, expand on it in greater detail, and discuss interactions with other subsystems. Specifically, the food system includes biophysical, socioeconomic, politico-institutional, and demographic environments within which the food supply chain operates to produces certain outcomes (e.g., contributions to the environment, the economy, human health and nutrition, etc.). These environments affect decisions within the food system activities, and food system activities in turn affect their environments. These changes alter the stock of resources, the institutions, the environments, and the stakeholder groups that will act in the food system in the future.

The Global Food System

Agents—or "stakeholder groups," as we call them in this book—in the food system include resource owners, farmers and farm laborers, traders, processors, consumers, investors, policymakers, policy analysts, officials in government and nongovernment organizations, and others from the public and private sectors and civil society. These agents respond to incentives (opportunities, challenges, and risks) and environmental constraints. As such, the food system is a dynamic, behavioral system that can be influenced by public policy through incentives, regulations, and knowledge generation (Pinstrup-Andersen 2006a). The food system must be perceived and understood as an economic, physical, and social system. The reader is referred to Goodman (2002) and Dixon (1999) for a detailed description of the links between the production and

FIGURE 1.1.
A conceptual framework of a food system.

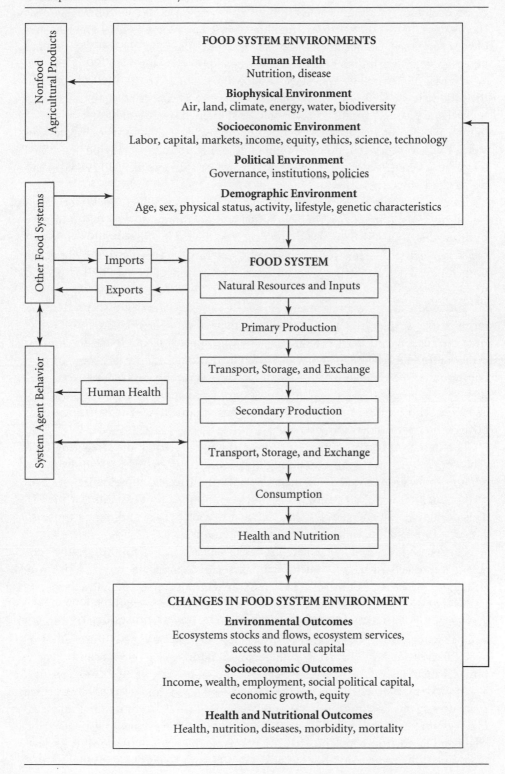

consumption sides of the food system, and to Gunderson and Holling (2002) for theoretical underpinnings. The food industry, which is defined by Nestle (2007) as "companies that produce, process, manufacture, sell and serve foods, beverages, and dietary supplements," occupies a large share of the total food system activities and possesses very large influence over its conduct and performance.

For ease of discussion, let us start with the food chain as traditionally delineated: the production, distribution, and consumption of food. The food chain starts with natural and planned production (chapter 7). Hunters, fishers, and gatherers harvest natural production, while farmers organize inputs (e.g., soil, fertilizer, water, livestock, feed) to produce food commodities. These commodities may be consumed by the producing household, stored for later use, or sold to other households or to traders and processors.

Processors combine and alter food commodities to reduce the time households must spend in such activities. Available food supply reaches consumers by multiple distribution channels (chapter 6). It is during the distribution stage that consumer demand meets producer supply, generating price signals that balance both forces. Food prices may be influenced by action taken by the public and private sectors.

The food chain may be relatively short (e.g., consumption of own production, farmers' markets), or food may pass through many links as it is traded, transported, processed in several different facilities, further transported to wholesale distribution centers, and sold at retail to households or to institutions that prepare food for final consumption. These institutions include hotels, restaurants and caterers, community centers, soup kitchens and food pantries, government facilities, hospitals, school cafeterias, and vending machines. Together these channels are often referred to as HRI: hotels, restaurants, and institutions.

The process of consumption includes not only acquiring and preparing food (chapter 4) but its distribution among household members, ingestion, digestion, and metabolization as well. Thus, the final stages of the food chain are the first stages of the nutrition cycle as the body turns prepared foods into nutrients (chapter 3). This occurs at different rates for each nutrient in each person at different times, so consumption and bioavailability are not synonymous.

The seemingly closed food chain just described is actually a communicative process that interacts with outside demographic, socioeconomic, biophysical, political, and international environments. The demographic environment includes the population's age distribution, gender composition, physical status, activity level, lifestyle, and genetic characteristics (chapter 4). The socioeconomic environment (chapters 5 and 6) includes labor, capital, markets, and social institutions and culture. The biophysical environment (chapter 8) includes physical forces (e.g., climate and energy), physical materials (e.g., soil and water) and biological factors (e.g., biodiversity). The policy environment refers to government regulations and policies, governance structures, formal institutions, and politics (chapters 2 and 9). For national and local food systems, there is also an outer environment that governs how a particular food chain and its environments interact with others, such as by international trade laws or competition between localities to host a new factory farm (chapter 10).

The interaction between food system activities and their environments can be illustrated by the example of a maize farmer in Mexico. The amount of maize that can be produced and the price received for it will be influenced by the physical environment (land quality, rainfall), market access to inputs (improved seeds, fertilizer, water), domestic laws and social norms on land tenure, potential government subsidies, transaction and market costs, and international trade laws, such as NAFTA.

Complexity

Despite the simple illustration (figure 1.1), the food system introduced above is complex, dynamic, filled with heterogeneous subsystems, and affected by nonlinear feedbacks (Ericksen 2007). The nonlinearity of its feedbacks means that a small shock may have one or several effects:

1. Amplification, as when increased production lowers prices, which spurs farmers to sell even more in an attempt to keep income stable, lowering prices further;
2. Proportionality, as when a farm laborer receives a wage increase that is then spent in the community so that other incomes in the community rise proportionately;
3. Dampening, as when increased demand for biofuels increases the amount of land devoted to growing maize and decreases the land for other crops, which in turn increases the prices for those other crops so that some farmers return some of the land to producing these other crops;
4. No effect at all, as when a government pollution mandate forbids a certain production technology, but firms respond by using a different technology that is just as polluting.

In contrast, linear system effects are always directly proportional to cause.

The global food system is made up of local and national food systems. Wilkins and Eames-Sheavly (2010) have defined a local food system as "a food system in which food production, processing, distribution and consumption are integrated to affect the environmental, economic, social and nutritional health of a particular locality." Local food systems are rarely completely self-contained: there are generally significant trade, labor, environmental, and technology links with other food systems. A food system may be defined geographically or politically (e.g., a neighborhood, province, or nation) or by other boundaries, such as by ethnic or religious groups whose social institutions create different interactions between elements. A national food system extends the concept of the local food system to a national level.

A holistic perspective of the global food system believes that significant information is lost when any national or local subsystem is considered in isolation from all others. Instead, these subsystems interact to exhibit novel properties at a higher (global) level that are not found in the subsystems themselves. The different component processes in the global food system also produce emergent properties together that would not be observed in isolation. Schroeter, Azzam, and Zhang (2000), for

instance, incorporate interactions between growing concentration in the meat processing industry with growing concentration in food retail, finding that the latter
offsets processors' possible market power (chapter 6).

Subsystem Diversity

The global food system is not a homogeneous entity. Nested food systems may be
as small as a household or as large as a nation. Even within a level, these subsystems
differ widely. For rural communities in developing countries, the local food system is still the dominant one, while usually interacting with outside food systems
in different ways. In most developing countries, food continues to be produced by
small-scale farmers (including livestock farmers or pastoralists and fishermen) to be
sold, processed, and consumed locally, providing the foundation of the community's
nutrition, incomes, and economies. The more integrated the locality is, the more
national and international factors ripple through to the micro level.

Local food systems differ based on the importance of food and agriculture. The
majority of the world's poor live in rural areas of developing countries and most of
them depend directly or indirectly on agriculture (World Bank 2007a; see chapters 5
and 7). Food expenditure accounts for a large share of their total income, often as
high as 60–80 percent. In contrast, budget shares for food in high-income countries
are low, often around 10 percent. The contribution of agricultural GDP to total
GDP[1] is much higher in developing countries than in high-income ones. It is not unusual to find more than half of the population of a low-income developing country
deriving their incomes from agriculture.

Local food systems also differ in their environmental contexts (WTO 2001): soil
fertility and climate, religious norms and traditional roles of women, land tenure
laws and labor costs are just a few examples. Some food systems may face more costly
or variable production conditions than others because of factors such as degraded
soils, low or erratic rainfall, small subsistence farms, underdeveloped infrastructure,
or limited access to new technologies. Differing production conditions alter the costs
of production even within small countries or areas.

These different conditions affect not only the production aspects of the food system but also how the food chain interacts with human health and nutrition, income
distribution, gender roles, and governance. For instance, the optimally efficient size
of a wheat farm is significantly smaller than for a sugarcane farm. This promotes
the development of household farms in areas that are biologically suited for wheat
and plantation-style farming in areas that are better suited for sugarcane. Easterly
(2007) demonstrates that this difference in agricultural suitability led to differences
in income distribution, government policies, and public goods provision that persist
today. In a similar vein, Boserup et al. (2007) argue that societies that adopted agriculture by plow developed predominantly male agricultural systems while societies
that did not use the plow feature significant female labor.

Agricultural development can more readily produce widespread poverty alleviation and income growth in areas where land is relatively abundant and evenly distributed (as in much of Africa and some parts of Asia) than where land is scarce or

concentrated (as in India or much of Latin America). Institutions develop to support landholders, whether they are relatively many (supporting equality) or few (preserving inequality). The distribution of agricultural development's benefits depends on which crops are grown and by whom within the household.

Food consumption behaviors tend to depend on income. Poor consumers spend a greater portion of their food budget on low-value staples, such as root crops and cereals. As incomes increase, people spend more on high-value food items, such as dairy and meat, and demand for food quality and safety increases as well. Increasing food quality similarly increases prices, so that "poor consumers may have to choose between safer but insufficient quantities of food and access to more food that is less safe. Poor people tend to prioritize quantity until their basic nutritional requirements are met, even if it implies lower levels of food safety" (Pinstrup-Andersen 2002a, 25). Many OECD countries have enacted stringent food safety requirements that increase prices for relatively small risk reductions.

In addition to higher food safety and health standards, higher-income consumers and societies are likely to pay more attention to the impact on natural resources. Sustainability goals become more prominent. Pollan (2006) refers to this as a movement from the industrial to the pastoral food chain, and Lang and Heasman (2004) argue that we are witnessing a paradigm shift from what they call a "Productionist Paradigm" to an "Ecologically Integrated Paradigm."

Different subsystems face different problems and to varying degrees. In some areas, the primary cause of hunger is a lack of food production, while in other areas what is lacking is the ability to purchase available food. The policy solutions to these two problems are vastly different. The policy solutions to hunger and obesity are also vastly different, making it difficult to combat the rising epidemic of obesity in many countries in Asia and Latin America where both undernutrition and obesity may be found in the same family. HIV/AIDS, malaria, and tuberculosis pose a more serious threat to the food systems in some African countries than in many other parts of the world.

The market and political power of farmers and consumers change with national income. In general, as countries become wealthier and the percent of the workforce involved in agriculture decreases, farmers organize themselves to lobby for government support. Poor countries' governments therefore tend to tax their farmers to benefit urban centers while wealthier governments tax urban areas and subsidize farmers. Even though farmers' political power tends to increase with national income, their market power decreases as consumer demands and processor requirements shape production choices (Pinstrup-Andersen 2002a).

Complex Systems Analysis

The issues now facing food policymakers are rooted in complex interactions inherent in the food system and the broader socioeconomic context within which it operates. Lang, Barling, and Caraher (2001) and Waltner-Toews and Lang (2000) propose that

issues related to food, agriculture, health, environment, and society cannot be satis-
factorily addressed unless considered in a holistic manner. This implies that policy
goals need to be considered jointly rather than in isolation.

Although many accept the existence of this complex system, few agree that there
is a good way to study it or apply it to real-world problem solving. This is largely
because experts tend to be specialists and to focus within their specialization. The
gains to multidisciplinary work are not seen in part because they are not considered.
As the World Bank (Gittinger, Leslie, and Hoisington 1987, 4) puts it, "Agriculturists
tend to focus on production, those active in the commercial food sector on market improvement, and physicians and nutritionists on clinical aspects of health and
nutrition." In similar fashion, economists focus on micro or macro economy, environmentalists on natural resources, and biotechnology researchers on the technical
aspects of GMOs. Government ministries and international agencies suffer from
similar disciplinary biases.

This book puts together several elements to assist in solving these complex problems. The case studies that support this book offer an opportunity to get a more
holistic understanding of policy issues and options available to the policymaker in
a manner that is readily accessible by multiple disciplines (Pinstrup-Andersen and
Cheng 2009). We encourage readers to approach complex problems with a strong
disciplinary background while being cognizant of how that discipline's tools and
particularly its biases and blind spots fit into the overall picture, open to the work
and insight from other disciplines, and prepared to work across disciplinary lines to
resolve complex issues. Such an approach is exemplified in this book as themes from
one chapter spill over into the other chapters, illustrating the interconnectedness of
food policy analysis. The next chapter provides additional tools to assist in solving
complex problems by considering food system problems from the point of view of
varying stakeholder groups, a methodology that underpins the rest of the book and
the case studies.

The Complex Systems Approach focuses specifically on the interactions and
relationships between elements of a system that would not be recognized by concentrating solely on the elements. It has its beginnings in the Austrian school of economics, arguing that market systems demonstrate "emergent orders"—systemwide
phenomena that are not present in any individual part, developing without a plan
or an overall decision maker dictating those results (Hayek 2007; Galea, Riddle, and
Kaplan 2009). The approach is dependent on an extended knowledge pool and peer
group for quality control (Funtowicz and Ravetz 1993). Emergent properties have
been found in flocks of birds and herd behavior (Reynolds 1987), in the fact that
the properties of water cannot be accounted for by the properties of hydrogen and
oxygen alone (Galea, Riddle, and Kaplan 2009), in the formation of communities
(Palla et al. 2005), and in political organizations (Cederman 2002). Indeed, Galea,
Riddle, and Kaplan (2009, 4) comment that "the appearance of emergent properties
is the rule and not the exception."

In his 1974 Nobel Prize lecture, Friedrich Hayek explained that scientific models
of complex systems could predict only patterns in emergent orders, not specific outcomes as is possible in simple systems:

Unlike the position that exists in the physical sciences, in economics and other disciplines that deal with essentially complex phenomena, the aspects of the events to be accounted for about which we can get quantitative data are necessarily limited and may not include the important ones. . . . In the study of such complex phenomena as the market, which depend on the actions of many individuals, all the circumstances which will determine the outcome of a process . . . will hardly ever be fully known or measurable. (Hayek 1974, 1)

Food systems, because of their complexity, likewise rely on a great deal of information that is not known or measurable even to an aggregate group of experts from the diverse fields that study the food system, let alone to those of only one profession. Because the immeasurable parts of a complex system cannot be verified empirically, it is common for analysts and policymakers to therefore ignore them. This can have tragic results.

The complex model thus offers a richer and potentially more effective basis for public policy than the single-discipline model, but also one that is more sober and modest. With fewer pretensions to understanding all facets of a problem, it can nevertheless provide readier policy guidance for supporting emergent orders and encouraging them to desired channels while harnessing their seemingly chaotic structure to improve efficiency and distribution.

Thinking in the food policy literature has been slowly moving in this direction, but it has been a very gradual change. Work by Schuh (1974) on exchange rates, and Krueger, Schiff, and Valdes (1988) on pricing policies, shows that macroeconomic policies may be as important for the food system as sectoral policies. An integrated approach to food policy that includes agricultural and resource policy will hold the most potential because of increased benefits from policy coordination (Timmer, Falcon, and Pearson 1983; Gittinger, Leslie, and Hoisington 1987; Just and Bockstael 1991). Epidemiologists have also called on their colleagues to make use of the complex systems methodology in studying public health (e.g., Koopman and Lynch 1999), particularly obesity (Hammond 2009; Galea, Riddle, and Kaplan 2009).

The central assumption for the new model is that an agrifood system should be treated as a complex system in order to be sustainable. Not only do practitioners of various disciplines need to work together to study complex systems, but scientific inquiry across disciplines needs to be brought into the same arena with public policy and management so that systemic feedback loops and trade-offs can be explicitly incorporated and negotiated.

In its simplest form, complex systems analysis begins with developing a conceptual framework, as in figure 1.1, that shows the primary elements and their linkages. This provides a reference and organizational tool to consider what factors interact with each other and how the most important feedback loops can be identified, as well as amplifying or dampening effects. From that vantage point, each element of the system can be examined with its connections included. Similarly, each chapter of the book delves into one portion of the conceptual framework deeply while recalling issues from other chapters that impact it.

Empirical complex systems simulations are generally accomplished through computer simulations. Stakeholders are modeled with relatively clear goals or rules of behavior: farmers maximize profits or minimize losses, consumers seek out food as close to them as possible or as cheap as possible, and the environment (pests, soil quality, water quality) responds in a certain way to fertilizer and pesticide application, for example. The computer then builds up macro-scale responses (population hunger and obesity rates, rates of soil decline, technology adoption rates, equilibrium farmer population, pest cycles, etc.). Researchers can calibrate the system using data on model parameters that have already been identified by previous disciplinary research where available, or can be calibrated so that outcomes match real-world data. By then introducing policy changes, it is possible to see how the patterns in the population develop and adjust to policy. Though they have their drawbacks—the most important of which is the ad hoc nature of the calibration if previous research has not established reliable parameter estimates—these methods can incorporate complex feedback effects, nonlinearities, psychological/behavioral models, social networking, ecosystem changes, temporal dynamics, and other features that would not be tractable theoretically, verifiable experimentally, or statistically measured. Modeled agents can be studied out of equilibrium, can demonstrate learning and evolving patterns of behavior as more information becomes available, and can be modeled with significant heterogeneity (Hammond 2009; Galea, Riddle, and Kaplan 2009). Readers interested in developing an analytical tool set are referred to Dickinson (1995) for physico-chemical complex food systems analysis, Miller and Page (2007) for complex systems in economics and social sciences, Allen and Holling (2008) for ecological complex systems, or the journal *Complexity Digest*.

Complex systems simulations have been applied successfully to the study of how infectious diseases are spread among people because they can account for social networks and their interactions (e.g., Ferguson et al. 2006). The theory has been regularly applied in economics under the name general equilibrium models (GEMs), differentiated from partial equilibrium models (PEMs) that focus on the effects in one sector only. GEMs have been known to completely overturn the results from PEMs. For instance, Jensen, Robinson, and Tarp (2004) show that while PEM indicated policies in fifteen developing countries were biased against agriculture, a GEM that includes exchange rate effects leads to a net positive bias in favor of agriculture in nine of them. Galea, Riddle, and Kaplan (2009) show that the effect of an antiobesity measure depends heavily on the extent to which individual diets are affected by those of their social network: the same policy had a powerful but shorter-lived effect when the influence of peers was weak, and a smaller but longer-lasting effect when peer ties were strong. Complex systems simulations have also been used to study civil violence (Epstein 2002), ethnocentrism (Hammond and Axelrod 2006), retirement decisions (Axtell and Estein 1999), tumor cells (Axelrod, Axelrod, and Pienta 2006), and terrorist attacks (Longini et al. 2007).

The costs when policymakers and analysts ignore the complexity of a system can be quite high. One example comes from an attempt to stock Lake Victoria with a nonnative species of fish in order to give fishermen in Kenya, Tanzania, and Uganda additional sources of income and protein in 1960. They did not take account of how the complex ecosystem would respond to the introduction of this species, however. The new fish decimated the population of a native fish that played an important role in reducing the incidence of schistosomes larvae, leading to a public health and economic crisis (Hammond 2009). This demonstrates both the importance of multidisciplinary, complex system modeling as well as the importance of maintaining modesty and avoiding policy overreach.

Organizations That Impact the Food System

During the twentieth century, the number of conventional international organizations increased from thirty-seven in 1909 to 251 in 1999 (Martinez-Diaz 2008). A summary of all of the international organizations that impact the food system and their governance is well beyond the scope of this book. In the interests of brevity, this section introduces only some of the largest and best-known of these organizations: the United Nations Food and Agriculture Organization (FAO), World Food Program (WFP), Children's Fund (UNICEF), and World Health Organization (WHO); the World Trade Organization (WTO); the Consultative Group on International Agricultural Research (CGIAR); the World Bank Group (WB); and the International Monetary Fund (IMF). Other chapters refer back to these organizations regularly, and chapter 9 in particular delves into their governance and the governance of the food system.

FAO's mission is to promote agricultural development, reduce hunger, and improve nutrition. It is the international organization most intimately involved with the global food system. The WFP focuses on providing food in a timely manner to victims of natural disasters and refugees, promoting development projects and raising awareness. UNICEF provides a forum where children's voices are heard, raises awareness of their needs, supports development projects, and produces research related to its mission.

WHO strives to control and prevent infectious disease outbreaks, produce policy-relevant research on health matters, and strengthen member government capacity for dealing with health issues. One of the key questions in the food system is how to balance the leadership of the FAO and the WHO, both of which impact human health and nutrition and comment on food policy. FAO and WHO formed another organization, the Codex Alimentarius Commission, to protect health and fair trade practices dealing with all food products. The Codex publishes nonbinding technical standards for food safety and best practices. This sometimes meets with opposition both from firms and more nationalistic policymakers who worry that these standards might be enforced on them and from NGOs opposed to corporate food because they perceive the Codex as being too aligned with industry interests.

The WTO took over from the General Agreement on Tariffs and Trade in the mid-1990s as an official organization to oversee the negotiation and enforcement of international trade laws. The intention was that the WTO's formation would make the international trade system more rules-based rather than power-based, improving transparency and accountability. The WTO's official mechanisms punish noncompliance and encourage commitment fulfillment. Though their efficacy in terms of punishing developed nations is questioned in chapter 9, the WTO is perceived as being the primary international organization "with teeth." This has led to calls for the WTO to take up enforcement of International Labour Organization (ILO) regulations, environmental standards, and human rights. Indeed, by focusing solely on trade issues, it is argued that the WTO undermines these other causes (case study 9-6). On the other hand, the mechanisms and training of the WTO do not put it in a strong position to speak with legitimacy on environmental or other nontrade issues. Instead, the WTO refers to other organizations as reference points, such as the Codex.

The largest, and most influential, international research organization is the Consultative Group on International Agricultural Research (CGIAR). Begun in the early 1960s with four founding research centers, the CG system was designed to undertake agricultural research that would generate international public goods—research for use by many developing countries that the private sector would not develop. Though its early successes were in rice, wheat, and maize, CGIAR has expanded to many other crops and production systems such as cassava, beans, potatoes, sorghum, millet, cowpea, leguminous trees, and indigenous vegetables and greens, as well as policy research undertaken primarily by IFPRI.

Agricultural technology developed by CGIAR in collaboration with national research systems brought high-yielding semidwarf wheat and rice varieties, developed with conventional breeding methods, to millions of small-scale farmers, initially in Asia and Latin America, but later in Africa as well (Evenson and Gollin 2003; Pinstrup-Andersen and Schiøler 2000; and chapter 7). The gains achieved during the early decades of this green revolution have continued and expanded to crops other than wheat and rice and to less-favored regions. The successes in creating high-yielding varieties and providing access to fertilizers, irrigation, and plant protection measures such as pesticides increased cereal production in Asia dramatically. Instead of the widespread famine predicted for parts of Asia and in spite of rapid population growth, cereal and calorie availability per person increased by nearly 30 percent, and wheat and rice became cheaper (FAO 2004d). Latin America experienced significant gains as well, but the impact in sub-Saharan Africa was much more modest. Poor infrastructure, poorly functioning markets, limited investment in irrigation, and adverse pricing and marketing policies resulted in high transaction and transportation costs that prevented the spread of the green revolution. IFPRI's policy research has been very instrumental in improving the understanding about policies to deal with these problems.

Emerging Trends and Driving Forces

Some of the changes in the global food system have been distinct improvements. Technological advances have enabled the world to feed many millions more people than it was previously believed possible while preserving marginal lands and forestry.

The percent of the world suffering from hunger has continued to decrease outside of occasional price spikes. The partial market liberalizations in China and Vietnam have been followed by the largest and fastest transition of people out of poverty and hunger the world has ever witnessed. A dietary transition has occurred in wealthier countries, encouraging healthier diets and lifestyle changes. Supermarkets and global food chains have enabled those people with access to achieve greater dietary variety, a trend now spreading to developing countries. Technological breakthroughs have also improved agricultural yield stability by reducing crops' sensitivity to pests and weather. Knowledge about the effects of micronutrients and how to eradicate diseases associated with micronutrient deficiencies has spread further than before. NGOs and microfinance institutions provide needed services to remote areas of the world. Other governance reforms in developing countries have laid the groundwork for ongoing agricultural growth, and international institutions could provide developing countries greater voice in global food policies.

Many other changes have been less promising. A significant dietary transition that includes increased consumption of meat, edible oils, refined sugars, and sweeteners in mostly middle- and high-income countries has led to rapidly increasing obesity worldwide. This has increased the ties between the food system and the health system. Even though millions of people have emerged from poverty, it appears that millions of others are becoming increasingly marginalized by and from the globalization of the food system, making it more difficult for them to emerge from poverty.

The ecological dimensions of the food system have received increasing notice. While technological progress and increased agricultural productivity have protected marginal lands, forestry, and biodiversity, the lack of productivity increases in other areas has exacerbated desertification, deforestation, and loss of habitat. Poor soil management techniques leave soils drained of nutrients (lack of fertilizers), burned (overuse of fertilizers), or salinated and waterlogged (over irrigated with poor drainage systems). Globalization has meant that food is shipped further and further between production and consumption, an environmental cost not borne by consumer or producer.

As mentioned above, serious debate rages about other changes that have both positive and negative aspects to them with well-meaning, well-informed, passionate advocates on different sides. Biofuels have promised a way to reduce fossil fuel dependence sustainably, but government subsidies to support them have increased food insecurity and may be causing more environmental harm on net in some areas. The increasing demand for meat and meat products has sparked a livestock revolution that also increases the demand for feed grains. Advances in animal husbandry have enabled the creation of so-called "factory farms" where thousands of animals can be raised at one time. While increasing feed efficiency,[2] there are many concerns about animal welfare, food safety, and the effects of concentrated manure and methane production on the environment. The green revolution—during which advances in plant breeding improved seed varieties, leading to much greater production—lifted millions of farmers and consumers out of poverty and hunger, but the increased intensive use of irrigation, fertilizer, and pesticides has prompted concerns about the processes' environmental sustainability. New technological advances in genetically modified (GM) foods have sparked intense controversy and fears of whether they are dangerous "Frankenfoods," as argued by some advocacy groups, or "substantially equivalent" to their nonmodified counterparts, as argued by the United States government. GMOs (genetically modified organisms) are addressed in chapters 7, 8, and 10.

Globalization has brought both opportunities and challenges, yet the world currently lacks the institutional infrastructure to guide the forces of globalization into the most positive channels (chapter 10). The dietary transitions in middle- and lower-income countries inflame worries about the "Westernization" of diets as U.S. and EU food firms can be found in nearly every country. The effects of multinationals' foreign direct investment in the food system, including investments by governments and corporations to gain control over land in low-income countries, and changes in trade patterns are also widely debated.

Urbanization is both a cause and effect of increased rural marginalization and the growing need for farmers to seek off-farm wages to support their families, particularly where agricultural productivity growth has been low. The growing urban demand for ready-to-eat meals has led to a larger processing sector that focuses on greater specialization, standardization, and food commoditization. There is concern that the growing concentration in food processing and retailing has led to increasing market power for a few international firms, and that the psychological distance between consumers and the people who produce their food is growing. More and more food is also being grown in urban garden plots. In the case of Russia, these garden plots produce most of the country's vegetables.

Advertising, marketing, and processing continue to claim larger shares of each dollar spent on food. This is a shift in both how food is sold to people and how we think about food. It has also created the popularity for the sensationalizing books discussed above. Food safety is as much an advertising concern as a health cause in advanced economies. The advent of widespread vitamin pills has brought the very nature of healthy eating into question as some agencies have needed to make a special effort to remember to include "food-based nutrition" as part of their health programs.

The increase in the share of the consumer dollar that goes to pay for advertising and processing has in part shielded consumers in more advanced economies from recent food price increases: the price of the food commodities went up, but since only a few cents of every dollar spent by the consumer actually went to the farmer, total costs to the consumer did not change as much in rich countries as they did in poor countries. Poor net food buyers were hardest hit. The last few years have ushered in a new era of increased global price volatility due to climate change, global market integration, increased politicization of food, and lower inventories. Globalization reduces the effects of local and idiosyncratic factors on food prices, but increases the ability of national policies to affect prices beyond their borders. On the other hand, open economies are able to spread the effects of national supply and demand changes across the international markets and thereby reduce the fluctuation in national prices.

Agricultural research has shifted from its largely public sector origins to include an increasing share of private research. Since private firms prioritize research for which there is economic demand (i.e., developing technology for wealthier farmers), many crops and areas of the world dominated by poor smallholders are ignored. This leaves smallholders, who are unable to translate their needs for technology into economic demand, increasingly marginalized and without the critical technology and knowledge they need to escape poverty and hunger. To solve that problem, there is a need for public and charitable investment. Public-private partnerships, which are becoming more widely used, may benefit poor farmers and consumers. NGOs are taking on an increasing burden of location-specific research to help develop solutions for poor people's problems. Recent increases in the financial support of international agricultural research and research by middle-income countries, such as Brazil, India and China, result in positive spillovers to other smaller and lower-income countries (chapters 7 and 10).

These changes were not directly planned by any one organization nor were they the products of chance. Decision makers are rational agents, responding to the changing incentives they face to produce the dizzying array of changes categorized above. Some of these forces impact the food system like the tides moving a ship: the food system can do little to affect them but must simply follow the larger trends. Other driving forces can be harnessed, as a ship does the wind, but it requires concentrated effort, knowledge, and guiding institutions to make use of them. Other driving forces are directly internal to the food system and readily subject to change. The chapter concludes by briefly discussing nine of the primary driving forces affecting the food system today and in the foreseeable future.

Urbanization and Economic Growth

Roughly 42 percent of the population of developing countries lives in urban areas, and by 2020 more than half will do so. Within developing regions, however, there is a wide disparity in terms of urbanization. In Latin America and the Caribbean, 76.8 percent of the population is classified as urban, while in both Asia and Africa it is only 39 percent (UN 2003). It is therefore not surprising that in the latter two regions urbanization is projected to increase the most. The urban population in China totaled about 524 million (41 percent) in 2003, and this figure will continue to rise. In west Africa, there will be over thirty cities of one million people by 2020. Poor performance in agriculture and nonagriculture rural activity has resulted in excessively rapid rural-to-urban migration.

As incomes increase, urban consumers demand higher food quality, more diversity, and more convenience food, and consumption shifts from grains to meat. These changes together with sedentary lifestyles in urban areas lead to growing obesity problems. With less time to prepare meals in urban settings, there is greater demand for preprepared ready-to-eat meals. This requires greater processing, which in turn leads processors to demand more uniformity among products they receive from producers. Income and globalization provide access to more foreign foods as well, leading to a gradual unification of diets across the world, though this is not as uniformly one-dimensional as some have claimed. The combined effect of these factors on diets can be summarized as a dietary convergence and a dietary adaptation (case 10-1).[3]

Demographic Shifts

Population growth, the aging of the farm population, and the feminization of agriculture, coupled with rural labor shortages caused by urbanization and the HIV/AIDS crisis, are likely to cause rapid changes in the structure of farming in many developed and developing countries over the next decades. HIV/AIDS takes the lives of many working-age people while leaving elderly and children on their own, creating new family structures, and requiring great adaptations. Small-scale farms are more vulnerable to these forces, particularly when coupled with globalization and domestic investment in infrastructure, which improves price transmission from other areas, changes relative prices, and makes capital available for larger production units.

Although population growth rates are falling, the current global population of 6.8 billion is expected to increase to about 8 billion by 2030 and between 8 and 10 billion by 2050 (World Bank 2007a; UN 2009, 18). As further discussed in chapter 4, almost all of this increase will occur in developing countries. The global labor force will increase even faster (World Bank 2007b). Current high rates of unemployment in both rural and urban areas of many developing countries cause poverty, hunger, and instability. Thus while some rural areas suffer from labor shortages, others have a surplus of labor and not enough labor demand. Where unemployment is high and labor plentiful, labor productivity and demand may be increased by expanded use of labor-using technology in agriculture instead of laborsaving technology and by investment in postharvest activities such as value-added processing.

Increasing Market Concentration and Globalization

The share of food products and commodities controlled by the largest firms has been growing steadily, both globally and within nations. Processors and retailers with greater market shares may capture economies of scale (the benefits of which may or may not be shared with producers and/or consumers), reduce competition, and/or increasingly dictate, or at least influence, production and consumption decisions.

With a few periods of interruption, globalization has been progressing over the last five hundred years. Improvements in transportation and telecommunications significantly reduce the market and transaction costs involved in international trade (capital, finance, knowledge, and to a lesser extent labor). The value of international trade in food and agricultural commodities has exceeded $600 billion annually, and is expected to continue growing (FAOSTAT 2005). Food-related foreign direct investment by U.S. companies in other countries totaled about $50 billion in 2002, and processed food sales from these companies were almost five times as high as the countries' processed food exports (USDA 2006). Benefits from additional exports have been captured by millions of farmers, but others have been left behind or pushed out.

While globalization and market concentration present opportunities to develop the food system, increase income, and reduce poverty, there are also risks. Globalization reduces domestic price volatility while exposing farmers to global variation in price, trade flows, and finance. There are risks of increased environmental damage as unsustainable systems of production are favored by short-term competitive pressures, and of increasing inequality within countries as some regions are better able to benefit from globalization while others stagnate.

The combined effects of market concentration and globalization can be seen clearly in the rise of supermarkets in the developing world. From a 50–60 percent market share in Latin America to 10 percent in India and China (case 6-2; Shepherd 2005), supermarkets' importance has been growing in developing countries. Within Africa, the experience is varied, where market maturity ranges from birth (Ghana) to a small niche market (Tanzania and Uganda with 1–4 supermarkets each) to increased importance (Kenya, Nigeria, and Zambia with over 100 each) to nearly saturated (South Africa). See case 6-11 for Uganda.

Sweeping Technological Change

Technological advances in information and communication technology (ICT) have the potential to dramatically alter rural market structures. Cell phone use has spread widely in particular African countries, granting farmers much more market access, information, and bargaining power. ICT can also form part of early warning systems and are becoming part of Africa's financial market infrastructure.

Agricultural research has similarly undergone many important changes. Molecular biology including biotechnology is widely used in plant breeding to raise and stabilize yields, to improve resistance to pests and weather, and to enhance the nutritional content of foods. Nanotechnology may provide even greater benefits. However, there are serious concerns about access for poor and food-insecure people, about food safety, and about effects on the natural environment. More agricultural research is privately funded, focusing primarily on nonpoor people in industrialized countries. Past agricultural research—tailored to solving problems of small-scale farmers and low-income consumers in developing countries—has been effective in expanding productivity, protecting the environment, reducing poverty, and increasing food security. Intellectual property rights laws are increasingly becoming important for the food system, particularly in terms of access, the widespread patenting of living organisms, and related "biopiracy." Without changes in policies and institutions, the current and expected future technological revolutions may leave groups of the poor and food insecure further behind.

Changing Roles and Responsibilities of Key Agents

From the 1930s to 1970s, governments intervened more and more in their economies. Government failures grew in importance in the public eye during the 1970s–1990s, leading to a scaling back of government's responsibility in food systems to the present time. The roles of private voluntary organizations, the for-profit private sector, and consumers have fluctuated as well, partly in response to—and partly causing—changes in governmental responsibilities. The role of the public sector has in general been shrinking over the last three decades, i.e. 1980–2010, while civil society and the private sector have taken on increasing importance.

While the ideal mix of power in the food system may be in constant flux, there are key roles that governments are uniquely suited to fill. Constructing a supportive legal framework of property rights and enforced contracts leads the list because no one else can formally put this sort of structure in place, though in the absence of government informal norms may develop. Public goods provision can be done by NGOs, and some public goods can be run by for-profit firms, but significant research and experience uphold the value of publicly provided goods. For the food system, some of the most important public goods include agricultural research to develop appropriate technology for small farmers, rural infrastructure, health care, education, and other supportive infrastructure (financial, energy, legal, market, etc.). Government is also needed to facilitate conflict resolution between other decision makers.

Degradation of Natural Resources and Increasing Water Scarcity

Failure to achieve yield increases on land that is well suited for agricultural cultivation has pushed farmers into areas less suited for agriculture, causing deforestation, desertification, land degradation, and unsustainable exploitation of surface and ground water. While modest fertilizer use is necessary to preserve soil integrity, overuse of fertilizer or improper timing can damage soil and water quality, affecting human health. Similarly, though chemical pesticides may be the only or the best crop protection methods, inappropriate and excessive use causes both health risks and soil degradation (Nelson 2010).

Natural resource degradation decreases production, food availability, and income for current and future generations. Soil quality is an essential input for farmers and farm laborers, while many of the landless poor rely on forestry as another source of income. The poor are often forced to make trade-offs between immediate household food requirements and environmental sustainability. Their negligible man-made capital assets, ill-defined or nonexistent property rights, limited access to financial services and other markets, inadequate safety nets in times of stress or disaster, and lack of participation in policymaking at all levels leave them few options but to draw down their natural capital in order to survive negative shocks, despite the harm it will cause them later. This then sets them up for lower returns later, which can lead to a vicious cycle.

In many countries, water use for agriculture is heavily subsidized, leading to overuse relative to its economic value. As a result, about 80 percent of the global use of water is accounted for by agriculture, and it is used inefficiently. Water scarcity is rapidly becoming the most limiting factor in agricultural production in more areas, and the demand for water in nonagricultural sectors is also increasing. There are many methods already devised that would increase water use efficiency and lower agriculture's water footprint.

Rising Energy Prices

Agricultural production alone uses about 4 percent of total energy consumption, mostly for irrigation (36 percent) and fertilizer manufacture (36 percent), with crop drying, tillage, and seeding using the rest (FAO 2000b). When the other steps in the food chain are included, the food and agricultural sector uses from 16 to 20 percent of all energy, depending on the level of development. The percent of agricultural costs due to energy (primarily fuel, fertilizer, and irrigation) varies greatly between regions, with developed country agriculture being more reliant on fuel prices. Agricultural producers have responded to higher energy prices by making trade-offs—replacing more expensive fuels with less expensive fuels, shifting to less energy-intensive crops, and employing energy-conserving production practices where possible.

Increasing oil prices have drawn the attention of policymakers to agriculture as a potential supplier of energy from plants and waste products, collectively called biofuels. Rapid increases in the use of land, water, and labor for biofuels production, heavily subsidized by several key governments, place additional pressures on natural resources, reduce food production, and raise food prices. Biofuels hold the promise to increase farm incomes, particularly in marginal lands that can grow jatropha trees. Rapidly increasing biofuel production in the United States in response to large government subsidies was one of the important factors responsible for the food price increase between 2005 and 2008.

Climate Change

As discussed in chapter 8, the impact of climate change on the food system is presenting itself as increasing weather volatility in the form of droughts, flooding, and strong winds. It is currently predicted that rising temperatures will further exacerbate such weather volatility. Natural disasters, particularly floods and droughts, have become increasingly common over the last fifty years and are expected to continue increasing in frequency. Rising sea levels threaten many coastal and island areas, and reduced rainfall in parts of the tropics will diminish yield potentials in many developing countries. The long time horizon over which these changes are expected, and their gradual nature, are both a blessing and a curse: it is easier to respond to them, but it is harder to gather support for preventative action.

Global warming may also have positive effects on agriculture. Colder climates will become more hospitable to agriculture, primarily benefiting northern countries that are already richer. Rising carbon dioxide (CO_2) levels fertilize many crops, which can improve growth rates and water use efficiency (FAO 2000a). Current estimates suggest that the next twenty years may see a period of global cooling before returning to the present warming trend again.

Agriculture may contribute to or reduce the concentration of CO_2 in the atmosphere. Rapidly increasing livestock production to satisfy increasing meat demand will increase greenhouse gases, as will expanded rice production and deforestation. However, reforestation and crop production also trap or capture carbon. Thus, while agriculture is seen by many as part of the global warming problem, it can also be part of the solution by binding CO_2.

Local and Regional Factors

Though the threat of conflict spilling across national borders threatens the global food system, the effects of conflict are most noticeably felt in particular local food systems. As discussed in chapter 9, this is not a one-way effect, but the ability of the food system to provide stable income, livelihoods, and food security impacts the probability of conflict erupting.

A number of health issues are also highly prominent factors in specific local food systems (Pinstrup-Andersen 2010; chapter 3). These include the unsolved crises of malaria, tuberculosis, and HIV/AIDS, which receive a great deal of media attention. Less noticed are the effects of sleeping sickness (African trypanosomiasis), river blindness, and widespread micronutrient deficiencies. There are also many livestock diseases that can affect food safety and endanger human health (Torrey 2010).

A number of "orphan crops" are crucial for specific regions, such as cassava, potatoes, plantains, teff, millet, sorghum, cowpea, and indigenous vegetables and greens. Because they are not traded internationally, however, they have received scant attention from researchers, policymakers, and NGOs. The focus on some crops and neglect of others often has subtle effects on food cultures. Herforth (2010a) discusses the nutritional value of traditional African vegetables that are looked down on in African society precisely because they are local and largely forgotten in the forces of Westernization.

Conclusion

There are two primary take-away messages from this chapter. The first is that food systems are complex, dynamic, and behavioral, aspects that will be expanded on in the next chapter. The global food system is a behavioral, social, economic, political, and ecological system. The primary objectives of the global food system are to make good human health and nutrition, food security, and environmental sustainability possible for all. These goals are determined by more than just how food is produced, processed, and distributed. They rely on the social and political rules that govern the system, the economic and ecological constraints and incentives, and their interactions at both a systemic and an individual level. A holistic approach is therefore necessary in order to understand and improve food policy.

The second message is that the global food system is facing diverse and complex challenges. The global food system is currently faced with five major problems that it is well positioned to address: continued rapid increases in food demand; widespread poverty, hunger, and malnutrition; overweight, obesity, and chronic diseases; mismanagement of natural resources; and marginalization of the poor. The challenge is to design policies and technologies that will alleviate and resolve these problems in a sustainable manner.

Eliminating widespread malnutrition (including hunger, micronutrient deficiencies, and overweight) in a sustainable manner—so that food for people today is not purchased at the cost of food for people in the future—is humanity's foremost challenge. Its place as the first Millennium Development Goal demonstrates the widespread acceptance of its prominence. As will be demonstrated in the remainder of the book, the foundation for a sustainable and equitable global food system is likely to be neither organic farming nor highly industrialized agriculture but a third option that incorporates and unifies technology and environment into sustainable development. Sound evidence-based policies are essential to allow decision makers at all levels to fulfill their roles in creating solutions, and sound evidence is critical to avoid misguided policy advice. Globalization, like government, can play a major role in achieving success but it also can make matters worse. As further discussed in chapters 9 and 10, the lack of appropriate international institutions to guide globalization poses substantial risks to developing countries. The marginalization of poor countries and poor individuals can persist where certain countries or societal groups are left out of the overall economic integration and growth process. Where this occurs, changes are needed in policies and institutions at the household, national, and international levels.

The conceptual framework introduced here is intended to strengthen the understanding of the consequences of dynamic change in the global food system during the past few decades. Such understanding can foster adaptive strategies to bolster the global food system's resilience in the face of rising challenges. Since the same effect (positive or negative) can be created, averted, lessened, or amplified with more than one approach, appropriate empirical and theoretical policy analysis should identify intervention points and adaptation pathways among different agents and institutions at multiple scales to identify the short-, medium-, and long-term consequences of different policies. These aspects will be taken up in the next chapter.

Notes

1. Gross Domestic Product (GDP) measures the total production of all residents of a country. Agricultural GDP is the value of production in the agricultural sector.
2. Feed efficiency measures how much feed it takes to increase an animal's weight by one pound.
3. Dietary convergence reflects a reliance on a narrow base of staple grains, increased consumption of meat, dairy, edible oil, salt, and sugar, and a lower intake of dietary fiber. Dietary adaptation signifies more foreign, brand-name, processed foods are being consumed, more of which is eaten outside the home (FAO 2004a; Hawkes 2006).

Chapter 2

Food Policy

Introduction

The fragility and flaws in the world's food and agricultural policies have become increasingly apparent during the first decade of the twenty-first century. Designing appropriate food and agricultural policies is essential in countries where food is barely enough for subsistence and rural poverty is widespread. In high-income countries, where agricultural subsidies and related trade policy have played an important role in the political arena for decades, new challenges have brought food and agricultural policies back to the front burner of policymaking. These challenges include the food crisis of 2007–2008 and the prospect of larger food price fluctuations in the future due to climate change, speculation, government policies, food safety concerns, environmental degradation, industrialized agriculture, genetic engineering, trade wars, and zoonotic diseases.

This chapter discusses the history of food policy and different theories about how it is created. The case for government intervention is put forward both from an efficiency-enhancing perspective and on the basis of other social goals. We show how to use political economy and stakeholder analysis to understand food policy formation in the complex food system introduced in chapter 1. We also examine food policy analysis, concluding that there is a real need to include macroeconomic and political economy concerns in analyses, and give recommendations to make future analyses more relevant and effective in influencing the making of food policy.

The focus of food policy historically has been on increasing productivity and either taxing or subsidizing farmers. Technological advance has increased agricultural efficiency and enabled farmers to keep ahead of rising population so that today enough food is produced to feed every person. Relieving this constraint has meant that other constraints—including in particular the driving forces discussed at the end of chapter 1 and ethically based food preferences—have become more relevant and require equally concerted action and a much more comprehensive, holistic approach to food system policymaking. This chapter introduces an integrated, long-term strategy for food policy analysis that links social, economic, political, and ecological dimensions, rooted in the food system conceptual framework laid out in chapter 1.

Governments have most often been modeled as monolithic, single-purposed entities that impose desired policies on food systems. Forgotten in such a characterization are the realities of interministerial conflicts; political lobbying; branches of government that have different rules, and constituencies with varying ideologies and political parties loyalties; the different horizons faced by bureaucracies and legislators; and the influence of different factions of stakeholders in different public agencies. Policies that emerge from this system rarely resemble the idealized versions considered in most policy analysis. This can lead to significant departures from expected policy results.

Government intervention is often motivated or legitimized by efficiency. Efficiency is most often defined as getting the most output per unit of input. Efficiency, however, can have multiple meanings depending on what the relevant goals are. Consider two cars traveling on a road. The first drives faster than the second, meaning it uses less time per mile. The first also has higher fuel efficiency, using less energy per mile. If, however, it is going in the wrong direction, the slower car that consumes more gas and is traveling in the right direction is actually the more efficient one at that time. An economy can produce many things, but if it fails to accomplish other societal goals, it is not very efficient. Once the first car is turned around and pointed in the right direction, however, it will again be the more efficient user of time and energy. One of the primary arguments in this book is that policy analysts need to understand the complete system and how food system elements interact in order to guide the various institutions—public and private, individual and group—in order for the food system to simultaneously meet its many social goals as efficiently as possible.

Economists have gone to great lengths over time to demonstrate under what conditions market systems will allocate resources efficiently using the standard definition of producing the greatest output using fixed resources. When one or more of these preconditions is not present, the market "fails," which is to say that market prices will not reflect the full societal costs and benefits of an intended action or will not aggregate the information of all market participants efficiently. The most common examples of market failure include cases when

- there are significant positive or negative effects on third parties (*externalities*);
- a firm is able to set prices or other market conditions and there are barriers to entry, preventing competition from correcting these actions (*market power*);
- vital information is not readily available to all participants (*asymmetric information*);

- there are significant nonmarket costs in doing business, such as searching for a buyer or seller, determining prices, paying bribes, and enforcing contracts to prevent fraud (*transaction costs*).

When markets fail, they may not succeed in allocating resources to their most productive use.

Government intervention is a possible solution, though not the only one. Entrepreneurs have been known, for instance, to develop new businesses (such as microfinance or telecommunications) based on reducing transaction costs and providing market information, and social institutions (such as community planning organizations or ethnic business networks) can develop to reduce transaction costs and internalize externalities.

Production efficiency is not the only, or even the most frequent, justification used for government intervention. The more responsive government officials are to organized interest groups, lobbying, or constituent stakeholder groups, the more heavily the benefits to that group will be weighed compared to societal costs (Grossman and Helpman 1994). Governments intervene in markets in response to ideological demands or ethical beliefs, such as concerns about income distribution, animal welfare, ecological concerns that go beyond sustainability, or beliefs about what kind of market structure (e.g., large firms versus small) will produce the most desirable food system.

Government policies often produce benefits and privileges for particular groups at the expense of overall efficiency and societal welfare. These benefits are called "rents" or "directly unproductive profits." Actions by government agents or market participants to claim a larger share of these rents are called rent-seeking activity. Government agents can, for instance, solicit lobbying and political contributions, market influence, or bribes in exchange for ensuring that one of the limited import licenses benefits the lobbying group or that new food regulations give the lobbying firm an advantage over competitors. Differentiating between bribes and appropriate licensing fees that are used to pay civil servant salaries is not a simple task.

Many macroeconomic policies, such as exchange rates, interest rates, wage rates, and fiscal and monetary policies, have significant impacts on the food system. These impacts are rarely considered when macroeconomic policy is made or analyzed, however. Similarly, food policy analysts often focus on microeconomic phenomena and miss the effects of the larger economic situation, leading to less effective policy prescription. The food system is sensitive to macroeconomic policy and an appreciation of this link is necessary on the part of analysts and policymakers who deal directly with the food system, and those who deal primarily with those macroeconomic policies (case 9-8).

As emphasized in chapter 1, the food system comprises the actions and decisions of numerous different agents, each with their own goals and constraints. Two key elements of a holistic food policy analysis are stakeholder analysis and the complex systems approach. Stakeholders are people who have an interest in the policy in question, whether because they will be affected by it, have knowledge needed in policy formation, or can influence its formation. Some stakeholders have more access to policymakers than others, making it imperative that analysts include in their analysis the voices of those who do not have access. The interactions among stakeholders produce a complex system, requiring specialized tools to understand.

Food policy analysts inform the policymaking process by collecting, analyzing, and interpreting data and communicating results to decision makers. Policy analysis can be divided into two very broad categories, normative and positive. Normative policy analysis specifies a judgment of "what ought to be." This type of analysis typically identifies optimum policies that maximize certain objectives given political and economic constraints. Positive policy analysis specifies "what is" and may estimate outcomes of various policy interventions without any value judgment of right or wrong outcomes. Although a large share of economic analyses claim to be positive and value-free, they are, in fact, based on a particular ethical system with strong assumptions. This choice is itself normative because it is one of several ethical foundations that could be selected (Pinstrup-Andersen 2005b). Although (ostensibly) positive economic analysis has been widely used in policy analysis, it may not explain policymaking processes and has been partially replaced by political economy, public choice, and institutional theories that offer additional insights in the determination of food policies. Institutional analysis is discussed in chapter 9, and the importance of alternative ethical structures in chapter 11.

Definition of Food Policy

Food Policy and Food Policymakers

A policy is a plan of action designed by one or more individuals to accomplish a given purpose (*American Heritage Dictionary of the English Language* 2000). Food policies, it then follows, are plans of action related to the food system. Most often, we refer to government policies, but the policies of the private sector and civil society are also important for the food system. More specifically, food policy consists in the setting of goals for the food system or its parts, including natural resources, production, processing, marketing, food consumption and safety, and nutrition, and determining the processes for achieving these goals. By setting regulations or changing incentives for different stakeholders, food policy shapes the structure and functioning of the food system in the direction of the intended goals, and sometimes toward unintended effects.

Food policy is often used as a generic term for government programs that directly or indirectly affect the food system. These programs include consumer and farmer subsidies, biofortification, food safety regulations, resource management, price stabilization, and trade liberalization. Though policies and intents differ across countries and across time, providing sufficient food (sometimes but not always of adequate nutritional quality) for each individual has been the most important food policy objective over time. Modern food policy also includes objectives such as farm income support, taxation of farmers, economic growth, poverty reduction, and environmental protection.

Defining policy as a plan of collective action aimed at the achievement of an agreed-on set of consistent goals, while theoretically correct, may not reflect realities. Public food policies are negotiated between government agencies, including not only finance and agriculture ministries but also health, commerce, trade, environment, and foreign affairs ministries, bureaucracies, and lobbies. Those involved in determining macroeconomic, labor, rural development, poverty relief, women's issues, transportation, and financial regulation policies also impact the food system. As a result, government action is likely to include conflicting goals and policy measures that may contradict each other. Furthermore, few governments pursue a consistent set of goals for policy intervention over time. Thus, proper stakeholder analysis considers the policies pursued by different organizations, individuals, or sectors and their impact on the relevant stakeholder groups.

The food policies of one country often influence policies of other countries. This is most noticeable with trade and other overtly international policies. Disputes over international food policies, whether violent or peaceful, have grown since the mid-1970s. This has led to the creation and development of various international organizations that also influence food policy, as discussed in chapters 1, 9, and 10.

Food Policy: The Change of Focus

Historically, food policy has meant *agricultural policy,* and agricultural policy focused primarily on (1) increasing farm output in order to guarantee sufficient food supply; (2) either assuring certain income levels for farmers or taxing them to subsidize other sectors; or (3) preserving the rights of land holders. This early emphasis on supply-side policies was necessary because hunger and malnutrition were caused by insufficient or unstable food production and because landownership played such a key role in income generation and social structure. It is still important for many developing countries to focus on increasing production because agricultural development is and will continue to be the ultimate driving force of overall economic growth (World Bank 2008; chapter 7). Agricultural productivity growth is necessary, though insufficient by itself, to achieve sustainable food security for current and future generations, and those countries that have experienced rapid growth in their agricultural sectors have typically reduced hunger and achieved economic development (Bayes 2007).

Government food policy has not only focused on increasing production. Roman law anciently aimed to provide bread for the masses, and the past governments of several countries including Egypt and Sri Lanka prioritized consumer access to basic food staples. However, Amartya Sen's work contributed to a more general shift in the thinking about food policy from agricultural production to effective consumer demand by emphasizing food entitlement and access (Sen 1981). Gradually the primary concern of the global food system changed from national food supply and food security to food demand, consumption, and individual and household food security (chapter 4). The objective of achieving food security for all has been a powerful driver of food policy design in both developed and developing nations.

Nutritional consequences of food policy have developed as another driver of the food system. In the pathbreaking book *The Nutrition Factor*, Alan Berg (1973) argued successfully for using nutritional goals to guide economic policy, and Pinstrup-Andersen, Londono, and Hoover (1976) and Pinstrup-Andersen (1981 and 1983) suggested how nutritional goals might be used to prioritize, design, and implement agricultural projects and policies. A fuller analysis of the development and current use of food security concepts is found in Pinstrup-Andersen and Herforth (2008).

The driving forces discussed in chapter 1 have also required a rethink about food policy. The food policy needs of urban dwellers are different from ruralists. Industrialized, integrated agriculture brings different challenges than subsistence, localized agriculture. The effects of globalization have called for a reevaluation of food sovereignty, and the food price crises of 2007–2008 and 2010–2011 emphasized the benefits of food self-sufficiency. Reliance on only a few crops has decreased biodiversity. Warnings about the environmental consequences of new technologies and agricultural practices raise an important question of how to continue the expansion of food production to meet future demand without negatively affecting the environment. The focus is increasingly on *sustainable* food policy, designed and implemented to ensure sufficient food supply and access in a manner that is also consistent with an ecologically sustainable management of natural resources. The changing nature of food policy issues as summarized by Maxwell and Slater (2004) is shown in table 2.1.

The Changing Role of Government in Food Policy

Government's role in food policy has gone through three distinct phases and may now be in a fourth. In broad terms, governments were expected to leave markets alone prior to the 1930s but to intervene heavily from the 1940s to 1970s. During that phase, governments around the world directed much of what went on in their food systems. The assumption was that markets were hampered by large, fixed investment costs, missing markets, high transaction costs, and imperfect information, which could all be resolved by government action. Food price stabilization and parastatal marketing institutions exercising monopsony pricing behavior toward farmers were pervasive.

It was gradually recognized that government intervention often did more harm than good. The parastatal marketing institutions tended to be corrupt, inefficient, and costly. Interventions distorted incentives, leading in some cases to more widespread hunger, poverty, and unemployment. Import substitution policies left many countries bereft of foreign currency and produced subsidized industries that still were unfit to compete with outside firms even after thirty years of protection. These policies were not sustainable, financially or environmentally, as the debt crises of the 1980s demonstrated. In many countries, criticism against government intervention was amplified by unemployment and underemployment despite economic growth and industrialization in the 1970s.

This induced the third phase, which saw "government as a problem." Since governments had so distorted the price signals that markets need in order to function,

TABLE 2.1.
Food Policy: Old and New

		Food policy "old"	Food policy "new"
1	Population	Mostly rural	Mostly urban
2	Rural jobs	Mostly agricultural	Mostly nonagricultural
3	Employment in the food sector	Mostly in food production and primary marketing	Mostly in food manufacturing and retail
4	Actors in food marketing	Grain traders	Food companies
5	Supply chains	Short-small number of food miles	Long-large number of food miles
6	Typical food preparation	Mostly food cooked at home	High proportion of prepared meals, food eaten out
7	Typical food	Basic staples, unbranded	Processed food, branded products, more animal products in the diet
8	Packaging	Low	High
9	Purchased food	Bought in local stalls or shops, open markets	Bought in supermarkets
10	Food safety issues	Pesticide poisoning of field workers, toxins associated with poor storage	Pesticide in food, adulteration, biosafety issues in processed food
11	Nutrition problems	Undernutrition	Overnutrition
12	Nutrient issues	Micronutrients	Fat, sugar
13	Food-insecure population	Peasants	Urban and rural poor
14	Main sources of national food shocks	Poor rainfall and other production shocks	International price and other trade problems
15	Main source of household food shocks	Poor rainfall and other production shocks	Income shocks causing food poverty
16	Remedies for household food shortage	Safety nets, food-based relief	Social protection, income transfer
17	Forums for food policy	Ministries of agriculture, relief/ rehabilitation, health	Ministries of trade and industry, consumer affairs, food activist groups, NGOs
18	Focus of food policy	Agricultural technology, parastatal reform, supplementary feeding, food for work	Competition and rent-seeking in the value chain, industrial structure in the retail sector, futures markets, waste management, advertising, health education, food safety
19	Key international institutions	FAO, WFP, UNICEF, WHO, CGIAR	FAO, UNIDO, ILO, WHO, WTO

Source: Maxwell and Slater 2004.

the neoliberal mantra became that "getting the prices right" would resolve the problems caused by government interventions. World Bank and IMF structural adjustment programs attempted to reduce fiscal unsustainability, remove price distortions, and reconnect global and local market prices. Retracting government interventions would help markets function more efficiently. It was assumed this would simultaneously increase food production and farmer incomes, reduce poverty and hunger, and improve welfare for most people. In the short run, however, many farmers lost access to needed inputs, which reduced food production and farmer incomes and increased hunger. The medium-term effects have been more positive thus far.

Government is more often seen in the beginning of the twenty-first century as a facilitator of successful markets through the creation of public goods, and an agent to reduce or eliminate negative externalities. That is, the failures of the original restructurings made it clear that there is an important role for active government involvement, but it is a role that is primarily supportive and complementary, correcting market failures rather than directly controlling market interactions. The focus has moved from "getting prices right" to "getting institutions right" in order to address market and government failures. The new institutional economics (see chapter 9), including the 2009 Economics Nobel Prize winners, have demonstrated the importance of reducing transaction costs, strengthening contract enforcement, and improving property rights (both private and communal). Given the long lag times for institutional changes to be debated, enacted, and finally begin to take effect, it will be some time before a final judgment can be made on the accuracy and effectiveness of the current development model.

Political Economics

Political economics can refer to the application of the tools of economic analysis to politics, or more generally to economists' policy advice. It is closely related to political science, though the tool sets and biases of the disciplines differ, with political economics focusing more on self-interested individual behavior, and political science more on institutions and group dynamics. Political scientists are more likely to make use of qualitative and comparative methods than economists, for instance. The use of economic tools to study political science topics is generally called "public choice theory" by economists and "positive political theory" by political scientists. Sociologists, public administration professionals, and philosophers also contribute to the field. For ease we will use the more generic term, political economics, throughout the book.

In political economics, government agents are assumed to have some objective they are attempting to maximize (e.g., citizen welfare, lobbying contributions, government legitimacy, length of term in office) subject to various political and economic constraints. Governments and public-sector agencies attempt to improve food security and nutrition for ideological, humanitarian, economic, or political reasons, including maintaining legitimacy, stability, and political power. Even when these rationales provide the initial impetus for policy formation, however, individual policies are amended during the policymaking process. Bureaucrats and politicians likely have their own, conflicting goals and objectives that may or may not be compatible with improved food security and nutrition, yet play an important role in the formulation of food and nutrition-related policies and programs. Different institutional arrangements and their effects on policy outcomes can be studied. Doing so explains the divergence between economic prescription and actual governmental practice. For a more political science approach to these questions, the reader is referred to Grindle and Thomas (1991).

Contemporary political economy models incorporate various assumptions about agent behavior and the institutions with which they interact. The origin of this type of political economy analysis can be traced back to the work of Downs (1957) on voter and politician behavior. Other influential foundational theories of political economy include the theories of Buchanan and Tullock (1962) on supply and demand of government policies; Olson's (1965) work on pressure groups; the theory of rent-seeking (Krueger 1974); the theory of directly unproductive profit-seeking activities (Bhagwati 1982); and Stigler's (1971) and Peltzman's (1976) theory of regulation. Literally thousands of books have been written on the political economy of agriculture.

Numerous studies apply political economy models to food and agricultural policy. Lobby group models explain, for example, why agricultural protection increases with per capita income: when the country is richer, there will be fewer farmers, and so there are lower costs to organizing, and larger and more uniform farm size, making lobbying more effective (e.g., Gardner 1987; Bates 1987; Krueger 1996). Baldwin (1985) uses a voter model to argue that the political equilibrium will favor free trade if the information is freely available and complete, there are no voting costs, and decisions are made by majority vote. Relaxing one of these conditions shifts the political equilibrium toward protectionism. Protectionist agricultural trade policies are argued to be the result of voting costs (Mayer 1984), imperfect information among voters (Magee, Brock, and Young 1989), and proportional voting (Hillman 1982). Other food and agricultural policy issues, such as why governments employ inefficient policy instruments in agriculture and why there appears to be a status quo bias, have been addressed within the political economy modeling framework (see De Gorter and Swinnen 2002, for a summary).

In parallel with the concept of market failure is that of government failure (Isani 1982). Government failure occurs when government intervention—or lack of it—makes the situation worse. It is not merely failing to produce utopian conditions, but a systemic problem that prevents efficient outcomes. Government failure is a relatively new concept taken up in new institutional economics and political economy (chapter 9). Examples of such failures include public spending crowding out private investment; rent-seeking activities; market distortions; unintended negative consequences (including environmental damage, adverse distributional effects, lower economic growth, and driving business activities "underground"); and the governance failures discussed at length in chapter 9. Causes of government failure include lobbying, capture of regulatory agencies by those they are meant to regulate, self-interested behavior on the part of public servants, poor institutional development and lack of government capacity, imperfect information, and short time horizons related to election cycles or the threat of extraconstitutional regime change.

Government food policy can also originate from response to the demands of organized stakeholder groups (defined in the next section). Governments are made up of a number of legislative and executive institutions, staffed by people who have specific powers and goals of their own and influenced by interest groups they either represent or to whom they are sympathetic. Policies brought forward may deal with efficiency or social welfare issues, or they may not.

The opportunity to lobby for a share of the rents created by policies can alter the shape of the proposed food policy as it moves toward implementation. Formally organized lobbyists are often successful in doing so because the gains from lobbying are concentrated while the costs are dispersed over a large number of consumers or producers so that opposition is rarely well organized. Market distortions resulting from food price subsidies, government interventions, food and agricultural marketing, foreign trade regulations, food stamp programs, and various types of social programs are examples of food- and nutrition-related government action that generates opportunities for economic rents. Basically, any time there is an opportunity for the government to determine how benefits will be distributed, there will be an opportunity for economic rents and incentives for organized groups to lobby for a larger share.

Economic rents may be distributed to a group directly or indirectly. Rents can be channeled indirectly by granting firms or groups exclusive rights to production or distribution of regulated goods. Transfer programs may increase political support for the government by the recipients. This gives governments an incentive to target transfers to groups from whom they need support, rather than groups most in need. In fact, increasing legitimacy may be one of the primary impetuses in the government's choice, design, and implementation of programs. An example of this was seen during the 2007–2008 food price swings during which several countries prioritized transfers to urban nonpoor consumers who threatened food riots and disrupted government legitimacy, even though the net food-buying rural poor had greater need.

Particularly in comparison to organized lobbying groups, individuals and households may have little influence on policy formulation. However, it is their participation and use of the system that will determine how successful government programs are. Particularly when households act in concert—whether acting collaboratively on purpose or not—they can wield enormous influence. Wolf (1990) suggests four types of power possessed by individuals: personal power, power of persuasion, power over group behavior, and power to change structures. Examples of these four levels of power in the food system include the buying behavior of individual consumers (personal power); individuals' attempts to convince others to buy organic food, to become vegetarian, or to avoid certain supermarkets (power of persuasion); the starting of or joining in consumer organizations through which power may be effective in changing food safety regulations (power over group behavior); and collective action to force governments to improve food system infrastructure (power to change structures). Case 3-4 suggests that the following characteristics lead to successful influence over the policy process: (1) relevancy; (2) correct timing; (3) stakeholder involvement; (4) credible information; (5) high degree of publicity; (6) good leadership; and (7) saliency relative to government goals (i.e., government political will).

Political Will: Government Priorities

One of the big frustrations confronting food policy advocates is the apparent low priority given by developing country governments to action aimed at reducing hunger and malnutrition. Watson (2009) measures the political will to reduce hunger in developing countries and finds that only a few countries demonstrate significant commitment and that commitment mechanisms are correlated with actualized reductions in hunger. Heaver (2005) identifies a number of reasons for weak government commitment to improve nutrition, many of which apply to other food system problems:

1. Micronutrient deficiencies may be invisible to malnourished families and communities so they do not advocate for nutrition programs.
2. When they do advocate, they may have little political voice (chapter 9).
3. Families and governments do not recognize the human and economic costs of malnutrition, underestimate the benefits of nutrition programs, or overestimate the costs of nutrition programs—a failure of cost-benefit analysis.
4. Governments may not know that other interventions can combat malnutrition more rapidly than economic growth and poverty reduction.
5. There are multiple organizational stakeholders in nutrition, each with their own agenda. This increases the costs of collective action.
6. It also means that there is not always a consensus about how to intervene, increasing the costs of collective action and weakening the effect of signals sent by policy advocates.
7. Adequate nutrition is seldom treated as a human right (chapter 11).
8. Some politicians and civil servants are not interested in whether nutrition programs are implemented well—it is enough that they are perceived as doing something, whether or not concrete results appear (chapter 11).
9. Governments sometimes believe they are sufficiently investing in improving nutrition when they are not.
10. Lack of commitment to nutrition leads to underinvestment in nutrition, which leads to weak impact, thus reinforcing lack of commitment (feedback effects).
11. Other serious problems may be perceived as requiring more immediate attention for limited financial resources and bureaucratic capacity.

Stakeholder Analysis

Stakeholder analysis is an important methodology used in political economic analysis and throughout the cases that support this book. Glicken (2000, 307) defines a stakeholder as "an individual or a group influenced by—and with an ability to significantly impact (either directly or indirectly)—the topical area of interest." Welp (2000, 9) identifies a stakeholder as someone who is affected by or responsible for an issue, "has knowledge or perspectives needed to develop good solutions or strategies, and/or . . . has the power and resources to block or implement solutions or strategies." This second definition is preferred because it includes anyone who is affected by policy, not only those who can significantly influence policy, so that it empowers underrepresented citizens. It also expresses the view of stakeholder dialogue as being a two-way flow of knowledge and information rather than merely a top-down process.

Stakeholders may be individuals, organizations, or unorganized groups. In most cases, food system stakeholders fall into one or more of the following categories: international actors (e.g., donors, international NGOs); political decision makers; public sector agencies (e.g., ministries, bureaucracies); organized interest groups; commercial/private for-profit firms ranging from part-time household shops to multinational corporations; nonprofit organizations; civil society organizations; farmers; workers; and consumers. These groups are themselves seldom homogeneous: vegetarian consumers have different policy preferences than meat consumers, farm laborers differ from urban factory laborers, and gender roles and household demographics alter farming interests, to name only a few types of subgroups. Exactly which mix of stakeholders needs to be included in policy analysis is context specific.

Stakeholder analysis involves gathering and analyzing qualitative and quantitative data about the people who have a "stake," or an interest, in the policy under consideration (Schmeer 2000; World Bank 2006a). Stakeholder analysis clarifies the microfoundations of the political economy and helps identify groups and individuals who should be incorporated in the decision-making process. It should therefore identify what stakeholders want, how influential they are, how interested they are, the group(s) to which they belong and how those groups interact, what impact the policy would have on stakeholders, how and why stakeholders' positions differ, ways to bring about greater consensus among stakeholders, and how to accommodate minority needs and rights (World Bank 2009). This information signals the capability a stakeholder has to block or promote a policy, join with others to form a coalition of support or opposition, and lead the direction of the policy. Knowing these facts enables policymakers to choose how to best accommodate the various stakeholders so that policies adopted are politically realistic and sustainable. Because stakeholders and their positions change over time, stakeholder analysis should be ongoing, allowing policies to adjust (World Bank 2009).

Readers interested in developing their stakeholder-analysis tool kit further are referred to Gomes (2007) on stakeholder analysis in local government; Batte's (2010) application of stakeholder analysis to agricultural development and ICT in Uganda; or Hajer and Wagenaar (2003) on governance networks and deliberative policy analysis. The business literature also contains many examples of stakeholder analysis.

In neoclassical political economy theory, stakeholders take an active role in policymaking if they expect that their influence on policy decisions will bring greater benefits than the costs of the effort. Agents differ in the timing of their interventions, their degree of access and influence, and the expected benefits and costs. Analysts must understand how each agent fits into the institutional, social, and political structure in order to come up with and promote feasible, effective recommendations.

Stakeholders favor policies for altruistic or more selfish reasons, ranging from broad notions of social justice (based on environmental arguments, religious or ethical principles, or consumer safety and awareness concerns) to their own monetary or political benefit. Lobbying groups may contain both types of stakeholders: grocery stores have promoted taxes on plastic bags alongside environmentalists in order to lower their costs, higher consumer-safety standards have been pursued by large corporations trying to reduce competition by increasing other firms' costs, and biotechnology is promoted by those interested in increasing production in developing countries as well as those who have invested heavily in it. Self-interested behavior by politicians, bureaucrats, and other political actors is also an important factor. It is interesting to note that whether the people requesting a policy change are referred to as "lobbyists" and "interest groups" or as "stakeholders" often depends on one's sympathy with the group in question rather than on objective criteria.

Food Policy in the Global Food System

The global food system includes highly diverse producers and consumers who are connected by social networks, including markets, which function in micro, macro, and international contexts. Often in developing countries these markets fail to operate efficiently, leading to a suboptimal allocation of scarce resources and/or distribution of costs and benefits that do not meet society's goals. Feedback mechanisms in the food system can amplify efficiency losses in one or more areas. By influencing the decision-making environment of food producers, consumers, and marketing agents, food policy interventions can improve market efficiency and achieve policy goals. Poorly designed policies can also make these problems worse or introduce new challenges. This is more likely when the effects of policies in one sector on another are not taken into account (e.g., the effects of biofuel policies on food prices).

Though different countries will rank these goals higher or lower depending on circumstance and history, food system goals include ensuring food security for all; improving and sustaining human health through food availability, safety, and quality; generating dignified employment, livelihoods, and income for farmers, transportation workers, processors, and retailers; realizing human rights; preserving biodiversity and soil quality; preserving natural beauty; and safeguarding animal welfare. There is both a short- and long-term focus in these goals. Short-run food policies intend to provide immediate solutions to problems such as hunger, malnutrition, and unsafe food. In the long run, policies attempt to ensure future food supply and access, employment, agricultural sustainability, and development.

In order to accomplish these goals, the food system needs to be efficient in the sense of generating desired quantities and qualities of these goals for the lowest cost possible, but efficiency is seen here as a means to accomplish these other ends rather than a goal in itself. From an efficiency perspective, the rationale for food policy intervention is the existence of market failures, which occur as a result of either external costs and benefits or suboptimal market structures.[1] As enumerated earlier, distributional, ethical, and purely political goals also prompt food policy interventions, often to the detriment of narrowly defined efficiency. This section discusses the main arguments that support food policy interventions from an efficiency or welfare perspective.

The Need for Public Goods

Pure public goods are nonrival and nonexclusive, meaning that once available, it is impossible to prevent anybody from consuming them (nonexclusive) and that one person's consumption does not diminish another's opportunity to consume (nonrival). In practice, most public goods fill these definitions only partially: roads are the classic example of public goods, but congestion can make roads rival and toll stations can exclude people from using the road. To the extent that certain goods are nonrival and nonexclusive, private firms cannot limit the use of them to only those who are willing to pay, and are therefore unlikely to produce sufficient quantities of public goods. This is not from mean-spiritedness. They simply will not be able to capture enough economic benefits to justify and afford the full investment. In some cases, it may be necessary to provide subsidies or have government or civil society provide certain public goods.

In the food system, public goods needed for efficiency reasons include roads and irrigation infrastructure, institutions and regulatory systems, environmental protection, and some types of agricultural research. Domestic food markets simply cannot function effectively in the absence of reasonable levels of infrastructure, commonly agreed-on standards and measurements, and a well-functioning legal system that, among other things, will assure enforcement of contracts and property rights. Hence, without these public goods in developing countries, globalization, markets, and economic development are unlikely to achieve society's goals. Investments in public goods may also be required to achieve welfare and distributional goals, as feeder roads and public agricultural research have been shown to significantly reduce poverty (cases 9-1, 9-2). These themes are addressed in chapters 6, 7, 8, and 9.

Externalities

In some cases, the full costs and benefits of some goods are not reflected in the costs paid or returns captured by the immediate participants. The result is either under- or overprovision of the good. Environmental degradation and health problems from inappropriate farming, processing, or storage techniques are chief among food system externality concerns. The decision makers do not bear the full costs of their actions, so market prices do not factor them in. Similarly, the social benefits from food system activities that preserve biodiversity and natural resources, or that produce additional health spillovers, are not remitted to farmers to incentivize these innovations. The loss of nutrients from soil degradation affects not only the farmer working the land but generations of farmers who own the land later as well.

Without food policy that deals with these externalities through interventions that incorporate environmental and health costs into private costs, the global food system will not be sustainable. Chapters 3 and 4 discuss externalities from the costs of poor health and malnutrition (see also Behrman, Alderman, and Hoddinott 2004; Finkelstein, Fiebelkorn, and Wang 2003). Chapter 8 deals with the need for policies to realign market prices with societal benefits and costs so that markets can function efficiently.

Monitoring and, If Necessary, Regulating Market Power

Trends in the global food system have shown an increasing market concentration in input supply, processing, manufacturing, marketing, and retail. The increase in concentration by itself is of concern since it is one of the primary factors correlated with amassing market power and reducing competition. As firms gain market power, they may take actions that improve their profitability at the expense of other stakeholders, such as by reducing the prices paid to input providers (monopsony/oligopsony power), increasing the prices paid by consumers (monopoly/oligopoly power), capturing more political rents, or engaging in anticompetitive behaviors.

A precautionary approach to market regulation would prefer to keep market concentration ratios small to prevent the possibility of market power accumulation—let alone the exercise of market power—while a reactionary approach waits until there is evidence of wrongdoing before intervening. At heart are the questions of whether firms are presumed innocent until proven guilty or whether it is more efficient to prevent problems from arising in the first place (chapter 6). Concentration in international markets affects developing countries through trade, technology transfer, and foreign direct investment. With a small number of large food firms dominating the world food industry, farmers and other producers face increasingly stringent requirements for quantity, quality, timeliness, and traceability. Small producers, in particular, find these demands difficult to meet. Food policy may be needed to address these market distortions. The U.S. Government Accountability Office (GAO 2009) concluded that concentration in U.S. food sectors was widespread but had not yet led to a rise of market power, or that any such exercise had been offset by efficiency gains. It is also likely that the GAO has not accounted for the effects of concentration on environmental well-being or examined local market trends where concentration ratios are higher and potentially more problematic.[2]

Imperfect Information

People choose whether or not to take part in various programs and may act differently if they have chosen to join than if they had not. If a program—inadvertently or deliberately—encourages people with particular negative traits to join more than people with offsetting positive traits, *adverse selection* occurs. For example, people who are most at risk of a loss are more likely to purchase insurance than low-risk, low-loss people, and the poorest people have more incentive to join a wealth-sharing system than the richest. The program itself may further incentivize negative behaviors, creating a *moral hazard* problem. If wealth or other rewards for work are distributed according to criteria other than the amount produced by a person, the incentives to work are reduced and may lead to shirking and decreased societal welfare. Once insured, a person may choose riskier behaviors, such as not exercising, or a farmer might not give livestock needed preventative medical care. These problems of imperfect and asymmetric information typically lead rural markets to fail to deliver insurance, credit, management, and supervision at optimal levels. Policy interventions may reduce or exacerbate these problems, as discussed in chapter 7.

Transaction Costs

Transaction costs are the costs related to carrying out transactions, including finding a buyer or a seller (search costs), negotiating a price, and obtaining payment; and costs related to risks, including the risks of being cheated (chapter 6). Eifert, Gelb, and Ramachandran (2007) estimate that, for the average firm in eighteen developing countries, marketing and transaction costs amount to 10–30 percent of the total costs of doing business. Governments can play an essential role in minimizing transaction costs by establishing and enforcing standardized weights and measures, constructing market-necessary public goods, promoting quality education, and ensuring the legal structure is fair, available, and predictable. Governments also engender transaction costs, such as the costs of negotiating and paying bribes, complying with regulations, and engaging in the political or legal systems (e.g., lobbying).

It has often been observed that large firms have an easier time responding to government regulations that involve fixed investment costs because they have a greater volume of product over which to spread the costs of compliance. Thus regulations have sometimes been blamed for the increasing market concentration as smaller firms are pushed out of the market because of the costs of complying with environmental, food quality, or food safety standards. The likely impacts on food market structure should be included in the analyses of proposed food policies.

Egalitarian Concerns

Most people, and hence most governments, share a concern for the least fortunate. In addition, many people are concerned when income distribution is very unequal. Some food policies are enacted in response to these concerns as well, such as providing food stamps or cash transfers (perhaps conditional on enrolling children in schooling, attending health classes, or for other desired behaviors). Income redistribution can be thought of as occurring either ex ante relative to production (i.e., before we know market outcomes) through asset redistribution or providing public health and education, or ex post (after the fact) through systems of taxes and subsidies. In a dynamic system, however, every transfer "after the fact" comes before the facts that will occur in the next period and so the distinction blurs. Neglecting the dynamic nature of the food system can lead analysts to forget the disincentive effects of redistribution.

A certain degree of inequality may naturally occur in a system that accomplishes society's other goals efficiently and where further redistribution would reduce society's ability to accomplish its other goals. In the case where there are efficiency gains from income redistribution—such as by improving the health and education of the poorest, resulting in increased production and economic spillovers throughout the economy—policy interventions can achieve political feasibility either if there are no losers or if compensation of losers by gainers can be managed. But when efficiency losses occur during the redistribution process, the political feasibility depends on the relative political power of gainers and losers. Identifying the incidence and magnitude of these gains and losses is fundamental to the success of implementing this type of food policy. These themes are further developed in chapters 5, 9, and 11.

Thus far the discussion has treated society's goals as if they were just one, fixed set of universally shared goals. As with models of a single-minded government, much can be gained by relaxing this assumption. Different stakeholders give each goal a different weight, and will often disagree on whether a goal should be pursued by society or through the instrumentality of government. Chapter 11 deals further with some of these ethical questions. The more the goals of individuals within a society differ, the more government policies are likely to be fractured and working at cross-purposes as different parts of government respond to the demands of different stakeholders. In more homogeneous societies, political processes will run more smoothly.

How Do Governments Intervene?

Food markets alone probably cannot achieve some important food policy goals. Without the support of needed public goods such as clear property and contract laws and legal structures that ensure equality under the law, they certainly cannot. As stated by the World Bank (2007b, xv): "Policy matters. The right domestic and international policies, sustained over long periods, have the power to raise incomes around the world. . . . Whether the underlying growth rates are low or high, the dynamics underpinning any likely scenario will generate stresses that require policy attention today." Governments have essential roles to play in ensuring that markets function in accordance with stakeholder goals and in striving to achieve them.

Food policy interventions can be divided into three types: policies that specifically regulate in a "command and control" style; policies that adjust incentives but neither proscribe nor prescribe particular behaviors; and policies that educate the public about their choices, but otherwise do not change incentives. Which variety of intervention is needed will depend on the problem to be solved, the market failures present, the risk of government failure, how precisely advisers can identify the correct action(s) to be taken, and the complexity of the subject. In general, the greater the risk of government failure and the greater the complexity of the subject, the more desirable it is for government to use a light hand; while the more certain it is that very specific action is required and the more pervasive market failures are, the more likely it is that direct regulation will be preferable.

Naturally, there are a variety of methods for each of these types of intervention and the lines dividing them are sometimes unclear. Conditional cash transfers that require a family attend health classes and send children to school in order to gain access to money have elements of all three. It is possible to tax a behavior so heavily that there is little difference between an economic incentive and an outright regulation prohibiting the activity. Incentive-adjusting policies can include not only money or in-kind transfers but also provision of additional services, perks, or other social benefits. Education may be formalized through classes or consist of advertising that is incorporated into public radio or television programming or delivered through handouts.

Interventions at the micro level need to take account of production, distribution, and consumption. Where hunger is widespread, it may be tempting to focus all efforts on increasing production. Ensuring that consumers have access to the food being produced and the income to purchase it, however, are also necessary conditions (World Bank 1987). On a global scale, the world produces enough food to feed everyone if it were distributed according to need. This does not remove the necessity of policies to increase production so that farmers can lift themselves out of poverty and reduce the need for transporting food to distant areas. As the world population continues to grow, increasing productivity continues to be important.

Individual differences and social and cultural contexts should be very important determinants of food policies at both macro and micro levels. For example, poor consumers may favor improved food security over higher food safety levels while wealthy consumers who may take their food security for granted clamor for increased food safety. The World Bank (1987) further identifies as difficulties at the micro level the problems that "small farmers may have more difficulty integrating into the supply chain than large ones; extension work may be directed toward men and not reach women, who are often the major food producers, especially in Africa; and the dynamics of decision making, time allocation, food distribution and nutrition status may be vitally different" among households and even within households. All these differences should be taken into account if sound food policy is to be designed.

Macroeconomic Policies and the Food System

Food systems analysts have focused primarily on the microeconomics of the food system. Timmer, Falcon, and Pearson (1983) recognized that the failure of traditional food policy to deal effectively with hunger, despite increasing world food availability, reflects a failure to understand the direct and indirect causes of hunger and their complex relationships in the food system. They proposed that macroeconomic policies that affect the food system should be integrated into policy analyses of a country's food system.

Two of the first attempts to integrate the agricultural sector into macroeconomic models of the economy were Lewis (1954) and Jorgenson (1961). In their dualistic economy, the agricultural sector is large relative to the more dynamic nonagricultural sector. The profitability of investment in the nonagricultural sector, and therefore the prospects for further investment and growth of the system, are dependent in part on the agricultural wage level. The implication was that agricultural wages should be kept low so that food for the urban population could be cheaper and investments in urban areas would increase.

Many countries followed this recipe for development, only to find rapidly increasing unemployment in urban areas. Harris and Todaro (1970) extended the earlier model to demonstrate that urban unemployment and mass urbanization are results of expected higher wages in urban areas than in rural areas. The solution in such an economy lies in rural, agricultural development: as conditions in rural areas improve, there is less incentive to move to urban areas, decreasing population and poverty pressure there.

These early efforts demonstrate that the agricultural sector in a predominantly rural, low-income society is much more than a collection of specific markets, villages, and farmers. It is a vitally important sector whose success or failure affects the success or failure of overall development. A brief and intuitive depiction of the macro/agricultural linkages is summarized in table 2.2.

Foreign exchange rates, inflation, governance structures (chapter 9), and interest rates affect the costs of investing in agriculture and the returns. Krueger, Schiff, and Valdes (1988) critically demonstrated that most developing countries' macroeconomic policies were significantly biased against agriculture, a finding supported in an update and revision by Anderson (2010): nonagricultural policies were three times as harmful to agriculture as were direct agricultural policies. Food price instability in the mid-1980s was three times higher than it would have been under free trade. Exports were taxed a portion of their foreign currency earnings, reducing the effective price farmers could receive for their products by 30 percent.

One tool of political economic theory that is readily applicable is the notion of a policy preference function. The basic insight is that governments must weight demands from competing stakeholders in order to resolve disputes. Observing policy outcomes gives the analyst information about how strongly governments weight the welfare of different groups. For instance, the policies discussed by Krueger, Schiff, and Valdes (1988) and Anderson (2010) showed that governments valued urban

TABLE 2.2.
Backward and Forward Linkages

Backward linkages: The agricultural sector provides the rest of the economy:	Forward linkages: The macro economy affects the agricultural sector through:
Food	Inflation rates
Manpower and materials	Interest rates
An internal market for domestic products	Wage rates
A source of saving and investment	Trade regimes
Foreign exchange earnings	Taxation and fiscal policies

Sources: Authors' extrapolation from data obtained by Johnston and Mellor (1961) and Glassburner (1985).

stakeholder interests more than the interests of rural stakeholders, but that this bias has decreased over time. An early example of this can be found in Rausser and Freebairn (1974), who examine U.S. beef trade and the trade-off between producer profits and consumer welfare, finding a much larger concern with the welfare of producers than consumers. Other examples include Wahl, Hayes, and Schmitz (1992) on Japanese beef policy, and Oehmke and Yao (1990) on U.S. wheat policy. Bullock (1994) provides important caveats.

Macroeconomic Stability Policies

Since the 1980s, there has been an increased focus on improving macroeconomic stability by reducing fiscal imbalances and inflation. Donor austerity programs from 1980 to 2003 reduced the average developing country's debt/export ratio from 157 percent to 90 percent, while the amount of money required to service debt fell from 330 percent to 72 percent of available reserves (World Bank 2004). Reducing the antiagricultural, trade-distorting macroeconomic policies increased global economic welfare by $233 billion per year, with more going to developing countries than developed (Valenzuela, van der Mensbrugghe, and Anderson 2009). Further reforms could net an additional $168 billion per year, two-thirds of which would accrue to developing countries. Farm incomes are roughly 5 percent higher than they would have been without these reforms (ibid.). Though these accomplishments and others have surely placed developing countries in a stronger position to weather unfavorable shifts in international finances, Hazell et al. (2007) echo concerns that austerity programs may have reduced governments' capacity to effectively govern and enact the programs and reforms that are needed to generate and sustain long-term economic growth. Kargbo (2000) shows that removal of government supports has increased food price volatility and food prices in many countries (chapters 6 and 7).

Macroeconomic policies often have unintended consequences for the food system, and vice versa. Many countries have followed an overvalued exchange rate policy in order to provide cheaper, imported food for urban workers to keep industrial wages low. Overvalued exchange rates make domestic farmers less competitive relative to foreign imports and make it more difficult for farmers to export their crops, so that agricultural output and employment decline. This reduces the value of land so that the farmers that remain have less wealth and less ability to raise capital, placing them at a further disadvantage—an amplifying linkage. Both landholders and landless agricultural workers are made worse off by overvalued exchange rates. In a seminal paper, Schuh (1974) demonstrated that if applied agricultural research is publicly available, the overvalued exchange rate can encourage land-enhancing, laborsaving technological adoption, which may partially or completely offset the negative pressures from the exchange rate. This process transfers wealth to landholders, encourages growth in average farm size, and reduces wages or increases unemployment for landless farmworkers.

Though it is clear that food prices are partially determined by exchange rates, money supply, and trade policies, it is an empirical question whether the combination of macro and sectoral policies in any given country are beneficial to agriculture

(Kargbo 2000). In Schuh's (1974) U.S. case study, the government simultaneously reduced direct agricultural subsidies and supported land conservation programs to artificially increase the value of land, supporting technological adoption and adaptation. These offsetting policies shared the fruits of technological progress between consumers and landowners. Cheng and Orden (2007) find that India's overvaluation taxed agriculture between 1985 and 1992, while China's undervaluation in 1999–2001 had a larger positive effect than its overvaluation in 1995–1998. Orden (2002) summarizes much of the literature on the effects of exchange rates on U.S. agriculture.

If the problem is overvaluation, devaluation is the cure. However, the short-run effects of devaluations may be very harmful for consumers. Devaluations make imports more expensive, increasing food prices and decreasing consumer purchasing power in countries such as Malawi (case 7-1) and Zambia (case 9-8). Since most low-income farmers in sub-Saharan Africa (SSA) are net food buyers, they tend to be worse off in the short run. As African countries rectified their overvalued currencies in the mid-1990s, hunger tended to increase in many countries, although the reforms in Zambia managed to stabilize the prevalence of hunger for the first time since independence.

In the medium to long term, however, liberalization of exchange rates and the trade system has provided many benefits. In Uganda, which also significantly reduced the level of inflation, agricultural production increased from 5.2 percent per year to 6.9 percent, and their exports became more diversified (case 9-1, also case 9-8 for Zambia). This growth brought many people out of poverty and hunger and prepared a solid foundation for future economic growth. Lachaal and Womack (1998) conclude that, had Canada reduced its budget deficit and encouraged greater price stability, its volume of trade would have increased 3 percent and agricultural prices would have been 8 percent higher.

Sri Lanka's liberalizations in 1978 included depreciating the currency and letting it float, eliminating or reducing price controls, increasing credit access, reducing import monopolies, reducing taxes, establishing free-trade zones, and targeting the remaining subsidies and tariffs to pro-poor sectors. GDP grew by more than 5 percent over the next five years compared with 1.8 percent in the previous decade. Unemployment fell rapidly. Sahn and Edirisinghe (1993) point out, however, that much of this may be due to the previous government's focus on supplying basic human needs and that the bottom quartile of the income distribution saw a decrease in their calorie consumption during the first five years of the liberalizations.

Panagariya (2005, 18) attributes the brief period of particularly high growth in India in the late 1980s to the liberalization of imports and depreciation of the exchange rate. He also argues that "a key message of the theory of distortions is that the larger the initial distortion, the greater the benefit from its relaxation at the margin." Thus it can be expected that liberalizations and deregulations will tend to have larger effects the larger the original distortion. These liberalizations have been highly controversial in India because the benefits of growth have not been equally shared.

These examples underline the importance of anticipating the effects of macro policies on agriculture and preparing safety nets and/or complementary policies that will mitigate the difficulties during transition periods without sacrificing the gains to be made in the longer term. Prior investments in education, health, roads and other infrastructure, and research and development will make it possible for the poor to gain more from reforms. Snell and Infanger (1991) discuss how extension agents can help farmers cope with macroeconomic policy changes.

Monetary Policies

In addition to exchange rate policies, monetary policies and inflation impact the food system. There is conflicting evidence on whether agricultural prices adjust more rapidly to inflation than nonagricultural prices. If the degree of price stickiness is different between commodities, even modest inflation can cause changes in real price ratios, making the more responsive commodities temporarily more expensive. High inflation hurts the poor, farmers, and the elderly more than other groups because savings are rapidly depleted and farmers receive income only at harvesttimes.

High inflation expectations can also spur speculative hoarding or encourage governments to block exports, as seen in the 2007–2008 food price hikes. World rice prices did not begin to skyrocket until India and Vietnam enacted export restrictions on rice, leading the Philippines to hoard it. This occurred without a significant shock to the availability of rice. Similarly, droughts in Russia and expectations of lower wheat production in 2010 caused the Russian government to stop wheat exports. The result was large international wheat price fluctuations.

Mozambique policy reforms to reduce inflation increased investment and exports, increasing GDP growth from 0.1 percent to 8.4 percent and decreasing the number of hungry people by one million during the 1990s (World Bank 2004). Vietnam's efforts to curb hyperinflation, invest in infrastructure, and reform property rights succeeded in cutting the poverty rate from 58 percent to 37 percent between 1993 and 1999 and reducing the number of hungry people by 7 million (ibid.). On the other hand, Brazil and South Africa have yet to see significant growth accelerations from their macroeconomic stability programs.

There are two theories of how the money supply and agricultural prices interact. The structuralist theory assumes that the money supply passively reacts to accommodate price level changes. The monetarist theory gives the monetary authority a more active role, assuming that if it did not increase the money supply when agricultural prices rose, aggregate demand would go down leading to a recession. To prevent this, the monetary authority injects more money into the economy, causing increased inflation but a stable demand system.

Barnett, Bessler, and Thompson (1983) analyzed which of these theories was more accurate for the food price crisis of the 1970s. Other studies had already demonstrated a correlation between the U.S. dollar devaluation and the food price spike, but could not determine whether it was the increase in the money supply that led to the dollar devaluation or if the food price spike led to an increase in the money supply. This study found that changes in the U.S. money supply two years before had led to significantly higher food prices, but that food price increases did not change the money supply, giving credence to the monetarist theory. Barnhart (1989) additionally finds that unanticipated increases in the money supply lower agricultural prices, consistent with an expectation that the monetary authority will tighten monetary policy. Baek and Koo (2008, 73) find that high exchange rates "may induce strong pressure for market interventions and thus undermine farm policy liberalization."

Other Macroeconomic Linkages

Tax and subsidy policies affect the food system by changing the relative prices of land, capital, and inputs; altering production incentives; changing food consumption patterns; and changing the returns to investment and technology adoption (Rausser et al. 1986). These effects may spill over into other countries. Policy analysis needs to take account of the differential effects feasible taxes can have on heterogeneous groups of people.

Policies that do not hamper farmer incentives are necessary but insufficient to bring about continued production increases by themselves. A thriving agricultural sector requires macrolevel public goods, such as infrastructure, more efficient technologies, and reliable water supplies (chapter 7). Ellinger and Tirupattur (2009) discuss how the 2007–2009 global financial crisis impacted agricultural production through credit access, agribusiness, and commodity markets. Research into locally adapted agricultural technologies is also vital to increase production and to reduce costs in the long run.

Many food policy interventions will only be as effective as the price transmission mechanisms in food markets. Without access to distant markets that can absorb excess local supply and knowledge about the prices offered in those markets, policy aimed at adopting more productive agricultural technologies typically can lead to a drop in farm-gate product prices, erasing all or many of the gains to producers from technological change, and reducing the number of farmers. It will often be the poorest farmers who were the latest to adopt new technologies who are forced out of the market. Just as infrastructure is necessary for farmers to access distant markets, low price transmission due to poorly functioning rural infrastructure and institutions may make policies to, for example, increase export prices irrelevant for farmers (chapters 6 and 7).

Mesolevel Policies and the Food System

Not only do macroeconomic policies affect the food system; policies in other sectors of the economy can also have important influences. Mesolevel policies may directly or indirectly tax agriculture relative to other sectors of the economy, decreasing the incentives to invest in increasing agricultural production.[3] Primary mesolevel policies include input markets, labor and wage laws, trade policies, migration, financial sector development, transportation and communication, and energy infrastructure. Input markets are directly linked to the food sector (chapter 7). The importance of microcredit and financing is discussed in chapters 5 and 7. International trade policies are covered in more detail in chapter 10.

Many countries have enacted a set of policies referred to as import-substitution industrialization (ISI). By overvaluing the exchange rate and tightly regulating imports, urban wages are kept low and competition with the manufacturing sector is reduced while encouraging local production of substitutes for regulated imports. It is hoped that by doing this domestic businesses will flourish and be prepared to compete with other firms outside the country when restrictions are lifted. ISI strongly biases country policies against agriculture, leading to stagnant rural growth in any country that had not simultaneously enacted countervailing measures. Resnik and Thurlow (case 9-8) point out that ISI can be very fiscally draining on a national budget. When copper prices collapsed, Zambia could not keep up the sectoral support. Jansen (1991) indicates that Zambia's policies had reduced agricultural output by 30 percent per year. Care needs to be taken in unraveling inefficient policies to ensure that the people left behind have other opportunities to support their families.

Labor market conditions strongly affect the food system. Farm wage rates are to a large extent determined by nonfarm wage rates (Gardner 1981). This is the case even if minimum wage laws or unions are not present in rural areas. When wages are higher in cities, people will leave rural areas and agriculture to seek out those jobs until farm wages rise sufficiently. If this moves surplus agricultural labor into areas with labor shortages, this can increase welfare broadly. Raising minimum wages can also reduce welfare if it results in high levels of urban unemployment and decreased rural food production.

Food policy interventions at micro, meso, and macro levels should be complementary to each other. World Bank (1987, 2) draws an analogy

> between the nutritional status of an individual and the food sector of a society. An individual with marginally inadequate food intake cannot build up reserves of energy and other nutrients to resist a crisis. Such an individual is thus vulnerable to infectious disease or variations in seasonal food availability, both of which can precipitate severe malnutrition. Similarly, a society in which a substantial proportion of the population receives only a marginal food intake is vulnerable to the food shortage and high prices resulting from a poor crop or an economic crisis. The result can be famine.

Food policy should therefore strive to prevent even marginal food deficiencies at household and national levels.

A Political Economy Analysis of Food Policy

Positive versus Normative and Endogenous Policy Analysis

Policy analysis tends to focus either on what is (positive analysis) or what should be (normative analysis). Normative analysis requires identifying a specific goal (e.g., maximizing a social welfare function, minimizing pollution, minimizing costs) and then demonstrating the best way to go about accomplishing that goal. The best policy course to follow depends crucially on the goal. However, reasonable people may disagree about what the goal of food policy ought to be: reducing hunger today versus long-term food security, ensuring food production processes are environmentally stable versus increasing land productivity, or employing the most workers versus increasing worker productivity.

In order to increase perceptions of its relevance and generalizability, economists and other scientists have tended to promote their work as positive sciences. Examples of positive analysis include identifying the impacts of alternative interventions, performing descriptive analysis, and modeling a process in order to predict out-of-sample outcomes. Ostensibly, the results are value free in the sense that the analyst is not advocating a particular policy, only describing what is or would be. However, the choice of what questions will be considered and what methods are deemed appropriate have important underlying effects on the outcomes of positive research.

Cost-benefit analysis is one example. On the face of it, cost-benefit analysis is a positive approach, tallying up the costs and benefits of a policy and comparing them. By comparing the ratio of benefits to costs for a range of policy options, analysts inform policymakers about which options are most efficient in producing desired benefits. This is one of the mainstays of applied policy analysis and is greatly in demand by governments, NGOs, and other employers of policy analysts. However, which costs and benefits are to be considered and how will they be weighted? Should the costs and benefits to future generations be included, and if so, how should they be weighted compared with the current generation? How should the costs and benefits to the environment be weighted compared to costs and benefits for human or animal stakeholders? A human rights ethic insists that trade-offs are not morally acceptable, which would make cost-benefit analysis inappropriate. But if a society does not have the resources to fulfill all human rights, or if a policy supports the attainment of rights for some stakeholders while reducing other stakeholders' capacity to meet their human rights, cost-benefit analysis can still be a useful tool. Positive and normative analysis and human rights are further considered in chapter 11. Campbell and Brown (2003) give practical examples to teach the methodology.

Another policy analysis dichotomy exists between exogenous and endogenous policy.[4] Exogenous policies are assumed to be simply imposed on a model society by an analyst. While convenient in dealing with analytical problems, assuming policies are exogenous is not always adequate, as it abstracts from the realities of politics. Since policies are the result of compromise, negotiation, and deal making between various stakeholder groups and policymakers, each with their own agendas, what emerges from the political process may bear little resemblance to the idealized exogenous policies considered by policy analysts. This perspective has given rise to the political economy view of public policy.

Presenting Food Policy Analysis to Policymakers

If food policy is largely determined by the expected payoffs for different social groups, then the main contribution of food policy analysis would be to identify these payoffs. This is technically demanding in part because policies have complex dynamic repercussions at all levels from individual welfare to macroeconomic aggregates. The political environment is influenced by political trade-offs and conflicting goals among stakeholders and parts of government, bureaucratic behavior and rent-seeking, and the demand of lobbies and pressure group politics.

Policy analysts rarely take explicit account of the policy environment. It is often assumed that public sector agencies behave as a monolithic entity that will adopt and implement food or nutrition-related policies either because they are cost-effective or out of a genuine concern for human welfare that overrides other policy goals.[5] When analysts' recommendations are not enacted, "politics" or a lack of "political will" is often blamed (Pinstrup-Andersen 2005b). Accounting for the different strategies, goals, and social norms of different public agencies will enable policy analysts to make more realistic, implementable, effective policy recommendations that are more likely to be adopted by policymakers.

Policymakers need information that is accurate, targeted, and holistic to guide food policies, particularly about what the costs and benefits of alternative policies are. Rather than focusing on aggregate costs and benefits, the distribution of those effects on different groups of people should become part of the policy analyst's arsenal, including not only beneficiaries but also groups that may support or oppose proposals. Ignoring conflicts among stakeholders or other related political economy aspects in analysis and advice may result in erroneous recommendations and policies to the detriment of the malnourished and other stakeholders. Furthermore, it will be frustrating for analysts whose recommendations are not taken up or are greatly altered because they ignored political realities.

In order for analysts' contributions to policy debates to be relevant, it is essential that they clearly present accurate, relevant, and comprehensive information on the issues and recommendations; take into account the political environment; and identify ways to mobilize external political support. Information on the extent and causes of food-related problems, the costs and benefits of possible treatments and policies, and the means of financing the "solutions" appeals to policymakers by allowing a grasp of the severity of the problem and the implications of alternative action or inaction. There is also a general consensus that policy prescriptions should be specific and direct. Policymakers often do not care about the refinements, caveats, concerns, weaknesses of methodology, and so forth, that interest academics. For a field to be successful in presenting needed interventions, consensus among practitioners is critical so that the message presented to policymakers is clear. Understanding the potential institutional or personal benefits of taking action can make it easier for policymakers to act. The outward appearance of policies is also important in gathering political support or defusing political opposition. For example, political support for in-kind transfers such as food stamps is likely to be broader than for pure cash transfers to households because households may be perceived as not spending the cash according to program objectives.

Gathering as broad a group as possible to pressure policymakers for needed change can be most beneficial. Coalitions can make the political or social consequences of inaction clear to decision makers and demonstrate that the resulting political support from action is broad based. For example, possible partners in a coalition to press for increased government action on nutrition for the poor include industry leaders who want to make additional sales, religious and private volunteer organizations that focus on the well-being of the poor, as well as the poor themselves. The more broad based the coalition, the greater are its powers of persuasion.

The politics of the policymaking process need to be incorporated into policy analysis. Policymakers take into account political and institutional considerations as well as economic, social, and ethical reasoning in designing and implementing policies and programs. Recommendations that do not take the political environment into account will almost certainly fail to be implemented in the manner described by analysts, not because they are wrong in a narrow technical or analytical sense, but because they are not feasible as constructed. Analysts also need to take into account the capacity of national and local governments to implement proposals and recommend ways to strengthen them where needed.

Policy and Program Implementation

A general critique that applies throughout the book is that perfectly well-designed policies and programs may fail because of faulty implementation. While certain policies may be successfully designed and implemented for a nation as a whole, most programs and some policies need to be tailored to the target communities. The question facing a government agency, NGO, or a private sector agent that has a small, successful program on their hands is whether and how it could be scaled up to reach more intended beneficiaries. This can be a very difficult process and is likely to fail unless the necessary space for context-specific elements and decision making is provided. A more detailed discussion is provided by Binswanger and Swaminathan (2003) and Marchione (1999).

Food system policies and programs are more likely to be effective and cost-effective if based on solid, relevant, timely information about the specific risks in specific cohorts, the causes, and impending changes. Early warning of impending problems such as droughts and floods resulting in local food shortages and poor sanitation, income shortfalls caused by abrupt increases in unemployment, infectious diseases, and a variety of other factors, is of critical importance to design and implement solutions in a timely fashion. International action against undernutrition is often caught in a vicious circle as well (figure 2.1).

Policy Trade-Offs

As illustrated throughout this book, there are ample food and nutrition interventions available to policymakers. However, identifying and committing to the most effective policy measures to address diverse issues is not an easy task. Stakeholder debate on which goal and approach to pursue is widespread and include such trade-offs as the relative importance of health versus food interventions, targeted versus nontargeted interventions, and supply-versus demand-side interventions. The most appropriate approach will vary across groups of intended beneficiaries and must be tailored to the circumstances. It does seem clear, however, first, that collaboration between sectors (e.g., food and health) is essential to achieve food system goals in a

FIGURE 2.1.
Core problems reducing the effectiveness of the international nutrition system. Source: Morris, Cogill, and Uauy 2008.

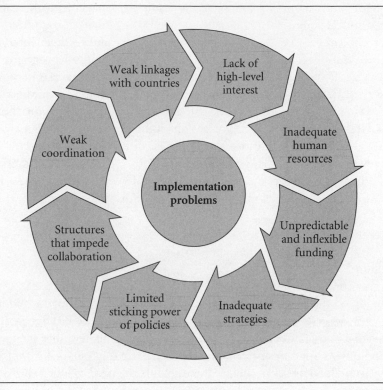

cost-effective manner; and second, that interventions should be implemented in an integrated way.

A key policy issue is how much to invest in indirect policies (such as women's education and many agricultural policies) that will take some time before the effects are noticeable but provide a more lasting solution, as opposed to more direct policies (such as micronutrient supplementation and conditional cash transfers) that will have an immediate effect but may not be financially sustainable. Should a government in a food-deficit country invest in rural infrastructure and productivity-increasing agricultural research that would provide a sustainable long-term food production increase beginning five to ten years from now? Or should the funds be spent on fertilizer subsidies that would increase food production next year but have no effect after that? The question of whether to pursue policies and programs that provide immediate solutions to existing problems but fail to be sustainable or never graduate from government support versus policies and programs that provide longer-term sustainable solutions but do not solve immediate problems is one of the most difficult issues facing government decision makers. It becomes an ethical question if viewed as a trade-off between the welfare of today's generation and the welfare of future generations. Do societies have a discount rate for current versus future deaths and current versus future health and nutrition problems? Although not usually explicit, such discount rates are implicit in many policy decisions. (See chapter 8 for similar issues related to natural resource management, and chapter 11 for related ethical issues.)

Policy choices also need to be made among direct and indirect interventions themselves (cases 3-4 and 3-5). Should food supplementation programs aim to solve shortages in dietary energy and protein or should the focus be on dealing with micronutrient deficiencies? Should programs and policies focus on the worst-off cohorts, which are probably the most difficult and costly to reach, or should the somewhat less affected but easier to reach cohorts be the target? Should aid focus on increasing economic growth or on alleviating the conditions of poverty until economic growth catches up? Chapter 3 provides, by way of example, an exercise that considers six different policy options for dealing with iron deficiency, comparing the conditions under which each policy is likely to be more effective and the trade-offs involved in each.

Conclusion

At the core of the twenty-first-century policy challenge lie some old goals—including the desire to ensure that there is not just enough food but that people have fair access to it and that it is produced ethically—and some new ones such as public health and environmental sustainability. This chapter suggests that a central challenge for future food policy to achieve these goals is the need to link policy areas too often dealt with in a disparate manner. We have mentioned in the previous chapter that the immense challenges of the future—including continuous hunger, malnutrition, and mismanagement of resources—require better understanding and linkage of agricultural, environmental, and public health policies. Although sustainable agriculture and food networks now have some experimentation with growing and distributing food in ways that at least recognize the enormity of the environmental challenge, the need to formulate a more integrated food policy model is still urgent. In order to address food policy adequately, we introduced in this chapter a complex framework for analyzing food policymaking that links social, economic, and ecological dimensions.

It is widely agreed that policy intervention in the food system is motivated by a number of objectives. However, there is much less agreement on how the actual governments' behavior can be explained. The view of government as an omniscient, benevolent planner that pursues policies to maximize productive efficiency by correcting allocative distortions in the food system regularly contradicts the realities of political economic structure in the food system. Furthermore, there are strong interactions between economic and political markets: the outcomes of economic markets influence how political power is shared, while the policy outcomes of political markets similarly affect the efficiency and distribution of economic outcomes.

It is now widely recognized among nutritionists, economists, and policymakers that past efforts to design, institutionalize, and implement multisectoral nutrition planning have failed, partly because of failure to explicitly consider the political economy, stakeholder, and institutional aspects of food policymaking. However, it is not yet clear that there is one ideal way to incorporate these diverse elements into a comprehensive framework. We reiterate our encouragement to readers, therefore, to be well versed in a particular disciplinary field while being cognizant of how that discipline's tools and particularly its biases and blind spots fit into the overall picture, open to the work and insight from other disciplines, and prepared to work across disciplinary lines to resolve complex issues. In addition to the reference materials that have already been cited, we recommend Babu and Sanyal's (2009) work on food policy analysis, which demonstrates how to apply statistical tools to specific food system problems we discuss in chapters 3–7; Timmer, Falcon, and Pearson's (1983) seminal work introducing economic and nutrition techniques for food policy analysis; and Pinstrup-Andersen's (1993) collection of essays studying the political economy of food policies.

Much more research has yet to be done to understand how improving food and nutrition status may be compatible with other goals and interests in the public and private sectors, and how to bring these united goals to the front of the policy arena. In the following chapters, we demonstrate a number of win-win situations and highlight other areas where trade-offs may be inevitable. Addressing these trade-offs requires taking the ethics of the food system seriously and explicitly. The next chapter begins by considering the primary goal of the food system, improved human health and nutrition.

Notes

1. Examples of external costs and benefits include the costs of pollution borne by those who do not cause it and the benefits of nationally supported agricultural research derived by farmers in other countries who did not have to pay for it. Monopoly power, incomplete markets, and information asymmetries are examples of suboptimal market structure.

2. http://www.ethicurean.com/2009/08/05/gao-report-on-concentration/.

3. The microeconomic level refers to individuals, households, and single firms. The macroeconomic level aggregates all these pieces. The meso-economic level incorporates only certain segments, such as at community or industry level.

4. Something is *exogenous* when it is determined outside the model, and *endogenous* when it is an outcome of the model.

5. For example, some advocates of improved nutrition feel so strongly about the overriding importance of alleviating malnutrition that their approach is nonnegotiable: trade-offs between cost-effectiveness and political factors are unethical, they feel, and should not be considered.

Chapter 3

Human Health and Nutrition Policies

Introduction

As mentioned in chapter 2, we believe that the global food system begins and ends with human health and nutrition. We take that position partly to emphasize that the food system is a means to an end rather than an end in itself and that the most important end is improved health and nutrition, and partly because health and nutrition are important inputs into the food system because of the critical role they play in food system labor productivity and food safety. Furthermore, the large majority of past and current human illnesses originated in the food system (Torrey and Yolken 2005; Torrey 2010).

Food systems influence human health and human health influences the food system. Thus government food system policies may impact health, while health policies impact the food system, whether intentionally or not. Failure to recognize this potential bidirectional causality may lead to forgone opportunities for improving human health and nutrition or even worse health outcomes (Pinstrup-Andersen 2010). Figure 3.1 illustrates some of the principal bidirectional pathways. Each of these will be discussed in turn. It is important to recognize that poor health and nutrition are caused by many factors, of which access to food is but one. Poor sanitation and hygiene, unclean water, poor child care, lack of primary health care, and household and individual behavior may be at least as important.

Efforts to improve human health and nutrition through government food policy require improved understanding of how such efforts influence food systems, how food systems influence health and nutrition, and how, in both the food and health sectors, government policy interventions may be effective. This chapter addresses both kinds of policies, with emphasis on how food systems influence health and nutrition. To provide a foundation for the policy discussion, the chapter begins with

FIGURE 3.1.
Interactions between food systems and human health and nutrition. Source: Authors.

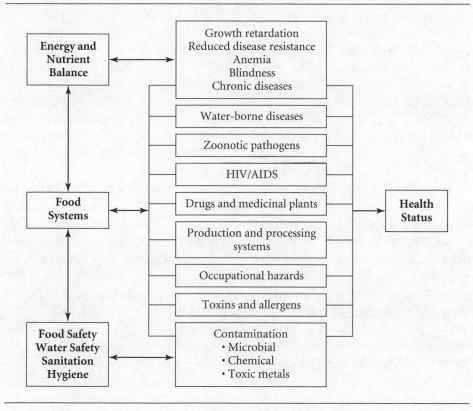

a presentation of selected conceptual relationships, followed by a summary of the magnitudes of the nutrition and health problems in developing countries and a brief discussion of the payoffs from improved health and nutrition in terms of public health and economic growth. The chapter then proceeds to present and discuss policy options and their expected health and nutrition implications within the context of household and individual behavior. The health and nutrition effects of government policies are closely related to food security and food consumption (chapter 4) and poverty (chapter 5).

An integrated, multidisciplinary approach to the solution of health, nutrition, and food system problems in a sustainable manner is much more likely to be successful than single-sector approaches (Pinstrup-Andersen 2010). The Giessen Declaration and the New Nutrition Science project are significant recent efforts that aim to expand nutritional concerns beyond the narrow nutrition science. (For more detail, see the special issue of *Public Health Nutrition*, vol. 8, no. 6A, September 2005.) Kataki and Babu's (2002) collection of essays link agricultural production and different solutions to nutrition problems, and Bhargava (2008) demonstrates a number of statistical techniques from nutrition, economics, psychology, and public health that apply to nutrition and health issues in developing countries.

Few would disagree that food systems are essential for good health. They produce the world's food, feed, fiber, medicinal plants, and a small but increasing portion of the world's energy. In most countries the food system is also an important source of income and livelihood among the poor. At the same time, the food system can be a causal agent for various health and nutrition problems among producers as well as the wider population, including malnutrition (hunger, micronutrient deficiencies, and obesity), malaria, food and waterborne illnesses, zoonotic diseases, chronic diseases, and occupational ill-health (Hawkes and Ruel 2006; ole-MoiYoi 2010; Torrey 2010; Gillespie 2010). Additionally, the food system interacts with other health and nutrition problems such as diarrhea, malaria, and human immunodeficiency virus/ acquired immunodeficiency syndrome (HIV/AIDS), making these problems more or less severe just as these diseases make malnutrition worse.

Food systems provide many human health and nutrition benefits (Pinstrup-Andersen, Berg, and Forman 1984; Kataki and Babu 2002). Increases in national income through agricultural development have had tremendous effects on the nutritional status of many people in developing countries. Changes in agricultural practices are shown to have improved nutrition, including crop diversification; breeding for micronutrient-enriched staple food grains; large-scale vegetable, fruit, and milk production and distribution; improved postharvest storage; small-scale vegetable production; and production of small animals, poultry, and fish.

Dietary Energy and Nutrients

The food system influences health through changes in the dietary energy and nutrition balance. This balance influences child growth, communicable disease resistance, and health problems due to micronutrient deficiencies, as well as several noncommunicable chronic diseases related to overweight and obesity. Each of these is discussed below.

The world population is faced with a triple burden of malnutrition: insufficient intake of dietary energy (hunger), nutrient deficiencies ("hidden" hunger), and excess intake of dietary energy (overweight and obesity). While individual and population dietary energy and nutrient balance is an outcome of household and individual behavior and the constraints they face (e.g., incomes and prices), the food system plays a pivotal role as a supplier of food and incomes for the large share of the populations of low-income countries that work in food system sectors. Hunger and malnutrition are associated with more than half of the 9.5 million preschool children who die annually (Pelletier et al. 1995). As shown in figure 3.2, interactions with the proximate causes of death, such as diarrhea and malaria, make malnutrition a primary cause of child death. More than half of the children who died of the diseases identified in figure 3.2 might have survived if they had been properly nourished.

As shown in figure 3.3, malnutrition manifests itself throughout the life cycle and perpetuates itself across generations with many wide-ranging repercussions unless the depicted cycle is broken. The vicious cycle from low birth weight, through stunted children with low resistance to disease, to low productivity of adults and

FIGURE 3.2.
Deaths associated with malnutrition. Source: WHO/UNICEF 2004.

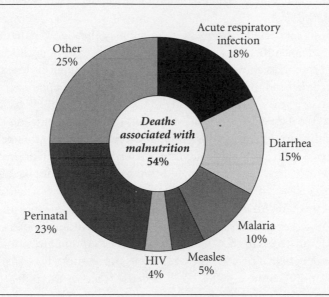

FIGURE 3.3.
Malnutrition and the intergenerational transmission of chronic poverty. Source: Benson 2004.

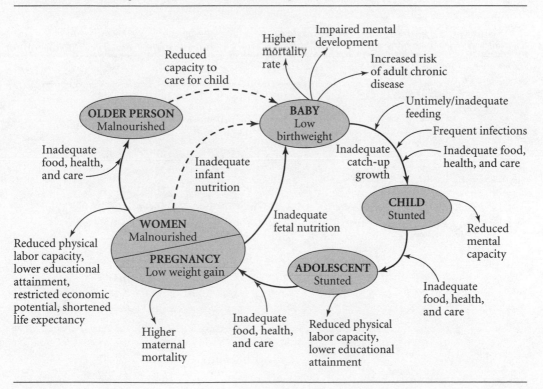

malnourished women giving birth to underweight babies can be broken by government policy and behavioral changes, including those discussed in this chapter and throughout the book.

The most critical period is from before pregnancy through the first two years of life of the baby. Poor nutrition prior to and during pregnancy may lead to low birth weight. Furthermore, as shown in figure 3.4, children's weight in developing countries rapidly falls behind their better nourished peers in developed countries during the first one to two years of life. According to the World Bank (2006b, 55), "There is consensus that the damage to physical growth, brain development, and human capital formation that occurs during this period is extensive and largely irreversible."

The choice of policies should take into account the underlying and proximate causes of malnutrition (figure 3.5). In addition to inadequate intake of dietary energy and nutrients, two other immediate causes are at play: infectious diseases and inadequate health care. All three are heavily influenced by household and individual poverty (chapter 5) and adverse living environments, including poor sanitation and hygiene and lack of access to clean water. The social, economic, and political contexts within which people live provide the overriding framework. This is an important consideration in the context of this book, because it shows the potential power of government intervention to improve health and nutrition by means of changing social, economic, and political contexts.

As further discussed later in this chapter and in chapters 4 and 5, policies aimed at changing these contexts may be as important to improve health and nutrition as

FIGURE 3.4.
The window of opportunity for addressing undernutrition. Source: Shrimpton et al. 2001. Note: Estimates are based on WHO regions.

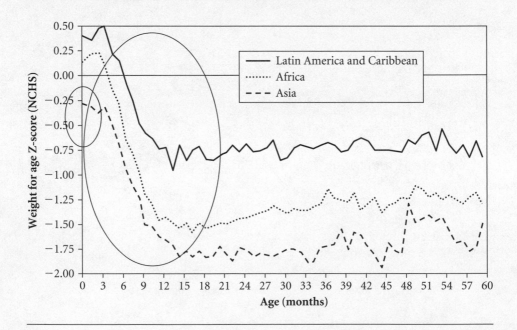

FIGURE 3.5.
Maternal and child undernutrition framework. Source: Black et al. 2008.

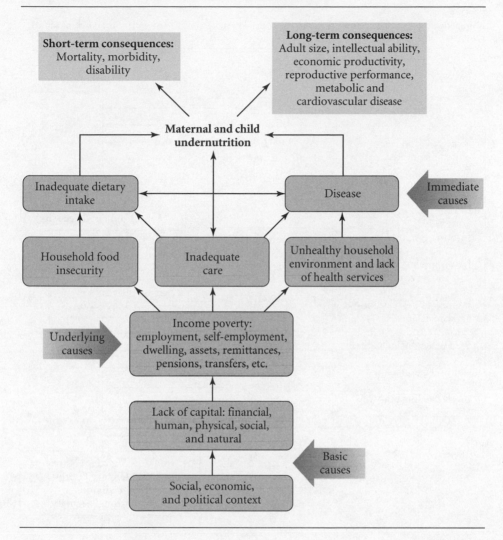

policies more narrowly focused on household food security, child care, and health services. Policies to improve access to a nutritious diet, good health care, clean water, and good sanitation are critically important. A combination of such policies is usually needed to improve the contexts within which the malnourished operate and to promote healthy behaviors from households and individuals.

Sufficient food availability is necessary but not sufficient to assure good nutrition. As shown in figure 3.6, the extent to which food availability is translated into good health and nutrition is influenced by a large number of factors, some of which are part of household and individual behavior while others are beyond the control of the households. Many are gender specific. Whether they are part of the household

FIGURE 3.6.
A simplified conceptual framework linking food availability, food security, and nutrition. Source: Modified from Pinstrup-Andersen and Herforth 2008.

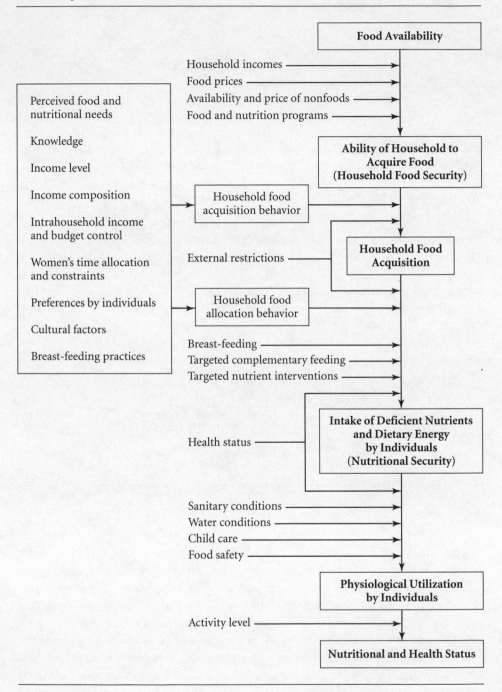

behavior or external to the household, these factors can be influenced by government policy. To be successful, however, such policies must be based on a thorough understanding of the factors, how those factors interact within the population of intended beneficiaries, and the motivations and goals associated with each. Failure to acquire such knowledge prior to the design and implementation of policies and programs is a major reason for disappointing outcomes.

Policies on animal production may influence nutrition through changes in the diet. Excessive consumption of foods of animal origin may lead to various chronic diseases while lack of access to such foods may contribute to risks of micronutrient deficiencies. Similarly, rapid increases in sugar and sweetener consumption are of particular concern because of the high energy content and lack of nutrients, leading to overweight, obesity, diabetes, and micronutrient deficiencies. In addition to the achievement of animal welfare and environmental goals, vegetarian diets eliminate health risks associated with excessive consumption of foods of animal origin but may increase the risk of deficiencies in certain micronutrients.

As discussed in chapter 4, an increase in available food (through production or trade) will result in improved household food security only if food-insecure households have access to the additional food. Access is influenced by household incomes, food prices, distance to markets, transaction costs, the availability and prices of non-foods, the presence of food and nutrition programs, and government policies. The extent to which households take advantage of increased food access is determined by household food acquisition behavior, which, as shown in figure 3.6, is influenced by a set of household-specific variables. These same variables may also influence household food allocation behavior, leading to intake of nutrients and dietary energy by individuals and thus the degree of nutritional security. Whether food consumption improves health and nutrition will be influenced by sanitary conditions, child care, food safety, and the quality of available water as well as the physiological utilization of the ingested food. According to Black and Fawcett (2008), 40 percent of the world's people lack access to adequate sanitation. Improving access to food in households with poor sanitary conditions may have little or no nutrition and health impact because diarrhea and other health factors may reduce absorption of ingested energy and nutrients and reduce appetite.

Other Food System Interactions with Human Health

Waterborne and Zoonotic Diseases

Returning to figure 3.1, the food system influences health and nutrition through waterborne diseases, bacteria, viruses, and parasites associated with poorly functioning irrigation systems and other water management problems in the food system. They may cause malaria, diarrhea, and other waterborne diseases. Rice production with continually flooded fields, for instance, are prime breeding grounds for malarial mosquitoes. Such diseases reduce labor productivity with negative implications for the food system.

Water contaminated with arsenic, cadmium, or other poisonous metals may cause illness through drinking water or the consumption of contaminated fish and plants. Arsenic poisoning is particularly problematic in south Asia, where irrigation has reduced groundwater levels. Overuse or untimely use of fertilizers and pesticides can also contaminate water resources, leading to health problems for food system workers and consumers (chapters 7 and 8).

"Animals and humans are intimately connected by diseases" (Torrey 2010, 58). Most of the microbes causing human diseases originated in animals (Torrey and Yolken 2005; Torrey 2010). HIV/AIDS, avian influenza, swine flu, mad cow disease and related Creutzfeldt-Jakob disease, Lyme disease carried by ticks from wildlife to humans, measles, tuberculosis, trypanosomiasis, and SARS, as well as microbial contamination of food by E. coli, salmonella, and other microbes causing diarrhea and other diseases, are but examples. Though rarely prioritized and often ignored, policies that would change the interactions between humans and animals, develop resistance in animals to certain diseases, and reduce the population of disease-carrying rodents and other wildlife could reduce the health risks associated with zoonotic diseases.

HIV/AIDS

HIV/AIDS influences the food system through reduced labor productivity—and the resulting poverty and malnutrition—and through impaired immune systems, increased vulnerability to infections, increased nutritional needs, and malnutrition (Gillespie and Kadiyala 2005). The interaction between food security and HIV/ AIDS is particularly important in rural areas of developing countries because of the debilitating effects on agricultural production. In response to death or sickness among adults, farming households may reduce the area cultivated, shift from high-value, labor-intensive crops to crops requiring less labor, such as cassava and sweet potatoes, and spend less time weeding, all of which tend to reduce incomes and increase the risk of poverty and malnutrition. HIV/AIDS is also likely to reduce off-farm incomes and increase expenditures for health care and funerals, leaving less money for the purchase of agricultural inputs (Jayne et al. 2006). On the basis of a review of available evidence, Gillespie (2006, 15) concludes that "decapitalization of highly afflicted rural communities, meaning a loss of savings, cattle assets, draft equipment, and other assets, may pose the greatest limits on rural productivity and livelihood for these communities." This is an important consideration for policy design because, instead of a sole focus on labor productivity, it implies a greater emphasis on making capital available to communities with a high incidence of HIV/ AIDS.

Drugs and Medicinal Plants

The food and agricultural system is an important supplier of medicinal plants and animal products used in both traditional and modern medicine to treat health problems. Such production provides additional income sources for farmers and others and thus contributes to better diets, nutrition, and health. A large number of plants traditionally grown in the food system possess medicinal characteristics and are used to prevent or cure health problems (Herforth 2010a).

Although illicit drugs (e.g., marijuana and cocaine) are not foods, they are an important link between the food and agricultural systems and human health. First, their production generates incomes among the rural poor in producing countries, which in turn may help them improve their health status. Second, drug use and drug markets cause negative health effects among users and produce negative externalities among nonusers. Like other nonfood agricultural commodities such as cotton and crops for biofuel, production of illicit drugs also influences the food system through the competition with food crops for land and water. Supporting alternative remunerative agricultural livelihoods, including through improved infrastructure and agricultural research, can be one method of combating illicit drug use, drug trafficking, and drug-related violence and conflict.

At the same time, the food system consumes drugs such as antibiotics, growth promoters, and synthetic hormones. As discussed later in this chapter, misuse of such drugs may increase health risks in food consumers. Demand for cotton, coffee, biofuels, and other nonfood agricultural production may similarly change nutrition among farm families, consumers, and others involved in agricultural production as incomes, relative prices, and available food choices change.

Occupational Hazards

According to FAO and ILO (FAO 2010), agriculture causes slightly more than half of all fatal workplace accidents and "is one of the three most dangerous sectors in which to work." "Agricultural work possesses several characteristics that are risky for health: exposure to the weather, close contact with animals and plants, extensive use of chemical and biological products, difficult working postures and lengthy hours, and use of hazardous agricultural tools and machinery" (Cole 2006, 1). Other parts of the food system, including processing and transportation, also exhibit health risks.

Health risks associated with the application of pesticides and other agrochemicals and the risks associated with pesticide residues in food have received considerable attention, and a series of policy interventions are in place to reduce such health risks. FAO has developed an international code of conduct for the distribution and use of pesticides (FAO 2003b). Unfortunately, many developing countries do not follow these guidelines, and where regulations exist, they are frequently not enforced. Agrochemicals outlawed in most developed countries are used in many developing countries and sound application methods are not followed. Trade-offs between yield losses due to pests and health risks associated with the application of pesticides are a key issue in policy decisions and farmers' compliance with existing regulations. As discussed in chapter 8, such trade-offs can be replaced with win-wins. Agroecological or organic production processes may reduce health risks associated with the use of inorganic pesticides but may, at the same time, have negative nutrition effects among low-income consumers because of lower yields.

Toxins and Allergens

Toxins and allergens found in foods may be naturally occurring or they may be introduced through the application of chemical pesticides, food processing, storage, or plant breeding. Production and processing research may remove toxins and allergens or introduce new ones. Testing of modified foods is critical before they are approved for commercial use.

Traditional plant breeding and genetic engineering can be used to develop pest resistance in plants to reduce the need for pesticides without yield losses. Much progress has already been made, for example, in rice production, where the use of chemical pesticides has decreased significantly (Nelson 2010).

Large price subsidies on pesticides in several Asian countries during the first phase of the green revolution resulted in significant overuse. In addition to reducing pesticide subsidies, policies that regulate the use of pesticides considered of greatest risk to humans would also help reduce the negative health effects. Organic and other agroecological production methods (e.g., integrated pest management) attempt to reduce health risks by using only organic pesticides and by using biological pest control and crop rotation. The potential of genetic engineering to reduce the need for chemical pesticides to protect plants is discussed in chapters 7 and 10, and the effects of input subsidies and price policies on pesticide use are discussed in chapters 6, 7, and 8.

Some sources of toxins, such as aflatoxin and other mycotoxins, may be difficult to avoid under adverse production and storage facilities, and may cause higher health risks than appropriate application of pesticides. Aflatoxin regulations and trade implications are discussed in case 3-11.

The choice of government interventions to reduce health risks associated with toxins and allergens in food is context specific. Agroecologically sound production systems that draw on science to develop host-plant pest resistance, biological pest control, and deliberate use of pesticides when no other option is available to avoid crop losses provide a starting point for policy design and implementation. Enhanced testing, incentives, and regulations of new foods complemented with certain chemical agents would also be useful to protect consumer health.

Food Safety

Food safety refers to the probability that consuming a particular food may cause illness. Powell (2010) colorfully and succinctly defines safe food as "food that doesn't make you barf." Food safety has grown in importance in consumer demand, particularly for wealthier consumers. Longer supply chains, in particular longer storage and transport routes, and novel production methods can lead to higher food safety risks caused by the use and misuse of conserving agents and contamination by microbial pathogens and unconventional agents (Nakimbugwe and Boor 2010). In addition to food safety, the impact of food systems on human health is heavily influenced by the degree of water safety, sanitation, and hygiene.

Food-borne diseases may cause diarrhea, fever, long-term health complications, and death (Nakimbugwe and Boor 2010). Diarrhea is a major cause of death in children (Lopez et al. 2006). WHO (2011) reports that about 1.8 million people die from diarrheal diseases each year, mostly caused by contaminated food and water. Contaminated food supplies also cause lower labor productivity.

Food safety hazards include food-borne pathogens (bacteria, parasites, viruses, and prions); chemical and medicinal residuals in food; growth hormones; and improper antibiotic use that supports the evolution of resistant bacteria (cases 3-11 and 3-12). Food contamination may occur in production, processing, storage, or transportation facilities and during such activities. The outcome may be microbial, chemical, and/or toxic-metals contamination. Case 3-12 delves into food safety issues with particular reference to salmonella control and related food security and food trade implications. Case 10-12 discusses food safety issues related to seafood production in Vietnam and export to the European Union.

Food safety standards tend to be more stringent in high-income than low-income countries (Caswell and Bach 2007). Assuming that higher food safety standards increase food prices, governments may face a trade-off between higher-priced, safer foods that high-income consumers want but low-income people cannot afford and less safe, lower-priced food. A segmented food system with dual safety standards may develop with more-safe food exported and less-safe food for domestic consumption. The ethical aspects of such a trade-off are discussed in chapter 11. As shown in figure 3.7, food safety hazards may be found in any of the elements of the food system.

FIGURE 3.7.
Potential points of contamination with food safety hazards along the farm-to-table food supply chain.
Source: Todd and Narrod 2006.

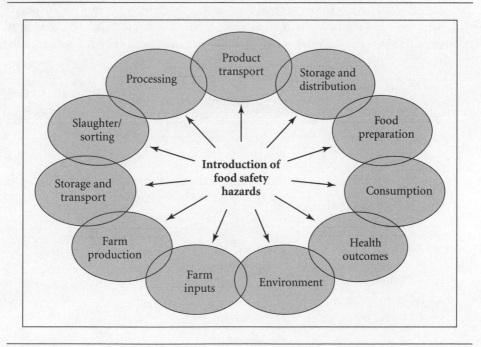

Current World Health and Nutrition Situation

During the last fifty years, increases in life expectancy and reductions in child mortality rates illustrate dramatic improvements in human health at the global level. However, this trend is marked by a clear divide between developed and developing countries. For example, life expectancy at birth is currently seventy-six and eighty-two years for men and women respectively in developed countries, and forty-seven and forty-eight years for men and women in sub-Saharan Africa (World Bank 2006b; Watson and Pinstrup-Andersen 2010). The average for developing countries disguises very large differences between countries, ranging from seventy-eight years in Costa Rica to thirty-eight years in Angola.

About 130 million babies are born annually. An estimated 4 million children die during their first four weeks of life and about the same number are stillborn (Lawn, Cousen, and Zupan 2005). Child mortality rates in selected regions and countries are shown in table 3.1. Sub-Saharan Africa (SSA) has the highest child mortality rate, followed by South Asia. During 1990–2005 SSA decreased its under-five mortality rate by only 12 percent compared to 35–44 percent in the other regions. In some African countries, such as Angola and DR Congo where accurate data is difficult to obtain, the very high mortality rates remained constant during the fifteen-year period. The highest reported mortality rate was in Sierra Leone where, despite some progress during the 1990s, twenty-eight of every one hundred children die before their fifth birthday.

Children's anthropometry is often used as a measure of health and malnutrition. A child whose height deficit is more than two standard deviations below normal for the child's age is considered *stunted.* A child whose weight deficit is more than two standard deviations below normal for that age suffers from *underweight,* and a child whose weight is two standard deviations below normal for his or her height is determined to be *wasted.* Underweight, overweight, and obesity in adults are usually

TABLE 3.1.
Under-Five Mortality Rates, 1990 and 2005 (per 1,000)

Region/Country	1990	2005	Percent reduction
High-income countries	12	7	42
Latin America	54	31	43
East Asia	59	33	44
Middle East & North Africa	80	52	35
South Asia	129	83	36
Sub-Saharan Africa	185	163	12
Niger	320	256	20
Angola	260	260	0
Sierra Leone	302	282	7
Congo, Democratic Republic	205	205	0

Source: World Bank 2006b.

measured by comparing weight and height, such as by calculating a person's body mass index (BMI). BMI is calculated by dividing a person's weight in kilograms by their squared height in meters. A BMI score of less than 18.5 indicates that a person is underweight for his or her height, while scores greater than 25 tend to indicate overweight and scores over 30 signal obesity.

Anthropometry data are useful for identifying malnutrition, both underweight and overweight, in a population, but its use for diagnosing individual health status is limited. Even in healthy, well-nourished populations, some children will be found who are more than two standard deviations from the average. BMI calculations need to be adjusted because men and women tend to have different percentages of lean mass, elderly people have less lean mass than young people, people who lift weights or do physical work have more lean mass than more sedentary people, and standard BMI calculations are inaccurate for very tall and very short people. Given these caveats, anthropometry data show when a population exhibits malnutrition because the percent of the population that is stunted or obese or wasted will be higher than one would expect statistically from an average, randomly selected, well-nourished population.

According to Black et al. (2008), 20 percent of children in developing countries are underweight and 32 percent are stunted (table 3.2). The prevalence of stunting is most severe in Africa, while average underweight rates are similar in Asia and Africa. However, both stunting and underweight rates differ greatly among Asian countries: 14.5 percent of children are stunted and 5.1 percent underweight in east Asia, but 40.7 percent of children are stunted and 33.1 percent underweight in south and central Asia (Black et al. 2008). Of a total of 112 million underweight preschool children in the world, 60 million (54 percent) are in south and central Asia. Similarly, 42 percent of the 178 million stunted preschool children are in that region.

Within-country variation in health status can be very large, a variation not identified by national averages. Thus, in a survey of forty-seven countries, WHO (2006) found that the child mortality rate in the poorest quintile of the population of these countries was 2.5 times that of children from the richest quintile, a slight increase from ten years earlier. Child mortality in households where the mothers had no education was more than twice that found in households in which mothers had some education and 50 percent higher in rural than in urban areas. The prevalence of child stunting was found to be more than four times higher in the poorest quintile than the prevalence in the richest quintile, and 60 percent higher in rural than in urban areas. As further discussed in case 3-2, indigenous populations, most of whom live in rural areas, are systematically marginalized in many countries, resulting in high levels of poverty, hunger, malnutrition, and suffering. Thorat and Sadana (2009) report that lower castes in India have worse nutrition and health than persons from higher castes, as well as higher mortality rates and poorer access to health care, even after controlling for other socioeconomic factors.

Deficiency in one or more micronutrients—including iron, vitamin A, iodine, and zinc—can cause or contribute to reduced labor productivity and a variety of diseases, as well as blindness, premature death, and impaired mental development (UNICEF 2004). Sufficient micronutrients in the diet can protect against infectious

TABLE 3.2.
Estimated Prevalence of Malnutrition among Preschool Children (Percent)

Region	1980		1990		2000		2005	
	Stunting	Underweight	Stunting	Underweight	Stunting	Underweight	Stunting	Underweight
Africa	39.0	23.5	36.9	23.6	35.2	24.2	40.1	21.9
Asia	55.1	45.4	41.1	35.1	30.1	27.9	31.3	22.0
Latin America and Carribean	24.3	12.5	18.3	8.7	13.7	6.1	16.1	4.8
Developing Countries	48.6	37.6	37.9	30.1	29.6	24.8	32.0	20.2

Sources: 1980, 1990, 2000: ACC/SCN 2004; 2005: Black et al. 2008.

diseases and reduce mortality (Catelo 2006). A 2004 global progress report states that 35 percent of the world population lacks adequate iodine, and 40 percent of people in developing countries suffer from iron deficiency (UNICEF 2004). Iron deficiency is particularly widespread in parts of Asia where 50–75 percent of pregnant women and preschool children suffer from iron deficiency anemia. In eight out of thirty-six SSA countries for which data were available, 80–85 percent of the preschool children suffered from iron deficiency anemia and more than half were affected in all but three of the thirty-six countries (IFPRI 2006). According to UNICEF (2004), more than a third of sub-Saharan Africa's population suffers from the debilitating effects of micronutrient deficiencies. The annual cost to these countries' economies is estimated to exceed $2.3 billion. Policy action to deal with micronutrient deficiencies with specific reference to Bangladesh and India is presented in cases 3-3 and 3-4. Case 3-5 discusses the development of a food fortification program for the Dominican Republic to address micronutrient deficiencies.

Nutrition Transition

Table 3.3 shows how the dietary transition has affected the percent of calories that are consumed from different food groups in developing countries between 1979 and 2006. The percent of a person's daily energy intake from cereals has decreased nine percentage points, while livestock products' (meat and dairy) and edible oils' shares have doubled—from admittedly low initial levels. This diet transition has been particularly pronounced in Asian countries experiencing rapid economic growth and in Latin America. Asia saw large increases occur in the consumption of milk, meat, vegetable oils, and vegetables (Pingali 2004). This transition has increased per capita fat intake in every region, which contributes to the rapid increase in overweight, obesity, and related chronic diseases. Eighty-five percent of the increase in cereal and meat demand over the next twenty-five years is expected to come from developing countries, with China alone accounting for 25 percent of the increased cereal demand and 40 percent of increased meat demand. While India is also expected to see a large increase in calories consumed, cultural factors are likely to keep meat demand much lower than income alone would predict.

The primary feature of the nutrition transition is the large increase in meat and edible oil consumption, leading some to conclude that a demand-driven "livestock revolution" is under way (Delgado et al. 1999). The trends alluded to in chapter 1—urbanization, Westernization, and population and income growth—are expected to continue, effectively doubling total meat demand in developing countries between 1995 and 2020, while increasing only by 25 percent in developed countries. Several developing countries in Latin America and east Asia (e.g., Brazil and China) have seen astronomical increases in meat consumption, although the levels are still well below those in industrialized countries. Meat consumption remained almost unchanged in south Asia, while in sub-Saharan Africa it has slightly decreased. In per capita terms, meat demand will increase four times as fast as cereal demand. Not all livestock sectors are expected to benefit equally (Delgado et al. 1999). Poultry

TABLE 3.3.
Contribution of Food Groups to Dietary Energy in Developing Countries (Percent)

Period	Cereals	Roots and tubers	Meat	Vegetable oils and fats	Sugar and products	Milk and products	Other
1979–1981	61	7	4	6	7	2	13
1989–1991	59	5	5	7	7	3	13
2004–2006	52	5	8	10	7	4	14

Source: FAOSTAT 2005 and 2009.

demand is expected to increase by more than 85 percent by 2020, while beef and pork will increase 50 percent and 45 percent respectively.

In much of the developing world, increased meat and dairy consumption represents an improvement in dietary diversity and macro and micronutrient supply (particularly iron, zinc, and vitamin A), leading to improved overall health. Consuming too much food of animal origin increases fat intake beyond recommended levels, potentially leading to obesity and related chronic diseases. Demand for livestock products tends to increase rapidly with income in developing countries. Adding to the consumption of fat, the amount of energy available in developing countries from edible oils nearly doubled between 1977–1979 and 1997–1999. Twenty percent of the increase in total energy available per person per day (from 2,152 kcal to 2,680) in developing countries has come from edible oils.

Increasing meat demand will double developing countries' demand for feed grains between 1995 and 2020, while demand for cereals for direct human consumption is projected to increase by only 40 percent. It has been estimated that raising livestock currently uses as much as 80 percent of the world's agricultural land either as housing or for growing feed (Stokstad 2010). As a result, maize demand in developing countries is projected to overtake demand for rice and wheat by 2020. The demand for maize for biofuel has also increased dramatically in the United States since 2005, reducing exports and increasing prices of maize and other cereals (chapter 8). This could provide an opportunity for sub-Saharan African smallholders to access world markets as maize exporters.

Fruits and vegetables are essential in obtaining sufficient quantities and varieties of micronutrients. Nutritionists today recommend that a person have at least five servings (or four hundred grams) of fruits and vegetables each day. Four hundred grams per day would translate into approximately 150 kg of fruits and vegetables each year, considerably more than the current consumption in sub-Saharan Africa and Asia (figure 3.8). Fruits and vegetables consumption has been above that level in industrialized and transitioning countries, North Africa, Mexico, and Oceania developing countries, though most surveys still show large portions of these populations consuming insufficient quantities and varieties of fruits and vegetables. The Latin America and the Caribbean region (LAC) met that goal only since the

FIGURE 3.8.
Consumption of fruits and vegetables (kg/person/year). Source: FAOSTAT 2005.

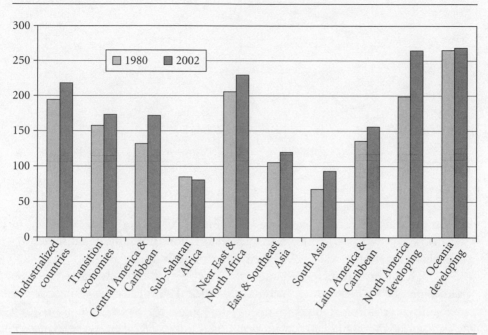

beginning of this century. Excepting sub-Saharan Africa, all regions have increased average fruit and vegetable intake since 1980.

Overweight, Obesity, and Chronic Diseases

Increases in overweight and obesity, resulting primarily from excessive energy intake relative to energy expenditures, are taking on epidemic proportions. The International Obesity Task Force estimates that about 1.1 billion adults are overweight—more than the number of underweight—including more than 300 million who are obese (Hossain, Kawar, and El Nahas 2007). Childhood overweight affects about 155 million school-age children, including about 40 million who are obese (ibid). Two-thirds of the U.S. population and more than half of the populations of several European countries are overweight or obese, and the prevalence of overweight and obesity is increasing globally, particularly among children and adolescents (Ogden et al. 2007). The prevalence of female overweight is particularly high in middle-income countries.

Overweight and obesity are leading contributors to chronic noncommunicable diseases, such as diabetes, cardiovascular diseases, stroke, and some cancers. Researchers have sought to measure the cost of these and other diseases and to find a meaningful way to compare deaths and morbidity costs. This is typically done by estimating disability adjusted life years (DALYs), which measure the number of years of healthy living a person enjoyed or is expected to have, equating death with disability. Disease burdens can then be measured in terms of lost DALYs due to illness,

TABLE 3.4.
Top Contributors to Lost DALYs, Global

Condition	Percent of DALYs	Condition	Percent of DALYs
1. Pneumonia	6.2	8. Low birth weight	2.9
2. Diarrhea	4.8	9. Birth trauma	2.7
3. Depression	4.3	10. Road traffic accidents	2.7
4. Heart attack	4.1	11. Neonatal infections	2.7
5. HIV/AIDS	3.8	12. Tuberculosis	2.2
6. Other accidents	3.7	13. Malaria	2.2
7. Stroke	3.1	14. Childhood diseases	2.0

Source: Data from WHO 2004.

disability, or death. Hossain, Kawar, and El Nahas (2007) report that 16 percent of the world's lost DALYs come from weight-related noncommunicable diseases. By comparison, fourteen of the largest specific contributors are in table 3.4.

The high and rapidly increasing levels of overweight, obesity, and related chronic diseases are not limited to high-income countries. The prevalence of overweight and obesity is growing rapidly in many developing countries. In China more than 200 million adults are affected, with a national adult overweight prevalence of 23 percent, one-third of whom are obese, while childhood obesity affects more than 8 percent of all Chinese children. Popkin, Horton, and Kim (2001) project that about one-third of the Chinese population will be overweight or obese by 2020. The prevalence of adult male obesity has tripled in Mexico since 1988, and almost one-third of men and more than half of women in South Africa suffer from overweight or obesity. In middle-income countries, overweight and obesity are the fifth most common causes of disease (Hossain, Kawar and El Nahas 2007). In west African countries, 10–30 percent of the men and 15–45 percent of the women are overweight or obese (Thiam, Samba, and Lwanga 2006).

The prevalence of overweight and obesity appears to increase with national income (WHO 2006). As noted by WHO (2006), some countries at the same level of national income have very different obesity rates, implying that factors other than those closely correlated with national incomes are important determinants of obesity. In high-income countries, the prevalence of overweight and obesity is highest among low-income population groups, while both high- and low-income individuals are affected in middle-income countries, and the prevalence is highest among the relatively well-to-do population groups in low-income countries (Pinstrup-Andersen 2007a).

Economic Payoffs from Health and Nutrition Improvements

The positive impact of improved health and nutrition on labor productivity and incomes has been affirmed by a large number of studies (e.g., Strauss and Thomas

1998; Fogel 2004; Sahn 2010; and World Bank 2006b). Sick and malnourished people's low labor productivity translates into lower wages, lower incomes, and lower food system efficiency. Poor farmer health and nutrition is also likely to reduce the motivation and incentives to adopt new technology, seek credit, and apply appropriate inputs. Greenwood et al. (2005) estimate that malaria costs Africa $12 billion annually.

Malnutrition hampers human capital accumulation during early childhood and adult capacity to work and earn income. Based on a review of available evidence, Victora et al. (2008, 340) conclude that "undernutrition was strongly associated . . . with shorter adult height, less schooling, reduced economic productivity, and—for women—lower offspring birth weight." They further conclude that stunting during the first two years of life leads to irreversible damage. In addition to energy and nutrient deficiencies, a large number of diseases, such as HIV/AIDS and tuberculosis, may contribute to low labor productivity and reduced motivation and incentives. HIV/AIDS is almost unique among diseases in its ability to incapacitate or kill working-age members of farming households, leaving the fields unattended and causing all remaining household members to face abject poverty, hunger, and—when all buffers have been exploited—death. Similarly, the symptoms of HIV/AIDS are much worse and the medicines less effective when a person lacks adequate nutrition. A large increase in the number of orphans, falling life expectancy, and high mortality rates among adults in parts of sub-Saharan Africa and increasingly in parts of Asia are a testimony to the tragedy (chapter 4).

While the first-best policy solution to health-induced low productivity is to improve population health status through direct health care interventions, it may not be a feasible solution. Food system policies may play an important role, as in improving the health of HIV/AIDS-infected individuals through better nutrition. With a focus on HIV/AIDS, Jayne et al. (2006) suggest several policy interventions, including research and extension programs to develop laborsaving technologies and production practices. Such programs are controversial because of existing labor surpluses in many developing countries. Interventions to increase both land and labor productivity, such as high-yielding crop varieties, would serve both labor-scarce and labor-surplus areas. Another potentially important set of policy interventions relate to gender biases in inheritance laws and practices, land tenure, and land rental markets. Gender equality in these and related areas is critical to protect material well-being, including food security for farm families, when individual family members die.

Policy Options to Improve Health and Nutrition

Virtually all the policies discussed throughout the book are likely to have an impact on health and nutrition, whether or not such an impact is explicitly sought. The subsections that follow discuss a set of policies and programs that either explicitly attempt to improve health and nutrition or that deal with other goals but that may be designed and implemented to have important health and nutrition effects.

Policy design and implementation should be based on a solution-free specification of the problems and opportunities to be addressed. Specifying the problems as the lack of a particular solution locks the decision maker into a particular solution that may not be the most appropriate. Specifying the problem in terms of its solution will only by chance lead to effective policies.

Consumer demand is influenced by preferences, household decision-making patterns, incomes and their sources, relative prices, advertising and promotion, and available food choices (chapter 4). A key policy question is to what extent food systems (supply factors) influence household and individual food consumption (demand factors) because the answer to that question will help design and implement effective policies. At the one extreme it can be argued that the food system responds to what the consumers want. Thus, policies to change diets should be focused on demand behavior. At the other extreme, some argue that supply decisions, particularly advertising and promotion by the food system, determine what is being consumed. If this is true, policies should try to change supply behavior. The answer is context specific but in most cases it is the interaction between supply and demand factors that determine what people eat and the related health implications. Another key policy question is whether to aim at changing the behavior of the intended beneficiaries or the constraints they face. The two aims are often interrelated. For example, promoting breast-feeding during the first year of a child's life would be an attempt to change behavior. However, working conditions for lactating women may have to be changed to facilitate breast-feeding. Similarly, nutrition education aimed at behavioral change may be successful only if certain constraints, such as lack of money to support the change, are removed. On the other hand, policies to increase incomes of families with unhealthy members may not improve health without the transfer of additional knowledge or access to health care clinics. Such complementarities are common among health and nutrition interventions, and the "lack of measurable effect of single interventions, such as food supplementation, access to improved drinking water, nutrition education, and improved sanitary conditions, is largely a result of failure to deal explicitly with complementarities and substitution in design and implementation" (Pinstrup-Andersen, Pelletier, and Alderman 1995, 337).

The first two years of a child's life are a particularly risky period for health and nutrition. Breast-feeding during the first year and the introduction of safe weaning food beginning at about six months of age are critical, as are good sanitation and hygiene and clean water. Targeting nutrition interventions to pregnant women and children below two years of age is much more effective in avoiding malnutrition than interventions later in the child's life (Ruel et al. 2008). Improved breast-feeding, introduction of safe weaning foods, and investments in clean water and good sanitation are merit goods, i.e., social benefits exceed the private benefits captured by the intended beneficiaries, but private benefits are still substantial. Healthy individuals mean a healthy and productive population for the benefit of society as a whole. This justifies a combination of public and private investment.

Severe acute malnutrition, which is defined as weight-for-height below 70 percent of the median, is, as the term implies, severe and acute. It is associated with between 1 and 2 million child deaths annually (Collins et al. 2006). A curative, medical approach in the form of therapeutic foods (i.e., nutrient-dense foods formulated for the treatment of severe acute malnutrition) may be the only feasible policy or program intervention (Greenaway 2009). Ready-to-use therapeutic foods are available, or the foods may be prepared in the community where they are used. While the use of therapeutic foods in hospitals is common, more recent approaches involve community distribution to outpatients.

While health and nutrition problems are caused by location-specific constraints and may require location-specific solutions, the following essential interventions to improve nutrition developed for India by an expert task force are likely to be relevant for other low-income and low-middle-income countries as well (Swaminathan 2009):

1. Timely initiation of breast-feeding within one hour of birth
2. Exclusive breast-feeding during the first six months of life
3. Timely introduction of complementary foods at six months
4. Age-appropriate complementary foods
5. Safe handling of complementary foods and hygienic feeding practices
6. Full immunization and biannual vitamin A supplementation with deworming
7. Frequent, appropriate, and active feeding for children during and after illness
8. Timely therapeutic feeding and care for all children with severe acute malnutrition
9. Improved food and nutrient intake for all, focusing on preventing anemia in adolescent girls and pregnant or lactating women

Other potential policy options for improved health and nutrition exist, including policies to interfere in the transmission of health problems from the food system to humans (see figure 3.1). Furthermore, every one of the factors shown in figure 3.5 to influence nutrition may be influenced by policies and programs. They may be designed with health and nutrition in mind or they may focus on other ends entirely. Cost-effective solutions must be tailored to the context and are likely to consist of a package of policies and programs rather than a single intervention. Further, an integrated approach is likely to be more cost-effective than separate sectoral policies.

Many of the policies in the remainder of the book will also improve human health and nutrition. Investments in rural infrastructure—particularly feeder roads—rural institutions, markets, and agricultural research, as well as policies that give the poor access to productive resources such as land and credit, are essential to help the rural poor out of poverty and improve their health. Such investments should be accompanied by improved public goods access. Improving governance can make many of these things more likely. As globalization progresses, national policies in one country may affect health and nutrition in others. As discussed in chapters 9 and 10, this is problematic because globalization has moved faster than the international institutions required to guide it for the benefit of human welfare.

Food Safety Policies

Food systems policies should help assure that the food available for consumption is safe. Food security refers not only to access to enough food but to enough food that is safe to eat. This is explicit in the FAO definition of food security (chapters 1 and 4). However, since food safety is a matter of relative risk rather than an absolute level, the degree of food safety (the level of risk) that a society desires becomes important in policy design and implementation. Higher levels of food safety (lower risk levels) usually mean higher costs and higher prices to the consumer. For poor households that spend a large share of their incomes on food, such price increases may mean that they cannot afford all the food they need. They may be faced with a trade-off between eating less food that is safer or more food that is less safe. Higher-income households are less likely to face such a trade-off, and may be willing to pay much more for food that is only a little safer, or perceived to be. Therefore, a positive correlation would be expected between household income and desired level of food safety. Furthermore, efforts to reduce food safety risks show diminishing returns: the additional risk reduction per dollar spent decreases as risk levels fall.

These relationships are illustrated by the desired food safety levels in the European Union and those in many developing countries. The policy question for the developing country governments is whether to pursue food safety standards at the level of the EU and risk increasing hunger and malnutrition as food prices increase, or seek a lower safety standard and thereby keep food prices lower but food safety risks higher. Countries that export food to high-income countries need to meet the importing country's standards. They may attempt to maintain the same standards in the food consumed domestically or they may maintain dual standards (case 10-12) The ethical aspects of these issues are discussed in chapter 11. Caswell and Bach (2007) conclude that full harmonization between food safety standards in rich and poor countries is an elusive and very costly goal. Instead, low-income countries should base their food safety standards on cost-effectiveness and cost-benefit analyses, taking into account the trade-offs between food safety and food access in achieving food security. Effective monitoring of the food system is critical (Nakimbugwe and Boor 2010).

With increasing concentration in the retail sector and the spread of supermarket chains in developing countries, food safety standards and monitoring may gradually move from the public to the private sector. Supermarkets may set standards that supersede those set by government, creating a dual standard between supermarkets and traditional wet markets (chapter 6). Although food safety risks should be perceived as a continuum with no scientifically based absolute level of acceptable food safety, government policy should focus on removing the most important sources of risk. Public and private investment in facilities for good sanitation and hygiene and clean water in all parts of the food system are critical, as is policy to change behavior and hygiene related to food handling.

Transfer Policies and Targeting

Transfer programs may play an important role in improving food security and reducing poverty, thereby improving health and nutrition. Such transfer programs may consist of cash (e.g., poverty relief), food (e.g., food supplementation), vouchers for food (e.g., food stamps), or health care. Transfer programs may be targeted to specific population groups or they may be available to all. They may include rationing or they may be available for unlimited amounts of food (e.g., a general food price subsidy). They may be conditional on certain behavior such as taking children to a health clinic periodically or sending them to school.

In the most comprehensive assessment of conditional case transfers, Fiszbein and Schady (2009, 3) conclude that such programs have improved the well-being of the poor. They found that conditional cash transfers "should be combined with other programs to improve the quality of the supply of health and education services." They conclude that "conditions can be justified if households are underinvesting in the human capital of their children" (2). As discussed in cases 3-8 and 5-1, conditional cash transfer programs can be very cost-effective. The Mexican Progresa/Oportunidades Program became a model for conditional transfer programs in a large number of countries, primarily middle-income ones in Latin America (case 5-1). They are discussed further in chapter 5.

If the goal is to transmit benefits to a particular group or cohort, targeting would be expected to reduce the fiscal costs per unit of benefit received because those not part of the group could be excluded from such benefits. However, perfect targeting is virtually impossible and, if possible, would itself be very costly. Thus, attempts to maximize cost-effectiveness would usually permit some leakage of benefits to non-target groups. Such leakage may also be politically expedient to get program support from stakeholder groups who have political power and partake in the benefit leakage. Targeting decisions should also take into account the errors of exclusion and inclusion. A very narrow targeting may leave out individuals and households who qualify (error of exclusion), while a broader targeting will increase the number of individuals and households who do not qualify but will receive benefits (leakage or error of inclusion).

As further discussed by Coady, Grosh, and Hoddinott (2004) and Pinstrup-Andersen (1988), there are many different targeting approaches and a long literature on targeting effectiveness. Food supplementation and other transfer programs may be targeted to poor households, an approach usually referred to as "means testing." Only households below a specified level of income or wealth qualify for the transfer. Transfers may be targeted to households with unhealthy or malnourished members or they may be targeted on these specific individuals in an attempt to bypass household resource allocation processes. Such attempts, as, for example, distribution of food to malnourished preschool children, often fail to achieve intended effects because households adjust intrahousehold food allocation accordingly and may share the food intended for the child among all household members (chapters 4 and 11). Many other household targeting approaches have been tried, including geographical targeting, distribution of inferior foods only the intended beneficiaries purchase, and targeting specific age groups (Pinstrup-Andersen 1988).

On the basis of a review of 122 interventions in forty-eight countries, Coady, Grosh, and Hoddinott (2004, 84) concluded that "the median program provides—approximately 25 percent—more resources to the poor than would random allocation." However, they found very large variation among the programs analyzed. A public works program in Argentina transferred 80 percent of program benefits to the target group, while about a quarter of the programs gave more to nontargeted households—the target group would have received a larger share of the total program benefits if the program had not been targeted. Both program design and implementation are important to achieve high cost-effectiveness of targeted programs.

Price Policies

A well-functioning food market is likely to result in food prices that reflect the most efficient allocation of scarce resources. However, most national governments intervene for a variety of reasons. The nutrition and health effects may be positive or negative. As discussed in chapters 6, 7, and 10, governments may intervene with the goal of increasing or decreasing farm incomes. To the extent that poor farmers are affected, the nutrition and health effects may be significant. Governments may intervene to reduce food prices to consumers in general (untargeted food price subsidies) or to poor consumers in particular (targeted food price subsidies). Such interventions and their impact are discussed by Pinstrup-Andersen (1988). Governments may also intervene to change relative prices among food commodities in an attempt to change diets. Taxes on energy-dense foods and price subsidies for fruit and vegetables may be introduced in an attempt to reduce overweight, obesity, and associated chronic diseases while increasing the intake of micronutrients. Governments also intervene to reduce externalities and to reduce transaction costs.

Governments may introduce a "wedge" between producer and consumer prices such that consumers pay less without reducing producer incomes or producers receive more without increasing consumer prices. The difference would have to be paid by the government, and fiscal costs of such policies can be very large as illustrated by past price subsidies in Egypt (Pinstrup-Andersen 1988). It is common for governments to introduce price policies for the benefit of one group at the expense of another. Maintaining market monopoly, parastatal food marketing boards discussed in chapters 6 and 7 and in cases 7-2 and 7-3, may fix low prices to farmers for the benefit of consumers and possibly rent-seeking public servants. Governments may also fix consumer prices at levels below the market price as was the case in many countries during the 2007–2008 food crisis. If consumer prices are fixed below market clearing prices, a black market is likely to develop.

Price policies to achieve one goal may cause negative effects on another. Thus, price subsidies to maintain farmer income in the United States promote expanded production and lower prices for cereals and dairy production but not for fruits and vegetables, contributing to obesity and chronic diseases. As mentioned in chapter 10, OECD farm subsidies and related import restrictions also contribute to poor nutrition in some developing countries by reducing export earnings by poor farmers. It is also important to consider the total effects of all government policies. The price effects of U.S. maize subsidies are partially or more than offset by other policies that increase demand, and hence prices, such as restrictions on sugar and biofuel imports (e.g., de Gorter and Just 2008).

Food Fortification and Crop Diversification

Nutrient deficiencies may be reduced through industrial food fortification—an approach to add vitamins or minerals postharvest widely used by the private sector (case 3-5)—or biofortification, an approach aimed at the incorporation of certain vitamins and minerals into the seeds of staple food crops, which is still mostly at the research and field-testing stage. The role of government may be to regulate the private sector to assure food safety and to provide financial support to make fortified foods available to low-income people. As illustrated by cases 3-6 and 3-7, biofortification offers promising opportunities for sustainable reductions of micronutrient deficiencies. Earlier research was successful in improving the protein quality in maize. While the ideal situation would be one where everybody could get access to a diversified diet that would meet all nutritional needs, widespread poverty makes such a situation difficult to attain. Biofortification, focused on staple foods affordable for the poor, appears to be an excellent second-best option. However, insufficient attention has been paid to research to improve the nutritional quality of staple foods in a number of areas. Vegetables, including pulses and oilseeds, can diversify crop strategies, increase farm incomes, and contribute to human health (Herforth 2010b; Kataki 2002).

Opportunities for changes in agricultural production that would achieve both health and environmental goals should be pursued. Agroecological approaches that reduce or eliminate the use of chemicals and antibiotics provide a step in the right direction. However, while reduced use of pesticides and other chemicals may have positive health effects, a systematic review of the evidence found that "evidence is lacking for nutrition-related health effects that result from the consumption of organically produced foodstuffs" (Dangour et al. 2010, 203).

Social Safety Nets and Public Goods

Governments may introduce social safety nets consisting of a combination of the policies and programs mentioned above (see chapter 5). Such safety nets sometimes aim to achieve health and nutrition goals explicitly, but often focus on poverty goals while either ignoring potential health effects or assuming a close positive correlation between poverty reduction and health improvements. The assumption may or may not be valid in a particular case because, as discussed earlier in this chapter, the health status of an individual is influenced by many factors of which income is one—although certainly an important one.

The supply of health care, clean water, and improved sanitation in the rural areas where most of the poor live is very limited and should be expanded along with primary education and income-generating activities within and outside the food system. Policies to eliminate gender discrimination in asset ownership and decision making should be pursued, with due consideration to the impact on time allocation by women and the associated health and nutrition implications.

Overweight, Obesity, and Related Chronic Disease Policies

Nutrition and health education, information sharing, and promotional campaigns strengthen the awareness of what constitutes a healthy diet and the negative health effects of overweight, obesity, and chronic diseases. Governments and NGOs could affect the food system environment by investing in productivity-increasing, unit-cost reducing technologies and production patterns that would expand the supply of fruits, vegetables, and other healthy foods at lower consumer prices while avoiding such policies for energy-dense, nutrient-poor food commodities. Taxes, subsidies, and price policies may provide health-friendly incentives to consumers, farmers, processors, and retailers. Regulation of food processing with respect to the content of sugar, sweeteners, and animal fat and their labeling may be considered.

Policy prescriptions are particularly difficult for middle-income countries because they show the coexistence of high prevalence of stunting in preschool children, high and increasing prevalence of obesity in both children and adults, and widespread micronutrient deficiencies. Attempts to address only one problem in isolation from the others are likely to have unintended adverse health effects.

Research Priorities

Agricultural research priorities should pay attention to both economic demand for agro-food commodities and health implications. Research funds should be targeted to increase productivity and reduce unit costs of food commodities with high content of deficient, absorbable micronutrients in the diets of the poor. Research priorities that should be pursued to improve human health and nutrition include biofortification of basic food staples, reduction of inorganic chemicals in plant protection through the development of resistant or tolerant plants, improvement of existing knowledge about the transfer of major zoonotic pathogens and how such transfer can be better managed or avoided, removal of important toxins and allergens from foods, and avoidance of the development of mycotoxins during production and storage.

Modern science offers tremendous opportunities for improving human health directly through curative and preventive measures and indirectly through improvements in the global food system. Unfortunately, the allocation of research resources is biased toward resolving health problems affecting the nonpoor. Opportunities for improving human health and nutrition and reducing child mortality are being forgone because of gross underinvestment in the application of science to solve poor people's health and nutrition problems. Recent investments by the Bill and Melinda Gates Foundation are helping to rectify this problem.

Comparing Alternatives: An Example of Efforts to Reduce Dietary Iron Deficiency

Identifying appropriate food and nutrition policies entails consideration of a country's financial and bureaucratic capacity as well as its domestic market and infrastructure conditions.[1] These and other context-specific conditions should be taken into account in policy advice. This section provides an example of the kind of policy debate that could occur around the main topics of this textbook and the associated case studies.

Consider as an illustration six alternative interventions that could be pursued to reduce iron deficiency, most of which have been discussed above: (1) adding iron to staple food postharvest (industrial fortification); (2) distributing nutrient supplements such as iron pills; (3) launching an educational campaign to change consumer behavior in favor of a diet that would meet the iron requirements; (4) incorporating iron into the seeds of staple food crops (biofortification); (5) reducing diarrhea or improving health in other ways that would enhance the absorption of ingested iron; and (6) creating incentives for consumers to change their diets (including the possibility of taxes, subsidies, or other price policies).

The choice among the six options will depend on the specific circumstances. While options 1 and 2 may be effective in urban settings and rural areas with good infrastructure, they are likely to be costly and unsustainable. They are unlikely to work among the rural poor in most locations because of deficient infrastructure and because most staple foods that could be fortified are either produced by the family that consume them or they are purchased on the local wet market. In those cases, the food is not likely to enter into a marketing process where such processing is viable, although village-level fortification may be an option in some cases. Distribution of supplements may be a short-term ad hoc solution until a sustainable approach is in place. Bangladesh, for instance, has made some progress toward controlling vitamin A deficiency by increasing the coverage of vitamin A capsules largely through foreign aid. However, there are concerns that if foreign assistance were to stop, the vitamin A program in Bangladesh could lapse and deficiency would increase again. More cost-effective and sustainable ways of reducing micronutrient deficiency are needed for this country. For a more detailed discussion of fortification and supplementation programs, see cases 3-3, 3-4, and 3-5.

Option 3 may help in cases where the deficiencies are a result of lack of knowledge rather than lack of income. However, in the case of low-income people, it is likely to be useful only in combination with increasing incomes and only by using new innovative communication approaches made possible by the information and communication revolution in developing countries. In this regard, it is useful to keep in mind that the food system is driven by the behavior of the actors in the system, including consumers and retailers, who do not necessarily prioritize improvements of health and nutrition over other goals. Thus information campaigns that promote good nutrition, such as ensuring sufficient iron intake, and regulation of advertising expected to have adverse nutrition effects may be useful instruments. From an advertising perspective, education programs are likely to be more effective when they discuss problems that their constituents care about, such as preventing named local diseases, rather than a vague promise of good nutrition.

Biofortification (option 4) offers exciting opportunities to help solve deficiencies of specific minerals or vitamins in the diets of people with severe income constraints and where the diet is dominated by one or two staples, such as rice or wheat in most of Asia; maize, cassava, or sweet potato in most of sub-Saharan Africa; and potatoes in most of the Andes of Latin America. Research aimed at the enhancement of the content of absorbable iron and vitamin A in rice and vitamin A in sweet potatoes has shown great promise. Ongoing research within the Consultative Group on International Agricultural Research system is attempting to enhance the content of iron, vitamin A, and zinc in several staple foods. It is reasonable to expect that these, and related research efforts, will be successful in making such biofortified foods available within a reasonable time frame if appropriate investments continue to be made.

Success or failure then hinges on economics and behavior. Can biofortified seed be made available to farmers at costs that are less than the expected benefits to the farmers? Must the price of biofortified food be higher than other food for the farmer to be interested, and will consumers pay more for biofortified food? In subsistence agriculture, how much more would farm households be willing to pay for the improved seed? These questions illustrate the importance of behavioral and economic responses to external influences and suggest the need for context-specific information for improving nutrition. While the global food system can be described as a set of physical activities, failure to recognize its behavioral aspects is likely to lead to disappointing outcomes of policy and research initiatives.

If the absorption of ingested iron and other nutrients is low in unhealthy persons, additional consumption may do little to reduce deficiencies. Thus option 5 offers opportunities for win-wins in the form of reduced micronutrient deficiency and other positive health effects. Investments to improve sanitation and access to clean water are critical in this regard.

The principal barrier to a diversified diet that meets all energy and nutrient requirements is poverty. Policies that help poor people out of poverty would make it possible for them to have access to a healthy and diversified diet (option 6). Many other policy measures discussed in this book might help low-income people obtain a better diet, such as investment in the development and dissemination of productivity-increasing, unit-cost-reducing knowledge and technologies for the food system, with emphasis on foods that are most likely to add the nutrients that are deficient in the diet; reduction of the costs of distribution through more efficient marketing and processing; and price policy. In addition to the reduction of iron deficiencies—the topic of this section—policies aimed at dietary changes should take into account the expected impact on other micronutrient deficiencies and both energy deficiency and excess energy intake.

Since any one policy measure is unlikely to achieve both reductions in energy and nutrient deficiencies and reductions in excess energy intake, and since both deficiencies and obesity are prevalent in an increasing number of developing countries—notably middle-income countries—the design and implementation of an appropriate policy package is a serious challenge. While poverty reduction is a necessary element, it is not likely to resolve all nutritional problems, nor does it work immediately. Complementary policies are also needed. It is also important that policy advice not let the best get in the way of the good in cases where the best is unlikely to be achieved within a reasonable time frame. It is also possible, however, for the good to get in the way of the best, reducing potential future gains in order to make smaller gains immediately. These are sometimes unavoidable trade-offs (chapter 11).

Conclusion

Sweeping technological advances in food and health systems have made significant contributions toward better health care and increased food supplies in developing countries. They have lowered food prices and improved access to food staples for the poor and malnourished. In spite of these successes, high levels of malnutrition remain major public health concerns. How serious are the health and nutrition problems worldwide? How are these problems related to the food system? What roles can food system policies and health and nutrition policies play in addressing these problems? How can we design and implement food system strategies that are more effective in reducing health and nutrition problems?

This chapter has attempted to answer these questions. Widespread health and nutrition problems continue to be the most challenging issue at the beginning of the twenty-first century. Undernutrition, micronutrient deficiencies, and infectious diseases are affecting the quality of life of millions in developing countries, especially women and children. Furthermore, while overweight, obesity, and resulting chronic diseases have traditionally been considered rich people's problems, such thinking is now outdated. Overweight and obesity are rapidly becoming an integral part of poverty in all but the poorest countries. In sum, developing countries are increasingly affected by a triple burden of malnutrition.

Health and nutrition problems are closely related to the food system (Hawkes and Ruel 2006). On the one hand, many of the world's major health problems—including undernutrition, food- and water-borne diseases, obesity, diet-related chronic diseases, and a range of occupational health hazards—are the result of improperly functioning food systems, while the effects of others—such as malaria and HIV/AIDS—could be mitigated if food systems functioned properly. On the other hand, food system workers in poor health are less able to work, denting productivity and income and perpetuating a downward spiral into ill-health and poverty. In a vicious cycle, this further jeopardizes food security and economic development for the country.

Societies can improve the health of the poor, reduce malnutrition and food insecurity, and promote pro-poor agricultural development through closer collaboration between the food and health sectors (Pinstrup-Andersen 2010). Although the relationship between the food system and health is clear, a more comprehensive treatment of their linkages has not yet been adequately addressed. We have illustrated existing food system policies and their impacts on human health, health and nutrition policies and their impact on the food system, and synergies between the two within a single conceptual framework. The emphasis is on incorporating these synergies in analysis and policy and fostering partnerships between the health and food sectors.

The links between the global food system and health and nutrition present an opportunity for stakeholders from diverse fields to work together to find solutions to the world's serious health and nutrition problems. Yet the food and health sectors and government interventions in both remain poorly coordinated. The message here is not that farmers and other actors in the food system should reorganize their activities to meet health goals if they conflict with market signals. The food system is part of the private sector, which depends on market demand to thrive. Thus, the role of the public sector is to design and implement policies that bridge the gap between societal goals and market signals. If market signals do not reflect the health and nutrition goals of society, there is a need for policy intervention. In so saying, it is important to stress that the goals of "society" are the varying goals of each individual member of society rather than the goals imposed on others by state or well-intentioned advocates: namely, the goals that enable people to live the healthy, balanced lives they seek through markets and collective public action. The next chapter delves further into food demand and consumption policies.

Human Health and Nutrition Policies Case Studies

Improving human health and nutrition is a key goal of food systems. The cases in this chapter describe the interactions between food systems, human health, and nutrition.* They illustrate how government action may improve human health and nutrition through a portfolio of direct interventions such as food fortification, biofortification, educational and food-for-education campaigns, and a variety of other government policies to address the needs of minorities and indigenous populations, deal with HIV/AIDS and food safety, and decrease the prevalence of overweight and obesity.

Case 3-1 adopts a gender lens to analyze how HIV/AIDS impacts agriculture and food security in sub-Saharan Africa because of the multiple levels of female vulnerability. Case 3-2 focuses on how different health and development policies are needed for marginalized populations. Cases 3-3 through 3-7 consider specific micronutrient shortfalls (hidden hunger) in different regions. Case 3-8 examines the potential of combining nutrition and education policies in a framework that is similar but distinct from conditional cash transfers. Cases 3-9 and 3-10 address the nutrition transition and obesity in middle-income and rapidly growing countries. Cases 3-11 and 3-12 ask students to identify how policy responses to food safety issues should differ for different groups of countries and how food safety policies in one country affect other countries.

---

* The case studies referenced here are presented in full in the three-volume work by Per Pinstrup-Andersen and Fuzhi Cheng, eds., *Case Studies in Food Policy for Developing Countries* (Ithaca, NY: Cornell University Press, 2009) and online via open access at http://cip.cornell.edu/gfs.

Notes

1. This section is based on Pinstrup-Andersen 2007a.

Chapter 4

Food Security, Consumption, and Demand Policies

Introduction

People's food choices are determined by many factors, of which meeting energy and nutrient needs is only one, and often not perceived to be the most important one. Food consumption is an important part of social behavior (influenced by culture, geography, and other social conditions) and differs across individuals and households (varying with incomes, preferences, cultural traditions, and local prices). In order to improve food consumption through government policy, it is important to understand the food consumption behavior of the target group and, as part of such understanding, to identify the factors that can be used as conduits for policy interventions. Food consumption is, of course, essential to meet energy and nutrient needs. Poor diets—whether too much or too little is being consumed—reduce life expectancy, increase the risk and severity of disease, and reduce productivity. Proper food consumption simply makes life better.

Food consumption patterns have changed markedly during the dietary transition introduced in the last chapter. Caused by accelerated industrialization, urbanization, economic development, market globalization, and Westernization, the dietary transition has been a force for both good and ill. People have enjoyed better access to food and a more diverse diet, and farmers who have been able to meet the new demands have enjoyed increased income security and well-being. For others, inappropriate dietary patterns and excessive net energy intake, coupled with decreased physical activity, have resulted in a significant increase in obesity and associated diseases. All three elements in the triple burden of malnutrition (hunger, micronutrient deficiency, and obesity) are present in all countries and can be found even within individual households.

Millions of the world's poor suffer from insufficient food consumption because they face structural constraints and stochastic shocks and because they lack effective coping strategies (see chapter 5). Problems associated with food consumption—both causing improper food consumption and caused by inadequate nutrition—are multisectoral, including political, socioeconomic, household, and environmental factors, and therefore need to be addressed through a multidisciplinary systems framework as elaborated in chapters 1 and 2 and discussed in detail in Pinstrup-Andersen (2010).

Food security refers to the ability of an individual, household, or nation to procure sufficient food for nutrition and preferences by legal, culturally approved means. According to FAO (2009a, 8), "Food security exists when all people, at all times, have physical, social and economic access to sufficient, safe and nutritious food that meets their dietary needs and food preferences for an active and healthy life." Food security also incorporates the notion of risk. A person who has enough food today but might not have enough tomorrow is not food secure. Food insecurity refers to the probability that a person will not have enough food over a specified period of time. Food security also often incorporates the concept of food safety: the food to which a person has access should keep a person healthy and have a low probability of causing harmful effects. Food insecurity tends to be concentrated among poor or socially marginalized people, and in areas remote from food markets. People above the poverty line may also be food insecure depending on their access to food.

Economic growth reduces poverty and tends to increase food consumption and food security for all. However, while increasing national incomes are of critical importance to alleviate hunger and undernutrition, a number of other factors must be considered. The distribution of the additional incomes is one such factor. Since hunger and undernutrition are closely associated with poverty, the extent to which income growth is captured by the poor is important. Even where the poor experience increasing incomes, complementary policy interventions will still be required to improve their food and nutrition situation (Haddad et al. 2002; Smith and Haddad 2002). Policies to increase agricultural production and market access, provide clean water, good sanitation, primary health care, and relevant knowledge are examples.

This chapter and the associated case studies discuss a set of potential policy interventions to improve food consumption and food security through poverty alleviation and complementary policies. The case studies illustrate that policy analysis and policy design and implementation must take into account economic as well as political and institutional considerations relevant for the particular country and target population. The political economy issues, which are frequently overlooked or assumed away in economic analysis, is of particular importance for sound and sustainable policies that are relevant, feasible and cost-effective.

The chapter begins with a brief overview of global and regional trends in food consumption and diets, followed by a conceptual analysis of why food consumption problems have persisted. We review the literature on individual and household food demand analysis and the importance of such analysis in food policymaking, focusing on the issues of inadequate food consumption and food insecurity in developing countries. We conclude by discussing food consumption policies. WHO (2010) provides additional discussion of the topics covered in this chapter.

The Food Consumption Situation

Global food consumption during the last three to four decades is characterized by four broad patterns: expanded per capita food availability, continuing widespread food insecurity, the nutrition transition with improvements in diet diversity, and dramatic increases in overweight and obesity combined with continued high prevalence of nutritional deficiencies. The first two are further discussed below. The last two were discussed in chapter 3.

Unprecedented improvements have been made in food availability worldwide over the past four decades. Global per capita food production has increased 15 percent in the past twenty years despite a 45 percent increase in the world's population over the same period, demonstrating both the strength of technological improvements in agriculture and their importance to food consumption. This also highlights the weakness of neo-Malthusian claims that growth in food production will be arithmetic while the population will grow exponentially, resulting in falling per capita food supply and increasing global food shortage. Large-scale and widespread famines caused by food shortages are largely a thing of the past (Ó Gráda 2007). Global food trade has likewise grown rapidly, making food more available in food-deficit regions. Real food prices in the world market declined sharply over a thirty-year period from the mid-1970s (Grilli and Yang 1988; Cuddington 1992). However, this falling price trend was reversed in 2005, and international food prices increased by 75 percent between 2005 and mid-2008. Large decreases between mid-2008 and the end of 2009 were replaced by new increases in 2010–2011 (chapter 1).

However, while average per capita food consumption has increased, unequal distribution of access to food has resulted in continued food insecurity. This is the second pattern: despite indisputable progress in food production, insufficient food consumption or food insecurity remains distressingly widespread. As discussed below, the absolute number of people suffering food insecurity has not fallen appreciably the last two decades, as widespread poverty and increasingly unequal asset and income distributions conspire to counteract the increased per capita food availability and falling food prices. The majority of people suffering from food insecurity reside in rural areas of developing countries and most of them are in south Asia and sub-Saharan Africa (see chapters 5 and 7). Even within regions, significant variation exists. Within central Africa, people in Gabon and Cameroon consume 300 more calories per day than in the Democratic Republic of Congo. Keyzer, Nubé, and Wesenbeeck (2006) estimate that average consumption varies within Cameroon alone from fewer than 1,800 kcal per capita in the north to over 2,500 kcal per capita in the south.

By 2020, developing countries are forecast to demand twice as much cereals and meat products as developed countries, but the average person in developing countries will consume only half as much cereals and one-third as much meat as the average person in a developed country. This disparity can be explained partly by lower incomes, greater dependence on roots and tubers in developing countries, and by much heavier use of cereals for feeding livestock in developed countries. In the case of cereals, while per capita demand in sub-Saharan Africa is projected to increase by 13 kg (9 percent) between 1995 and 2020, in east Asia it is projected to increase by 66 kg (21 percent) by 2020, mostly for feed grain. Oil crop demand is expected to grow faster than demand for cereals (WHO 2010). Meat demand is expected to increase greatly as part of a livestock revolution (discussed below). The increase in demand for cereals and meat products in developing countries is not likely to be met by increased production without significant agricultural investment (chapter 7). The difference will have to be imported, resulting in a growing trade deficit for net food importers. For the world as a whole, food demand is expected to increase by about 70 percent between 2010 and 2050 (FAO 2006a).

Food Security: Millennium Development Goals and the World Food Summit

In 1996, the FAO gathered leaders from over 180 governments to a World Food Summit (WFS) to pledge their "political will" and "national commitment" to reduce the number of people suffering from hunger to half of its 1990 level by 2015. That would mean a reduction from 845 million to 422 million people. This goal was supported and weakened in the year 2000 Millennium Development Goals (MDGs), in which governments pledged, among other things, to reduce the percent of the world suffering from hunger to half of its 1990 level by 2015. That would reduce the percent from 16 to 8, or approximately 590 million people. These goals focus solely on the number of calories consumed, ignoring micronutrient deficiencies.

Progress toward the WFS goal was initially hopeful but was ultimately short-lived, and even though the number of food insecure people decreased by 40 million from 1990 to 1998, the decrease was much less than what was needed to stay on a linear trend toward achieving the goal. Since the late 1990s, the number of food insecure people has increased, and the increase has been particularly severe since 2004 due largely to increasing food prices (figure 4.1). In addition to depicting FAO's estimates of world hunger since 1991 and the trend needed to meet the WFS goal, figure 4.1 shows two linear time trends comparing the overall trends from 1991–2005 and from 1991–2009 respectively. These are not projections of how many hungry people there will be in 2020, but are illustrative of the lack of progress over the last two decades, highlighting the negative impacts of the food price crisis.

During the period 1990–2005 the number of people suffering from food insecurity decreased by 100 million in China, yet increased in the Middle East (93 percent), central Asia (45 percent), and sub-Saharan Africa (26 percent). As detailed in Watson and Pinstrup-Andersen (2010), however, most of the increase in sub-Saharan Africa was due to increases in the Democratic Republic of the Congo. The number of food insecure people remained relatively constant in most of the other countries of sub-Saharan Africa. From 1991 to 2005, the number of people suffering from hunger decreased

FIGURE 4.1.
Progress toward meeting the World Food Summit goal. Source: Watson and Pinstrup-Andersen 2010;
Observations from FAO 2009a.

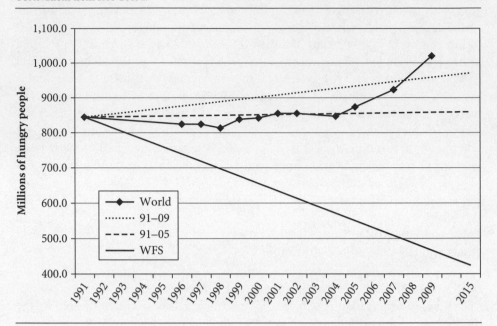

most in western Asia (66 percent), east Asia (26 percent), and South America (20 percent). If the trend from 1991 to 2005 were to continue, there would be 15 million more
hungry people in 2015 than there were in 1991. However, if the trend based on the
period 1990–2009 is the likely outcome, the increase will be closer to 100 million.

Progress toward the MDG has been more promising. The percent of hungry people decreased from 16 percent in 1991 to 13 percent by 2004. If those trends were
to continue, 12 percent of the population would still be hungry in 2015. The world
would be only halfway toward accomplishing the MDG. Country performance has
varied substantially. Remarkably, however, before the food crisis, sub-Saharan Africa's high population growth rate and the fact that most countries saw no change
in the number of hungry people has meant that the region excluding the DRC was
almost on track to accomplishing the MDG for reducing hunger. The combination
of these facts means that there is much more hope for African countries than is typically believed, but the region as a whole will not be able to achieve these goals unless
the situation in the DRC improves dramatically. Of course, achieving the MDGs
primarily through rapid population growth instead of reductions in the number of
hungry people is not a desirable outcome.

A Conceptual Evolution and Its Data Requirements

Although aggregate food availability has improved markedly over the past half century and is predicted to continue to grow in the next few decades, insufficient food
consumption and food insecurity resulting in hunger and malnutrition remain

widespread. As discussed in chapter 2, the concept of food consumption policy has changed during the last ten to fifteen years from a primary interest in national food availability to household food security, although the 2005–2008 food price increases brought back some of the earlier concerns about national food availability and desires to pursue food self-sufficiency goals. The increasing emphasis on household-level access means food consumption policy analysts must take household decision making, uncertainty and risk, market infrastructure, labor markets, terms of trade, and individual food access into account. Sen's (1981) concept of "entitlements"—the food that a person may legally claim through one's own endowment, production, trade, or charity—and the potential for "entitlement failure" was very influential in bringing about this shift. However, food production (chapter 7) is still an important part of food security, particularly increasing average productivity where it is low or where low incomes prevent relying on food imports, and reducing production volatility that leads to consumption instability (Diakosavvas 1989; Sahn and von Braun 1989).

National food balance sheets (FBSs) provide the most widely used data to assess the national and global food availability. They are produced by FAO in partnership with national governments, usually on an annual basis. FBSs estimate total national food availability (production, storage, and imports) and its allocation to direct human consumption, livestock feed, industrial nonfood uses, exports, and storage. They take account of food lost during storage, food used for pets, or nutrient losses through spoilage or cooking processes. The FAO measures of food insecurity are largely measures of food availability with a correction for income inequality to proxy for food access. For this reason, data on "food consumption" or "food intake" reported in this chapter should be considered as "food available for consumption" and the estimates of the number of food insecure (FAO uses the term "undernourished") people are likely to contain large error margins.

Food consumption is usually measured in kilocalories (kcals) per person per day, which is typically abbreviated as a person's daily energy supply (DES). Such data are not available for all countries but are typically estimated. To minimize random errors and smooth out the effects of temporary shocks, it is customary to present three-year averages instead of annual numbers. Table 4.1 shows that average DES has increased by 25 percent in developing countries from 1969–1971 to 2003–2005. Averaging can mask significant variation, however: DES has increased by only 3 percent in sub-Saharan Africa and decreased in the transition countries while soaring by 27 percent in east and Southeast Asia. This underscores the importance of improving agricultural productivity and food consumption in sub-Saharan Africa (chapter 7).

One of the difficulties faced in combating food insecurity is that, while a conceptual change has occurred, data collection has not followed suit. As Pinstrup-Andersen and Herforth (2008) put it:

> While measuring food security consistently over decades allows us to track changes in that indicator over time, a suboptimal indicator can lead to actions that fail to address the real problems. The way food insecure people are counted frames the problem, and the data collected inform the solution. (53)

TABLE 4.1.
Global and Regional per Capita Food Consumption (kcals/person/day)

Region/World	1969/71	1979/81	1989/91	1999/01	2015 (proj.)	2050 (proj.)
Industrialized countries	3,046	3,133	3,290	3,446	3,480	3,540
Transition countries	3,323	3,389	3,280	2,900	3,030	3,270
Developing countries	2,111	2,308	2,520	2,654	2,860	3,070
East and Southeast Asia	2,012	2,317	2,625	2,872	3,110	3,230
Latin America and the Caribbean	2,465	2,698	2,698	2,836	2,990	3,200
Near East and North Africa	2,380	2,830	3,010	2,974	3,080	3,190
South Asia	2,066	2,084	2,329	2,392	2,660	2,980
Sub-Saharan Africa	2,100	2,078	2,106	2,194	2,420	2,830

Source: FAO 2006a.

Nutrient deficiencies are disregarded in the food security estimates reported by FAO, as are any measure of the depth or severity of calorie shortages or the probability that someone could suffer from transitory food insecurity. Even including these factors in an improved measure of food insecurity would not address the difference between whether households have access to food and whether they actually choose to acquire food, nor how food is distributed among household members. Pinstrup-Andersen and Herforth (2008) discuss some emerging attempts to get at these factors through enhanced household surveys, dietary diversity scores, and anthropometry.

Household food consumption surveys often ask participants to recall what they ate over a specific time period. The longer the time period, the less accurate memories are likely to be; the shorter the time period, the more concern there is of not capturing dietary variations over time. Recall accuracy is also better for food consumed in the home than outside. Even people who have been prepared and trained to measure the food they eat have a tendency to underestimate portion sizes, introducing important biases into measures of food consumption. Consumption data may be improved by precisely measuring the food while being consumed or comparing the difference between foods available in the home on two consecutive days, but these introduce additional expense, time, and intrusiveness that may affect behavior and the composition of household samples.

Other household surveys that attempt to measure food security ask more general questions about whether households have felt vulnerable over a specific time period, whether there was a day when they had to go hungry because they could not access food, whether there has been a time when they did not know where they would get food for the day, and whether they made use of government or charitable food sources. These provide a more qualitative assessment that can capture temporary food insecurity, but this in turn makes quantitative assessments of how to affect the probability of food insecurity more difficult.

Anthropometric data provide easy-to-collect evidence of malnutrition. Stunting (low height for age), underweight (low weight for age), and wasting (low weight for height) for children, and low or high body mass index (BMI) scores for adults, provide evidence about the prevalence of malnutrition in a population.[1] Comparing these scores for a population over time or between populations and ignoring health problems not linked to nutrition allow one to identify where malnutrition is most prevalent. Keyzer, Nubé, and Wesenbeeck (2006) use anthropometric surveys for fourteen African countries to estimate undernourishment. They find significantly less food insecurity in central and eastern African countries than FAO data suggest, so that the total number of hungry people in sub-Saharan Africa in 2000 may have been 125 million instead of over 200 million. They conclude from this that agricultural productivity has been higher in Africa than previously estimated.

The Global Hunger Index (von Grebmer et al., 2009) includes three measures of food insecurity in one index: the percent of the population suffering from food insecurity, the percent of children under the age of five who are underweight, and the under-five mortality rate expressed as a percentage. Each measures a different dimension of food insecurity and may be influenced by factors other than food insecurity.

Threats to Food Security: Famine

Famines have proven difficult to define precisely. It is generally accepted that famines occur when there is severe, prolonged hunger over a large area, leading to at least two to five deaths per 10,000 people from starvation directly or from hunger-caused diseases. As with conflicts, many more people die from diseases during and after famines than from starvation during the actual famine. Had they not been malnourished, the diseases would not have been as deadly. Famines do not occur suddenly. There are many early warning signs of severe food shortage, such as declining food production, rising food prices, and increased migration. Sen (1981) found that famines can occur during a food production boom as well as during periods of low productivity; that famines are as much a failure of government and civil society as they are a lack of food; and that it is possible for farmers to be "hit" by drought, but "decimated" by the market mechanism. While natural catastrophes may have been the main culprit in the past, in modern times it is the failure of markets, governments, and humanity to assist people in times of trouble that turn regional economic or agricultural problems into famines. Risks associated with climate, markets, and government action and idiosyncratic risks contribute to the probability of famine.

Ó Gráda's (2007) outstanding summary of famines in the twentieth century is most instructive of how hunger and food security have changed. Famines have more often been caused by conflict and lack of democracy than poverty, and even the largest famines of the last century killed a smaller percent of their populations than previous famines. He reviews the literature also on how markets have both relieved and exacerbated different famines and the increased importance that government policy has had in mitigating or sparking famines, focusing on the Chinese famine of 1959–1961, which had perhaps the highest absolute death toll of any famine in history; the Bengalese famine of 1942–1944 diagnosed by Sen (1981) as caused by market forces; and Stalin's famines aimed at controlling the Ukraine from the 1920s to 1940s. The periodic mass starvation in North Korea is an example of famine caused directly by government policies. Devereux (2008) summarizes:

> Amartya Sen's *Poverty and Famines* taught us that where access to food is mediated by markets and purchasing power, vulnerability to famine is determined by market supplies and prices of food. Haggard and Noland's *Famine in North Korea* teaches us that where access to food is mediated by government allocations and politically stratified claims, vulnerability to famine is determined by public distribution failures or discretionary shifts in allocations of food. (1038)

Failures of government food entitlements when governments are not accountable to their people have also been indicted in the Soviet and Chinese famines mentioned above, and Ethiopia's mid-1980s famine. Malawi's 2000/01 famine (cases 7-1, 7-2, and 7-3) had its roots in natural causes (drought and low production) but was exacerbated by government policies and poor international relations and coordination.

Ó Gráda (2007) concludes that the eradication of famine risk is easier today than it ever has been, but that much depends on the international community: "Today, world public opinion alone may not eliminate underdevelopment but, unless civil strife intervenes, it can prevent harvest deficits from producing mass mortality" (32). Similarly, Devereux (2008) claims that "the fight against famine is a fight against the callousness of unaccountable regimes and the indifference or impotence of the international community" (1039).

Several institutions have been important in reducing the probability of famines. Sen (1981) emphasizes the importance of democratic accountability and free press so that citizens can hold politicians accountable for failing to act promptly at the first signs of impending famine. Well-integrated world markets can be an important part of eradicating famine: while one particular area may experience a severe food availability shock, other areas will be able to transport food there without decimating their own food access. Securing entitlements and rights to food through wage stability and low unemployment, public and private charity, and government programs (discussed below) provides multiple layers of protection for households and communities. Food stocks or cash reserves to purchase food in times of emergency can be effective, but are expensive to maintain and require good governance to work efficiently (chapter 7). Insurance and other risk management, and microfinance are discussed in chapters 5, 6, and 7, and in case 7-5. Ongoing commitment to agricultural research, infrastructure, and other needed public goods investment also serves to increase average food availability and reduce volatility, further reducing the probability of mass starvation.

Food Markets

Barrett (2002) identifies three primary groups whose food security is particularly vulnerable to market conditions and other external factors: traditionally vulnerable populations, wage earners, and smallholder farmers. Marginalized and traditionally vulnerable populations include the very young and very old—who must rely on savings, the generosity of their household and society, and social safety nets for food—and minorities and indigenous populations (chapter 5; case 3-2). Wage earners' food security is highly dependent on how high food prices are relative to their wages. In cases of price and inflation uncertainty, wages paid in kind (e.g., food) can reduce food insecurity (Ito and Kurosaki 2009). Many governments' food and trade policies have been directed to reduce the prices of agricultural goods in order to keep manufacturing wages low so that manufactured goods would be cheaper for export. Even for those who have enough food on average, volatility in either income or food prices can cause temporary food shortages, potentially leading to long-term health problems.

Smallholder farmers are also highly dependent on weather fluctuations and food price volatility, though in this case it is decreases in the prices of the foods they sell and increases in the prices of foods and inputs they purchase that matter. Among this group, pastoralists face a somewhat unique situation in that their livestock supply food and income and are a store of wealth and cultural status (case 7-6). Forced sales of livestock during drought may trap a family in poverty for generations.

Wages are heavily dependent on labor productivity, which itself is partly determined by health, technology, labor market regulations, financial market development, relevant market sizes (including labor, domestic goods, and trade), and individual access to education and health care options. For people with few assets, labor is their primary endowment. Ensuring the social conditions necessary for people to make fullest use of that labor is a primary role of government. Governments also set the rules that govern labor and financial market transactions, enact and enforce property and contract laws, and protect human and minority rights.

Food prices are an integral part of food security. They are also complex. Just as with wages and the prices of any other good, there is no single right price for any food commodity or meal that will satisfy everyone. Net food buyers prefer lower prices unambiguously. Individual net food item sellers prefer high prices. Smallholder farmers who are net food buyers would gladly accept income-maximizing, potentially high prices for the foods they produce and very low prices for those they buy. Because of these conflicting desires for food prices, any price determined by a government, marketing board, or firm, rather than the market, will be based on the relative strength of various stakeholders' voices in decision making. Food price policies are discussed in a separate section below.

Agricultural production volatility and socioeconomic and political stability matter for the poor and their long-term food security. As discussed in more depth in chapter 7, rainfall patterns—including its timing and variability within a season—pests, and diseases greatly affect crop and livestock productivity and value. Particularly in arid and semiarid regions, even farmers who are typically net sellers can face sudden sharp losses. Lack of financial market development (insurance and credit markets particularly) prevent smallholders and pastoralists from diversifying their risk, smoothing their consumption, and avoiding catastrophe sell-offs that leave families impoverished for years afterward (case 7-5). Sociopolitical stability includes securing property rights against theft, arbitrary nationalization, and conflict. Weak states and conflict are mutually reinforcing, both harming food security and food markets. Stability and the food system are further discussed in chapter 9.

Those who routinely suffer shortfalls in purchasing power or nontradable food availability regularly depend on transfers. The flow of international remittances is already larger than official development assistance (ODA) and foreign direct investment (FDI) if China's FDI is excluded (Klein and Harford 2005; chapter 10). Remittances show less variance than ODA or FDI. People who give private charity or remittances may give for a variety of reasons, but rarely provide either an entitlement or an enforceable right to food or income (chapter 11; Webb and Reardon 1992; Townsend 1995).

Guaranteed entitlements and social security systems may be either public or private. Among the difficulties with relying on transfers is that private donations and government income tend to decrease during recessions when the poor are likely to need the transfers most. Social norms regarding familial responsibility to care for the elderly have tended to weaken both with increasing average incomes and public social security systems. Designing policies that provide social safety nets without reducing private transfers and social networks or that ease labor mobility and remittance flow can support this source of income for the poor.

Household Choices: Coping and Adaptation

Even the most vulnerable people are not merely passive victims of the circumstances in which they find themselves. Food systems are behavioral systems. People respond to the incentives and risks they face to mitigate negative risks before they are realized and to cope with problems when they arise. Chapter 7 discusses at length the importance of agricultural risk for determining smallholder agricultural practices. Government policies intended to assist in mitigating risk may have both positive and adverse effects as people change their strategies in light of the new resources and incentives they face. For example, the poor might not do enough to mitigate risks when they know they are insured by the public sector—a moral hazard problem.

Government policies affect how people choose to allocate their limited resources and time. A lack of secure property rights and high taxes on capital gains dampen the incentive to invest in improving land, homes, or other capital. Income taxes do not tax being wealthy as much as trying to become so, and therefore change the incentives to invest in human capital and productivity enhancements. From a livelihoods perspective, government policies may focus on preserving current livelihoods or on making it easier for people to change livelihoods if they choose.

When negative shocks occur, there are a limited number of coping strategies available to the poor (Barrett 2002). If transfers and loans are unavailable and households do not have sufficient nonproductive assets such as jewelry to sell, the remaining options involve trading future well-being for current survival. Farm families may engage in unsustainable exploitation of natural resources with negative long-term consequences for both the environment and food security (chapter 8). People may draw down their health capital by reducing food and nonfood consumption, or sell productive assets, reducing future income possibilities. Either option may have serious, long-term consequences, trapping a person in poor health or poverty. Such distress sales usually only happen when there are few other options remaining, leaving sellers with little flexibility or bargaining power to get the highest return possible.

When other avenues have been exhausted, people may take desperate measures, such as migrating, turning to crime, or selling themselves into servitude or prostitution. Depending on the options for migration and the labor conditions there, migrating may be an excellent opportunity to escape from poverty at the expense of the psychological and transportation costs of moving, or it may trap a household in a worse situation than before. If the decision to migrate has been put off long enough, a family's only option may be to go to a refugee camp, urban homeless shelter, or other area that will provide a meager safety net but few opportunities for future employment. Chapter 5 discusses the social marginalization that accompanies bonded labor or migration.

Reducing dietary diversity and calorie or micronutrient consumption can be either a coping strategy or part of a mitigation strategy designed to increase cash savings in case of a negative shock in the future. Households may also consume less desirable foods, called, in economics terms, "Giffen goods," and in other literatures, "famine foods," including leaves and roots, unsafe or spoiled foods scavenged from elsewhere, and animals not normally consumed in that society (Corbett 1988).

Small short-term changes in diet diversity or calorie consumption may not affect a household's health status over the long run, or not to the extent that distress sales or forced migration would. However, as discussed in chapter 3, large decreases in food consumption can cause permanent health problems, retard children's physical and mental growth, or leave a person susceptible to death from otherwise nonfatal diseases. Changes in household food access are not likely to affect all household members equally. "Lifeboat ethics" refers to a situation where resources are given to the strongest or most able members of a group to ensure the survival of at least some of the group, leaving the weakest in a more precarious position. Lifeboat ethics may be seen at household, communal, or national levels as favored groups receive privileged access to scarce resources (e.g., the Ukraine famine of the 1930s).

Government or community policies that provide effective safety nets can prevent many of the worst coping mechanisms and consequences. Communal food pantries, school feeding programs, and other in-kind transfers of food can obviate the need to reduce food consumption while freeing up limited resources for other needs. On the other hand, it can be difficult to target such benefits only to particular family members if the household decision makers change the allocation of in-home foods as a result of food eaten outside the home (Pinstrup-Andersen 1993b).

Population Growth and Demographic Transitions

Demographic transitions also have important implications for the food system. If agricultural production does not grow at least as fast as population, per capita food availability decreases. In such a situation, it is possible to be continually producing record harvests with a population that slowly starves. Thus agricultural-productivity-enhancing investments and other food security investments are most needed in areas with the highest population growth.

Writing in 1798, Malthus is credited with first postulating a population poverty trap (chapter 5). Since population grows exponentially but agricultural productivity increased only arithmetically at the time, he argued that conflict, famine, and disease would keep human populations at a constant level that ensured their subsistent survival. If people ever rose temporarily above the subsistence level, they would have more children and this would put too great a strain on the environment and production possibilities, leading to conflict, famine, and diseases that would reduce population back to its steady-state level. Many environmentalists follow a neo-Malthusian argument (chapter 8).

Oddly enough, however, Malthus himself was not "Malthusian" (Emmett 2006). His most famous work was written in response to a proposal to eradicate institutions such as private property and the family. Malthus (1798, 3) argued that private property and the family provided households with incentives to self-regulate their numbers: "Impelled to the increase of his species by an equally powerful instinct, reason interrupts his career, and asks him whether he may not bring beings into the world, for whom he cannot provide the means of subsistence."

This alternate view was also expressed by von Mises (1979, 5–6), who argued that one of the indicators of the success of capitalism has been the "unprecedented increase in world population. . . . The mere fact that you are living today is proof that capitalism has succeeded." That is, today's population is the result of past improvements in incomes and food production. When poor people experience economic improvements, some of those resources go toward more children but a larger portion goes to improving quality of life and investments in the children that already exist. Von Mises further argued that where mortality rates have declined without economic growth because of medical technology transfer, population growth has occurred without the corresponding improvements in living standards that support the neo-Malthusian view.

Novartis (2010) argues that the population growth rate may soon reach its peak and begin to slow as population growth rates in developing countries begin to slow. After the population growth rate peaks, it could be within this century that global population peaks as well. Policies that enable households to choose the number of children they want and at what spacing provide people greater freedom and control. Choosing the size and composition of one's family has been deemed a universal human right by the United Nations.

Eighty-five percent of the population growth since 1900 has taken place in developing countries, and it is expected that 97 percent of the world's population growth from 2000 to 2050 will take place there as well (Novartis 2010). At the same time, the populations of several OECD member countries have already begun to decline, and declines are expected in many other wealthier countries and China in the coming decades. This means that the average age of people in wealthier countries is likely to increase significantly, while the average age in developing countries will remain lower.

This change in the age distribution can already be seen in the aging of U.S. farm populations, who are concerned that very few people from younger generations are interested in farming. The demographic transition will impact the foods that are demanded and the income and spending habits of consumers in OECD countries. Harris and Blisard (2002) and previous research have identified significant food consumption and expenditure differences among groups of elderly people in the United States. From age sixty-five to seventy-four people spend more on beverages, meat products, and sweets than households whose head is over seventy-five, but less on fresh fruits.

Aging populations will also have a harder time affording the pension, welfare, and social safety net programs in place because there will be fewer working-age people for every person receiving benefits. This is likely to impact OECD migration policies, encouraging more young people from developing countries to live, work, and pay taxes for government programs that benefit older domestic citizens. Chapter 10 discusses both the benefits and concerns this poses for people from developing countries.

China's one-child policy is particularly noteworthy. It exacts a heavy fine from most urban families, approximately 36 percent of the total population (Xiaofeng 2007), that choose to have more than one child, who may also be shut out of certain occupations or positions. Another 53 percent of the population may have a second child if their first was a girl. Fertility had already fallen in China from five births per woman in 1970 to three in 1980 when the policy came into full effect. The government maintains that the policy has spurred the country's economic growth, reduced environmental damage, and reduced social population pressures in its urban areas. Because sons have been favored in many countries, the one-child policy has also created a large gender imbalance, which the Chinese government estimates will result in 30 million more men than women in 2020 (BBC 2007).

For further reading on the demographic transition and development, Galor (2005) provides a useful summary of the research on the relationships between population and economic growth and compares the various explanations for the initial demographic transition in OECD countries. He finds that the growing importance of human capital determines both reductions in fertility and increased economic growth. Lorentzen, McMillan, and Wacziarg (2008, 81) find that risk of death during the adult years has an independent effect on fertility and investment beyond the effects of infant mortality, and that this adult mortality "explains almost all of Africa's growth tragedy." Boucekkine, Desbordes, and Latzer (2009) expand this analysis, demonstrating that increased adult mortality on average decreases fertility in Africa while child mortality increases total fertility but not net fertility. Thus, the HIV/ AIDS epidemic tends to lower African fertility.

Consumer and Household Demand Analysis

Introduction to Consumer Demand

Knowing why and how consumer and household food consumption behavior will change as the external environment changes—markets, governments, and demographics—is essential to designing effective policies. Economic theories on consumers and households are vast and are beyond the scope of this book. This section introduces a few fundamentals of consumer demand and summarizes two primary models of household decision making: the unitary model and the collective model.

Economics is the study of decision making in the face of scarcity and, as mentioned in chapter 1, the foundation of food policy as presented in this book. There is only so much money available, so much time, so much energy, and far more potential demands on our time, money, and energy than we could possible fill. The steel used to build a bridge cannot simultaneously be used to build a hospital. Food consumed by a child cannot simultaneously be consumed by a parent. A policymaker has only twenty-four hours each day to divide between the demands of constituents, lobbyists (including donors, NGOs, and policy analysts), colleagues, community (including social networks and religion), family, and self. A government or household budget can stretch only so far. How can people make decisions among so many competing demands?

The basic primitive from which economic theory is built is the notion of rational preferences. In order for preferences to be rational, they must meet only two criteria. First, given a choice between any two outcomes, a person can choose one or the other or be equally happy with either. It could be as simple as a choice between eating bananas and cassava, or as complex as a choice between a societal pathway toward less income inequality, more public goods, less individual freedom, and higher taxes or a society that moves in other directions. Second, these choices should not obviously contradict each other: if a person prefers eating a pound of bananas to a pound of oranges and also prefers eating a pound of oranges to a pound of cassava, then that person's preferences are rational only if he or she would rather eat a pound of bananas than a pound of cassava.

Economists assume that people are rational. They know what they want and are able to choose between available options. Economists assume that people make choices based on what will make them happy, including giving charitably to someone else if that other person's happiness or the simple act of giving makes the giver happier. The happiness a person receives from their choices is generally referred to as "utility." Economists have demonstrated that if a person tries to maximize his or her utility, the best way to do this is to equate the amount of utility a person would receive from different outcomes "at the margin"—from just a little more of each thing. It is not the total amount of utility that is the focus, but the utility from the next doughnut, the next bit of exercise, the next hour spent working or playing. If the marginal utility from eating one more doughnut is greater than the marginal disutility of exercise or of weight gain and increased probability of chronic diseases, then a person will choose to eat the doughnut.

Nutrition education attempts to help people make more informed decisions, by explaining, for instance, what the risks of chronic diseases from obesity are, but it is possible that people may still rationally prefer the risk of diseases in an undefined future to forgoing passing pleasure now. Nutrition policies (chapter 3) need to take account of these behavioral factors to be effective at improving health and nutrition.

Rational parents balance the welfare of themselves and existing children in making a decision whether to have one more child. For the poor, children are often assumed to increase the utility of other household members and to be an investment in future income, social safety nets, and future utility from interacting with grown children. Child creation and rearing decisions are also based on physical and social constraints, expected lifetime income of parents and children, and gender norms.

It is generally, but not universally, assumed that the pleasure of any activity diminishes the more it is done. In the jargon, this is referred to as the law of diminishing marginal utility. One doughnut will not have much effect on a person's long-term health and may taste very good, but eating an entire dozen at one sitting may have both short-term and long-term impacts on a person's health and well-being while that twelfth doughnut just doesn't taste as good as the first.

Whether a household member, a government official, or a politician, decision makers act as if they were constantly weighing and balancing thousands of these choices every day, from the mundane to the profound. Should the small amount of money a parent received from an NGO be spent on improved nutrition for his or her children, on furthering their education, on medical care, on paying off a loan to improve farm productivity, on savings for possible future needs, on cultural obligations, on maintaining social networks, or on something else? Where would a small amount of additional government spending be best directed and what would be the intended beneficiary's response?

Another of the basic tenets of economics is that, while we cannot observe preferences directly, the choices people make reveal what their preferences are. The amounts of different foods people purchase at different prices indicate their relative demand for each. Policymakers demonstrate their relative political will for various causes based on how they allocate their time and the resources they control (Wood and Peake 1988; Watson 2009).

Individual food preferences depend on a number of factors. Some are physiological, such as the size and timing of meals, blood sugar changes, hunger for specific nutrients, diseases that come from a lack of specific micronutrients, addictions, and cravings. Physiological needs depend on a person's height, age, gender, occupation, activity level, ability to metabolize different nutrients, and past and current health history. Psychological wants are equally important in determining individual food demand. Individual taste perceptions vary both between individuals and within an individual over time. Some foods are "an acquired taste," implying that future desire depends on current decisions. Cultural factors matter as well in determining what is eaten, how it is prepared, and with whom it is eaten. Wansink (2006) has done important research showing how unconscious framing effects change how much a person eats, such as taking larger portion sizes when the serving dish is larger or gauging how full a person is by whether they have emptied their plate. Advertising plays a critical role in food perceptions as well. Food consumption analysts need to understand how these factors interrelate in order to design food policies that improve health and nutrition.

Household Demand

Identifying preferences empirically is not necessarily simple. There is a difference between the hypothetical demand functions that relate the maximum amount a person would be willing to pay for given quantities of a good and the price a person would be willing to pay in an experimental session when nearby stores provide an outside option. Surveys can provide another guide to understanding preferences, but when no actual decisions are being made, the margin for error is relatively large and it can be difficult to know what is being communicated. Actual purchase decisions will differ from both of these depending on how households make purchasing decisions.

There are two primary models of household decision making. The unitary household model posits one of several assumptions: either all household members have identical preferences, all of them are altruistic in the sense of caring about the others' preferences as much as their own, or the household head acts dictatorially and may or may not care about the preferences of other members of the household. Models based on any of these assumptions will arrive at substantively similar results. When individual preferences differ, there have been efforts to aggregate preferences or average utility functions, which would then indicate the level of well-being of the whole household (a social welfare function, chapter 11), which describes how a benevolent dictatorial household head makes decisions (Alderman et al. 1995).

Much evidence has been presented on the unequal distribution of resources and commodities within a household. However, the issue did not receive much attention in the past, partly because of the difficulty of applying the traditional economic tools such as the unitary model to its analysis. Fortin and Lacroix (1997) claim that with the unitary model, it is impossible to review individual preferences of household members or the parameters that characterize the internal processes determining the observed outcomes. Consequently, it is also impossible to analyze intrahousehold inequalities or external transfers to intrahousehold resource allocation with this model. As Chiappori (1992) points out, traditional models can be inadequate and misleading in such policy issues as the welfare of individuals because they focus on income distribution across households not within the household, even though the within-household distribution is central to individual welfare (see also Haddad and Kanbur 1990).

The collective model attempts to resolve these concerns by modeling how competing interests are resolved in a household. Collective models are sometimes divided into two types: cooperative and noncooperative. Cooperative models assume that individuals form a household if this option is more beneficial for each party than remaining unattached. One cooperative model, the efficient cooperative model, views household decisions as efficient in the Pareto sense so that no one can be made better off without someone being made worse off (see Chiappori 1988). Another cooperative model is the bargaining model, which applies the tools of game theory in its analysis (see McElroy 1990). Noncooperative models posit that individuals have separate economies within one household and they do not enter into enforceable contracts with each other (see Lundberg and Pollak 1993). Intrahousehold decision making and allocation are discussed by Quisumbing and Smith in case 4-5.

Collective models are regularly invoked to justify targeting program benefits to mothers, who are deemed to be more willing to spend marginal income on children's welfare than fathers. Even when programs give in-kind transfers, household decision-making rules matter. A household that tries to share all resources may distribute food designated by a donor for infants among all family members. Another household may give all the designated food to an infant while redistributing other nutritive inputs to other family members as another sharing mechanism. If households value other interventions more than the one being given, they may also attempt to trade in-kind transfers for cash. On this there is a debate on whether public transfers targeted toward children are largely neutralized by the household, as the theory of altruism implies, or whether there is an intrahousehold "flypaper effect" whereby such transfers "stick" to the children. Empirical evidence is mixed since the exact outcome depends heavily on the interactions and resource reallocations among household members (Anderson et al. 1981; Beaton and Ghassemi 1982). Failure to understand household decision-making rules can reduce the effectiveness and efficiency of nutrition interventions (Pinstrup-Andersen 1993b).

One recent example is You and Davis (2007), who model how parental and child food decisions determine child obesity rates. Their empirical analysis rejects the unitary model and finds that targeting program benefits to mothers may impact obesity less than previously believed. Another example is Shimokawa (2010), who shows that Chinese households who have limited access to capital respond differently to negative shocks than positive ones, with female children bearing more of the costs in urban households and elderly household members in rural areas. He also shows that these effects matter more in households with less than median income than in households above the median.

Food Prices

Food prices are an essential factor mediating food choices and are necessary for understanding group food decisions. People respond to price incentives. This does not mean that every person robotically and automatically responds the same way to a change in prices, but that when prices change, a large proportion of people will change behavior in a predictable way, leading to observable changes in group behavior.

From 1974, the end of the last major food price crisis, to the beginning of the 2000s, there was a trend to lower food prices as technology, increasing global food trade, and agricultural subsidies in rich countries increased food production and availability faster than demand. Around this trend, however, there has been significant variation. A food price spike in 1996 led many commentators to predict the end of historically low food prices, as many have predicted based on the more recent food crises (2007–2008 and 2010–2011). Where markets are not competitive or not well integrated, where production is more dependent on variable rainfall in a given year, or where government policies are less predictable, there can be significant price volatility in local markets as well. Market integration tends to lower food price variation due to local factors, but increases volatility based on far-off factors. Large food price swings are unambiguously harmful because they reduce the ability of food system agents to plan and prepare and can wipe out a household's ability to achieve food security and adequate nutrition. Chapters 6, 7, and 10 further discuss the importance of food price volatility for markets, producers, and traders.

Increases in price tend to reduce the amount that people purchase while decreases tend to have the opposite effect. That is not the end of the story, however. When prices change, there are two effects, called the income and substitution effects. A price increase effectively reduces a person's real income: they can buy less of that good with the money they have available, and if they continue to buy the same quantity, then they will have to buy less of something else. Price decreases act similarly to increases in income: a person can now buy more of anything when something they already purchase is cheaper. The substitution effect captures the change in consumption of other goods whose prices have not changed.

People may change purchases by a large amount when prices change or they may not respond much at all, continuing to consume almost the same as before the price change. Their demand is more or less "elastic" in response to price changes and is estimated by the "price elasticity of demand." Estimates of price elasticity are an important part of understanding how people will respond to food consumption policies.[2] Demand for other foods may also change a lot or a little when the prices of a particular good changes, reflecting the "cross-price elasticity."

Consider what happens when a tax is imposed on an unhealthy food. The taxed good rarely bares the full brunt of the tax. For most goods, people will consume not only less of that food, but less of other goods as well. However, if there are ready substitutes, the tax may shift consumption to those substitutes. Notice that a tax on one food may increase or decrease demand for other foods depending on how responsive a person is to price changes. Price changes on staple foods are likely to decrease demand for other foods while price changes on more luxury foods are likely to increase consumption of other goods. The adjustments in the demand for the taxed food and the adjustments in all other foods result in what is really important from a food security and nutrition point of view: the change in the diet. For example, a tax on sugary foods may encourage people to eat foods with more fat and businesses to use less sugar and more fat in their products.

Subsidies on healthy foods can have perverse impacts. By reducing the price of a healthy food, consumers effectively have more money to spend. They may choose to consume both more healthy foods and more unhealthy foods! In fact, recent research has shown that this is a very real possibility (Epstein et al. 2010). It is not enough to demonstrate that lowering the price of healthy foods increases consumption of those healthy foods. Food policy analysts need to consider the entire set of food choices in order to understand what effect taxes and subsidies will have on the diet. From a health and nutrition perspective, it is important to also understand how food taxes and subsidies would affect household expenditures on health care, sanitation, and access to clean water. This is one of the reasons for more multidisciplinary policy analysis so that economists, nutritionists, health professionals, and others can examine the total effects of proposed policies.

Food Consumption Analysis

So far, our discussion has been on the food decisions of individuals and households. Food consumption analysis also needs to be able to examine higher-level aggregates, including communities, minority groups, geographic (provincial, national, regional, global) aggregates, and occupational groups. A useful analysis of food consumption must also recognize the complementarities and trade-offs between food and other variables, notably education, caregiving, and health; capture behavioral dynamics; understand uncertainty and risk; and capture irreversibilities and threshold effects that make the threat of an adverse nutritional state so worrisome. This section will discuss each of these issues in turn (see also Barrett 2002).

Aggregation masks variation. Positive and negative shocks within a group cancel each other out: for instance, an intrahousehold variation in food consumption can mask child hunger (Pitt and Rosenzweig 1985; Rosenzweig 1986; Behrman 1988; Haddad and Kanbur 1990 and 1992; Pitt, Rosenzweig, and Hassan 1990; Rogers and Schlossman 1990; Haddad and Reardon 1993; Haddad and Hoddinott 1994; Kanbur and Haddad 1994; Doss 1996; Behrman 1997; Haddad, Hoddinott, and Alderman 1997; and case 4-5).

Complementarities and trade-offs affect food consumption. It is one thing to say that every person has a human right to food, education, shelter, and/or health. It is quite a different thing to understand how individuals or societies that lack the capacities and entitlements to fulfill all of them deal with inherent trade-offs between how much they fulfill each one, no matter how ethically unacceptable those trade-offs appear (chapter 11). Because the poor face a variety of urgent needs, economists have identified a surprisingly low increase in food purchases with income increases (e.g., Behrman and Deolalikar 1987; Bouis and Haddad 1992; Alderman 1993; Strauss and Thomas 1995).

Most people try to stabilize or smooth their food consumption over time. If there is a low probability of negative shocks, this means that people will not change consumption by much in response to a problem. As the probability of negative shocks increases, there is an increased motive for precautionary saving. People may choose to consume less now so that they have more money as a cushion in case of a future negative shock. On the other hand, people may choose to eat more now so they have a body mass cushion in case of a future negative shock. Either strategy can be bad for their long-run health. Effective safety nets that reduce the severity of negative shocks and macroeconomic stability that reduces the probability of negative shocks are important parts of helping people smooth food consumption in healthy ways. Food policy analysts tend to focus on the chronically food insecure and need to be more cognizant of people with transitory food shortages who are nevertheless food insecure. The policy goal is to reduce downside systematic risks and enable households to reduce idiosyncratic risks more than to compensate households after problems have arisen. Barrett (2002, 7) describes how "behaviors may change radically as one approaches the threshold of adverse, irreversible states, thereby introducing important nonlinearities into many economic and nutritional relationships."

Implications for Policymaking

Since many food interventions take the form of an implicit or explicit subsidy, either by altering the price facing households or by transferring real income, an important question is how food or nutrition intake changes when incomes change or when food prices change. On this subject, there has been an active debate on the magnitude of the income elasticity[3] of calorie intake compared with the income elasticity of food expenditures. As the income of poor people rises, it is likely that they will trade quantity for quality of food and substitute away from calories toward health and nonnutrient characteristics of foods such as taste and variety. If this is the case, the income elasticity of calorie intake could be significantly lower than the income elasticity of food expenditure or of nutrients such as iron, zinc, and vitamins. Income transfers would thus have a much smaller impact on energy intake and would require much larger transfers to the poor to achieve a given level of improvement (compare Behrman and Deolalikar 1987 and 1990, with Subramanian and Deaton 1996).

A key issue in studying a country's food subsidies is to determine which commodities to subsidize in order to minimize the budgetary cost to improve the nutrition of the malnourished. To achieve this, an ideal commodity for distribution is one consumed in large quantities by the poor and little by those with adequate diets, thus minimizing leakages toward the latter (Timmer, Falcon, and Pearson 1983; Kanbur 1987). Subsidizing one commodity may create not only direct nutritional gains through increased consumption of that commodity (an income effect) but potential indirect gains or losses as well, as the consumption of nonsubsidized foods or other goods change (a substitution effect). Assessing the total nutritional effect of a subsidy thus requires capturing the complex reallocation of consumer expenditures across commodities in response to the price change. Food prices may be reduced through direct price interventions or through the allocation of public budget to reduce unit costs of production and marketing (chapters 6 and 7) of specific foods. For example, a country may tailor its agricultural research strategy to its nutritional improvement objectives by prioritizing some commodities and research goals over others (Pinstrup-Andersen, Londono, and Hoover 1976).

Knowledge of demand structure is essential for sector and macroeconomic policy analysis. In the very short run, food supply cannot readily respond to changes in market structure because of the long duration of the production cycle, meaning that prices can fluctuate rapidly and only demand can respond. As the time horizon increases, changes in supply become increasingly salient. High prices for one food commodity will lead farmers to produce more of that food and less of others, as has been the case with increased demand for maize for biofuels. Complete systems of demand equations need to be estimated that satisfy budget and consistency constraints. Mittal (2006) identifies some of the more popular demand and market system models: the linear expenditure system (Stone 1954), the almost ideal demand system (AIDS) (Deaton and Muellbauer 1980), the general AIDS (Bollino 1990), the Rotterdam model (Barten 1969; Theil 1976), the translog model (Christensen, Jorgenson, and Lau 1975), and IFPRI's IMPACT system (Rosegrant et al. 2008).

Food Consumption Policies

Government policies can impact food security by altering markets, governments, or consumer mitigation and coping strategies. Of course, the dividing lines between categories are not always clear: labor productivity is an important factor that responds to individual choices, but is constrained or enhanced by market realities and government policies. There are also three key elements to successful food consumption promotion strategies according to Barrett (2002):

> (i) stable employment and high labor productivity to provide a regular
> means of sufficient income to subsist; (ii) access to finance, food markets,
> and storage technologies that permit consumption smoothing in the face
> of shocks to purchasing power or food supplies; and (iii) safety nets to pro-
> vide transfers to those who suffer adverse shocks that the economic system
> cannot allay itself. At an aggregate level, there is also a need for continuous
> technological and institutional progress in food production, processing, and
> distribution, so as to ensure non-declining per capita food availability and
> declining, real prices. (30)

Policies that improve food consumption over the long run generally take effect only with significant time lags, while policies that aim to improve food consumption immediately can have very deleterious effects if continued beyond a short time frame. Chapters 5–10 largely focus on longer-term solutions to consumption problems: reducing poverty, improving market infrastructure, investing in public goods such as agricultural research, pursuing environmental win-win situations, improving governance at each level of government, and making globalization work for the poorest. Strategies directly attacking such root causes of poverty as unemployment, landlessness, and poor infrastructure can be most effective in ensuring the sustainable eradication of hunger.

Policies generating income growth have an important role to play in alleviating hunger and other food-related problems, since the poor spend a large share—as high as 70 percent—of their income on food. Empirical studies in support of this view demonstrate that increases in income translate to a rise in the nutritional status of the poor (Subramanian and Deaton 1996; Haddad et al. 2002; Smith and Haddad 2002; chapter 5). In developing countries, increases in income for the poor enable the undernourished and malnourished to purchase more calories to provide sufficient energy and a greater variety of food to provide better nutrition. In developed countries, it is often the least healthy foods that are the cheapest so that increases in income enable households to consume more fruits and vegetables and thus reduce micronutrient deficiencies that may coexist with obesity, though this response is not guaranteed.

Figure 4.2(a) indicates that countries with higher per capita GDP have a lower incidence of hunger. Grouping countries based on their success in reducing hunger during the 1990s, we can see that those with increasing hunger registered the worst economic performance (figure 4.2(b)). Paradoxically, figure 4.2(b) also indicates that countries that registered the highest economic growth only made slow progress in reducing hunger, while those progressing rapidly in reducing hunger achieved only moderate economic growth. This finding and other research (e.g., Haddad et al. 2002; Smith and Haddad 2002; World Bank 2007a) indicate that additional policies beyond those that promote general economic growth are needed to combat hunger.

FIGURE 4.2.
Economic growth and hunger. Source: FAO 2005a.

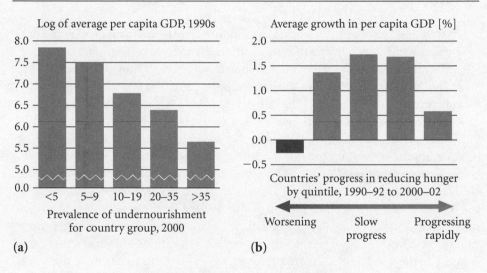

(a)   (b)

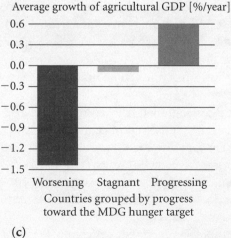

(c)

Chapter 7 discusses how economic growth that is centered in rural areas and agricultural development has a greater impact on hunger and is more likely to reduce inequality.

Figure 4.2(c) supports this last argument. It shows that the countries that made progress toward the MDG hunger reduction target were where the agriculture sector grew. Indeed, in most poor countries with agriculture employing over half of their population, income from growing food is a main source of food entitlements. It can readily be argued that increased agricultural production that generates sufficient self-employment income to ensure food entitlements should be the key to food security, until enhanced farm growth followed by successful diversification has reduced employment dependence on farming. As Muralidharan (1994, 26) puts it: "It is good to have an industry that provides food to millions. But it is better to have an industry which does the same thing and at the same time provides employment to millions of people."

Chapter 5 discusses the literature on improving economic growth for poverty reduction. At present, there is little consensus about the extent to which food security and nutritional status improve with increasing incomes. However, Barrett's (2002) summary of the current state of thought is quite reasonable: it appears that macroeconomic stability helps maintain economic growth and support market investments, but either does not spur growth by itself or only does so with a long lag. Access to public goods (especially education, roads, agricultural research, and a functioning, transparent legal system) and productive assets are essential to enable individuals to produce economic opportunities. Credit and financial markets are both part of a wise investment strategy and help people cope with temporary shocks. Well-integrated food markets reduce price volatility from local weather and conditions, in turn stabilizing food consumption, though they introduce other sources of volatility beyond an individual's control.

Food Assistance Programs

Markets in low-income settings are often complex, typically involving personalized relationships, high transaction costs, and asymmetric information (chapter 6). These factors reduce market access for the vulnerable and induce higher price and income volatility. The food insecure people are disproportionately concentrated in areas with weak markets and considerable exogenous risks. In these areas, government policies are required to keep people from suffering chronic or transitory food insecurity. Food assistance programs may attempt to enhance the poor's access to food (e.g., food price subsidies, food stamps, conditional cash transfers) or improve people's ability to make use of the food available (e.g., nutrition education, micronutrient fortification, biofortification).

Existing policies vary significantly across countries with different income levels. Richer countries tend to target their food assistance programs more directly than poorer countries. The latter may favor untargeted food subsidies or price controls. The harm that price controls cause to long-run market development and the difficulty of running food subsidies sustainably will be discussed in chapter 6.

Notwithstanding the long-term harm these policies can cause to proper food system development, they make more sense for poorer countries than for wealthier for four primary reasons: (1) they are less costly to administer in terms of bureaucratic capacity; (2) they are politically attractive since many of the benefits spill over to people who do not strictly need them but may have more political power than the poor; (3) they can be administered and benefit populations quickly, while waiting for economic growth and market development may leave many people hungry today; and (4) since hunger is more prevalent in poorer countries, targeting is simply less of an issue. Related policy options and issues are discussed in cases 4-2, 4-3, and 4-4, and in chapter 5.

Public food policies are negotiated between government agencies, and are influenced by policies in seemingly unrelated fields and by lobby groups representing stakeholders with very different needs and perceptions. As a result, government action may include conflicting or contradicting goals and policy measures (chapter 2). For instance, food aid from developed countries is often legitimized by ethical arguments, while the specific food provided is determined by the surplus crops created as a result of farm subsidies and international strategic considerations rather than the health needs of recipients (Barrett and Maxwell 2005). While some policy analysts would gladly remove the political and agricultural lobbying from the determination of food aid policies, without their support the food aid program would shrink. In-kind transfers have more political support than cash transfers and conditional cash transfers more than unconditional because it is easier to argue that aid is going only to donor-approved goals (chapter 5). Whether food assistance contributes to obesity or whether families can reduce their expenditures on the in-kind transfer to spend on other desired items is often forgotten.

Similarly, because untargeted food subsidies benefit nonpoor urban consumers more than the urban or rural poor, the nonpoor urban citizens will oppose efforts to reduce or target food subsidies in ways that would shift more benefits to the poorest. This is not because they are mean-spirited, but simply because the removal of the policy directly harms them. Food riots have weakened and even removed governments who have attempted subsidy reforms without complementary policies to make them politically feasible. Hence, untargeted food subsidies persist, despite increasing evidence of their financial instability, poor ability to target poor households, and poor effectiveness or efficiency in improving nutritional outcomes (Pinstrup-Andersen 1988 and 1993).

Thus, stakeholder analysis needs to identify the different possible constituent groupings to support or oppose a measure and take account of their incentives to participate in the political process. Effectiveness and efficiency can be at cross-purposes in this regard: adding another stakeholder group to the coalition may improve the chances of policies being enacted or expand coverage of needed programs, but at the expense of lower efficiency (chapter 9). Identifying how to improve efficiency (e.g., targeting) without sacrificing effectiveness and legitimacy, stabilize needed programs, and find creative long-term solutions to food consumption problems is a major task for context-specific research.

Conclusion

In addition to the pain and suffering inflicted on the food insecure, insufficient or excessive food consumption leads to substantial productivity losses, diminished work performance, and lower human capital accumulation. The world's poor are disproportionately affected because they face structural constraints and excessive risk exposure and because they rely heavily on a narrow set of coping strategies that are progressively injurious. Excess energy intake results in overweight, obesity, and chronic diseases, and has become a serious public health and development problem in many developing countries (chapter 3).

Our understanding of what food security means has expanded in recent decades, progressing from mere food availability to include food access, acquisition, entitlements, and utilization. Data collection needs to address these additional dimensions in order for policy analysts and makers to properly address food consumption problems.

Barrett (2002, 3) notes that "most nations have implemented food policies, but many of these have proved expensive, ineffective, or both, and may increase obesity." There are many issues involved in increasing food consumption for the undernourished that are dwelled on in the remainder of this book: poverty reduces food intake (chapter 5), lack of market access prevents consumption smoothing (chapter 6), increasing food production is necessary (chapter 7) but must be sustainably managed (chapter 8), the efficiency and effectiveness of government programs is often questionable due to poor governance (chapter 9), international trade issues have powerful effects on the structure of domestic food production and consumption (chapter 10), and different ethical viewpoints provide diverging instructions for how societies should combat food insecurity (chapter 11).

The food consumption problems now facing the world are therefore multidimensional and require multidisciplinary efforts. Developing countries are making efforts to solve these problems, but they face difficult choices due to budgetary and institutional resource constraints. Typically, these countries rely heavily on a narrow set of policy instruments while few employ an optimal policy combination that calls on multisectoral efforts. Improving policy combinations requires a careful analysis of the characteristics of a country's food consumption, the nature of food insecure population, resource availability, and institutional capabilities. An optimal set of policies should achieve both effectiveness, ensuring an adequate and balanced dietary intake for all individuals without exposing them to excessive risks in attaining that intake, and efficiency, costing as little as possible and being sustainable in the long run.

Since the dimensions, causes, and consequences of food consumption problems differ widely from country to country, and even within the same country, a general blueprint for setting policy priorities cannot be suggested or even considered. Therefore, the search for the optimal combination of policies has to be country specific. Pinstrup-Andersen and Herforth (2008) conclude that most country policies will have to deal with similar elements: address improving food security, environmental sustainability, and poverty reduction simultaneously; focus on rural areas where most of the poor are located in most countries; identify and confront underlying causes of food insecurity rather than try to repair damage once it has occurred; place greater emphasis on proper nutrition; and end trade distortions.

Poverty and malnutrition are intimately linked. Poor people are more likely to be chronically undernourished, to have fewer coping mechanisms to prevent periods of food insecurity when exposed to negative shocks, and to have less knowledge about proper nutrition. Similarly, poorly nourished people will have lower labor productivity and potentially permanent physical damage that makes it more difficult for them to escape from poverty. The next chapter discusses poverty issues in greater detail.

Food Security, Consumption, and Demand Policies Case Studies

Food security is defined as access to sufficient food to meet the energy and nutrient requirements for a healthy and productive life.* The majority of food insecure people live in rural areas of developing countries. Their food security is heavily influenced by poverty, lack of access to resources, and fluctuations in weather patterns and markets. Household and individual food security is also influenced by household behavior in general and intrahousehold allocations in particular, which, in turn, are influenced by knowledge, promotion, and advertising. The cases in this chapter explain how government policies can reduce food security caused by poverty and fluctuations in weather patterns and markets, change household allocative behavior, and regulate external influences such as food advertising by retailers and wholesalers.

Case 4-1 focuses on food advertising to children, debating the roles of parents, teachers, government, and industry. Cases 4-2 through 4-4 discuss various forms of safety nets. Case 4-2 does this most directly, with case 4-3 focusing on food aid and case 4-4 questioning the role of genetically modified food in food aid and agricultural development. Case 4-5 deals with household decision-making rules and how women's roles in society and the home affect food security.

* The case studies referenced here are presented in full in the three-volume work by Per Pinstrup-Andersen and Fuzhi Cheng, eds., *Case Studies in Food Policy for Developing Countries* (Ithaca, NY: Cornell University Press, 2009) and online via open access at http://cip.cornell.edu/gfs.

4-5   Intrahousehold Allocation, Gender Relations and Food Security in Developing Countries
Agnes R. Quisumbing and Lisa C. Smith

Notes

1. It should be noted that these anthropometric measures actually reflect past and current health status of people, which may be influenced by factors other than nutrition.

2. Direct price elasticity measures the percentage change in the demand for a good in response to a 1 percent change in the price of that same good. Cross-price elasticity measures how demand of a good changes with a change in the price of a different good.

3. The income elasticity estimates the percentage change in the demand for a good in response to a 1 percent change in incomes.

Chapter 5

Poverty Alleviation Policies

Introduction

One billion men, women, and children struggle to survive on less than $1 per day per person. Roughly half the world's population lives on less than $2 per day. Persistent poverty is the central problem of economic development and, as discussed in chapter 4, a key consideration in efforts to understand and improve the global food system and derive food security for all. The greatest share of poor people is found in south Asia, while sub-Saharan Africa has both the greatest incidence of poverty and the fastest growth in numbers of poor people. Sub-Saharan Africa also has a very high prevalence of the ultra poor (those earning less than $0.50/day). Combined with the fact that poverty has in general been decreasing in much of the rest of the world, at least up to 2005, poverty is concentrating in Africa.

People who do not have sufficient income frequently suffer want in multiple dimensions. They are or are susceptible to becoming deprived of basic consumption goods such as food and shelter; malnourished and unhealthy; illiterate; unemployed; clinically depressed; socially marginalized (e.g., excluded from markets); vulnerable to natural disasters; vulnerable to threat of crime and unable to use the legal system for redress; victims of corruption; and unknowledgeable about their rights and about ways to escape from poverty (Banerjee, Benabou, and Mookherjee 2006). These forms of poverty can be not only lifelong but transmitted across generations.

But what is poverty? For more than a century, poverty has been considered mainly in monetary terms—as levels of income or material wealth below a poverty line. Sadly, poverty lines are largely arbitrary because there is no overarching theory that can permanently, in all societies and all times, divide the poor from the non-poor. Adam Smith wrote that poverty was lacking both the necessities of life and the ability to fulfill certain cultural obligations (Smith 1776).

The most widely used measure in international development today is the $1 per day criterion adopted by the World Bank in 1990. One dollar per day was chosen because eight of the world's poorest countries used that as their poverty line under the logic that anyone who was considered poor in the poorest country must indeed be poor. That $1 per day has been occasionally updated: $1.08 in 1985 dollars, $1.13 in 1993 dollars, and today $1.25 in 2005 dollars. This line has been used in setting the Millennium Development Goals (MDGs). The median poverty line among all developing countries, $2 per day, is also frequently used.

Increasingly, poverty is perceived as a multidimensional concept of deprivation. Lack of health, education, and human dignity have been emphasized as key aspects of poverty. Studying the multidimensionality of poverty is particularly important because the poor are not a homogeneous group. They did not become poor for the same reasons, different factors keep them poor, and they require different solutions to enable them to escape (Hulme and Shepherd 2003).

Even among the chronic poor, understanding why people differ in their poverty experience is difficult because of multiple overlapping and interacting factors that lead people into poverty and keep them trapped in this situation. At an individual level their constraints include lack of human or physical capital and lack of opportunities. Groups of people may be excluded or discriminated against, limiting opportunities at a meso level. Government policies that favor one group over another (e.g., that support manufacturing and tax agriculture), lack of public and merit goods, poor governance and institutions as well as natural disasters and lack of economic growth are often cited as causes of national-level poverty. International factors, such as trade policy and ineffective institutions, also slow people's rise out of poverty. The available evidence so far indicates that poverty rarely has a simple "single cause." Rather, different forces, from the individual, household, communal, national, and global levels, interact and may trap people in poverty or repeatedly bring them back down into poverty after escaping.

Hunger and poverty go hand in hand. Poverty prevents the food system from fulfilling its primary mandates of improving human health and nutrition and providing livelihoods that enable people to leave poverty. Poverty reduces household access to food even where it is plentiful, causing a lack of dietary energy and protein. Poverty similarly reduces the dietary diversity needed for micronutrient sufficiency. These deficiencies in turn harm human health by increasing the incidence and severity of disease and by stunting growth and reducing the benefits of education that lead to lifelong reductions in health and income. Food production and trade is supposed to provide smallholders with needed income to escape from poverty. The lack of energy and increase in disease decrease smallholder food production. Traders' market power—if any (chapter 6)—is greater when bargaining with poor people, weakening the poor's ability to escape poverty by market means.

Poverty also affects the environments in which the food system takes place. As further discussed in chapter 8, poor people may have few options outside of using up their natural resources unsustainably—deforestation, soil mining, and desertification are all partially consequences of poverty. Poor people have less voice in government, a greater probability of being victimized by predatory institutions, and less recourse to the law for protection or redress (chapter 9). Poor people have fewer opportunities to harness the forces of globalization for their benefit and may be cut off from international markets, leaving them further marginalized.

The primary purpose of this chapter is not to provide one grand explanation for poverty or one definitive solution to all poverty. It is rather to gain a greater appreciation for the complexity of what poverty is, what causes it, and how it interacts with the food system. After a discussion of the extent of income-poverty worldwide, we examine in more detail different aspects of the conceptualization of poverty, and discuss the measurement issues associated with the multidimensional definition of poverty.

We conclude the chapter with a framework of policy intervention for poverty alleviation. Acknowledging the multidimensional nature of poverty, we propose that effective poverty reduction strategies should focus on three important areas: (1) promoting opportunity by expanding pro-poor economic growth and building up poor people's assets while increasing the returns on these assets through a combination of market and nonmarket interventions, including agricultural research and infrastructure investment (chapter 7); (2) improving governance (chapter 9) by increasing participation of the poor—particularly marginalized groups—and government accountability; and (3) reducing risk through strategies such as safety nets, access to primary health care and education, and law enforcement that reduces the risk of crime (see also World Bank 2001c). We argue that, while making progress on all three fronts is important for poverty reduction, policy design should be context specific. We therefore avoid providing specific policy recommendations in this chapter.

World Poverty Situation

Defining and Measuring Poverty

Poverty is a state where people do not have enough in some key dimensions of well-being. Most often, people think of poverty purely in monetary terms: the lack of money. A person is poor if his or her income, consumption, expenditure, or wealth falls below a certain threshold or poverty line. Poverty lines may be set either with reference to living standards (absolute poverty) or in comparison to a reference population (relative poverty). An example of a relative poverty line is the European Union poverty line, which is 60 percent of the median income. Considering that large parts of the populations of developing countries survive with the bare minimum, reliance on an absolute rather than a relative poverty line often proves to be more relevant. Unless otherwise stated, this chapter refers to absolute poverty.

Even if one has decided to focus on absolute poverty, there is significant debate about whether to measure monetary poverty based on income, consumption, expenditure, or wealth.[1] Each has its advantages and none is truly superior to the others. Income data is the most easily comparable with wage data and national statistics and it can be broken down by source, which may be important either as a check for data quality or for understanding income dynamics among the poor. Income, however, is volatile, particularly for farmers and those who have nonwage income. People tend to smooth their consumption over time relative to income, so consumption data may provide a more accurate reflection of the resources a household feels it has at its disposal. Expenditure data is less time and cost intensive to obtain than consumption data, but some precision is lost compared to direct consumption data (e.g., a household purchases a certain amount of food and it is measured as an expenditure, but much of the food may be wasted and not consumed). It is also possible that while incomes are temporarily low, wealth levels may be high, shielding a household from the worst effects of poverty.

There are important ethical questions underlying this choice. For example, if a person has enough income to afford a basic food bundle but chooses not to (i.e., income measures indicate a household is not poor while food expenditure and consumption measures say the opposite), is the household poor? As discussed in chapter 3, the interaction between ability to acquire enough food and the household behavior related to the use of that ability makes food security estimates very difficult. Is a household food insecure if it could but chooses not to allocate sufficient household resources to food? For ease, we will refer to low income throughout the chapter, but the reader should keep in mind that other measures may be more salient.

Because of the methods by which poverty data are collected, there is significant measurement error in any estimate of poverty. Official statistics cannot see informal wage income. Methods for imputing streams of income, particularly from housing and own-labor, differ widely between studies and countries. Survey data may rely on faulty recall—and the further back the survey goes, the larger that error becomes—and household dynamics may introduce further measurement errors. Any measure is at best a snapshot, and even panel data is merely a string of widely spaced snapshots that potentially hides many of the salient dynamics. Surveys introduce further complexities that, though well-known, make the work of interpreting results more difficult (e.g., selection bias and nonrandom attrition).

Ghana is a case in point. Ghana's GDP was estimated for years using an early 1990s survey that determined the relative sizes of various sectors of the economy. GDP, population, and inequality data were combined by international agencies to estimate the number of poor or hungry people. In 2010, the results of a new survey were released which showed that the finance and communications sectors had grown rapidly. This changed the estimates of per capita GDP by over 60 percent overnight. This in turn significantly reduced estimates of poverty and hunger in Ghana for the last decade, ushered Ghana into the ranks of middle-income countries, and highlighted just how much uncertainty there is in estimates of GDP and poverty in even relatively well-governed poor countries.

Absolute poverty lines come from several possible sources: research, politics, convenience, and social norms (see Fields 2001). In the United States and India, researchers identified the cost of a minimal food basket depending on household size and added to that an allowance for nonfood needs. Though political discussion adjusted those lines, they have remained relatively stable over time. Political processes often affect which poverty line is chosen, such as in budget debates (the poverty line determines who is eligible for benefits, so lowering it reduces government expenditures) or elections (politicians may promise to raise poverty lines so that more people are eligible for benefits to secure their vote). In Brazil the poverty line is the minimum wage. Whenever the government changes the minimum wage, it simultaneously changes the measures of poverty.

Communities may also set subjective absolute poverty lines as formal and informal debate identifies the characteristics of a poor household. This has the advantage of most readily incorporating qualitative and nonmonetary factors. Other poverty lines have been chosen as a matter of convenience, such as Korea's line: 100,000 won. The $1 and $2 per day World Bank poverty line came by aggregating the poverty lines from the poorest countries, sharing elements of all four methods.

Poverty measures translate indicators of household well-being and the chosen poverty line into one aggregate number for the population as a whole or a population subgroup. Many alternative measures exist, but three are most commonly used: the headcount index, the poverty gap or depth, and the severity of poverty. The headcount index is simply the proportion of a population below the poverty line. The poverty gap measures how far below the poverty line the average person is, with a person above the poverty line measured as zero. While headcount poverty can be used for any nonmonetary measure of poverty, the poverty gap is meaningful only if there is a sensible metric for the "distance" from a poverty line, such as number of calories needed (Greer and Thorbecke 1986) or number of years of schooling. Squaring each person's shortfall gives additional importance to those who are furthest from the poverty line. Hence the squared poverty gap measures the severity of poverty.

These measures and others complement each other because each looks at poverty from slightly different ethical value systems (Watson 2009). To the extent there is a common poverty experience of exclusion or lumpiness in consumption (e.g., above a certain income level, a person gains access to significantly improved housing and education opportunities), the headcount index will be most meaningful. If the experience of poverty gets increasingly bad the further from the poverty line one gets, other measures will be more appropriate.

Each poverty measure has a different implication for how poverty reduction resources should be allocated. If the goal is to reduce the poverty headcount, funds should be allocated to the richest of the poor, those just barely below the poverty line. By contrast, if we intend to reduce the severity of poverty, funds should be allocated to the poorest of the poor to alleviate the most suffering rather than lifting the most people above the poverty line. Kanbur (1987) demonstrates that it also depends on how well the funds can be targeted. Barder (2009) and Watson (2009) discuss the importance of these trade-offs for development assistance and antipoverty programs.

Poverty maps can be a useful tool in targeting antipoverty funds. Poverty maps are generated by first econometrically determining the relationships between household characteristics (e.g., demographics, education, housing conditions) and poverty from household survey data, then estimating finely detailed poverty incidence figures from census data with these basic household characteristics. Benson, Epprecht, and Minot (2007) provide several examples. A Malawi poverty map, for instance, increased the number of geographic units that could be considered from the thirty-two large districts and urban centers covered by household surveys to 360 subdistrict units and demonstrated that poverty was lower in areas with greater crop diversity and nonfarm employment. A Mozambique poverty map showed that income inequality largely stemmed from inequalities within a subdistrict and only 15 percent from differences between administrative units. A Vietnam poverty map showed that poverty was greater on agricultural land with a steeper slope, poor soil quality, and greater distance from small towns, and where there were significant ethnolinguistic boundaries. They cite studies in Cambodia and Tanzania that also consider hunger maps, mapping data on child stunting and wasting, though the connection between census household characteristics is weaker for malnutrition than for poverty.

Vulnerability

The depth of poverty is one important dimension; so also is its duration. Fundamentally different policies are needed when considering temporary poverty, chronic poverty, and repetitive poverty or poverty vulnerability. Table 5.1 from Krishna (2007) and von Braun and Pandya-Lorch (2007) depicts the percent of the poor in each subgroup that identified a particular need as its most pressing. As can be seen, the most important deprivation depended on how long a person had been poor: the persistently poor value improvements in wage labor most, while the newly poor value health and housing improvements and those who have recently escaped poverty most value investments in irrigation and education. It is also important to differentiate between poor people who are unemployed, underemployed (those who would gladly work more but are unable to find additional work), and fully employed but still poor, and the nonpoor who are vulnerable to becoming poor.

Vulnerability is the probability that a person either enters poverty or becomes more impoverished in the future.[2] Risk and uncertainty are inherent elements of vulnerability that affect the incentives for households to work and invest and choose livelihood strategies. Chapter 7 discusses how risk and uncertainty affect farmers' decisions regarding credit, input use, technology adoption, and farming strategies.

The probability that an individual might become poor is inherently difficult to measure. Measurement error may make it appear that a person enters and leaves poverty when only the error term has changed, necessitating checks and confirmation measures. On a population level, however, the determinants and probabilities of entering and exiting poverty and of income dynamics may be profitably analyzed.

TABLE 5.1.
Major Demands by Subgroups (Percent within Each Subgroup)

	Health	Housing	Irrigation	High school	Wage labor
Persistently poor	8	9	9	3	46
Newly poor	34	24	9	6	8
Escaped poverty	7	3	28	25	5

Source: Krishna 2007 and von Braun and Pandya-Lorch 2007.

FIGURE 5.1.
The chronic poor, transient poor, and nonpoor: A categorization. *Depending on data availability, poverty could be assessed in terms of household expenditure, income, consumption, a poverty index, or an assessment of assets/capital. Source: Hulme and Shepherd 2003.

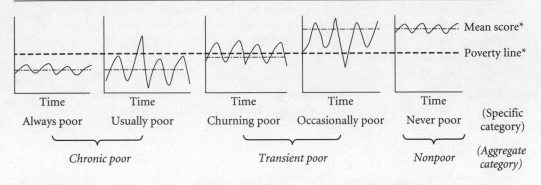

The amount of time between a household's entry into and exit from poverty is typically referred to as a poverty spell. Policies may attempt to decrease the frequency of poverty spells, their duration, or their severity.

Hulme and Shepherd (2003, 405) categorize five groups of people depicted in figure 5.1:

> The *always poor* whose poverty score . . . in each period is below a defined poverty line; the *usually poor* whose mean poverty score over all periods is less than the poverty line but are not poor in every period; the *churning poor* with a mean poverty score around the poverty line but who are poor in some periods but not in others; the *occasionally poor* whose mean poverty score is above the poverty line but have experienced at least one period in poverty; and, the *never poor* with poverty scores in all periods above the poverty line.

These five groups may also be aggregated into three groups: the chronic poor who are usually poor, the transient poor who are sometimes poor, and the nonpoor.[3]

The mix of chronic and transitory poverty will vary between countries and across time. Baulch and Hoddinott (2000) summarize ten studies from thirteen countries that found anywhere between 3 and over 50 percent of the surveyed population was consistently poor, 20 to 66 percent were sometimes poor, and 12 to 72 percent were never poor. Two studies of India, one from 1968–1971 (Gaiha 1998) and one from 1975–1984 (Gaiha and Deolalikar 1993), found very different patterns of poverty: the earlier identified roughly one-third of households suffering chronic poverty, one-third transitory poverty, and one-third no poverty; the latter found 22 percent in constant poverty, 12 percent experiencing no poverty, and the remainder in between. Such dynamics make it most difficult to know where to draw the cutoff lines between chronic and transient poverty.

When the number of poor people is measured at a given point in time, the measurement provides a "snapshot" that blurs the distinctions between these categories.

Assuming that a representative sample is taken, the study will likely identify as poor most but not all of the chronically poor and only some of the transient poor. Consider as an example a country with 20 percent of the population in each of the five tiers, with a probability of being poor of 100, 75, 50, 25, and 0 percent respectively. In such a case, 80 percent of the population is vulnerable to poverty, 40 percent is chronically poor, but approximately 50 percent will be identified as being poor at any given time, reflecting neither chronic poverty nor vulnerability.

Glauben, Herzfeld, and Wang (2006) refer to previous studies in China that report on chronic poverty from different base populations: 20–25 percent of poor households are chronically poor, but only 6 percent of all households and 60 percent of poor rural households. Their own work showed that on average 24 percent of farm households had less than $1 each day, but less than 1 percent remained consistently below that line through 1995–2000. Combined, these results suggest that poverty in urban China tends to be temporary and that income stabilization programs and short-term safety nets would be most effective at alleviating poverty, while rural poverty is more likely to be chronic and to require changes in underlying factors.

The August 2000 issue of the *Journal of Development Studies* gathered a series of studies on poverty and vulnerability in Ethiopia, Zimbabwe, Chile, Pakistan, China, and South Africa. Baulch and Hoddinott (2000) summarize the findings as indicating that the transient poor make up "by a considerable amount" the larger group; improvements in the economic returns to assets that the poor own and to the general stock of capital can significantly reduce poverty; and temporary, negative shocks can have effects that last a long time. Krishna (2007) breaks down the reasons households enter poverty and the reasons they escape in three Indian provinces, plus Kenya, Uganda, and Peru, demonstrating that health-related expenses and debt are important features for most people entering poverty, while other factors (e.g., negative agricultural shocks or household composition changes) vary more between areas; and most people who escaped from poverty in five out of six areas diversified their income, while government assistance helped a small portion of people out of poverty.

Global and Regional Poverty Pattern and Evolution

In 2008, better data on prices in developing countries (particularly China) became available, leading the World Bank to update its poverty data sets collected since 1980. The international poverty line was updated to $1.25 and $2.00 per day in 2005 purchasing power parity (PPP) terms. Table 5.2 gives the estimates of the headcount indexes for $1.25 and $2 poverty lines (hereafter simply $1 and $2). Table 5.3 gives the corresponding counts of the number of poor for each poverty line.

Between the start of the Millennium Development Goals in 1991 and 2005, the incidence of $1 per day poverty was nearly halved, falling from 42 percent to 26 percent. The number of poor fell by almost 300 million.[4] There was clearly more progress in some periods than in others, (e.g., less progress was made between 1985 and 1995 because of lower growth in China and India) though a significant long-run declining trend in the global poverty rate has emerged. The rate

TABLE 5.2.
Percentage of Population Living below $1.25 and $2 per Day

	$1.25 per day at 2005 PPP				
	1981	1990	1999	2002	2005
East Asia	78.8	56.0	35.6	29.6	17.9
Of which China	84.0	60.2	35.6	28.4	15.9
Eastern Europe and central Asia	1.6	1.5	5.4	5.6	5.0
Latin America and Caribbean	12.3	10.7	11.5	10.1	8.2
Middle East and North Africa	8.6	5.4	5.8	4.7	4.6
South Asia	60.3	51.3	44.1	43.8	40.4
Of which India	59.8	51.3	44.8	43.9	41.6
Sub-Saharan Africa	50.8	54.9	56.4	53	50.4
Total	52.2	41.7	33.7	31.1	25.7

	$2.00 per day at 2005 PPP				
	1981	1990	1999	2002	2005
East Asia	92.9	80.1	61.5	53.1	39.7
Of which China	97.8	84.6	61.4	51.2	36.3
Eastern Europe and central Asia	8.2	6.7	13.5	12.6	10.6
Latin America and Caribbean	24.5	21.4	22.3	21.0	17.9
Middle East and North Africa	28.7	22.0	23.7	19.6	19.0
South Asia	87.0	82.3	77.4	77.1	74.0
Of which India	86.6	82.6	78.4	77.5	75.6
Sub-Saharan Africa	72.0	73.5	75.6	73.7	72.2
Total	69.5	63.1	57.0	53.6	47.6

Source: Chen and Ravallion 2008.

of decline—not counting recent food price volatility or the global recession—has roughly been what is needed to meet the first MDG of reducing poverty by half by 2015.

There have been notable changes in regional headcount poverty rankings over this period. In 1981 79 percent of east Asians (84 percent of Chinese) were poor. South Asia and sub-Saharan Africa had the next-highest poverty rates, with other regions having far lower poverty rates. Twenty-four years later, sub-Saharan Africa has the highest incidence of poverty at 50 percent, followed by south Asia. Sub-Saharan Africa has the same headcount index as was measured in 1981. The greatest gains were attained by east Asia where the percent of the population falling below the $1 level fell from 79 percent to 18 percent (table 5.2).

TABLE 5.3.
Millions of People Living below $1.25 and $2 per Day

| | $1.25 per day | | | | |
	1981	1990	1999	2002	2005
East Asia	1,071.5	873.3	635.1	506.8	316.2
Of which China	835.1	683.2	446.7	363.2	207.7
Eastern Europe and central Asia	7.1	9.1	24.3	21.7	17.3
Latin America and Caribbean	42.0	42.9	54.8	58.4	46.1
Middle East and North Africa	13.7	9.7	11.5	10.3	11.0
South Asia	548.3	579.2	588.9	615.9	595.6
Of which India	420.5	435.5	447.2	460.5	455.8
Sub-Saharan Africa	213.7	299.1	381.6	390.0	390.6
Total	1,896.2	1,813.4	1,696.2	1,603.1	1,376.7

| | $2.00 per day | | | | |
	1981	1990	1999	2002	2005
East Asia	1,277.7	1,273.7	1,104.9	954.1	728.7
Of which China	972.1	960.8	770.2	654.9	473.7
Eastern Europe and central Asia	35.0	31.9	67.6	56.8	41.9
Latin America and Caribbean	82.3	86.3	108.5	114.6	91.3
Middle East and North Africa	46.3	44.4	51.9	50.9	51.5
South Asia	799.5	926.0	1,030.8	1,083.7	1,091.5
Of which India	608.9	701.6	782.8	813.1	827.7
Sub-Saharan Africa	294.2	393.6	508.5	535.6	556.7
Total	2,535.1	2,755.9	2,872.1	2,795.7	2,561.5

Source: Chen and Ravallion 2008.

The greatest changes over time have occurred in China where there were 630 million fewer poor in 2005 than twenty-four years earlier. It is widely understood that this was caused by governance reforms beginning in the late 1970s, including privatization, the decollectivization of agriculture, allowing food market prices to adjust to market forces, and government support for needed intellectual and physical infrastructure (Chen and Feng 2000). This process began with one village whose members divided up their land into family parcels. As the success of the venture became apparent, it was supported by the provincial and then the state government and spread to other regions. Central government support for irrigation and many of the interventions associated with the green revolution greatly supported this transition. When the government increased its grain procurement price, this served as a transfer from urban to rural areas, temporarily decreasing poverty by another 200 million people (World Bank 1997).

Global poverty figures excluding China have increased between 1981 and 2005. In sub-Saharan Africa alone, the number of poor people has nearly doubled with the headcount index remaining constant. Thus Africa's share of the world's poor has increased from 10 percent to over 25 percent.

The percent of the global population that earn less than $2/day has fallen from 70 percent in 1981 to 48 percent in 2005 (table 5.2). However, far more people have risen into the $1–$2 range than have advanced out of the $2 range. Thus the number of people in this less severe level of poverty doubled during these years from about 0.6 billion to 1.2 billion (table 5.3). Most of these people are found in south and east Asia. This bunching up between the $1 and $2 poverty lines should serve as a warning that many of these people are vulnerable to returning to extreme poverty during recessions (Chen and Ravallion 2008).

New research has shown that there are now more poor people living in middle-income countries than in lower-income countries (Sumner 2010). This is largely due to the ascendancy of China and India to middle-income status. This has far-reaching implications for understanding the causes of poverty (clusters of poverty within growing economies rather than a "bottom billion" of people in economies trapped in poverty) and how development assistance can and should be operated.

In practice, poverty gap and squared poverty gap measures show similar trends to headcount poverty indexes. The regions with the largest percent of poor people also have the poorest people. Table 5.4 shows average incomes for people below specific poverty lines, which is equivalent to showing the poverty gap while being more intuitive. Over time, the income of the poor has been growing in east Asia and India and remaining relatively constant elsewhere. Sub-Saharan Africa's and the Caribbean's poor people are the poorest on earth.

The low average income among the poor in sub-Saharan Africa is a reflection of a high prevalence of what IFPRI calls "ultra" poverty, incomes of less than $0.50/day (Ahmed et al. 2007; von Braun and Pandya-Lorch 2007; figures 5.2a and 5.2b). In 2004, there were an estimated 121 million ultra poor in sub-Saharan Africa out of 162 million ultra poor worldwide (one in six poor people). In comparison, only 4–5 percent of the people earning less than $1/day in east and south Asia fell below $0.50. While accounting for 48 percent of the ultra poor in 1990, sub-Saharan Africa was home to 76 percent of the world's ultra poor in 2004 (Ahmed et al. 2007). In contrast, most of the poor between $0.50/day and $1.00/day live in south Asia.

Who Stays Poor?

People who are poor are not a homogeneous group although they tend to concentrate in the same regions. They become poor for different reasons, have different priorities at different points during a poverty spell, and those who remain

TABLE 5.4.
Mean Income of the Poor in Dollars per Day

| | Earning below $1.25 per day | | | | |
	1981	1990	1999	2002	2005
East Asia	0.68	0.83	0.87	0.83	0.95
Of which China	0.67	0.82	0.86	0.87	0.94
Eastern Europe and central Asia	0.97	0.84	0.86	0.91	0.89
Latin America and Caribbean	0.82	0.79	0.77	0.78	0.77
Middle East and North Africa	0.99	0.99	1.00	1.01	0.98
South Asia	0.84	0.88	0.92	0.92	0.93
Of which India	0.84	0.88	0.92	0.93	0.93
Sub-Saharan Africa	0.72	0.68	0.70	0.72	0.73
Total	0.74	0.82	0.85	0.86	0.87

| | Earning below $2 per day | | | | |
	1981	1990	1999	2002	2005
East Asia	0.80	1.05	1.17	1.20	1.31
Of which China	0.79	1.03	1.17	1.19	1.33
Eastern Europe and central Asia	1.55	1.51	1.31	1.29	1.25
Latin America and Caribbean	1.22	1.23	1.21	1.24	1.26
Middle East and North Africa	1.44	1.48	1.48	1.50	1.50
South Asia	1.05	1.14	1.20	1.20	1.22
Of which India	1.06	1.15	1.20	1.21	1.22
Sub-Saharan Africa	0.98	0.91	0.92	0.95	0.99
Total	0.94	1.08	1.15	1.16	1.21

Source: Chen and Ravallion 2008.

poor do so for a variety of reasons that go beyond simple correlations between poverty status and personal characteristics. Explanations for persistent poverty tend to fall into one of three categories: individual or microlevel explanations (the reason this person is poor); mesolevel explanations (the reason this group of people is poor); and macrolevel explanations (the reason the people in this country are poor).

Micro Explanations: Assets and Choice

Poverty alleviation policies may focus on preventing people from becoming poor in the first place, reducing job search or retraining times, providing income or

FIGURE 5.2A.
Millions of ultra poor (<$0.50/day) by region in 1990. Source: Ahmed et al. 2007.

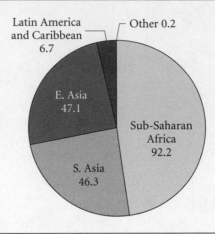

FIGURE 5.2B.
Millions of ultra poor (<$0.50/day) by region in 2004. Source: Ahmed et al. 2007.

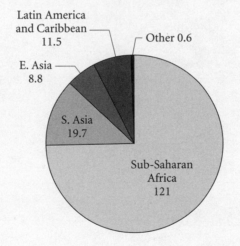

in-kind supplements (e.g., public housing, food stamps), fostering community building, or initiating other public goods projects that enable people to lift themselves out of poverty, such as agricultural research and feeder roads. Policy needs differ depending on which population is targeted and where the population is located. Geographic and community factors (e.g., natural resources, rainfall, population density, public goods, and area government) can be just as important as household factors in promoting either chronic poverty or escape therefrom (Ravallion and Wodon 1999).

The chronically poor typically have low levels of capital assets (physical and human), low returns to those assets, and are vulnerable to negative shocks (Baulch and Hoddinott 2000). These factors reinforce one another: owning few capital assets makes one more vulnerable and lowers returns; bad shocks may induce families to make irreversible disinvestments (reducing capital) that make them more vulnerable and yield lower returns in the future; low returns make it more difficult for households to accumulate capital or prepare for bad shocks. Government policies can be most effective at reducing covariate or aggregate risk (e.g., droughts, recessions), such as by providing safety nets, but do relatively poorly at reducing risk at an individual level.

Household composition is correlated with poverty status. Glauben, Herzfeld, and Wang (2006) find that the risk of chronic poverty in China increases with the number of nonworking household members. Kirimi and Sindi (2006) similarly show for Kenya that families with more children under six years old and those in areas where HIV/AIDS is prevalent are more likely to fall into poverty. Female-headed households are also more likely to be poor.

Access to economic opportunities is a primary factor in whether households are able to escape from poverty. As an example of spatial marginalization, the presence of district and local roads in Kenya makes it much less likely that a household enters poverty as well as more likely that they leave poverty afterward (Kirimi and Sindi 2006)

Income depends in part on age and the stage of the life cycle a person is in. During most of the life cycle, potential earnings increase as human capital is accumulated in education, physical strength, and experience. Eventually, advancing age tends to reduce income and opportunities. Thus children and the elderly are particularly vulnerable, as are young households just beginning their career paths and families with many children. According to UNICEF, of the world's 2.2 billion children, 1 billion grow up in absolute income poverty (UNICEF 2005).

In a very different vein, poverty may be an individual's choice rather than something that happens to them. Some religious persons take vows of poverty, hoping it will make them more pure and holy. Such people are not looking for outsiders to come free them from poverty. Another hypothesis for why some people are poor indicates that they may prefer to enjoy more leisure rather than work. This situation is extremely unlikely when discussing people living below $1 per day but could be more common when generous welfare and entitlement systems permit it.

It is sometimes claimed that there is something "ennobling" about subsistence agriculture, and that it is better to leave the poor alone rather than burden them with Western "progress" and the corruption of wealth. Rather than romanticizing subsistence farming, policy analysts should keep in mind that subsistence farmers who lack interactions with input, output, and labor markets are exposed to severe risks, caused by their dependence on weather fluctuations and adverse production factors such as pest attacks, and lack of effective coping mechanisms. The consequences are felt in terms of large fluctuations in their living standards causing periodic or chronic hunger, malnutrition, and high child mortality rates. While many farmers prefer farming to other ways of making a living, very few would prefer subsistence farming, as practiced in most developing countries, over some degree of commercialization of their farming operation if given the choice. Farmers should be informed about alternatives and assisted in making knowledge-based decisions about their future endeavors including, of course, a continuation of subsistence farming if that is their choice.

Meso Explanations: Labor Conditions, Social Marginalization, and Conflict

In contrast to the asset approach, a livelihoods approach takes another step toward holistically understanding individual poverty (Chambers and Conway 1992; Wood and Salway 2000; Francis 2000, 2006). It incorporates, for instance, how local labor and product markets function, social networks, gender power relations, and access to work and working conditions. The livelihoods approach is therefore more likely to address the mesolevel characteristics described in the next section while incorporating but minimizing individual factors.

Between 70 and 75 percent of the world's poor are in rural areas and depend on agriculture. Chen and Ravallion (2007) report that 37 percent of the developing countries' rural population earns less than $1/day compared to 14 percent in urban areas. In China, the prevalence of poverty in rural areas is twelve times the urban prevalence. In Latin America, rural poverty is about three times urban poverty. Chen and Ravallion (2007) demonstrate that it will be decades before there are more urban poor globally than rural poor. This is the context for case 5-1.

Labor conditions are often worse for the poor than for other groups. Migrants, even within-country migrants, are generally employed in unstable or seasonal sectors at low wages in rural areas (e.g., case 5-3 in China; de Haan and Rogaly 2002). The grueling jobs offer low wages and poor working conditions and create a situation of high vulnerability to shocks.

Forced and bonded labor[5] and human trafficking are particular egregious forms of poor labor conditions. There were an estimated 20 million bonded laborers early in the twenty-first century. Most bonded labor takes place in south Asia, particularly among low status castes and tribes. In these countries, bondage is most common in agriculture, but it is also found in sectors such as mining, textiles, and domestic service (Daru and Churchill 2003). Bonded laborers lack the freedom to choose where they live and work or their working conditions. Similar to bonded laborers, people who have been trafficked are also vulnerable to deprivation as they are often treated as outsiders and illegals, and completely dependent on their captors for survival.

Conflict creates, exacerbates, and prolongs poverty. It destroys productive private assets and public goods and creates greater insecurity that reduces investment by siphoning off resources into protection. Time spent in conflict also reduces the hours available for labor, leisure, and human capital accumulation for participants on any side of a conflict. More people are killed due to diseases incident to conflict than from conflicts themselves, and those who aren't killed may be weakened by the diseases as well. When the risk of conflict is high, a community or region can become trapped in poverty. Chapter 9 discusses the linkages between conflict, poverty, and governance in greater detail.

Social marginalization plays an important role in keeping many people from exiting poverty by limiting economic opportunities. People may be marginalized because of a group to which they belong (e.g., ethnic, caste, gender, age), stigmatized health conditions (including tuberculosis, depression, cancer, and sexually transmitted diseases), lifestyle choices (including religion, sexual practices, and political orientation), or because they are seen as not belonging to the community (e.g., migrant laborers and refugees).[6] Socially marginalized people may face discrimination in hiring practices or in labor conditions once hired, be unable to access public entitlements such as basic education or health care, lack recourse to the legal system to secure their rights, face higher risks of crime or state confiscation, and be at a bargaining disadvantage in markets. Social marginalization is a particularly thorny issue for women, who may live in poverty even though their household income would be sufficient to prevent it. Easterly (2006) discusses how the informal institutions of networks formed around ethnic minority groups hinder market reforms, promote static inequality, and exclude and marginalize at the same time they include members of their own minority. Case 3-2 discusses the difficulties faced by indigenous minorities who commonly suffer from multiple forms of marginalization.

Ethnic minorities tend to be grouped in the poorest areas. In China, 40 percent of the poor are ethnic minorities who make up less than 9 percent of the total population (World Bank 2001b). Vietnamese ethnic minorities' share of poverty is twice as high as their population share (Baulch et al. 2002). Ethnic fractionalization has been shown to be connected to low growth and mobility in Africa (Easterly and Levine 1997).

Like migrant communities in general, refugees and internally displaced people tend to suffer high levels of discrimination and exclusion, have few economic opportunities, and are vulnerable to forced labor, violence, and eviction. In most cases, the displacement caused by conflict exacerbates conflict's effects, leaving refugees and internally displaced people poor, both within camps and outside them. Personal documentation lost or destroyed during displacement further undermines access to state and relief services.

Children may suffer poverty because their household is poor or because they have few bargaining rights within a household. Other children do not have the benefits of supervised care, and may become orphans, street children, working children, child sex workers, and child heads of households. Child abuse and child trafficking are serious problems that can leave lifelong physical and emotional effects and significantly reduce children's ability to escape from poverty later in life. Chapter 11 discusses child labor.

Macro Explanations: Systems and Poverty Traps

Macro and international explanations tend to be the most politically charged. Fine (2004) argues that persistent poverty is inherent to capitalism, while Dollar and Kraay (2004) claim the exact opposite: it is lack of capitalism that causes long-lasting poverty. The World Bank and IMF have dedicated much time and many resources over the years to reducing poverty and instability, while their critics retort that structural adjustment programs directly caused poverty for millions. Though one theory of development or another has been in vogue at particular periods, there never has been a true consensus. This section can present only the barest introduction to ideas that have been vigorously debated for generations.

The primary model explaining underdevelopment in the 1950s–1970s was one of underinvestment. This theory made good sense in Europe and other industrialized areas that had suffered from World War II and previously productive areas that suffered from the Great Depression. At low levels of capital and human investment, the returns to additional investments are high, so that investments in physical infrastructure, public goods, and so forth, would enable poor countries to catch up or converge with more advanced countries. While particular interventions like the Marshall Plan for Europe or the green revolution are hailed as largely successful in reducing poverty, most of the world's population and countries did not catch up. Government was believed to have a pivotal role in reducing poverty.

The turbulence of the 1970s caused by unsustainable government interventions and the bursting of many Keynesian theories brought into ascendancy the theory that government was more of a hindrance than a help. Retrenchment, decentralization, privatization, deregulation, macroeconomic stability, and a host of other pro-market reforms became the order of the day. Chapters 2 and 9 discuss these changes, finding that—as with aid—there were notable successes (e.g., China and Vietnam), notable failures (Eastern Europe shock therapy), and mixed results in Africa. At the least, the high levels of economic growth expected from freeing up markets have not been witnessed in most areas.

In the meantime, the hypothesis of the 1950s that lack of capital was the principal bottleneck to economic growth has been updated and enlarged by the poverty trap literature (e.g., Carter and Barrett 2006). The various models posit economic situations that could give rise to multiple equilibriums: some countries settle at a higher level of income and growth while others stagnate, unable to overcome large fixed costs, to break out of feedback effects, or to take advantage of increasing returns to scale. Dasgupta (2007) presents a poverty trap model based on undernutrition. There could be two equilibriums or there could be hundreds of stopping points. The important point is that it will take a large shock to an economy to move it forward (or backward) to a new equilibrium in order to overcome constraints in multiple dimensions simultaneously. A "Big Push" of aid may allow countries to overcome their structural deficits and begin growing (Sachs 2005).

One of the most vigorously debated questions has been whether or not aid is effective at reducing poverty and producing economic growth. The focus of research in the last decade has been to respond to two very influential papers by Boone (1996) and Burnside and Dollar (2000). Their primary conclusion was that aid was only effective where policies were "good." Debate over what is meant by "good" and expanded panel data sets (longer time series and more countries) have shown that their results are not robust. The macroeconomic evidence for aid effectiveness has not been conclusive (Tarp 2006).

Collier (2007) and Easterly (2006) determine that aid does a better job ameliorating suffering than producing economic growth. Easterly focuses on the importance of bottom-up governance improvements based on feedback from the poor, increased NGO and government accountability, and the realignment of donor incentives to send aid to projects that have a demonstrated track record of success. Growth and poverty reduction will come organically, Easterly believes, as long as incentives are not redirected to rent-seeking behaviors as market and political "searchers" fulfill needs they identify.

Collier (2007), in contrast, identifies several factors that combine with poverty to keep the poorest countries trapped in poverty: conflict, poor governance, being landlocked with "bad" neighbors, and developed governments' trade policies. Depending on the type of trap involved, he advocates a mix of support, including improved international norms and charters that would give reformers a standard to hold up, the promise of military support to prevent coups and civil conflict, appropriate international standards for foreign militaries, and preferential trade access for African countries. While these may not by themselves break the traps, they improve the international environment in which the poorest countries find themselves.

Other ideas have included allowing freer labor mobility across countries to increase remittances; allowing skilled people to escape poverty by leaving their country, and, by reducing labor supply, increase wages in that country; establishing "Charter Cities" similar to export zones in developing countries that would be governed using the laws of a developed country; and reforming and adding to the existing international institutional structure to make each institution more responsive to developing countries' needs.

Causes of poverty at different levels interact and reinforce each other. If someone experiences a negative income or health shock that sends them into poverty, is socially excluded, and lives in a country with weak safety nets and poor governance, it may be much more difficult for that person to gain access to the resources they need to escape poverty. IFPRI's 2020 Vision initiative found that elements from all three levels are important for understanding poverty, including access to markets and assets, education, minority status, landownership systems, and poverty traps (Ahmed et al. 2007).

Conceptual Issues of Multidimensional Poverty

Income has been the preferred unidimensional metric for poverty in part because a household with sufficient income ought to be able to acquire nonmonetary dimensions of well-being, such as health, education, security, and social connectedness. Additionally, it readily allows the application of sophisticated quantitative methods in poverty analysis. However, some nonmonetary attributes cannot be purchased because markets do not exist. For example, you can purchase health care, but not health. The use of income to pinpoint poverty presupposes that markets exist and are efficient for all attributes of human welfare. While efforts have been made to translate some of these attributes into monetary terms (i.e., monetize them), these efforts will remain provisional estimates and subject to great measurement error.

Second, even if it were possible to specify the minimum thresholds of each basic need, monetize all of them, and aggregate across minimum thresholds to derive a more inclusive monetary poverty line, this only reflects a monetary capability to acquire each good, rather than actual access or desire. Spending money on alcohol or tobacco instead of nutrition is the example used most stereotypically. A less patronizing example is that money may be used to fulfill cultural obligations, such as to bury the dead or maintain familial connections, which could be valued more by the household than additional nutrition. Whether governments and donors should enforce their own ideals on recipients and whether recipients are somehow bound to spend money only as donors intend are important ethical discussions. In any event, in the money-metric approach, such households and others with the same income would all be classified as nonpoor, whereas in reality some members of a household may be deprived of some basic needs despite having otherwise adequate income and therefore should be considered poor.

Other studies that focus on only one measure of well-being as a measure of poverty—such as hunger and malnutrition, morbidity, incidence of specific diseases (e.g., diarrhea, malaria), literacy, life expectancy, or dietary diversity—provide a useful complement to monetary poverty studies, but ignore the importance of their interactions and combinations. They also suffer from the potential confusion between access and behavior mentioned earlier.

Another option is to create a composite poverty index incorporating multiple dimensions, as operationalized in various issues of the Human Development Report of the United Nations (e.g., UNDP 1997) or the Multidimensional Poverty Index (MPI) (Alkire and Santos 2010). The Human Development Index (HDI) combines the average life expectancy at birth, education, and GDP within a country to rank countries based on their citizens' capacity for development. The MPI measures ten factors correlated with poverty and declares a person is poor if they meet at least three criteria. It finds that material poverty is greatest in sub-Saharan Africa while malnutrition contributes more to poverty in south Asia.

Again, however, each element of well-being must be put on a standardized, comparable scale of measurement, so the HDI is really a relative measure against the most developed countries rather than an absolute development standard; a country that does not grow as fast as the richest countries falls behind even though growth may be occurring. Further, there is no theoretical limit to how high GDP can temporarily grow, while there is an upper limit to the measures of educational attainment.

Any relative weighting assigned to different attributes will be arbitrary, with alternate weightings implying different ethical standards. Because of the way the weights are currently established, the HDI implicitly assumes that the value of an extra year of life is higher in a rich country than in a poor country. The MPI equates household malnutrition with having a dirt floor or lacking electricity.

One of the ongoing difficulties of understanding multidimensional poverty is how the dimensions interact. Clearly a person with less education and less health is poorer than someone with more of each, but what if someone has more education and less health? Are different dimensions substitutes for each other or complements? In how many dimensions must someone be below the respective poverty line in order to be considered poor? Thorbecke (2008) and Bourguignon and Chakravarty (1999) discuss these issues and others.

Sen's Capability Approach

Amartya Sen's *capability approach* is one of the leading alternatives to the standard monetary framework (Sen 1985). Building on a long history of moral philosophy, including Adam Smith and Karl Marx, Sen considers a person's scope of action—what he or she manages to do or to become—called "functionings" (see Clark 2006). Examples of functionings are being alive, being in good health, being employed, being educated, and taking part in the community.

The various combinations of functionings make up an individual's "capability." It is thus the individual's choice set, and could be interpreted as an augmented budget set. From these definitions, one can see that, in contrast to the monetary approach, the capability approach explicitly takes into account nonmarket goods and services, the intrinsic value of choices, and heterogeneous preferences and needs.

In Sen's framework, goods are considered based on how they contribute to a person's capabilities, such as a bicycle's ability to provide transport depending on a person's health and the state of the roads. Food provides nutritious capacity, which is converted into "being well nourished," depending on physical circumstances such as the metabolic rate, presence of parasites, and so forth. The individual's capability includes, then, the freedom to be well nourished, to fast for religious reasons, or to go on hunger strike for another's sake.

The capability approach takes its own share of critiques. There is little agreement on what functionings are truly valuable and which capabilities should be included (e.g., Williams 1987; Nussbaum 1988; Sugden 1993; Qizilbash 1998). The approach is also extremely data-heavy. The data requirements for monetary or epidemiological measures of poverty are stringent enough, let alone collecting data on every tool at the household's disposal, its condition, and the environments in which it could be used. Furthermore, gathering data on counterfactuals—nonactualized choices that could have been made—and differentiating them from capabilities that a person could not achieve borders on the impossible. As with monetary poverty, the problem of differentiating between actualized functionings and potential functionings arises: Is a household poor if some members' needs are not fulfilled, or only if they could not be?

The capabilities approach further fails to resolve many of the problems that have plagued monetary and other multidimensional measures: Where should poverty lines be set and by whom? How do different functionings and capabilities interact? Are they substitutes or complements? These questions are fundamental to being able to utilize multidimensional analysis effectively. The lack of an organized theory of how to do so quantitatively has thus far prohibited multidimensional poverty measures' widespread use. See Tsui (2002), Bourguignon and Chakravarty (2003), and Duclos, Sahn, and Younger (2003) for detailed discussion of measurement issues related to multidimensionality.

Among nonquantitative measures of multidimensional poverty, sociology has used factor analysis to classify particular groups of poor people who share common sets of traits. This identifies clearly defined stakeholder groups, narrows the focus on antipoverty efforts for each group, and is readily computable. Understanding the "distance" between groups, measuring improvement in conditions, and comparing individuals across groups are problematic given the qualitative nature of the analysis, however.

Poverty and the Food System

Poverty reduces human health and nutrition through several channels. Lack of income and wealth reduces access to both preventative and curative health care. Poverty is also correlated with less knowledge about health, nutrition, and behaviors that improve health. Poor people have less access and means to purchase a diverse diet, affecting micronutrient balances. In more developed economies, poverty is also associated with combined obesity and micronutrient deficiencies as nutrient-poor, calorie-rich foods are cheaper than healthier alternatives. Hunger and malnutrition in turn harm the body's ability to deal with disease.

Gentilini and Webb (2008) construct a composite index using five indicators for the first MDG to consider how changes in hunger and poverty are connected. They find that patterns can vary greatly: poverty went down while undernutrition increased in Guatemala, poverty increased while undernutrition decreased in Bolivia, and Brazil showed progress in both. They find that inequality is not significantly correlated with changes in undernutrition or underweight and agree that reductions in poverty or improved food supply by themselves will not automatically translate into improved nutrition without changes in household behavior.

Individual-level poverty traps are particularly important for food system livelihoods. Hunger reduces productivity and human capital accumulation, increasing household vulnerability over the long term. Though poor people have often reduced consumption in order to invest in their livelihoods to reduce future poverty, when poor people are already hungry such sacrifice becomes increasingly painful. In agropastoralist systems, Lybbert et al. (2004) have shown there is a threshold level of livestock holdings necessary to avoid poverty. Households with livestock above that threshold are able to cope with drought and rebuild herd size after. Below that level, households are highly vulnerable and likely to lose their remaining animals over time.

Chapter 8 discusses in detail how lack of other income options and negative shocks induce poor people to draw down their environmental capital. Deforestation, soil mining, and selling off parcels of land reduce the land's productive capacity in the future, making it more likely that households will be poor in the future and more vulnerable to the next shock. Efforts to reduce poverty in such cases can produce win-win situations. Chapters 9 and 10 discuss how governance and globalization impact poverty through food systems.

Poverty Reduction Policies

Economic Growth and Poverty

Achieving economic growth is of significant importance in reducing poverty. Kraay (2004) shows that 70 percent of the short-run variation and 97 percent of the long-run variation in poverty is explained by different rates of per capita GDP growth. Dollar and Kraay (2004) argue that, on average, the incomes of the bottom 20 percent improved one for one with those of the population as a whole as a result of economic growth. Ravallion and Chen (1997) find that nearly all countries either experience rising incomes and falling poverty or falling income and rising poverty. Figure 5.3 from Pinkovskiy and Sala-i-Martin (2010) shows that poverty correlates very strongly with economic growth in sub-Saharan Africa.

However, a focus on the poor as a homogeneous group can miss important changes in well-being for different segments of the poor. Most of the world's poor work in agriculture, so it is reasonable to argue that agricultural growth will reduce poverty by more than growth in high-skilled technology sectors. On the other hand, the more growth is focused on only one sector, such as during commodity booms, the more growth will have to trickle through to other sectors via multipliers to reach a broader cross-section of the poor. To the extent that booming sectors are controlled by elites rather than the poor, poverty reduction will be slower. Labor market frictions partly determine how quickly growth translates into poverty reduction as well.

FIGURE 5.3.
$1/day poverty and growth in sub-Saharan Africa, 1970–2006. Source: Pinkovskiy and Sala-i-Martin 2010.

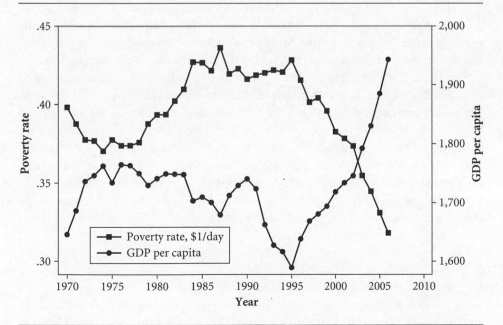

The effects of economic growth reach the unemployed through different channels. As economic growth increases employment opportunities—and vice versa—previously unemployed people are brought in to share the benefits of growth directly. For those who remain unemployed, private and public charity flows depend in part on economic growth and the policy stabilizers in place. Private charities and governments receive additional funds thanks to economic growth that can be channeled to the poor. If they are spent during boom times, the well-being of the unemployed poor improves and worsens along with the business cycle. To the extent private charities and government programs save some resources during good periods to distribute during economic downturns, this will smooth transfers and reduce the negative aspects of downturns. Investments made during good times to improve education and health services for the poorest can produce long-term improvements in people's ability to exit poverty in good times and bad.

There are different definitions of what constitutes "pro-poor growth." Is growth pro-poor because the poor's absolute level of income or wealth increases, no matter how little? This is a pretty low standard: economic growth must only avoid harming the poor. A more restrictive requirement would be that growth is only pro-poor if the growth of poor incomes is larger than the growth of rich incomes in percentage terms (e.g., each poor person's income increases 5 percent while each rich person's income increases 3 percent). The rich might still gain more in absolute terms, but the poor's growth rate is higher. A very high standard would require the poor to gain more in absolute terms than the rich (e.g., each poor person gains $1,000 while each rich person gains $500.) Often clarity is needed in poverty debates.

The available evidence indicates that no growth, low growth, and narrowly based growth increase the probability of people being trapped in poverty and transferring that poverty to the next generation. Hence, promoting broad-based economic growth is important for reducing poverty, and the absence of growth is a severe constraint to reducing poverty. Patterns of growth that make use of the labor of the poorest, expand demand for the services and goods they produce, support traditional livelihoods and open up jobs and livelihoods in new sectors that poor people can access, and enable them to increase their labor productivity need to be fostered (von Braun and Pandya-Lorch 2007). In many economies, this means focusing on and investing in agricultural and casual laborers and the labor markets they depend on, and prioritizing trade opportunities that increase employment and improve working conditions and wages. Much more research needs to be done to understand the channels by which economic growth reduces poverty in different settings so that policies can better influence growth to be more pro-poor. Research is also needed to better understand the roles that development assistance, remittances, FDI, and other capital inflows play in reducing and alleviating poverty.

Inequality

Suppose that economic growth is distributed according to the inequality of the country. That is, if a group of people controls 10 percent of a country's wealth, they also get 10 percent of the benefits of growth. In such a case, it has been argued, higher inequality means that economic growth will benefit the poor less than it would if inequality were lower. Ravallion (2004) estimates that an increase in per capita GDP of 1 percent could decrease poverty by between 0.6 percent and 4.3 percent depending in part on whether the initial level of inequality was high or low.

Numerous economic models show that redistributive policies reduce work incentives of both the poor and non-poor, which could lead to lower rates of economic growth. This produces a potential trade-off between poverty and inequality reduction today versus poverty reduction and increases in living standards in the future. Even small changes in growth rates produce very large average income differences over twenty-year horizons. On the other hand, if inequality hinders economic growth from reducing poverty, reductions in inequality today could increase the poverty-reducing power of future economic growth enough to compensate: lower rates of economic growth that benefit the poorest more may be more beneficial for them than higher rates of growth that do not reach them. (See also chapter 11.)

Kuznets (1955) hypothesized a possible relationship between economic growth and inequality. Rich countries tended to have low inequality; middle-income countries (mostly in Latin America) tended to have high inequality; poor countries (primarily Asian) tended to have low inequality. He suggested a simple mechanism of modernization that would lead to increasing inequality over the early stages of economic growth and later decreases in inequality as more and more of the populace entered the modern sectors of the economy. This would form an inverted-U relationship between income levels and inequality. Rapid economic growth in China has been associated with increasing inequality, and it could be argued that this growth has been of the kind Kuznets hypothesized, as rural workers have entered a more modernized sector (case 5-2).

A very extensive literature has tested the Kuznets curve but has failed to find evidence to support it. Growth has increased and decreased inequality even within the same country without a recognizable trend. Changes in inequality do not appear to depend on how fast economic growth has been (Ravallion and Chen 1997; Deininger and Squire 1998). Ravallion (2007) posits that growth is less effective at reducing poverty in countries where there is both high poverty and high inequality. The effect of growth on inequality appears to depend on a number of context-specific factors.

Recent literature has concluded that institutionalized inequality slows growth (e.g., Acemoglu, Johnson, and Robinson 2001; Easterly 2007). Ethnic fractionalization has also been shown to affect inequality in a way that reduces growth. In each of these cases, the real story is about institutions that entrench inequality and prevent upward mobility. Institutional reforms, however, have not been shown to promote the kind of rapid growth proponents have claimed. As chapters 2 and 9 discuss, this may be because reforms were not deep enough or were gone about in the wrong way, or there may be significant lags between institutional reform and growth opportunities. What is clear, however, is that good governance is part of maintaining economic growth once it has started, providing social and economic stability, ensuring that the benefits are spread throughout society, and enabling entrepreneurs to create opportunities.

Evidence has shown that on average countries with well-developed markets experience higher growth and poverty reduction (World Bank 2001c). Many poor people are too distant from the markets that could enable them to reduce risk and create opportunities to exit poverty (chapter 6). There are many individual markets whose effective operation is important for the poor: markets for the goods they sell, labor markets, financial markets to provide the capital they need, health care markets, and what may be termed political markets where they are able to trade their political support for policies they need. Making markets work for the poor requires social integration—particularly in labor markets—and numerous social norms and formal government policies. Effective public goods provision, particularly ensuring education and health for the poorest, have been credited with making market reforms work for the poor in Sri Lanka (Sahn and Edirisinghe 1993). Reducing gender inequality and marginalization are essential for reducing societal and community factors acting against poor households, while public support for agricultural research, safety nets, and education strengthens poor households' asset allocation.

Risk Mitigation and Safety Nets

Risk mitigation and enhancing the poor's coping skills against adverse shocks is essential. That includes reducing risk created by governments' macroeconomic instability, policy reversals, procyclical government spending, corruption, and unreliable entitlements. Governments also need to be actively involved in preventing or managing shocks at the national and regional level, such as economic downturns and natural disasters; minimizing the impact on poor people when they occur; supporting the range of assets of poor people; and supporting the institutions that help poor people manage risk and enable them to pursue the higher-risk, higher-return activities that can lift them out of poverty. Some possible tools include health insurance, old age assistance and pensions, unemployment insurance (Vodopivec 2009), workfare programs, social funds, microfinance programs, and cash transfers. Safety nets should be designed to support immediate consumption needs, protect the accumulation of human, physical, and social assets by poor people, and encourage asset accumulation (Alderman and Hoddinott 2007). Illustrations of government interventions in these areas are provided in cases 4-2, 5-1, and 7-5.

Cash transfers have received increased attention thanks to the recent successes in Mexico's Progresa/Oportunidades program (case 5-1) and Brazil's Zero Hunger transfer, Bolsa Familia. In 1997 there were only three conditional cash transfers (CCTs) worldwide, but by 2008 there were twenty-eight (Fiszbein and Schady 2009, 4). CCTs provide households with a cash stipend provided the members fulfill certain criteria, such as vaccinating and making sure children attend school or mothers attend nutrition and health classes. CCTs may be an easier political sell than unconditional cash transfers (UCTs), and conditions can be tailored to provide additional targeting/ screening devices or provide education to complement the financial incentives being provided. They are also increasing in popularity compared to in-kind transfers that provide the poor with the least freedom in how to allocate donations but give donors/ taxpayers the greatest perceived degree of control over how funds are spent.

Preliminary evidence suggests that even UCTs may be more effective at reducing poverty and more likely to be spent on socially desired activities than has been supposed. Cash transfers are providing a change in the way some program-impact evaluations are carried out. Normally the comparison used in evaluating impact is to compare an intervention to the option of doing nothing if for no other reason than the counterfactuals are usually easiest to foresee and justify. However, a more meaningful comparison would be between using the same resources in a UCT: Did the program reduce poverty or accomplish other goals more than spending the same resources in a UCT would? This sets a higher standard and could potentially reallocate aid to more effective programs by simply transferring money from less effective programs to cash grants.

Hulme and Shepherd (2003, 404) discuss the importance of context in identifying appropriate poverty reduction policies:

> Different poverty reduction strategies should be pursued for different mixes of chronic and transitory poverty. In a country where poverty is more transitory than chronic, where "the poor" at any particular time have a high probability of improving their position, policies should focus predominantly on social safety nets that help people to avoid descending into chronic poverty. . . . In a country where a significant proportion of the poor are chronically poor, then policies to redistribute assets, direct investment toward basic physical infrastructure, reduce social exclusion (from employment, markets and public institutions) and provide long-term social security will be necessary if poverty is to be significantly reduced. In these two cases, quite different national development strategies, roles for the state and forms and levels of international support are needed.

The importance of international factors has been increasing over time. This was seen most dramatically in the rapid increase in food prices from 2005–2008 as government import and export policies spilled over to affect the poor of many nations. International corporate governance, intellectual property rules, international public research, labor norms, environmental regulations, and governance norms similarly impact the ability of poor people to extricate themselves from poverty. International cooperation is thus needed to reduce industrial countries' protectionism and avert global financial volatility. The growing importance of such international public goods as agricultural and medical research calls for a shift in the focus of development cooperation. Furthermore, because of the importance of international actions in poverty reduction, the voices of poor countries and poor people should be strengthened in international forums (chapter 9).

Conclusion: Reducing Poverty

Poverty is a key factor in the global food system. Poverty causes hunger, micronutrient deficiencies, and in some cases obesity. Poverty's causes and correlates reduce people's productive capacity and hence their ability to escape poverty. Poverty affects the biophysical and political environments of the food system as well. While there is much potential for food system activities to reduce poverty by providing secure livelihoods and better nutrition, feedbacks throughout the food system tend to enhance and prolong poverty (Dasgupta 2007).

Poor people are not a homogeneous group. They do not become poor for the same reasons, they have different needs when poor, and different factors prevent them from exiting poverty. Any serious attempt to reduce poverty must understand the context in which a group of poor people find themselves, identify the binding constraints that prevent them from improving their condition, and work *with* them in a participatory manner to remove those constraints. Some transitory poor do not need interventions to leave poverty so much as they need interventions to prevent their falling back in once they escape.

The goal is to empower the poor—enhancing their capacities, capabilities, and functionings to alleviate and reduce poverty. This includes empowering them politically so they can demand the policies they need. This includes providing the public goods they need through whatever mechanism necessary, particularly education, basic health, roads, and agricultural research (chapter 7). It also means removing the barriers—political, legal, economic, and social—that work against the poor.

Much of the debate around empowerment in recent years has focused on rights-based approaches to development and poverty reduction. As discussed in chapter 11, a rights-based approach means that clear duties are identified that different institutions must fulfill as duty-bearers in order to combat poverty. Therefore, empowering poor people is part of the broader agenda of sound governance and accountability of state institutions to their citizens (chapter 9). Ambler et al. (2007) discuss gender empowerment in Bangladesh, El Salvador, Mali, and Mozambique. Stewart (2007) addresses integration policies.

Analysis of poverty points to the need to invest in human capacity, support the acquisition of assets, and strengthen people's capacity to assert their rights. Internationally, efforts to reform global governance and international trade need vigorous support if the poor are not to be further marginalized and impoverished by globalization. In the short term this is challenging and costly, but it is essential to achieve the MDGs.

Market-based economic growth has done more to reduce poverty in the world than any other factor over the world's history. By itself, however, it is not sufficient to bring *all* people out of poverty. In many cases, the poor are socially marginalized and unable to take advantage of the benefits of growth and markets. Labor markets that are oppressive—particularly bonded labor, the worst forms of child labor, and human trafficking—and restrictive migration laws that prevent people from moving to improve their situation reduce the scope of opportunities for poor people to escape poverty. Conflict, serious health problems, lack of productive assets, low human and social capital, and poor governance all interact to keep millions of poor people trapped in poverty in ways that markets alone cannot address.

Though there are many problems market access cannot solve, lack of access to markets and uncompetitive market structures prevent millions of people from being able to escape poverty. Markets that lack necessary public goods and supportive governance can be as inefficient and ineffective in producing social welfare and poverty reduction as overly regulated markets. These topics are taken up in chapter 6.

Poverty Alleviation Policies Case Studies

The cases in this chapter address the interaction between income distribution, poverty, food security, and nutrition.* They show how government action can influence all of these factors through conditional transfer programs (case 5-1), policies to facilitate migration out of agriculture (case 5-3), and a series of other policies that influence income distribution and poverty (case 5-2).

5-1   PROGRESA: An Integrated Approach to Poverty Alleviation in Mexico
       Leigh Gantner
5-2   Income Disparity in China and Its Policy Implications
       Fuzhi Cheng
5-3   Migration in Rural Burkina Faso
       Fleur Wouterse

Notes

1. In standard welfare economics, well-being is measured by utility. Since utility is directly linked to income in applied research, income is routinely used as the basis for welfare judgment. The tradition of using utility or monetary representations thereof in welfare analysis has been dominant for the last two centuries and is referred to as *utilitarianism* (chapter 11).

2. Vulnerability also means the probability of being exposed to a number of other risks such as violence, crime, and natural disasters.

3. This categorization needs further development. For example, a dramatic, short-term downturn or "spike" in the welfare of a transient poor household could lead to an event (e.g., wasting of children, a preventable impairment or death) that has long-term negative implications for an individual or household and is thus chronic.

4. The slower progress in reduction of the number of people in poverty is in part due to population growth.

5. Laborers are bonded to their employer through various means—often through indebtedness, but also through violence, and through feudal type systems whereby households are dependent on landlords for their basic needs.

6. In addition to those displaced by armed conflict, many millions of people have been forcibly relocated by state and paramilitary forces attempting to control insurgency movements or resource-rich territory; by states attempting to reconfigure the ethnic makeup of particular regions, such as in Indonesia and Bangladesh; and even by "development" itself, in the form of, for example, large-scale dams or exclusion from forests or national parks.

---

* The case studies referenced here are presented in full in the three-volume work by Per Pinstrup-Andersen and Fuzhi Cheng, eds., *Case Studies in Food Policy for Developing Countries* (Ithaca, NY: Cornell University Press, 2009) and online via open access at http://cip.cornell.edu/gfs.

Chapter 6

Domestic Market Policies

Introduction

Trading in markets has characterized humanity for millennia. Europe and China were connected long before the European Age of Discovery "rediscovered" the East with profitable land and sea trade routes reuniting cultures and people. Markets were no less important in small communities. Though American folklore has celebrated rugged frontiersmen who produced all their own goods, most people throughout time have lived in communities and drawn on each other for economic support through markets.

Over time, products have become increasingly complex, making it more difficult for any one individual or group of individuals to produce all the products they consume. Read's (1958) seminal pamphlet shows how many different people's effort has to be organized in order to produce even a pencil. The organization of economic activities has therefore become more and more specialized, requiring ever greater reliance on markets and trade.

Since World War II, food supply chains have grown longer, including more processing and marketing than before. The increasing importance of these "value added" activities has significantly changed the food system. Less and less of every dollar of food expenditures has gone to farmers or primary product producers, leading farmers to worry about processor market power (see case 6-1). It has also changed consumers' relationship with the food they consume. Research on markets and marketing attempts to understand the producer-market-consumer relationships in the supply chain.

This chapter discusses how markets impact food systems and identifies the primary policy challenges. These challenges tend to arise from market deficiencies in terms of high marketing and transaction costs, excessive risks, externalities, wide marketing margins, lack of clear contract or property laws, and failure to meet the needs of producers and/or consumers. These challenges arise in both developed and developing countries' food systems, though they are more prevalent in the latter. Government intervention may be needed to achieve economic and social objectives and keep markets functioning as they ought. Another recommended resource is Mc-Cullough, Pingali, and Stamoulis (2008) on the impacts of changing global food systems on smallholders.

Food markets in developing countries are evolving rapidly. Market dominance is shifting from basic grains and commodities to higher-value products, from farmers to processors and retailers, and from spot markets to horizontally and vertically organized decision makers. Supermarkets' procurement systems have led to a growing concentration in manufacturing, processing, and distribution (cases 6-2 and 6-11). Increasing concentration has brought fears that firms may abuse market power, leading to loss of efficiency and consumer and smallholder farmer welfare (cases 6-1 and 6-7). Imperfect markets weaken the power of prices to signal information between producers and consumers.

As has been discussed in chapter 2, there is a growing realization that governments need to take an active, supporting role so that food markets can work properly. This primarily includes investing in public goods, particularly building and maintaining infrastructure (e.g., roads, electricity); crafting laws and institutions that will reduce marketing and transaction costs, increase stability, and provide a level playing field for market participants; supporting financial capital; funding public research to increase productivity; disseminating that research and market information to distant areas; and providing opportunities for basic education and health care. This chapter will focus on the first two of these factors: the physical and legal infrastructure necessary for markets to function.

Ineffective or unsustainable government policies have also had negative impacts on food markets. Historically, developing country governments frequently set food commodity prices below market levels to subsidize consumers and urban industry. This was an implicit tax on the agricultural sector, creating disincentives to invest in increasing agricultural productivity (chapter 7). Many governments established state-owned enterprises or parastatal marketing boards to govern the sector by using monopoly and monopsony power to set the prices at which farmers could sell and consumers purchase food. They often set prices to channel benefits to urban elites, the industrial sector (low food prices keep wages low), and rent-seeking policymakers and bureaucrats, and were generally inefficient, costly, and corrupt.

By the 1970s, evidence had mounted that some government interventions in food markets had done more harm than good to society, producing stagnant agricultural sectors and large fiscal and trade deficits. Other markets also impact food systems, such as health care markets, land markets, markets for environmental services, political markets, and international trade. Government policies regarding these markets impact food markets indirectly.

A Marketing System

The term "market" is widely used, and most economists regard it as frequently misunderstood. A common view of the market is that it is a physical or online location where buying and selling takes place (a "marketplace"). While not incorrect, economists take a much broader view. A market is any physical or institutional arrangement within which (1) the forces of demand and supply are at work, (2) the ownership of some quantity of a good or service is transferred, and (often) (3) the price is determined or modified (Cochrane 1957).

Some of these markets bear little resemblance to a marketplace. Economists discuss "marriage markets" as being analogous to labor markets, where demand and supply for spouses results in a matching equilibrium. This views marriage as a contract between two people specifying the "price" paid to remain married, such as a division of labor or household privileges. In "political markets," support for elected officials might be traded for favorable legislation or legal action. "Aid markets" might describe the demand (developing country governments) and supply (donors) of limited aid money and the actions required by governments to receive aid, or the demand (donors) and supply (developing country governments) of limited government capacity specifying the amount of aid that must be paid for governments to act.

Markets are made by people. It is easy to think of markets as impersonal "market forces" beyond control, but such a perception is faulty. You are part of many markets and the conditions in those markets are partially determined by your choices. Because markets are made by people, people can shape markets to serve them and government policy affects markets by regulating, informing, or incentivizing people so that they behave differently. Firms make money only by providing a service or product to someone that values it more than the money they pay for it. Those firms that provide the best products—which could mean highest quality or lowest price or most convenient access or most environmentally friendly and socially conscious, depending on the consumer—receive more money from consumers for their services. Your choices as a consumer partially determine what the "best" products are and which firms will be rewarded. In a real sense, you are an integral part of the market.

A different but related term "marketing" is also widely used. In most contexts, marketing refers to how companies present themselves and their products to customers. In food markets, this includes advertising that targets different age and income profiles, arranging product appearance to highlight perceived health benefits while hiding health risks, and connecting product consumption with values of acceptance, security, fun, or attractiveness. If at its best marketing is understood as influencing production to meet consumer demand, at its least attractive it is perceived as manipulating consumers.

This chapter refers to marketing as a different concept sometimes called "macromarketing" that examines the markets themselves both as created by society and as an influence on society (Oliver 1980). Business-oriented "micromarketing" described above is discussed in a voluminous literature (see Kotler 1994). This chapter is more concerned with understanding the behavior and functions of food markets and related government policies.

Marketing refers to all the activities involved in the functioning of the market. It is "the way in which any organization or individual matches its own capacities to the need of its customers" (Christopher, McDonald, and Wills 1980). The production and market sectors should not be thought of separately even though there appears to be a natural dividing line between the two. The market is not necessarily an institution to which firms turn their attention only at the end of the production. Rather, it is best seen as an integrative force that directs production in ways that would match customer needs and satisfaction.

This can be illustrated by the case of the Ford Motor Company. From its beginning until the mid-1920s, production managers informed sales managers how much they had to sell and it was up to the marketing arm to find ways to unload the vehicles that had been produced. Competition determined that such a system was unsustainable. Within a decade, it was the Ford sales manager informing the production manager how many cars should be built and at what specifications to meet expected consumer demand.

A marketing system comprises all of the actions that move goods and services in some orderly fashion from producers to consumers and the agents who perform those activities (chapter 1). The components of a marketing system are interdependent. A change in any one of them impacts on the others as well as on the system as a whole.

Marketing systems are open, existing in biological, socioeconomic, and political environments that influence how markets function. This is true whether the ways and means of production are owned privately or publicly; whether prices are determined by the interactions of a large number of atomistic consumers and producers, by a monopoly's executive board, or by government mandate; and regardless of the extent to which governments intervene in markets. Thus, a marketing system is a separate concept from "the market system," which is widely taken to be synonymous with capitalism. Though the marketing activities described throughout the chapter are discussed as if they were taking place in a market system, many of the principles are readily adaptable to situations where government takes a more controlling role in marketing decisions.

Marketing systems, unsurprisingly, are made up of markets. Understanding how markets function depends crucially on how large or small each individual market is. In some cases, it is sufficient to talk about a market for "grains" versus "other foods," while for other purposes it might be necessary to separate the market for "hard red winter wheat" from the market for "soft spring wheat" because they have different characteristics. In practice, markets are differentiated according to some easily observed characteristics such as locations (e.g., the Saint Louis market), product types (e.g., the wheat market), time (e.g., the May soybean market), or institutional levels (e.g., the retail market). For references on theoretical determinations, see Houck (1984), Cochrane (1957), and Papandreou and Wheeler (1954).

Introductory Theory of the Firm

Understanding how markets and food markets function requires a basic level of understanding of how for-profit firms are believed to operate. Just as markets are often misunderstood, so are firms. Firms are not just multinational corporations or supermarkets. Every farmer operates a firm. Additionally, it is not possible to separate people into those who are only producers (firm owners and workers) and everyone else as consumers. Every working person is simultaneously part of a firm and a consumer.

Most firms try to maximize expected profits, their revenue from sales minus their costs. There are two types of costs: fixed costs and variable costs. *Fixed costs* include the cost of establishing the business and receiving legal permission to enter the market and anything that cannot be changed over the time horizon being considered (e.g., property taxes or rent and land use cannot be changed quickly but can be adjusted over a longer time horizon). *Variable costs* are the costs that vary by the quantity produced. *Marginal costs* are the variable costs of producing one more unit, including wages, materials, marketing, transportation, search, and bargaining costs, among others. So long as firms are able to pay the variable costs of production, they are liable to stay in business in the short run, even if they cannot cover their fixed costs. The next sections introduce the concept of marketing and transaction costs, which are part of the costs firms attempt to minimize. Firms organize around, and market structures therefore adapt to, changes in transaction costs. Chapter 7 discusses what happens when downside risks force farmers to depart from this model.

In a competitive setting with low barriers to entry, economists have demonstrated that prices will tend to equal the marginal cost of producing one more unit of a good or service. Why would this be? Consider what would happen if one firm out of many decided to raise its price. Consumers would buy less from that firm and buy more from the other firms, reducing its profits. By returning its price to the market price, the firm could increase profits. If that firm lowered its price below marginal costs, it would lose money on every additional item sold, which is not a winning proposition.

In noncompetitive frameworks, such as a monopoly, prices will not necessarily equal marginal cost but are likely to be higher. If prices are too high and barriers to entry are low enough, however, this will spur other firms to enter the industry and lower prices again. Some people combine this insight with the large profits announced by multinationals to demonstrate that they cannot be working in a competitive framework. This comes from a misunderstanding of the difference between "accounting profits" and "economic profits," which include the "opportunity costs" of doing business. It is economic profits that go to zero, rather than accounting profits.[1]

Market Functions and Costs

Marketing activities add value for consumers by changing the form of the goods to match consumer expectations, transporting goods for consumers' convenience, providing centralized places and times for people to meet, and facilitating the transfer of ownership (Kohls and Uhl 2002). Market transactions require the transfer of ownership of goods and services, even if no goods move locations (e.g., in the futures market). The costs associated with packaging, handling, transporting, wasting, storing, processing, and maintaining deteriorating capital are called marketing costs.

One of markets' key functions is to store products for when they are needed and to transport them to locations where they are needed. Because food products are perishable and produced only seasonally while demand is continuous, markets' storage function assumes greater importance than for manufactured goods. Many areas are unsuitable for growing food and hence must import food from the surrounding areas, requiring someone to transport the food where it is needed.

Middlemen or traders are often vilified for buying food during times of plenty when prices are low and holding on to these stocks until supply is low and they can command a high price. The fact that traders often come from minority backgrounds in most areas does not help their popularity. What is seldom seen is that, without these traders and this storage service, price fluctuations would be even larger. While there are doubtless traders who take unfair advantage of their relative scarcity in the market (only one or a few buyers during harvest and one or a few sellers during hungry months), one of the simplest solutions to this problem is to entice more traders into the system rather than fewer. The competition among traders reduces the market power of any individual trader, reducing price instability further. By making trading more profitable, infrastructure investments that reduce transportation and storage costs induce lower price variation and may reduce traders' market power by enticing more traders into the market.

Some food products require substantial processing before they can be sold to customers. Others may need minimal processing or can be delivered directly to market after harvest. As incomes increase, food processing takes on increasing importance and the value-adding activities are responsible for an increasing share of the consumer price. The more processed a food is, the larger the share of food money that accrues to processors. In the United States, about 16 cents of every dollar spent on food goes to the farmer for the raw food inputs, while the other 84 cents covers the cost of marketing (USDA 2010). Farmers receive a larger share of food expenditures for foods that are not highly processed, but to the extent that processing encourages people to spend more, it is possible for farmers to increase their revenue by selling foods that will be more highly processed. The relationship between farmer and processor will be discussed in greater detail later in the chapter.

FAO (2007a) provides an interesting and informative illustration of how marketing costs affect the difference between the retail price and the farm-gate price of agricultural commodities (the marketing margin). In their example, a farmer sells tomatoes to a trader for $0.50/kg. The trader transports the tomatoes to a distant retailer who purchases the tomatoes for $0.90/kg and sells them to a consumer for $1.19/kg. The natural reaction is to assume that the farmer received 42 percent of the total price, the trader 34 percent, and the retailer 24 percent. Such a calculation ignores marketing cost. For the trader, FAO calculates marketing costs of $0.26 and waste costs of $0.09, so that traders actually receive only $0.05/kg in profit (table 6.1) and retailers $0.04/kg.

TABLE 6.1.
Example of a Trader's Marketing Costs per Kilogram of Tomatoes

Purchase of tomatoes	$0.50
Packaging	$0.05
Labor	$0.02
Transportation costs	$0.15
Road blocks	$0.01
Market fees	$0.01
Market agent fees	$0.02
Wastage	$0.09
Total costs	$0.85
Profits from sales price of $0.90/kg	$0.05

Source: Adapted from FAO 2007a.

Market Power, Market Failure, and Imperfect Competition

Market structures determine equilibrium market prices and quantities and impact the allocative efficiency of resources. In perfectly competitive markets, resources end up distributed such that it is not possible to make one person better off without making someone else worse off (also known as Pareto optimality, see chapter 11). Adam Smith's formulation of the "invisible hand" theory demonstrated that a system that preserved maximum human liberty would be not only ethically appealing but efficient in a Pareto sense. To the extent that market transactions are entered into voluntarily by both parties, reliance on the economic self-interest of individuals and firms results in desirable social outcomes: neither side would agree to the transaction if it did not make them better off.

This conclusion does not, however, mean that markets will ensure equal division of resources, that all poverty will be eradicated, or that other social goals will be promoted. Some social goals are simply not addressed by markets because that is not what they were created for.

The standard assumption in the economics literature is that of perfectly competitive markets where there are numerous buyers and sellers who are small relative to the size of the market. No individual person or firm has the market power to influence the price in such a case—they are "price takers" rather than "price setters." When these assumptions are violated there is "imperfect competition" or market failures (chapter 2). Imperfect competition and market failures reduce market efficiency so that markets may fail to do those things they are supposed to do.

Extensive research has examined cases of imperfect competition where there is only one buyer or seller (monopsony or monopoly, respectively) or only a few (oligopsony or oligopoly), or where many firms sell imperfectly differentiated products (monopolistic competition) such that no other firm can produce exactly the same product that another one makes, but they make close substitutes (e.g., car brands, cell phone providers, processed food products). The more buyers and sellers in a given market, the "thicker" the market is, while a market with few buyers or sellers or infrequent transactions is said to be "thin." Thin markets are problematic because they are more likely to have participants with much market power and weak price-discovery mechanisms for transmitting market information to all participants.[2]

Individual farmers or consumers are very unlikely to have market power and are more likely to be subject to market power. If there is only one trader in an area, for instance, that trader likely has the ability to influence prices with each farmer. Producer and consumer groups can counteract some of this because cooperatives and other groups can have a greater market influence than the sum of their members' market power, which can reduce inequality. Cooperatives' governance structures may undermine this, however, if they serve primarily to benefit a few elites within the group.

A fundamental question is whether the various market deficiencies discussed above constitute "market failures" or "government failures." Markets in developing countries are not as efficient as they could be and hence fail to deliver the promised benefits. To the extent markets fail because governments have created rent-seeking opportunities that favor some at the expense of others, have failed to enact proper legislation, uphold contracts and property laws that are passed, or provide public goods, and have intervened in ways that hamper market performance, however, it is more accurate to say these are the results of government failures.

Is environmental degradation of common property resources a market failure because private individuals caused the damage or a government failure because governments did not adequately establish accountable stewardship (as through property rights) for those resources? These questions matter because the answer in part determines whether analysts look for ways to reform markets or reform governments, and government failure may prevent it from being able to fix market failure. Chapter 9 discusses government failure in detail, while the rest of this chapter examines interventions to improve market performance.

Transaction Costs and Market Structure

Market structures evolve to reduce marketing costs and to provide additional services involved in reducing transaction costs. Transaction costs are the costs related to carrying out transactions, including finding a buyer or a seller (search costs), negotiating a price, obtaining payment, and costs related to risks, including the risks of being cheated. Coase (Coase 1991), whose introduction of the notion of transaction costs in the 1930s earned him the Nobel Prize, defined transaction costs as the costs of making an exchange. Some transaction costs are fixed (e.g., market entry costs) and some are variable (e.g., managerial oversight). The legal environment has a pivotal effect on transaction costs, particularly laws regarding property rights, contracts, and standardized weights and measures. Another Nobel Prize winner, Williamson (Williamson 2000) provides an excellent introduction to transaction cost economics.

Furubotn and Richter (1998) break transaction costs into three primary kinds. Market transaction costs are the prices paid for using market mechanisms, including searching for buyers and sellers and bargaining or price determination (analyzed by

Coase). Management transaction costs are the costs associated with decision making within a firm, including valuating in-firm services and goods for which there is no market and monitoring employees (analyzed by Williamson). Political transaction costs include the costs of complying with political requirements and lobbying politicians to change institutions in ways that favor the company or industry (analyzed by North [1990]). Market transaction costs are part of marketing costs, while management and political transaction costs are not. The new institutional economic (NIE) theory on which these strands are based is further discussed in chapter 9.

Eifert, Gelb, and Ramachandran (2007) estimate that, for the average firm in eighteen developing countries, marketing and transaction costs amount to 10–30 percent of the total costs of doing business. These costs constitute a smaller percent of total costs in somewhat wealthier countries, such as Bangladesh, India, and China, than in poorer countries. Gabre-Madhin (2001) finds that search costs account for 19 percent of the market and transaction costs of Ethiopian grain traders. In terms of fixed costs, de Soto (2000) demonstrates that it takes from thirteen to twenty-five years to formalize an informal business in the Philippines, six to fourteen years in Egypt to secure property rights on desert land, and more than eleven years to obtain a sales contract in Haiti. These transaction costs keep many firms from joining the formal sector, preventing their owners and workers from accessing its attending privileges. De Soto (2000) estimates that over $9.3 trillion of capital are owned by poor people just in real estate alone to which they lack a formal title because the transaction costs of formalizing it are too high.

Marketing and transaction costs are an important determinant of market delimitations. Markets are defined geographically when it costs time and money to purchase things and transact business over distance; markets are defined by time when storage and spoilage costs prevent reallocating production or consumption decisions over time; and by product classes depending on the costs of substitutes. Transaction costs also come about because of (1) imperfect information: the buyer or the seller or both may have a lack of information they need to negotiate the terms of the transaction; (2) bounded rationality: even if the buyer and seller had all the relevant information, they would not have the time or capacity to analyze it thoroughly (chapter 9); and (3) opportunistic behavior: the buyer and the seller may have short-run incentive to misrepresent the truth and violate the terms of their agreement.

Transaction costs depend on the nature of the market, the product involved, and the policy environment. In some situations, a spot market will be a low-cost way of conducting transactions, but in others, contracts or vertical integration[3] will be more efficient. Governments can lower marketing and transaction costs through institutional arrangements, such as public weights and measures that define quality and facilitate negotiations, infrastructure that reduces transportation costs, good radio or cell phone coverage that reduces informational costs, and a legal system that enforces contracts and limits opportunistic behavior. In developing countries where these institutions are not well established, the issue of high marketing and transaction costs is acute.

Mass production requires high levels of standardization. Standardized production simplifies purchasing decisions and reduces market and transaction costs. It also makes it easier for consumers to communicate what product qualities they value, makes product enjoyment more reliable, and can create brand loyalty. Standardization requires an effective set of standard weights and measures that may be imposed by individual firms, by industry agreement, or by legislation. The less uniform standards of weights and measures are, the larger are the transaction costs for consumers to make informed purchasing decisions, so formulating agreed-on standards can be one of governments' important facilitating roles. Standardization has also affected the relationship between farmer and processor, which will be discussed later in the chapter. Food safety standardization between countries is discussed in cases 3-11 and 3-12, and export policy is discussed in chapter 10.

Markets provide financing to ensure firms can survive during the time between investing and receiving payment for the sale of the product. For consumers, financing can enhance their purchasing power and enable them to smooth consumption when negative shocks hit.

Markets also enable risk sharing between farmers and processors, between investors and firms, and between producers, traders, retailers, and consumers (chapter 7). Risk bearing is important because the possibility of incurring losses is always present, whether because of natural disaster and weather fluctuation or because the value of the product changes unexpectedly (e.g., during the food price crisis or as a result of a food safety warning). These risks increase transaction costs, which risk sharing reduces.

Vertical Integration

Marketing and transaction costs determine market structure. Whether a meat-packing firm should purchase land, hire farmers, and own the livestock that will be slaughtered or contract with farmers who are already there or only purchase livestock as needed at spot markets depends on the costs of each method of coordination. Coordination between supply and demand and between different participants in the supply chain is called *vertical integration*.

The least vertically integrated market structure is the "spot market," where buyers and sellers settle a transaction "on the spot" and make no commitment outside the transaction itself. At the other extreme is control or ownership of the complete flow of products and information during all stages of a supply chain. In this case, vertical coordination follows a corporate scheme rather a negotiating-parties scheme and all transactions are internalized. Contracts take an intermediate position, allowing market participants to conduct transactions according to formal or informal agreements that specify terms of transaction including price, quantity, timing, and product attributes.

Vertical integration in developed markets has transformed relationships between processor and producer. For example, a modern poultry firm now grows the grain that will be fed to the livestock and performs functions that cover hatchery activities, poultry feed manufacturing, growing of broilers, egg production, veterinary and pharmaceutical services, slaughtering, and rendering of slaughtering wastes. Direct firm control of the different processes can reduce the transaction costs of coordination, ensures more stable (low risk), uniform, high-quality inputs, and allows firms to quickly change any step of the production process to respond to consumer demands. These efficiency gains lead to gains for both the firm and consumers, though estimates of how large consumer and producer surplus differ.

Developing country food markets are becoming more vertically integrated through contracts. As illustrated by cases 6-3, 6-4, and 6-6, contracts exist throughout the food-marketing channel—for example, between processors and wholesalers and between wholesalers and retailers. The greatest focus recently has been on the relationship between farmers and the buyers of the agricultural output.

Contract farming can be attractive for farmers when contracted prices are stable and guaranteed for a reasonable period, credit and other inputs are provided at favorable terms, risk is shared between the farm and processors, and/or profits are high enough and stabilized. Contracts make sense for processing firms when longer-term relationships between farm and firm reduce transaction costs and outright farm ownership would be too expensive; when contract terms allow firms to tailor farm output to variable consumer demand; when farmers have demonstrated an ability to provide consistent, high-quality output; and/or to ensure farm prices do not suddenly spike when purchasing decisions are made. Relative to other coordination schemes, contract farming also makes more sense when (1) the buyers are large scale; (2) agricultural products are high value, perishable, and technically difficult to produce; (3) the destination market has high demand for quality and food safety; and (4) public policies do not hamper contract farming by poor contract enforcement (Key and Runsten 1999).

Among the advantages of contracts is that farmers engage in them willingly because the terms of the contract are more attractive to them than other available alternatives. The voluntary nature of entering into contracts is not always recognized by some commentators who see only that contract terms are often dictated by processing firms and worry that, just as contracts protect farmers from low farm prices, they also prevent farmers from taking advantage of higher than normal farm prices. On the other hand, if processors are local or regional monopsonists, farmers may have very few other options than to sign contracts or move to another area. In such a situation, the relevant market is very thin and market power may significantly harm farmers who opt to make the best of a bad situation.

The least detailed type of contract specifies that a firm agrees to purchase at least a certain quantity of produce or livestock from the farmer at a given time at a given price. Instead of agreeing on a particular price, contracts may specify a price range or a formula for determining the final price or quantity at the time of sale. Farmers are free to choose production methods and reduce the risk of their investments. Production management contracts may also specify elements of how the farm is organized—for instance, requiring that chicken coop sizes be larger than a particular minimum or requiring that only organic fertilizers and pesticides be used. Resource-providing contracts tend to specify every feature of the farming process, with firms providing inputs and most management decisions while farmers act as pseudoemployees. Tournament-style contracts place farms in competition with each other such that the best-run farms (in terms of cost efficiency, highest production, or highest quality) receive a price premium when purchasing time comes.

Food Markets

Food commodity markets (usually referred to as agricultural markets) and processed food markets (or simply food markets) are structurally different. In agricultural markets, there are often numerous farmers supplying the same undifferentiated food products. These agricultural commodities are usually unbranded, largely unprocessed, and are handled and sold in bulk. Buyers can switch to different suppliers with few additional costs except transportation costs. National agricultural markets with many buyers and sellers closely resemble a perfectly competitive market (leaving aside pervasive government involvement). However, it is possible for regional monopolies or monopsonies to exist within a competitive national market.

Processed food markets tend to be less competitive. Products are often differentiated by their attributes, making markets thinner by reducing the number of sellers and endowing them with potential market power.

Food Markets and Human Health

Both food and agricultural markets impact human nutrition and health because marketing strategies directly impact people's food purchasing and eating habits (see case 4-6). Positive examples may be found in health advertisements that increased high-fiber cereal consumption and decreased red meat consumption in the United States in the 1970s–1980s. Currently, food advertising disproportionately promotes energy-dense fast foods, carbonated soft drinks, sugary breakfast cereals, salty snacks, and baked goods that tend to be high in fats, sugars, and salt and low in nutrients. Food advertising primarily targets children and adolescents who have limited cognition but tremendous spending power and influence on parental purchases. The health impact of such advertising is discussed in cases 3-9, 3-10, and 4-6.

Opinions diverge about whether supermarkets or traditional food markets (e.g., open markets and farmers' markets) serve human health and nutrition needs better. Supermarkets tend to promote greater dietary diversity; they rely on reputation, advanced food sourcing, and government oversight to ensure food safety standards are met; and they provide higher food quality than traditional food markets. This food quality largely manifests itself in appearance (uniform size and color; lack of visible bruising or insect damage; etc.), which is maintained in part by pesticides. While food appearance does not directly translate into food's nutritional content, it is a quality valued by consumers that supermarkets are better able to provide than traditional markets. It may also be the case that individual farmers and small markets do not have as strong incentives, scale, or government oversight to make the large, fixed cost investments to ensure food safety.

However, with heavy consolidation in growing and processing, large-scale contamination becomes easier in the supermarket chain, so that while food safety standards may be more likely to be enforced in supermarkets, an outbreak can do more damage. Since most produce takes longer to reach supermarket shelves than local markets, there is a risk of biophysical decrease in food quality, as sugars can turn to starches, plant cells shrink, and produce loses its vitality. Farmers' markets based on locally produced food are expanding rapidly in high-income countries (case 6-10).

Food markets also influence the environment. Increasing market integration has contributed to geographic specialization in food production and processing. Regional concentration and large production units lead to an accumulation of animal wastes and pesticide residues that may contaminate ground or surface water. The distance food travels from the time of its production until it reaches the consumer (food miles) has attracted much attention to the environmental impact of food. These issues are further discussed in chapter 8.

Lack of Food Market Integration

Food markets in developing countries suffer to varying degrees from poor infrastructure, lack of effective competition among market agents, restricted access to commercial finance, limited rule of law, and weak contract enforcement (chapter 9). Poor market institutions and infrastructure increase the costs that buyers and sellers incur in executing a transaction because they have to search for and screen potential suppliers or buyers, negotiate and contract with them, and monitor and enforce their adherence to the contract. Social, ethnic-based networks and personalized, trust-based exchange lower these costs, but it may still be more cost-effective for many people to avoid markets and produce only for home consumption (Fafchamps 2004; Easterly 2006).

Poor infrastructure and low market integration lead to large price variation (Jayne, Zulu, and Nijhoff 2006) and high marketing margins (Ahmed 1988). If markets are not well integrated, increases in production lead to significantly lower prices locally. This reduces the welfare of farmers who do not adopt improved techniques and limits the benefits of technology adoption for others. Local prices shift more due to idiosyncratic and local weather shocks. When communities are better integrated into surrounding markets, local variation matters less for price determination because food can be brought in or sent out to other areas. However, as seen in food price crises, it can also expose areas to shocks from far-distant areas and government policies well beyond their control.

Empirical studies documenting commodity price variability in developing countries suggest that lack of market integration, high transaction costs, and entry and mobility barriers have created enormous price variation over time and between regions. Ethiopian maize prices tripled from 1997–1998 to 1999–2000, then fell by 80 percent in the next two years. The price of maize in Malawi quadrupled between April 2001 and April 2002 (Pinstrup-Andersen and Shimokawa 2007). Geographic price variations are especially high in Tanzania, Ethiopia, Benin, and Ghana (Badiane et al. 1997; Delgado and Minot 2000).

Poor market integration reduces the extent to which changes in world prices are transmitted to consumers and producers. Thus, production increases in other countries may not benefit net-food buyers in poor countries if price decreases do not work through the system. Poor market integration also makes it easier for certain stakeholders to gain market power and change prices. This is usually examined empirically by testing whether price decreases and increases pass through the system to producers equally quickly, also known as testing for asymmetric price transmission (Meyer and Cramon-Taubadel [2004] review the literature). If processors, for instance, have market power, they can reap the benefits of price increases without increasing prices paid to farmers while the costs of price decreases are quickly passed through.

When markets and governments fail to provide the mechanisms for risk mitigation, farmers typically lose their incentives to invest for future productivity increases. Supply has been shown to be twice as responsive to price changes in areas with good market infrastructure as in areas with poor infrastructure (Chhibber 1998). Poor financial market development reduces the extent to which traders can stabilize prices. In Ghana, where smallholders have limited financing for storage, prices vary in real terms by over 90 percent during the year. In contrast, seasonal price variation is only 11 percent in Indonesia where financing exists to promote effective storage (Ellis, Trotter, and Magrath 1992). These price fluctuations have important spillover effects on rural employment, merchants, and processors and can be detrimental to all market participants, particularly when shocks are area-wide or systemic. The importance of risk mitigation for production is further discussed in chapter 7.

The effects of poor market infrastructure are not equally felt: those who have better access to market infrastructure and information—such as through government connections granting an import or export license exception—can lower their costs and enjoy a competitive advantage over others. Rural smallholders are often considered prey to extortion by monopsony or oligopsony behavior among traders and processors who collude to keep prices low (for alternate views, see Bauer 1957; Schultz 1964; Bellemare and Barrett 2006). The concern is that thin markets and unstable supply might not support efficient price discovery while physical and institutional barriers limit new entrants into the market and preclude the development of competitive market structures.

Structural Change in Food Markets

New Market Trends and Driving Forces

Reardon and Timmer (2007) discuss the many differences between developing and developed country food markets and how developed country food markets are changing and adapting to new market realities. Change has not been uniform across countries because of differing regulations, particularly regarding foreign direct investment (FDI) and foreign ownership of firms, and in some cases because of cultural factors (e.g., India's meat sector). Most changes have been demand driven, as introduced in chapter 1.

In developing countries, food marketing chains have traditionally been short and direct, requiring only basic logistics systems and inefficient compared with developed country marketing chains. Rural households produce a significant part of their own food, and much of what is purchased comes from local production. Most food marketing activities deal with undifferentiated raw commodities. Firms are usually household enterprises with low volume and profits. The market attracts little investment in modern facilities or business practices. While this represents an environmentally friendly pattern of low "food miles," the costs in terms of human health and nutrition, livelihoods that keep people out of poverty, and reliable food supply are quite high in many developing countries.

In developed countries and the faster-growing developing countries, market liberalization has stimulated substantial private investment in agricultural production and marketing, rapidly developing the agro-food industry and increasing farm productivity. Urbanization has accompanied the concentration of agricultural production in locations with abundant resources, frequently distant from consumers. Elaborate and efficient logistics systems have evolved in product processing and transportation. More and more food preparation is handled within the food marketing channel.

Food products are becoming increasingly differentiated and food markets more concentrated. Large-scale processors, wholesalers, and retailers have emerged in the distribution channel in many developing countries, with scale economies playing an important role in driving the changes. One of the linguistic ironies is that the shift of food markets away from commodity markets toward product markets is termed by many commentators as the "commoditization of food" because food is seen as merely a product, another way for large firms to make money, rather than being appreciated in the context of food culture and its impact on human health and nutrition.

The shift from commodity market to product market necessitates changes in public rule setting regarding grades and standards (weights and measures), food safety, and market information. In the traditional food market there exists a minimum of rules: quality control is done by the consumer, and producers build a reputation for quality and consistency. As consumers become more disconnected from the farm, there is greater stakeholder pressure for government controls on firms to ensure that food safety, animal welfare, and other consumer concerns are managed.

However, many consumers find these public standards inadequate, leading many firms to offer additional services, such as ensuring higher food safety or environmental friendliness. Generally, government imposition of food standards has resulted in increased concentration of food markets because large firms are able to spread the costs of complying with regulations over a larger product, giving them a cost advantage over small firms. Much of the high concentration of U.S. meat processing, for instance, occurred during the 1980s immediately after the government raised quality standards, causing smaller firms to leave the market.

Technology has had myriad, diverse impacts on food markets. Some technological innovations, such as cold storage freight trains, led to increasing firm size and market concentration of meatpacking firms. Other innovations, such as cold storage trucking, reduced the advantage of large firms, enabling a new generation of meat-packing firms to become prominent. Both developments served to lower the cost of transporting meat to distant markets, allowing higher food safety and food quality with decreased costs—a win for all.

While some technological breakthroughs have permitted increased environmental degradation, others are now promoting more environmental stewardship, such as satellite imagery that is able to pinpoint when crops need water or pesticides, reducing the need to apply either in as great quantities as they once were ("precision farming"). Farmers' technology adoption decisions are discussed in chapter 7 and the impact of biotechnology in chapters 7 and 10.

Globalization affects domestic markets in developing countries more through FDI than through agricultural trade (Reardon and Timmer 2007). While global trade in food and other agricultural products has increased both in volumes and values, their shares in consumption and output in domestic markets have remained low and literally unchanged (15 percent for cereals, meat, and produce) from 1980 to 2001 (Regmi and Gehlhar 2005). In contrast, FDI increased from $8 billion in 1980 to $36 billion in 1990 and $211 billion in 2001. FDI and agricultural trade are discussed in greater detail in chapter 10.

Supermarkets and Smallholders

Supermarkets have had a profound impact on food chains and marketing structure. One of the primary differences between supermarket food chains and traditional chains is innovation of centralized procurement systems. Purchasing in bulk through centralized procurement makes sense when it lowers the transaction costs of coordination by more than the increase in transportation costs (Reardon et al. 2003). Costs of coordination are further lowered when supermarkets can deal with a few, large wholesalers because of lower search costs, monitoring costs, and contract enforcement costs. This supports growing upstream concentration and potentially large efficiency gains.

Supermarket growth has been impressive in Africa since the 1990s and highly concentrated. The four largest supermarket chains in South Africa control 90 percent of all supermarket receipts (Weatherspoon and Reardon 2003). Each focuses primarily on upper- and upper-middle-income Africans in urban areas. The number of supermarkets in Africa varies widely between countries: in the mid-1990s, Kenya boasted 206 while Uganda had but one and Tanzania four (Fafchamps and Gavian 1997). The top supermarkets in Kenya are preemptively moving into the rest of eastern Africa hoping to beat the South African stores to the punch. Fafchamps and Gavian (1997) opined that most of western or central Africa will see little growth in supermarket chains for some time yet because of political instability, poverty, and low rates of urbanization. Nigeria with 102 supermarkets is an exception.

Fafchamps and Gavian (1997) note three possible scenarios for emerging economies as supermarkets develop. In countries like South Africa where there are already medium- to large-scale growers operating, supermarkets draw principally on them, assisting to form them into associations for export and domestic sale. Where small farmers can improve their services with outside assistance or by banding together in a collective agreement to meet the needs of supermarkets, chains have appeared ready and willing to accept them, as in Zambia. Where this is not possible, supermarkets rely on imports, such as importing Israeli orange juice to Kenya. Case 6-11 provides a detailed description of supermarket developments in Uganda.

The advantages of working with large-scale wholesalers and farmers resulting from scale economies in the marketing sector, can shut out poor smallholder farmers from gaining access to modern food channels.[4]

Several supply-side (farmer) factors may also prevent smallholders from escaping poverty through selling to supermarkets. Low levels of capital, technology, input quality, access to credit, and low capital flexibility prevent them from investing in improvements or changing products to meet supermarkets' demands. These demands include greater food safety, quality, and traceability. Additionally, high transportation and transaction costs as a result of poor infrastructure (e.g., roads and market information) restrict smallholders access. Contracts that provide farmers with technology, improved inputs, and shared risk would enable many farmers to dramatically increase production and potentially improve income and food security (Glover 1984; Key and Runsten 1999). Contracts with retailers can also provide farmers additional access to banking credit.

Contract farming, however, is not free from controversy. Several authors argue that contracts could be a way for large firms to take advantage of the land and poverty of small farmers, effectively paying them below the minimum wage and "taking control" of their farms (Glover 1987; Glover and Kusterer 1990; Grosh 1994; Little and Watts 1994; Porter and Phillips-Howard 1997). The costs associated with establishing and maintaining contracts still favor larger farms. The disadvantages associated with contracts pinpoint the necessity of public policies that would promote pro-poor contract formulation. Cases 6-3 to 6-7 provide evidence on the workings of contract farming.

The research on food retailers' monopsony power as buyers from wholesalers, manufacturers, and farmers in developing countries is more recent and partial. Instead of analyzing monopsony pricing effects, the literature has focused on the participation and performance of upstream agents in the market chain. The findings in this area are also mixed, though the overall picture is not positive for smallholders. First, there is a relatively unambiguous picture of traditional wholesalers and small food processing firms being rapidly excluded from the modern food system. Their function has been fulfilled by a relatively small number of medium to large firms. Second, in some countries small farmers are found to be excluded from the formal markets, while in others good participation is observed. Third, small farmers, even those successfully integrated, are increasingly challenged to meet the volume, cost, quality, and consistency requirements set by the dominant purchasers (supermarkets directly or through the mediation of processors), and there is a tendency for the buyers to source products from medium and larger growers.

Market Concentration

On both national and international scales, food market concentration has been rapidly increasing in the last decades. That is, an ever-increasing share of the world's food consumption has come from a smaller number of increasingly large companies. This has generally been a cause of some alarm as increasing concentration leads to greater risk that firms will acquire and exercise market power to the detriment of consumers, workers, and farmers. Limited research has been conducted on the topic of food retailers' monopoly power in developing countries, and the empirical evidence from developed countries shows mixed results (see Digal and Ahmadi-Esfahani 2002 for a survey).

Several European-based food manufacturers such as Nestle and Unilever are among the largest food corporations in the world. The concentration ratio of the four largest firms (CR4) in retailing is similarly high: around 50 percent in the United States and 60 percent in the EU. The world's largest food retailers include Wal-Mart (United States), Carrefour (France), Ahold (Netherlands) and Metro (Germany). The control of food markets by the top firms is even impressive on the global scale, where the CR15 is over 30 percent for total world food sales.

It can be difficult to know when concentration levels have risen too much. Consider the increasing concentration in the U.S. meatpacking sector. Most economists who study the issue are reasonably confident that a CR4 less than 40 or a Herfindahl-Hirschman Index (HHI) of less than 1,000 signals a healthy competition. While the CR4 in the U.S. broiler processing industry—one of the least concentrated U.S. food industries—was almost 60 in 2006, its HHI was only 884 (GAO 2009). Regional concentration ratios are likely much higher: since individual processing plants rarely purchase from more than twenty to fifty miles away, they may be able to exercise monopsony power even if there were no evidence of market concentration at the national level.

Studies on the concentration of the meatpacking industry in the United States have failed to demonstrate conclusively that meatpacking firms have exercised market power to lower farmer prices and increase consumer prices (e.g., Azzam 1999; Goodwin and Holt 1999; Muth and Wohlgenant 1999; Whitley 2003). However, this could be in part because retail sector concentration acts as a counterweight to meatpacking concentration (Schroeter, Azzam, and Zhang 2000).

Another issue deals with how markets are defined: Is the relevant competition for a beef packer other beef packers or all meatpacking firms? If beef and chicken are close enough substitutes, then the level of beef concentration is less important than the level of total meat concentration. Azzam (1998) also demonstrates that, while the increasing concentration levels may not be perfectly competitive in a static, neoclassical framework, they may be dynamically competitive if innovations rather than price differentials signal the degree of competition. That is, if firms need to constantly update their methods and products in order to compete with each other, a market may still be competitive even if there are high levels of concentration. Markets could also be competitive in the presence of high concentration rates if the top firms are regularly changing, implying a high degree of "creative destruction." Azzam concludes that any government intervention to artificially change concentration levels or to affect the structure of the market in order to maintain a neoclassical concept of price competition could make consumers worse off.

Grandin points out another difficulty associated with the standard assumptions of the benefits of classical competition in meatpacking (in MacLachlan 2001). Government regulation and consumer demand in the United States and Canada have led the large meatpackers to increase the quality of inputs and the humanity of slaughter and sanitation practices. By contrast, small firms usually accept the old and sick, nonuniform cattle, and are less likely to have state-of-the-art machinery and equipment for humane slaughter or the prevention of contamination, despite the fact that these small firms fit the classical model of atomistic sellers much better. This supports the conclusion that the industry may be better off in the control of a few large firms providing much higher quality output under better conditions when properly regulated.

Others have found a lack of positive association between concentration and price (Kaufman and Handy 1989; Newmark 1990). As the above discussion of U.S. meatpacking shows, the presence of competitive features almost unique to the food industry may alter the competitive balance of power. For example, the tendency for large distributors (e.g. Walmart) to offer low price, private-branded products in competition with the products of large manufacturers mitigates the market power that would otherwise accrue to manufacturers. In addition, the determined focus of food manufacturing competition on new product development and introduction reduces the likelihood of oligopolistic collusion. With the complex structure in the food industry, the assessment of market performance with regard to consumer price is difficult and multidimensional.

Information and Communication Technology (ICT)

Information and communication technology (ICT) has sparked a revolution in many developing countries' food markets. Cell phones and access to radio, TV, and the Internet have enabled farmers to gain accurate, current information about market conditions in diverse areas, expand to new markets, make contracts, improve government accountability and participation of the poor, reduce marketing and transaction costs, increase economies of scale, gain access to services and research, and even provide limited banking services.

Cell phone coverage has expanded rapidly in several countries in sub-Saharan Africa, such as Kenya and Tanzania, which are bypassing the infrastructural necessities of landlines altogether in favor of satellite connections. Even owning a cell phone can be part of a firm as cell phone time can be sold to others nearby. Forty-eight percent of the African cell phone market is supplied by local operators, and two of the six multinationals who supply the rest are based out of South Africa (African Economic Development, n.d.). Only a handful of landlocked African countries still have very poor cellular penetration.

For remote farmers, market information can be quite limited. Farmers may have to take their food to the nearest market or deal with a trader without knowing about prices in other areas at that time, decreasing their bargaining and planning power. Cell phones provide access to up-to-the-minute market information so farmers can know whether it is worthwhile to travel to distant markets or bargain with traders. Easterly (2006) provides the example of "one illiterate fisherwoman" who keeps her fish in the water on the line until a customer orders a fish via cell phone because she has no freezer to store the fish otherwise. Cell phones in this case are improving food safety and quality and providing her access to a wider market than would be possible otherwise.

Radio is another excellent source of market information, including in countries like Mali and the Democratic Republic of Congo. Radio has been used to improve awareness of gender issues, reduce marginalization, provide market information and adult education, and improve community awareness.

The Africa Partnership Forum in 2008 declared that improving ICT infrastructure and access investments were of pivotal importance. They highlighted regional coordination in investment, supporting community public access facilities, supporting freedom of expression, and allowing private competition in ICT.

Food Marketing Policies

Food Price Policies

As has been made clear in other chapters, governments have many, often conflicting, motives for intervening in food markets. Supporting producers' price is often in conflict with providing cheap food to urban populations, for example. The purposes pursued by governments and how they are pursued depend on the political power of the stakeholders that may benefit or lose from proposed interventions.

In many developing countries, urban elites are the most vocal group and have been favored by market policy through a combination of cheap food prices (to lower urban food consumption costs), overvalued exchange rates (to lower imported food prices), and commodity export taxation (to finance urban infrastructure development) (see case 9-8). Policies have often been biased against the rural poor, due to their geographic dispersion and limited or nonexistent lobbying power. During the food price riots in 2007–2009, the most vocal group were urban lower-middle class who were not poor themselves, but also not elite.

Antirural food policy biases are often rationalized using Lewis's (1954) theory by which economic development relies crucially on the growth of the modern urban sector rather than the traditional agricultural sector (chapter 2). The general expectation among these governments is that rapid economic growth and development can be achieved only by transforming the largely agrarian state into an industrial economy by extracting revenues from agriculture through market policies that serve as direct or implicit taxes. Unfortunately, these policies are most detrimental to long-term, sustainable agricultural growth, which other economic development theories have shown can be as important to long-term economic growth (chapter 7).

Perhaps the most harmful policy in terms of agricultural production and market development is directly setting food prices. "Government interventions in the pricing of food and in the determination of entitlements to food are so pervasive that it is impossible to analyze the nutritional status of a population without an understanding of the politics of food policies and their economic consequences" (de Janvry and Subramanian 1993, 3).

Case 6-8 discusses the primary means of regulating agricultural prices used in developing countries in the 1960s and 70s: state agricultural marketing boards that kept prices low for consumers by obtaining an import monopoly and setting low prices (Eastern Europe and Africa), dual pricing policies that paid farmers a high price while selling at a low price to consumers (Asia), and public storage policies that supported marketing board price policies. Low food prices may also occur as a side effect of import substitution policies, as practiced throughout Latin America and parts of Africa.

During colonial times, marketing boards were established with the key objectives of generating revenues, facilitating the export of agricultural commodities to colonizing countries, and stabilizing prices faced by settlers. In some countries, marketing boards were relatively small and operated within the market structure in competition with private traders (e.g., Benin and Ghana), while in many other African countries private trade was banned, granting the parastatal monopsony power (e.g., Ethiopia and Madagascar). The Asian experience outside of China was very different because they allowed the private sector to operate, did not impose production quotas on farmers, and invested heavily in infrastructure and input subsidies as part of the green revolution. Case 7-2 discusses the marketing board in Malawi.

The long-term effects of price-setting policies are fairly straightforward. Artificially lowering prices transfers welfare from producers to consumers and stunts agricultural development by reducing adoption of new technologies and decreasing the use of credit, irrigation, and other necessary inputs. Farm incomes tend to stagnate or decline, rural poverty increases, and opportunities for economic growth and poverty reduction outside agriculture are forgone because the multiplier effects are absent. Furthermore, when agricultural prices are artificially low, governments have less incentive to make the necessary investments in rural areas. If black markets develop to provide people with additional sources of food, this undermines government legitimacy; the long lines for food have much the same effect, leaving the government as well as farmers and the poor worse off than originally.

Policies that attempt to artificially raise food prices or provide production subsidies benefit producers at the cost of consumers and/or taxpayers (chapter 10). These policies have resulted in food aid programs devoted to removing excess supply from the domestic market and selling or dumping it in other markets to the detriment of foreign farmers (Barrett and Maxwell 2005).

When world market food prices are low and decreasing, as grain prices were from the mid-1970s to the end of the century, it is easier for governments to maintain prices at a fixed low level. However, when world prices rise sharply, as they did in 2007–2008, fixed price regimes rapidly become unsustainable. Their instability has been criticized since the 1980s (Bates 1981; Pinstrup-Andersen 1988). One-third of the USSR's expenditures went to purchasing food from farmers at high prices and selling them to consumers at low prices, a policy that could not be sustained and contributed to the regime's eventual downfall (case 7-7). Because the instability occurs just at the time that food prices are rising and the protection for poor households may be most needed, this forces governments to make very difficult choices over spending priorities and civil unrest.

The short-run effects of pricing policies on production depend on the relative price elasticities of supply and demand. The short-run food supply is price inelastic. That is, even large changes in price produce only small changes in output because the amount of land cannot be practically changed after the planting has taken place. This was the logic behind the policies advocated by the Economic Commission for Latin America in the 1950s and 60s: governments could set artificially low prices for food through exchange rate manipulation and still maintain high levels of production. In the medium to long term, producers have the opportunity to sow a larger or smaller field, purchase additional inputs, seek other livelihoods, and make other adjustments, making supply more elastic. When prices are artificially low, production levels decline over time, sowing the seeds for price increases later.

The distribution of gains and losses from price or subsidy policies depends on the mix of policies used (Pinstrup-Andersen 1988). Agricultural support polices in Ivory Coast and Kenya were beneficial to smallholders, ensuring a ready supply of requisite inputs and timely procurement of output, construction of rural infrastructure, and organization of agricultural research (Gbetibouo and Delgado 1984). Timmer (1996) finds that the Indonesian marketing board was successful in making the country self-sufficient in rice and reducing price volatility.

The Egyptian food subsidies have been quite complex. Before 1973, Egyptian food subsidies transferred wealth from farmers to urban consumers. As input subsidies and meat policies changed after 1973, the overall transfer benefited rural households more than urban and transferred wealth from large-scale farmers to smallholders and the landless, but wealthy consumers have benefited more than poor consumers (de Janvry and Subramanian 1993; Pinstrup-Andersen 1988). Egypt's policies reduced income inequality because they included agricultural development strategies that offset low product prices. However, the sharp rises in food prices during 2007–2008 tested the sustainability of Egypt's wheat subsidy and rationing program. The cost of the subsidy increased dramatically despite a tight household rationing program that caused hours-long lines for bread. It is estimated (Saleh 2008a, 2008b) that 20 percent of the subsidized flour was stolen through corruption, while countless additional loaves are wasted or fed to animals.

Since the 1970s and 1980s, evidence had mounted that many interventions had done more harm than good to the economy, either by distorting incentives or by creating skewed market power. Black markets had grown ever larger, increasing crime, decreasing government legitimacy, and decreasing governments' ability to fund urban development from a shrinking rural base. Parastatal marketing channels were not only inefficient but also costly to national budgets that had to bear the transportation and transaction costs. In many cases they were also a byword for corruption and rent-seeking activities. Many marketing boards experienced severe financial difficulties during 1980s and early 1990s, and some eventually went bankrupt. The failure of government interventions in food markets was considered one of the key reasons for the stagnating agricultural sector, unsustainable fiscal deficits, and serious balance of payment problems. Massive pressure from the urban sector, combined with that from international donors, triggered reform efforts in many of these developing countries (Kherallah et al. 2002).

De Janvry and Subramanian (1993) conclude that, on average, "cheap-food policies and programs have often benefited groups not at nutritional risk, while bypassing or injuring the neediest" (12). They further assert that "extractivist cheap-food policies should be restricted, because they have ultimately contractionary effects on economic growth, while policies that seek lower food prices through technological change and irrigation in agriculture are expansionary" (21).

Unfortunately, low price policies are politically "addictive" and difficult to reduce or remove once in place. Numerous attempts to increase the prices farmers received in Sri Lanka's untargeted food support system were prevented by urban food riots. It required a new government to enact changes, introducing them as part of a larger reform package targeting larger food subsidies to the poorer half of the population (Sahn and Edirisinghe 1993).

Direct price interventions are blunt policy instruments at best, in part because of the difficulty of targeting benefits to the poor (chapter 5). The government's ability to prevent black-market transactions, endure changes in terms of trade and exchange rates, and legitimize income transfers from producers to consumers will determine the limits for how extensive and long-lasting price policies can be (de Janvry and Subramanian 1993). They are capable of doing more harm than good, particularly in the medium and long run. Governments should be extremely wary before enacting price controls.

Market Reforms

The accumulated weight of these forces pushed many countries to accept much-needed market reforms in the form of structural adjustment and stabilization programs sponsored by the IMF and the World Bank. These included reducing inflation and government spending on subsidies and the parastatal marketing boards, removing price restrictions, and opening food markets to private investors. These reforms were generally designed to correct the previous biases against agriculture to enhance marketing efficiency and increase domestic prices to import- or export-parity price levels. It was hoped that doing so would increase food prices and improve the incentives for greater investment in agricultural production. The supply response would reduce rural poverty and establish long-term economic growth through increased reliance on markets.

The results from these reforms have varied among countries and time periods but have generally resulted in improved macroeconomic stability and increased food prices—planned and desired consequences of the reforms—but the predicted agricultural takeoff failed to materialize in some areas, leading to increased hunger and poverty (chapter 2; Kherallah et al. 2002). As discussed in chapter 9, one of the reasons for these disappointing results was that reforms were often partial, discontinued before completion, and sometimes reversed. Lack of political will to full market liberalization due in part to poor stakeholder participation, to resistance from existing patron-client relationships, to mistrust of markets by policymakers—particularly in formerly socialist states—and reduced government revenue for public purposes and private gain were some of the factors that stymied reform programs. The fact that reforms were needed because of instability during hardship times correlated market reforms with hardship in many people's minds. These factors are discussed more fully in chapter 2.

Even though reforms were partial, they increased competition and reduced marketing margins in a number of countries. In the more successful cases, market liberalizations significantly increased private trader entry in food and export crop markets and improved macroeconomic stability by reducing deficit spending and inflation. The increase in competition in the private sector lowered marketing margins and improved market efficiency so that farmers received a greater share of the retail or export price.

In other countries, the private sector was unable to fill the vacuum left by government withdrawal because of prohibitive risks, poor infrastructure, high entry barriers, lack of access to information, lack of transparency, and absence of contract and property rights laws, all of which foster high marketing and transaction costs. The agricultural sector's response was constrained by lack of research, extension, and transportation, storage, and communications infrastructure. The lack of prior investment in public goods is seen prominently in this list. The lack of supporting institutions also played a pivotal role: inadequate laws and regulations for contract enforcement, quality control, standardized weights and measures, and property rights. Markets require a host of other innovations and institutions to function properly.

The structural reforms attempted to "get prices right," either by reforming price policies (liberalizing input and output prices, eliminating subsidies, reducing tariffs, allowing prices to vary more between seasons and regions, and reducing exchange rate overvaluation) or restricting marketing boards, allowing private entry to food markets, and liberalizing quotas and licensure. Reforms that dealt with poor infrastructure and lack of market institutions were largely absent during this episode but are beginning to be addressed more today (see the following subsection).

Even though many reforms were partial and did not begin in earnest until the early to mid-1990s, considerable liberalization has taken place. In sub-Saharan Africa, fifteen countries classified by the World Bank as undertaking reforms had lifted the primary restrictions on market participation between 1980 and 1994 (Jones 1995). Price restrictions and parastatal marketing are still present in a number of countries (e.g., Indonesia, Kenya, Malawi, Zambia, and Zimbabwe), though they now operate in at least a semicompetitive environment with private, commercial traders and processors. They now focus more on providing public goods, such as market information, or reducing price variation (Akiyama et al. 2001, 2003) than directly controlling prices.

Although private traders have responded to increased market opportunities, dismantling marketing parastatals does not guarantee widespread entry of private agents or the emergence of efficient market structures, institutions, and operations (Badiane et al. 1997). One part of the problem relates to governance problems (chapter 9). When there is insufficient participation and policy changes are not explained to stakeholders, as was often the case with the market reforms of the 1990s, citizens can come to believe that policies were imposed only from outside and resent the impositions from international financial institutions. When governments' responses are not planned and announced ahead of time and there are few checks on governments to prevent backsliding—a lack of transparency, commitment mechanisms, and rule of law—traders cannot rely on governments not to undo or appropriate their investments, so they have less incentive to enter the market despite favorable reforms.

Market entry has as a result tended to be limited to certain marketing niches not suffering from capital, information, or relationship barriers, with much more limited private trader activities in areas with poor infrastructure (Kherallah et al. 2002; Barrett 1997). In addition, limited access to credit, continued uncertainty about the state's commitment to reform, lack of public goods, institutional deficiencies, and policy reversals have significantly constrained the willingness of the private sector to invest in marketing channels. State-owned enterprises are still the dominant actors in input markets in many countries and it is often unclear to the private sector how and when the government will act, such as at what price or time of year governments will begin selling or rotating grain reserves and how much. Small traders have emerged, but their participation in markets has been largely informal.

The impacts of reforms on market efficiency, agricultural production, and social welfare in developing countries are also mixed, with much more favorable outcomes in Asia than in Africa. Market reforms have generally improved price integration and reduced transaction costs (Badiane et al. 1997). Food prices increased, often dramatically, resulting in immediate gains to food producers and increased hunger and poverty for net food buyers (Singh, Squire, and Strauss 1986; Pinstrup-Andersen 1988; Peters 1996; Chilowa 1998). Over time, food production has increased, reducing prices and rural poverty. The largest impacts have been in export-oriented cash crop sectors that were previously the most heavily regulated. There is considerable debate whether smallholders selling export crops or agribusiness firms have gained more from market reforms (Reardon and Barrett 2000).

On the other hand, since one of the primary goals of marketing boards was to provide price stability, there is little wonder that price liberalizations have increased price volatility. Higher price variability offsets some of the potential gains from increased production, which may explain why supply responses have not been as large as predicted in African countries (Jayne and Jones 1997; Seppala 1997). Marketing boards had also subsidized many of the marketing and transaction costs involved in reaching farmers who were distant from markets, so market reforms actually reduced the market access for more remote smallholders who may not produce enough to make it worthwhile for private traders to reach them. Credit, which had also been provided by marketing boards, has also not been extended as widely as before to remote areas, reducing input usage and crop output in the areas that were already the poorest.

Infrastructure and Other Public Goods

The chapter has emphasized numerous factors that affect market transaction costs. High transaction costs reduce resource use and allocative efficiency, promote segmented markets with greater vulnerability and marginalization of the poor, and prevent economic growth. Through these effects, the poor are more likely to suffer from hunger and malnutrition—particularly during droughts or other adverse shocks—and less likely to escape from poverty. Infrastructure and public good provision are essential to reduce transaction costs in pro-poor ways.

Developing countries need to invest in market infrastructure and institutions such as transportation, warehousing facilities, public provision of market information and advice, market regulations (including standardized weights and measures), and credit institutions to reduce marketing and transaction costs, distribute market power more evenly between farmers and intermediaries, facilitate farmer associations, and increase agricultural production. In addition, barriers to the entry of new enterprises need to be lowered, while alternative marketing channels, public-private partnerships, and greater coordination between smallholders should be promoted. ICT investments, particularly in mobile telephony, can have significant roles to play in bringing market information to far-flung communities, strengthening farmer bargaining power, and providing additional employment without requiring significant, upfront capital expenditures. This reduces information asymmetries and market failures. (See Pinstrup-Andersen and Shimokawa 2007, for a review of the literature.) The role of research and extension are discussed in chapters 7 and 10.

Cases 6-9, 9-1, and 9-2 discuss the immediate impacts of improved physical infrastructure for poverty reduction. Feeder roads and agricultural research have the largest benefits in terms of reduced poverty in many areas, and in some areas expanding the electric grid also has high dividends as it improves storage and processing.

Public investment in infrastructure should not "crowd out" private investments, which have been increasingly significant in the past two decades. In many developing countries, publicly provided infrastructure services often deliver poor quality and inadequate coverage. Private companies have been contracted in an increasing number of areas to provide public goods with government regulation or oversight or market feedback. Private roads, private water provision, and private ICT investments have brought large dividends, such as reducing government expenditures and speeding the process of development in a number of areas. It is unlikely that private investment will reach everywhere or be universally equitable, but it can serve as a potential check to improve government service provision, improve efficiency, and strengthen private sectors that must grow if development is to be ongoing. The ICT revolution in Africa has been almost entirely privately driven.

Markets adapt to high transaction costs by increasing reliance on personalized trading networks, which reduces the scope of marketing activities. Limited rule of law and uncertain and unenforced property rights create substantial risks that inhibit private investment to develop more reliable markets. All these have redirected the focus of food market reform agenda from "getting prices right" to "getting institutions right."

Narayanan and Gulati (2002) review the literature on supermarkets and smallholders. They find that supermarkets are most likely to be a positive influence for smallholders with vertical coordination, low transaction costs, high human capital, and low physical capital constraints. Government policies that support these conditions can enable smallholders to take the greatest advantage of globalization and modernizing food chains.

Conclusion

This chapter has emphasized the importance of improving market institutions and infrastructure and a set of other public goods to get markets working for the poor and increasing agricultural productivity. The development of financial markets, labor markets, and health care markets also matters for food market development. Access to credit is an essential part of agricultural production (chapter 7) and an essential coping strategy (chapter 5). Microcredit and microfinance can stimulate small business opportunities, but by themselves cannot solve the multifaceted constraints faced by smallholder agriculturalists. Low-volume traders also lack credit facilities. Public finance corporations have tended to be plagued by governance and moral hazard problems, but government action is still needed in order for credit markets to develop in pro-poor ways.

Improving the rule of law to ensure that financial intermediaries, microfinance firms, and other credit market agents can anticipate government reactions is an important part of developing this crucial sector. Public investment in roads has been shown to attract private banks and lead to other improvements in marketing systems.

Effective public and private market institutions need to (1) channel information about market conditions, goods, and participants; (2) define and enforce property rights and contracts; (3) be incentive compatible so that rewards and penalties lead to desired behavioral changes; (4) be either internally or externally enforceable; (5) reduce marketing and transactions costs; and (6) encourage participation of the poor in market and policy activities (World Bank 2002). Chapter 9 discusses institutional development in greater detail. Some institutional arrangements that can be utilized include regulatory measures that set low barriers to entry (e.g., by streamlining registration procedures, limiting licensing requirements, and lowering unnecessarily high capital requirements) and a fair, transparent tax code. Governments should also improve the institutional framework for foreign investments in the food market so that it encourages inward FDI while limiting risks to food safety and the livelihoods and food security of the poor.

There is growing evidence that private institutions such as cooperatives, producers' associations, contract farming, and vertical integration have considerable potential to strengthen market linkages for small farmers and reduce transaction costs. The exact mix of institutions cannot be simply imposed from the top down, nor will the same institutions develop in different countries. If market participants are informed, they can be relied on to find the lowest-cost means of transacting business available.

Government investment and institutional development can expand the vista of opportunities that private individuals can seize. If government barriers to market entry are too high, or if contract enforcement is too weak and the poor do not feel they will be able to rely on the legal system to fairly handle grievances, markets will remain highly inefficient, trapping people in poverty. Support for greater legal and market education can make markets more effective at reducing poverty as well. In some cases, a large-scale farmer or agribusiness firm can serve as a link between small farmers and the marketplace. There is a lot of room for experimentation in how governments can support market activities for the benefit of a larger segment of society than currently benefit.

Well-functioning private institutions must be accompanied by appropriate public institutions (chapter 9). Grades and standards need to be clear and enforced to facilitate communication and negotiation between buyers and sellers. The development of the rule of law and contract and property law reduces transaction costs and strengthens people's trust in the system. Policies that limit market power and reduce barriers to entry promote competition. These public institutions are broad in the sense that they affect all kinds of private institutions and can be adapted to many contexts. That adaptability comes at the cost of there not being one single set of institutions that will work in all contexts, countries, or cultures.

Experimentation by political entrepreneurs is needed. The importance of public institutions does not necessarily imply a need for heavy involvement of government in markets or marketing activities. Rather, the rule of law is about government actions and reactions being predictable and applying the laws impartially to all people. Effective marketing sectors are essential for agricultural production, discussed in chapter 7.

Domestic Market Policies Case Studies

The cases in this section illustrate the role of food markets and food marketing in the economy and discuss the links between farmers and markets.* These cases discuss

---

* The case studies referenced here are presented in full in the three-volume work by Per Pinstrup-Andersen and Fuzhi Cheng, eds., *Case Studies in Food Policy for Developing Countries* (Ithaca, NY: Cornell University Press, 2009) and online via open access at http://cip.cornell.edu/gfs.

policies needed to help integrate small farmers into the market economy, with an emphasis on the facilitation of contract farming, collective bargaining, farmer associations, food price stabilization, and the successful development of high-value agriculture on small farms. The increasing concentration in food retail and wholesale and the role of government are discussed, along with the importance of infrastructure to promote market-based poverty reduction.

Case 6-1 deals with addressing market power in Danish food markets. Cases 6-2, 6-10, and 6-11 concentrate on various forms of food retailing: in India (6-2), where large-scale retailing is being introduced; in the United States (6-10), where small-scale retailing is being reintroduced through farmers' markets; and in Uganda (6-11, exclusively online), where supermarkets are rapidly spreading. Contract farming is discussed in depth in cases 6-3 and 6-6, and to a lesser extent in cases 6-4, 6-5, and 6-7, which focus on smallholder access to retail markets. Case 6-8 addresses food price stability in the context of landlocked African countries with poor infrastructure. Case 6-9 focuses on the role of rural infrastructure in agricultural development and poverty alleviation.

Notes

1. For example, if the firm could earn $50,000 by renting a piece of equipment to another firm, they have to make at least $50,000 in accounting profit on that piece of equipment or else it would make more sense for them to rent it out to someone else. Economic profits include these opportunity costs as well as accounting costs. Thus accounting profits can exist, and be quite large, even in a competitive equilibrium where economic profits are close to zero.

2. The term "thin market" is also used to describe a situation where only a small share of the world production is traded.

3. Vertical integration describes a market relationship where one firm directly controls multiple production stages, as, for instance, a meat processor firm that also owns or directs the production from livestock farms.

4. The literature has directed more attention to small farmers rather than small wholesalers or processors because smallholders represent a high percentage of the population in developing countries whose well-being has critical implications for food security, economic development, and equity.

Chapter 7

Food Production and Supply Policies

Introduction

Approximately three-fourths of the poor people in developing countries—883 million people—live in rural areas, more than half of whom are directly employed in agriculture while the rest are dependent on the agricultural economy (ILO 2005; World Bank 2007a). Although the percent of the population involved in agriculture decreases as national incomes increase, many of the poor remain in rural areas, even in transition and urbanized countries. These facts imply that agriculture is, without exception, the predominant industry and source of income for the poor and that increasing agricultural productivity is a major component of a balanced, just development (Pinstrup-Andersen and Schiøler 2000; von Braun and Pandya-Lorch 2007).

Agricultural development effectively encourages broad-based economic growth, reduces poverty, and increases food security (von Braun and Pandya-Lorch 2007). Increases in GDP based on agricultural growth increase the incomes of the poorest members of society two to three times as much as growth in nonagricultural sectors (World Bank 2007a). There is a general consensus that neglecting agriculture constrains the development process. "Economic development needs industrialization but, in many economies, industrialization also requires the development of the agricultural sector" (ILO 2005, 27). New investments in human capital, rural infrastructure, research and technology, irrigation, and input markets are necessary to sustainably ensure food security for a growing world population, expected to reach 9 billion by 2050.

Government policies play an important role in encouraging needed investments. Government policies influence producer behavior directly and change the environment in which producers operate. Examples of direct effects include food and input price policies and policies that affect incomes directly. Governments adjust producers' decision environment through laws on land tenure and gender roles; public goods investments in roads, education, health, credit provision, electricity, and irrigation; and macroeconomic rules that govern trade, labor markets, money supply, and research.

Farmers face a large number of risks, both natural and market related, and often the first issue at stake for producers is to ensure a base level of production/income/ nutrition for the household. This may lead farmers to choose production methods that provide lower average yields but that promise lower variability. Unfortunately, such a risk-reducing strategy can keep them trapped in poverty (see chapter 5). Elimination of risk may not be desirable either, however, as lack of downside risk can encourage socially suboptimal, risk-seeking behavior. Multiple interventions are needed to reduce downside risk and provide safety nets without removing the incentives for people to help themselves or compelling them to engage in overly risky behaviors (Hazell 2003).

Subsidies of all kinds, whether for food commodities, farm inputs, or credit, are often problematic. There are three sustainability tests that subsidies (or any government policy) need to pass: economic, political, and environmental sustainability. Untargeted subsidies are nearly always unsustainable economically because the high costs they engender cannot be borne over long periods of time. Furthermore, subsidies tend to erode production incentives. Targeted subsidies to households sufficiently poor that they could not participate in markets in the first place will tend to avoid or mitigate both these problems (chapter 3). Macro policies such as artificially low exchange rates, import or export tariffs, inflation, and tax credits are additional forms of untargeted subsidization or taxation that affect the balance between industries and change production incentives (chapter 9).

The difficulty with appropriately targeting subsidies is generally a question of political sustainability. If only disorganized groups benefit from a policy, it is more likely that the policy will be discontinued when a new government comes to power. This is why many subsidies are given more broadly than is economically sustainable: if the less-poor, middle class, and/or elite do not benefit in some way, they may not support the subsidy. Overcoming both of these constraints is a difficult challenge in policymaking.

The final issue is that subsidies often lead to environmentally unsustainable practices. Large subsidies on fertilizers and pesticides have encouraged farmers in Asia to use too much, which then leech into and contaminate water sources. Farmers in developed and developing countries regularly do not have to pay for the irrigation water they use, leading to unsustainable water management practices. Subsidized insurance and credit schemes encourage herders to expand their holdings beyond what the land can carry since their losses will be restored by the government should something go wrong.

Other policies can increase agricultural production without distorting incentives unsustainably. Two of the most important of these are rural infrastructure and agricultural research (cases 9-1 and 9-2). Many of the smallholders in rural areas are cut off from significant markets, increasing input costs and preventing them from reaching larger markets. Building roads can be a powerful tool in increasing agricultural productivity and reducing rural poverty. Improving rural health and education can also provide significant dividends in increasing agricultural productivity.

Agricultural research and development has been and remains one of the most effective tools for increasing agricultural productivity sustainably. Research needs to be targeted to the areas, circumstances, and people that need it most. A participatory research environment that brings researchers and other stakeholders together can increase its effectiveness and adoption rates. Credit constraints can seriously hamper the adoption of new technologies, as can ineffective extension services or a lack of trust between farmers and governments. There is a growing need for more publicly funded agricultural research. Private and public research systems serve different needs, products, and farmers. While they are strong complements (FAO 2004d), they are poor substitutes.

The Economic Importance of Agricultural Production

Despite the stigmatization of rural areas as being "backward," agriculture is a dynamic, integral component of most economies when not being hampered by adverse policies, providing employment and income directly and indirectly to more than half the world population. The International Labour Organization (ILO) declared that agriculture "is about employment opportunities and chances for poor people to work themselves out of poverty," (ILO 2005, 128). This is especially pronounced for women, who perform much of the agricultural labor in the developing world today: 60–80 percent in Africa, 35–60 percent in Asia (FAO 2003c). Agricultural growth has been shown to be more effective at reducing poverty than other types of growth. This section elaborates on each of these arguments.

The areas of the world with the lowest agricultural labor productivity also have the largest number of poor people (ILO 2005). As seen in table 7.1, agriculture provides employment for a larger share of the population in poorer countries than in more advanced. In a number of countries, such as Ethiopia and Uganda, agriculture employs more than 80 percent of the total population, while agricultural productivity is low. Even where incomes are higher and populations more urban, a disproportionate share of the poor live in rural areas. It will be decades before there are more poor people living in cities than in rural areas (Hazell et al. 2007). Figure 7.1 demonstrates that increasing cereal productivity was associated with lower poverty in south Asia, while stagnation in poverty has accompanied stagnation in cereal yields in sub-Saharan Africa (SSA).

Agricultural growth promotes greater gender equality and women's empowerment (ILO 2005). Planting, collecting water, weeding, gathering and applying fertilizers, harvesting, processing, transporting, and marketing food tend to be assigned to women, while men are deemed responsible for plowing or raising large livestock (FAO 2003c). Production methods that reduce the time spent on these activities are liberating and relax women's time constraints. Similarly, empowering women and improving their access to secure land holdings and credit should increase growth (Bayes 2007). Gender also partly determines what crops are grown. Herforth (2010a)

TABLE 7.1.
Agriculture's Share of GDP and Employment

	Type of country		
	Agricultural	Transition	Urbanized
GDP per capita	< $400	$400–$1,800	$1,800–$8,100
% GDP from agriculture	29	13	6
% labor force employed in agriculture	65	57	18
Total rural population (millions)	417	2,220	255
Share of rural poor in total poor ($1.08 a day)	70%	82%	45%
Principle regions	Sub-Saharan Africa	South Asia, east Asia, ME/NA	Europe, central Asia, Latin America

Source: World Bank 2007a.

describes how men in rural Kenya and Tanzania had strong preferences for growing dairy, maize, coffee, and tea because they had large single payoffs. Women preferred crops with multiple, smaller harvests that provided smaller amounts of money on a daily basis to meet daily needs.

Assuming that agricultural growth causes poverty reduction rather than the reverse, a 10 percent increase in agricultural output led to a 1.3–2 percentage point decline in African poverty and a 1–6 percentage point decline in Asia from 1970–1990 (ILO 2005). By contrast, manufacturing growth did not affect poverty in either area. Additional increases in agricultural productivity should cause a 7.2 percent decrease

FIGURE 7.1.
Cereal yields and poverty rates in south Asia and SSA. Source: World Bank 2007a.

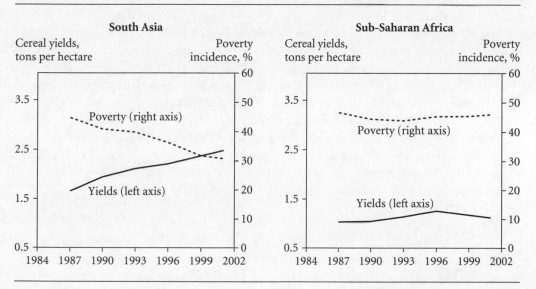

in poverty in Africa and 4 percent in India over the short term, and a 12 percent decrease over the long term (IFPRI 2004).[1]

The amount of poverty reduced in a particular case will depend on the extent to which social, political, and economic structures are pro-poor. As one example, the fact that land is distributed much more evenly in western SSA than in Latin America implies that improving the productivity of land would have a greater poverty-reducing power in SSA than in Latin America (World Bank 2007a).

Agricultural growth lowers poverty through several channels. Increasing yields and lowering unit costs benefit farmers directly. This decreases food prices, making consumers better off. Higher yields additionally give farmers an incentive to hire more labor, increasing rural wages and employment. As farmers spend their increased incomes, they boost the nonfarm rural sector, increasing nonfarm wages and employment. Agriculture also strengthens the rest of the national economy as an employer, demand sector, and source of revenue. Increasing rural incomes strengthens the market for domestic products, supporting industrial and services growth, especially in nontradable sectors (ILO 2005). Particularly during economic downturns, agriculture provides employment to millions of displaced persons because the need for food is constant and universal. Agricultural exports provide 90 percent of the foreign exchange earnings many countries have (Oygard et al. 2003).

The extent to which additional agricultural income results in higher incomes elsewhere is called a *multiplier*. Table 7.2 lists estimates of this multiplier in Asian and African countries. There is a significant difference between the multiplier in high-productivity rural areas, where $1 of agricultural income produces an additional $0.93 of rural income (for a multiplier of 1.93), and low-productivity areas, where the increase is only $0.46 (Hazell and Haggblade 1990). Infrastructure and research play significant roles in determining this magnitude. Economies where more goods are traded are likely to experience smaller multipliers due to agricultural productivity increases than those with larger nontradable sectors. Delgado, Hopkins, and Kelly (1998) determine that 47 percent of additional income would be spent on nontradables in Niger and 33 percent in Senegal, indicating significant opportunities for nonagricultural sectors to grow with agriculture.

Agricultural productivity is closely tied to increased productivity in the economy as a whole. In agricultural economies, productivity growth has been higher in agriculture than in industry sectors (World Bank 2007a; case 9-2). Significant poverty reduction has never occurred in history without higher productivity on small farms (Lipton 2005). More recently, China, South Korea, Taiwan, and Thailand invested in agriculture by improving institutions and technology adoption prior to the strong economic growth and poverty reduction they experienced in the 1980s–90s (Bayes 2007). Hazell et al. (2007) conclude that agriculture has been central in the development process as both the sector leading development and through effects on other sectors.

Food and Nutrition Security

As important as these economic factors are, they neglect perhaps the most important and unique facet of agriculture, one that compels an interest in the sector even

TABLE 7.2.
Estimates of the Agricultural Multiplier

Country or Region	Study	Time	Multiplier
Asia	Delgado, Hopkins, and Kelly 1998	1970s	1.80
India	Rangarajan 1982	1961–1972	1.70
	Hazell and Haggblade 1990		2.35
	Hazell, Ramasamy, and Rajagopalan 1991		1.98
Malawi	Simler 1994		1.66
Malaysia	Bell and Hazell 1980		1.80
	Bell, Hazell, and Slade 1982		1.83
Burkina Faso	Delgado, Hopkins, and Kelly 1998	1984/85	2.88*
Madagascar	Dorosh and Haggblade 1993		2.0–2.7
Niger	Delgado, Hopkins, and Kelly 1998	1989/90	1.96*
Senegal	Delgado, Hopkins, and Kelly 1998	1989/90	2.24–2.48*
Zambia	Delgado, Hopkins, and Kelly 1998	1985/86	2.48*
Worldwide	CGIAR 2005		1.5–2.0

* Estimates are an upper limit. Actual multipliers may be up to 30 percent lower.

if another sector in a particular economy is more effective at reducing poverty and producing broad-based growth. No other sector can fulfill the primary role of agriculture, that of providing food and nutrition security.

Food production is not an end in itself, but is a means to improving the health, nutrition, and welfare of individuals and the world (chapter 3). Similarly, unhealthy, malnourished workers can neither grow enough food to feed themselves and others nor invest in human or physical capital to increase their limited productivity, creating a cycle of malnourishment. The ILO (2005, 157) concludes that "ensuring that the world's poor receive adequate nutrition is absolutely essential."

The UN Food and Agriculture Organization (FAO) estimates that 1 billion people do not have enough food to meet their caloric needs. While some of these people have been so malnourished for such a long time that the effects are visible in stunted growth and/or underweight, many more people lack important micronutrients (hidden hunger), putting them at risk for serious diseases and a higher chance of dying from preventable diseases. The U.S. Government Accountability Office (GAO 2009) determined that almost 15 percent of all U.S. households—and 20 percent of households with children—experienced hunger at some point during 2008.

Increasing agricultural productivity reduces hunger and malnutrition. The average food production of a Malawi smallholder would only provide enough food for ten months if they consumed all of it (case 7-2). However, in order to pay off loans or purchase needed inputs, farmers sell off about half of their production at a time when other farmers are doing the same. This means that farmers sell most of their food when prices will be lowest and they are left with food for only half the year. The cash they save may also be rapidly depleted by inflation. Nonfarm income becomes then the difference between life and death, providing 40–45 percent of average rural household income in SSA and Latin America (ILO, 2005). Doubling rice yields reduces the hungry period by a third and dramatically increases food security (World Bank 2007a).

Food Production Situation

Most developing world agriculture is either staple crops grown largely for household consumption or nonstaple crops produced for export. A few key crops provide food for most of the world's population: rice, maize, and wheat. Half of the people in the world rely on rice as their staple food, which is grown in more than one hundred countries (CGIAR Science Council 2005). Almost 40 percent of the cereals produced in Africa are maize varieties for human and animal consumption. Wheat is grown almost as plentifully as rice and maize, with over 600 million tons produced of each annually since 2004, an increase of over 150 percent since 1960.

The next most produced crops (200–300 million tons) include potatoes, cassava, and soybeans. In recognition of the potato's importance and to increase awareness of the need for research to increase its stagnant yields, the UN declared 2008 the Year of the Potato. Despite being fifth in terms of production volume, cassava is the third-largest source of calories in the world. Because cassava is generally produced for household consumption, increasing productivity could lead to significant reductions in hunger in western and central Africa (Thomson 2001; World Bank 2007a). Other crops of which at least 100 million tons were produced globally in 2006 include oil palm fruit, barley, tomatoes, sweet potatoes, and watermelons (FAOSTAT 2008). Additionally, bananas provide more than one-fourth of the calories consumed in west/central Africa (Thomson 2001), while millet and sorghum are primary staples in the Sahel (World Bank 2007a).[2]

Crop yields vary greatly depending on region, with Africa bringing up the rear in every category. Grain yields tend to be half as large in east Asia as in developed countries, and half as large in south Asia as in east Asia (Pinstrup-Andersen and Schiøler 2000). Rice yields in Africa are only 30 percent of the yields in other countries with improved rice varieties and techniques. In 1961 the difference between Africa's agricultural productivity and the rest of the developing world was small, but while Africa's production has increased by 80 percent, production in Asia and Latin America has increased by 150 and 200 percent (figure 7.2).

Much of the improvement in African cereal yields took place from 1997–2007, though the smoothness of the curve in figure 7.2 implies that these are predictions rather than data points. The overall African agricultural productivity index (API) has grown 62 percent since 1990, but once its high population growth rate is included, it has experienced below-average growth in agricultural productivity over the 1990s: 10 percent growth in SSA compared to 20 percent in Asia and 30 in Latin America.

Regional aggregates mask significant variation (figure 7.3). Northern and western Africa experienced significant gains in per capita API during the 1990s, equivalent to Latin America. Eastern, southern, and central Africa experienced prolonged

FIGURE 7.2.
Cereal yield (kg/ha) by region: 1961–2007. Source: FAOSTAT, downloaded March 2008.

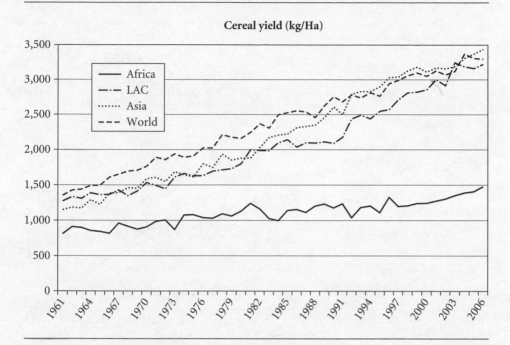

Cereal yield (kg/Ha)

declines, particularly in war-torn areas. Thus the regional average resembles none of its subregions. Only four countries have maintained per capita food production growth above 2 percent since 1980: Nigeria, Mozambique, Sudan, and South Africa (World Bank 2007a).

The per capita API has grown by over 30 percent in Latin America and the Caribbean together while plummeting by 30 percent in the Caribbean. Even as east Asia experienced 35 percent growth from 1990–1998, central Asian agricultural productivity shrank by 35 percent. Thankfully, central Asia is recovering, so that it now has 90 percent of the productivity it had in 1990. At the same time, western Asia declined slowly to 90 without any signs of takeoff or recovery. Even though central and western Asia have the same ending index levels, their histories and trajectories tell completely different stories, and both are buried in a regional average of 20 percent growth. Productivity growth has also been negative in Eastern Europe since the fall of the Soviet Union and has recovered only 10 percent of its 40 percent decline.

Meat production has steadily increased across the world, particularly in Asia where production has increased 600 percent since 1961 (figure 7.4). This increase is strongly demand led, and has been called part of a livestock revolution (Delgado et al. 1999; chapter 4). The increase in production has come from increasing the number of animals rather than improving yields. Even as the number of animals has increased, milk yields have shown significant periods of stagnating with sharp adjustments up or down. Farmers in Latin America and the Caribbean receive five to seven times more milk per animal than African farmers and twice as much as Asian.

FIGURE 7.3.
FAO API per capita by African subregion: 1990–2006. Source: FAOSTAT, downloaded March 2008.

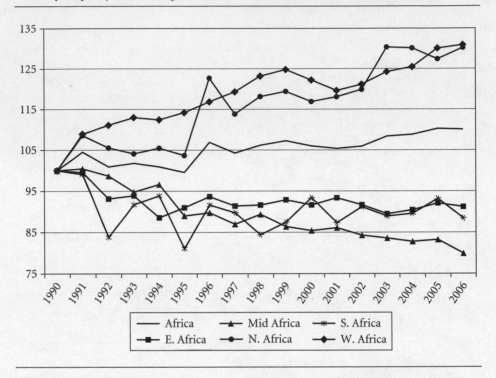

FIGURE 7.4.
Meat production (tons) by region: 1961–2007 (1961 = 100). Source: FAOSTAT, downloaded March 2008.

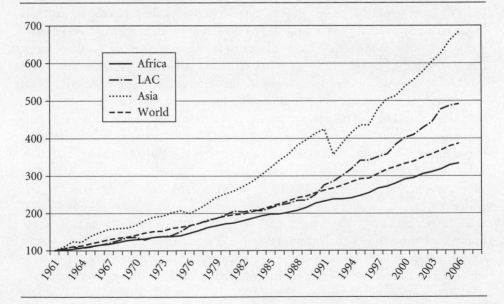

Food Prices

Following the world food crisis in 1973–1974, a sharp downward trend reduced real food prices by 75 percent from their 1974 peak by 2000 only to see a dramatic price increase between 2005 and 2008 (figures 7.5 and 7.6). During this three-year period, nominal international wheat and soybean prices doubled and rice prices tripled. By the middle of 2008, real food prices had once again entered a new long-term downward trend although at a higher level than where the previous trend ended and with large price volatility as illustrated by a 60 percent increase in international wheat prices due to a combination of adverse weather and speculation. The reasons for these price developments are discussed in chapter 1.

Even though real prices have in general decreased, there have always been ups and down (figures 7.5 and 7.6). By mid-1996, for example, wheat and maize prices had increased by 50 percent over mid-1995 levels, leading commentators to predict that the era of low food prices had ended (Rosegrant et al. 2001). Producers responded to the higher prices by increasing production, bringing prices back down. This demonstrates the importance of focusing on long-run trends in populations, incomes, and technological progress as well as price volatility in appropriately formulating development policies.

During the 1970s, average developing world grain yields increased 3 percent per year. This slipped to 1.6 percent between 1982 and 1997, and it is expected to decrease further to between 0.9 and 1.5 percent per year from 1997 to 2020 (Pinstrup-Andersen and Schiøler 2000; Rosegrant et al. 2001; Lipton 2005). The cause of this slowdown differs between regions. Delinking some farm support from production reduced the incentives to increase production in OECD countries (Rosegrant et al.

FIGURE 7.5.
Real food price index: 1900–2008 (1900 = 100). Source: IMF 2006.

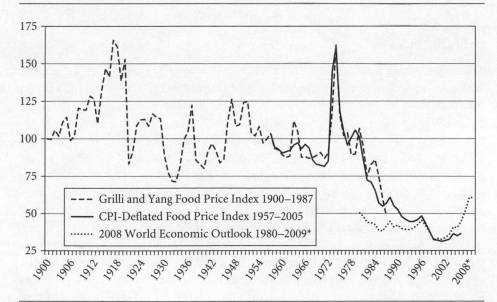

FIGURE 7.6.
Cereals price index: 1990–2009 (2002–2004 = 100). Source: FAO (2009a).

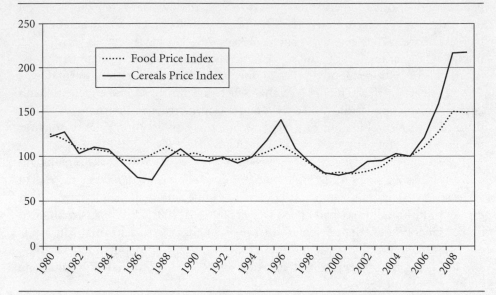

2001). The collapse of the Soviet Union reduced yields in much of Eastern Europe and central Asia. Perhaps most importantly, world investment in agricultural research and development has slowed considerably.

Together, these facts present a picture of guarded optimism. Overall production levels are increasing, but many areas are being left behind, leading to increased food insecurity, poverty, and environmental deterioration. Increasing agricultural research will be essential in maintaining food production growth above population growth.

Food Distribution

Although enough food is being produced to feed everyone, there are several important reasons why the proposal to solve world hunger by redistributing food is not feasible.[3] First, it is too expensive for the poor to be able to purchase traded food, particularly in landlocked countries with poor infrastructure. Maize imports in Africa cost up to five times more than locally grown maize (case 7-3), and even food aid costs 2.5 times as much as that grown by smallholders (Hazell et al. 2007). That means it would have to be given to the poor. Second, the majority of the people that do not have access to enough food depend on agricultural and food production for a large share of their incomes. Bringing free food into the countries where they reside would remove their livelihood and increase poverty and dependency. Third, the declining percentage of GNP given by developed countries as development assistance is indicative of the fact that the political will does not exist to gift that much food to the poor of the world. Fourth, the international infrastructure does not exist to transfer that much food from food-surplus to food-deficit areas, even if donor governments wanted to. Fifth, even if the will and the way existed to give the poor that much food, the "surplus" food does not actually exist: it is being eaten by the nonpoor and by the animals people eat.

Hazell et al. (2007) identify three groups of countries that would be particularly harmed in such an arrangement: large countries whose food needs are larger than trade volume, landlocked countries with high transportation costs, and countries with limited foreign exchange earnings to spend on either food or development. The additional food to feed the millions who are currently hungry and who are mostly rural will have to be grown there, and that means increasing food production and agricultural productivity in areas with hunger.

Currently, 5.5 percent of global food production is traded across borders. Africa will have to increase grain imports by 40 percent by 2020, while grain imports will have to more than double in east Asia without increases in domestic production (from 31 to 71 million tons) (Pinstrup-Andersen and Schiøler 2000). Meat imports could increase 700 percent. At current trends, this would mean that 7.5 percent of food produced will have to travel across borders (Pinstrup-Andersen and Schiøler 2000). These imports will further increase the average "food miles"—the distance food travels from its point of origin to its eventual consumption—and cause further emission of CO_2 (chapter 8).

Increasing Food Production and Productivity

Without improving agricultural productivity, the primary means of increasing food production is increasing the amount of land under cultivation. As populations swell, often the only recourse for smallholders is to open new, marginal lands for farming. Since 1970, the amount of land used in agriculture in Niger has increased over 600 percent, leading to increased desertification, topsoil erosion, and other environmental problems (case 7-6). It is projected that the area being used for cereal production will increase in Africa by 27 percent and 15 percent in Latin America by 2020, but there is very little additional land available in Asia (Rosegrant et al. 2001). The FAO and the European Bank for Reconstruction and Development (2008) estimate that 13 million ha of land in Kazakhstan, Russia, and Ukraine that were abandoned during the last two decades could be brought back into production with limited environmental impact.

Even if these lands were brought under cultivation, adding land is not environmentally sustainable as a long-term solution. The best agricultural land has already been appropriated for use. As more land is needed, the new land has lower productivity and potential for improvement. Farming practices that do not account for environmental constraints cause soil nutrient depletion and desertification, further decreasing the land base. Furthermore, as populations increase, the amount of land available per person decreases. It is simply impossible to perpetually increase the amount of land being used per person while the population continues to grow.

The miracle of the past four decades is that today's farmers are feeding almost twice as many people with better quality food from virtually the same land base (Pardey and Beintema 2001). By increasing yields on the land that is best suited to agriculture, farmers have been able to leave vast areas untouched, preserving forests and biodiversity (CGIAR Science Council, 2005). Land use for agriculture would have needed to increase by 80 percent—an area about the size of India—from 1961 to 1993 in order to produce the same amount of food without increases in agriculture productivity (Goklany 1998). Because of the advances in research, input use, and other increases in productivity, only 8 percent more land was used during those three decades.

On the farm itself, increasing productivity is usually accomplished through better production methods and better use of inputs such as fertilizer, irrigation, and higher quality seeds. This section of the chapter will focus on these factors. Investments to facilitate yield increases, such as infrastructure, human capital, and research and development, will be considered later on in the chapter. Market access was considered in chapter 6.

Fertilizers

Fertilizers are any substance used to make land more fertile. Judiciously used fertilizers can significantly and sustainably increase agricultural output and labor productivity without harming the environment. Small amounts of chemical fertilizers increased average maize yields in Malawian farms by 50 percent and in Kenyan by 70 percent (case 7-2; Duflo, Kremer, and Robinson 2009). When complementary practices and seeds are available, the increase can be even larger.

There are several examples of natural fertilizers. Livestock-cropping systems rely on livestock manure to fertilize fields, which then provide additional feed for the livestock. Certain leguminous plants may also be grown as "green manure." Green manures not only provide increased soil nitrogen but also give pollinating insects additional food, assist in weed control, and when plowed back into the soil, increase the soil's organic content and ability to handle water effectively. The system of letting part of a field remain fallow for a period of time was in essence making use of green manures. Unfortunately, livestock and green manures require additional time resources, and are often considered "women's work," adding to the time constraints faced by poor women. Nitrogen-fixing trees (NFTs) and legumes have the distinct advantage of growing in difficult climates, improving soil quality both by increasing nitrogen content and by bringing nutrients from the subsoil up into the soil area. NFTs can be grown from shoots cut off from the parent tree, making them inexpensive to spread, and additionally provide shade and mulch.

Fertilizers have shaped the agricultural trends of the last forty years. Fertilizer use increased 700 percent and tractor use 500–600 percent in China from 1970–2000, contributing to an increase in agricultural output of more than 400 percent (ILO 2005). Fertilizers in Asia are credited with 20 percent of the increase in agricultural output, where its use has increased from 6 kg/ha in the early 1960s to 143 kg/ha in 2000. This is more than is used in the OECD countries (World Bank 2007a). Fertilizer use is much lower in Africa (around 10 kg/ha) and has increased very little. Von Braun and Olofinbiyi (case 7-4) indicate that only 14 percent of the farmland used for cereal production in Ethiopia had the benefit of fertilizers in 2000.

African farmers are aware that fertilizers increase yields. The chief difficulties, though, are that chemical fertilizers are expensive for cash-constrained farmers, organic material is very limited, and green fertilizers would occupy land and time needed for food production. One bad year can wipe out the fertilizer investment, leaving the family unable to pay back credit or purchase fertilizer in the next year. When yields decrease in the next year due to the lack of fertilizer, farmers' ability to afford them erodes further. Duflo, Kremer, and Robinson (2009) consider a behavioral model of time inconsistency: people know they want fertilizer in the future, but may or may not realize that, when the time comes to purchase and apply fertilizer, they will prefer to avoid the additional effort involved in acquiring the fertilizer, leading to suboptimal fertilizer application rates. They show that subsidizing fertilizer *delivery* induces time-inconsistent farmers to use optimal amounts, while failure would lead them to forgo fertilizer use altogether. Delivery subsidies are much cheaper to maintain than general fertilizer subsidies while providing significant improvements in production.

Integrated soil fertility management (ISFM) can be an important alternative to increasing chemical fertilizer use where fertilizers are expensive or risky. ISFM uses both organic and inorganic methods to improve soil quality, such as dual cropping complementary crops (e.g., maize–pigeon pea or maize-groundnut) that can fertilize each other and improved fallowing. Sauer and Tchale (2009) review eight estimates, and produce another one, all of which demonstrate that ISFM provides greater productivity, profits, and sustainability than chemical fertilizers alone for African smallholder farmers.

Pesticides

In addition to low soil fertility, low agricultural yields are often caused by pests, plant diseases, and weeds. Examples in SSA include cotton weevils, banana bacterial wilt, east coast fever in cattle, and maize "witchweed," each capable of decimating its respective crop. While native crop and animal varieties have developed some immunity to their respective problems, improved varieties resistant to the pests are likely to be the best solution (see chapter 8).

In the past, heavy use of pesticides and herbicides was deemed the best method to try to eradicate these problems. This can be quite expensive, as well as creating health risks for farmers, consumers, and water. Pesticides are indiscriminate, killing the pests' predators as well as the pests, so that if pests return there is less to stop them (Huang, Pray, and Rozelle 2002). Because it is nearly impossible to eradicate a pest or weed, it is likely that a new race of superpests and superweeds breed from the survivors that are more resistant to the chemicals, requiring ever-greater pesticide/herbicide usage. Regulations have proven ineffective in this regard (chapter 8; Nelson 2010).

Integrated pest management (IPM) attempts to reduce, if not eliminate, this problem. By taking steps to prevent pests before they are born, monitoring where and when infestations occur, and only using chemicals when infestations go above a certain tolerance point, much expense and time can be saved while preserving yields. This reduces infestations to acceptable levels in a cost-effective manner. In Bangladesh 80 percent of the farmers using IPM no longer use pesticides (Pretty

2001). This has allowed farmers to raise fish in rice fields, providing a second crop and source of protein.

The push-pull system developed by the International Center for Insect Physiology and Ecology provides a natural means of reducing losses to insects and weeds. By intercropping maize with nitrogen-fixing legumes and particular grasses, insects are repelled from the maize by the legumes (the push) and drawn to the grasses that will trap and kill them (the pull). The legumes also cause "suicidal germination" in witchweed—causing weeds to germinate before the maize crop exists to support it, so that weeds die before the crop is in danger. The legumes also improve soil fertility and the grasses may be harvested for livestock fodder, so that farmers gain three crops instead of one and have a greatly reduced need for pesticides and fertilizer. These methods have been shown to increase maize productivity by 60–70 percent in western Kenya (Pretty 2001).

Organic Production

Health and environmental risks associated with the use of chemical pesticides (chapter 8) and concerns about future availability of such chemicals and farmers' dependence on them have led many people to advocate organic agricultural practices, which specify that no inorganic chemicals are used during production. It also excludes the use of GMOs and animal growth hormones. Ninety-five percent of the $25 billion organic food products sales occur in the United States and European Union, and the demand has grown at double-digit rates for the last decade (Laux 2006). Though much of the demand for organically produced food is based on the assumption that it is healthier or safer, this has not been demonstrated (FAO 2003c). Organic methods are also intended to be more environmentally friendly, though the increased land needed to grow green manure and the methane emissions of livestock offset at least some of these gains.

The primary incentive for farmers to switch to organic production methods has been the price premium, ranging from 34 percent for organic beef to 182 percent for poultry and 102 percent for grains (Laux 2006). Whether organic methods would be more affordable, profitable, and pro-poor for developing nations than more input-intensive methods is an empirical question. Though yields are higher in the "modern" system than in the organic system, yields are higher in an organic system than in traditional systems. The cost of fertilizers in both systems—either purchased chemical fertilizers or the time and land needed to grow green manures—affect the calculation.

One of the difficulties preventing smallholders from entering the market is being certified by an accredited agency. Providing such certification opportunities and encouraging the development of private certifiers is one way that developing country governments could support smallholders moving into upscale food products.

New Farming Techniques

Making farming both more efficient and sustainable is necessary for achieving food security now and in future generations. New production methods that have been shown to significantly increase yields, reduce costs, and make agriculture more environmentally sustainable include precision farming and zero tillage, as well as the IPM and push-pull systems already discussed.

In precision farming, farmers apply water, pesticides, or other inputs only as needed to increase efficiency and reduce the harm to natural resources. While large commercial farmers may use satellites and GPS units to track how particular areas of their farm are doing, low-income smallholders may achieve similar results through more labor-intensive methods. Geographic information systems improve the targeting of research and policy planning.

In standard farming techniques, the soil is cleared and plowed up to prepare it to receive new seeds and reduce weeds in the next crop. This can increase soil erosion, decreasing the soil's long-term fertility, and release large amounts of carbon into the atmosphere. By planting seeds for the next crop just before or after the last is harvested using zero-tillage methods, seeds are able to germinate up to fifteen days sooner, leading to larger and earlier harvests, increased carbon capture, reduced soil erosion, and increased nitrogen fixation as the previous crop's roots and organic material are returned to the soil. The practice has been integrated on 20 million hectares in Brazil and Argentina (Pretty 2001). It has also been a proven success in Argentina and the Indo-Gangetic Plains (Spielman and Pandya-Lorch 2009). Several complementary practices—such as cover cropping, green manure, and appropriate crop rotation—need to be adopted at once in order to make this method as effective as possible, making extension work increasingly important. Overall, the expectation is that yields will not increase significantly at first, and in fact may decrease slightly in the first year, but that costs in terms of time and machine use will decrease. As several years go by, the improved soil quality will begin to manifest itself in higher yields and yet lower input costs, so zero-tillage practice has much to offer smallholders.

Increasing Yields through Research and the Green Revolution

After World War II, the focus of most agricultural research was to increase productivity. This sparked what came to be known as the *green revolution* in which advances in plant breeding led to a dramatic increase in yields particularly when improved seeds were combined with irrigation and fertilizer use. Though the research started in Mexico in the 1940s, the techniques were most famously applied to south and east Asia since the 60s and are credited with lifting millions of people from poverty and alleviating the suffering of many of those who remain impoverished.

The benefits of high-yielding varieties (HYVs) for farmers and consumers have been significant. India increased the area cultivated with HYVs from 17 percent in 1970 to 40 percent in 1980 and 55 percent in 1994, increasing the average real incomes of smallholders and the landless by 90 and 125 percent, respectively (ILO 2005; case 9-2). East and south Asian governments promoted HYVs, increasing their spread from 10 percent of farmland planted in 1970 to 80 percent in 2000 (Pinstrup-Andersen and Schiøler 2000; World Bank 2007a). HYVs are credited with approximately half of the increase in agricultural output in China, the other half coming from improved institutions (World Bank 2007a). If complementary inputs are present, HYVs can significantly reduce producer risk and increase incomes of poor farmers. Foster and Rosenzweig (1995) demonstrate, however, that returns to HYVs were quite low, and sometime negative, at the beginning of the green revolution in India because of the lack of complementary inputs and practices.

Agricultural research is highly cost-effective. The benefits of CGIAR research worldwide outweigh the costs at a rate of at least nine to one, and possibly as high as seventeen to one (Raitzer 2003). That is, for every dollar invested in agricultural research by the CGIAR, $9–17 in additional agricultural output were generated. When this is added to the agricultural multiplier effect, the impact of agricultural research can double. Without the research contributions by CGIAR alone, world food production would be 4–5 percent lower than it is now and cost 18–20 percent more, with the resulting impacts on increased poverty and hunger in poor areas that have received the greatest benefits (Evenson and Rosegrant 2003). Pinstrup-Andersen and Schiøler (2000) report that the returns to increasing yields in the worst areas of Africa could be as high as 40 percent per year.

One of the primary criticisms of the green revolution has been that it spread first to large farmers with the best situations in terms of irrigation, market access, and other assets. Increases in production on large farms drove down prices and reduced the income of farmers who had not been able to increase their production to compensate. Huang, Pray, and Rozelle (2002) point out, however, that smallholders in Asia benefited from the green revolution before they had access to the seeds because lower food prices reduced poverty for net buyers of food and the increased productivity strengthened the demand for labor on large farms, increasing rural employment and wages. Ensuring access to future technologies and their rapid spread will still be vital in increasing production sustainably to reduce poverty and feed the hungry of the world, particularly in Africa, where only 10 percent of farms have adopted improved seed varieties (AATF 2007).

New research is needed to increase output per unit of input to meet the rising demands of population growth and to give poor farmers the opportunity to get out of poverty as well as relieving environmental pressures on marginal lands (Huang, Pray, and Rozelle 2002). As food prices began to decrease after the 1974 food crisis and the green revolution successfully doubled and in some cases tripled rice and wheat yields (case 9-1), researchers became complacent and funding moved to other areas (Pinstrup-Andersen and Schiøler 2000). Even though benefits from the previous research are still being reaped, the growth rate of agricultural productivity worldwide is decreasing as many areas of the world have reached the limits of what irrigation, fertilizer, and the already developed HYVs can accomplish. In recent years, scientists have expressed the concern that the present use of chemicals in farming may not be sustainable. The great diversity of land conditions within countries in Africa has made spreading the benefits of the green revolution to Africa difficult.

There have been several recent successes in bringing a new green revolution to Africa, however. New Rice for Africa (NERICA) combines the drought and weed resistances of local African varieties with the high-yielding varieties from Asia. This has not only increased yields by 25–250 percent in parts of Africa, but has been laborsaving for women and reduced the need for rice imports as exemplified by an analysis for Guinea where rice imports were reduced by $13 million (CGIAR Secretariat 2005). In Uganda, cassava varieties resistant to a local virus have increased yields by 10 tons/ha, providing farmers with an additional $140 million in income after a research investment of $5 million (CGIAR Science Council 2005). Introducing aquaculture and vegetable growing has also produced significant gains in nutrition, health, and income for many poor farmers in Africa and Asia. Hybrid bananas increased yields by 3.5 kg/tree because the bananas are larger and more resistant to pests (Nkuba, Edmeades, and Smale 2006). This increase allows farmers to consume more of their crop and have more available to sell, improving both nutrition and incomes.

Technology Adoption

A number of constraints can hinder technology adoption. HYVs that require large amounts of fertilizer and good water management to be effective will be of limited usefulness to farmers in rain-fed areas or who lack access to fertilizer. Access to credit services determines whether or not farmers can bear the start-up costs of buying fertilizers and improved seed. Adoption depends not just on a technology's availability to farmers but also on the scalability of production to other regions (Bayes 2007) and the economic and environmental sustainability of the technology (AATF 2007).

Hallman, Lewis, and Begum (2003) found that there were significant problems in bringing new opportunities to the poorest. Nongovernmental organizations and credit services, including microcredit, assisted the $1/day poor, but did not reach the $0.50/day ultra poor. Government extension workers are sometimes distrusted, perceived as being corrupt, uninterested in the situation of the poor, and rarely available. Often the primary constraints on aquaculture adoption were institutional failures. When governments have offered to trade new, improved seeds for the old seeds poor farmers had available, it greatly increased dissemination and, by targeting seeds to the poorest farmers who would not be able to purchase new seeds without assistance, had minimal negative impacts on markets in existence (Pinstrup-Andersen and Schiøler 2000).

Farmers have developed intricate, informal networks to disseminate technology, though they take time. In Uganda, new varieties of banana plants were introduced into an area through informal networks from other parts of Uganda, Tanzania, Rwanda, Burundi, and Kilimanjaro (Smale et al. 2006). After improved banana varieties were introduced to Tanzania in 1997, 29 percent of households surveyed in 2002 had used at least one improved variety with significant variation depending on pest problems: all farmers in areas with rampant pest problems had tried an improved variety, while only 6 percent had in areas with lesser problems (Nkuba, Edmeades, and Smale 2006).

Farmers have also proven inventive in disseminating plant material through new community and incentive structures. In one system, farmers were required to pass on one hundred free plantings to their neighbors, who were required to spread the technology as well, before being allowed to sell further plantings after the first one hundred (Smale et al. 2006). It seems important to recognize the universal truth that things provided for free are seldom valued, but when some cost or effort is required in order to obtain them, farmers are more likely to take proper care of them.

Adoption rates can be improved by using a more participatory innovation systems approach to designing new technologies. Local farmers who are involved in the design of improved varieties or methods, and particularly in the field trials, can both be more ready to adopt new technologies as they become available and influence the research agenda so that it better meets their needs, making each project more effective. The International Potato Center in Peru, for instance, involved farmers in on-farm field schools to inform them about ways to control potato blight and potato weevil, increasing their incomes on average by nearly $400/ha/year (CGIAR Science Council 2005). At the same time, researchers gained detailed information about the effects of various methods in the different soil types and circumstances faced by different farmers, enabling them to focus their research in the most productive channels.

Since most agriculture in the poorest households is undertaken by women, efforts to reach women in particular are crucial in technology dissemination. However, men and richer households are more likely to adopt technologies if they are not specifically targeted to women, lessening technology's impact or even causing a negative impact on women (Hallman, Lewis, and Begum 2003).

Smallholder Agriculture

Approximately one-third of the 6.5 billion people in the world live on small farms with less than two hectares of land. Their average income is only $46 per month and they own $35 worth of durable goods (Bellemare and Barrett 2006; James 2006). They produce most of what they eat, but very little for sale, hence smallholders employ mostly family labor with low technology and capital inputs. Half of the world's undernourished people and most of the people living on less than a dollar a day are smallholder farmers and their families (Lipton 2005; Hazell et al. 2007). Two-thirds of the people in sub-Saharan Africa live in rural areas, and the majority of them are involved in subsistence agriculture (ILO 2005). Furthermore, both the number of smallholder farms and the area under cultivation are increasing as the average size of farms decreases (Hazell et al. 2007).

Smallholder agriculture is not a special case but is the norm for most countries and most rural people. Despite this, too little attention is paid in devising policies and interventions to the particular circumstances facing smallholder farmers as stakeholders. Smallholders are often on marginalized land disconnected from markets.

What constitutes "small" varies from region to region (Hazell et al. 2007). Nearly all rural Malawians are smallholders, most of whom have less than one-fourth of a hectare though the mean landholding is just less than 1 ha (case studies 7-1 and 7-2). Millions of Indians have no access to land, while one-third of the rural population operates a farm with less than 1 ha (James 2006). The average Russian working

FIGURE 7.7.
Farm size (ha) in select countries. Source: FAO data from agricultural censuses.

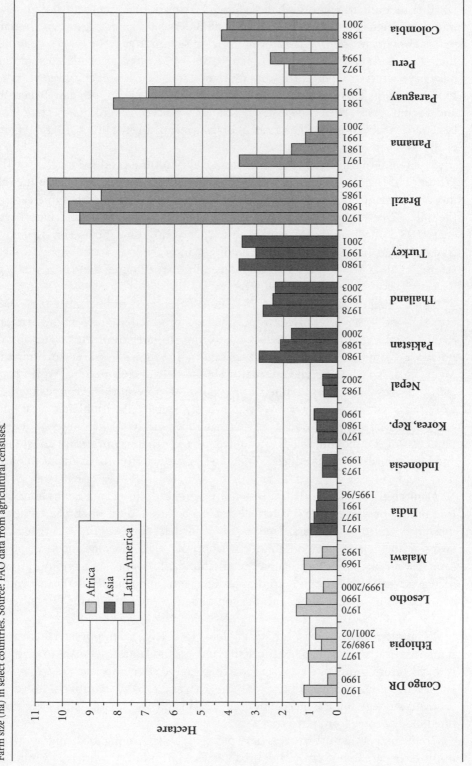

on a "household garden" has between 0.15 and 0.36 ha to work with depending on whether they are urban or rural, though small farms of six hectares are not uncommon (tho Seeth et al. 1998). Ethiopian smallholders have an average of one hectare that they cultivate, but the laws forbid them to sell, mortgage, or otherwise utilize their latent nature as collateral or capital (case 7-4). In Kenya, smallholders nominally have access to 1.4 ha of land, but much of it will lie fallow in any given year due to lack of rainfall, so they subsist on less than $0.24 per person per day (Bellemare and Barrett 2006). Even though those farmers would consider a ten-hectare farm large, such a farm would still be small in Brazil while fitting the other criteria (Hazell et al. 2007).

Smallholder farms are important for total agricultural production. Despite the existence of large, mechanized farms, Russia's household garden plots produce almost 40 percent of its agricultural output: 42 percent of the meat, 44 percent of the milk, 82 percent of the potatoes, and 90 percent of fruits and vegetables (Seeth et al. 1998). Smallholders are more likely to spend additional income on local non-tradables than farmers with larger holdings, increasing agricultural multipliers (Hazell et al. 2007). The landless also depend on smallholder farms for wages at harvesttimes.

Most smallholders are net buyers of food—that is, they buy more food than they sell—so lower food prices from increased productivity help many of them (Sahley et al. 2005; Hazell et al. 2007). Less than 10 percent of the population of Bolivia, Ethiopia, and Bangladesh are net sellers of food, while one person in five in Madagascar is a net seller, and one in three in Vietnam and Cambodia (World Bank 2007a). Prices that are kept artificially low, however, prevent them from using their work to rise out of poverty and are significantly correlated with higher rural poverty among net sellers of food (Fan, Zhang, and Zhang 2004). The key is to reduce unit costs of production, which can contribute to both lower prices for consumers and higher incomes for producers. That is why productivity-increasing technology is so important.

Yaujirao (2005) argues that subsistence-oriented producers are not as bound by tradition as previously—and paternalistically—believed, but respond to economic incentives and opportunities. Lipton (2005) further discusses the fact that small farms, with their reliance on abundant labor, make more economic sense when capital accumulation is low than in capital-abundant nations. As economic growth increases wages, larger farms become more efficient, supporting both the movement of workers out of agriculture and the consolidation of family farms (Hazell et al. 2007).

What other options exist for smallholders to emerge from poverty? Increasing nonfarm rural wages would help both the landless and landowners. Another option is to shift from producing staple crops to high-value cash crops such as fruits, vegetables, livestock, or aquaculture (cases 6-3, 6-4, and 6-5). There are risks involved in such a strategy, but it is an economically sustainable way forward that has already lifted many people from poverty.

To the extent that urban areas have plentiful, better-paying jobs, migration can improve welfare in both rural and urban areas. Lipton (2005) warns, however, that "it is wishful thinking" to believe that mass urbanization will reduce poverty without growth in agricultural production. Very few countries have successfully industrialized without preexisting agricultural growth, and many have failed for the lack of it. The World Bank (2007a) further estimates that 81 percent of the rural poverty reduction worldwide came from improved conditions in rural areas, and only 19 percent from migration.

In order to understand how government policies affect producer behavior, it is necessary to understand producer goals. Chapter 6 introduced the concept of firms that maximize expected profits. Many developing country farmers face a large number of risks, both natural, such as drought and pest attacks, and market- and government-related risks, such as international price volatility. Often the first issue at stake for producers is to ensure a base level of production/income/consumption for the household (Jordaan 2005; Low 2008). A useful concept from behavioral and game theory economics is that the poor may choose production and livelihood strategies that ensure the family the best possible income in the worst possible world (maximin), even if those strategies produce lower average expected profits. This problem has even been dubbed "the farmer's dilemma" (Jordaan 2005). Particularly during times of crisis, rational short-term survival strategies of farmers and pastoralists may severely restrict future growth. At very low income levels, farmers will be highly risk averse and policies will need to address risk before development can take off.

Livestock Smallholders

Smallholders suffer from low efficiency in meat production and processing. Despite this, traditional livestock production systems—also referred to as "backyard" production, which enable year-round employment of family labor and utilize other slack household resources while fostering crop-livestock interactions within smallholder farming systems that rely on domestic breeds—remain a key and vital technological option widely relied on in nearly every developing country (Farrelly 1996). Cases 7-5 and 7-6 discuss the situation of the pastoralists and agro-pastoralists in Africa's Sahel region in depth, particularly in regard to land tenure. Pastoralists provide about 70 percent of all meat and milk produced in sub-Saharan Africa.

Livestock do more than generate income in many pastoralist societies. They also act as a source of savings or investment, define social status, and fill important cultural roles in religion, marriage, and festivals. Policy analysts should try to understand what effect the cultural significance of livestock may have as they make recommendations.

In between the traditional production systems and large-scale commercial production of the developed nations is a medium-scale or semicommercial system, specializing in one commodity, though without the intensive technological innovations found in full commercial enterprises. These ranchers often purchase additional feed and limited outside labor.

In most countries, meat is a luxury consumption good among the poor, with an income elasticity greater than 1. This means that the demand for meat and meat products increases faster than incomes. Over the period from 1970 to 1995, meat consumption increased almost three times as fast in developing nations as in developed countries (Delgado et al. 1999). Making sure that smallholder livestock growers are able to take advantage of this opportunity is an important part of formulating effective developmental food policy.

Most increases in domestic meat supply in developing nations over the last three decades have come from increased herd size and pasture utilization rather than from improved technologies or shifts between production systems (Delgado et al. 1999). As demand continues to increase in the face of fixed land constraints, techniques, technologies, and genetic resources will have to improve in order for productivity to increase sustainably.

The proper role of government in these situations is a matter of debate, and there is hardly a consensus on the issue. Delgado et al. (1999) opine that it would be "foolish" for governments to adopt a laissez-faire attitude, while Jarvis (1986), Jahnke (1982), and others point to many failed government policies or ill thought-out programs that have made matters more difficult for poor livestock smallholders. Whatever role governments decide to take, livestock smallholders form an important stakeholder group that should be included in policy analysis and formulation.

Mechanization Policy and Economies of Scale

In light of these facts about smallholders, should countries actively pursue a policy that encourages the mechanization or "modernization" of agriculture, speeding the removal of smallholders to other sectors of the economy? There are many factors that would speak against rashly applying the same production methods in every country that are used in much of the West, though in other areas it might prove most beneficial.

In countries where capital is expensive and labor cheap, economies of scale[4] in farming are usually low and often absent. That is, larger farms may not have an advantage over smaller ones in terms of cost-effectiveness. The cost of producing one ton of potatoes in Mexico is the same for large and small farms because of the high levels of agrochemicals used on the large farms and the risk of inbred diseases in the seeds on small farms (Pinstrup-Andersen and Schiøler 2000). Laborsaving mechanization here would not reduce unit costs and could result in many poor smallholders losing their livelihoods. Panin (1995) finds that tractor use in Botswana decreased smallholder income.

Agricultural growth led by labor-enhancing productivity is more effective than labor-replacing growth (ILO 2005). As Muralidharan (1994, 26) puts it, "It is good to have an industry which provides food to millions. But it is better to have an industry which does the same thing and at the same time provides employment to millions of people." Lipton (2005) also argues that, though the question for an individual farmer on whether or not to mechanize production is one purely of production cost efficiency, for a government to choose to support mechanization, or other laborsaving technology, it must be shown that it is a cost-effective means of cutting poverty.

On the other hand, Nweke (2004) claims that mechanization would efficiently increase cassava production by alleviating labor bottlenecks that have doubled farm wages and slowed production. Increasing production would reduce the price of cassava, which could serve to reduce food insecurity in much of Africa where it is a staple crop, but replacing this labor with mechanization would reduce food security for the newly surplus labor (Nweke 2004). Large economies of scale may exist in some production enterprises, such as chicken, particularly if small farmers have difficulties in meeting food safety and uniformity standards required by the market (chapter 6). Jackman (1994) argues that, even in areas where infrastructure is scarce, it is more cost-effective to use refrigerated trucks to transport chickens from centralized factory farms over long distances than to try to grow an equivalent number on small farms in unfavorable conditions.

Many countries' food systems are dualistic, with both modern and traditional sectors. The modern sector is highly sensitive to macroeconomic policies, but the traditional sector is also dynamic, particularly for mass employment and consumption. Properly designed policies could energize the traditional sector to reach key development goals. Ultimately, the decision on whether to actively support the commercialization and modernization of the traditional small-scale sector or move toward mergers and large-scale farming and the speed by which such transitions are desirable, will depend on the relative cost of capital and labor, the population pressures, the market structure and demand, including food safety and uniformity standards required, the policy goals, the stakeholders involved, and the physical environments. Over the longer term, as outmigration from rural to urban areas proceeds, the two options may reach the same endpoint. The policy question may be one of speed and nature of the transition rather than the ultimate goals. However, given the context specificity of the relevant factors, specific policy analysis will be needed in each case.

Policies for Production and Supply

Risk Management Policies: Insurance

Government intervention could either reduce risk or provide additional incentives for smallholders to act in a manner more consistent with their long-term interests. In case 7-4, von Braun and Olofinbiyi argue that market integration and price stabilization policies must be in place in order for other development projects to work effectively (see also cases 7-5 and 6-8). Once a subsistence level of consumption has been assured, producers will attempt to maximize their income. Producer preferences for biodiversity will tend to change with development, and it is also important to recognize the unintended side effects many policies can have on biodiversity.

The UN and many governments have begun to establish early warning systems to alert policymakers and locals about the warning signs of disasters before they happen. Weather monitoring stations can gather and provide information on likely rainfall patterns, and the preconditions for tornadoes, tsunamis, and other disasters can forewarn people to prepare for the events. As only one example of a traditional warning system, the Moken people who live along the coasts of Thailand and Myanmar taught their children that when the ocean receded, the "Laboon"—a wave that eats people—would come. When village elders saw that happen shortly after the earthquake off the coast of Indonesia in December 2004, they gathered their people to higher ground. When the tsunami came, the villagers were safe (Wirthlin 2005).

One of the greatest risks during famines is that poor households must sell off what little land, livestock, or other capital they have to survive. This makes them even more vulnerable than before and reduces their prospects for long-term growth (case 7-4). During difficult times, though, the price of livestock tends to fall because distress sales expand supplies in local markets, so that the returns to livestock can be negative.

This situation has led governments to provide various forms of drought assistance. The difficulty with many of these interventions, though, is that they create moral hazard problems, encouraging production methods for farms and livestock that exacerbate their losses during drought and their dependence on government assistance, and which could in fact increase the severity of a given drought by encouraging environmental degradation. While single interventions can bring great benefits, frequent and expected intervention can exacerbate moral hazard problems. Hazell (case 7-5) recommends that policymakers should not try to eliminate downside risk, which would disincentivize basic safety measures, and instead focus on supporting insurance markets and providing targeted subsidies for those who cannot afford to pay for insurance.

The rural poor engage in a variety of occupations or livelihoods as a means of diversifying their income sources. While protecting them against severe losses, this reduces producers' willingness to embrace new, untried technologies, particularly those that require expensive inputs. Hallman, Lewis, and Begum (2003) reported that many of the very poor with whom they worked to introduce aquaculture as an additional source of income indicated they could not spend the time and resources for it unless they could ensure a base level of consumption for their families by income, cash, or credit. Indeed, one of the great differentiators between producers who feel vulnerable and those who don't is access to cash or credit (see also Birol, Kontoleon, and Smale 2005).

Subsidized credit and insurance programs often fail due to moral hazard problems, corruption, and emphasizing crisis recovery rather than prevention. Colombia's credit subsidy is one case where the program worked well because the subsidy was effectively targeted to only the most poor who would not have obtained private insurance from the private sector, so that there was very limited market distortion (Mosquera 1993).

Because formal banking rarely extends into rural areas, microcredit and microinsurance have been effective public and private sector answers to some of these concerns. Microcredit schemes can alleviate cash constraints so that the poor can invest in their businesses, while microinsurance attempts to use market mechanisms to reduce the chance of catastrophic losses, making investments less risky. These two methods attack the same problem in different ways, so that each will be effective for different stakeholders. They can reinforce and complement each other. Unfortunately, they can also undermine one another. It is important to plan both simultaneously (von Braun and Pandya-Lorch 2007). Even microcredit schemes have difficulty reaching the ultra poor, who live on less than fifty cents a day. BRAC, a development-oriented NGO in Bangladesh, has found that providing short-term grants to the ultra poor has often allowed them to become microfinance clients (von Braun and Pandya-Lorch 2007).

One of the difficulties of providing private insurance in such areas is the covariate nature of the risks: if the rains don't come for one farmer, they don't come for any farmer facing the same microclimate. Small-scale insurers would then have to pay out to everyone at the same time, making the group a bad risk. A larger, regional insurance framework based on rainfall patterns that pay off in cases of catastrophic drought would be relatively inexpensive to monitor and manage and would be one effective means of introducing the private sector into the solution of this problem (case 7-5).

Hallman, Lewis, and Begum (2003) identify additional sources of vulnerability among the poor or ultra poor: gender inequality, lack of knowledge about different opportunities, and poor governance. A lack of good governance affects producers through law and order problems, such as theft and threat of violence; corruption that denies access to services that ought to be provided; low trust in government that reduces participation in programs that could be beneficial; and lack of access to justice.

Output Price Volatility Policies

The risks arising from market and government mechanisms are no less severe than natural risks. Because farmers are often cash constrained and have urgent loan repayments to make, more than three-fourths of the grain harvested by farmers may be sold immediately after harvest (e.g., case 7-4). This drives the price of grain down after harvest, and, by leaving many people without sufficient reserves during what are termed "the hungry months," leads to high prices prior to the next harvest as there are many buyers but few sellers. Even with increasing globalization that should dampen such price variation, the coefficient of variation for grain prices within a year has been quite high over the 1980s and 90s (case 6-8). High price volatility reduces farmers' incentives to invest or take needed risks and causes civil unrest, as illustrated by food riots in more than thirty countries in response to rapidly increasing food prices in 2005–2008. Timmer (1997) estimated that reducing price volatility in Indonesia increased economic growth by 14–16 percent from 1969–1979.

Rashid (case 6-8) identifies infrastructure, institutions, and information as key ingredients in ensuring that market liberalizations lead to stable prices. Without adequate infrastructure, it is costly for food to travel from food-surplus to food-deficit areas. Institutions, such as commodity and futures markets, and effective market information allow prices to adjust much more smoothly and in advance of problems, reducing variability and vulnerability. It is argued that market liberalizations were much more successful in China and Vietnam than in Africa because of Asia's better infrastructure and institutional network (case 6-8; Dollar 2004).

Governments sometimes reduce price volatility by purchasing farm products at harvest when the price is low and storing it up for emergencies. This can seem to be a good solution because individual farmers experience high storage losses and lack the inputs to improve their storage techniques. By facilitating storage, more of the grain can be preserved. This can be an expensive proposition, however. Rashid (case 6-8) indicates that conservative estimates of the cost to store grain—not including storage losses, transportation costs, administration costs, or corruption losses—are $30 per ton per year. Since one ton provides only three people with the world average amount of grain for a year, it would cost $50 million to store enough grain to feed half of the people of the median developing country for one year. If disasters happen only every several years, the cost of preparing for each emergency is accordingly multiplied. The fact that there is no agreement on how much governments should store compounds the difficulty of accurately measuring the costs of this policy.

Cases 7-1, 7-2, and 7-3 demonstrate that government storage proved to be very ineffectual in Malawi during the 2001/2002 famine. Prior to the famine, the IMF had recommended a partial sell-off of the expensive grain stocks. Instead the government sold the entire stock, and it is suspected that corruption and poor governance were important factors in determining who benefited from the sales. Hence, government failure can be as crucial as market failure, undermining well-intentioned policies.

Malawi's government failure also harmed market development and perpetuated market failures. Unpredictable changes in policy reduced the incentives and ability of private traders to perform the same actions, exacerbating the famine. In general, the more food stored and the less policy can be predicted in advance, the greater the market distortions. Some policies that can reduce these distortions include announcing the sale price or release conditions before the planting season; rotating the stock by selling some of it at import prices; and strengthening the legal framework to minimize corruption, such as collusion between traders and officials (case 6-8). Sauer and Tchale (2009) further implicate devalued currency and inflation that makes fertilizer more expensive to purchase, reducing market incentives. When the government maintained price policies and made its own imports transparent, it reduced risk to private traders who were able to acquire sufficient grain outside the country at a lower price than the one set by government, and the food shortage the next year was much milder.

One alternative means of national saving for emergencies is for a government to hold foreign currency reserves or to run budget surpluses in good years so that it can import food or increase spending in bad years. This smoothes consumption and reduces price volatility. Such a foreign reserve policy means that governments spend less on food storage, but may be faced with high international food prices as was the case in 2008. This can also have significant effects on exchange rates, affecting other export industries when there is increased volatility and uncertainty already.

Other government interventions can reduce price volatility through supporting market mechanisms. This can include overcoming coordination failures to set up public access storage areas that reduce the costs to individual farmers of storing their grains, increasing the availability of credit and cash during harvest periods so that farmers do not need to sell off so much of their harvest immediately, and supporting the development of futures and options markets (cases 6-8 and 7-3).

Simply relying on market mechanisms does not guarantee lower price volatility. Liberalizing agricultural markets in the 1990s increased crop production and reduced the price differential between food-surplus and food-deficit areas, but price volatility remained (case 7-4). Improving infrastructure and market information, monitoring the weather, fostering private trade, and improving input markets would reduce long-run price variability in market-friendly systems, but are not immediate solutions.

Government food price policies were discussed in chapter 6. To summarize, many governments' primary objective has generally been to keep food prices low to reduce urban unrest and support urban industry. This reduces the incentives for agricultural investment and production, reduces incentives for traders to enter the market to dampen price volatility, and transfers income from producers to consumers—often increasing income inequality. They also tend to be quite expensive (case 7-7), reducing macroeconomic stability, leading to more black market or informal activity, and can create or exacerbate severe food shortages. Cases 7-1, 7-2, and 7-3 demonstrate the importance of transparency for encouraging private traders as governments transition away from direct price control.

Input Price and Availability Policies

There may be a vicious cycle in African agricultural input markets: their supply is low because there is little incentive for private firms to invest in sparsely populated rural areas where demand is low, but demand is low in part because input prices are high due to the small quantities traded. On average in SSA, farmers remove 52 kg/ha of soil nutrients every year while restoring only 10 through fertilizers (World Bank 2007a). Weak credit markets and the threat of default under such conditions add to the problems. Growth in either supply or demand would ease the other constraints, but both find it difficult to move first in the current setting.

In much of Asia during the green revolution, governments actively promoted fertilizer and improved seed use, as well as making the necessary investments to ensure that their use would be as effective as possible, including roads and irrigation. The mix of policies succeeded in increasing farmer productivity significantly, and by increasing incomes created a larger market for private input suppliers, thus breaking the vicious cycle.

Input distribution programs in SSA have been fraught with difficulties (e.g., cases 7-1, 7-2, and 7-3 on Malawi and Zambia). When subsidized fertilizer was provided near universally, production increased dramatically, improving food security for many households and reducing seasonal price fluctuations. However, the subsidies benefited the larger, wealthier farmers more, increasing inequality. Procurement delays in the public sector programs also reduced the effectiveness. The cost strained the budget, and international donors (who were funding much of the program) insisted the subsidies be reduced and programs be better targeted, run more effectively, and cut back to allow private firms greater entry. This, however, meant increasing prices and lower usage of inputs precisely where they were most needed: in remote rural areas with poor farmers, where the private sector could not make a profit. The cutbacks greatly decreased crop productivity, contributing to widespread hunger and famine. As the cases in Malawi demonstrate, there were many other factors involved in turning the drought into a famine, but the unsustainability of the earlier policies, the poorly designed changes, and poor governance throughout exacerbated the situation.

Regarding subsidies' financial sustainability, it is sometimes argued that it is less expensive and better in the long run to subsidize fertilizer than to distribute food aid (case 7-1). Levy, Barahona, and Chinsinga (2004) demonstrate that it is more effective, where politically feasible, to target the input subsidies appropriately to those who need them most and are least able to afford fertilizer on their own, thereby causing the least distortion to fertilizer markets and ensuring that benefits accrue to the poor for whom they are intended. Relying on targeted vouchers redeemable at private input sellers has greatly improved the efficiency and equity of the fertilizer program in Malawi. Vouchers were sold to farmers in Kenya at harvesttime when cash was available as a commitment device to ensure that the money would be used for inputs (World Bank 2007a). Other options include supporting alternative soil fertility practices discussed earlier in the chapter. Doing so means that governments will need to provide more support for their extension programs to educate and train farmers.

Overlooked by these policies are the important public goods that could make markets more efficient in the long run. Investments in roads, social networks, and spreading market information reduce the costs of supplying inputs as well as increase demand, leading to a synergistic improvement in conditions.

Other supply-side policies include training networks of small-scale, local "agro dealers" who are able to make a profit selling small amounts of fertilizer and seeds because they are able to purchase in bulk as a network. Farmers' associations can also purchase in bulk and distribute to members. Training and appropriate credit policies have enabled such public/private partnerships to thrive in SSA (World Bank 2007a). In deciding which of these input policies to pursue, the question becomes which will be the most effective and least distortionary means of achieving efficiency and equality in an ethical manner that is politically feasible and sustainable. This will likely differ between countries and within countries over time.

Income Support Policies

If giving consumers food aid harms farmers by reducing the demand for their food, and giving input subsidies to farmers harms input producers by reducing the demand for their products, why not just support incomes? By giving cash to farmers, they demand more fertilizer, benefiting both the farmers and the input producers. Similarly, giving income or food stamps to the poor consumers increases their demand for food products, making both the poor and the farmers better off. As with the other policies discussed, this one too has its merits and demerits (see case 6-8). Whether income incentives should be linked to production or not is discussed in chapter 10.

There are potential difficulties that cash transfers run into: fungibility and macroeconomic effects. Money is fungible, which means that even if funds are earmarked for spending on one thing (e.g., food for children or agricultural inputs), that frees up money that would have been spent on those goods for other purposes. Both the good and the bad thing about cash transfers is that they can be spent on anything. The good part of that means that the recipient is free to determine how best to spend the money to accomplish his or her goals. If givers (be they donor organizations, government programs, or individual philanthropists) trust the recipients to "spend the money well," there is no problem with unconditional cash transfers. When givers are concerned, perhaps paternalistically, about how recipients will spend the money, fungibility is a major stumbling block. Givers may then prefer donations to be "in-kind," such as giving food or inputs directly. Unless the conditions are nontradable—i.e., they cannot be exchanged for money or other goods and services—these transfers are still fungible, but by introducing transaction costs it makes it more difficult to "funge." For example, farmers who receive free or subsidized fertilizers may sell the fertilizers to other farmers for cash.

Conditional cash transfers have been an increasingly popular option with the success of the programs in Mexico and Brazil. Funds are given only to households that meet certain requirements, such as attending health and nutrition classes, sending children to school, or working on public works projects (targeting the poorer households that would be willing to do this poorly paid work). With the proper infrastructure in place and when properly managed—which may be a difficult undertaking for a poor state with limited bureaucracy—they can significantly improve nutrition, education, and rural incomes.

The other difficulty with cash or in-kind transfers deals with macroeconomic effects. Other than the money they print, governments do not actually have or earn money. The funds to operate policies have to come from somewhere else, usually in the form of distortionary taxation. The ILO (2005) and de Janvry and Subramanian (1993) point out that cash subsidies can have negative effects on credit markets, overvalue exchange rates, subsidize mechanization processes, and take resources from more efficient uses to less efficient. Though some of these effects are mitigated when the money comes from financial aid, Scobie (1983) finds that increased subsidies of any kind lead to higher inflation, which can slow investment and impoverish farmers.

It is essential that transfers be appropriately targeted if they are to be effective (chapter 4). If the money doesn't get to poor farmers, transfers can increase inequality. Investments in roads and market infrastructure remain critical to ensure that policies work as they are intended. The secondary effects of transfers on prices are also critical. If some of the poor population is not assisted by the transfers, then when the prices of inputs and food increase, they are made worse off.

Contextual Policies

Land Tenure

Many policies affect the context in which farmers make production decisions, such as land tenure policies, support for nonfood land uses, irrigation policies, and core public goods. Without nutrients, water, and light, crops will not grow. The laws that govern land use are among the most important ways that governments influence agricultural production. There are four primary land tenure issues: the lack of registered land ownership, unequal land distribution, conflicting traditional rights in common property areas, and attempts by multinational corporations and middle-income countries that are net food importers or fossil fuel importers to obtain ownership or control over land in low-income countries, a phenomenon referred to as "land grabbing" (Robertson and Pinstrup-Andersen 2010).

The poor are often unable to register and claim ownership to their land. This restricts their access to credit, reduces their ability to invest in improving their land, and prevents many millions of people from improving their land and livelihoods. There are often multiple layers of traditional land rights that have developed over hundreds of years. Modern Niger (case 7-6) and America's Wild West (de Soto 2000) are two cases where much effort has been put into harmonizing the diverse traditional systems. Assuring legal rights to land need not be limited to private titles. In many countries, collective landownership has functioned well over long periods of time. But in those cases, it is critically important to clarify the communal landownership and cultivation rights for individuals or groups. Unclear ownership and cultivation rights lead to insecurity because of the risk of losing the land, leading potentially to failure to invest in increased productivity.

Unfortunately, it can be very difficult to appropriately craft and enforce new land tenure laws in ways that will be efficient, equitable, and ethical. Granting specific land rights to some people may disenfranchise others, who will unjustly lose their traditional rights to land without compensation (Meinzen-Dick, Kameri-Mbote, and Markelova 2007). In many countries farmers who have cultivated the same land over long periods of time may not have any tenure security either because private landownership is against the existing government policy or because land titling institutions are ineffective or absent. In such cases, particularly where the land belongs to the state, governments may enter into agreements with middle-income country governments or corporations for control over large extensions of land, ignoring the consequences for the farm families that live off the land but have no legal recourse (Robertson and Pinstrup-Andersen 2010). There is also the essential matter of gender equality: Do women have the same rights and access to land as men, independent of their husbands? Ignoring the social, cultural, and religious purposes of land can lead to opposition against even well-planned land reforms that focus only on its economic value and fail to include land users in the deliberative process. Rodrik (2008) and Easterly (2008) discuss the difficulties of top-down land tenure decisions that do not account for social structures. There is no single land tenure system that will work universally.

In most developing countries, many of the poor have either no land or else not enough to sustain themselves and their families. In general, the more equally land is distributed, the greater the prospects for pro-poor agricultural-led development (ILO 2005). In addition to the titling and distribution of the land, reforms are also needed to form well-functioning land markets so that landholders, individually or in groups, can obtain credit, reallocate land to its most effective use, rent or sell it, and fully utilize it as capital (de Soto 2000; case 7-4). This may also require legal literacy campaigns (Meinzen-Dick, Kameri-Mbote, and Markelova 2007).

Shortly after the Second World War, Japan, South Korea, and Taiwan were each able to enact very successful land reforms that significantly reduced inequality and poverty while increasing agricultural production by transferring often unused land from wealthy landowners to the people working the land. Similar reforms in many other countries have failed. Hayami (2005) concludes that at least some of the preconditions for this type of land reform to be successful include a displaced elite who could not oppose the measures, an established bureaucracy with accurate historical land records, and favorable demand and supply for *that particular* reform.

Case 7-7, which discusses land tenure issues in depth for Russia, identifies the additional precondition that the newly minted landowners need to be able to make efficient use of the land. In Russia they had lost the capacity for individual farming, heirs to particular plots of land could not be found, the infrastructure was designed for large farms rather than individual plots, and processing was not competitive. Many of these same conditions were present in Zimbabwe during its land reform that has taken place since 2000. In both cases, land reforms led to a large reduction in agricultural output.

It is important that the landless be included as stakeholders in debates on new land tenure rules. More than 30 percent of Africa is common property, and community forests provide up to 29 percent of poor households' income (Meinzen-Dick, Kameri-Mbote, and Markelova 2007). Land rights adjustment is most particularly needed in clarifying the relationship between farmers and pastoralists in the Sahel. Historically they had developed a cooperative system, with pastoralists providing manure or services tending farmers' livestock in exchange for grain. Recent population and farmer-biased attempts to turn community properties into private property without stakeholder participation have strained these relationships (cases 7-5 and 7-6).

Nonfood Uses for Agricultural Land: Biofuels, Biodiversity, and Living Space

In assigning rights to land, governments must balance not only the various claims different farming and landless stakeholders have but also the claims for other land uses. These include production of other agricultural goods like biofuels or cotton, the preservation of biodiversity and the environment, roads, industrial uses, and the provision of adequate housing.

Farmers have long grown cash crops they would not consume in order to earn money to purchase the food and other goods and services they need. Biofuels have added a new dimension to this as governments have erected high subsidies and tariffs to encourage domestic farmers to grow crops that can be turned into alternatives to fossil fuels. Over two hundred policies are in effect in the United States alone to support biofuels production, amounting to a $0.40–$0.50 per liter subsidy (World Bank 2007a). Such policies divert large amounts of land to biofuel production, reducing the availability of maize, soybeans, and other biofuel feedstock for food and feed; reallocate land and other resources away from food production; and contribute to the rapidly rising prices witnessed during 2005–2008.

The U.S. Department of Energy estimates that soybeans can produce 3.24 units of energy for each unit consumed in their production. However, the cost of producing biofuels is $0.53/liter against $0.35/liter for gasoline (case 7-8). The cost in terms of forgone food is higher: the same maize that it takes to fill an SUV with ethanol could feed a person for a year (World Bank 2007a).

It is estimated that sugarcane in Brazil is one of the only examples of a country where biofuel production is currently economically sustainable, and even there it required years of direct subsidization before the industry grew to become competitive (World Bank 2007a). Other countries are also actively promoting biofuels production, such as palm oil in Indonesia and Malaysia, sugarcane in Mozambique and some Latin American countries, rapeseed in Canada, and oil-rich plants in India (case 7-8). Russell (2008) reports that China hopes to increase its biofuel output from 3.6 billion liters in 2002 to 15 billion by 2020, replacing 9 percent of the projected gasoline demand, and that India plans a similar expansion. China and India are expected to make up the lion's share of increased demand for oil in the next twenty-five years.

The agricultural hope of biofuels is that, because they are labor intensive, they will increase rural wages and farmers' incomes, and that the rising relative prices for agricultural products will enable more farmers to become net sellers of food (Bayes 2007). Unfortunately, it seems likely that most of the gains will be captured by large farms and very large processing plants that are able to take advantage of government protection and large economies of scale. Furthermore, in order to produce biofuel, multinational corporations and middle-income country governments may enter into agreements with governments of poor countries for the control of land currently used for food production. Some farmer cooperatives have made inroads in Brazil. Biodiesel is a more likely means for small-scale farmers to enter the market competitively (World Bank 2007a).

The total environmental impact of biofuels is difficult to determine, but it is looking bleaker than originally forecast (chapter 8). In 2006, one-fifth of the U.S. maize crop was diverted to ethanol production, which displaced only 3 percent of fossil fuel consumption (World Bank 2007a). In Brazil, by comparison, there has been a 40 percent replacement of gasoline by ethanol (Russell 2008). Even then, the production of biofuels produces new emissions, so the gasoline reduction is being offset by increases elsewhere in the economy—a 50–60 percent reduction in Brazil, but only 10–30 percent in the United States (World Bank 2007a). Biofuel production also requires large amounts of water: 90 liters of water for 1 liter of ethanol in Brazil, but 2,400 liters in China and 3,500 liters in India (Russell 2008). Water use on the scale they envision by 2030 is simply not environmentally sustainable. Increasing the land available for biofuels is another environmental concern as large sections of forest and wetlands are being clear-cut to make room for sugarcane and palm oil farms (chapter 8).

Though future technological breakthroughs could increase the production of biofuel and reduce their emissions, this will take years of dedicated private and public research to discover and make commercial. The development of enzymes that could transform plant cellulose into biofuel is not an economically viable commercial technology unless oil prices increase very significantly. Some dryland crops, such as sweet sorghum or the shrub *Jatropha curcas,* could also replace some of the water-intensive crops, and may be more pro-poor because they can be grown on more marginalized soils, but again, it will take time and serious investment to move any project like this forward to an economically relevant size.

ICRISAT (International Crops Research Institute for the Semi-Arid Tropics) has also been moving forward with public-private partnerships to bring the advantages of biofuel production to the poor in India, with new projects beginning in the Philippines and SSA as well. In these partnerships, distilleries provide farmers with improved seeds, training, transportation for the goods, and a contracted price for the goods (Russell 2008). Another partnership works to give landless women access to community lands to plant biodiesel species to use in their local villages or to sell.

Rhoads' (case 7-8) analysis demonstrates the difficult trade-offs between these issues. He praises the Indian government's efforts to promote public-private partnerships as "the best mix of market incentives and public direction," while simultaneously indicating that "the market alone should direct the development of biodiesel tech" and calling for the government to make greater public interventions. While advocating that the government should consider the needs of poor stakeholders in formulating policy, he also warns that too great a focus on the poor will drive away private investors to make the whole thing sustainable.

Preserving biodiversity is another goal that has its claims on land and agriculture. The green revolution's focus on monocultures has reduced biodiversity on farmers' fields and, in some cases, increased risks that a few well-adapted pests or diseases can reduce yields to a greater extent than before (Lipton 2005). However, the higher yields reduced the need to bring in new lands, thus protecting biodiversity on those lands. New research projects, such as NERICA, recognize the inherent value in landraces and have been actively promoting their inclusion in research to improve native varieties rather than replacing them. Chapter 8 discusses to what extent farmers will protect biodiversity, and to what extent government incentives will be needed to preserve this public good.

There is the further issue of the need for land for people to live on. In 1961, there was approximately 0.44 ha/person in the world. By 2000 that had dropped to 0.26 ha/person, and it is expected to decrease to 0.15 by 2050 (Pinstrup-Andersen and Schiøler 2000). One of the major constraints to future agricultural growth in China is that local governments are able to create significant rents from selling public land to nearby cities so they can continue their rapid growth and expansion (World Bank 2007a). This is another reason for the importance of focused rural development: it will slow the rate of urban sprawl and leave more land available for agricultural production and biodiversity.

Irrigation and Water Management

Agriculture is a major part of the water system, consuming 85 percent of the water used in developing countries (World Bank 2007a). Irrigated crops yield on average

2.5 times as much as rain-fed crops (Pinstrup-Andersen and Schiøler 2000). Since intensive fertilizer use is effective only if there is sufficient water available, many of the green revolution's benefits came through increased public and private investment in irrigation (ILO 2005). China invests ten times as much on irrigation and water control as on agricultural research (Fan, Zhang, and Zhang 2002). Case 7-4 discusses irrigation projects in depth.

In some areas of the world, the ability to increase irrigation sustainably has not yet been exploited. One-third of Malawi is covered with fresh water that could be used for irrigation (case 7-2). Ethiopia has utilized only 11 percent of its irrigation potential (case 7-4). Throughout Africa, only 4 percent of farmland enjoys the benefits of irrigation, compared with 34 percent in Asia (World Bank 2007a).

The reliance of governments on intense irrigation in some areas of the world during the green revolution has lowered water tables, and it is estimated that up to one-third of the productivity gains in China and Pakistan have literally eroded through soil and water degradation (World Bank 2007a). Almost 40 percent of Asia's dry irrigated land is being affected by salinization because of overwatering and poor water management practices (Pinstrup-Andersen and Schiøler 2000; World Bank 2007a). As water becomes scarcer in many areas of the world, yields will decrease and human health may suffer by increasing the incidence of diarrhea and infectious diseases (Huang, Pray, and Rozelle 2002).

Future projects must increasingly focus on the total effect in areas downstream, or else the externalities of upstream projects may be greater than the initial benefits. Increasing population will increase demands on scarce water resources, which need to be harvested and managed responsibly to ensure their long-term continued availability. It is expected that climate change will decrease average water available in many places while increasing its variability (chapter 8).

Essential also is altering the governance structures that encourage an overuse of water, such as inflexible water delivery systems, bureaucratic rigidities, oversubsidizing, and poorly targeted subsidies to farmers who then do not internalize the costs of the water they use. Political processes matter in reforming water systems because these are among the most entrenched policies in many states where water is regarded as an entitlement or a right.

Infrastructure and Other Core Public Goods

Governments need to expand infrastructure and create other core public goods as an essential part of making agriculture more productive and bringing about equitable, poverty-reducing growth in both the short and long run. Only agricultural research is more effective at reducing poverty than building more roads (ILO 2005; cases 9-1 and 9-2). Roads make markets more effective by reducing marketing costs, and increase rural wages and employment. Cases 9-1 and 9-2 discuss their relative importance at some length, demonstrating, for instance, that building new feeder roads were the most important factor in reducing poverty in India from 1970 to 1995. Thirty percent of Africa's rural population lives more than five hours from a market town, and there are fewer roads in SSA today than there were in Asia forty years ago (World Bank 2007a). Roads are an essential part of enabling farmers to sell their goods.

Creating well-functioning education and health systems that provide primary services universally are two of the Millennium Development Goals to which countries agreed in 2000. Primary education (generally measured by literacy or years in school) and basic health interventions tend to have a greater effect on productivity and well-being than more advanced care, and are much more cost-effective (ILO 2005; cases 9-1 and 9-2). Sahn and Edirisinghe (1993) propose that government investments in health and education are necessary conditions for free markets to work efficiently and equitably.

Electricity access increases agricultural production and rural employment opportunities. Bringing more people onto the grid and providing electricity to those too far from the grid by alternate means also provides opportunities to improve rural health and education, and reduces the amount of time women spend in fuel collection. More fuel-efficient cooking stoves save women seven days of labor each year in India (Pachauri and Mehrotra 2001). Photovoltaic technology is a cost-effective means of bringing small amounts of electricity to areas more than 5 km from the main electricity grid.

Other infrastructure projects in developing countries include disseminating market information to distant areas via radio, cell phone, or the Internet; establishing livestock cooling and storage stations at ports; maintaining trade routes; developing market and legal literacy programs; investing in agricultural extension services; improving rural credit, insurance, and financial services; and providing good governance.

Research and Development

Agricultural output growth will be unsustainable without labor-enhancing technological progress. Anywhere agricultural productivity has gone up, poverty has gone down, and the more these productivity enhancements encouraged employment, the more poverty was reduced (ILO 2005). An investment of $179 in agricultural research and development (R&D) would lift one person out of $1/day poverty, a higher rate of return than any other investment, with the possible exception of roads in some areas (ILO 2005). There is no evidence that the benefits of new agricultural research in developing countries has reached a point of decreasing rates of returns, implying that high returns continue to be available for the foreseeable future (CGIAR Science Council 2005).

While investments in roads lowered poverty in India more than investment in agricultural research, this was because most research in India was not aimed at increasing agricultural productivity (case 9-2). The portion that is focused at improving productivity was more effective than anything else, decreasing poverty 2.5 times more than education investments and ten times more than irrigation investments (ILO 2005). For smallholders who consume or sell most of their crop, increases in agricultural productivity will affect poverty and malnutrition directly, while landless rural workers benefit from the indirect effects of increased employment and wages.

Estimates of the exact impacts of specific technologies are difficult to assess, but Adato and Meinzen-Dick (2007) present seven case studies of the impacts of different technologies in six countries. To briefly summarize some of the results:

- Bangladesh: Improved rice varieties increased production from 1.52 tons/ha in 1965 to 3.48 by 2000, approximately 70 percent of which can be attributed to the improved seed and 30 percent from improved input use. For a smallholder on an average of 0.67 hectares, this amounted to an increase of $237 per year in income, a 20 percent increase.
- Bangladesh: Improved fishpond techniques tripled fish sales and increased profits over 50 percent.
- Bangladesh: Introducing vegetable cultivation to women with very little access to land increased incomes, health, social standing, and equality (see also Hallman, Lewis, and Begum 2003).
- Kenya: Nutrient-fixing shrubs and biomass transfer increased maize output by 55 percent, though time costs to gather biomass from other areas to bring to the farm (considered women's work) increased. This gave a return to labor of more than $2/day, an increase of over 33 percent, and provided firewood that could be sold.
- Zimbabwe: Second-generation hybrid maize varieties that focused on pest resistance increased average yields and decreased output variability, but by less than the first-generation hybrids that focused on yield production.

Spielman and Pandya-Lorch (2009) present twenty-one further case studies on proven successes in agricultural development. Many are on efforts to increase production: improved maize in Kenya, Malawi, Zambia, and Zimbabwe; rice in Bangladesh and China; pearl millet and sorghum in India; mung bean in Asia; smallholder dairy in India; aquaculture tilapia in the Philippines; and homestead food production in Bangladesh. Other cases focus specifically on technologies to reduce pests, including containing wheat rusts, creating pest-resistant cassava in Africa, and eradicating rinderpest in cattle. Institutional and environmental reforms are also discussed.

Despite the large benefits that have been achieved through agricultural research, there is a great need for further research. Eighty percent of the farmers in developing countries already use HYVs, but new varieties that are drought tolerant, resistant to insect attacks and diseases, and compatible with changing climate must be developed in order to reignite agricultural productivity growth (Pinstrup-Andersen and Schiøler 2000).

Biotechnology and nanotechnology and their impacts on smallholder agriculture are discussed at length in chapter 10. But who benefits from these technologies? Falck-Zepeda, Traxler, and Nelson (2000) attempt to identify who benefits from GM crops in the United States. Farmers using Roundup Ready (RR) soybean seed in 1997 pocketed 48 percent of the estimated benefits, with consumers receiving 21 percent through lower prices, leaving 9 percent for seed companies and 22 percent for the multinational corporation (MNC) that developed the product. Similarly, for Bt cotton in 1997, farmers received 42 percent of the benefits, with 35 percent going to the MNC, and most of the remainder going to consumers. Publicly funded research promises even greater reward shares for farmers and consumers. It is estimated that three-fourths of the gains from a disease-resistant variety of sweet potato in Kenya would go to farmers and the remaining one-fourth to consumers (Pinstrup-Andersen and Schiøler 2000).

Conclusion

It is possible for countries to significantly increase food production in a short amount of time. Between 1970 and 2000, twenty-eight countries managed to increase average food consumption by at least 22 percent, and nine of these managed to accomplish this feat with slow or negative income growth rates (FAO 2003c). For many developing countries, a greater focus on the agricultural sector will provide "the fastest and surest way out of poverty" for many millions of poor people (ILO 2005, 171). Differing circumstances between countries and over time will call for different appropriate policy measures. As noted in the section on pricing policies, the same policy may be beneficial to producers in one country—or in one part of a country (tho Seeth et al. 1998; Rodrik 2006)—but harmful in another because of the different circumstances they face. Government interventions that were necessary in the early stages of development may need to be phased out later as markets are able to take up some of the functions. Regulations and programs need to adapt to changing global realities and market conditions. No one policy is going to address the varied needs of the poor, implying a need for complementary policies.

Though some attempt has been made to indicate under which circumstances specific policies would be more effective, the policies discussed above are to be viewed more as a menu of options that policymakers could consider than a prescription of what all policymakers should do right now. However, some general principles can be gleaned that will apply in most countries at most times: the importance of investment in core public goods such as infrastructure and research, the need for active governments to support market development, and the necessity of balancing short-term relief and long-term development objectives.

There are large marginal effects from investments in core public goods and many countries have not yet reached the point where these returns are diminishing. Even though agriculture accounts for over 30 percent of the GDP of many African countries, it receives only 4 percent of government expenditures. The proportion of public expenditures allocated to agriculture varies greatly among African countries, and only a few have achieved the 10 percent target agreed on by CAADP (Comprehensive Africa Agriculture Development Programme). Fan (case 9-1) contrasts this with Asian countries during the green revolution, which allocated 10–15 percent of government expenditures toward agricultural development.

Where will these additional funds be most effective? Several authors argue that there is an essential first phase of "establishing the basics," with investments focused on providing core public goods—research, infrastructure, education, health, and equality of access to land and water—followed by a second phase to "kick-start markets" that concentrates on improving farmers' access to input and output markets and government withdrawal to allow private markets to function efficiently (Sahn and Edirisinghe 1993; Timmer 1997; Huang, Pray, and Rozelle 2002; Dorward et al. 2004; Lipton 2005; Hazell et al. 2007; case 6-8). Hazell et al. (2007) also mention improved marketing systems and stable macroeconomics and institutional innovations among their three central elements to promote growth and equity for smallholders. These institutions should recognize both market and government failures and make participatory use of the knowledge and expertise of all the relevant stakeholders (farmers, NGOs, private firms, researchers, government). See also chapters 6 and 9; Lipton 2005; and von Braun and Pandya-Lorch 2007.

Which of the core public goods is needed first will depend strongly on country specifics. Bayes (2007) contends that Thailand needs more education to ensure migrant workers can get access to better jobs with higher remittance potential while Laos needs rural roads to give farmers access to more liberalized markets. Fan (cases 9-1 and 9-2) compares the effects of several policies in different countries, and finds that agricultural research that is targeted to assisting smallholders and the landless has the highest poverty-reducing potential, with feeder roads and education providing significant benefits as well (table 7.3). Rosegrant et al. (2001) point out that, even though irrigation improvements have had relatively low rates

TABLE 7.3.
Comparative Effectiveness of Public Goods Investments

Investment	Benefit-cost ratio			
	Uganda	Tanzania	China	India
Agricultural R&D	12.38	12.46	9.59	n/a
Education	2.72	9.00	8.68	n/a
Feeder roads	7.16	9.13	8.83	n/a
Improved roads	n/s	n/a	n/a	n/a
Health	0.90	n/a	n/a	n/a
Electricity	n/a	n/a	126	n/a
Irrigation	n/a	n/a	188	n/a

Number of poor people raised out of poverty (per million expenditure in local currency units)				
Agricultural R&D	58.39	40.39	679	914.0
Education	12.81	43.10	880	317.0
Feeder roads	33.77	26.53	322	165.0
Improved roads	9.7	n/a	n/a	n/a
Health	4.60	n/a	n/a	4.0**
Electricity	n/a	141,962*	227	2.9**
Irrigation	n/a	n/a	1330	7.4**

Source: compiled by authors from Fan (cases 9-1 and 9-2).
Note: * denotes the number of poor reduced for 1 percent increase in connection; ** denotes not significant at 5 percent level; n/s = not significant; n/a = not available.

of return, cutbacks in spending on proper irrigation projects can have strongly negative outcomes on worldwide productive capacities.

The ideal mix of policies will depend on the pattern of landholding: the poor in Uganda benefit directly from growth in agricultural productivity, while India's landless poor benefit most from lower food prices, and both groups gain from increased employment opportunities (World Bank 2007a; case 9-1). Health, education, and research benefits are most likely to be seen over a long time horizon, so in calculating expected benefits in a particular country, much will depend on how far into the future the benefits are calculated.

Pardey and Beintema (2001) conclude that a "sizable and sustained effort" to reinvigorate developing country science is "unquestionably the top priority." One of the reasons for this is the need for locally relevant research for the soil and societal conditions faced by smallholders in a particular country. Both Lipton (2005) and the ILO (2005) describe two "tightropes" that science-led agricultural growth needs to walk in order to most effectively reduce poverty. The first is that productivity must increase faster than prices decline, which requires a sufficiently price-elastic demand—including household demand—to slow price declines. Increased trade liberalization will assist by reducing the responsiveness of many domestic prices to individual farm productivity increases. The second is that productivity per hectare should increase faster than productivity per worker. If workers are made more efficient without commensurate increases in land productivity, fewer workers are needed on the same amount of land, lowering employment and wages for those still hired. Mechanization tends to make labor more effective, but the land still produces as much food as before.

Concerning both biotechnology and nanotechnology, due care must be taken to ensure public safety before products are brought to market (chapters 10 and 11). With any new technology, extension work to educate farmers on how to maintain their crops remains important. But the right to choose whether or not to make use of a given technology should belong to individual countries and individual farmers and consumers. Millions of lives depend on it.

While focusing on the provision of so many public goods, governments need what might be termed an "exit strategy." Rashid (case 6-8) describes studies in six Asian countries (Bangladesh, India, Indonesia, Pakistan, Philippines, and Vietnam) where, because of previous investment in agricultural development and core public goods, farmers are well integrated into markets and have adopted improved technologies, and countries have sufficient currency reserves. In each case, continued government-controlled price policies "have resulted in staggering increases in costs," while well-planned liberalizations have improved conditions for farmers.

There is a natural tendency during crises for governments to focus on short-term solutions that are politically attractive because politicians can be seen to be "doing something" about the problem. As important as safety nets are for temporary problems, they have heavy long-term costs associated with them and are not economically sustainable. On the other hand, initiating a new program of agricultural research will not bear fruit for years, and is unlikely by itself to placate the demands of urban rioters. In figure 7.8, von Braun, Teklu, and Webb (1998) demonstrate that not all

FIGURE 7.8.
Trade-off between safety nets and public goods investments. Source: von Braun, Teklu, and Webb 1998.

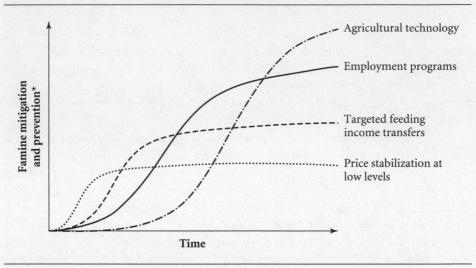

Note: It is assumed that there is a similar amount of resources spent on each of the alternative programs.
*Measured, for instance, in terms of number of people prevented from famine risk.

government spending is created equal. Spending that favors long-term growth from which the poor can benefit will often work only with a delay, while short-term government spending that may be effective in limiting a crisis can hobble a government when continued as a permanent feature of the political landscape. The point is that different tools are needed for different purposes, and an important part of guiding agricultural policy so that it benefits the poor is to understand and take account of these differences. A sound stakeholder analysis is important to guide the design and implementation of government policy for the food system.

Food Production and Supply Policies Case Studies

The cases in this chapter present policy options to help farmers expand production, increase income, improve food security, and manage production and market risks. The emphasis is on policies that mitigate threats facing small farmers and pastoralists, such as the negative effects of potential or actual famines and droughts.* Land distribution policies, research and technology policies, and policies to facilitate the production of biofuel without negative effects on food security are also discussed, along with policies to facilitate urban agriculture.

Cases 7-1 through 7-3 discuss the 2001 famine in Malawi, while case 7-4 focuses on famine in Ethiopia. Cases 7-6 and 7-10 focus on the needs of agro-pastoralists and other livestock farmers. Case 7-9 deals with cotton farming. The remaining

* The case studies referenced here are presented in full in the three-volume work by Per Pinstrup-Andersen and Fuzhi Cheng, eds., *Case Studies in Food Policy for Developing Countries* (Ithaca, NY: Cornell University Press, 2009) and online via open access at http://cip.cornell.edu/gfs.

cases address specific policy interventions: insurance (7-5), land holdings (7-7), biofuels (7-8), fertilizer subsidies (7-11), and urban agriculture. Cases 7-9 through 7-12 are available exclusively online.

Notes

1. Note the critical difference between a 1 *percentage point* decrease and 1 *percent* decrease. The first refers to a decrease from 30 percent poverty rate to 29. The second implies a decrease from 30 percent to 29.7.

2. The Sahel region is the area immediately south of the Sahara Desert, stretching across Africa from the Atlantic Ocean to the Red Sea.

3. The reader is referred to Pinstrup-Andersen and Schiøler 2000, chapter 4, for a more detailed discussion of these points.

4. Economies of scale imply that the unit costs of production go down as the quantity produced goes up. This could happen because of decreased transaction costs, improved technology, specialization, or other means. Economies of scale give larger producers a cost advantage compared to smaller producers.

Chapter 8

Climate Change, Energy, and Natural Resource Management Policies

Introduction

Natural resources are food systems' foundation. Similarly, the management and sustainability of natural resources are heavily influenced by the food system. The two-way causal interactions between them show that food systems will be sustainable over time only if sustainable natural resources management is assured and vice versa. That is not currently the case at the global level, as exemplified by widespread deforestation, soil erosion and soil mining, waterlogging and salinization, contamination of surface and ground waters, drawn-down groundwater levels, and increased emission of greenhouse gases. Furthermore, increasing international trade of agricultural commodities has expanded the use of energy in the transportation of food and related contributions to global warming.

Estimates of the social cost of natural resource degradation caused by agriculture are scarce. Norse, Ji, Leshan, and Zheng (2001) estimate that the total environmental costs of rice production in China were between $1.6 and $5.9 billion in 1995, and project an increase to $5.7–$12.1 billion by 2020. The largest share of these environmental costs comes from air pollution caused by agrochemical production. Smil (1997) estimates the environmental cost of agriculture related to soil erosion, forest ecosystems damage, and grassland degradation in China to be between $9.8 and $21.2 billion in 1990. De Haen (1997) reports that 1.2 billion hectares of agricultural land were degraded in the early 1990s, of which wind and water erosion accounted for 280 and 748 million ha, respectively. Maxwell and Slater (2004) estimate the environmental costs of modern agriculture in the UK at £2.3 billion per annum, or £208/hectare.

In addition to food, natural resources provide many other ecosystem goods and services. These include forestry products, natural beauty, improved health, and biodiversity. The food system affects the quantity and quality available of these goods and services for both good and ill.

The objective of this chapter is to provide a foundation for designing policy interventions aimed at sustainable natural resource management (NRM) and a sustainable food system. A conceptual description of the interaction between natural resources and food systems is followed by an analysis of the environmental externalities related to the food system. The chapter then discusses how climate change may be expected to affect the food system and analyzes trade-offs between natural and human-made resources as well as complementarities and trade-offs between the goal of sustainable NRM and other goals, such as poverty alleviation and expanded food production. The chapter ends with a discussion of policy options, with emphasis on those aimed at the internalization of environmental externalities associated with food systems and promoting multiple win situations.

A sustainable food system can be achieved at reasonable food prices only if environmental externalities are internalized in decisions related to the food system. This will require government incentives and regulations and collective action by various stakeholder groups that assure full-costing of environmental damage, payment for environment services, and allowance for trade-offs between natural and human-made capital.

Full-costing is a concept that assures that the social costs of environmental damage as well as the social benefits of environmental services are incorporated into private costs and benefits. In other words, society—as represented by the government, policy analysts, and scientists—will estimate the value of environmental costs and benefits associated with action by private and public agents and transfer those costs to the private agents in the form of explicit or implicit taxes and subsidies. Policy analysts from many disciplines are indispensible in making such a system work efficiently and fairly. The revenues from such taxes and subsidies should be used to remedy any negative environmental effects, thus maintaining a sustainable stock of natural resources.

It is further argued that the triple goal of producing enough food for current and future generations, reducing poverty and hunger, and maintaining sustainability in NRM can be achieved simultaneously by exploiting multiple-win synergies. For the very poor, most of whom are in rural areas of developing countries, it is rational to damage natural resources—such as cutting down trees to grow food on slopes that subsequently erode—if that is the most effective or the only way to survive. Short-run needs and private benefits and costs are likely to take priority over long-term goals and social benefits and costs. In such situations, policy interventions to reduce poverty would be needed to reduce or eliminate unsustainable use of natural resources. If poverty is reduced by helping the poor farmer enhance productivity on a piece of land well suited for cultivation, progress toward the triple goal may be achieved.

The Food System and Natural Resource Management

Sustainable NRM is understood by some as the protection of natural resources in their current or improved conditions, while others argue that NRM is sustainable if their productive capacity is maintained or augmented. The former, which in its extreme definition implies the sustaining of nature itself for its own intrinsic value (National Research Council 1999), does not permit any exchange of natural capital for human-made capital. The Brundtland Commission report (World Commission on Environment and Development 1987), on the other hand, declares that development is sustainable if human needs today are satisfied "without compromising the ability of future generations to meet their own needs." A focus on natural resources as a means to support human needs permits trade-offs between food system and environmental goals and between natural and human-made resources,[1] which a "deep ecology" ethic that values resources intrinsically would not (see chapter 11).

The food system is both a consumer and producer of ecosystem goods and services. Soil nutrients, water, land, air, sunshine, genetic resources, forest stock, and marine fishery stock are all essential food system assets. Climate change has the potential to significantly affect agriculture and other elements of the food system, particularly through changes in rainfall patterns and average temperatures.

In exchange for natural and human-made resources, the food system provides food, fiber (including timber, cotton, hemp, and silk), fuel (wood, biofuel, and biogas), medicines, a cultural heritage of which many nations are justly proud, reduced pest infestations, income for farmers, stronger rural economies, and foreign exchange. In addition to these environmental goods and services, the food system also purifies water, reduces the damage from natural disasters, protects biodiversity, sequesters carbon, and provides sustainable alternatives to fossil fuels. Carbon sequestration refers to the fact that as plants take in carbon dioxide (CO_2) and expel oxygen (O_2), the carbon is captured in the plants' structure and the soil. This removes carbon from the atmosphere, reducing global warming.

Agricultural intensification—achieving greater production of food and other agricultural commodities per unit of land, water, and labor—is critical to achieving sustainable NRM while meeting growing future food demands (chapter 4) at affordable prices. Contrary to what is sometimes believed, agricultural intensification need not cause environmental degradation. It is rather the mismanagement of resources and inputs, including inefficient use of water, overgrazing, and overuse or untimely and insufficient applications of fertilizer and pesticides, that causes damage to the environment.

By facilitating productivity growth on existing cultivated land, the green revolution reduced the expansion of agricultural cultivation into more land to meet food demands. It has been estimated that the area of land under cultivation would have had to increase by 80 percent from 1961 to 1993 to meet present food demand without these productivity enhancements (Goklany 1998). The resulting deforestation and soil erosion on land poorly suited for agriculture would have had severe environmental and humanitarian consequences.

At the same time, poor water management and excessive and inappropriate use of pesticides and fertilizers caused serious harm to the environment in some locations (Pinstrup-Andersen and Schiøler 2000). The negative environmental effects of the green revolution and other agricultural intensification efforts are caused in large measure by a failure to incorporate the social costs of such effects into private costs and inappropriate government incentives. Price subsidies for pesticides and free and open access to water, for example, result in overuse of both. Policy options to deal with such problems will be discussed later in the chapter.

Environmental Externalities Related to the Food System

Economic externalities refer to consequences of economic transactions that are experienced by a party not directly involved in the transaction. In the case of the environmental externalities, the consequences of the damage done to the environment may not be experienced by those who cause the damage. Where externalities occur, market prices do not reflect the full cost (if the externality is negative) or benefit (if it is positive). In a market economy without government intervention, the presence of externalities will cause private costs and benefits to differ from social costs and benefits with negative social consequences. Furthermore, as illustrated by the ecological disaster in central Asia discussed in case 8-6, government intervention may cause severe environmental damage. The next subsections discuss each of the main groups of natural resources, and it will be seen that environmental externalities are common.

Deforestation

Forests cover more than twice as much land area as agriculture and contain two-thirds of all plant species (National Research Council 1999). Pinstrup-Andersen and Pandya-Lorch (1994) report that about one-third of tropical deforestation is due to logging and city growth while two-thirds occurs to prepare land for agriculture. Of that new agricultural land, 30–50 percent subsequently loses more than half of its soil quality within the first three years. FAO (2006c) indicates that 70 percent of former Amazonian rainforest land is now used as pasture for animals and that most of the remainder provides fodder for animals.

Deforestation decreases carbon sequestration as the carbon stored in trees is released into the atmosphere. It also reduces income and livelihood options for many poor people who depend on forest products, while temporarily adding to others' incomes (e.g., farmers and developers) who get access to the land. It also raises levels of soil erosion, salinization, and flooding, reduces barriers against natural disasters, and decreases biodiversity. Deforestation forces women, who are the primary agricultural producers in much of the world, to travel further to gather firewood, decreasing their time available for other activities.

According to FAO (2005d), the global forested area decreased by 8.9 million hectares per year during the 1990s. These annual losses correspond to about 0.2 percent of the total forested area. The losses were largest in Africa, which lost 0.6 percent of its forested area annually during the period 1990–2005, while east Asia experienced an annual increase in its forested area of 0.8 percent during 1990–2000. Global deforestation slowed during 2000–2005 as east Asian forestry grew by 1.6 percent per year.

Elmqvist et al. (2007) indicate that the highest loss of forest cover occurred in low human population density areas with long distances to markets, while forest covers remained stable in the area with the highest population density and good market access. Loss of forest cover occurred mainly in areas characterized by insecure property rights, while areas with well-defined property rights showed either regenerating or stable forest cover. Even marginal forestland can regenerate when pressures are reduced and institutions permit stability. Forest regrowth in Madagascar during the 1990s occurred without specific replanting efforts.

Fairhead and Leach (1998, 1) warn that many estimates of deforestation may be exaggerated because of the assumptions made to estimate the base level of forestry for years when data are not available, particularly that "everywhere that forest *could* exist today . . . it originally *did* [and] that this loss was principally caused by people's land use activities" (emphasis original). Recent estimates tend to be one-third lower than earlier estimates. The hopeful conclusion from this is that deforestation may be much less of a factor than has been previously believed and that improving market access, property rights, and institutions can further slow or even reverse deforestation.

Soil Degradation

Soil quality is determined by the soil's physical structure, organic matter content, water-holding capacity, nutrient balances, depth, salinity, and acidity (Pretty and Hine 2001; Stocking 2003). Soil degradation refers primarily to reduced soil quality and decreased agricultural yields due to a loss of soil nutrients (soil mining), erosion, waterlogging, or salinization. Overgrazing, deforestation, and faulty agricultural practices, including soil mining and inappropriate water management, account for more than two-thirds of worldwide soil degradation since 1945 (de Haen 1997).

Soil degradation is widespread and severe in many locations. The estimates vary from 22 percent of the world's agricultural area (Bridges and Oldeman 2001) to 38 percent (Scherr 1999). Although wind and water erosion occur on uncultivated lands, the vast majority of soil erosion is caused by agricultural activities (see table 8.1). There are large yield losses at even low levels of soil losses because of the high value of topsoils (Stocking 2003).

Oldeman, Hakkeling, and Sombroek (1991) estimated that close to two-thirds of Africa's agricultural lands were degraded between 1945 and 1990 and that the degradation caused major yield losses on one-fifth of the land. The estimates of yield losses vary widely. Thus, Scherr (2000) estimates yield losses of 40 percent due to soil degradation in sub-Saharan Africa, and Jansky and Chandran (2004) estimate that land degradation reduces the value of sub-Saharan Africa's annual agricultural production by 3 percent. Soil erosion is also widespread in Latin America as shown in cases 8-1 and 8-2. To a large extent, soil degradation is caused or exacerbated by inadequate property rights; poverty; population pressures; inappropriate government policies; and lack of access to markets, credit, and technologies appropriate for sustainable agricultural development (Pinstrup-Andersen 2002a).

TABLE 8.1.
Causes of Soil Degradation, 1945–1995 (Percent)

Region	Deforestation	Overexploitation	Overgrazing	Agricultural activities
Europe	38	n/s	23	29
N. America	4	n/s	30	66
Central America	22	18	15	45
S. America	41	5	28	26
Africa	14	13	49	24
Asia	40	6	26	27
Oceania	12	n/s	80	8
World	30	7	35	28

Source: Pinstrup-Andersen and Pandya-Lorch 1994.
Note: n/s = not significant.

Plants need nutrients for growth. Soil mining occurs whenever more nutrient is taken out of a soil than is put back in over an appropriately defined cycle. When farmers are forced to ignore fallow periods or when organic or chemical fertilizers are insufficient to restore fertility or replace soil erosion, soil mining occurs. At high rates of soil mining, agricultural productivity can plummet and desertification can set in. Though it can take years and be expensive, soil mining is largely reversible.

The International Fertilizer Development Center (IFDC) estimates that 45 percent of sub-Saharan Africa's farmland loses 30 kg/ha in nutrients annually, and another 40 percent loses 60 kg/ha or more (Henao and Baanante 2001). The estimated losses vary from 9 kg/ha in Egypt to 90 kg/ha in Somalia. Land tenure issues, a lack of markets for agricultural land, and lack of fertilizers are the primary culprits. The reasons for low fertilizer use in SSA have been covered in chapter 7. Nkonya et al. (2008) estimated annual nutrient losses of 179 kg/ha in eight districts of Uganda. The value of fertilizers needed to replace these losses was estimated at one-fifth of the annual household incomes from agricultural production. While this is likely to be a larger expense than poor households can afford, these households can also scarce afford not to replace nutrients as continuation of such losses leads to falling productivity and increased future vulnerability.

This raises the question of whether efforts to maintain soil fertility can be considered a merit good, to be paid for or subsidized by governments. The answer would be yes only if there are societal costs or benefits over and beyond the costs or benefits captured by the farmer. Drechsel and de Vries (2001) estimate the cost of replenishing the lost nutrients in the soils of sub-Saharan Africa to be 7 percent of the value of the region's annual agricultural output. In view of the importance of increasing agricultural productivity in efforts to generate economic growth in sub-Saharan Africa, a case could be made for cost sharing between farmers and the public (chapter 7; Duflo, Kremer, and Robinson 2009). Alternatively, public investments in improved rural infrastructure, credit institutions, and domestic fertilizer markets might reduce fertilizer prices to the farmer and make public subsidies unnecessary.

While soil mining is common in sub-Saharan Africa, excessive fertilizer use causes environmental problems elsewhere. Overuse of fertilizer burns soils and pollutes water because the nutrients cannot all be absorbed by the plants. Vitousek et al. (2009, 1519) report that a "low-input corn-based system in Western Kenya in 2004–2005" resulted in soil mining to the tune of 52 kg/ha of nitrogen. A "highly fertilized wheat-corn double-cropping system in North China" resulted in an addition of 227 kg/ha of nitrogen. A negative environmental impact is likely in both cases.

Low-cost technologies already exist that can profitably reduce soil erosion by up to 90 percent, resulting in win-win strategies. Zero tillage methods leave the last crop as a cover for the next one, increasing water saturation, reducing soil erosion, and sequestering additional carbon while reducing the need for fertilizer. In Laos, zero tillage improved harvest productivity and reduced the number of days spent on crops significantly: twelve fewer days in field prep, fifty-three fewer weeding, twenty-two fewer planting the main cereal crop, and twenty-one fewer in harvest (Maglinao and Valentin 2003). Zero tillage methods may increase weed and pest problems in some cases, however.

Much land degradation is irreversible and may eventually result in desertification, although there are no reliable estimates of the extent of desertification. Haarsma et al. (2005) indicate there may be a trend toward greater rainfall in the Sahel over the last twenty years, increasing vegetation and reversing desertification. Such trends, however, only create additional marginal, fragile lands that will be very sensitive to use intensitivity.

Water Availability and Degradation

In addition to being an essential resource for the food system, water is essential for drinking, cooking, and sanitation and of critical importance for industry. Contrary to oil, which may be replaced by other energy sources, water is indispensable. Yet, with population growth and economic development, fresh water is becoming scarcer in many parts of the world. About 1.2 billion people live in places that are short of water (Lundqvist, de Fraiture, and Molden 2008). Depletion of groundwater, reduced surface water, changing rainfall patterns due to climate change, water pollution, and waste are closely related to the food system and influenced by government policies (Rosegrant, Cai, and Cline 2002).

Agricultural irrigation accounts for 80 percent of the world's and 86 percent of developing countries' fresh water consumption (Rosegrant, Cai, and Cline 2002). Use efficiency is low. A large share of irrigation water is lost to leaky irrigation channels, evaporation, and improper drainage.

Water subsidies and failure to internalize the scarcity value of water in private costs are among the prime causes of this waste. In places where farmers have to pay market prices similar to industry for the irrigation water they use, investments occur that significantly improve water efficiency, including drip irrigation, leak repair, and layers of mulch that improve seepage and reduce evaporation.

Even without market prices and with even low-technology irrigation projects built from mud, rock, and wood, community-based irrigation projects have been shown to improve agricultural yield and sustainability over nationally built and managed, concrete irrigation in Nepal (Lam 1998; Ostrom 1999). During Soviet times, farmers in Uzbekistan were given a fixed allocation of water. When they were free to choose how much water they needed, even without price controls, water usage dropped 30 percent (case 8-6). Abdullaev et al. (2009) discuss the importance of how trade policy affects Uzbekistan's agricultural water use.

The amount of water needed by 2050 is estimated to be 50–90 percent higher than current use, largely because of population growth and increasing demand for livestock products. Global meat production currently consumes 8 percent of the total consumption of fresh water (FAO 2006c) and is projected to at least double between 2000 and 2050 (Steinfeld et al. 2006). As shown in figure 8.1, each kg of beef requires 15,500 liters of water, compared to 3,900 for chicken and 900 for maize. If farmers needed to pay for the water they use, the cost of animal food products would increase relative to plants, encouraging consumers to move to a more environmentally friendly diet, which could also contribute to lowering obesity rates and chronic diseases.

As water becomes more scarce, and population growth and higher incomes cause demand to increase, the competition for available water among potential uses (e.g., household and industrial) will become stronger. Agriculture will be unable to maintain its current share and there will be stronger incentives for governments to change water policies to promote efficiency.

Where can additional water come from? The costs of dam construction and other efforts to develop new water sources for irrigation are increasing. The cost of seawater desalination is decreasing thanks to technological innovations and expanded production that capture economies of scale (Solomon 2010). Its use may be economically viable for high-value crops in areas near the sea (Yermiyahu et al. 2007).

FIGURE 8.1.
Liters of water per kilogram of product. Source: Waterfootprint (A. Y. Hoekstra and A. K. Chapagain, at http://www.waterfootprint.org).

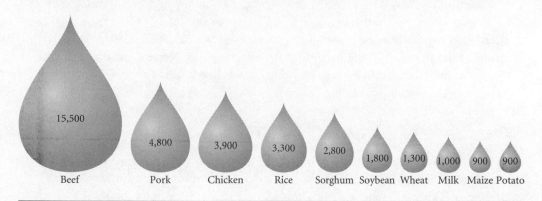

While bottled drinking water is transported over long distances to meet consumer demand, the transportation cost of water for irrigation over long distances is still prohibitive for most localities. With so few options, increasing water-use efficiency is essential.

Climate change is likely to add to the uncertainties about the future water situation. The UN Intergovernmental Panel on Climate Change (2007) recently predicted that 3 billion people—half the world's current population—could face a shortage of clean water by 2080 because of climate change. Changing weather patterns caused by climate change will change seasonal and regional water availability, with positive and negative impact on food systems.

A Turkish proverb says that "when one man drinks, while another can only watch, doomsday follows" (Solomon 2010, 412). Water shortages and increasing competition may result in conflicts within and between nations, and result in "water wars" (Cooley 1984; Gleick 1993). Wolf (1998, 262) concludes on the basis of a review of the evidence that only one war was ever fought over water and that was "between the Sumerian city-states of Lagash and Umma" 4,500 years ago. He also concludes, however, that lack of fresh water has caused political instability and violence, the latter mostly within individual countries. There is therefore more concern about intranational "water conflicts" than international "water wars."

In designing more effective systems, it should be kept in mind that farmers tend to perceive surface water and groundwater differently (Gill 1995). Farmers treat surface water as common property, and since competition is easily seen, communities create conflict resolution institutions. Groundwater is treated as private property, and of infinite supply. Because competition between farmers is unseen, negative externalities are rarely dealt with.

Improper irrigation and drainage techniques can raise the groundwater table, preventing needed oxygen from reaching plant roots (waterlogging), and/or leave large salt deposits in soils as water evaporates instead of being properly channeled away (salinization). This can cut yields severely and decimate incomes (Pinstrup-Andersen and Pandya-Lorch 1994). Bridges and Oldeman (2001) estimate that 15 percent of the earth's arable land is at least minimally degraded due to salinization and waterlogging, 2 percent to an extreme level and 3 percent enough to reduce food productivity.

Salinization and waterlogging are largely avoidable through technical or management solutions. On the farmer side, more irrigation water is often used than is needed, primarily because water is free or available at very low costs. More care needs to be taken in constructing irrigation projects to reduce seepage from canals and improve drainage. Gersfelt (case 8-4) discusses policy options and their efficiency and distributional implications.

Chemical Contamination and Agroecological Farming Methods

There are four main approaches to pest control: host-plant resistance (the plant is resistant to a particular pest either by nature or as a result of agricultural research), biological control measures (maintaining a balance between pests and their natural enemies), ecological production systems (employing production systems that reduce losses from pests), and chemical pesticides. Oerke (2005) estimates that global crop losses due to pests are about 29 percent of total production. He further estimates that pest control measures by farmers brought the losses down from a potential loss of 50 percent. The use of pesticides, including herbicide and fungicide, increased 12 percent per year during the 1960s, though the growth rate fell to 3–4 percent by the early 1990s (Pinstrup-Andersen and Pandya-Lorch 1994).

Implicit and explicit government subsidies have encouraged indiscriminate overapplication as a form of insurance in Asia and some OECD members (Pinstrup-Andersen and Schiøler 2000; Nelson 2010). In addition to improved seed varieties, much of the initial yield gains and reductions in production risks during the green revolution stemmed from a significant increase in pesticide applications. However, subsequent research on the development of host-plant pest resistance has dramatically reduced the needs for pesticides in rice and other crops. Private sector research has also successfully developed host-plant resistance. Thus, the use of Bt cotton seed developed by Monsanto reduced the use of pesticides by 80 percent in China, 77 percent in Mexico, 58 percent in South Africa, 47 percent in Argentina, and 39 percent in India (James 2009; chapter 10). Biological control measures have also been successful in several cases and improved integrated ecological production methods show great promise (Nelson 2010).

Indiscriminate pesticide use kills pests' predators, reducing the natural boundaries against pests. Because it is nearly impossible to fully eradicate any given pest, the pests that survive gradually build up immunity, forcing the creation of stronger or different pesticides. Overuse can also threaten local biodiversity, though as it is very difficult to fully eradicate the pests being targeted, it would seem equally unlikely that other animals and plants are made extinct.

The job of applying chemical pesticides and the pesticide residues in food threaten serious health risks for workers and consumers. Paoletti and Pimentel (2000, 279) report that the "use of pesticides for pest control results in an estimated 26 million human poisonings, with 220,000 fatalities, annually worldwide." Thus, decisions about plant protection methods are complicated by significant trade-offs: failure to protect crops may have severe income, nutrition, and health consequences, while the use of chemical pesticides may result in important health and environmental risks.

Alternatives to chemical pesticides, such as integrated or biological pest control, are knowledge intensive and may be difficult for the farmer to manage, while the development of host-plant resistance requires research for which funding is lacking or, in the case of the use of genetic engineering, may confront popular resistance (chapters 10 and 11).

Policies to incorporate the social costs from overuse of fertilizer (discussed above) and pesticides into private production costs and training in the timeliest fashion to apply fertilizer would be expected to reduce these environmental problems.

Organic production methods (chapter 7) use no chemical fertilizers or inorganic pesticides, do not permit the use of genetically modified seed and animals, and follow specified cultivation practices such as composting and crop rotation. While they are an attempt to assure sustainable NRM, composting and animal waste on intercropped organic farms are insufficient to fully replenish soils, forcing farmers to "import" nutrients onto the farm from other sources. Nitrogen fixation by legumes from the air can play an important role, but other plant nutrients such as phosphorous may still have to be obtained from chemical fertilizers. Green manure offers another source of plant nutrients and organic material for the soil but this requires reallocation of land, water, and labor away from food production or other household uses.

One of the concerns about organic production is that the yield per hectare—although higher than in most traditional systems in developing countries—tends to be lower than that obtainable using modern techniques and inputs. This lower yield in developed countries means that organically produced food tends to cost more and organic systems' economic sustainability is dependent on consumers being willing to pay a premium. Full-costing methods (discussed below) penalize negative externalities and pay for positive ones, reducing and possibly eliminating the cost disadvantage for commodities that can be more sustainably produced.

Is the goal to be organic for the sake of being organic, or is the goal to promote the long-term environmental sustainability of a food system that provides food for human health and well-being? Full-costing would increase the sustainability of food processes, irrespective of whether they comply with the narrow definitions of "organically produced" existing in the European Union and the United States. These definitions and the related certification requirements are ideological, political, and arbitrary from a sustainability perspective. What is important is that natural and regenerative processes are integrated (Pretty and Hine 2001). This may include nutrient cycling, nitrogen fixing, soil regeneration, and protection of natural enemies of pests.

Organic production methods, which by definition do not permit the use of inorganic pesticides and chemical fertilizers, may result in soil mining, large losses due to pests, and low yields. A more pragmatic approach to sustainable food production would achieve the stated goals for sustainable farming methods and meet future food demand by promoting the use of modern science, including genetic engineering to increase yields; protecting the environment and reducing risks; and permitting the use of inorganic fertilizers when needed as well as timely, limited use of pesticides to reduce health risks from microtoxins (chapter 3).

Biodiversity

In an agricultural setting, biodiversity includes not only the natural flora and fauna found in an area but also the additional species that have been bred or genetically modified by humans. One of the important tasks the international research organizations in the CGIAR system have undertaken is the preservation of many indigenous species in situ and ex situ in gene banks.[2] Preserving these species has led to important discoveries, such as twenty unique genes from the Silent Valley in India that can be used to improve disease and pest resistance in rice (Bridges and Oldeman 2001).

The global food system relies in particular on soil biodiversity. Microorganisms in the soil can break down pollutants, recycle plant material into soil nutrients, oxygenate the soil, and reduce the prevalence of diseases and pathogens. Overuse of broad-spectrum pesticides can harm this essential part of the agroecosystem.

Recent agricultural production expansions have focused on monocropping: the use of only one crop—and often only one variety of that crop—over large areas. While this allows large economies of scale, it has also left the food sector vulnerable to potential pest epidemics. A wider genetic base can protect against this. Research by Herforth (2010a) shows a positive causal relationship between crop diversity and dietary diversity, the latter being critically important for nutrition. With proper policy incentives, farmers can be active partners in supporting biological and crop diversity, thereby improving nutrition.

Biodiversity may be an important part of a risk management strategy (Birol, Kontoleon, and Smale 2005). Even if the pests harmed one crop variety, farmers wouldn't be wiped out. As high-yielding varieties of selected crops become available, it may be necessary for governments to provide incentives to safeguard their national biodiversity. Governments could provide farmers with cash incentives to follow agrobiodiversity-preserving techniques, which would be less distorting to production than production-linked subsidies.

Bioenergy

Firewood, charcoal, crop residues, manure, and other biomass are the most important sources of energy for the majority of the rural poor in developing countries, particularly for the poorest (Karekezi and Kithyoma 2006). Population growth and other sources of increasing bioenergy demand have contributed to severe deforestation, land degradation, and increases in greenhouse gas (GHG) emission in many developing countries (Ogg 2009). Furthermore, according to Kammen (2006), pollutants from biomass fuels cause very serious health problems and large numbers of deaths every year.

Production of liquid bioenergy—biofuel—has gained much attention in response to rapidly increasing fossil fuel prices during 2006–2008, increasing fuel price volatility, concerns about GHG emission, and attempts to develop alternative income sources for farmers. Global biofuel production in the form of ethanol and biodiesel—most of which is based on sugarcane, sugar beets, maize, soybeans, rapeseed, and palm—tripled during 2000–2007 (Coyle 2007). Other potential sources include nuts from jatropha trees, algae, and animal waste. Case 7-8 discusses a specific case of bioenergy production in India. The net energy and GHG balance in biofuel production and distribution varies according to the biomass used and the processing approach, but energy used is generally slightly less than the energy produced. However, the net balance of GHG emission may be negative if all sources are considered, including transportation (Fargione et al. 2008; Scharlemann and Laurance 2008).

Unlike energy derived from fossil fuel, energy from biomass may be renewable if the resources used for its production are managed appropriately. Bioenergy production competes with food production for access to land, water, labor, and other inputs. The result is likely to be increasing food prices. Von Braun et al. (2008) estimate that about one-third of the large food price increase that occurred during 2007–2008 was due to the expansion of biofuel production on land that was removed from food production.

Hazell (2006) suggests six ways to reduce the trade-off between biofuel and food production. First, develop high-efficiency bioenergy crops (i.e., high energy yields per input); second, breed food crops with large amounts of by-products that could serve as a source for biofuel (e.g., corn husks); third, use less-favored areas that are not well suited for food production; fourth, enhance research to develop economically sound approaches to the production of biofuel on the basis of cellulose-rich biomass; fifth, increase food crop yields to free up land and water for biofuel production; and sixth, remove barriers to international trade in biofuels. Effective biofuel policies should integrate policies to protect ecosystems and reduce GHG with policies to support food security and improve health and rural incomes.

One of the key policy considerations is the close coupling of energy markets and food markets through competition for common resources, which has implications for food prices and food security. Since biofuels account for a very small portion of total energy consumption, relative oil/food prices that favor the use of common resources such as land, water, and labor for biofuel production over food production open up an almost unlimited demand for biofuel and opportunities for large increases in returns to these resources. This, together with expected high food prices and desires for more control over food and fuel supplies by middle-income food-deficit countries, is causing widespread interest by multinational corporations and governments to acquire control over land in low-income countries for the production of biofuel and food.

Climate Change and the Food System

Climate change may affect the food system through changing temperatures, higher atmospheric greenhouse gas concentration, changing rainfall patterns, and greater volatility in weather patterns. Temperature changes affect the quantity and pattern of rainfall, evaporation, and temperature ranges. Rainfall and evaporation affect soil moisture, water management, plant and animal health, and pest attacks, which, together with altered heat maxima, may amplify or reduce existing biotic and abiotic stresses and introduce new ones. Changes in such stresses affect yields, the conditions of natural resources, and the degree to which the food system is sustainable. GHG emissions increase the atmospheric CO_2 concentration, which, in turn, may increase yields. Increasing volatility in weather patterns, with more severe adverse weather events, could cause more droughts, floods, forceful downpours, and strong winds, all of which will reduce yields, increase production risks, and damage natural resources, not to mention the increase in risks associated with loss of life and property damage.

There is considerable uncertainty about how the food system is going to be affected by climate change over time, not least because nature and humans will try to adapt to the changing circumstances. In the first case (figure 8.2), an increase in a particular activity (e.g., livestock production) causes a proportional increase in environmental degradation (e.g., methane production). In the second, the costs of polluting activities may increase the more harm is done, a more than proportional effect (e.g., low levels of chemical pesticide application have few effects on human health, but the negative effects can ratchet up rapidly). The buildup of consequences may also result in a stepwise impact in which a relatively slow linear impact will periodically be replaced by a much steeper impact (e.g. expansion of extractive industries into new sites). In the last case, environmental costs are initially very low but reach a critical threshold when further actions produce significant, potentially irreparable harm (e.g., loss of biodiversity leading to extinction). Some actions contain features of each, such as having no effect at low levels followed by quadratic increases after a certain threshold. The scariest scenario is the one with a future tipping point as shown in figure 8.2.

Because food and ecosystems are highly complex, the impact of climate change on the future food system is very difficult to estimate and existing estimates are highly tentative. However, there is general agreement that crop yields will decrease in tropical regions and increase by roughly the same amount in temperate zones (e.g., Parry et al. 2004; Cline 2007). If the estimates turn out to be correct, climate change will enhance the already existing maldistribution of available food between rich and poor countries. Furthermore, Cline (2007) projects large intracountry differences, particularly in large countries spanning several agroecological zones. Based on past experience, large-scale redistribution of food from surplus to deficient areas is not

FIGURE 8.2.
Hypothetical patterns of negative impact of climate change on agriculture. Prepared by authors.

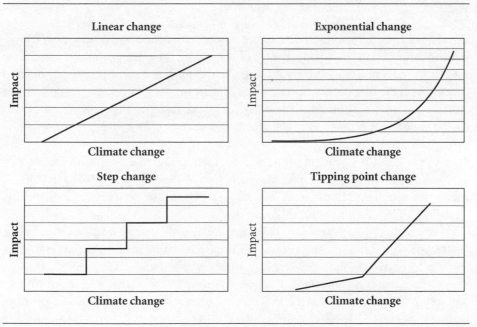

likely to take place. A more likely scenario is increasing prevalence of hunger in deficit regions and obesity in surplus areas, particularly if governments enact price controls or antitrade (domestic or international) policies.

Projections of climate change's impact on hunger vary widely: from 5 million to 170 million additional people at risk of hunger by 2080 (Schmidhuber and Tubiello 2007). Morton (2007) concludes that the rural poor are particularly vulnerable to the negative aspects of climate change partly because they are mostly in tropical areas and partly because they have limited capacity to adapt. However, he also stresses that smallholder farmers in fragile environments have adopted livelihood strategies to reduce overall vulnerability to climate shocks as well as coping strategies to deal with the impact ex post. While the international debate about climate change has intensified during the last few years, smallholders in fragile environments have lived with climate risks for as long as they have farmed. Their adaptation and coping mechanisms—risk management—include income and crop diversification, integrated livestock-crop production systems, on-farm storage, and reduced use of credit and purchased inputs (chapter 7).

According to IPCC (2007), agriculture contributes more than a quarter of all global greenhouse gas emissions, compared to the sector's 4 percent contribution to the global GNP. This compares to industry's 19 percent and transport's 13 percent contribution to GHG emissions (IPCC 2007). The five largest sources are the removal of forest cover, methane from cattle and manure, timber burning, rice production, and fertilizer production. Land tillage and other food production activities involving the use of carbon-based energy are also important sources, as is energy use in postharvest activities such as processing, storage, and transportation.

Food Miles

There is an increasing interest among consumers and advocacy groups, primarily in high-income countries, to consume locally produced food. In addition to arguments related to freshness, traceability, and relative food safety risks, the concept of food miles is being used to justify the emphasis on consumption of food that is produced close to where it is consumed. "Food miles"—the distance that food travels from the farm before it is finally consumed—are used as an indicator of GHG emissions through transportation.

However, recent research questions the widely accepted assumption that locally produced food has few environmental costs (see case 6-10). It is during agricultural production itself and home storage that most of the natural resource damage, including GHG emissions, occurs (Olesen 2008).

Assessments by Pretty et al. (2005) for the UK and Saunders, Barber, and Taylor (2006) for New Zealand demonstrate the importance of considering the total environmental costs of food in a systems approach, rather than isolating transportation. The former paper demonstrates that the environmental externalities from import and export of food are dwarfed by the environmental costs of domestic production out of season. The latter similarly shows that the total energy use—and the associated GHG emission—of producing food in New Zealand and shipping it to the UK is 30 percent lower for onions, 40 percent lower for apples, 50 percent for dairy, and 75 percent for lamb. That is, the New Zealand food system is much more efficient in environmental terms than the British system, so that even when accounting for the environmental impact of transporting food from New Zealand to the UK, it is more environmentally friendly for the UK to import the food products studied when they are not in season in the UK.

According to Coley, Howard, and Winter (2008, 154), "The food consumer is not confronted simply with a choice between 'local-good' and 'global-bad.'" On the basis of their research results, they conclude that "the concept of food miles, as typically used, is of little value per se and that it is carbon emission per unit of produce over the transport chain that really matters." They recommend that the concept of "food miles" be replaced by carbon accounting life cycle assessments. On the basis of an analysis of the U.S. food supply, Weber and Matthews (2008) come to a similar conclusion.

Trade economists have worried that the focus on food miles could be simply used as another form of agricultural trade distortion (chapter 10). There have been few mentions of the environmental impact of "furniture miles," for instance, even though concerns about the environmental impact of international trade should focus on all trade and not just food. The ideal is neither to try to limit all production to the geographical area where it is consumed nor to maximize international trade, but rather to include environmental costs in determining where goods may be most efficiently produced. Including the environmental costs of production, processing, and transport in the price of foods and other tradable products would soon lead the market to appropriately allocate production where it is most efficient. It would enlighten the debate about globalization versus national self-sufficiency and it would specifically help guide the debate about locally produced food.

GHG emissions depend on the food commodity produced. Livestock production is a major source of GHG emission, estimated by FAO to contribute 18 percent of all GHG when measured in CO_2 equivalent (Steinfeld et al. 2006). Olesen (2008) reports that each milk cow produces about twice as much CO_2 equivalent per kilocalorie of food as a sow and more than four times as much as many crops (table 8.2). Other large farm animals, such as dairy buffalo in India, are seldom mentioned but produce large amounts of methane as well. Full-costing would increase the price of beef relative to plant-based foods and bring private costs closer to social costs.

Positive Effects and Responses to Climate Change

Food systems contribute to global warming. They may also be part of the solution. Agriculture and forestry capture GHG by sequestering carbon. Reforestation and changes in agricultural production toward more ground cover, perennials, and conservation tillage are examples of activities that may help capture additional GHG from the atmosphere and reduce emissions. As mentioned above, biofuel production may also be helpful in the fight against climate change if it reduces fossil fuel consumption.

TABLE 8.2.
Climate Impact of Foodstuffs

Food in supermarket	CO_2 kg equivalent per 1 MJ
Beef	1.47
Firm cheese	0.84
Low-fat milk	0.59
Pork	0.46
Chicken, whole, fresh	0.41
Eggs	0.31
Onions	0.20
Rye bread, fresh	0.09
Wheat flour	0.08
Carrots	0.08
White bread, fresh	0.07
Potatoes	0.06
Oatmeal	0.05

Source: Olesen 2008.
Note: 1 megajoule (MJ) is roughly 239 kilocalories.

Policies and programs to reduce the negative effects of climate change on the food system may attempt either to reduce and prevent climate change or to adapt and cope with the negative effects of climate change that has happened. Carbon sequestration, emission reduction during rice cultivation or animal production, and improvement of land management fall into the first group. Research to develop crop varieties with higher yield response to high CO_2 concentration in the atmosphere or that tolerate or resist drought, periodic floods, saline soil conditions, and pests brought about by climate change and species are examples of action that would help the food system adapt. Coping mechanisms would include safety net programs of various kinds, including those discussed in chapters 4 and 5, and risk management policies (chapter 7).

Poverty, Hunger, and Sustainability Goals: Trade-Offs and Policy Implications

Two sets of trade-offs are of policy importance in the context of this chapter. First, if the global food system is to meet increasing demands for food and nonfood agricultural commodities on the basis of a fixed or falling stock of natural capital, substitution between natural and human-made resources must take place.

Second, trade-offs between sustainability goals and other food system goals must be considered. Does sustainable NRM imply that no degradation of the stock of natural capital must take place, even if the degradation is reversible and can be rectified at a later time? Or does sustainability refer to the capability of the total capital (natural, human, physical, financial, and social) to meet future demands? This raises several other important policy questions, some of which are of an ethical nature (chapter 11). Do natural resources, such as a beautiful landscape or a rare bird, have intrinsic values that cannot be compensated for by human-made capital, or should these resources be considered merely as part of the total input into the economic growth process? Must the stock of natural resources be maintained at any cost, or can some be forgone and replaced with human-made resources? If natural and human-made resources are highly substitutable, then imposing strict conservation restrictions could actually reduce sustainability and future growth (Ruttan 1997).

An analysis of the trade-offs between the goals of expanding food availability, reducing poverty and hunger, and maintaining a sustainable productive capacity must specify a time frame. If the trade-off is between reducing hunger and poverty now versus sustainability for the foreseeable future, the question becomes one of comparing the welfare of current versus future generations. The social discount rate or time preference becomes important as well. Should hunger and child death today receive a higher social value than hunger and child death fifty or a hundred years from now? Like many of the other questions raised in this section of the chapter, this is an ethical question without a unique answer (chapter 11).

It could be the case that improving the welfare of people today is the most important part of the foundation for higher future welfare (e.g., improving mothers' nutrition in order to improve their infants' health). Some ethical traditions further regard a person's relative sphere of influence to be important in determining responsibility. The further in the future we are considering, the less direct influence any one person can wield and hence the less responsibility. A food system based on natural resource degradation is prioritizing current generations over future ones, unless the degradation is fully compensated by enhanced efficiency of natural resources and/ or human-made resources.

Rapid yield increases caused by the green revolution undoubtedly provided such compensation for damage done to soils by protecting forested and fragile soils and by an increasing economic surplus generated by higher yields. It is less likely that the damage done to water resources was fully compensated. A full-costing approach would surely have placed more emphasis on improved water use efficiency. Furthermore, while the damage done to soils may have been compensated in terms of net social gains, the compensation has not been used to rectify the damage. This is an important consideration in full-costing. Unless the revenues from higher consumer prices that reflect the cost of damage to the productive capacity are actually allocated to cancel out the damage, future generations will still be subsidizing the living standards of current generations and productive capacity will not be protected. Full-costing will assure sustainability only if revenues are used to protect or enhance productive capacity.

One of the key questions deals with the time horizon used by decision makers. Market advocates have generally assumed that the people who work the land have very long time horizons, particularly if they have clear land tenure and the land market is functioning well. If they don't internalize the future costs of their environmental activities, they or their children will be the ones to pay the price. Certain indigenous cultures have also placed long time horizons as a characteristic ideal.

Supporters of greater government intervention argue that private individuals and corporations have short time horizons resulting in very high discount rates. Therefore, future generations, which by their absence cannot be active stakeholders in current policy decisions, must be represented by self-appointed, enlightened, forward-looking, current stakeholders that will guide policy action by current governments.

Governments' commitment to environmental stewardship cannot be taken for granted. If politicians or bureaucrats expect to remain in power for an extensive period of time, they may internalize the needs of stakeholders over a longer time horizon or they may feel protected and give less attention to long-term issues. If they look forward only to the next election cycle, their effectiveness as environmental guardians should certainly be questioned. It is worth noting that events of great environmental damage have occurred in impoverished developing countries, in the relatively more free-market United States, in totalitarian USSR and Germany, and in the modern social democracies of Europe.

The Environmental Kuznets Curve and Full-Costing

Must policies to achieve the dual goals of poverty alleviation and sustainable NRM necessarily confront trade-offs between the two, or are there policies that can achieve one without sacrificing the other? Can poverty alleviation be achieved only at the expense of natural resources and sustainability, or are win-win strategies possible? Knox, Meinzen-Dick, and Hazell (2002, 33) state that concerns about trade-offs are "perhaps overstated." Most poor people live in ecologically vulnerable areas, and "environmental risks go hand-in-hand with socio-economic deprivation," implying no trade-off between the two (Songsore and McGranahan 1993, 33). However, Vosti and Reardon (1997, 64) conclude that "reducing poverty will not necessarily protect the environment, nor will protecting the environment necessarily alleviate poverty."

Therefore, policy advice should be context specific and based on a thorough understanding of the nature of local poverty and environmental problems and how they interact. The environment-poverty trap hypothesis supports not only the notion that poverty causes natural resource degradation but the idea that poverty and degradation enter into a vicious cycle (Nkonya et al. 2008). By reducing their stock of natural capital to survive, the poor are likely to have a lower average income in the future and be even more susceptible to future negative shocks. As their environment becomes ever more degraded, their opportunities to lift themselves out of poverty continue to diminish, particularly when poverty feeds back into greater environmental degradation (e.g., Sahelian agro-pastoralists in Barrett 2008).

Even the rural poor who are not in an environment-poverty trap may engage in unsustainable behavior to reduce their poverty, hunger, and other human suffering. People facing very severe risks such as hunger and death would be expected to employ very high discount rates in their behavior. This is supported by evidence from a survey of several studies undertaken by Nkonya et al. (2008, 13), who conclude that "poor rural households discount the future heavily." Cutting down trees on sloping land, which may erode within a few years, may be the best option available to grow enough food to fight hunger in the short term.

In such situations, win-wins are possible only with external intervention. Access to plant nutrients, improved crop varieties, better market access, access to credit and risk insurance and primary health care are examples of such interventions. Triple wins are possible when poor farmers in areas with soil mining get access to fertilizers or improved crop varieties or both. Food production increases, poverty is reduced or eliminated, and the soils are improved.

The existing literature on the relationship between incomes and environmental degradation seems to overlook such relationships. Instead, it tends to focus on the traditional environmental Kuznets curve (EKC) illustrated in figure 8.3, which assumes that increasing incomes result in more degradation at lower income levels, while shifting to a win-win scenario of declining degradation at higher incomes.

Grossman and Krueger (1995) have proposed and demonstrated that, at least for some environmental indicators such as air and water pollutants, the relationship between economic growth and environmental degradation does form such an inverted U. In the early stages of development, it was hypothesized, scale effects tended to dominate, implying that increasing production leads to increasing degradation. Beyond the tipping points that they estimated as occurring well before \$8,000 per capita, the changing composition of the economy and technological progress dominate, reducing the environmental harm associated with economic growth.

Grossman and Krueger (1995) argue that this relationship is not an automatic or natural process but a policy response: as incomes increase beyond a certain level, citizens demand more environmentally conscious policies and products, which in turn prompt technological innovation that uses natural resources more efficiently. Bulte, Damania, and López (2007) show that this is not the only possible development path: wealthy farmers may trade political contributions for subsidies that

FIGURE 8.3.
The environmental Kuznets curve. Prepared by authors.

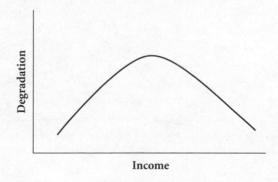

encourage environmentally harmful, inefficient agricultural practices, as they find for nine Latin American countries. Andreoni and Levinson (2001) demonstrate that the inverted-U correlation can also result simply from there being increasing returns to pollution abatement technologies or large fixed costs to their adoption.

On the basis of reviews of the empirical literature on the EKC, Webber and Allen (2004) and Lee, Chiu, and Sun (2009) conclude that the shape of the relationship between pollutants and income per capita is not uniform across pollutants. This implies that each measure of environmental quality needs to be considered separately. Ehrhardt-Martinez, Crenshaw, and Jenkins (2002, 240) find evidence that deforestation followed an inverted U from 1980 to 1995 based on changing rates of urbanization, changing importance of service industries, and the emergence of democratic processes. They conclude that this "points to the possibility of combining development with policies and forest practices that slow deforestation, perhaps creating environmental sustainability alongside development." In other words, win-wins are possible.

The following discussion is focused on deforestation and soil mining, two important elements of environmental quality on which agricultural activities have a strong impact. Keeping in mind that about 75 percent of the world's poor live in rural areas and that about half live in marginal areas with poor soils, irregular rainfall, and poor infrastructure, we hypothesize that the relationship between deforestation and income may be described as having a sideways-S relationship with income, such as that depicted in figure 8.4.

The concept in stage 1 is that the combination of numerous factors—poverty, an increasing population on fixed land constraints, lack of technologies that would produce sufficient food without damaging the environment, and particularly negative shocks (e.g., drought, illness)—places enough immediate pressure on poor people to leave them few options for survival that do not involve weakening their resource

FIGURE 8.4.
Hypothetical relationships between income and deforestation/soil mining. Prepared by authors.

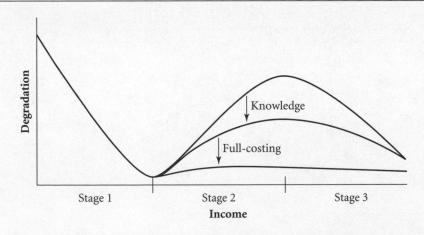
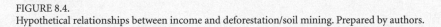

base. It is in this context that Pinstrup-Andersen and Pandya-Lorch (1994) identified absolute poverty as the most serious cause of environmental degradation. Poverty forces them to eat their seed corn, as it were, in the form of deforestation, soil
mining, and unsustainable water management.

The first stage of the sideways-S function implies win-win possibilities. Efforts to
reduce poverty may reduce the need and desire by the poor to engage in unsustainable behavior. Safety nets and input provision programs help lower the curve so that
less environmental damage occurs at low levels of income while simultaneously alleviating or reducing poverty (moving along the curve to the right). Pro-poor development policies, such as research and technology to enhance agricultural productivity
on small farms, reduce deforestation and the expansion of agriculture into marginal lands and resulting soil degradation. Granja e Barros, Mendonça, and Nogueira
(2002) found evidence that focusing on reducing poverty and providing education
and other social capital assets to the poor could create similar win-win outcomes.

As farmers become better off and move into stage 2, they may get access to markets and chemical inputs and engage in practices that result in increasing degradation and/or increase their consumption of natural resources, unless they are asked
to pay the costs of such degradation (full-costing). That explains the top curve of
the second stage of the graph. As communities further improve their material well-
being, forces mentioned above in the standard EKC literature increase the priority
of sustainable resource management, thus resulting in stage 3. Research into cleaner,
more efficient technologies and increasing consumer awareness can lower the EKC.
Full-costing in addition can lower the curve even further because the cost of polluting activities increases with the damage they do—perhaps eliminating degradation
altogether.

There is some evidence for this first shift downward. The shape of the EKC for the
water and air pollutants that have been studied has been shown to shift downward
over time. Lomborg (2001) demonstrates that the peak level of environmental degradation occurring in developing country metropolises is significantly lower than
the past peak seen in developed countries' metropolises, although not necessarily occurring at an earlier level of development. This could occur because of the increased
spread and availability of environmentally friendly technology and international
public goods, increased political pressure from the international community, or a
decrease in the costs of acquiring financing for environmental projects. The green
revolution, for instance, greatly reduced the demand for agricultural land, reducing thereby the rate of deforestation with economic growth. These changes, labeled
"Knowledge" in figure 8.4, represent improvements in the trade-off between growth
and the environment.

Much degradation still occurs, however, because private costs and social costs are
not properly aligned. Full-costing would further reduce the environmental costs of
economic growth: farmers would not overuse fertilizers, pesticides, or water because
they would pay the full social costs of using these inputs, they would not mine the
soil because it would not be economical for them to do so, and deforestation of
indigenous trees would slow as consumers of wood products pay the full costs of
environmental damage. The lowest curve in figure 8.4 illustrates such a scenario.

In order to ideally study these hypotheses empirically, data would need to be aggregated by community rather than by nation in order to capture the far left portion of the relationship between environmental degradation and poverty. It should be noted that the data sets most prevalently used in the EKC literature are unable to address these issues because of their focus on different environmental issues, such as particles of air pollution that are not likely to be produced by the extremely poor.

Policy Options to Maintain Sustainable Use of Natural Resources

Full-Costing

This book maintains that full-costing would be the most effective way to assure sustainability. Full-costing involves aligning private costs and benefits with social costs and benefits. The first half, aligning costs, is known as the "polluter pays" (PP) principle while the second half is called "payment for environmental services" (PES). In addition to incentivizing changes in the behavior of farmers, consumers, and other food system agents, full-costing would induce innovation in product, research, and technology development and public policy. Vehicles for implementing full-costing include CO_2 or other green taxes and subsidies, water pricing, tiered fertilizer pricing, and payment for land restoration or reforestation, and payments for other environmental services.

Just as with environmental regulation, full-costing requires effective government enforcement, but has the advantage that firms also have incentive to police their suppliers. To the extent that private incentives can be brought into line with social marginal costs and benefits, an environmentally and economically efficient solution can be achieved by market forces. It has the advantage over direct regulation that it allows entrepreneurs to search for the most efficient means of lowering environmental costs, which may differ between firms or industries and would not be readily apparent to the bureaucratic authority.

The PP principle entices firms to proactively find the least environmentally damaging solution while direct regulation can only reactively stamp out individual fires. For example, it was discovered in the 1980s that chlorofluorocarbons (CFCs) found in many aerosol products reduced the ozone layer. CFCs were summarily banned in many countries and the ozone has as a result begun to recover. However, it has only recently been determined that the replacement technology creates more global warming than the CFCs did.

PES does the same thing for the positive externalities created by the food system, paying farmers and other food system actors for preserving biodiversity, water quality, and landscape beauty and for sequestering carbon. Transparency and tracking technologies are becoming increasingly widespread, making it more feasible for companies to certify that their products are organically produced or their livestock were treated with higher standards of animal welfare (chapter 11).

If agricultural activities harm the environment in a roughly linear fashion, a simple tax on production can achieve full-costing. Simple taxes will not solve problems that increase quadratically or that have threshold effects (see figure 8.2 above). They may harm the poor (at low levels of activity) while providing insufficient conservation incentive at high levels of income. Instead, more inventive tax schedules or taxes with rebates for poor households need to be considered (see Hellegers, Schoengold, and Zilberman 2008 and Bontems 2008 for details).

Dellink and Ruijs (2008) have argued that both PP and PES can be followed within the same system, but that it is critical to get appropriate threshold levels to determine whether the stick (PP) or the carrot (PES) is the proper instrument. In either regime, they stress that it is important that compensation (punishment) should be large enough to encourage action, but not larger than the social benefit (cost).

Policies to reduce unsustainable agricultural water use are urgently needed. Possibilities include removal of unsustainable and inefficient water subsidies, water pricing, water markets, and allocation of water by collective action. Public support of sustainable production methods in the form of additional research and knowledge dissemination deserves priority.

Implementation of Full-Costing: Difficulties to Overcome

There are several difficulties in applying the full-costing approach. The most important is whether the approach is politically and technologically feasible. Are governments and the stakeholder groups supporting them ready to move toward equating private and social costs? Second, the estimates of environmental costs differ widely, from the catastrophic to the negligible. Solid research is needed to sort out the varying claims and come to a true consensus of the costs involved.

A third difficulty is that it is hard to enforce penalties on the poorest individuals who damage natural resources, both because they are poorly integrated into markets and government outreach and because of the problematic ethics of punishing the absolutely poor. A positive approach to subsidize behavior that would lead to positive environmental effects, such as fertilizer subsidies that reduce or eliminate soil mining, might be more appropriate. A fourth difficulty is that the environmental science literature has seldom dealt with the issue of whether certain systems are better approximated as being linear, quadratic, or affected by significant threshold effects, as already discussed.

Property Rights

Open access to natural resources is likely to result in the unsustainable use of those resources, referred to as the tragedy of the commons (Hardin 1968).[3] The lesson is that sustainable NRM will occur only when the agent that uses or rents out the resource also will be held accountable for the consequences of such use. Appropriate property rights institutions are of critical importance (Tiffen, Mortimore, and Gichuki 1994).

Three primary forms of property rights are possible: private property, state property, and communal property. Though each can potentially be used to organize

resources in a more sustainable manner, several preconditions are necessary to ensure that they function as intended.

Private property rights can be highly effective in preserving ecosystems while
achieving the other goals of the food system. Farmers with a long-term interest in
the land and its resources for their future needs will most likely be able to identify
the trade-offs over which they have control and sustainably manage their property.
Full-costing measures provide incentives for property owners to internalize social
costs to reduce negative externalities, and effective extension services can improve
farmer knowledge of sustainable technologies.

However, this presupposes a well functioning land market and that landowners
have a long-term interest in the land. One of the primary concerns about private
property systems is that farmers may be induced to sell their property rights to,
for example, an MNC whose primary interest is to exploit the land for short-term
profits.

Though it is often assumed that state ownership and management of land resources
can effectively resolve the tragedy of the commons, state-managed lands have often
fallen to some of the worst degraded states (Pinstrup-Andersen and Pandya-Lorch
1994; Gill 1995). The Volga River became so polluted during Soviet times that ships
had to carry a sign informing passengers not to throw cigarettes overboard because
the water was flammable. Cases 8-6 and 7-9 illustrate how policies by the former
Soviet Union to promote irrigated cotton production caused environmental disasters
in central Asia. Further, if the regulatory authority is captured by the businesses it is
supposed to regulate, little good may be accomplished, and if the state is unable to
properly control a region, state ownership can be equivalent to open access.

Community property is not synonymous with open access. Gill (1995) and Dellink and Ruijs (2008) cite numerous case studies where communal organizations
have established institutions that prevent the overuse of resources while ensuring
an equitable distribution of benefits. The cases where state property management
has not failed in south Asia were because de facto resource management was under
community control (Gill 1995). However, it requires a high degree of social capital, relatively equal power distribution within a community, and the local enforceability of traditional institutions in order to keep this system politically sustainable.
The imposition of further state controls, even if for private property mechanisms,
can undermine successful communal systems. It is therefore important to empower
communities and local participation in national policy discussions (Meinzen-Dick
and Bruns 2000).

Elinor Ostrom won the 2009 Nobel Prize in economics for her work on community institutions to govern common property assets. Her work has shown that people
do more than maximize short-term benefits and are able to cooperatively manage
common resources (Vollan and Ostrom 2010; Ostrom, Gardiner, and Walker 1994;
Ostrom 1990); that designing fair rules for sustainable NRM is a complex, difficult process at which national governments frequently fail (Ostrom and Crawford
1999); and that ecosystems management is best treated as a complex, adaptive system (chapters 2 and 9). The probability of communities forming sustainable NRM
institutions depends on at least ten factors (Ostrom 2009):

- the size of the resource system (moderate size is most likely);
- productivity (users need to observe some scarcity, but the resource cannot already be exhausted);
- predictability of the effects of user actions;
- mobility of resources (trees and lakes are easier to manage than wildlife and rivers);
- group size (smaller is easier to manage, but larger makes it easier to generate management resources);
- leadership;
- common moral and ethical standards;
- common, accurate knowledge about natural resources;
- importance of the resource for livelihoods; and
- transaction costs of forming and managing resources.

One concern with changes to property laws is that the imposition of formal, governmental property laws that do not take account of preexisting traditional property relationships can take away land rights that others have had without compensation, harming the environmental balance of the system, as has happened to pastoralists in some parts of arid and semiarid sub-Saharan Africa (case 7-5). This top-down approach to institutional change can reduce sustainability and increase poverty, as has been recognized by Rodrik (2008) and Easterly (2008). On the basis of a review of relevant literature, Meinzen-Dick and Bruns (2000, 33) conclude that "state action to regulate water, forests, fisheries and other resources may support or undermine user self-governance."

Conclusion

Natural resources are the foundation of food systems. Sustainable management of each is essential for the sustainability of the other. Past successes in food production have been obtained in part by unsustainable exploitation of natural resources, offset in part by alleviating pressures on land poorly suited for agriculture and on biodiversity and wildlife through rapidly increasing agricultural productivity.

Future food system sustainability requires internalizing environmental externalities into private costs, a process this chapter calls full-costing. If such full-costing is implemented and the revenues captured by the state are used for investments to repair natural resource damage and create other human-made resources to compensate for natural resource losses, major structural and behavioral adjustments would take place in the food system, moving it closer to sustainability.

There are many multiple-win policies that can reduce poverty and improve environmental quality in stage 1 of what we have termed the modified environmental Kuznets curve for some measures of environmental quality. More research is needed in order to identify other multiple-win strategies and increase the sustainability of the food system.

The per capita stock of natural resources, such as land and water, available to the food system is decreasing due to previous unsustainable practices and competition from other sectors such as industry, residential housing, and household demand that is expected to continue increasing. Thus, public policies that increase natural resource productivity are essential to assure sustainability (see chapter 7). Such policies should include reducing water subsidies and increasing public investment in research, technology, and government policy to increase productivity of land, water, and labor. Current investments by most developing countries are grossly insufficient.

Traditional agriculture should not be romanticized as being in perfect harmony with nature and in opposition to improved production practices and technologies (Gill 1995). Many improved technologies reduce a farm's dependence on the local environment and can free up important resource constraints to help improve the environment and reduce risks. Action by the public sector and NGOs is needed to help farmers and other food system agents improve production and marketing practices to conserve and increase the productivity of scarce natural resources and to avoid degradation of the total productive resource base. In particular, there are tremendous opportunities for increasing water use efficiencies. Such public interventions should be supported by changing production and market behavior brought about by full-costing.

Multiple-win technologies and policies exist that promote economic growth, poverty alleviation, expanded food production, and environmental improvements. Improved irrigation technologies (particularly sprinkler and drip systems) tend to increase yields and reduce water use. They also reduce the large percentage of applied water that is not consumed by plants. For those able to afford the large setup costs, biogas plants can significantly reduce costs and environmental impact, while potentially increasing revenue (Olesen 2008; Bishop and Shumway 2009). Wani et al. (2003) demonstrate that integrated pest management, soil and water conservation initiatives, and green manure reduced water runoff by 45 percent in years of heavy rainfall and 30 percent with little rain; doubled or tripled production per hectare; cut annual soil loss by two-thirds; increased groundwater 27 percent; and reduced dependence on purchased chemical fertilizers and pesticides. At a municipal level, recycling city wastewater for use in industry or agriculture costs one-third less than desalinization and can be used to reduce pollution.

Multiple-win strategies discussed in chapter 7 also include: planting nitrogen-fixing trees and crops, particularly during fallow periods, to restore soil fertility and reduce the need for chemical fertilizers; applying productivity-increasing technology, such as improved crop varieties, that increases farm incomes; and intercropping push-pull systems that provide additional sources of revenue while reducing dependence on pesticides. Research into improved crop varieties that are more pest resistant, require fewer chemical inputs, and that have a more reliable output in years with little rain can significantly increase farm production and income while simultaneously reducing risks and dependence on chemical fertilizers and pesticides.

While there are still many technocratic solutions that can make the global food system more sustainable, Ostrom's research shows that there are few clear, universally applicable policy configurations. Crafting effective environmental policy requires understanding the needs and situations of the particular resources and the prevalent social norms and institutions currently in operation. Thus, political economy and governance are essential to understanding food system and environmental policies. This will be discussed in chapter 9.

NRM Policies Case Studies

The interaction between natural resource management and food production, as well as the role of government, is illustrated in these cases.* Policy options through which government and civil society can fight soil degradation are presented, along with an illustration of how government policy can best be used to deal with strong interactions between human and environmental health in the context of expanded food production. These cases also present several policy options for allocating scarce water supplies.

Cases 8-1 and 8-2 discuss soil conservation in Peru, with the former concentrating on NGOs and the latter on governments. Case 8-3 challenges students to integrate environmental, agricultural, and poverty policies. Cases 8-4 through 8-6 deal with water rights and management. Case 8-7 addresses soil quality and irrigation. Cases 8-5 through 8-7 are available exclusively online.

8-1   Civil Society Strategy to Fight Soil Degradation in Peru
       Lesli Hoey
8-2   Incentives for Soil Conservation in Peru
       Helena Posthumus
8-3   Environment and Health in Rural Kazakhstan: Linking Agricultural Policy
       and Natural Resource Management to Rural Welfare
       Andrew Jones
8-4   Allocating Irrigation Water in Egypt
       Birgitte Gersfelt
8-5   The Economic Benefits of Fisheries Management: The Case of Western
       Channel Sole
       Trond Bjørndal
8-6   The Aral Sea: An Ecological Disaster
       Inna Rudenko and John P. A. Lamers
8-7   Managing Soil Salinity in the Lower Reaches of the Amudarya Delta: How
       to Break the Vicious Circle
       Akmal Akramkhanov, Mirzakhayot Ibrakhimov, and John P. A. Lamers

* The case studies referenced here are presented in full in the three-volume work by Per Pinstrup-Andersen and Fuzhi Cheng, eds., *Case Studies in Food Policy for Developing Countries* (Ithaca, NY: Cornell University Press, 2009) and online via open access at http://cip.cornell.edu/gfs.

Notes

1. Such resources include financial, physical, human, and social capital.
2. "In situ" means "in the natural place," while "ex situ" means "out of the natural place."
3. Similar problems can also occur when resources are privately owned but assumed to be inexhaustible, or where land tenure systems are weak, such as when spouses have few rights to land if their partners die.

Chapter 9

Governance and Institutions

Introduction

Market mechanisms have shown themselves time and again to be effective means of promoting voluntary win-win transactions. Where significant informational, coordination, or external costs are involved, public assistance may be needed to facilitate them. Most of the issues that come before governments, however, involve winners and losers. Governance deals with how these conflicting interests are resolved.

Institutions comprise formal laws and informal social norms that affect human choice (Alston 2008; North 1998). They are the "rules of the game" (Friedman 1962; North 1990). All policies are institutions, but not all institutions are policies. The market mechanism is itself an institution that includes myriad lower-level institutions (Samuels n.d.). The formal institutions of a free press, an independent judiciary, and fair elections by secret ballot are part of the foundation of modern democratic societies. Informal social norms that are no less important to the functioning of a modern democracy include the institutions of civic responsibility, publicized debates, and whether and how religious opinion should influence policy. Formal and informal institutions affect transaction costs and production within organizations and firms through the incentive structure, turnover rates, and human capital generation (chapter 6). Different societies devise different institutions and varying policies to support or change them. Organizations are entities that may implement action.

Governance is the exercise of authority or management of resources through institutions, policies, traditions, cultures, and societal norms. It is distinct from the ends governments pursue (goals), the desire to achieve these goals (political will), the means by which competing groups reach binding collective decisions (politics), and specific government interventions in the food system such as input subsidies, nutrition programs, and tax schedules (policies).

Indeed, there is more to governance than governments. The governance of non-governmental organizations (NGOs), multinational corporations (MNCs), and international organizations also affects the global food system. For-profit organizations are governed not only by their boards of directors and shareholders but by credit-rating agencies, unions, civil society organizations, internal rules and institutions, media, and by market mechanisms through which consumers express their approval or disapproval.

In this chapter, governance is said to be good when resources are managed and institutions function in accordance with a notion of broad stakeholder welfare. It might reasonably be supposed that a government's political will reflects the goals of those stakeholders who have access to the political process, a contest that disadvantages the poor. Stakeholder-focused governance can be thought of as the extent to which all stakeholder interests are reflected in political will, politics, and policy formation. Good governance is essential for the food system to function well and deliver the benefits desired by society. Several elements of governance are believed to be particularly valuable in ensuring patterns of broad-based development: participation and consensus, effectiveness and efficiency, transparency and accountability, lack of corruption, rule of law, equality, stability, and freedom.

Institutions define the sociopolitical environment in which the food system operates. They interact with the food system at every level of the global food system and at every point in the diagram from chapter 1 (figure 1.1). Global institutions provide the framework within which international trade is carried out, just as national institutions provide the framework for intranational production, trade, and consumption. Local norms determine what practices are acceptable in natural resource management, production, and consumption patterns. Institutions can encourage investment, productivity, equality, and social cohesion or drive economic activity underground, constrain farmers into subsistence agriculture, and spark divisiveness and conflict. Whether government is perceived as being productive or predatory by actors has enormous importance at every point in the food system.

Governance affects the food system indirectly through economic growth and the distribution of its benefits, poverty reduction, health and nutrition, use of natural resources, appropriate use of foreign assistance, and land tenure. Chapters 2–8 have detailed many ways that local and national governments and their policies affect the food system.

There are additionally many issues in international governance, particularly regarding accountability and participation. Unless international agreements exist, national governments are not held accountable for any effects of their policies on people in other countries. This enables governments to choose beggar-thy-neighbor policies (such as banning or taxing food exports when prices are increasing, distorting trade and subsidy policies, or polluting rivers upstream while the costs are borne by people in downstream countries) without facing either the economic or political fallout. The divergence of government systems and inability to coordinate policies around the world makes it possible for multinational corporations (MNCs) to evade onerous laws by moving their headquarters or capital flows to different countries or establishing a "race to the bottom"[1] in corporate taxation and responsibilities, labor laws, and environmental regulations.

Institutions in Economics

Institutional economics unites efforts from many branches of economics and from other disciplines, including law, political science, sociology, psychology, and anthropology. New institutional economics (NIE) viewpoints influenced the preceding chapters as we argued that policy analysts should incorporate political economy concerns, and recognized that there are important limits to what can be accomplished by either markets or government alone, particularly without proper checks and balances.

Chapter 6 introduced the theme of transaction costs. Coase's (1937) Nobel Prize–winning work on transaction costs demonstrates that "all solutions have costs and there is no reason to suppose that government regulation is called for simply because the problem is not well handled by the market or the firm" (Coase 1960, 18). Rather, governments and markets function best when institutions are designed to minimize transaction costs and externalities. The usual complaint that government oversight of certain activities is inefficient because of weak incentives, greater bureaucracy and regulation, and less responsiveness to market forces is in some cases a *virtue* because these same factors can provide greater stability in a highly uncertain environment (Williamson 2000).

The NIE generally follows the neoclassical framework while making some important departures, such as in the concepts of bounded rationality and rational ignorance (see North 1990; Eggertsson 1996; Alston and Ferrie 1999); people attempt to maximize utility but face informational, psychological, time, and cognitive constraints that may result in suboptimal outcomes. People use decision heuristics ("rules of thumb") in making complex decisions that should be "close enough" to optimal. Bounded rationality implies that contracts and markets are unavoidably incomplete in contrast to mainstream economics that assumes complete markets.

Rational ignorance implies that individuals sometimes choose to not be perfectly informed about legislation: the costs of doing so outweigh the expected benefits. This gives special interests greater influence over the political system than the general public, leading to more distortionary policy than is optimal. Rausser (1992), for instance, estimates the distributional effects and deadweight loss[2] of U.S. commodity support programs in 1985, reproduced in table 9.1. In each case, the gains are concentrated among a few who have an incentive to lobby for increased support, while the consumer and deadweight losses are diffuse, reducing the pressure to reduce the supports. Rausser (1992) estimates that between $2 and $6 billion were lost from the U.S. economy in 1985 alone because of these interventions, not including the effects on farmers and consumers globally.

In a clear summary article, Williamson (2000) depicts four levels of institutions: (1) the embedded informal institutions of a society that change only over the course

TABLE 9.1.
Range of Annual Domestic Welfare Gains and Losses from Support Programs
under the 1985 Food Security Act, 1985–1988 (Billions of Dollars)

Crop	Consumer loss	Producer gain	Taxpayer cost	Deadweight loss
Wheat	0.24–0.30	2.62–3.22	3.67–4.27	0.69–1.95
Corn	0.68–0.76	7.23–7.62	7.30–8.10	0.36–1.63
Cotton	0.19–0.21	1.20–1.46	1.40–1.60	0.13–0.61
Peanuts	0.36–0.40	0.29–0.35	0	0.01–0.11
Dairy	1.80–2.90	1.50–2.20	1.13–1.72	0.73–3.12
Sugar	1.35–1.55	1.15–1.25	0	0.10–0.40

Source: Rausser 1992.

of centuries if at all; (2) the institutional environment that identifies the proper roles and limits of government and the divisions of power among actors through constitutions, property laws, and/or societal norms that require decades to amend; (3) the governance level where individual laws, contracts, and negotiations among different stakeholders take place over a period of years; and (4) the actual production, transportation, and consumption level where most economic analysis takes place and changes occur continuously. The NIE focuses primarily on the second and third level of institutions, and more particularly on property and contract law, because the first level is very poorly understood and the fourth is already the focus of many literatures.

Outcomes and the set of feasible options today depend on the history of previous actions, a concept known as path dependence. Institutions may be viewed as exogenous constraints on the choice set or as endogenous and subject to reform. Endogenous theories of institutions are being divided into two basic worldviews: one wherein institutions emerge from a blank slate that can be readily rewritten in a "top-down" approach, and another that recognizes the "bottom-up," gradual evolution of standards and norms in society that are eventually codified into institutions and policies (Easterly 2008). This latter is usually favored by the NIE, though it recognizes that there are sometimes radical breaks and departures from history that favor the former.

The degree to which institutional formation can be described as bottom-up or top-down has important consequences for the extent to which international donor agencies, national policymakers, or NGOs can influence institutions, and for how to best go about doing so. Easterly (2008) and Rodrik (2008) point to formal land titling in Africa (chapter 7) as an example of a top-down process that has been ongoing for seventy years without adequately resolving many of the conflicting practices that hinder development while weakening informal local institutions that have maintained peace and social order.

Feige (1998) discusses the perception after the fall of the USSR that there was a chance for a dramatic break from former rules. Instead, many of the initial reforms granted legality to unjust divisions of property, and people with special access to the earlier system used that influence to gain more wealth and influence in the new system, crafting rules for their benefit. This ensured that similar social orders would prevail. Rausser (1992) explains that a number of U.S. agricultural policies were justified by efficiency arguments—making "wastelands" more productive, reducing soil erosion as a public good, and so forth. Over time, however, special interests were able to gain influence over subsequent changes to the legislation, making them more and more redistributive.

Governance Situation

Defining governance is a difficult exercise because it has many different facets. The Kaufmann, Kraay, and Mastruzzi governance series defines it as "the traditions and institutions by which authority in a country is exercised" (2009, 5), while Huther and Shah (1998, 2) consider "all aspects of the exercise of authority through formal and informal institutions in the management of the resource endowment of a state" before moving to a more operational definition. UNDP refers to governance as "the exercise of economic, political, and administrative authority to manage a country's affairs at all levels" (Birner 2007).

Official World Bank publications have used several definitions at differing degrees of precision and breadth, such as the dictionary's definition: "the manner in which power is exercised" in managing resources (Webster's New Universal Unabridged Dictionary 1979). This chapter defines governance in its broadest sense: the exercise of authority or management of resources through institutions, policies, traditions, cultures, and societal norms.

Under what circumstances governance can be said to be "good" or not is debatable. Is governance good because government practices are those recommended by aid agencies, or because certain outcomes occur regularly and efficiently? Should those outcomes refer mostly to economic growth, to the Millennium Development Goals, to human rights, or to other outcomes (chapter 11)? Must the quality of governance be defined in terms of particular stakeholders or can general definitions hold for all stakeholders? There is a need for greater integration of stakeholder analysis and ethics in research on governance.

Kaufmann and Kraay (2008) warn that defining good governance as the state where desirable development outcomes regularly occur can confound a proper understanding of both governance and development. The World Bank (2004, 6) could almost be describing poor governance instead of its effects:

> Many countries with poor institutions and weak governance are beset by poorly designed and weakly implemented policies, shoddy infrastructure and public services, and state harassment of citizens and business. Legal systems are neither effective nor predictable. Contracts are only weakly enforceable. And crime is widespread.

Only the shoddy infrastructure mentioned in that catalog would count purely as an effect of poor governance rather than an oft-used measure of governance.

For practical purposes, most researchers restrict their attention to particular facets of good governance they believe should be correlated with desirable outcomes. While they may be based on a general sense of societal welfare, there is little attempt to identify particular stakeholders benefited or excluded.

The World Bank's Kaufmann, Kraay, and Mastruzzi (2009) (hereafter KKM) governance index is one of the most widely used governance measures, incorporating measures of the presence of free and fair elections, media independence, political stability, the quality of public services, the incidence of market-unfriendly policies, the independence of the judiciary, and perceptions of corruption. Freedom House produces two measures, one of political freedoms and one of civil rights such as the right to express personal beliefs in politics, religion, and academia, gender and ethnic equality, and the freedom to organize.

Transparency International's Corruption Perceptions Index (CPI) details corruption levels, while the Heritage Foundation and the Wall Street Journal put out a further index specifically to measure the extent to which governments interfere with the market. Rather than focusing on one topic, the Ibrahim Index of African Governance examines only SSA countries, comparing them on how citizens experience fifty-seven indicators of safety and security; rule of law, transparency, and corruption; participation and human rights; sustainable economic opportunity; and human development.

Many measures indicate that there are serious governance problems in Africa. This has led Tupy (2005, 18–19), among many others, to exclaim that, as important as it is for OECD members to liberalize trade with Africa, "blaming African poverty on forces beyond the control of Africa's political elites takes the spotlight away from decades of failed economic policies, wholesale looting of Africa's wealth, and loss of countless lives to political repression and ethnic conflicts."

In opposition are voices complaining that the concept of "governance" is an attempt to imperialistically impose Western ideals on Africa. In either case, there is great variation in any region: Ibrahim rates countries between 18.9 (Somalia) and 85.1 (Mauritius); KKM indicates that Zimbabwe and Eritrea experienced large declines in governance during the last decade while Liberia, Rwanda, and Tanzania made significant progress; and Freedom House ranks one in four SSA countries as being free, which compares well with central Asia.

One of the potentially most important efforts to improve governance this decade was the inauguration of NEPAD—The New Partnership for Africa's Development. Based on principles of good governance and African ownership of the development process, NEPAD works to achieve the MDGs in Africa by improving coordination among African countries, giving Africa a greater voice in global debates, and holding African leaders accountable for the promises they have made.

This last goal is accomplished through the Africa Peer Review Mechanism (APRM). The APRM grades the twenty-nine member states on democracy and political governance, economic governance, corporate governance, and socioeconomic development. While the plan has been to conduct a base review followed up by additional reviews every two to four years, the first five years of the organization's life have seen the implementation of six base reviews and no follow-ups. The six governments to complete the base review are Ghana (2005), Rwanda (2006), Kenya (2006), South Africa (2007), Algeria (2007), and Benin (2008). The reports identify good practices from each nation that could be profitably emulated by others and suggest ways to improve governance and move forward on international commitments. The question has been asked, however, whether European leaders would be willing to be held to the same comparative evaluation.

Governance and the Food System

This chapter divides governance into seven concepts: participation and consensus, effectiveness and efficiency, transparency and accountability, corruption, the rule of law and equality, stability and conflict, and freedom. The concepts are general enough to apply not only to national governments but also to local governments, NGOs, projects, and even households. The following sections describe each, their connections to the food system, and suggestions for improving them.

This discussion uses these concepts of good governance rather than "democracy" for three reasons. The first is that democracy is generally understood as being desirable because it encourages participation, makes leaders more accountable and politics more transparent, strengthens the rule of law, and so forth. Rather than concentrating on one particular institutional system for encouraging these facets of governance, the focus should be on the primal features.

The second reason is that democracy encompasses many different institutions that differ between countries, and the specific forms of democracy matter (Dixit 2008). Parliamentary and presidential democracies function in very different ways with important economic and governance implications (Persson 2005). Working on the primary governance concepts rather than an overarching system allows one to evaluate different institutions for how they contribute to participation, stability, equality, and so forth.

Third, it is not necessary for a government to be democratic in order for it to provide opportunities for meaningful stakeholder feedback, be transparent and accountable, preserve individual freedoms, and reduce corruption and conflict. In general, it is believed that democratic systems foster these qualities. Collier (2009) demonstrates that the extent of these governance qualities matters far more than the veneer of democracy. Rodrik (2007) explains at length that the policies recommended by good governance and good economics do not map neatly into specific policies, but that many policy constellations can produce these higher-level governance elements.

Participation and Consensus

Participation is typically measured by the existence of free and fair elections and independent media. It also includes the extent to which stakeholders can influence the policies and laws that affect them between election cycles at all levels of government. Participation gets to the heart of the question, for whom is governance good?

If governance institutions receive high marks from surveys of foreign investors, but smallholders are denied participation, can governance be said to be good? Giving disadvantaged people greater voice increases the political will of the government to deal with their problems (Pinstrup-Andersen 2003).

In many countries, participation is practically unknown as there are no opposition parties or free professional organizations that could serve to bring different viewpoints to policymakers' notice. Elite firms in Russia have significantly more access to politicians through lobbying than geographically dispersed farmers or consumers, enabling them to influence laws and policies in their favor (case 7-7). African land tenure reforms were carried out without the input or participation of pastoralists affected by them, in most cases leading to a loss of land rights without compensation (case 7-6). Government and development reforms are most effective when there is meaningful participation from stakeholders at many levels (Heidhues et al. 2004). Case 9-5 discusses the participation of consumer groups and sugar producers and processors in evaluating WHO recommendations and performing research. It emerged that the sugar industry had contributed significantly to an early WHO report on the link between sugar intake and diabetes—enabling the industry to select the experts and scientific editor. The conflict of interest this represents is another major hurdle that needs to be overcome in improving national and international governance to promote a healthy and sustainable global food system profitably.

One of the challenges to improving participation is that poor people are often perceived as mere recipients or passive targets of government interventions, rather than economic agents with knowledge, assets, and goals that policymakers may be unaware of (case 9-1). Another is that stakeholder participation might be undesirable to those in power because of hidden—or not so hidden—agendas to exploit certain stakeholder groups (e.g., cheap labor).

Most program evaluation procedures are organized hierarchically with a very top-down structure. Each level evaluates the one below it, leaving little room for bottom-up feedback to improve the evaluation processes. Including ground workers and implementers in the planning stages would improve the sustainability and effectiveness of projects, whether run by governments or NGOs (Lefèvre and Garcia 1997). Introducing more feedback mechanisms into programs and policies allows civic stakeholders greater voice, which can lead to greater efficiency and effectiveness. Farmer and consumer organizations can also bring forward stakeholder issues during planning stages, though their governance is itself pivotal.

Participation determines whether local stakeholders continue with a project, how much effort and how many resources they dedicate to it, and how long the project continues to function after the instigating agency leaves, affecting effectiveness and stability (Lefèvre and Garcia 1997). Case 9-3 demonstrates the importance of ensuring broad-based support for long-term reforms from civil society, the private sector, and different government institutions and parties.

Democracy and participation of all stakeholders are not synonymous. As early as the mid-1800s, the English philosopher John Stuart Mills (1863, 12–13) wrote that the "self-government" promised by representative democracy was "not the government of each by himself, but of each by all the rest," leading to a "tyranny of the majority." This is why the principle of participation needs the principle of consensus: for the input of minority-interest stakeholders to be relevant, solutions should optimally be found that satisfy all stakeholders, and not merely 50.1 percent. This is similar to protecting minority rights: the rights of the individual should not be made subservient to the convenience or whim of the majority (see chapter 11).

Politics may be formed by compromise, but it enforces conformity. Thus there is a good reason for making as many decisions as possible consistent with society's goals outside of the political process. The market mechanism, alternatively, "permits unanimity without conformity," preserving freedom and diversity (Friedman, 1962, 23).

The challenge is to bring about consensus solutions that are meaningful in a timely manner. Stakeholders rarely seek to agree with those who disagree with them, but rather attempt to maximize the gains that accrue to their group or increase their power and position for future policy debates. As discussed in chapter 5, poor people are not homogeneous. Their different circumstances, needs, and preferences make consensus difficult to reach.

Participatory governance may make change difficult and time-consuming, while dictatorship and/or limited participation by stakeholder groups may introduce and implement change in short order. Furthermore, reforms reached by full consensus will only be as deep as the political will of the least-interested party (Rajan 2008; Berglof et al. 2008). This fact can significantly slow down needed reforms and has led the EU to move from unanimous decision making to 70 percent for an increasing number of policy areas (Baldwin 2008; Berglof et al. 2008). As one of the areas in the world where policy coordination has progressed furthest, the results of the EU experiments in multinational democracy both foreshadow and provide lessons for future attempts at international governance.

Effectiveness and Efficiency

"For most of the poor, governance means just getting access to the services they are promised" (von Braun and Pandya-Lorch 2007, 13). Participation of the poor may establish appropriate priorities, but if the results never materialize, of what use was the exercise? Is government spending effective in producing desired results? Effectiveness is concerned with the amount of output produced. Hunger reduction programs are effective to the extent that hunger is reduced. Though often used as if it were a binary term ("Are conditional cash transfers effective?"), it is often more appropriate to describe relative effectiveness ("Are conditional cash transfers more effective at reducing hunger than food stamps?"). Even when a binary question is being posed, the implicit comparison with the status quo should be made explicit.

While effectiveness addresses only the amount of output produced, efficiency considers producing the greatest output using a given amount of inputs. The World Bank and IMF's Structural Adjustment Programs in the 1980s stemmed from the realization that government policies and institutions implemented by specific developing countries were not sustainable, in part because the public sector over-extended public services relative to revenues and partly because of inefficient public monopolies that could be potentially better managed through competition in the private sector (see cases 7-1, 7-2, and 7-3). Though the means employed by the Bretton Woods institutions have been criticized, concerns about resource use efficiency are nevertheless often considered to be another essential part of governance. Cost-effectiveness is a measure of efficiency frequently used in project design and evaluation.

The efficiency of government spending can be considered either intrinsically (How much output is produced per unit of government input?) or extrinsically (Could inputs be used more efficiently privately?). Recall from chapter 2 that both effectiveness and efficiency rely heavily on the goal being pursued. Is an agricultural policy the most effective one if per capita GDP increases more than it would under other policies, if total food production increases the most, if food insecurity or poverty decreases the most, if food self-sufficiency increases the most, or if the government is able to secure the most votes? Each and all of these goals may play some role in policy formation, despite the fact that they can conflict with each other. Hence, there are real drawbacks to using GDP or GDP per capita as the primary means of measuring development and government efficiency.

One way to identify the most cost-effective means of, for instance, reducing the under-five mortality rate (U5MR) is to compare the costs of different interventions that improve child health. Studies of individual interventions place the cost of saving one more child's life between $10 and $1,000, suggesting that it is relatively inexpensive to reduce the U5MR (Jamison et al. 1996). However, macroeconomic cross-country studies using public health expenditures put the cost between $50,000 and $100,000 per life saved (Filmer and Pritchett 1999).

To explain this discrepancy, Filmer and Pritchett (1999) point out that the macro studies include not only the effectiveness of a given intervention but also the efficiency of public spending and the extent to which private spending is crowded out by public spending. Gupta and Verhoeven (2001) analyze health and education spending in eighty-five governments, finding high levels of waste and loss and that the level of cost-effectiveness declines rapidly as spending increases.

Many studies identify only the gross output of government programs rather than the effect net of crowding out. If government spending merely re-creates output that was being produced by the private sector using the same inputs, the net societal benefit is zero. Furthermore, unpredictable and unreliable government expenditures adversely affect private investment in those areas (Feng 2001; see also cases 7-1, 7-2, and 7-3). The fact that government funds come from confiscation should also be included in net impact calculations because raising funds bears a cost that is greater than the amount raised.

Fan, Saurkar, and Shields (2007) report one estimate that each dollar of public expenditure raised in Africa reduces national income by $1.17, implying that government expenditures should minimally have at least a 17 percent return on investment in order to be socially acceptable. In the United States, the opportunity cost of government spending may be between $1.20 and $1.50 per dollar spent (Alston and

Hurd 1990). As Alston and Hurd (1990) argue, the deadweight loss of any particular tax is an empirical matter that needs to be decided on a case-by-case basis. There are also reasons for funding many public goods that go beyond their economic value, and the intrinsic, moral, and societal benefits of having a healthy, educated populace should also be included in cost-benefit or cost-effect analyses.

Fan (cases 9-1 and 9-2) finds that agricultural research and rural infrastructure tend to have the highest benefit-cost ratios and the largest number of poor people released from poverty per fixed amount spent. Spending priorities change over time, implying the need for continual updating and reliance on the most recent research to identify spending priorities.

In African political discourse, agriculture is regularly referred to as the "backbone of the economy," yet the share of national budgets devoted to agricultural development remains consistently below that in Asia (Fan and Rao 2003). While government spending in developing countries has increased on average by 7 percent per year since 1990, spending on agricultural development has increased only half that much, and the percent of government spending that goes to infrastructure has decreased significantly (Fan, Saurkar, and Shields 2007). What spending has been allocated pays for subsidies instead of investments in public goods (Hazell et al. 2007).

Transparency and Accountability

Where organizations are not perceived as accomplishing the things they promise, it is essential that citizens are able to both identify how and by whom decisions were made and hold decision makers accountable. The ability of stakeholders to identify how decisions were reached and carried out is called transparency. Accountability reflects the extent to which officials may be held responsible for the choices and actions they make as part of their duties. Both are essential in curbing corruption.

Transparency affects participation. If stakeholders do not have information about how decisions are made and by whom, how can they participate effectively? Access to information about laws that cover government expenditures, voting records, campaign contributions, and the minutes of significant meetings is as important to ensuring participatory government as a free and independent media that can disseminate such information without fear of reprisal.

Transparency enables government and the private sector to work together as seamlessly as possible. When, for example, a government privatizes an agricultural parastatal, is the real decision making done behind closed doors with the possibility of bribes, or is there an open and fair bidding process (Kaufmann 1997)? Case 7-2 records how uncertainty about the conditions under which government would release stored food reduced private traders' willingness to enter the market, worsening Malawi's food crisis. As Jayne, Zulu, and Nijhoff (2006, 338) report:

> The phenomenon of subsidized government intervention in the market, or the threat of it, leading to private sector inaction, is one of the greatest problems plaguing the food marketing systems in the region. Effective

coordination between the private and public sector would require greater consultation and transparency with regard to changes in parastatal purchase and sale prices, import and export decisions, tariff rate changes and stock release triggers.

To the extent that government, corporate, and NGO processes and actions are transparent, actors can be held accountable. In addition to electing people out of office or bringing forward legal proceedings, accountability includes the internal rules and proceedings that provide checks and balances on a regular basis, independent auditors, and monitoring by civil society organizations.

Much of the literature on the principal-agent problem[3] deals with the question of accountability and how to overcome conflicts of interest between donor/citizen (principal) and politician (agent) or citizen/politician (principal) and bureaucrat (agent). The literature finds, for instance, that electoral systems where citizens vote for individual candidates are more likely to keep corruption in check and increase accountability than systems where votes are cast for party lists (Persson and Tabellini 2002; Persson, Tabellini, and Trebbi 2001).

If accountability is about keeping governments in check, why would any government increase accountability? Accountability increases legitimacy, enabling them to enact otherwise unpopular reforms. Sahn and Edirisinghe (1993) explain the ability of the new Sri Lankan government to enact major reforms and unpopular food subsidy cutbacks in 1978 in terms of the gross mismanagement of the previous government. The accountability of the new administration gave it greater latitude to enact reforms. Case 9-8 details a similar example in Zambia where the incoming government lowered food subsidies despite riots. A strong sense of accountability can provide both the opportunity to remove poorly functioning governments as well as greater legitimacy for those governments that allow themselves to be held accountable.

Marketlike mechanisms help keep companies and governments accountable: if people don't buy the products of corporations that engage in improper practices, they will either go out of business or be forced to change. Allowing the private sector to enter a market that has been served only by a government monopoly can introduce incentives for improved efficiency and help the government identify where its services are needed most and which ones can be let go.

Government is similarly needed to keep companies and individuals accountable for their actions, particularly when public services are contracted out to private firms or when they pose dangers to public safety. The legal system is heavily involved in ensuring that members of society are accountable. Accountability strengthens a country's rule of law by constraining government officials, private corporations, civil society organizations, and individuals to act according to the prescribed laws.

The history of meatpacking in the United States exemplifies the importance of transparency and accountability in the food sector. Upton Sinclair's book *The Jungle* provoked a reaction to the quality of the meat being sold. Businesses lobbied government to regulate and inspect their industry to assure domestic and foreign consumers that their products were safe. The increased transparency and account-ability of the industry served to calm markets.

Increasing transparency and accountability is currently the focus of a number of projects (e.g., Kaufmann 2003; Svensson 2005). Informing school districts in Uganda of the timing and amounts of textbook disbursements increased the amounts that actually arrived in the district from a mean of 13 percent, where more than half of the districts received nothing, to a mean of 80 percent (Reinikka and Svensson 2004). Similar programs have been effective in the Philippines.

Even though such citizen monitoring has grown in popularity, there are impor-tant free-rider problems that need to be dealt with. Free-rider problems are a form of externality problem that exist when collective action requires voluntary individ-ual contributions, but the final results are not very sensitive to any one individual's contribution. Everyone benefits if someone monitors the government, but the in-dividual gain is small relative to the costs. People who choose to not contribute or reduce their contribution to get the societal benefit from other people's efforts are called free riders.

Corruption

Corruption is the element of governance that has received the most attention and has often been treated as if it were synonymous with governance. The abuse of public power for private gain, corruption is a classic case of government failure with devastating consequences for the global food system. Relea (2002) reports that northeast Argentina "has been devastated by corrupt governments" where thou-sands of children face severe malnutrition and high risk of dying of hunger, despite abundant foreign food aid in a middle-income country that supplies more food to the rest of the world than it consumes. More corrupt countries tend to have lower GDP/capita, lower human capital, longer time to obtain legal status to operate a firm, and less freedom of the press, and they are generally less open to imports (Svensson 2005).

Corruption is typically measured using ordinal perceptions data produced by Political Risk Services,[4] Transparency International's CPI, and the World Bank KKM index. Cardinal measures include the EBRD-World Bank Business Environment and Enterprise Performance Survey, which surveyed over ten thousand firm managers between 1999 and 2002 about their experiences with corruption in twenty-six tran-sition countries, and UN surveys (International Crime Victims Survey, ICVS), which ask residents of the capital city if a government official asked for or expected a bribe in the last year. The ICVS is highly correlated with the ordinal measures discussed above, but most highly correlated (negatively) with GDP per capita.

Svensson (2005) argues that stealing from public funds and ignoring health and safety regulations are among the worst forms of corruption. Feige (1998) believes the greatest costs occur when many independent decision makers in the government have veto power, allowing each to act as a monopolist in setting bribe prices. Case 7-1 demonstrates that corruption allegations had worsened international relations to the point that famine disaster relief came slowly because donors did not believe the government's claims. The brunt of these evils from corruption falls on the poor and the marginalized.

In opposition to the "moralists" who argue that all corruption is wrong and costly, and should therefore be eradicated, many "relativists" contend that the removal of corruption has important societal costs as well. Where laws and regulations are too restrictive, it is argued, a little bribery "greases the wheels" and ensures a more efficient outcome because those investments that are more likely to succeed will be more likely to get through the red tape (Leff 1964; Leys 1965; Huntington 1968). Furthermore, corruptive rents can entrench needed programs, making it difficult for future governments to remove them. "Relativists" also point out that it is difficult to objectively determine which actions count as corruption, particularly when cultural norms and standards change over time and differ between societies.

Empirical investigations into this hypothesis have generally found, however, that corruption does more to "sand the wheels" than grease them. Numerous studies, such as those by Kaufmann and Wei (1999) and Lambsdorff (2002), find that corruption reduces growth and investment, particularly where other governance indicators are low. This indicates that corruption does not ameliorate poor governance, but exacerbates it.

Dreher and Gassebner (2007), however, find that corruption reduces the negative impact of regulatory barriers to firm entry in countries with high barriers. Part of the problem with this hypothesis is that it assumes that regulations are exogenous. It is likely that corrupt governments will craft onerous regulations that provide greater opportunities for bribery. Kaufmann and Wei (1999) report that bribe payers end up spending *more* time with government officials, rather than less, and face higher costs for capital. There are also the risks to social health: the same bribe that can be used to overcome an excessive barrier to firm entry can also overcome a needed public health measure, grant monopoly rights, protect against proper oversight, and degrade the environment (Kaufmann 1997).

Corruption tends to be worse in countries with greater market regulation, particularly where the bureaucracy has discretionary authority. De Soto (1989) and Shleifer and Vishny (1993) propose that the less authority individual bureaucrats have, the less they will be able to extract. Reducing discretionary barriers, strengthening the rule of law, and increasing competition among civil servants would then be appropriate responses.

The Rule of Law and Equality

UNDP (2008) declares that 4 billion people live without the protection of the rule of law. The rule of law is typically understood as the extent to which a country is governed by predictable and effective laws, contracts are enforced, and the justice and police systems are effective and impartial. The important point is not so much that the court system is used, but that recourse to the law is possible (Alston 2008). The rule of law stands in contrast to discretionary rules, insisting that those responsible for writing and executing the laws also adhere to them and that the rules are predictable.

In cases 9-3 and 9-4, Cheng discusses the effectiveness of attempts to make the World Trade Organization's (WTO) accession and dispute resolution (DR) mechanisms more transparent and rules-oriented. He points out that there are many portions of the accession process that have yet to be codified, effectively granting current members bargaining power with applicant countries to reduce the benefits of accession (WTO−) and increase the costs (WTO+). The primary means of encouraging compliance with WTO rulings is the threat of allowed retaliation by the wounded country. The smaller the wounded country, however, the less effective that threat is (Anderson 2006). Another concern underscored by NIE theory is that constructing a new rules-based system is liable to codify the original power-based inequalities present in the old system. In more recent years, developing countries have brought forward more cases and, as in case 9-4, have successfully won some against larger powers. Whether they submit to the WTO rulings and demonstrate effective rule of law has yet to be determined.

One of the important parts of the rule of law related to these examples is the notion of "equality under the law." In understanding the role of equality in governance, there are two primary questions that must answered: First, equality of what? Second, is equality a means to another end or an end in itself? The answer to the second question intimately depends on the answer to the first. This section has touched on equality of access to legal processes and protections. Alternate definitions include equality of outcomes and equality of opportunities.

It has long been argued that inequality contributes to economic growth and poverty reduction. Since the relatively wealthy are more likely to save and invest, and investment leads to growth, initial inequality can be seen as a precondition of future growth and equality. Another argument was developed in the Kuznets hypothesis: as workers moved from the traditional agricultural sector into the higher-paying modern sector, inequality would initially increase, only to decrease again as most of the population moved into the modern sector. These two scenarios acknowledge equality as a desirable end, but focus more attention on the absolute living standards of the poor, which are assumed to rise faster with higher economic growth, than on whether or how fast they catch up to the living standards of the wealthy. Friedman (1962) points out that income inequality can also preserve freedom of expression by producing patrons who can fund ideas outside of the mainstream, funding which would be otherwise unavailable.

Other theories link inequality to slower income growth. Inequality fosters unproductive rent-seeking, increased instability that reduces investment, poorer median voters who support higher distortionary taxes, and reductions in human capital investment that perpetuate poverty (Thorbecke 2007). High inequality can also give wealthy elites greater control over the political process, leading to policies that reduce mobility and prevent the trickle down of economic growth to the poor. If these processes dominate, then equality is desirable as a means to bring about additional desirable development objectives including economic growth and poverty reduction. Recent empirical work has supported the notion that structural inequality and institutions that foster inequality and lack of mobility are bad for growth and development (e.g., Acemoglu, Johnson, and Robinson 2001; Easterly

2006). Understanding equality as both a desirable end and a means to growth can help justify difficult political choices.

Equality of opportunity is an implicit part of this discussion. Income inequality may be so great that it prevents or hinders poor people from having the opportunity to improve their condition. On the other hand, too great a focus on redistributive policies can likewise weaken opportunities and incentives to improve the human condition. Equality under the law asks if poor people have the same access to legal redress, government benefits, and other public goods as more privileged citizens. Hallman, Lewis, and Begum (2003) detail that in all communities studied, the poor saw government agents as being remote and primarily there to serve the rich. They also report that a culture of fear prevents poor people from reporting criminal activities because of the perceived biases and corruptibility of police and judiciary.

These governance problems are most likely to reduce pro-poor growth and agricultural investment. The poorest people, minorities, and women are often excluded from government services, and NGOs that strive to reach the poor are often unable to reach the ultra poor who suffer from social exclusion. In such cases, lack of income equality is both the problem and the cause of additional problems. Failing to account for social inequalities can lead well-intentioned interventions to exacerbate them, leaving the ultra poor further marginalized.

Equality under the law is subtly different from the rule of law, and the relationship between the two can be complex: supportive, conflicting, or complementary. Laws can be—and often are, whether intentionally or not—designed to provide benefits to some groups while excluding others. Ostensibly designed to serve the poor in outlying communities, many government institutions and organizations, particularly agricultural parastatals, were accused by the international community of being "corrupt, rent seeking and subsidizing industry or cheap prices for urban consumers, while not paying farmers based on the actual production costs" (case 7-1). Pan-territorial pricing policies, in which all farmers were offered the same price independent of transportation costs, were common in past state marketing monopolies. Even though sponsored by the government legally and predictably, such policies harm market efficiency and subsidize one group at the cost of another.

Should the justice of a policy be judged by its intended ends or by the means used (chapter 11)? Often the perceived justice of a policy that gives explicit benefits to one group depends on the viewer's perspective and sympathies about the recipient. Occasionally, authors take on seemingly contradictory positions: first, that developing country governments should not tax their agricultural sectors, but instead subsidize them as rich country governments do; second, that rich country governments should not subsidize their farmers. If a practice is unjust when used in one circumstance (e.g., subsidizing OECD farmers), why would it not be unjust to use it in very similar circumstances?

Financial equality and the rule of law can also come into conflict when the law does treat each person equally. Consider the enforceability of contracts. Ying (2000) discusses how some Chinese farmers would renege on contracts with a foreign company if they could find a better price elsewhere, putting local officials in the difficult position of choosing whether to support the rule of law to the detriment of their poverty-stricken locals. This problem is not unique to China by any means. Case 7-7 discusses the effects of weak land contract enforcement on agribusiness development in Russia, while case 7-4 describes how a lack of transparency in Africa reduces farmers' trust that contracts will be enforced, in both cases reducing investment.

Hayek (2007) argues in fact that equality under the law, or the rule of law, and government policies designed to equalize economic outcomes are completely incompatible:

> Any policy aiming directly at a substantive ideal of distributive justice must lead to the destruction of the Rule of Law. To produce the same result for different people, it is necessary to treat them differently. . . . It cannot be denied that the Rule of Law produces economic inequality—all that can be claimed for it is that this inequality is not designed to affect particular people in a particular way.
>
> To say that in a planned society the Rule of Law cannot hold is . . . not to say that the actions of the government will not be legal. . . . It means only that the use of the government's coercive powers will no longer be limited and determined by pre-established rules. The law can . . . legalize what to all intents and purposes remains arbitrary action. If the law says that such a board or authority may do what it pleases, anything that board or authority does is legal—but its actions are certainly not subject to the Rule of Law. By giving the government unlimited powers, the most arbitrary rule can be made legal; and in this way a democracy may set up the most complete despotism imaginable. (Hayek 2007, 117, 119)

Stability and Conflict

Instability and armed conflict are among the greatest hindrances to agricultural, economic, and human development. Feng (1997) finds that constitutional regime change has a positive effect on economic growth, but that the probability of unconstitutional regime change has a significantly negative impact. Economic growth likewise tends to increase the probability of the government in power remaining so (Collier 2007). At the same time, widespread food insecurity is currently one of the greatest threats to stability. As Norman Borlaug (1970, 2), Nobel Peace Prize recipient and acclaimed "father" of the green revolution, has often stated, "We cannot build world peace on empty stomachs." Historically, the governments of today's developed countries began by providing their citizens security and protection and only later moved in to providing health, education, and other public goods, while today's developing countries are encouraged by international organizations to provide other public goods first, with very little donor attention being paid to security (Blattman and Miguel 2010).

Conflict clearly causes food insecurity. FAO (2000c) reports that $121 billion of agricultural output was lost to conflict in developing countries from 1970 to 1997, and that conflict in Africa between 1980 and 2000 destroyed agricultural output worth more than half of all the continent's aid receipts. Conflict can destroy up to 90 percent of GDP (Pinstrup-Andersen and Shimokawa 2008). Heidhues et al. (2004) and UNDP (2008) indicate that conflict can undermine decades' worth of development. Conflicts further compound the problems of infant mortality by encouraging governments to divert funds from social priorities to military spending.

The effect of food insecurity on conflict is less well understood, but very important. Collier et al. (2003) declare that low and unequally distributed per capita income is "the key root cause of conflict." Messer and Cohen (2007) conclude that most of the armed conflicts of the last fifty years have been "food wars." That is, food has been one of the sources of conflict, it has been used as a weapon during conflict, and the destruction of food systems during conflict leads to lasting food insecurity in the aftermath. They discuss how problems in the food system trigger conflict through natural disasters (Shepherd 1975); through economic channels, such as sudden shifts in market prices (Uvin 1996; case 9-7); or through political and land access issues (Collier and Quaratiello 1999; von Braun and Pandya-Lorch 2007). They further demonstrate that government revenues from taxing the export of cash crops—particularly sugarcane, cotton, and coffee—have been extensively used for arms purchases. Case 9-7 discusses a food conflict in Mexico, demonstrating that pockets of poverty within middle-income countries are significant as well because "although poverty itself does not cause violent conflict, it does provide a basis for it."

A 2003 UN Security Council report identified two main sources of the current conflicts in the central African states: poverty and lack of good governance. The World Bank (2004) similarly indicates that poor nations are three times as likely to experience civil war as middle-income nations. As seen in table 9.2, a comparison of sixty-seven countries that experienced conflict between 1980 and 2005 with forty-four developing countries that did not reveals that those in conflict had, in the period before conflict began, on average half the gross national income (GNI) per capita and negative economic growth, twice the poverty, less education, greater food insecurity, greater inequality between men and women, less access to improved water sources, and twice the under-five mortality rate (Pinstrup-Andersen 2006b; see also Pinstrup-Andersen and Shimokawa 2008). In addition, conflict countries had worse scores on the Freedom House Political Rights Index than those without conflict. The localized riots these relationships can spawn can spread into national and international conflicts, and support international terrorism. For more information, Blattman and Miguel (2010) review the theoretical and empirical literature on the causes of civil wars and civil conflict.

None of this is meant to imply that impoverished, marginalized, or hungry people are terrorists. The cross-country research and case studies demonstrate that exclusion, poverty, and related grievances provide a "moral and political foundation" for those who propagate violence (Pinstrup-Andersen and Shimokawa 2008). Miguel (2008) argues that the desperation of poverty makes violence or crime more attractive. Reducing poverty, hunger, and inequality between groups of people can significantly reduce the probability of conflict and terrorism (Pinstrup-Andersen 2003).

Much of this book has highlighted needed public goods investment that would increase stability and reduce the risk of conflict, including investment in research,

TABLE 9.2.
Means of Selected Socioeconomic Indicators for Countries in Conflict and Countries Not in Conflict, 1980–2005

Indicators	Means of MDG and economic indicators	
	Countries in which no conflict started in the next period	Countries in which conflict started in the next period
Headcount poverty index	13.0 (99)	17.1 (9)
Poverty gap index	5.4 (100)	8.5 (10)
Child mortality	61.6 (528)	124.5 (57)
Child malnutrition (HAZ)	22.8 (106)	34.3 (20)
Undernutrition	17.3 (157)	25.1 (19)
Access to improved water source	87.2 (62)	50.0 (4)
GDP per capita	9,357.9 (389)	3,569.4 (48)
Annual GDP growth rate	3.2 (400)	1.7 (49)

Source: World Development Indicator Online (World Bank 2010a). The number of observations is given in parentheses.

infrastructure, and human capital. Halting natural resource degradation to ensure that gains are not literally eroded away over time will provide long-lasting benefits to stability. Reducing the under-five mortality rate by 10 percentage points reduces the likelihood of armed conflict each year by 3 percentage points; reducing the headcount poverty index by 5 percentage points reduces the probability of conflict by 2.5–3.0 percentage points (Pinstrup-Andersen and Shimokawa 2008). Since economic crises can be ignited by unexpected changes in rainfall, early warning systems, insurance, and safety nets can help prevent conflict (Miguel 2008).

Miguel (2008) and Collier et al. (2003) propose that foreign aid should be targeted to states with fragile governments before conflict happens:

> Tracking current rainfall levels and commodity price movements is a good way to figure out which countries should receive the aid. The hope is that using more of the existing foreign aid pool as *insurance* for the poorest African countries in this way could pay off by preventing armed conflicts that jeopardize whole regions. (Miguel 2008, 11)

Freedom

The preservation of freedom may be regarded as one of government's highest and most difficult aims. The great difficulty lies in the fact that a government strong enough to preserve freedom is strong enough to take it away. Part of ensuring that governance is good for all stakeholders is securing to them the maximum level of liberty consistent with maintenance of a harmonious society and the fulfillment of all social goals.

Several of the major measures of governance are explicitly about freedom, such as the Freedom House political and civil liberties index, the Economic Freedom in the World index, and de Soto (2000). Freedom from gender discrimination was enshrined as one of the Millennium Development Goals. Many of the UN human rights are about individual freedom. Food sovereignty is the freedom of an individual or a nation to provide sufficient food for itself as it chooses.

Other freedoms have also been proposed whose execution is far from certain. Freedom from hunger is closely tied with freedom to life or freedom from want, but the mechanics of ensuring everyone a right to food are troublesome. Can hungry people sue their government for food? Can urban poor sue rural poor for not producing enough? Does a right to food translate into a right to own land on which to produce the food and/or costless inputs? Chapter 11 considers trade-offs between freedoms and between freedom and other societal goals.

U.S. President Franklin Delano Roosevelt talked about a freedom from fear. If freedom from fear is interpreted as freedom from risk, this is an impossibility. Freedom from risk implies total control over every variable and contingency, and would erase all freedom of expression or choice in order to ensure total control. There is additionally the problem that fear is by nature subjective and the cure for one person's fear (e.g., building a dam to prevent flooding) may excite another person's fear (e.g., loss of biodiversity).

Closely related, the precautionary principle seeks to avoid changes that might cause harm even though a causal link between the change and harm has not been empirically shown. The application of the precautionary principle in policymaking is somewhat controversial in cases where a policy measure that is likely to be of benefit to some stakeholder group is not implemented because of the risk of unsubstantiated harm to another. The former stakeholder group's desire for freedom from want may collide with the latter's desire for freedom from fear. Most countries are still trying to determine how to reconcile these various freedoms when the freedom from want or freedom from fear so often conflicts with economic freedoms, and when freedom from discrimination conflicts with freedom of expression. There are likely to be no simple answers that satisfy all parties, but collective action as well as government incentives and regulations may have an important role to play. Case 9-6 discusses international agreements on GMOs and the precautionary principle, highlighting the importance of stakeholder analysis for understanding national and international policy formation. The WTO agreements on GMO stipulate that an importing country must provide solid scientific reasoning for a health or environmental trade barrier and treat all producers equally regardless of point of origin. The Cartagena Protocol, by contrast, not only allows much greater latitude in setting "precautionary" trade barriers, but also permits governments to protect domestic GMO producers while blocking foreign producers or producers from specific regions as strictly forbidden under WTO rules.

Governance and Growth

Does improved governance lead to higher economic growth (North 1990; Barro 1991; Mauro 1995; Knack and Keefer 1995; Burnside and Dollar 2000), and/or does economic growth lead to improved governance (Rosenberg and Birdzell 1986; Eggertsson 1990; Mauro 1995; Clague et al. 1996; Keefer and Knack 1997)? If improved institutions develop only as the social need for them develops, then attempts to create them prior to that point may be ineffective. Chong and Calderon (2000) test both models simultaneously and find that both effects are important, and that economic growth tends to affect institutions faster than institutions affect growth. Their results further suggest that "the poorer the country and the longer the wait, the higher the influence of institutional reform on economic growth" (80). Rodrik (2006) further argues that improving institutions might be better at sustaining economic growth than igniting it.

The link between governance and poverty is strong. Many African peasant farmers avoid corruption by producing only enough to subsist on. Such behavior is a major barrier to increasing productivity and reducing poverty (Bates 1981). Governance reforms are credited with the enormous reduction of poverty in China, where the number of poor people decreased by 600 million from 1970 to 2007 (Chen and Ravallion 2008; case 9-2).

Recent Trends in Governance

Objective, quantitative measures of these elements of governance either do not exist or have fundamental flaws. There may be a wide difference between the independence of the judiciary or central bank in law (de jure) and in actual practice (de facto), so relying on de jure measures is problematic. Measures of corruption that rely on self-reporting by victims must deal with self-selection problems, while the number of corruption prosecutions does not differentiate between an increase in corruption and an increase in enforcement and ignores the measurement problems that exist without a free and independent press or judiciary. Similarly, if election districts have been sufficiently gerrymandered, voter turnout may not be a significant indicator of participation.

This has led most researchers to rely on subjective perceptions-based measures of governance. Corruption perceptions are an excellent case in point. Surveys of corruption perceptions are collected from three to sixteen experts with experience in multiple economies and surveys of domestic business leaders and citizens to form the CPI. The CPI is used by some of the surveys that it uses (e.g., Freedom House), implying that there will tend to be high degrees of correlation between different governance indexes. High correlation coefficients should not be confused with objectivity.

Trends in governance need to be interpreted with caution. Social norms on corruption and the proper role of government vary across nations and across time within the same nation. Knack and Azfar (2000) point out that in addition to these difficulties there is a selection bias in terms of what economies are covered by which data sources: those ranked for business purposes tend to be either well governed or large, but small corrupt nations will generally not be included. As more of the smaller and more corrupt regimes are added over time, this creates spurious time trends on average worldwide governance while making it appear that larger countries are more corrupt because large corrupt nations are included in the data set while small corrupt nations are not. Furthermore, the margins of error in measuring governance tend to be fairly large, and it is also difficult to ascertain to what extent changes are based on changes in the country, on changes in perceptions, or on the increase in the number of data sources available over time (KKM 2009). As such, the following trends should be interpreted with caution.

The six KKM (2009) measures of governance between 1996 and 2007 show that very little change appears to have occurred overall in SSA or in the Middle East/ North African regions. Compared to south Asia, which on average has seen stability and the effectiveness and quality of regulation decrease, this is relatively good news. The United States has also seen large decreases in almost every governance measure since 1996. Eastern Europe and the Caribbean have seen significant improvements in a number of areas.

Freedom House's indexes of political and civil rights demonstrate that governance improved in sub-Saharan Africa, Asia, and Latin America between 1991 and 2001, and stayed constant or worsened in Europe and the Middle East. Table 9.3 shows governments that have demonstrated improved governance by region. In every region there are governments that have improved and weakened their governance structures significantly. This demonstrates that progress is possible in every region—belying the notion that some areas are "culturally" impossible to reform. Similarly, even very well-governed countries can experience significant reversals.

Policies to Improve Governance

Unfortunately, there are more suggestions for what should be improved than there are solid answers for how to go about it. This reflects different path histories, social norms, and complementary institutions (Rodrik 2006). Many of the proposed solutions to reduce corruption—such as increasing bureaucrats' salaries, making decision making more transparent, and providing increased protection and encouragement to whistle-blowers—have prerequisites in order to be effective that may not hold

TABLE 9.3.
Countries Demonstrating Improved Governance by Region, 1991–2001

Asia	Africa	Eastern Europe	Latin America	Middle East
Bangladesh	Cameroon	Croatia	Honduras	Jordan
China	Central Africa	Latvia	Nicaragua	
India	Madagascar	Lithuania	Panama	
Indonesia	Mali		Paraguay	
North Korea			Venezuela	

Source: Freedom House.

true in all countries. Reliable third-party monitoring or effective and impartial judiciaries are but two examples. Proposed solutions to improve one ideal sometimes vie with other ideals: reserving seats in the national legislature for marginalized groups increases their participation but makes these same legislators less accountable.

Different dimensions of good governance interact with each other. Concentrating on only a single aspect of governance may actually worsen the overall situation. For instance, the quality of health, education, justice, and public service provision can actually go down as transparency and punitive accountability are increased unless bureaucratic incentives are simultaneously realigned (Prendergast 2002; Dranove et al. 2003; Bar-Isaac, Caruana, and Cuñat 2008; Gavazza and Lizzeri 2007). A more holistic approach that accounts for the total effects, including unintended consequences, of planned changes is required. Public-private partnerships can play a significant role in bringing stakeholders together to find mutually agreeable solutions.

Many sources recommend increasing civil servant wages to reduce corruption. Unfortunately, as Svensson (2005) points out, much of the evidence on its actual effectiveness is conflicting and appears to rely heavily on other conditions, particularly effective third-party monitoring. Kaufmann and Kraay (2008, 8) discuss the problem:

> It is difficult to know which rules should be reformed and in what order. Will establishing an anticorruption commission or passing legislation outlawing bribery have any impact on reducing corruption? If so, which is more important? Should, instead, more efforts be put into ensuring that existing laws and regulations are implemented or that there is greater transparency, access to information, or media freedom? How soon should one expect to see the impacts of these interventions? Given that governments typically operate with limited political capital to implement reforms, these tradeoffs and lags are important.

Good governance is both an outcome of the various institutions in a society and a philosophy about "the right way of doing business" within any given institution, including NGOs, MNCs, and international organizations. Improving governance, then, is in part about installing new institutions, such as guaranteeing freedom of the press or creating new research organizations. It is also about changing the mindset of current organizations, linking them more closely with stakeholders (Krishna 2002) and ensuring access to information at all levels of government as part of the operating philosophy of the organization. This orientation toward good governance can make NGOs, MNCs, and other nongovernmental bodies more effective and improve overall governance.

Birner (2007) divides governance reforms into demand- or supply-side changes. Economists and sociologists tend to focus on the demand side with initiatives to increase citizen participation and government accountability so that citizens can demand the policies they want. These initiatives include reserving seats on governing councils or advisory boards for disadvantaged groups (Chattopadhyay and Duflo 2004), implementing citizen initiatives, establishing feedback mechanisms for users of government services, and pursuing democratization or political decentralization. Strengthening civil society groups is a high priority.

Political scientists tend to focus on the supply side: the responsiveness, efficiency, power, and capacity of the agencies supplying reforms. There are many recommended methods for trying to introduce private-sector-like incentives to public good provision, including reorienting bureaucracies to view citizens as clients or customers and outsourcing to the private sector or having private sector oversight. Public-private enterprises, user-management systems, and e-government movements can work on both supply and demand sides simultaneously.

The five primary types of reform encouraged over the last thirty years are decentralization, deregulation, privatization, improved macroeconomic stability, and trade liberalization. Macroeconomic stability was discussed in chapter 2. Trade liberalization will be addressed in chapter 10. The rest will now be discussed in turn.

Bringing government services closer to the level of consumers—decentralization—enables citizens to oversee operations (transparency and accountability) and tailor programs to community needs (participation). Hazell et al. (2007) argue for more decentralization for agricultural policies. More localized services can help bring formal and informal institutions into closer alignment in highly diverse societies.

Some of these reforms have been successful at maintaining access for the neediest members of society to necessary services while lowering costs, while many others have failed. Uganda's health care system was devolved to local councils on the grounds that they had better information on needs. Despite budgeting appropriate amounts to support the councils, inputs often did not reach the facilities, preventing them from working efficiently (case 9-1). Von Braun and Pandya-Lorch (2007) point out that local elite capture and lack of incentive can still be problematic at local levels just as at national, and they propose several reforms that can improve decentralization efforts.

In cases 9-1 and 9-2, Fan argues that decentralization can be profitably carried one step further. Rather than putting local government in charge of programs, communities themselves can be effective owners and managers of infrastructure projects. Costs can be significantly lowered this way while providing sustainable access. The risk of elite capture is still present, however.

Deregulation has been a prime feature of governance changes in recent decades. Countries in southern Africa with relatively open markets are better able to fill food gaps than countries where the government is directly involved or restricts private sector trade (Mano, Isaacson, and Dardel 2003; cases 7-1, 7-2, and 7-3). In 2003 the private sector in Malawi imported about 80 percent of the amount the government imported that year (Mano, Isaacson, and Dardel 2003). With the proper incentives (or lack of disincentives), the market can be quite active in importing grain even in landlocked economies with high transportation costs.

Public sector enterprises (PSEs) have proven significantly difficult to reform by themselves, making privatization attractive. Fan (cases 9-1 and 9-2) encourages governments to consider a range of options for encouraging private sector engagement in order to reduce corruption, waste, inefficiency, and government expenditures. In the best case, this will enable services to reach more people at higher quality with lower costs.

There have been many cases where privatization attempts have failed to improve market efficiency. Partial reforms that do not adequately resolve constraints are often fingered as the culprit in these failed reforms. As discussed in cases 7-1, 7-2, and 7-3, because Malawi's marketing board was only partially privatized, Malawi suffered "all of the instability of the market but [reaped] none of the benefits" (Rubey 2003, 3). A chicken-and-egg scenario is being played out by the private sector and many governments. The government is reluctant to fully privatize the PSE until it knows that the private sector has the infrastructure and capacity to respond to demand, fearing price volatility and famine. However, the private sector is unwilling to invest as long as the PSE exists and creates an uncertain environment for the traders.

Feige (1998, 33) discusses a similar problem in postcommunist Russia:

> Incomplete liberalization—the maintenance of arbitrary gaps between buy and sell prices—produces incentives for rent-seeking and acquisitive behaviors. Incomplete privatization—the maintenance of valuable assets in the public domain with amorphous property rights—produces incentives for predation. Incomplete legalization—the maintenance of arbitrary discretion in place of the rule of law—sustains high levels of uncertainty and transaction costs, and discourages the reallocation of resources to productive activities.

International Governance

There is a growing list of reasons why increasing international cooperation is becoming more desirable. The macro-, meso-, and microeconomic policies of national governments discussed in chapter 2 have effects that extend beyond their borders. Stakeholders in other countries are unable to participate in the choice of policies that impact them. Without enforced international agreements, politicians are not held accountable for the effects of their choices on people in other countries. Preferential access rules deny the principle of equality under the law. Despite international agreements on corruption, firms are rarely held responsible by either their host or recipient country for paying bribes. Food riots and food-related conflicts can rapidly spread beyond national borders, and there is no means to effectively intervene to stop conflict or prevent it on a regional or international level in many instances.

Economic burdens are also imposed across borders. As monetary policies change, short-term capital flows rapidly adjust, forcing outside governments to adjust their macropolicies to offset the gain or loss in capital. Rajan (2008) refers to this as "exporting inflation." The ability of finance traders to destabilize a currency can be seen as both a necessary check against improper government policies and a source of dangerous risk to the livelihoods of millions. The escalating tariff system in developed countries that taxes manufactured products more than raw materials changes the balance of trade in developing countries and reduces their range of development options (chapter 10). Biofuel subsidies in a few countries are partially to blame for the rapid increase in world food prices in the 2004–2008 period. The ability of food-exporting countries to instantly and without warning remove export foods from international markets generates significant food system instability and food insecurity for millions.

Basu (2006) argues that national policies were sufficient for dealing with poverty in the past, but that international capital flight weakens national government policy effectiveness to the point that international cooperation and coordination is necessary. Baldwin (2008) similarly notes that EU members exhibit increasing desires to integrate their policymaking as unilateral policymaking becomes less and less effective. Many international public goods, such as agricultural research and technology transfer, are undersupplied, while international public bads, particularly pollution and crime, are oversupplied. The same efficiency arguments that support government intervention on a national scale apply internationally, as do the same cautions that warn against too much government interference.

In many cases the institutional and organizational framework for addressing these spillovers and externalities does not exist. Without effective international institutions—formal and informal—to deal with these and other spillovers and externalities, globalization could continue to reduce the ability of governments (and their citizens) to determine their own policies, world income inequality may rapidly increase while the poor are marginalized, and inefficient risk management could hamper global productivity.

International Governance Questions

The question of what constitutes good governance, and for whom, is more difficult to answer in an international context. The most desirable governance qualities in specific international organizations may not be the same qualities that are vital in ensuring good national governance. Though the concepts of transparency and accountability translate directly to international organizations, participation, equality, the rule of law, and democracy likely do not mean the same things when speaking of nation-state members as when discussing the rights of individual citizens in those countries. There are far more questions currently than solid answers.

One of the most important questions concerns what form international democracy should take. The institutions of democracy have changed greatly over the course of history as the size of the governed body grew. A pure democracy, where each enfranchised person votes on each issue and each vote has equal weight, was satisfactory in the city-states of ancient Greece. With the formation of the nation-states, however, it was seen that it was infeasible for each citizen to vote on every issue. A more representative form of government was created that a citizen of ancient Athens would never have recognized as democracy. It has been argued similarly that international democracy is not likely to resemble the national democracies with which most people are familiar today. The representative bodies in the UN are appointed by elected officials rather than elected directly, for instance. It is still largely undetermined how our concept of democracy will be altered in the decades and centuries to come.

Should we be most concerned about the participation of individual stakeholders or governments? More broadly, should countries be treated equally or the citizens within those countries? The difference between a one-country/one-vote rule and a one-person/one-vote rule is the difference between whether China controls 0.5 percent or nearly 20 percent of world voting power, and whether the voices of the residents of small island nations are heard at all. The United States has faced these competing notions and the EU grapples with them anew now. At the time the U.S. Constitution was formed, the individual states were seen as independent nations. In exchange for sacrificing their state sovereignty to a larger, regional government, they agreed to the formation of a bicameral legislation with one chamber's representatives selected by population weights and democratic vote and the other chamber's selected by state governors or legislations under the principle of sovereign equality (Watson 2009).

One of the primary arguments against the formation of additional international organizations is that of national sovereignty. If people from other nations can influence domestic policies, it lessens domestic citizens' voice and ability to control how they choose to live. A similar argument can be, and has been, made for local versus national government and for individual freedom versus any government control at all. It is the same argument that compels one to find systems of coordination between citizens to produce public goods, reduce public bads, and generate greater stability and order in society at each level of organization.

The challenge is to find the right level of governance (personal, local, state, national, regional, or global) for each challenge. Purely interpersonal exchanges can and should still be made at that individual level. When those exchanges significantly affect others, there is a need for interventions to provide more efficient outcomes. When these spillovers cross national borders, there is a need for international coordination.

Should the rights of nation-states within international organizations be dependent on their own governance? Is it ethical and equitable to treat equally governments that are not democratically elected, that are corrupt, that support terrorism, or that torture and abuse human rights, with more benevolent, "better" governed countries? Alternatively, is it ethical that the citizens of those countries be punished for the corruption of an unelected tyrant? These questions were brought up during the FAO World Food Summit, when nations from South America, Africa, and the Middle East decried placing conditionalities on food aid, restricting the spread of agricultural technology, and restricting food trade with poorly governed countries as policies that use "food as a weapon."[5]

These questions are relevant to the global food system, such as when considering the formulation of international food policy (chapter 2), food safety legislation (chapters 3 and 4), the proper role of markets and governments (chapter 6), and food trade regimes (chapter 10). Can health and quality standards be left to private industry and civil society or is government intervention needed? If governments intervene, can the regulations, incentives, and knowledge be effectively enacted by national governments or must there be a set of global organizations and institutions to guide the process? The record to date gives very mixed evidence supporting each proposition. Miguel (2008) implies that when NGOs are sufficiently capable of performing the "watchdog" role, market mechanisms can be an effective tool to ensure health and safety standards.

Even where civil organizations are effective, however, there are concerns that they are more reactive than preventative. Governments may be better placed to establish consistent, stable standards that prevent problems from arising before they happen. Governments are also more susceptible of capture by lobbying organizations, including the businesses they are supposed to regulate, and their stability can make them ill equipped to deal with new technologies, such as nanotechnologies in food (chapter 7).

There is also the issue of exporting regulation (Baldwin 2008). One example, discussed in chapter 4 and case 3-11, is that the EU standards on the aflatoxin content in foods are set higher than the international standards, with the result that many African economies are unable to gain access to the EU markets. This higher standard is estimated to save one person in the EU from death by liver cancer each year at a cost of over $500 million to African cereal, nut, and fruit farmers compared to CODEX standards. The number of lives that could have been saved with that $500 million in Africa shows an implicit valuation of African lives vis-à-vis European lives. Another example of exporting regulation occurs when MNCs adopt the higher standards of another country and lobby their home governments to adapt domestic laws to match those of foreign countries to ensure that purely domestic competitors don't have an advantage in the home market. Resolving any of these concerns involves international cooperation and coordination.

International Organizations

In a critique of IMF governance, Martinez-Diaz (2008) discusses four roles that the executive boards of international organizations could play: political counterweight, strategic thinker, performance police, and democratic forum. Each of these is necessary in ensuring good international governance, but because they involve significant trade-offs, it may not be possible to effectively pursue all of them within one organization.

Political counterweights ensure that the interests of member nation-states are represented in the decision-making process, so board members should identify with the interests of the country (or countries) they represent rather than with the organization and watch over its activities closely through extensive bureaucracy and frequent meetings. Almost in opposition to this role, an executive board tasked with being a strategic thinker should be distant from the day-to-day decision-making process, meet infrequently to discuss the organization's broader context and goals, and be composed of independent experts. As performance police, boards should set out transparent standards of accountability against which agency performance can be measured whether or not that performance is currently in the interests of particular nations or not. In order for the governing board to be a democratic forum, it must be inclusive and allow each member the opportunity to express dissenting opinions. Democratic forums and political counterweights place the highest premium on participation and consensus, while transparency, accountability, and the rule of law are best protected by performance police. With the exception of democratic forums—which focus more on processes than outcomes—each is concerned with the efficiency of resource use, but approaches efficiency from very different perspectives.

FAO, UNICEF, and similar organizations have convened conferences of world leaders on a number of occasions, encouraging them to pledge their political will to resolve the problems of hunger, lack of education, gender discrimination, and others. Once made, however, these promises have generally fallen by the wayside unfulfilled. One of the several reasons for this is that these organizations have no enforcement mechanism to ensure that governments keep their promises. In matters of enforcing compliance, the national sovereignty complaint is less troublesome because the goals being encouraged are ones to which governments themselves agreed. Many international agreements, however, have built-in escape clauses that allow governments to avoid fulfilling their obligations whenever they are inconvenient. For instance, the United States has exempted itself from the methyl bromide protocol, designed to reduce application of an ozone-depleting chemical pesticide, because of the economic harm to California's strawberry and tomato industries (Avgerinopoulou 2005).

Chapter 8 discussed the importance of adopting a full-costing approach to reduce environmental externalities. One of the key issues preventing such a policy is the lack of international agreement on dealing with environmental issues. Suppose only one country enacted a series of full-costing laws on its own firms but not on firms that export to it. This would give foreign firms a competitive advantage, prompting the exodus of domestic firms to other countries. That implies that these full-costing laws would have to apply to all firms doing business in that country. Applying full-costing laws, however, requires great knowledge about the specific production conditions and their spillovers, information that will be very difficult to coordinate with countries that do not share that policy framework and difficult to gather without extensive, expensive bureaucratic support. Even if that could be worked through, some governments would complain that the full-costing measures represented trade-restricting policies and challenge them at the WTO. Without an international framework to work through these issues, full-costing is unlikely to become a reality.

As mentioned in chapter 2, some commentators have called for the WTO to take up enforcement of environmental standards for just these reasons. Given that the WTO staff are trained in trade-related policy rather than environmental policy, however, others urge governments to reduce the scope of the WTO in environmental matters and support a new forum to take explicit account of international environmental law. Esty (2008) proposes a possible structure for a Global Environmental Organization that would focus on strategy and enforcement rather than on being a democratic forum. Rajan (2008) opines that the WB and IMF could fill the roles of such an organization, but it would require significant reorganization to improve their environmental capacity and governance.

One of the primary difficulties in establishing such a competing international organization is to determine which will have jurisdiction when environmental and trade matters collide. It is likely that complainants would choose whichever international body was most likely to uphold their argument, possibly to the detriment of justice and, ironically, the rule of law. Avgerinopoulou (2005) focuses on changing the governance structures of existing international organizations that have some environmental competence—such as the International Civil Aviation Organization for air travel and the International Maritime Organization for fisheries—to improve government and NGO compliance with environmental safeguards.

Among the primary concerns about the WB Group and IMF's governance are that the organizations are accountable to shareholders and stakeholders, their primary focus and missions are decreasingly relevant, and they can undermine government accountability to their own citizens. The WB and IMF affect the food system primarily through their funding of development projects and changes to trade, macro-, and mesolevel policies. The recent Poverty Reduction Strategy Paper initiative has been an attempt to give national governments more control over their development process. There are concerns that governments have not been giving sufficient attention to agriculture in their PRSPs.

Multinational corporations influence the food system for both good and ill. To the extent that private corporations improve market functions and undertake research and technology development that enables farmers to increase production, reduce hunger, and escape poverty, they do much good. As further discussed in chapters 6 and 10, public-private partnerships are of critical importance to support agricultural and rural development. While the private sector cannot be expected to invest in the development of public goods for which they cannot capture sufficient returns to cover costs and reasonable profits, it plays an important role in the creation of technology for which they can obtain exclusive rights. Attempts by some private corporations to reduce competition and generate monopoly or monopsony profits in the markets for agricultural inputs and outputs may harm farmers, consumers, and private traders. There is at present no international organization charged with the oversight of MNCs to prevent global monopolies or cartels, punish corruption, ensure workers' rights are respected, or forestall races to the bottom in labor and environmental standards. What is needed is an effective international organization that serves as political counterweight and democratic forum where policies can be coordinated.

Conclusion

Governance is the exercise of authority or management of resources through institutions, policies, traditions, cultures, and societal norms. This chapter has presented a model of good stakeholder governance that is broad enough to be applicable to local, national, and international governments, NGOs, and other civil society organizations. That generality rests on fundamental principles of ensuring that all stakeholder groups are able to participate in decision making in a meaningful way, to receive promised benefits, and hold decision makers accountable. In doing so, it has been argued, as many decisions as feasible should be rules based and transparent to promote the equal treatment of all stakeholders. At the same time, policies and institutions should attempt to preserve notions of freedom, equality, and stability. Because these principles of governance transcend particular institutions, organizations, and systems, they are widely applicable and adaptable to different contexts.

Demand-side governance reforms increase citizen participation and government accountability so that citizens can demand the policies they want. Supply-side reforms emphasize the responsiveness, efficiency, power, and capacity of the agencies supplying reforms. The exact mix and timing of reforms that should be implemented are highly sensitive to an area's history, culture, and factors currently constraining development. Chinese market reforms, for instance, were phased in gradually over years, with market prices taking effect only after farmers had met their quotas. This created both a government safety net and incentives to increase production in a unique institutional structure fit for Chinese history.

On the international front, several critical governance institutions are very weak or missing altogether. Among them are organizations and mechanisms capable and responsible for providing international public goods, dealing with international environmental externalities, and unifying private corporation governance. These factors are of critical importance to the global food system and are likely to become more so over time.

However, the structures of international institutions tend to differ greatly from their national counterparts. The UN system, for instance, functions at the will of its member states, who are free to opt out of agreements at any time. Neither countries nor the people in them are weighted equally. By trying to work from consensus as much as possible, the least willing states have great latitude to alter international agreements and weaken them. This makes any kind of international governance reform remarkably difficult to effect. As the costs of continued lack of public goods and international governance grows, however, these questions will have to be addressed. Chapter 10 follows by considering international trade governance and trade's effects on the global food system.

Governance and Institutions Case Studies

Although the term "food policy" is often interpreted to mean sectoral micro- or mesoeconomic policies, food systems are strongly influenced by macroeconomic policies and governance institutions, as shown by cases in this section. Institutions enter into food systems in a variety of ways at local, national, and international levels, and institutional innovation is a critical element of effective policy design and implementation.* These issues and the related role of governments are discussed, along with the impact of instability and armed conflict on food security.

* The case studies referenced here are presented in full in the three-volume work by Per Pinstrup-Andersen and Fuzhi Cheng, eds., *Case Studies in Food Policy for Developing Countries* (Ithaca, NY: Cornell University Press, 2009) and online via open access at http://cip.cornell.edu/gfs.

Cases 9-1 and 9-2 examine the impacts of large-scale public goods investment on poverty reduction and economic growth in different contexts. WTO governance is addressed in Cases 9-3 and 9-4. Cases 9-5 and 9-6 discuss how international agreements are made in the case of health (9-5) and environmental regulation (9-6). Case 9-7 focuses on the feedbacks between the food system and conflict. Case 9-8 shows the impacts of different macroeconomic development strategies on the Zambian agricultural sector. Case 9-9, available exclusively online, deals with labeling genetically modified foods and the extent to which this is best carried out by private or public institutions.

9-1   Linkages between Government Spending, Growth, and Poverty in Uganda and Tanzania
       Shenggen Fan
9-2   Linkages between Government Spending, Growth, and Poverty in India and China
       Shenggen Fan
9-3   Cambodia's WTO Accession
       Fuzhi Cheng
9-4   The WTO Dispute Settlement Mechanism and Developing Countries: The Brazil–U.S. Cotton Case
       Fuzhi Cheng
9-5   The Sugar Controversy
       Fernando Vio and Ricardo Uauy
9-6   Biosafety, Trade, and the Cartagena Protocol
       Fuzhi Cheng
9-7   Coffee, Policy, and Stability in Mexico
       Beatriz Ávalos-Sartorio
9-8   Development Strategies, Macroeconomic Policies, and the Agricultural Sector in Zambia
       Danielle Resnick and James Thurlow
9-9   The Role of Government in the Labeling of GM Food
       Camille Emma

Notes

1. A "race to the bottom" refers to any situation where an agent—a person, firm, or nation—takes an action to improve its own position relative to others that hurts those others and encourages them to engage in the same action. When a new equilibrium is reached, all are worse off than originally.

2. Deadweight loss refers to the loss of efficiency or consumer/producer surplus from an economy that is not at a Pareto equilibrium. To take a simple example, if a policy increases one person's taxes by $10 and distributes $5 to another person, the deadweight loss is $5. Whether or not this is an acceptable trade-off is an ethical question discussed in chapter 11.

3. A principal hires an agent to do certain tasks where the agent has more information about the effort expended or underlying shocks and the two do not necessarily have the same

priorities. This can lead the agent to shirk responsibility to the detriment of the principal. The goal of principal-agent problems is to devise a payment system that encourages the agent to act in the manner desired by the principal.

4. http://www.prsgroup.com/countrydata/countrydata.html.

5. See the interventions made by the representatives of the Gambia, Guyana, and Iran, http://www.fao.org/wfs/index_en.htm.

Chapter 10

Globalization and the Food System

Introduction

Globalization is a powerful force in the world economy. It may improve or harm food systems and food security. The term "globalization" usually refers to increasing economic integration and flows of goods and services across national borders. Von Braun and Mengistu (2007a, 1) define globalization of the agro-food system as "the integration of the production and processing of agriculture and food items across national borders, through markets, standardization, regulations, and technologies." Four increasing cross-border flows are of particular importance for food systems:

1. Trade in goods and services resulting from liberalized food and agricultural trade policies, improved information and communications technology, and reduced transportation costs
2. Capital flows including foreign direct investment (FDI) and remittances in food systems
3. Food system knowledge and technology flows
4. Food system labor flows

Interactions between food systems and each of these flows, along with an analysis of their implications for poverty, health, and nutrition, will be discussed in this chapter.

Globalization offers opportunities for economic growth and development. According to the World Bank (2007a, 102), "Globalization, coupled with technological change, has driven growth in the world economy, bringing new employment opportunities and enabling millions of people to escape absolute poverty." Dinello and Squire (2005) find no evidence of increasing income inequality within countries, but present data showing that globalization increased inequality between countries simply because some countries (such as many east Asian countries) experienced a much higher growth than others (such as most African countries). They conclude that "globalization and growth eventually translate into poverty reduction in most regions and countries" (Dinello and Squire 2005, 25). However, "the risks and costs brought about by globalization can be significant for fragile developing economies and the world's poor" (Nissanke and Thorbecke 2007, 3).

Three aspects are responsible for much of the opposition to globalization, expressed through peaceful and violent street demonstrations and much debate (Bardhan 2006). First, highly valued local and indigenous cultures are perceived to be at risk of being harmed by global mass production and cultural homogenization. Second, large-scale, volatile, short-term movements of capital in and out of countries cause serious economic disruptions to countries. Third, international trade and FDI change the demand for labor in different sectors of national and local economies, leading to job losses, wage reductions, and hardships for certain groups and new opportunities for other groups. Losing groups are seldom compensated.

Globalization is multifaceted and complex, and takes place in varying circumstances. Therefore, questions such as "is globalization good or bad for the poor?" and "does globalization have positive or negative effects on the global food system?" cannot be answered abstractly. The outcomes of globalization depend on which part of globalization is considered and the socioeconomic and political environments at different levels of organization. The specific impacts of globalization are heavily influenced by national policies. This chapter outlines the most critical links between globalization and food systems and identifies policy issues and options to guide globalization to improve the food system and enhance the benefits for low-income people.

Globalization influences food systems through changes in governance, capital availability, employment, incomes, relative prices facing producers and consumers, access to dietary diversity, advertisement, labor mobility, women's status, lifestyle, and energy expenditure. These changes in turn impact diet diversity and composition, food safety standards, food quality, human health and nutrition, poverty, food production, the environment, child care and time allocation, and access to knowledge and technology. While globalization improves global economic efficiency by allocating production according to comparative advantage, the distribution of the benefits and costs from efficiency gains is extremely important from a welfare and policy perspective (Stiglitz 2002). The magnitude and distribution of these benefits and costs among various stakeholder groups depend on a number of factors, including the following seven:

1. The degree of price transmission: Are price changes at the border fully transmitted to all market agents? The degree of price transmission depends largely on the domestic market structure, government policy, and particularly the condition of domestic infrastructure.
2. The domestic market structure and conduct. The main issues are relative market power, relative market efficiency, domestic price transmission, trade policy, and the institutional framework (chapter 6). For example, a market

with few large-scale traders and many independent smallholders likely distributes globalization's benefits very differently from a market with many small-scale traders and strong farmer organizations such as marketing cooperatives.

3. Physical infrastructure, including roads, ports, rails, electricity, communications networks, irrigation canals, and storage. Market efficiency and stakeholders' ability to benefit from the opportunities presented by globalization are heavily influenced by infrastructure. Poor roads and rails produce high transportation costs; insufficient ports create bottlenecks and high costs; lack of access to a sufficient and continuous supply of energy increases production costs and risks; and poor communications infrastructure such as lack of access to radios, telephones, Internet, television, and satellite coverage causes high transaction costs and poor market information dissemination (see chapter 6). Most of the needed infrastructure is of a public goods nature. Countries that fail to make the corresponding public investments may be bypassed by the opportunities offered by globalization.

4. Access to knowledge and technology. Transfer of knowledge and technology offers great opportunities for improvements in low-income countries' food systems. Technology transfer may be linked to FDI or to exchange between universities and research institutes. As discussed in chapter 9, the creation of global public goods and institutions is extremely important to guide globalization to create efficiency gains sustainably and distribute benefits and costs ethically. At the same time, intellectual property rights regimes, including those included in WTO/TRIPS (Trade-Related Aspects of Intellectual Property Rights), play an important role in the access to technology for the domestic food systems (discussed below). A significant portion of the chapter discusses the international research system and the pros and cons of biotechnology.

5. Human resource conditions. Countries with a poorly educated, unhealthy, malnourished labor force are not likely to be major beneficiaries of globalization. They could actually be marginalized and made worse off. While globalization offers new employment opportunities and efficiency gains, people with few skills and low productivity will be relegated to low-paying jobs or simply bypassed. Exposure to global competition has sometimes formed a dual food system, in which the high-income minority integrates with the international market through imports and supermarkets, while the poor majority is left to its own devices. Public investment in increasing worker productivity at the lower end of the income distribution (e.g., health care, good nutrition, primary education, and skill development) is critical not only on humanitarian grounds but to bring the poor into the global economy and avoid armed conflict (chapters 9 and 11).

6. Access to capital. The vast majority of private capital flows have been to middle-income countries, where expected returns are higher and perceived risks are lower. FDI in many of those countries has improved the domestic food systems' efficiency and enhanced the penetration of globalization benefits

in the population. Low-income economies with poor infrastructure, poorly functioning food markets, a low-productivity labor force, and adverse public policies have been all but bypassed, except for small amounts of development assistance and the more recent foreign investment in gaining control over land for the production of food and biofuel. As a result, their relative competitive position in the global economy is weak and deteriorating.

7. Asymmetric globalization. Negotiations within the multinational framework hosted by the World Trade Organization (WTO) have been unable to remove or significantly reduce trade-distorting agricultural policies in most OECD and several developing countries. Thus, countries that remove food trade distortions (e.g., member countries in NAFTA and CAFTA) are faced with competition from countries where agricultural subsidies permit export at prices below the cost of production. Such artificially low food prices are beneficial for consumers and disadvantageous for farmers (chapter 6). Bilateral and multilateral agreements restrict the policy response that participating developing countries may pursue, an issue referred to as reduced policy space (Page 2007). Protective import tariffs are usually not permitted under the WTO regime. Tokarick (2008), Tutwiler and Straub (2007), and Hoekman, Ng, and Olarreaga (2002) provide useful summaries of the sources of OECD agricultural protection and who would benefit most from which form of trade liberalization.

The current wave of globalization offers developing countries significant new opportunities for broad-based economic growth, poverty alleviation, and improved human health and nutrition. However, despite significant efficiency gains, perceptions and empirical evidence about the distribution of benefits and costs have raised serious concerns in many quarters about the desirability and ethics of globalization as currently practiced.

The current failure to compensate the perceived or documented losses by groups of low-income people through safety nets and retraining programs strengthens popular opposition to globalization and political pressures to return to a situation of more closed economies protected by trade-distorting policies. The large international food price fluctuations during 2007–2011 and the beggar-thy-neighbor policy responses of some nations added political pressures on many national governments to pursue protection through trade distortions. While there is ample evidence about the overall economic gains from globalization, the news media and other opinion-forming groups tend to focus on those who lose rather than those who gain. Chapter 9 argued that there is an urgent need for institutional innovation to guide globalization toward a more acceptable distribution of benefits and costs.

As shown in chapter 3, global food market integration has shifted diet structure in developing countries. Globalization has reduced the consumption of traditional, low-cost diets, rich in fiber and grain, and increased high-cost, energy-dense diets that include more refined sugar, sweeteners, vegetable oils, and animal fats. Together with changes in lifestyles toward less manual labor, these diet changes cause increasing overweight, obesity, and chronic diseases. Aggressive promotion of energy-dense and processed foods by producers and distributors and rapid increases in FDI in developing countries' food systems have contributed to these dietary changes (cases 10-1 and 4-1).

In this chapter, we go beyond those nutritional concerns and illustrate several other policy challenges brought about by globalization. First, most industrial and many developing nations still significantly protect agriculture, while substantial trade reforms have reduced the protection of the manufacturing sector. In fact, as further discussed in cases 10-2 and 10-3, agricultural protection continues to be among the most contentious issues in global trade negotiations, with high protection in industrial economies as the main cause of periodic breakdowns in multilateral trade negotiations. This is what we referred to in point 7 above as asymmetric globalization.

Second, the increase of FDI and the penetration of multinational corporations (MNCs) into developing country markets have changed the competitive structure of developing country food markets, providing new opportunities for some private traders, smallholder farmers, and rural poor while bypassing others who are made relatively, and sometimes absolutely, worse off. For instance, rapid increases in the market share of supermarkets, brought about largely by FDI, have made safer, higher quality food available, usually at somewhat higher prices. This alters the competitive position of traditional wet markets and small-scale grocery stores.

Third, very limited investments by most developing country governments in food systems research and technology development, together with enhanced opportunities for the private sector to obtain exclusive property rights to plant varieties and other live organisms, have generated rapid increases in MNC investment in food systems research and technology. While some such research is aimed at the solution of poor people's problems, much of the technology needed by smallholder farmers is of a public goods nature and will be developed in sufficient quantities only if public funds are available.

Furthermore, low-income farmers may not have the capital or access to credit to be able to purchase private technology. The result is very limited economic demand for technology that would benefit poor farmers even though it would be developed by the private sector if farmers could express their technology needs in economic demand (chapter 7). Recent developments in biotechnology and the rapid global expansion of GM crops have raised concerns among some stakeholder groups, including some transnational advocacy groups, on the grounds that the knowledge about the impact on human and environmental health is insufficient (chapter 11).

Finally, sharp increases in migration of both low- and high-skilled workers from the South to the North have resulted in large flows of remittances and caused "brain drain" in the home countries. Low-skilled and illegal immigrants have led to substantial political debate. These and related challenges and policy options will be discussed in the rest of the chapter.

A brief clarification should be made early on: trade occurs between individuals and between firms, even occasionally between governments. Sometimes that trade involves two people who live in close proximity to each other, and sometimes that trade spans hundreds or thousands of miles, possibly crossing multiple state or national borders. Despite the distance, trade occurs between people; international trade occurs between individuals who happen to live in different countries. It is cumbersome, however, to repeatedly use phrases such as "trade between people who live in industrialized economies" or "trade between people who live in Africa and people who live in Europe." It is much easier and therefore common to refer to trade *as if* it occurred between countries and regions: "trade between the United States and China," or "trade between Africa and Europe." This chapter will be no exception.

Whether trade takes place over short or wide distances, it is not a zero-sum game. Trade itself adds value to both parties (chapter 6), but it is not the case that changes in trade policy do not create losers as well as winners. The governance issues discussed in chapter 9 are very important for determining trade policy. Losses from changes in trade policy tend to be concentrated while benefits are dispersed widely, setting up larger incentives for negatively affected groups to lobby for changes than for benefited groups. Foreign multinationals are likely to be able to put their policy issues forward, while foreign workers or consumers affected by changes in trade policy are not likely represented. Chapters 3 and 11 discuss national food safety standards and how they impact trade, and chapter 8 discusses environmental standards.

The International Food Trade Situation

World food trade almost doubled over a twenty-five year period from $243 billion in 1980–1981 to $467 billion in 2005–2006. The European Union is the largest trader, followed by developing countries as a bloc. Trade between people in industrial economies dominates global food trade. Trade within trade blocs, such as the EU and NAFTA, accounts for more than a third of global food trade, a share that is growing over time. Intra-EU food imports increased from 51 percent of total food imports in 1980–1981 to 66 percent in 2005–2006, and intra-NAFTA from 29 percent to 44. This increase illustrates how removing tariff barriers stimulates trade.

Trade among developing countries is also increasing, with almost 50 percent of their food imports coming from other developing countries in 2005–2006. Only 39 percent of their food exports are to other developing countries, however, showing the continuing importance of industrial country markets for their exports.

Large differences in food trade performance persist among developing countries. For low-income developing countries (especially small ones), the 1980s were a period of declining trade, while the 1990s and early 2000s were periods of major expansion. Their overall food trade surpluses have risen from $7.4 billion in 1980–1981 to $10.5 billion in 2005–2006. Middle-income countries such as Argentina (soybeans, wheat, maize, and edible oils), Brazil (soybeans, meat, orange juice, sugar, and coffee), and Thailand (fish and rice) are becoming major food exporters. These countries, which do not usually have highly distorted agricultural trade regimes, are often considered as potential gainers from global liberalization (Dollar and Kraay 2004).

The upper-middle-income manufacturing exporters in east Asia are becoming major importers of agricultural commodities, as Japan is. Of these, South Korea and Taiwan (China) have distorted trade regimes, while Hong Kong (China) and

Singapore have liberal trade regimes. With liberalization, China and India, with one-third of the world's population, are emerging as major global exporters and importers. While they have trade surpluses, the surpluses have not increased significantly since 1990. The remaining middle-income countries experienced rapid trade growth during the 1990s and early 2000s, but their trade surpluses shrank considerably during this period. Trade liberalization among developing countries since the 1980s could explain some of their expanding imports.

The structure of world trade in food has changed since the 1980s along with overall trade. To examine the detailed flows, UN Comtrade (2007) separates food products into four groups.

1. Developing country tropical products, such as coffee, cocoa, tea, nuts, spices, textile fibers (mostly cotton), and sugar and confectionary products. This group's share of world trade value has been steadily decreasing since 1980.
2. Highly protected temperate zone products of industrial countries, such as meats, milk and milk products, grains, animal feed, and edible oil and oilseeds. Trade in this group has generally remained constant, though developed country grain exports have been cut at least in half.
3. Dynamic nontraditional products, such as seafood, fruits, vegetables, and cut flowers, for which global protection rates are lower. Seafood sales from developing countries tripled and other nontraditional exports increased by over 50 percent since 1980.
4. Other products, including processed agricultural products such as tobacco and cigarettes, beverages, and other processed foods. Exports of these products from developed countries have almost doubled, and developing country exports of beverages more than doubled, within the last decade.

Product groups that have expanded include fruits and vegetables, which now have the largest share of world exports at 19 percent; fish and seafood, at 12 percent; and alcoholic and nonalcoholic beverages, at almost 9 percent. The largest declines between 1980–1981 and 2005–2006 took place for grains, from 17 percent to 10 percent. These and other declines result from a combination of price declines, low demand elasticities, product substitution (e.g., synthetic fiber for cotton), and, in the case of sugar and grains, expanded developed country production (FAO 2007b).

For developing countries the biggest decline in export shares has come in their traditional tropical products, such as coffee and cocoa, while the biggest gains have come in nontraditional exports, such as seafood and fruits and vegetables. For products with high OECD import tariffs, such as grains, the increase in export shares since the 1990s is due exclusively to expanding trade among developing countries; these products lost shares in industrial country markets and gained them in developing country markets (FAO 2007b).

Commodities such as seafood, fruits, vegetables, cut flowers, and processed products constitute about 40 percent of the exports of developing countries, while the traditional products that have received most of the attention in the literature now constitute only 19 percent of the exports of developing countries. Attention has to be placed on efforts to reduce tariff escalation in processed foods (case 10-11) and on further expanding trade within developing countries in temperate zone products such as milk, grains, and meats. These developments show that many developing countries can compete in the product categories historically dominated by industrial countries and that trade reforms in industrial sectors could lead to a large expansion of exports from these developing countries.

An increasing share of global trade consists of similar products. China both imports and exports chicken from and to the United States, for example. How is this possible? Trade is based on economies of scale and slightly differentiated products: chicken feet and beef offal that are not valued in the United States are considered delicacies in China, whose citizens do not value breast meat as much as Americans. This type of trade equalizes food prices across countries and reduces price volatility.

Differences in production methods and market structure (chapter 6) also produce trade opportunities. The U.S. hog sector is designed to mass-produce very similar cuts of meat, while the Danish hog sector's emphasis on small cooperatives in production and processing can adapt to and supply high-quality niche markets around the world.

Trade-Distorting Policies

Trade-distorting policies are pervasive in global food markets. The experience with trade policy reforms in market access, export subsidies, and domestic support indicates that the Uruguay Round Agreement on Agriculture (URAA) has had modest impacts at best (Anderson and Martin 2006). Within OECD nations, producer support in agriculture was about $230 billion in 2000–2002, or almost 45 percent of the value of production (evaluated at world prices), down from approximately 63 percent in 1986–1988, but still very high.[1]

Of producer support, about two-thirds came through higher prices associated with border protection (tariffs and nontariff barriers) or "market price support," and one-third from direct subsidies or "budgetary payments." Both domestic subsidies (except those absolutely decoupled from production decisions) and border protection contribute to large trade distortions that increase fluctuations in international prices and impede trade flows, depress world prices, and discourage market entry or delay exit by noncompetitive producers. (Cases 10-2 and 10-3 provide additional details on the OECD agricultural policies.)

Domestic support in OECD nations has substantial negative effects on producers in developing countries. Cotton subsidies in the United States and European Union, for example, reached $4.4 billion in a $20 billion market in 2001–2002. Such large subsidies shield noncompetitive producers in developed countries from exit decisions but drive efficient producers in developing countries out of the market. If U.S. cotton subsidies were abolished, revenues for cotton farmers in west and central Africa would increase by some $250 million (case 10-5). International agreements to gradually reduce import tariffs for textiles and reach their complete elimination by January 1, 2005, resulted in major changes in trade flows. Within less than a year, the EU and the United States introduced new trade restrictions (case 10-7).

Protective measures (tariffs in particular) for agricultural commodities are usually kept in place to accommodate domestic support policies.[2] Although the average agricultural tariff in developed countries has been cut to relatively low levels (11 percent for the United States, European Union, Japan, and Canada), its structure remains complicated and nontransparent. Case 10-13 addresses the effects of reduced rice tariffs in Haiti.

Relatively low average agricultural tariffs in industrial countries hide tariff peaks that reach up to 500 percent. Tariff peaks usually apply to commodities produced domestically, while lower tariffs are imposed on commodities that are not produced locally. This is why the OECD measure of protection that compares local and international prices shows much higher rates of protection than do average tariffs, and why average tariffs can underestimate the real degree of protection given to local producers.[3] Tariffs also increase by the degree of product processing, creating an escalating tariff structure that impedes access to processed-food markets (case 10-11). In addition, almost 30 percent of OECD production is protected by tariff rate quotas—a measure that permits limited market access but causes more complexity in tariff regimes (case 10-4).

Although lower tariffs and the move toward decoupling production subsidies from production are beginning to reduce the need for export subsidies in agriculture in order to remove the resultant domestic surpluses, export subsidies continue to distort world markets. The European Union accounts for almost 90 percent of all OECD export subsidies. With usage levels low early in the implementation period, when world prices were high, several countries carried forward unused export subsidy credits for later use. High food prices during the period 2005–2008 provide similar opportunities. Circumvention, through the subsidy elements of export credits, export restrictions, and revenue-pooling arrangements in major products, remains a concern. Implicit export subsidies lend unfair advantage to industrial country producers. In the United States and the European Union, export prices of cotton are less than half the average cost of production (Oxfam 2002).

In WTO terms, subsidies are identified as belonging to "boxes" on the basis of their expected trade distortion. The amber box contains support measures that are considered to be trade distorting; the blue box covers subsidy payments that are directly linked to production quotas or land retirement; the green box includes policies that cause very limited or no trade distortion (Ingco and Nash 2004).

Decoupled payments, considered to be green box measures, play an important role in recent efforts by the United States and the EU to reduce trade-distorting agricultural subsidies (cases 10-2 and 10-3). In addition to decoupling, numerous one-time buyouts have taken place, including New Zealand's exit grant in 1984, the buyout of Canada's grain transportation subsidy in 1995, and the buyout of the U.S. peanut-marketing quota under the 2002 Farm Bill. Whitaker (2009) finds that decoupled payments are more successful at helping farmers reduce the volatility of their consumption over time than payments that depend on market conditions, making them attractive farm-income support policies.

Developed country tariffs on both agricultural products and processed products harm developing countries more than the massive subsidies (Tutwiler and Straub 2007). Hoekman, Ng, and Olarreaga (2002) find that reducing tariffs by 50 percent would raise developing country income by $2.3 billion, compared to $273 million for reducing subsidies by 50 percent. Removing either policy will affect countries in different ways, however. Since the subsidies keep international prices lower than otherwise, food importing countries and urban people are benefited by them, but at the cost of their agricultural sectors.

In contrast to developed countries, many developing countries historically taxed the agricultural sector. They levied export taxes on agricultural products to generate revenues while protecting manufacturing through high tariffs and other import restrictions. These countries also used price controls, exchange rate policies, and other restrictions to keep agricultural prices low for urban consumption (chapters 6 and 7).

This pattern of disincentives began to change with market reforms over the last two decades as many developing countries have moved from taxing agriculture to protecting it (Anderson and Martin 2006). They eliminated import restrictions, devalued exchange rates, abandoned multiple exchange rate systems that penalized agriculture, and eliminated almost all export taxes. Instead, developing nations reacted to OECD agricultural subsidies by enacting high average tariff rates. These measures increased incentives for agricultural production. However, without compensating reductions in protection in upper- and some middle-income countries, the result was overproduction (beyond competitive, undistorted market levels) and declining commodity prices, reducing opportunities for competitive lower-income countries to expand exports and rural incomes. Rapid price increases during the period 2005–2008 opened new opportunities for exports by efficient developing countries, while increasing the cost of food imports of particular concern for the least developed, food-deficit countries.

The European Union's "Everything but Arms" (EBA) program permits exports of everything but arms from the least developed countries to the EU, initially with time-bound exceptions for a few foods such as bananas and rice. However, EBA includes a safeguard clause, which reserves the right of the EU to reduce or halt imports if EU firms are threatened by, for example, strong pressure on domestic prices (Koning and Pinstrup-Andersen 2007).

The United States designed a similar program for selected African countries (African Growth and Opportunity Act, AGOA). A number of other special and preferential trade arrangements, themselves trade distorting, serve to compensate selected developing countries for the negative effects of trade-distorting policies for agricultural commodities (Blandford 2007; Rodrik 2007; case 10-9). Furthermore, a large and increasing number of bilateral trade agreements influence global and national food systems. Fair-trade initiatives have benefited low-income farmers in developing countries as well as marketing agencies, but the extent of fair trade is still very limited (case 10-8 and chapter 11).

In addition to tariffs, nontariff barriers in the form of health, safety, and quality standards are widespread. These standards should be addressed in a way that upholds public confidence in food safety and product standards while preserving the benefits of an open food system (case 10-10). Three relevant agreements have been established within the Uruguay Round: the Agreement on the Application of Sanitary and Phytosanitary (SPS) Measures, the Agreement on Technical Barriers to Trade (TBT), and the Agreement on Trade-Related Aspects of Intellectual Property Rights (TRIPS, discussed below). These agreements stipulate that safety and quality standards as potential barriers must achieve legitimate objectives and not constitute disguised import restrictions. Countries are to adopt only those sanitary and phytosanitary (SPS) measures (related to protection of plant, animal, and public health) that are justified by objective scientific evidence.

These agreements attempt to strike a difficult balance between the concerns of importers and exporters. New knowledge and better measurement tools may tilt the balance. Even where risk levels are known with scientific accuracy, their acceptability varies over time and between societies. Therefore, while greater international collaboration and harmonization of standards may be necessary to facilitate globalization, desirable food safety standards tend to be a function of income level and to differ between high- and low-income countries and between poor and nonpoor households (Caswell and Bach 2007; chapters 3 and 11).

Other standards that influence international trade include food quality, plant and animal health, animal welfare, environmental effects, and labor practices. One topic of concern has been whether developed countries have lowered their pollution emissions by technology improvements and changes in demand or whether polluting industries have merely been transplanted to other countries, effectively exporting the pollution. Levinson (2009) finds that only 10 percent of the decrease in U.S. air pollution from 1987 to 2001 came from exporting polluting industries. While national governments set standards through negotiations within the framework of the WTO and the Codex, increasing concentration in food retail and wholesale has facilitated rapid increases in private standards, which may be more binding.

Private standards are expected to reflect transportation and transactions costs, other commercial interests, and consumer values and demand. They may conflict with government standards, the latter presumably being set on the basis of scientific risk assessment although influenced by various stakeholder groups. Private standards, on the other hand, may reflect consumer values regarding, for example, labor practices, animal welfare, and the perceived impact on the environment (chapter 11).

For instance, consumers may be willing to pay a premium for food that can be traced back to the primary producer. In an environment of rapidly increasing global market concentration, the potential collision between value-based, science-based, politics-based, and business-based standards may render standard-setting activities by WTO and Codex irrelevant or relegate the two institutions to a role of setting minimum health standards, which may or may not be incorporated into private or domestic standards. More nontariff barriers and disorderly trade over which WTO has little or no influence is likely to result. Furthermore, private standards aimed to meet increasingly demanding consumers may make it impossible for small farmers to compete with larger, subsidized farmers.

The International Capital Market

Alongside the expansion of trade flows, global food markets have experienced rapid growth in capital flows. MNCs have driven this development by investing directly in businesses in other countries (foreign direct investment, or FDI). Through FDI, MNCs affect production levels and composition, production technologies, labor markets and standards, and eventually also trade and consumption patterns. Through their control over resources, access to markets, and development of new technologies, MNCs have the potential to integrate countries into global markets. They can also be powerful political lobbyists.

The flow of FDI to developing countries' food systems increased from about $3 billion in 1990 to $8 billion in 2007. This accounts for less than one-half of one percent of the total worldwide FDI. The fastest relative increase occurred in agricultural production, where FDI increased fivefold from $0.6 billion to $3 billion annually between 1990 and 2007 (UNCTAD 2009). China received almost a quarter of the FDI inflow for agriculture in 2007, and Malaysia and Brazil together received more than one-third. Africa received only 7 percent, while 15 percent went to Latin America and 78 to Asia.

The FDI stock in developing countries' food systems has also increased significantly, growing from $4.6 billion in 1990 to $18 billion in 2007 in agriculture, forestry, and fishing, and from $10.4 billion to $46.9 billion for food and beverages manufacturing. About one-third of the FDI stock in agricultural production in 2007 was in China.

According to the United Nations Conference on Trade and Development (UNCTAD 2009), the largest agriculture-based and plantation MNC in the world—Sime Darby Berhad, headquartered in Malaysia—employed one hundred thousand people with assets of about $11 billion and sales of more than $10 billion in 2007. The second- and third-largest MNCs are the U.S.-based Dole Food Company Inc. and Fresh Del Monte Produce. The largest users of FDI in agricultural input supplies (seed, fertilizer, and agrochemicals) are BASF AG, Bayer AG, and Dow Chemical Company; in food and beverages, Nestle SA, Inbev SA, and Kraft Foods Inc.; in wholesale and retail, the supermarket chains Wal-Mart, Metro AG, and Carrefour SA.

FDI can be a powerful catalyst for overall economic development (UNCTAD 2006). Reardon and Barrett (2000) suggest that FDI may support much-needed agro-industrialization by improving technologies, transferring skills, providing capital, and increasing foreign exchange. Government policies can guide such agro-industrialization to help expand employment in underemployed regions, reduce poverty and food insecurity, protect natural resources, and meet food safety standards. Principles to guide FDI for agriculture have been developed by a group of international organizations (World Bank n.d.). These principles include respecting land and resource rights and ensuring food security, good corporate and country governance, responsible agro-enterprise investing, and social and environmental sustainability.

The increase in FDI to agriculture has been offset in part by decreasing inflow of development assistance to the sector. The large food price increases during 2007 and the first half of 2008 renewed bilateral donors' and international institutions' interest in providing such assistance, and some increase occurred during 2009–2010. Food aid has also contributed to the inflow of resources although the impact on sustainable economic growth is not clear.

A recent surge in efforts by MNCs and governments of middle-income food-deficit countries to acquire control over land suited for food or biofuel production (so-called land grabbing) may involve foreign landownership or long-term lease. In both cases, the MNCs or representatives of the foreign government are likely to bring into the country the investments and technology needed to support production. In some cases, the investor will also bring in some or all of the management and labor needed. The food or biofuel raw material produced is usually the property of the investor and exported wherever the investor wishes. Instead of taking ownership or lease to land, the MNCs may enter into contracts with existing farmers for delivery of certain commodities that have to meet agreed-on standards and specifications.

Land grabbing offers both risks and opportunities for countries with ample land resources (Robertson and Pinstrup-Andersen 2010). The principal risk is that land resources currently cultivated by poor farmers are turned over to foreign investors with little or no compensation to the farmers. Furthermore, while large-scale capital-intensive farming methods introduced by foreign investors are likely to increase production, the additional food and biofuel raw material is likely to be exported, leaving the host country with less food. Since most land grabbing takes place in low-income food-deficit countries, food security will suffer, particularly for subsistence farmers. The principal opportunity is that land-grabbing arrangements will bring foreign exchange and technological improvements into countries that desperately need it. Lessor governments have important roles to play in setting the terms for these land acquisitions in ways that can maximize the benefits for the poor, but that will depend on country governance and capacity (chapter 9).

International Technology Transfer

International technology transfer is an integral but differentiated part of FDI. Half of the agricultural productivity gains in recent years have come from technology spillovers, whereby research intended for a particular area is adapted, formally or otherwise, for use in other areas (Alston 2002). This spillover effect is not just from developed country to developing: developed nations have also greatly benefited by the improved varieties created for developing countries. This creates national and international externalities, making a case for publicly funding international research (chapter 7).

Public investment is needed to develop public good technologies. The question of who pays for the research investment should be viewed in the context of which stakeholders are likely to capture the benefits. In the case of a closed economy, where prices are determined by domestic demand and supply, the majority of the benefits from productivity-increasing (and therefore supply-increasing) agricultural technology are likely to be captured by consumers in the form of falling prices. Producers may capture a major share of the benefits generated in a small open economy because increasing supplies should have little or no impact on international prices. Research that benefits only a certain group of producers (e.g., export commodities) would produce what is called "club goods," and one would expect the "club members" to pay for the research. If transaction costs are low, club members should be able to work toward a joint solution without intervention. The higher transaction costs are, the greater are potential benefits from government policies that reduce them and improve coordination.

In addition to national public research and private research undertaken by firms, international research systems include a host of NGOs as well as regional, subregional, and interregional research centers simultaneously at work with different agendas, methods, and funding opportunities. Within nations, the focus is less on national agricultural research organizations (NAROs) than national agricultural research systems (NARSs) that include public and private institutions, NGOs, regional and subregional research centers, universities, and farmers' organizations.

Even though most spending on R&D is concentrated in a few large economies, developing countries began spending more than developed countries on agricultural R&D during the 1990s (CGIAR Science Council 2005). This included a tripling of expenditures in China and India from 1981 to 2000 as most rich countries decreased their public expenditures on agricultural research. The Consultative Group on International Agricultural Research (CGIAR) system (introduced in chapter 1) today has a budget of around $500 million, which is about 0.9 percent of the total global spending on agricultural research. The share of official development assistance for agricultural research decreased from 16 percent in 1980 to 4 percent in 2003.

Private Agricultural Research and Intellectual Property Rights

Private agricultural research has grown in importance, accounting for more than half of the R&D funds in the developed nations and more than one-third globally (Huang, Park, and Rozelle 2002; CGIAR Science Council 2005). The ten MNCs most involved in agricultural research spend more than the CGIAR, Brazil, China, and India combined, even though public funding doubled between 1976 and 1995.

Private research is a complement to publicly funded research rather than a substitute simply because they focus on different activities (Pardey and Beintema 2001). Most private research in OECD nations focuses on issues of interest to large farmers, using capital-intensive methods, reducing the extent to which it produces cross-country spillovers. Even though only a small portion of the R&D spending in developing nations is undertaken privately, it is expected to play an increasing role as more profitable markets for new technology develop.

The UN Declaration of Human Rights recognizes the right of individuals to benefit from the protection of their intellectual property. It also recognizes the importance of disseminating knowledge. Human rights to health, education, food, development, and other rights (chapter 11) are significantly affected by intellectual property law, which attempts to balance the rights of those who created the knowledge and the rights of those who need it.

More work needs to be done to find a proper balance between these rights. The tools used by publicly funded research groups are increasingly protected, making it more uncertain whether publicly funded research can use those tools and still make the research results available to the public as a public good (CGIAR 1998). The TRIPS agreement (Trade-Related Aspects of Intellectual Property Rights) is part of the multilateral trade agreements with which WTO members must comply. It stipulates that all members must make available patent rights or, in the case of plant varieties, either patent rights or other intellectual property rights regimes such as plant breeders' rights (Pinstrup-Andersen and Mengistu 2007).

Although one of the perceived advantages of the private sector is that competition can increase the speed and efficiency of many endeavors, R&D is an unusual case: all firms pay the costs of research, but only the first one to patent gets the benefits. This is a remarkably inefficient system, with room for improvement. One means of harnessing market incentives and the powers of the private sector for public means is for public entities to offer contracts to develop particular improvements that will raise smallholder productivity or reduce risk, with ownership going to the public entity for widespread dissemination (Lipton 2005). This is currently being done in some areas of health research against malaria, and could be a profitable public-private partnership that would combine the best of both systems. Another possibility is for public organizations to guarantee a market for certain products (e.g., vaccines) at predetermined prices and quantities, assuring private firms an immediate return after investment and granting them ownership rights.

The Role of Biotechnology

Until fifteen years ago, most progress in improving plant yields came from a laborious process of crossbreeding different plant varieties with known desirable traits in the hopes of fostering an improved variety. As advances in molecular biology allowed scientists to map different plants' genomes, they were able to determine the specific function of many simple genetic sequences. *Biotechnology* refers to any of the techniques using substances from living organisms or the organism itself to "produce or alter a product, cause changes in plants or animals, or develop microorganisms for specific purposes" (Pinstrup-Andersen and Schiøler 2000, 36). This can include enhancing or repressing a particular gene already inside the organism or transplanting a gene from the same or different species. The organisms or products derived from this process are commonly referred to as *genetically modified organisms,* or GMOs.

GM crops appeared in 1996, and by 2009 14 million farmers in twenty-five countries had planted biotech crops on 134 million hectares (James 2009). As shown in figure 10.1, the rate of adoption was high worldwide. Developing countries that have planted GM crops are, in descending order of hectarage, Brazil, Argentina, India, China, Paraguay, South Africa, Uruguay, Bolivia, the Philippines, Burkina Faso, Mexico, Chile, Colombia, Honduras, Costa Rica, and Egypt. Pakistan and Myanmar began using GM crops in 2010 (James 2010). Even though a little more than half of the area used for GM crops is in the United States, over 90 percent of the farmers planting GM crops are smallholders from developing countries, primarily growing insect-resistant (Bt) cotton (James 2009).

Bt cotton is credited with contributing to a doubling of yield, halving insecticide usage, increasing farmer income by $220–$250 per hectare in Asia, and helping India transform itself from a cotton importer to a cotton exporter (Bennett et al. 2004; James 2009). In Argentina, where farms are larger, agricultural employment has increased by 1 million new jobs, while some farmers in South Africa report more than doubling their output of maize and cotton while reducing insecticide sprayings by 80 percent and reducing water usage (James 2007).

Although many other crops and traits are now included in genetic engineering research, initial efforts concentrated on a few crops: soybeans, maize, cotton, and canola. The two primary means of modifying the plants has been to make them either herbicide tolerant (so that the plant is resistant to chemical weed killers) or insect resistant (requiring fewer or no pesticides) or both. These few combinations are used on 72 percent of the total world area planted with GM crops, and were developed in large measure by the private sector (CGIAR Science Council 2005).

Large productivity gains and reduced risks are not something unique to GM methods. Research using more traditional methods has produced very high rates of economic returns (chapter 7). For example, traditional plant breeding as part of a public-private partnership succeeded in developing herbicidal resistance in maize seeds so that when the *Striga* weed—a weed that is responsible for large production losses in Africa—attached to the modified maize, the weed would be infected with

FIGURE 10.1.
Global area of biotech crops (million hectares). Source: James 2009.

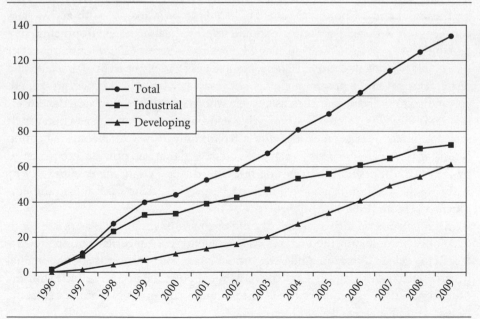

the herbicide and die while the crop lived on. Application of the technology in 2006 succeeded in doubling average maize yields, with some farmers indicating it was their best crop in seventeen years (AATF 2007). Trials also demonstrated a greater effectiveness of weed removal using the improved seed than could be attained by better weed and soil management techniques alone. However, the research took twelve years. Could it have been done faster with genetic engineering and other molecular biology methods?

In some cases genetic modification offers no advantage over more traditional methods. In other cases, the desired research outcome can be achieved with a shorter research time, and in still other cases, the problems cannot be solved with traditional methods. Marker-assisted breeding, which does not insert new genetic material but only a genetic marker, enables scientists to identify whether the offspring plant has the particular traits for which it was bred without growing the plant to full maturity. Alpuerto et al. (2009) estimate that it could save three to six years in the time to breed rice that is tolerant of soils with high salt and low phosphorous, at a cost of $1 million more than conventional breeding methods, while increasing economic benefits by $50 to $900 million in Bangladesh, India, Indonesia, and the Philippines.

New waves of research attempt to solve problems facing farmers and consumers, including combining higher-yielding traits with landraces that are accustomed to local conditions and ideally suited to the pests, diseases, and problems in that locality; making foods healthier, such as adding beta-carotene (that the body turns into vitamin A) to reduce the prevalence of blindness or reducing the level of saturated fats in oils; reducing the allergenic effects of certain foods; improving feed grains so that less will be needed for livestock; and enabling crops to produce a more consistent yield under adverse weather conditions so that a poor rain season does not decimate farmers' investments (Pinstrup-Andersen and Schiøler 2000).

Despite the many potential benefits, there have been many health and welfare concerns too. Reduced pesticide use should improve health and environmental sustainability. As expected, Wang, Just, and Pinstrup-Andersen (2008) found that after three years of using Bt cotton in China, pesticide use had dropped by 70 percent, and farm earnings were 36 percent higher. A few years later, however, farmers growing Bt cotton had to spray just as much as farmers who grew other cotton varieties, lowering net incomes by 8 percent compared to conventional cotton farmers because Bt seed cost three times as much. Benefits lasted for only a few years because Bt cotton is resistant to only some pests. Other pests flourished that had previously been killed by the chemical pesticides. Herbicide resistant varieties could increase poverty by reducing the amount of labor required on farms, decreasing rural wages and employment (Lipton 2005).

Although no evidence of negative health or environmental effects associated with GM foods currently on the market has been identified, concerns continue to surface in the debate (Pinstrup-Andersen and Schiøler 2000). Concerns about potential negative effects are as legitimate as concerns about potential negative effects with any other innovation. The importance of the precautionary principle for policymaking is discussed in chapters 9 and 11.

Before any such new developments, including new crop varieties, are released to the public, they must be tested and approved by an entity representing or trusted by the public. In the case of biological innovations, a biosafety regime capable of science-based testing, risk assessment, regulation, and approval is essential (case 9-6). National and international biosafety programs are essential to support such decision making. It should also perhaps be kept in mind that many of the practices now considered traditional were once new and the subjects of massive public outcry (Pinstrup-Andersen and Schiøler 2000).

Current national legislation on biotechnology and GM products ranges from "limited regulation" in many developing countries (addressing certain aspects of biosafety), to "specific regulation" in the EU (involving premarketing approval and mandatory labeling regimes for GM products), to "existing regulation" in the United States (simply applying the instruments developed for conventional foods) (Eggers and Mackenzie 2000). Substantial differences in domestic biosafety regulatory measures have increasingly affected international trade in GM products and led to trade disputes and, as discussed in case 9-6, inconsistencies between the Cartagena Protocol and the WTO.

Even as some groups in Europe and elsewhere call for the abolition of biotechnology methods and products in the area of food and agriculture, FAO (2004d) has called for biotechnology's continued use as a complement to traditional research. Forgotten in much of the clamor is the issue of national—and indeed, individual—sovereignty. Consumers, farmers, and governments should continue to have the right to choose whether they want to make use of this technology or not, and to what extent. The then minister of agriculture for Nigeria, Hassan Adamu, put it well:

> We do not want to be denied this technology because of a misguided notion that we do not understand the dangers or the future consequences. We understand. . . . We will proceed carefully and thoughtfully, but we want to have the opportunity to save the lives of millions of people and change the course of history in many nations. That is our right, and we should not be denied by those with the mistaken idea that they know best how everyone should live or that they have the right to impose their values on us. The harsh reality is that, without the help of agricultural biotechnology, many will not live. (Pinstrup-Andersen and Schiøler 2000, 107–108)

Nanotechnology

Nanotechnology is another area where significant potential gains for consumers and producers are expected, but there are many factors about which not enough is known. It is estimated that nanotechnology—technology dealing with manipulation of particles on an atomic scale—could be incorporated into $20 billion worth of consumer products within a few years, and there are over one hundred known projects in development to apply nanotechnologies to food and agriculture that could result in marketable products by 2020 (Kuzma and VerHage 2006). Middle-income countries have also begun research programs into nanotechnology, such as

Argentina, Chile, China, India, Mexico, the Philippines, and South Africa (CGIAR Science Council 2005).

Kuzma and VerHage (2006) report that some of these projects deal largely with consumer issues: nanomaterials could be used in packaging to notify consumers when a product has become unsafe or in foods to allow vitamins to reach parts of the body they had not reached before or to prevent cholesterol buildup. Farm applications could increase productivity and decrease agriculture's environmental impact: pesticides that become active only once the pest has eaten them; nanomaterials that would increase the effectiveness of growth hormones so that less is required, or that eradicate animal pathogens, such as campylobacter in poultry; sensitive devices that could help researchers stop runoff from crops or prevent animal waste pollution from contaminating nearby rivers. There is additionally discussion of turning leftover crop materials into biofuel through nanotechnology.

However, almost no research has been done to understand what unintended impacts nanotechnologies might have on humans, animals, and ecosystems. Farmers, consumers, and workers need to understand what risks, if any, the new technologies pose. Firms interested in developing nanotechnologies (nearly all of the major food MNCs) need to remember and take a lesson from the history of the catastrophic public relations strategy followed for GMOs. As Kuzma and VerHage (2006, 11) put it: "Ten years from now, companies do not want a situation in which consumers are attracted to products because they claim to be 'nano-free.'" Firms have an essential role in identifying these risks before products are marketed, or else they will bear the consequences of poor product preparation. Governments have not been proactive in identifying what standards will be set to determine the safety of nanotechnology products. As long as firms are uncertain about what regulations will be in place, there will be less innovation and the studies that are performed will lack the guidance and rigor that accepted standards can provide.

The International Labor Market

The global labor force will increase from 3.1 billion in 2001 to 4.1 billion by 2030, growing faster than the total population (World Bank 2007a). Most of the increase will occur in developing countries, putting strong pressures on labor migration to high-income countries that will have new pressures to accept immigrants because of the aging of their population structures. Although restrictions on labor flows across country borders are much more severe than for capital flows, massive movements of labor have been a feature of globalization.

Migrants account for about 3 percent of the world's population, or about 190 million people (World Bank 2006c). There has been a persistent increase of international migration worldwide since the 1970s. The stock of immigrants in high-income countries increased about 3 percent per year from 1980 to 2000, up from the 2.4 percent pace in the 1970s. Because of this growth, the share of migrants in high-income countries' population almost doubled over the thirty-year period to historic highs.

Like FDI, accurate data on international migration directly linked to the food sector are scarce. However, there is substantial evidence that many immigrants are involved in food-related industries. A large share of the migrants working in agriculture, the food-processing industry, and other parts of the food system come from low-income families, to whom remittances flow.

Migration reduces poverty and income inequalities. In theory, the influx of low-wage labor puts downward pressure on low-skilled wages in immigrant regions, while raising wages in the poorer emigrant nations. The empirical literature has not found conclusive evidence for the first effect. Moreover, wealth is also redistributed when and to the extent that emigrants send back remittances to their countries of origin. Lindert and Williamson (2001) conclude that migration was overall a more important equalizing factor than either trade or capital movements. Clemens (2010) demonstrates that immigration policies have had enormous impacts on poverty and argues that immigration policy should be a pivotal element in development policy agendas. For example, the vast majority of Haitians earning more than $10 per day are emigrants.

Migration's impacts depend on the size of emigrant flows, the kinds of migrants (e.g., high-skill versus low-skill), and labor and product market conditions. The stock of low-skilled emigrants who moved from developing to industrial countries in 2000 averaged only about 0.8 percent of developing countries' low-skilled, working-age residents. Therefore, the effects of South-to-North migration on working conditions for low-skilled workers in the developing world as a whole might be small. In individual countries, however, large scale emigration may contribute significantly to poverty alleviation.

The increased emigration of high-skilled workers from developing countries is partly due to the growing importance of selective immigration policies first introduced in Australia and Canada in the 1980s and later in other OECD nations. Developed countries have moved from being passive recipients to active recruiters of skilled migrants, relaxing their criteria relating to labor market testing and job offers, introducing new programs (e.g., Germany, Norway, and the United Kingdom), and offering fiscal incentives to attract talent to specific sectors (e.g., Austria, South Korea, the Netherlands, and Sweden) (OECD 2005). These programs, and the migrants themselves, are responding to rising skill premiums in industrial countries that have tightened global competition for skilled workers.

Like its low-skilled counterpart, high-skilled migration can benefit migrants and their families through remittances and help relieve labor market pressures in home countries. In addition, a well-educated diaspora can improve access to capital, technology, information, foreign exchange, and business contacts for firms in the country of origin.

However, the "brain drain" hypothesis claims that high-skilled emigration reduces growth in the origin country because (a) other workers lose the opportunity for training and mutually beneficial exchanges of ideas; (b) opportunities to achieve economies of scale in skill-intensive activities may be reduced; (c) society loses its return on high-skilled workers trained at public expense; and (d) the price of technical services (where the potential for substitution of low-skill workers is limited) may rise. Highly educated citizens improve governance, the quality of debate on public issues, child education, and state administrative capacity—all of which may be reduced through emigration of the highly skilled. Clemens (2009, 1) addresses some of these concerns, concluding that "regulating skilled-worker mobility itself does little to address the underlying causes of skilled migrants' choices, generally brings few benefits to others, and often brings diverse unintended harm." In addition, emigration can improve stability by allowing the most discontented citizens a way to leave.

Agricultural migration is primarily a movement of low-skill labor, so it is unlikely to be associated with many of the typical brain-drain concerns. Moreover, agricultural migrants seldom sever their ties with their households after emigration. Family members who remain behind (often parents and siblings) reorganize both their consumption and agricultural production activities in response to the migrant's departure and remittances. Remittances or savings accumulated abroad can even create the basis for future investments in the economies of their home countries. Remittance flows are larger and less volatile than official development assistance (ODA) or FDI (excluding China) and tend to be more concentrated on the poorest countries, communities, and households (Klein and Harford 2005). Unlike ODA or FDI, there are no intervening mechanisms separating donors from recipients, though there are still policy levers that can reduce transaction costs and increase remittances.

The impacts in the countries of agricultural immigration are often more ambiguous. While an inflow of unskilled workers from developing countries benefits the highly skilled workers in host countries (their jobs are not threatened by these immigrants, and the presence of immigrants will lower the costs for food production and services, and hence the prices that the skilled workers pay), the same inflow reduces the real wages of unskilled agricultural workers. Such competition has brought about political tensions within many host countries even where there are few native, unskilled agricultural workers, and has often resulted in increasingly restrictive immigration rules. Government plays a key role in integrating immigrants and determining to what extent they are entitled to government programs and social structures. Chapter 5 discusses the high rates of migrant poverty caused by marginalization.

Policies to Guide Globalization

Globalization is a tool. Like any tool, its effects depend on how it is used. The impact of globalization on national food systems and food security depends largely on national policies and international institutions. The key policy point therefore is that globalization offers an opportunity but not a certainty for developing countries and poor people within them to benefit. Opening up the borders for goods, services, capital, and labor is not a substitute for good national policies. It can be a complement.

Globalization has moved faster than the needed innovations in international institutions (chapter 9). International agreements and/or organizations are needed that can regulate the cross-border flows of goods, services, labor, and capital—including protecting intellectual property, preventing abuses of migrant labor, preventing increased financial volatility without hampering productive FDI, and dealing with food safety and advertising—resolve environmental externalities, produce public goods, and ensure access to the benefits of globalization for countries and people currently being marginalized. Without appropriate international architecture, globalization's benefits are likely to increase global inequality and make some preventable problems worse even as other benefits are produced.

In few arenas has policy exportation been more important than those dealing with genetically modified foods. While some consumers and governments would prefer to not buy them or even allow them into their country, other countries' rights of food sovereignty need to be preserved (chapter 11). Preserving the maximal level of individual food sovereignty likely requires some form of labeling so that consumers who do not want to purchase them have the ability to differentiate products. The firms using biotechnology, nanotechnology, and other nontraditional scientific methods to improve food production have responsibilities to ensure that their products will not harm consumers or the environment. It has been seen that perceived failure to fulfill these duties can be a public relations disaster, so it may just be good business practice. Greater international cooperation and clarification is needed to deal with the precautionary principle motivations regarding GMOs as well.

At the national level, policies are needed on the same issues to facilitate domestic competition and competitiveness. Because changes in policy produce both winners and losers, policies are needed to assist in the transition from a closed to an open economy, such as safety nets for the poor and hungry during the transitions. Of particular use are skill development, retraining, and education programs to reduce structural frictions as one sector profits and another shrinks in response to global competition. Research and government support for risk management in small-scale national private sectors is also needed to facilitate the transition from national to international markets and from nontradable to exportable goods and services. Policies to reduce marketing and transaction costs, such as investments in infrastructure and marketing facilities as well as investments in productivity increases in agriculture, are essential to strengthen the competitive position of the developing country. Most if not all of the national policies needed for a country to benefit from globalization have been mentioned in earlier chapters.

Economic theory suggests strongly—indeed it is one of the few topics on which a large majority of economists agree—that the country that benefits most from reduced barriers to trade is the country that lowers its own barriers. However, the benefits to the developing countries, and to the world's poorest people, from reducing OECD agricultural subsidies and associated trade distortions are significant. Bilateral and multilateral trade agreements in which developing countries agree to open up their markets for food from OECD countries at subsidized prices are harmful for developing countries' rural poor, though helpful for the urban poor because the subsidies lower food prices.

The effects on net food buyers who also rely on food sales are complex and may be positive or negative depending on local price transmission, relative price changes, the size of imports, and how quickly they enter the country. WTO has been encouraging countries to move their farmer income support policies away from production support to nondistorting, decoupled policies. Food aid policies that are largely farmer income support policies dumping excess food stocks on other countries also need reformation.

One of the major policy fronts for OECD countries is ensuring intellectual property rights protection in developing countries. It is unlikely at present that a deal will be reached to remove OECD agricultural subsidies and trade barriers without progress on intellectual property rights protection. Ensuring that such policies are just and beneficial requires policies to facilitate credit to small farmers so they can purchase technology from the private sector, or public investment in the development of technology for free distribution to them.

Food safety standards harmonization is another important area where globalization affects food systems. As discussed in chapter 9, national food safety regulations affect farmers in other countries who have no voice in policymaking. In addition, private food safety standards are changing market structures as international retailers enter new markets (chapter 6). Sometimes these factors work in concert. The current system seems to support governments setting minimum standards with firms free to set higher standards as part of their product differentiation and advertising. Minimums differ across countries, however, making the system more complex. The ethics of the current system are debated in chapter 11.

Demographic changes in developed countries are likely to increase pressures to allow more migrant workers to enter (chapter 4). Policies in migrant-accepting countries will need to consider how to incorporate the new workforce into society in an equitable manner. Policies in both recipient and home countries should lower the transaction costs that impede remittances. At the same time, education policies may need to be adjusted to take account of trained people leaving their countries, reducing the public goods aspect of public education.

Conclusion

It is clear that globalization may reduce or increase poverty and hunger, depending on its specific content and implementation. Furthermore, it is likely that some groups of poor and food insecure will be affected positively while others will be harmed. Thus, while globalization is likely to improve global resource-use efficiency, the key policy question is how to balance potential efficiency gains with the distribution of benefits and costs desired by society. In this regard, the interaction between globalization and national policies is critical.

Winters (2002, 29) suggests that answering the following eleven questions is necessary to understand the impact of international trade reform:

1. "Will the effects of changed border prices be passed through to the rest of the economy?" (See chapter 6 on price transmission.)
2. "Is reform likely to give poor consumers access to new goods?" This includes both goods newly introduced to the country and increased access by

poorer households as prices fall. New highly processed, calorie-dense foods becoming available at low costs due to the opening of imports are a case in point: new goods can be both positive and negative.

3. "Is trade reform likely to affect different household members differently?" New employment opportunities for women might enhance women's status and decision-making power within the household, while placing additional pressure on women's time.

4. "Will spillovers be concentrated on areas and activities that are relevant to the poor?" An example would be expansions in smallholder agricultural production from new export opportunities that increase their incomes and, through the multiplier effects discussed in chapter 7, raise incomes among the rural poor that provide goods and services to farmers. Such second-round effects reduce poverty and hunger but are frequently overlooked in the debate.

5. "What factors are used intensively in the most affected sectors?" The question here is which groups benefit the most (e.g., wage earners, land or capital owners, or high-skilled workers).

6. "Will the reform actually affect government revenue strongly?" Tariff removal reduces government revenues, a critical consideration for many impoverished nations. However, if the trade reforms replace nontariff barriers with tariffs, as pursued by the WTO, tariff revenues actually increase. Taxes on remittances or international capital flows are additional opportunities to increase government revenue, though they are not without offsetting costs. The goal is not to maximize government revenue but to understand what programs will be added or cut with changes in revenue.

7. "Will reform lead to discontinuous switches in activities? If so, will the new activities be riskier than the old ones?" Spreading risks among national and international activities lessens overall risks. However, if national activities are replaced with international ones, risks may increase or decrease. Trade distortions to maintain a high degree of food self-sufficiency are regularly justified on the grounds that no country should depend on imports for its food supply. The perception that self-sufficiency implies lower risks than free food trade is widespread among policymakers but is often wrong. Spreading the risk across an international food market is likely to reduce the risks associated with a closed food economy. Food self-sufficiency is not necessary for low food insecurity, as seen in Japan.

8. "Does the reform depend on or affect the ability of poor people to take risks?" The consequences of losses by the very poor are so severe (death of a child, e.g.) that the poor are usually reluctant to take on new risks (chapter 7). If participation in new opportunities offered by globalization implies higher risks than nonparticipation, government policies such as safety nets or other risk management tools may be required to generate the income and efficiency gains from globalization.

9. "If the reform is broad and systemic, will any growth it stimulates be particularly unequalizing?" Economic growth is critical to poverty and hunger

alleviation, but the way growth occurs and government policies influence its impact on the poor (chapter 5).

10. "Will the reform imply major shocks for particular localities?" Removing import barriers for certain goods and services may have disastrous effects on poverty and food security in certain regions and sectors in which many poor derive their incomes (case 10-13). Government policies may be needed to compensate the losers and facilitate an orderly transition or provide offsetting supports.

11. "Will transitional unemployment be concentrated on the poor?" As mentioned above, compensatory schemes such as food safety nets and retraining may be needed.

It should be clear from the above that globalization offers great risks and opportunities for the alleviation of poverty and food insecurity. Modeling alternative trade liberalization scenarios in case studies from twelve countries, Anderson, Martin, and van der Mensbrugghe (2006) conclude that trade liberalization's impacts are likely to be modest. Outcomes will be context specific.

Winters, McCulloch, and McKay (2008) conclude that the outcome of trade liberalization depends on many factors including the starting point of the liberalization, the specific trade reforms undertaken, and the particular group of poor people and how they receive their incomes. They further conclude that "there is strong evidence for the beneficial impact of trade liberalization on productivity" (ibid., 107) and that the impact on poverty depends on accompanying national policies. They point out that poor people have less buffer to carry them through transitory economic shocks, and that safety nets and other forms of social protection are important components of national policies to promote pro-poor globalization. Their overall conclusion is that "with care, trade liberalization can be an important component of a pro-poor development strategy" (ibid., 108).

The importance of "with care" is demonstrated by a set of case studies all of which show serious negative effects on certain groups of poor people, particularly small farmers (Madeley 1999). Potential benefits from trade liberalization were forgone by failure of national governments to implement appropriate accompanying policies. Rodrik (2007, 3) similarly encourages policymakers to frame the question as "how should the institutions of economic globalization be designed to provide maximal support for national developmental goals?"

International governance and policy harmonization is an essential topic. For instance, a Kenyan NGO lowered marketing costs for export crops, resulting in a 32 percent income gain for participants. One year later, however, new EU regulations closed the market to these adopters, nullifying the gains of research, extension, and investment (Ashraf, Giné, and Karlan 2009). Trade links the policy frameworks of multiple countries, as discussed in chapter 9.

The pathways by which globalization affects food security and nutrition were discussed in the beginning of this chapter. Focusing specifically on how globalization affects the diet transition (chapter 3) and the related prevalence of overweight, obesity, and chronic diseases, Hawkes (2006) concludes that MNCs affect diets both directly through the products they produce, market, and promote, and indirectly through their influence on domestic food markets and their competitive structure.

The debate about the dietary impact of globalization tends to focus on the promotion of hamburgers, soft drinks, and other energy-dense, nutrient-poor processed foods that leads to obesity, chronic diseases, and international convergence of diets toward a small number of homogeneous diet components. Hawkes (2006) argues that the integration of global food markets also generates greater diet diversity. Thus, food market globalization causes both convergent and divergent dietary outcomes. Recent and current trends show convergence toward less healthy but cheaper foods among low-income people and divergence toward more healthy, safer, more expensive foods among the rich. The health consequences are very visible in the rapidly increasing prevalence of obesity and diet-related diseases among the poor, and pressures for more food safety and nutrition regulation of the food market by the rich (chapter 3). The ethical dimensions of these questions are taken up in the next chapter.

Globalization and the Food System Case Studies

The cases in this chapter address the effects of trade and agricultural policies in both high- and low-income countries, as well as the impact of other elements of globalization, such as the international expansion and concentration of the private food sector.* The impact of trade and domestic agricultural policies in OECD countries on low-income countries and low-income people are discussed, and available policy options for alleviating negative impacts are identified. The impact of tariff escalation and nontariff barriers is also considered.

Case 10-1 addresses the effects of globalization on the nutrition transition (chapter 3). Cases 10-2, 10-3, 10-5, and 10-13 discuss subsidy policies in developed countries and their global impacts, and 10-11 does the same for developed country tariff policies. Bilateral and multilateral trade agreements are the subjects of cases 10-4, 10-7, and 10-9. Cases 10-6 and 10-13 focus on the effects of trade liberalization within a single country. Case 10-8 examines the potential for fair trade to resolve globalization's inequities. Cases 10-10 and 10-12 return to the topic of international food safety regulation. Cases 10-12 and 10-13 are available exclusively online.

10-1   Globalization and the Nutrition Transition: A Case Study
         Corinna Hawkes
10-2   Producer Subsidies and Decoupling in the European Union and the United
         States
         Maria Skovager Jensen and Henrik Zobbe

---

* The case studies referenced here are presented in full in the three-volume work by Per Pinstrup-Andersen and Fuzhi Cheng, eds., *Case Studies in Food Policy for Developing Countries* (Ithaca, NY: Cornell University Press, 2009) and online via open access at http://cip.cornell.edu/gfs.

Notes

1. The OECD defines its measure of producer support as an indicator of the annual monetary value of gross transfer from consumers and taxpayers to agricultural producers (Portugal 2002).

2. Restrictions caused by safety and quality standards are becoming more apparent and determinant for an exporter's market access. In recent years, in response to an increasing number of food safety problems and rising consumer concerns about food-borne hazards, developed country governments are intensifying their efforts to regulate their food sectors and strengthening their domestic food safety and quality standards. Rising standards create obstacles to the exports of agricultural commodities from developing countries and have led to numerous trade disputes (case 10-10).

3. This is in contrast to developing countries, which protect commodities that are not produced locally more than commodities that are.

Chapter 11

Ethical Aspects of Food Systems

Introduction

Ethics are the rules or principles that dictate whether certain actions or ends are considered virtuous, right, good, moral, responsible, or proper. "Ethics . . . is the rational defense of virtue" in a world that does not always reward virtuous behavior, where hunger, poverty, and inequality are pervasive (Sison 2010). Ethical beliefs have profound, yet often unnoticed, effects on our attitudes, actions, and achievements. While personal ethical beliefs influence many of our daily decisions, our ethical understanding is in turn influenced by family and friends, social norms, religious beliefs, governance structures, and media.

As demonstrated throughout this book, many of the most important questions regarding the food system are ethical questions. How can the extreme hunger and deprivation of hundreds of millions of poor people be ethically reconciled with the abundant opulence displayed in the world's richest countries (chapter 5)? Are the tools of genetic engineering ethical, and is denying GM foods to hungry people ethical (chapters 7, 9, and 10)? How should the rights of unborn generations be considered when making decisions that will affect the natural resource base they inherit (chapter 8)? By what methods could food be better distributed—not only globally, but within communities and households—to ensure food security and better nutrition for all (chapters 3, 4, and 7)? When national and individual food sovereignties collide, how can this conflict be resolved (chapter 9)?

These questions cannot be resolved by appeal to objective, scientific methods. Sadly, this often means that these questions and others raised in this book are rarely discussed explicitly in empirical or theoretical studies of the food system. For policy analysts, the danger is that implicit value judgments could render research and policy recommendations ineffectual. As mentioned in chapter 2, focusing too much on average effects without specifying distributional outcomes or identifying how winners can compensate losers ignores the realities of the political process and can prevent reforms. Because of the subjective nature of ethics, it may be difficult coming to a consensus without acknowledging the values that underlie our positions. Likewise, economic and political factors are critical to actually implementing ethical ideals (von Braun and Mengistu 2007b).

The purpose of this chapter is to specifically discuss these concerns, identifying situations where differences in ethical beliefs can have a significant impact on the food system and where action has failed to live up to ethical rhetoric. The first half introduces several competing schools of moral thought, identifying where and how they differ and the importance of those differences for the food system. The latter half of the chapter delves into ethical questions dealing with specific parts of the food system, such as food sovereignty, equality, biotechnology, animal welfare and environmentalism, and trade. Much of the chapter will introduce questions rather than provide general solutions. Readers are encouraged to ponder these questions in order to find answers for themselves and to learn how to understand and work with people who embrace different ethical backgrounds.

Ethical Systems

Consequentialist Schools

Ethical systems can be readily classified as being either consequentialist (focusing on outcomes) or nonconsequentialist. Within consequentialist ethics we will primarily consider utilitarianism and rights-based ethics, while the principal nonconsequentialist ethics used here are deontology and virtue ethics. Each approaches ethical questions from fundamentally different positions. Though they often agree on the most basic ethical questions, different ethical principles can lead to different policy conclusions.

In *consequentialism* (or teleology), the determining factors in understanding what actions are ethically right or wrong are the outcomes or the consequences of the action (hence, consequentialism). Actions that further desired outcomes are good, and actions that harm them are bad. What matters is the outcome rather than how that outcome was reached or the intentions or characters of decision makers unless the process is itself the desired outcome. In one sense, whenever a goal is invoked to justify an action, a form of consequentialism is in effect. Exercising in order to lose weight is consequentialist. Profit maximization is also: whatever improves the bottom line is good.

For consequentialists, the question "Do the ends justify the means?" is one of serious and deep contemplation. Means are rarely considered in and of themselves. Chapter 9 introduced the view that if bribery and corruption could "grease the wheels" of progress, ensure more efficient government actions in the face of heavy regulation, and preserve efficient, pro-poor programs during regime changes, it might be good. Whether it is good or not is then an empirical question. In chapter 3, it was argued that the food system itself is a means to an end, and that end is human health and nutrition. To the extent that the food system provides adequate nutrition for billions of individuals, it is good; to the extent that hundreds of millions still suffer from intense hunger, millions more from hidden hunger, and an increasing number from obesity, the food system needs reform.

In most of economics, the outcome of concern is human well-being, or utility. In its broadest sense, *utilitarianism* (also welfarism) means that the only factor that is important in making a decision is the effect of different actions on individual utilities. The primary utilitarian goal is creating "the greatest happiness for the greatest number of people." This has created an efficiency bias in economic thinking: the larger the economy, the greater its capacity for improving the human condition for as many people as possible.

Contrary to the stereotypes invoked by other ethicists, however, utilitarianism readily admits a wide variety of ethical concerns, including the Benthamite goal of producing the greatest happiness for the greatest number of people (discussed below); Rawlsianism, which seeks to make the least happy person in society as happy as possible (discussed below); egalitarianism, which seeks to make every person equally happy (discussed below); human needs; psychological models of how individuals actually behave versus how they think they ought to; and intergenerational equity.[1] Each of these could be thought of as different theories about how to create the greatest good for the greatest number. Jeremy Bentham (1789) and John Stuart Mill (1863) were particularly influential in utilitarianism's early development. Peter Singer (1972) is one of its strongest advocates today, particular as it relates to world hunger. Utilitarianism will be discussed at some length in the next section.

The human rights perspective is also a consequentialist ethic. Certain outcomes are defined as being morally essential, implying obligations and options to act or restrictions preventing certain actions. Marinoff (2007, 45) clarifies that these rights are not "laws of nature that somehow should be operative without individual intervention, social cost, or political process," but that there are responsibilities and duties attached to each of them. Jonsson (2007) explains that every right has to have a duty bearer, without which rights are only privileges that can be given and taken away. While an individual possesses rights because he or she is a human being, entitlements generally have prerequisite conditions based on, for example, income, household size, gender or racial characteristics, or geographical location. Even though people have rights to food, it would be difficult to argue that a person has rights to food stamps, an entitlement program used in many countries to fulfill the right to food. Jonsson (2007) also differentiates between human rights standards and human rights principles: standards can be met as a privilege that can be taken away without a process that keeps the standard in place as a principle.

Rights are generally categorized as either negative (preventing action) or positive (encouraging or requiring action). For example, a negative right to life means that an individual should not kill another, while a positive right to life requires that a person proactively supports the life of other people. Another important differentiation is made between intrinsic or unalienable rights that cannot be taken away and alienable rights that may. This distinction became a focal point during the American

Revolution: if the colonists were granted privileges rather than rights by the British government, then that government had the authority to take those privileges away. If human rights stem not from government or the pleasure of another person but from God or, as in the humanist argument, nature, they cannot be taken away. The protection and preservation of one's rights then becomes a moral imperative.

Rights may or may not be enshrined in legislation and may or may not have a self-acknowledged duty bearer (see table 11.1). The Indian constitution declared that each person had rights to food, but until 2001 there was no one who accepted the duty of ensuring that right would be fulfilled. As discussed in case 11-1, the Indian Supreme Court determined in late 2001 that the government had an obligation to fulfill its populace's right to food. At that moment, the various food programs from various states became official entitlement programs. The third column represents the many countries where there is no legal right to food, but a combination of self-production, markets, government programs, and private charity work together to fulfill the right to food for many millions of people. In some cases, NGOs have taken on the role of duty bearer for the right to food, a subtly different stance in terms of accountability than simply providing charity. There are individuals in each of the four cases considered in table 11.1 who have their right to food fulfilled and people who do not. It is hoped that introducing legal rights and appointing duty bearers could increase the realized right to food for those who do not have their rights met yet.

One of the greatest differences between a rights-based perspective and utilitarianism is that there is little to no acknowledgment of trade-offs between rights. Building on Sen's work on human capabilities, Nussbaum (2007) has identified ten inherent rights, all of which must be fulfilled to a basic level simultaneously regardless of the capacities of poor countries (Dasgupta 2005). To Nozick (1974), rights impose rigid constraints on what individuals or societies may do, while Rawls (1971) establishes a lexicographic[2] hierarchy of rights and suggests that societies fulfill the most basic rights first, and then are able to move on to fulfill additional rights. If someone truly has an intrinsic right to something simply by virtue of being a human being, it is difficult to argue that political realities, budget constraints, or conflicts between rights imply that individuals and societies must make trade-offs between achieving their various rights or between rights and other desired goods. This provides policymakers little guidance (Arnold 2007).

Even when few rights are put forward, they can be problematic. Nozick (1974) asks what the difference is between appropriating a person's time by taking away goods earned by work and appropriating a person's time by forcing a person at

TABLE 11.1.
Legally Codified Rights and Acknowledged Duty Bearer Cases

	Legislative right	No legal right
Acknowledged duty bearer	India post-2001	Potential NGOs
No duty bearer	India pre-2001	Markets, self-production, charity

leisure to work for no pay. The first is called taxation and the second slavery, but both accomplish the same thing without consent, leading Nozick to equate rights to property with rights to life and freedom from slavery. On the other hand, it is claimed that Gandhi said that people "have no right to anything . . . until these [millions of poor people] are clothed and fed better" (Gilbert 2007), indicating that an individual could have rights to some property (some of their time/self) but not all. Arnold (2007) also points out that focusing on individual rights over responsibilities or collective rights could endanger environmental, economic, and social sustainability.

Over time, the number of rights deemed to be intrinsic has increased, and it has been recognized more and more generally that they apply to all people regardless of gender, ethnicity, or other factors, making them more truly *human* rights. The UN Universal Declaration of Human Rights in 1948 is perhaps the most famous codification of widely accepted human rights. That declaration includes the statement: "Everybody has the right to a standard of living adequate for the health and well-being of himself and his family, including food, clothing, housing and medical care" (UN 1948). Libertarian and autarchistic ethics are based heavily on the notion that individual liberty and the right to life and property are among the highest intrinsic rights, implying that governments do not have authority to appropriate one's property or restrict what can be done with it without consent (e.g., Williams 2009). Others take the right to food or the right to a basic standard of living to be of higher importance than rights to liberty, implying a greater degree of latitude in considering government policy.

Nonconsequentialist

In contrast to results-oriented consequentialism, deontologists focus on the inherent morality of actions and intentions. *Deontology* literally means "the study of duty." The notion is that some actions are simply wrong and should not be done by an ethical person. Duty likewise obligates a person to do other inherently good actions. One of deontology's great strengths is that it sets clear guidelines for behavior and action, while utilitarian recommendations are susceptible to regular change with changing preferences and circumstances. Deontologists reject that ends justify means: corruption is wrong regardless of the outcome, for example. Immanuel Kant was one of its leading philosophers, so deontology is also known as Kantian ethics.

Though divine command theory[3] is deontological, religion is not the only source of these duties, nor of ethics in general. Most organized professions have established rules of conduct that define what is and is not ethical practice in their field. The most famous of these are medical ethics, legal ethics, and business ethics. In other atheistic ethical traditions, the natural order is taken for a moral guide about how humans ought to behave, though these traditions have also been accused of conflating the way things are with how they ought to be.

Another branch of deontology focuses on intentions more than actions. That is, what makes an action virtuous could be a person's intent. Someone who lies in order to escape punishment is dishonest, while someone who lies in order to protect a friend from punishment when that friend is believed to be innocent is loyal. This branch of deontology is closer to consequentialism in that outcomes are important, though there is a significant difference: it is not the actual outcome that matters, but the desired outcome. In the last example, it is not the actual innocence or guilt of the friend that matters, but that the friend was believed to be innocent.

The final branch of ethics considered in this chapter is *virtue ethics*. Virtue ethics was widely promoted by Aristotle, Buddha, and Confucius. The most famous statement defining virtue ethics came from Friedrich Schiller (1793), who wrote that the purpose of life "is not to perform individual virtuous deeds but to become a virtuous person. . . . And virtue is nothing other than 'an inclination to duty.' . . . Desire and duty should be brought together. Reason should be obeyed with joy."[4] The focus is on becoming a person characterized by desirable virtues, for whom fulfilling Kantian duties is natural and desired, while Kant had emphasized the virtue of fulfilling a duty when one wished not to. However, the values cherished by a society are likely to change over time and to differ between societies. There are also sometimes conflicts between values, as between mercy and justice or freedom and responsibility.

In Comparison

The practical differences between these perspectives can be highlighted with a few short examples. Consider the case of an altruist who gives money to an organization representing poor individuals. A utilitarian considers this to be good only if someone is made happier by the gift—which could include the giver (Andreoni 1989; 1990). A human rights ethicist would take a more narrow view: only if the money went to reduce hunger or improve some other human right would this be good. An action-oriented deontologist would consider the action to be good and charitable regardless of outcome (it is the right thing to do), while an intent-oriented deontologist or a virtue ethicist would consider the action to be good only if the altruist gave from the right motives: out of a sense of duty or compassion, for instance, instead of trying to impress someone else.

This example scales up to national levels as well. Consequentialists will think foreign aid is good only to the extent that results are produced, while deontologists and virtue ethicists will argue that it is good to give regardless of outcome in order to fulfill the continually neglected promise of providing 0.7 percent of GNP in aid.

In another example, a deontologist would view a policymaker who enacts food price ceilings in order to reduce hunger as having acted ethically even if the lower food price has the unintended consequence of decreasing food production and increasing hunger. If (being perceived as) doing virtuous actions is important to policymakers, it will be harder for utilitarian-centric economic policy to prevent price ceilings (Pinstrup-Andersen 2005b).

Though each ethical system approaches moral questions from a different vantage point and there are many other examples where they disagree, they are in general not opposed to each other. O'Connor (2006) goes further and claims that someone who strictly follows deontological ethics would eventually become the kind of person virtue ethicists would hold up as ideal. Similarly, it has often been argued that social welfare would be maximized (utilitarian) if people chose to act more in accordance with deontological or virtue ethics. Robinson (2007) speaks of reframing the development debate to one of human rights in order to make policymakers' duty (deontology) clearer.

In general, the choice between ethical systems is not either/or. Even while encouraging the adoption of a rights perspective, Robinson (2007) admits that "human rights alone won't provide all the answers," indicating that the perspective is better at identifying problems than applicable means to resolve them. Kelly (1990) argues that Bentham's utilitarian theories presupposed the legal and social framework within which actions can be taken, implying that deontological or virtue concerns provide additional constraints to utility maximization, and that he did not favor sacrificing the welfare of a few people in order to benefit many. Sen (1977) introduced the concept of "meta-preferences," or preferences about what our preferences *should* be, allowing a deontological perspective to control a consequentialist one.

The extent to which each is individualistic or collective also differentiates ethical stances. Ethical systems derived from evolution may focus on the survival of the individual's physical and cultural offspring—in which case duties to others are based on creating a society favorable for self-promotion—or on the survival of the society. Confucian and Ubuntu virtue ethics are more collective than Aristotelian virtue ethics, emphasizing the interconnectedness of individuals, establishing self-identity in a group context, and prizing openness, generosity, and cooperation. Utilitarianism tends to fall somewhere in the middle: the focus is generally on the welfare of individuals in isolation from each other, but total social outcomes are also emphasized. Most rights are based on notions of individual rights, though some have posited group rights or societal rights. For example, UN laws allowing or requiring countries to intervene to prevent genocide presuppose additional protection for preserving ethnicities above preventing the deaths of ungrouped individuals, such as the five million children who die each year from hunger and malnutrition worldwide (Pinstrup-Andersen 2007b).

"Feminist ethics" contends that women develop different value systems than men, based more on nurture than justice and on interpersonal relationships than individuality. Wilber (2004) mentions feminist ethicists' focus on "particular others" rather than the broad welfare of a mass of undifferentiated others, the importance of feelings over logic in motivations, an emphasis on survival of children, and a desire that sacrifices not be in vain.

One final set of questions deals with the relationship between ethics and the law. In order to support a pluralistic society, not all ethical views can or should become law. However, ethical viewpoints do and should inform the creation of laws and governance structures. Regardless of whether the source is religious or not, ethical beliefs inform our views of the proper roles of government, the admissible processes for it to accomplish its roles, and the relationships between citizens and between citizen and society.

Legality similarly informs ethical beliefs. Utah Supreme Court Justice Dallin H. Oaks wrote that "the law declares unacceptable some things that are simply not enforceable, and there's no prosecutor who tries to enforce them. We refer to that as the teaching function of the law" (Oaks and Wickman 2008). Most people, including Oaks, agree, however, that legalizing a behavior does not make it ethical.

Pinstrup-Andersen (2007b, 20) worries that laws based on answering one set of ethical concerns (e.g., anticorruption or illegal drug laws) can hinder the accomplishment of other ethical goals and how we should react: "If [illegal drugs were] produced by small farmers, might [it] help millions out of poverty, hunger, and child death? . . . What if millions of child deaths could be avoided at the expense of the lives of thousands of drug addicts?" From a utilitarian perspective, these laws and their consequences imply that the life of each developed country drug addict is valued thousands of times more than the lives of starving children in developing countries. Is this an ethical valuation? Do individuals have rights to a livelihood that claims the lives of other people even to save their own lives or those of their family members? Pinstrup-Andersen (2007b) also points out that the laws and rights that are enforced tell us much about the ethics of those in power: property rights are enforced and laws against robbery and fraud are enforced while public failure to act, leading to death by hunger and malnutrition, is not prosecuted.

Social Welfare Functions and Pareto Efficiency

Utilitarianism forms the backbone of most economic analysis, which has led to a focus on Pareto efficiency. The Pareto principle says that if we can make someone better off without making anyone else worse off, we should. In a Pareto efficient outcome, the only way to make one person better off would be to make another person worse off. If a situation is Pareto inefficient, then it is possible to make at least one individual better off without making anyone else worse off.

One of the primary complaints against the Pareto principle is that it is unconcerned with distribution. A static economy where one person has all the wealth and everyone else has nothing is Pareto efficient. It is possible—indeed, likely—that such a distribution would not be Pareto efficient in a dynamic economy because transfers of wealth to the poorest (everyone) would increase their productivity sufficiently to compensate the original owner. This disregard for distributional concerns is one of the chief problems preventing economists and other policy analysts from having a greater impact on policymaking. Another problem with the Pareto principle is that if any concern other than individual utilities is included, situations arise that violate the Pareto principle by optimally creating situations where everyone has lower utility (Sen 1970; Kaplow and Shavell 2001).

The Pareto principle does not say utility transfers *should not* be made, as recently enunciated by DeLong (2009). The Pareto principle is a minimal criterion that a large subset of utilitarians should be able to agree on. The insight is that one needs more ethical structure in order to justify transfers, such as by specifying social weights for each individual's utility. It does not claim that the current income distribution is the best of all possible worlds.

Specifying social weights for each individual's utility creates a social welfare function (SWF). SWFs rank different states of society. SWFs can be highly individualistic or collective; specific (e.g., every person receives a weight of one, and utility is measured by the natural log of income) or more generalized (e.g., all SWFs embodying the Pigou-Dalton transfer principle register an increase in social welfare when income is transferred from a richer person to a poorer person); and can include social goals other than individual utility. However, von Neumann and Morgenstern (1946) warn that it is mathematically impossible to simultaneously maximize two variables: trade-offs are ever present.

The most common utilitarian SWF is simply the sum of each individual's utility with income standing in as a univariate proxy for utility (see Thorbecke 2007 for an explanation and modest defense of this practice). With u_i standing for the utility of the i-th individual and w_i that person's weight or importance in the SWF, this can be represented mathematically as $\sum w_i u_i$. It is most commonly assumed that everyone has equal weight in the SWF (i.e., $w_i = 1$ for all i) because otherwise you have to explain why one person's welfare deserves to be counted more than another's. This SWF will be notated as SWF1. It is sometimes claimed that SWF1 makes no statement about welfare distribution. If utility is marginally decreasing with income, however, SWF1 is maximized for a given level of resources by equalizing incomes.

The *World Values Survey* finds that increases in annual individual income lead to increases in happiness directly up to approximately $13,000, after which the correlation is much less significant, implying large gains to world utility with redistribution (Gilbert 2007). If income redistribution affects production decisions, a certain degree of inequality would be more acceptable in order to increase the resources available for consumption by all people later.

Other popular weighting systems include focusing solely on people below a certain income level (i.e., the nonpoor receive a weight of 0), weighting utility inversely with income, or including other notions of inequality in the weighting system. Atkinson (1970) and Sen (1973) argue that social welfare is the average income in society multiplied by the degree of equality in society. Thus increases in average income are good (they increase social welfare), but an increase in income that simultaneously increases inequality is less preferred to one that decreases inequality as well (see chapter 5 on pro-poor growth). These functions are still utilitarian because only individual utilities are used, but they incorporate more distributional concerns and are explicitly in favor of equalizing incomes.

More general social welfare functions can also be constructed that do not rely solely on individual utilities. Fields (2001) discusses a class of SWFs that rank changes to the underlying income distribution similarly. For instance, one might believe that, holding all else constant, per capita GDP growth is good and higher inequality and poverty are bad. In comparing two income distributions, either in the same country over time or between two countries, if one distribution has higher income and lower inequality and poverty, we can say with confidence that a large class of SWFs (and hence a wide range of people with differing ethical concerns) would agree this income distribution was better. If one distribution has a higher income, but also higher inequality, then there would be disagreements, with some SWFs saying the high income distribution was better and some indicating the opposite.

Compared to the Pareto principle, one must make a large number of relatively subjective assumptions in order to construct a SWF. Some of the questions that must be answered include the following: Is individual income an appropriate proxy for utility (Pinstrup-Andersen 2007b)? Is per capita GDP an appropriate proxy? How should inequality and absolute or relative poverty enter in? If one person's utility depends on another person's well-being, should that dependence be included in the SWF? Does it make a difference if the first person cares about the second or hates the second (i.e., is marginal utility positive or negative)?

It is well known that individuals adapt to difficult circumstances. Should the chronically ill be weighted using the utility that would be expected for someone who did not have to live with the disease, or using the utility that members of the afflicted group report after rationalization and adjustment have helped them adapt to their suboptimal situation? How should we weight different generations of people? If there is no ethical difference between how we should treat people who happen to be alive today, people who will be born within twenty years, and people born seven generations from now, what implications does this have for natural resource management?

Pinstrup-Andersen (2005b) argues that, for the most part, these questions are swept under the rug in policy analysis. Ignoring the subjective, normative parts of ostensibly positive analysis does not make them go away nor make the analysis more objective. By not answering deontological or virtue concerns that policymakers or their constituents have, policy analysis that uses exclusively utilitarian ethics may fail to achieve its stated objective, making it, ironically, a poor choice of method according to utilitarianism. In addition, Pinstrup-Andersen (2005b, 1098) points out that the choice of ethic itself will bias the questions asked and the methodologies used:

> If I am a utilitarian, I am also likely to focus on options that I believe will
> be most cost-effective. If, on the other hand, my ethical perspective is closer
> to deontological ethics . . . , I will bias my work toward what I believe is the
> right thing to do. . . . Or, maybe I simply subscribe to the ethics that freedom
> from hunger is a basic human right thus overriding any other considera-
> tion, including opportunity costs. While claiming positivism because I am
> not making recommendations, I am in fact biasing the allocation of research
> resources and the likely government intervention to conform to my ethical
> values.

Dasgupta (2005) defends against the frequently made accusation (e.g., Sen 1987, 1999; Nussbaum 2003) that economists and economic analysis lack ethics. The ethical foundations of economics are broad enough to accept and incorporate criticisms while simultaneously being so long ago settled that further rehashing of why they follow this pattern is likely of little benefit. Scarcely one year after Rawls's (1971) work on distributive justice, for instance, Atkinson (1973) demonstrated that the optimal tax code for a society attempting to follow his recommendations would not be much more progressive than the optimal tax code for a society maximizing SWF1. Publications such as *The Journal of Markets and Morality* and *The Review of Social*

Economy regularly publish articles on economics and ethics, and entire subdisciplines examine economics and religion from varying religious backgrounds.

Equity and Equality

In the SWFs considered up to now, the primary distributional concern has been with inequality aversion:[5] society is better off the less inequality there is. The ethical belief that a fair income distribution is one where each person has the same income is called egalitarianism. An egalitarian would argue that if individuals are inherently equal, why would it be just for them to have different levels of income? Most world religions have emphasized at least a certain degree of self-denial and sacrifice in order to benefit the poor and reduce inequality (Gilbert 2007). However, Marinoff (2007) points out that, while there are many theoretical notions of how humans are equal (e.g., equal under the law, deserving of equal rights, children of one God), people differ widely in the actual opportunities afforded them, skills (genetic and acquired) to make use of those opportunities, tastes, and in the shocks they face. Thus humanity is characterized by great inequality of outcome in many key dimensions of human welfare that do not match the ethical notions of an equal humanity.

Is equality of outcome desirable primarily as an end in itself or as a means to other ends? Some theories of development (chapter 5) held that a certain degree of inequality is necessary for development because only the wealthy are able to afford to save and invest in order to build needed infrastructure. Others, such as the Kuznets hypothesis, held that increasing inequality is a temporary phenomenon that occurred during development and that further economic growth would subsequently resolve the inequality. More recently, the economics literature (e.g., Acemoglu, Johnson, and Robinson 2001; Easterly 2007; Thorbecke 2007) has focused on how inequality leads to political impediments that reduce economic growth and poverty reduction. From this perspective, reducing inequality is also a means to the end of reducing poverty and spurring future economic growth.

Equality of outcome is not the only ethically justifiable distribution. There are many notions of fairness, or equity, among which equality of outcome is only one. Yaari and Bar-Hillel (1984) summarize the philosophical literature as providing six main reasons why an equitable distribution might differ from one of strict equality. These exceptions tend to be based on one or more of the following criteria:

1. Needs. If two individuals have the same income, but one has a chronic medical condition requiring expensive medicine, income is unequal relative to needs. Similarly, the sufficiency and equality of household income depends on the number and genders of members in the household, their ages, cultures, and the distribution of income and expenditure among household members.
2. Tastes and preferences. If one person does not enjoy eating a particular food and another does, there is no reason to force the first to consume any of it, let alone equal amounts. If one person chooses to consume more leisure

than another or to enjoy consumption today instead of saving, is it just to transfer wealth from the harder working, thriftier person?

3. Beliefs. In dividing a parcel of land of unknown quality between two individuals, does the difference in their belief about land quality matter for the distribution? Closely related, if one claimant believes in an environmentalist ethic while the other does not, should that affect the equitable land distribution?

4. Endowments. In dividing an amount of money between two individuals, how do their initial wealth levels matter in determining what is equitable? To what extent do people have rights to their initial endowments (Nozick 1974)? Does it make a difference whether these endowments were genetic, inherited, or acquired in a previous period by hard work, thrift, and wise investment? On the other hand, to what extent is accumulated wealth based on luck, expropriation, or unjust social factors?

5. Effort, productivity, or contribution. If one worker contributed two-thirds of the work to a particular project, and both workers were equally capable, would an equal distribution of the gains from that project be equitable?

6. Rights or claims. If someone has a prior claim to something, the resolution of that claim often trumps other distributional concerns.

In each of these cases, notions of equity and equality diverge, though some concerns merely reflect a more refined understanding of equality. Do we "deserve" certain goods and services based on needs, rights, contributions and productivity, membership in a historically advantaged or disadvantaged group, or on some other basis? Most utilitarians say very little about the processes that generate well-being or its distribution—whether income was gained by work or transfer is considered completely neutral—and would appear to abstract from many of these considerations.

John Rawls (1971) imagined the governance structures and outcomes that a group of people would develop if they were to decide on the rules before knowing who would end up in which position (i.e., who would be rich and who poor). He demonstrated that such a social contract would establish an equitable society that sought to maximize the welfare of the least well-off person. If two distributions gave the least well-off person the same utility, then the next worst-off would be considered, and so on lexicographically. This result depends on assuming that people are somewhat risk or inequality averse: a risk/inequality neutral group of people would establish rules that maximized one's expected outcome, and a risk-seeking group would want the richest people to be as wealthy as possible.

Rawls's max-min rule (aka Rawlsianism) is not the same as seeking to equalize all incomes. Inequality as such is never addressed. The focus is rather on making the worst-off members of society as happy as possible. Imagine, for example, a society with only two individuals who have to choose between one income distribution where both are equally poor (say, $2 per day) and a distribution where one is slightly less poor and the other is fabulously rich (say, $2.50 per day and $100,000 per day). Following the max-min rule, they would prefer to establish the second society where the poorer person—whichever of them it turned out to be—received a higher income. Rabin (1998) demonstrates through several experiments that many people identify Rawls's max-min principle as the most equitable when compared with various notions of egalitarianism or utilitarianism.

Ethical considerations may also dictate allowable methods in order to arrive at desired distributions. Adam Smith's argument in *The Wealth of Nations* was that a system of individual liberty was not only just but could be efficient as well (Smith 1863). In promoting its justice, Smith wrote: "To hurt in any degree the interest of any one order of citizens for no other purpose but to promote that of some other, is evidently contrary to that justice and equality of treatment which the sovereign owes to all different orders of his subjects" (Smith 1863, 295). Smith wrote at a time when income inequality among the working class was relatively small so that the appropriate focus was on removing impediments on what they could do for themselves. Despite his focus on distribution, Rawls also emphasized individual liberty, placing it lexicographically before distribution as his "First Principle," even though most of his writings were about the distribution side of the equation in his "Second Principle." Buchanan (1976) points out that Rawls focused on the premarket distribution of endowments, leaving the market to efficiently arrange for mutually improving trades. This ordering, however, denies trade-offs between liberty, distribution, and efficiency.

Gilbert (2007) proposes one means for overcoming some of these difficulties by considering the negative impact of inequality on freedom: a more mild reduction in freedom for some (via taxation, for instance) could secure much greater degree of freedom and human capability for someone suffering from hunger and poverty. Equality of freedom could be united with equality of opportunity and outcome.

Another modern philosopher, Nozick (1974), believed that if the rules determining how initial endowments are obtained and those governing exchanges thereafter are fair and just, the resultant distribution will also be equitable regardless of the eventual inequality that may emerge. However, if no one person has an inherent right to own natural resources, redistribution could address prior injustices. Some religious traditions emphasize the principle of stewardship, claiming that all things belong to God and that individuals are accountable for what they do with their stewardships. Islamic law regards wealth beyond what is necessary to sustain life as a bounty from God and indicates that it should be used to assist the poor (Gilbert 2007).

For the most part, however, religions work from the bottom up, enjoining adherents to voluntary action. How often should top-down redistribution be done? Is it possible to have one grand redistribution that adjusts everything to a Rawlsian (or egalitarian or rights-based or any other ideal) distribution for all time, or does each generation have a new grand redistribution, or must this be done every year? Yet again, how would this ideal distribution change if future generations are taken into account? Every new day is a new initial period from the point of view of the people there. Nozick (1974) discussed this problem, positing a situation that starts from an egalitarian distribution, but where each individual decides that one member of the society is particularly deserving and freely gives money to that person. This results in one person having significantly more wealth than anyone else and a nonegalitarian income distribution. This demonstrates the inherent tension in enforcing a particular ideal distribution in a society where free exchange is allowed.

Mill, as mentioned in chapter 9, demonstrated that democracy is less the rule of self by each person than it is the rule of each person over everyone else. It is easy for the rights, circumstances, and desires of minorities to be overlooked or even trampled in the name of the "common good." The diversity of situations, opinions, practices, and ethics makes it in most cases impossible to identify one single "common good." This also ties in with the above quotation from Smith: if governments have a duty to protect each citizen, that duty includes protecting their rights from being infringed on by other citizens through the government. One of the strengths of the human rights framework is the emphasis placed on ensuring every human has access to needed capabilities. Case 3-2 deals specifically with addressing the issues faced by indigenous minorities.

Households and Other Actors

So far this discussion has been at an aggregate level. Of primary concern for policy analysts should be how households are modeled (see chapter 4 on household choice theory). Do we assume that households act rationally and benevolently within their constraints, or that social planners are much better informed about how households *ought* to act? If households don't act that way, is it due to a lack of knowledge, to constraints, to different maximands, or other issues? Could and should policymakers attempt to force certain choices on households? Does the household run by bargaining between members, or is the structure more dictatorial, and how does this difference inform society's duties? What limits define when society should intervene in a household? We are often warned that paternalistic policies may actually reduce household welfare if households are rational, but what is meant by household welfare? Is it the sum of the utilities of household members or the extent to which their basic needs and rights are fulfilled? Do parents' needs count more or less than children's do?

Consider the example of child labor laws. If children who currently work were prevented from working by child labor laws, is the alternative activity education or starvation, and how should that alternative inform the debate on them? Should child labor laws be identical across countries or are there valid reasons why they might differ? Is there a difference between working outside the household and child labor on a home farm? Should we assume that national governments and/or parents are trying to do the best thing for their children within the context in which they live, or should international agreements and trade restrictions dictate child labor laws at the local and national levels? Should the pursuit of children's education always override short-term needs for family survival? How could both goals be achieved?

Very similar questions apply to areas of human health and nutrition. Is obesity the result of rational lifestyle choices or does it stem from a lack of self-control so that obese people would be thankful for higher taxes on sugar and fat, and so forth, to help them commit to live healthier lives? The chronic diseases that stem from obesity may be a drain on others in the society (a negative externality) to the extent that medical care is paid for by taxes. Does this give society the right to dictate food or activity choices for obese individuals? What about mentally handicapped people who also use societal resources? What about the elderly or the poor?

One of the difficulties in crafting policies to affect household and individual behavior is sometimes called the law of unintended consequences. Subsidies on particular foods encourage overeating and obesity. Improved subsidy targeting can result in secondary markets where poor people sell food to the rich in order to fill other needs or wants. Food stamps may be used for nonfood purposes or sold in order to purchase other things (Pinstrup-Andersen 2007b). Even barring these avenues, household resources are fungible. School lunch programs aimed at providing food to schoolchildren may lead households to provide schoolchildren less food at home so that it may be freed up for other family members, or to use the money that would have been spent on food for other purposes. Similarly, infant nutrient supplements provided to a household are often shared among all household members because of notions of intrahousehold distributional equity and equality.

Whose ethics should be regarded? In all these examples, the household might be addressing needs or wants that are different from those of government agencies or other donors. Is it ethical for households to make other use of donated goods than was intended, and is it ethical, on the other hand, for donors to impose their value structures on households? Does it make a difference if those donors are foreigners or fellow citizens from other regions or different social castes? Attempts to circumvent household preferences through targeting of donated food or cash to individual household members may fail, wasting the cost of targeting. Similarly, attempts to change household behavior by targeting transfers to specific foods or to food as opposed to nonfood frequently fail because of fungibility within the household.

Policy analysis needs to take such household decision making into account when calculating the real costs and benefits of programs. In the remainder of this chapter we turn our attention to specific areas of policy where our ethics play an important role in determining how policy analysis and policymaking operate. The order of topics roughly follows the chapters of the book.

Poverty, Hunger, and Nutrition

> If I accept the responsibility that I *should* act; if I have the authority that I *may* act; and if I have the resources so I *can* act; then I can be held accountable for my action or non-action. (Jonsson 2007, 119)

At the 1996 World Food Summit and at the Millennium Summit in 2000, government representatives declared that each person has rights to adequate food that is safe and culturally appropriate. They accepted the duty to reduce hunger to half of its 1990 level by 2015. There are three primary obligations resting on governments as a result of this right: to identify at-risk groups, ensure they can obtain food in the immediate term, and assist them to become self-reliant; to protect their own citizens against actions by other governments, citizens, or corporations that might threaten their food security; and to itself do no harm. This amounts to ensuring access and availability for all people, rather than providing everyone free food (Robinson 2007). The Millennium Declaration itself is more than the eight goals, but includes agreement on the processes by which the goals are to be achieved, including support for democracy and human rights (Jonsson 2007). Case study 11-1 discusses the Right to Food Campaign's efforts in India to use litigation to ensure that the poor's right to food is honored.

Singer (1972, 1997) presents an ethical question nearly all people answer affirmatively: If you could save someone's life or avert great suffering without sacrificing anything of (comparable) moral significance, is it an obligation? Singer argues from this that to ignore hunger in other countries is morally wrong and unjustifiable. He has argued at different forums that people should give at least 5 percent of their income to the problem of hunger, that people should give until they are reduced to the same level of utility as those they help, and that people should simply do more. He reports giving 20–25 percent of his income for hunger relief efforts (Harris 2003). In contrast, most Kantians and virtuists tend to see helping those in other countries as good, but neglecting to give such aid is not morally equivalent to ignoring a drowning child near you.

One of the effects of globalization and telecommunications progress has been to increase the ability of the ordinary person to have an influence for good far beyond their normal circle. In past times, news of a famine or other natural disaster would not reach people until long after it was too late to help. For the first time in human history, the prosperity of the West has placed vast majorities in a position to contribute charitably. Plentiful NGOs reach out to the poor and children to relieve immediate suffering. The Internet enables anyone to examine an NGO's track record to ensure money goes where it is supposed to and to easily give money for support.

And yet. And yet news media do not find it worthwhile to report on the annual demise of 10 million children under five from hunger and other preventable causes. Bryce et al. (2005a and 2005b) implicate hunger and malnutrition as a culprit in over half of the cases, and find that 60 percent of those deaths could be prevented in forty-two countries for as little as $1.23 per person living in them. Pinstrup-Andersen (2007b) asks, could "the richest 10 percent of the populations of those countries . . . afford to pay US$12.30 annually without sacrificing anything of comparable moral or material significance? Of course they could. Do they? No." The same amount of money could be raised by donations of as little as $40 from the richest 50 percent of the United States, approximately 0.08 percent of the median household income.

In partial defense, it should be noted that (1) this is in addition to what individuals may already be giving, which in some cases may be zero but in many cases is already substantially more; (2) Bryce et al. (2005b) do not take account of the cost of scaling up health care provision to a universal level, nor the cost to increase uptake from the demand side, only the cost of providing necessary interventions once that scaling up has already occurred (i.e., the real cost is much larger); and (3) once these children's lives have been saved, much more will be needed in order to bring them out of poverty, to educate them, and so forth. If one takes a positive rights-based approach or Singer's utilitarianism, however, such distinctions become less meaningful: what matters is the unfulfilled outcome. From a Kantian or virtuist perspective, how much of a donation is needed to fulfill one's duty or how much a virtuous person should give is likely correlated with the cost but differs significantly from a rights-based perspective.

Our very definitions of poverty and poverty reduction have important implications for how aid should be apportioned and how much is needed. Barder (2009) differentiates between aid that is broad (reaches many people) and deep (affecting the poorest); between helping individuals who are poor today (e.g., food aid) and preventing poverty in the future (e.g., agricultural research); and between sustained aid and temporary aid. Recalling the Foster, Greer, and Thorbecke (1984) measure of poverty discussed in chapter 5, if we only care about whether a person's income is below a certain threshold, aid will be most effective when given to the least poor, requiring very little aid per person. The more concerned we are about the depth of poverty, the more aid should go to the most chronically and deeply impoverished. This impacts program and intervention allocation. Barder (2009) also notes a political preference for thinking of aid as a temporary means of increasing economic growth, rather than a perpetual global redistribution of wealth. He posits that donors would perceive aid agencies as coming closer to fulfilling their missions, reducing donor fatigue, if they explicitly indicate they are merely lessening the misery of the poor while waiting for development to catch up to them.

Aside from the regularly discussed question of how, there is also the question of why. Is reducing poverty a moral imperative only, or is it also enlightened self-interest for wealthy individuals and nations? U.S. President George W. Bush acknowledged that global inequality and poverty create a world that is not only unjust, but unstable (Pinstrup-Andersen 2007b). Chapter 9 covered the correlations between poverty and inequality on the one hand, and conflict and terrorism on the other. Reducing poverty in the South can also mean important new markets for the products of the North and can reduce illegal immigration. There are therefore political and economic reasons for poverty reduction in addition to the ethical arguments.

Recall from chapter 3 that the global food system begins and ends with human health and nutrition. That is its ultimate goal, and human health and nutrition in turn affect food production and distribution around the world. Reducing hunger, poverty, and malnutrition is therefore instrumental in producing a better global food system, and improvements to the food system will result in reduced hunger, poverty, and malnutrition.

Numerous studies have demonstrated that economic growth plays an integral part in poverty reduction. Dollar and Kraay (2004) document that the income of the poorest fifth of the population has tended across countries to grow at the same rate as average economic growth, leading to significant poverty reductions. Aziz (2007) reports on studies that reveal that 60–70 percent of poverty reduction in China, Vietnam, Korea, Chile, Malaysia, Uganda, and Tunisia came from economic growth. These findings imply that pursuing economic growth brings important dividends for the poor. The remaining reductions in poverty from the above-mentioned countries came from specific, targeted pro-poor policies. Jonsson (2007) further points out that lack of resources by both individuals to claim their rights and governments to fulfill their duties is one of the primary reasons that human rights are not being met more widely.

There is an important difference between meeting human rights standards and fulfilling human rights principles. The first can be accomplished with stopgap measures, food aid and other charities, and other efforts to address what might be termed symptoms. Fulfilling human rights principles attacks the underlying causes of hunger, poverty, malnutrition, and other societal ills so that individuals can support themselves (Pinstrup-Andersen 2007b). Jonsson (2007), case study 11-1, and chapter 9 have argued that this includes establishing democracy and good governance structures so that individuals can claim their rights.

Food Safety

If asked whether any person should have to eat unsafe food, most people would answer no. If asked whether all people should have access to safe food, the answer would likely be yes. There are a number of difficulties hidden behind these seemingly innocuous questions, however.

How safe is safe? The uncomfortable fact is that the cost of removing the last parts per million of organic material from water or pests from food are prohibitively high (chapter 3). From a utilitarian perspective, the money that would have to be spent to ensure 100 percent purity could alleviate much more suffering if spent elsewhere. How much food safety is a human right and how much is preference? One hundred percent purity is likely unattainable. The same is true of eliminating *all* risk. It simply isn't possible. There are decreasing returns to standards—that is, the number of lives saved and the improvements in health for an additional dollar spent on food safety decreases as expenditures go up. As high-income populations demand more food safety, the marginal cost-effectiveness may become very low: very limited increases in food safety for very high costs. Though the discussion is typically cast in terms of finding objective standards of safety, subjective ethics lie behind deciding which standards to apply, which methods to use to obtain them, and how universally to apply them.

Increasing food safety potentially requires different production and storage techniques, different inputs, and the expenses of testing or cleaning. These factors increase the costs of production, thereby decreasing food affordability for the poor. Trade-offs thus need to be considered between safety and price, and hence between food safety and food security. Demand for food safety tends to rise with income both at an individual and national level. Rich country governments are liable to set higher food safety standards than poorer countries even though both have the goal of ensuring their citizens can consume safe food. In some cases, these standards are used as nontariff barriers: the methods required to pass inspection may be prohibitively expensive to poor farmers from developing countries, effectively serving as a protectionist barrier in disguise (Caswell and Bach 2007).

A second issue occurs when farmers sell their high-quality food to the North and low-quality food domestically, producing a two-tier food system that is found in many developing countries attempting to meet the food safety standards of importing countries. Improved food safety systems spread to domestic markets very slowly and are likely to increase domestic food costs to the detriment of the poor (Caswell and Bach 2007).

There is a great need for harmonization of food safety standards across countries. For the reasons already discussed, it is highly unlikely that one set of standards could be applied to all countries with all tastes at all income levels. However, minimal standards for health and safety could be developed from a rights-based perspective. Caswell and Bach (2007) maintain that the first priority is for the needs and food security of developing countries to have a place in the food safety policies of rich countries, rather than being disregarded.

There is also a fierce debate over the extent to which food safety standards may be left to the private sector. MacDonald (2006) points out that all firms and industries must self-regulate to a certain degree when their specific case has not been judged by the government. In some cases, private standards set by supermarket chains are well above national standards, and to the extent consumers are willing and able to pay, this could be a key marketing niche. Consumer groups and NGOs can also play an important role in keeping firms accountable. The need for firms to develop relationships of trust is one force pushing private standards up, but the harm that could be caused by neglect of food safety for short-term profits and by unscrupulous people justifies some precaution. A combination of minimum standards that are rights based and freedom to exceed those standards for those who have greater food safety preferences seems optimal, though it may increase the inequality of food safety (von Braun and Mengistu 2007b).

Food Sovereignty

Three levels of food sovereignty are often confused: individual, household, and national. While food safety refers to the health quality of the food consumed and food security its sufficiency and reliability, food sovereignty is the right of an individual, a household, or a nation to determine its own food-related behavior. It is different from food self-sufficiency because a household may not grow all its own food (i.e., be self-sufficient) but still be enabled to choose what foods they will eat and under what circumstances (sovereignty). The principle might be stated as "No one person, household, or country has the right to choose the food policies of another person, household, or country."

Primarily this is a negative right, restricting other individuals, households, or nations from intervening. Food sovereignty is usually framed as an important part of food security, but the two could come into conflict, such as when a household exercises its food sovereignty to choose a food allocation that violates a household member's food security. Those who regard individual food security as the higher right would justify society intervening, while those who value household food sovereignty more highly would object.

The principle of national food sovereignty both protects and weakens individual and household food sovereignty. The policies of one country often impact citizens of another country, in which case the citizens of the affected country should have a say in those policies that affect them (chapter 9). This is a large part of the call for greater international cooperation and coordination in setting policies for the global food system. Yet opponents of the WTO argue that power structures enable rich countries to impose food and trade policies on poorer countries in violation of national food sovereignty, so greater international cooperation can have the opposite effect (Sharma 2007).

National food sovereignty weakens individual food sovereignty, though, when it is taken to mean that one group of citizens within a country can dictate the food policies of another group. This conflict is seen when a national government restricts agricultural trade with another country—whether in the name of protecting domestic farmers, increasing food security, or for ethical concerns—even though some citizens might be willing to purchase food from individuals in that other country.

Like governments and households, some claim that nongovernmental organizations (NGOs), multinational corporations (MNCs), and other businesses and civil society entities are groups of individuals that acquire new sets of rights and responsibilities as a group that the members of the group individually did not possess. Business ethics, which also affect NGOs, deal primarily with the relationships between the firm and consumers, between employers and employees, between owners (shareholders) and operators (managers), and between the firm and the social and physical environment.

One of the primary ethical concerns about NGOs and MNCs was summarized by Ambrose Bierce (1911), who sardonically defined a corporation in his *Devil's Dictionary* as "an ingenious device for obtaining individual profit without individual responsibility." That is, the firm itself is responsible, but often no one person, from the workers on the ground to the topmost board of directors or CEO to the shareholders who own the company, is responsible and accountable for the actions and policies of the firm. This is a serious governance lapse that makes it difficult to precisely define what a firm's or NGO's social responsibility is or to whom it is accountable.

Markets and Morality

There is a heated, ongoing debate over the morality of markets and the market system. Wolf (2003) contends that markets are a highly moral institution: no other social system has been found that has lifted so many people out of hunger and poverty; reduced diseases and premature deaths; preserved and maximized individual liberty in political and socioeconomic realms; nor granted so many people the economic and social freedom for self-discovery, development, and expression. Markets produce happiness in a very real sense: individuals will only trade with each other voluntarily when both have something to gain. I give up something I value less than you in exchange for something you value less than I do. People "vote" with their money every day, supporting causes, goods, and people they deem good and denying that support to things they believe are less deserving. Systems of private property promote individual accountability, and some conservationists have claimed that legalizing markets for ivory or other animal products from endangered species would give entrepreneurs an incentive to preserve them—no one is concerned about the extinction of the cow, after all.

If these are the primary outcomes we care about, and if we adopt a consequentialist ethic, then markets have achieved and could achieve what no other system has, and should be properly heralded. Markets are often defended most vigorously by those who believe most fervently in human rights to freedom that free market systems preserve. Markets also deserve praise to the extent they incentivize service to others, hard work, creativity, and other virtues.

Others have argued that, far from saintly, markets are fiendish: they commoditize not only food but humanity itself as "labor inputs," and permit explicit slavery and implicit "wage slavery." They marginalize those unable to compete, produce and promote gross inequality, permit selfishness and greed, and dehumanize interpersonal relationships. Globalization has masses of critics (chapter 10). The relationship between market systems, economic growth, and inequality has been under intense scrutiny without coming to definitive conclusions. Walzer (2008) argues that all competition, economic or political, forces people to compromise their values. Even the existence of some markets, such as human trafficking, pornography and prostitution, illicit drugs, or human organs, is repugnant to many individuals following Kantian and virtue ethics. Market imperfections may also lead to irreversibly negative environmental consequences.

A third line of argument holds that markets are neither moral nor immoral, but amoral (Krugman 2010). Markets are mirrors, reflecting the values of their participants. Where markets produce inequality by allowing one individual to exercise market power and exploit another person, it is not the market that has caused it, but the greed and lack of feeling of the exploiter (Sacks 2009). If there were no demand for slaves or sex workers, the markets for them would disappear. To the extent people care about environmental consequences of their actions, they will be willing to pay more for goods and services that preserve the environment. Markets then appear as mere reflections of the ultimate expressed preferences, values, and virtues of the members of society. Whether free, regulated, or controlled, markets reflect the values of the people who have decision-making power. Indeed, one of the benefits of the private ownership of property is that it separates the public and private, reducing problems of conflict of interest when the government makes policy (Wolf 2003). Free markets come closest to reflecting the values of the most people, both the most virtuous and the lowest common denominator, while command systems reflect only the values of those with political power. Though wealthy individuals have more influence, even the poor have some ability to shape the market and their society.

Wilber (2004) and Anderson (1990) point out, however, that markets are not value-neutral because there are basic assumptions that must be in effect for markets to function. "A good is properly traded on the market if its value is successfully realized by the norms of the market" (Wilber 2004, 437). Market norms are highly individualistic, impersonalize transactions, emphasize personal advantage over other factors—no one is forced to act to their own advantage, but there are no countervailing market institutions to suggest other courses of action—and allow people to express their discontent only with silence rather than participation in decision making. As such, encouraging markets and using market incentives for social engineering can undermine nonmarket norms (Sacks 2009), turning charitable donations that foster community into self-interested tax breaks and replacing parental love and concern with monetary incentives to attend school or turn children over to day care so the family can have another material possession. Promoters of a "deep ecology ethic," discussed below, reject the use of markets for environmental decision making for just these reasons. (Beckerman and Pasek [2003] respond to these concerns.)

These are not easy questions to untangle. People have differing values, so they will arrive at different conclusions over whether and the extent to which free markets or regulations should be used in order to fulfill society's ultimate goals. The Templeton Foundation (2008) collected brief, memorable statements from thirteen social scientists, politicians, philosophers, and writers at the dawn of the 2008 financial crisis on this fundamental question, and each one drew different conclusions from different arguments and ethical positions. From an individualist ethic, in fact, there are no societal goals, only the summation of the goals of the individuals in that society. If there are transcendent societal goals, who is to decide what they are and how to achieve them? Governments have generally taken it on themselves to answer this question, and international bodies have convened many summits of government leaders in the last century to identify common ethical principles and norms, particularly regarding hunger, poverty, and human rights.

For policy analysts, most questions will not be about the grand shapes of society, but rather about individual policies. What sorts of behavior will this policy incentivize? Do the outcomes justify both economic and moral costs? What trade-offs are acceptable and which are not?

Animal Welfare and Environmental Ethics

Primarily to this point we have considered only ethics relating to the self and other human beings. This anthropocentric view has come under increasing challenge in recent decades (Sandøe and Jensen 2008) as different perspectives argue that animals, plants, and/or the global ecosystem as a whole should be included in ethical considerations as well. *Extentionists* claim that the reasons put forward for caring about other humans could be extended to include sentient animals or plants as fellow living beings. *Holists* reject the individual focus of modern ethics and focus attention on the interdependency of entire ecosystems of which we are a part. *Deep ecologists* go further and emphasize the unity of nature and all living things. *Ecofeminism* claims that feminine virtues would be more environmentally friendly and unifying. These views are in stark contrast with *moral antinaturalism,* which argues that only humans are capable of ethical thought: the natural world is decidedly amoral (Marinoff 2007).

Any of the ethical systems in this chapter could be expanded to consider animal welfare and environmentalism. Do humans alone have intrinsic rights, or do all sentient animals, all life, or the ecosystem as a whole also have intrinsic rights? Does only the welfare of human beings enter into the SWF, or do we include animals because they are capable of feeling and reacting to pleasure and pain? Some traditions hold that the earth itself is alive and feels pain. Should this enter into the SWF directly, or only to the extent that the welfare of humans is dependent on certain types of environmental health? What are our moral duties toward animals and the environment? Environmentalist virtue ethics often places environmental consciousness as one of the primary virtues to be pursued by the good person.

There is an important distinction to be made between intrinsic and extrinsic virtues in relation to animals and the environment. Intrinsic virtues or rights are ends in themselves while extrinsic virtues or rights are means to other ends. Compare the following sample arguments from different ethical traditions regarding intrinsic and extrinsic environmental issues:

1. Animals should be free from cruel forms of death because it is a denial of their right to life, and the defining principle for inclusion in a SWF is not the ability to reason but the ability to suffer (Bentham 1789; also Singer 1975).
2. Animals should be free from cruel forms of death because animal stress harms the quality and safety of the meat, harming human health and nutrition (Grandin 1997).
3. Appropriate measures should be taken to limit carbon output because climate change will harm the poorest people more than the richest, which is unjust (Vanderheiden 2004).
4. Humanity is one part of an interconnected whole in the fabric of life. We thus have a moral duty to reduce our carbon emissions and avoid harm to the ecosystem (Zimmerman 1989).

As in the above cases, though intrinsic (2 and 3) and extrinsic (1 and 4) reasoning support carbon emission reductions and animal welfare, the amount of effort proposed will differ widely, as will how trade-offs are discussed and managed. For instance, developing countries adhering to point 3 argue that reducing their emissions now would hamper their development and the ability of poor individuals to lift themselves out of poverty. Environmentalists supporting point 4 would not agree.

What trade-offs are permissible between human and animal welfare? Sharma (2007) notes that while over 1 billion people live below the $2 a day poverty line, the EU subsidizes their dairy industry to the tune of $2.70 per cow and Japan spends $8.00 per cow. When one takes into account the methane produced by each cow and the additional cows supported by OECD subsidies, understanding how to balance the needs of the poor, the environmental damage, the preferences of consumers, and animal welfare becomes a difficult ethical puzzle.

328 Food Policy for Developing Countries

The question of how we should weight the rights and needs of people in future generations against present needs is important for policies related to the natural environment. For a utilitarian, if that weighting could be agreed on, it would be possible to identify the costs to future generations of environmental actions today and determine explicitly the trade-offs between production and consumption (including enjoyment of natural beauty) today and in any future period. Such information is useful for devising full-costing measures that price into today's decision making the effects of purchases on future generations and the environment. If all people that have yet to be born are equal with those living today, principles of stewardship and sustainability take on greater importance. Ultimately, therefore, determining appropriate carbon taxes, cap and trade systems, payments for environmental services, or other elements of a full-costing policy approach (chapter 8) is deeply ethical in nature. Without resolving the ethical dimensions behind them, it will not be possible to identify a satisfactory set of policies.

Trade and Aid

Many trade policies of OECD countries have long been a thorn in the side of development and social justice (chapter 10). Mimicking the behavior of former colonial powers, OECD countries emphasize imports of raw materials from developing countries through little or no import tariff on these raw materials and tariffs that escalate with increasing degree of processing. The purpose of such policies is that the value addition and employment creation associated with processing and manufacturing will take place in the importing, high-income countries, leaving low-income countries as providers of raw materials, failing to create the employment they so badly need. The same OECD countries may provide development assistance domestically to promote processing and manufacturing of goods for export. Clearly, there are ethical issues to be considered here.

Barrett and Maxwell (2005) present an important vision of how food aid has been changing over the last fifty years and what further changes are needed in order to improve its ability to help in crisis situations and prevent the most adverse consequences. U.S. food aid benefits are supported by three stakeholder groups in the United States: agricultural interests represented by members of Congress, NGOs whose incomes come from monetizing food aid, and U.S. maritime shipping because U.S. food aid has to be transported primarily on U.S. ships. This iron triangle provides strong support for the continuation of U.S. food aid. Barrett and Maxwell (2005) provide evidence that the cost-effectiveness of food aid could be enhanced significantly by replacing U.S. food with food acquired in developing countries closer to where it is needed and by pursuing competitive shipping rates. While food aid may be the most appropriate form of aid in certain cases, including abrupt large-scale natural catastrophes, large-scale monetizing of food aid depresses domestic food prices, harming poor rural people. Gelan (2006) considers food aid in Ethiopia and finds that cash grants would likely increase household welfare by more than food itself, but warns that cash grants can increase the price of food and harm those who do not receive the cash benefits.

Large agricultural subsidies in OECD governments present another ethical dilemma. They depress agricultural product prices, making it difficult for developing country farmers to compete in international and domestic markets and reducing the incentives to invest in rural areas and agricultural development, including agricultural research, in developing countries. The competitive advantage of poor farmers, whose costs of production are often lower than those in OECD countries, is wiped out by the OECD countries' subsidies and import tariffs. The outcome is continued rural poverty and hunger. Theft of genetic resources (biopiracy) from poor communities that are then threatened with legal action for patent and copyright infringements is yet another ethics issue requiring urgent policy action at the national and international levels.

On top of the harm done by developed country governments is the harm done by the trade policies of the developing countries themselves. Most developing countries have followed trade, exchange rate, and other macro policies that have harmed their agricultural sectors, leading to increased levels of hunger, poverty, and unemployment. Removing these barriers would be of primary benefit to the developing countries themselves. Tutwiler and Straub (2007) point out that keeping those barriers in place because of developed countries' barriers may be an appropriate trade negotiation strategy, but that does not make it ethical.

Von Braun and Mengistu (2007b) argue two important points regarding these issues. The first is the necessity of a rules-based trading system for creating an ethical food system where the rules are designed as much by and for the stakeholders in poor countries as they are for those in rich countries. Ensuring that minority views, poor individuals, and poor countries have appropriate participation in the process and that all actors are held accountable for their actions in a transparent manner is a great challenge (chapter 9). They secondly argue that removing negative ethical incentives—such as those that promote a race to the bottom in environmental or labor standards—is insufficient. Because past histories and institutional memory matter, it is also important to provide positive incentives for ethical behavior, at least for a time. Where these positive incentives are the only incentive, Kantians and virtue ethicists will likely be concerned that they are not virtuous acts, even if consequentialists are satisfied. Trade-offs between ideals, rights, and ethics are likely to come into play.

In any of the changes proposed above, there will be winners and losers. People and industries that have been protected may experience loss of income, structural unemployment, and other economic and psychological losses. SWF1 is satisfied if the winners gain more than the losers lose, but it is clear that these are not Pareto changes. It is not enough to say that the winners *could* compensate the losers. For politicians who desire to be perceived as doing what is right, analysts would do well to discuss the distributional ramifications of their proposals and how to compensate the losers or mitigate their anger.

Fair trade schemes have been a popular means for consumers to express preferences for social equity (case 10-8). These actions are readily understandable from a utilitarian perspective: people enjoy the thought that their choice of coffee, chocolate, or woven rug is helping a poor individual and their utility increases by the thought. It is less certain that people have a moral duty (Kantian or virtue ethical) to purchase fair trade coffee over other brands, in part because it is uncertain that individuals who do not purchase any coffee have a moral duty to do so.

Whether fair trade purchases are a more effective means of helping the distant poor than charitable donations is not empirically certain. Fair trade coffee growers have been shown in a number of studies to experience increased incomes, more stable prices, better access to credit, training, and education, and improved political participation, though production costs also increased (Murray, Raynolds, and Taylor 2003; Eberhart 2005; Jaffee 2007). Enabling individuals to work their way out of poverty and hunger has a great deal of appeal. Not all fair trade schemes deliver real benefits to the farmers involved, however, and Cheng (case 10-8) points out that by increasing prices, oversupply may be exacerbated for extended periods of time, the distribution of benefits may be at odds with social justice, and the long-term sustainability of fair trade programs is questionable. Further, fair trade efforts are not designed to provide public goods that are needed for long-term, widespread poverty reduction.

Implicit Normativity in Research

It should be clear from the foregoing discussions that the issue is not that agricultural, economic, biotechnological, or political science research lacks an ethical base, but that it remains implicit and rarely discussed. This has led to widespread distrust and anger. It is essential for analysts both to respectfully consider the ethical arguments put forward by the opposition and to consider a variety of perspectives explicitly (Thompson 2007).

Without delving into the well-established questions on the ethical treatment of human and animal subjects, there are several implicit ethical judgments being made in any research project. Wilber (2004, 426) points out that "the questions asked, the problems considered important, the answers deemed acceptable, the axioms of the theory, the choice of relevant facts, the hypotheses proposed to account for such facts, the criteria used to assess the fruitfulness of competing theories, [and] the language in which results are to be formulated" are all normative, value decisions (see also Millstone 2006). Is the goal to avoid harm or to promote good? When should policy and behavioral advice be given, and how strongly worded should it be, considering that it is based on research that is seldom if ever conclusive (Folker, Andersen, and Sandøe 2008)?

In addition to individual or institutional biases behind these types of assumptions are the biases of discipline. Economics focuses on utilitarian ethics, objective quantitative data, and primarily statistical methods to evaluate falsifiable hypotheses. Sociology is much more likely to view subjective qualitative data and case studies as forming the basis of knowledge, concerned that economists' utilitarianism sweeps people and important facets out of sight. Multidisciplinary work can help cover many of these blind spots and provide a more holistic picture.

Folker, Andersen, and Sandøe (2008) discuss in a compelling way the difficulty of determining which segment of the population to emphasize in a research project. Should research and policy advice focus on the mythical "average" person—who is half-male/half-female, with an above-median income, lives in all parts of the country simultaneously, works part-time in multiple occupations, and so forth—or on specific target groups? Their example concerns advice on optimal sugar intake, which would be lower for obese groups than for the average person. The optimal amount of fertilizer and water inputs depends on soil quality and other farming practices, which will be different for smallholders than for the average farmer. Should poverty reduction research focus on the urban or rural poor? The differences in these cases are inherently ethical and have important political ramifications in terms of program feasibility and sustainability, yet at present researchers and policy analysts have no outside guidance on which to rely.

Biotechnology

The original U.S. risk assessments on the effects of genetically modified (GM) foods (chapters 7 and 10) are a glaring example of the importance of explicitly discussing these ethical questions because they considered only the effects on commercial agriculture rather than human health or the environment (Millstone 2006). Thompson (2007) avers that, in general, the biotech industry and even many unaffiliated proponents of GM crops as one weapon in the fight against hunger and poverty have been dismissive of the ethical concerns raised against biotech processes and applications, an attitude that has not recommended the cause or its proponents to the general public. He identifies four primary concerns that will be addressed in this section: unnaturalness, the precautionary principle, social justice, and food sovereignty.

One of the first complaints is that the genetic modification processes themselves are "unnatural." Combining plant DNA from different species, or injecting animal DNA into plants and vice versa, strikes many people as going against the natural order. Chapman (2005) defines natural processes as those where humans observe what happens and adapt their behavior accordingly, while in unnatural processes humans change nature to suit their needs at the time. According to this definition, however, the difference between genetic engineering and traditional plant-breeding methods is one of degree rather quality. Indeed, when direct plant breeding was introduced in the twentieth century, many of the same unnatural arguments were applied against it. Thompson (2007) thus notes that our concepts of nature and natural processes adapt over time, providing no objective foundation for policy bans. There is an important discussion that needs to take place on why one level of unnaturalness (deliberate cross-pollination, artificial insemination, or Chapman's [2005] example of artificial clothing fibers) is an acceptable alteration of nature while another is not.

Though the precautionary principle (PP) has had several formulations in international law (chapters 8 and 9), the primary notion behind it is that if something could reasonably cause severe or irreparable harm, extreme caution is warranted, even if scientific evidence has not yet demonstrated that such harm is likely. The

1992 Rio Conference held that the PP should be applied to environmental harm as well as human harm, though it permits countries to consider the cost-effectiveness of interventions. Of primary concern is the difference between risk, where probabilities can be measured or estimated, and uncertainty, where they cannot. It is the very fact that we do not know whether the probability is high or low that justifies the PP.

Regarding GM products, there is no evidence that GM foods have harmed consumers in any way. Given that the crops have existed for only fifteen years, however, there are no long-term studies of the effects on consumers, and the effects on ecosystems when modified genes are spread to the wild are also understudied. These are the underlying uncertainties for GM foods.

There are also benefits forgone by banning GM crops. Increasing food production and nutrient quality could reduce hunger, malnutrition, and the millions of deaths to which they contribute every year. There are also environmental benefits, including reduced chemical pesticide use and reduced need to expand onto marginal lands thanks to increasing production, resulting in improvements to water quality, carbon capture, and soil quality (Goklany 2000). This highlights that any PP against action needs to also consider the possibility of a PP against doing nothing. How to weight certain and/or uncertain benefits relative to certain and/or uncertain costs—and indeed, determining the moral culpability that accrues to someone who halted processes that might have saved a life because of concern that they might take someone else's life—are as yet unsolved questions in ethical thought. They apply to the situation in case study 11-1, where the government of India was accused of sitting on massive stockpiles of food during a prolonged drought without sufficiently fulfilling citizens' rights to food.

The costs and benefits—known, risky, and uncertain—are liable to accrue to different stakeholders. Some critics of agricultural research, the green revolution, and biotech are concerned about the social justice ramifications of the research. Chapter 7 discussed in detail the possibility that new technology may be adopted first by wealthier farmers, driving down prices for nonadopters, potentially forcing them out of business. In essence, these arguments are not about the research as such, but rather how it is applied. Thompson (2007) argues that questions about ethical practice tend to establish how agricultural research should be carried out in order to be considered legitimate. Ensuring that agricultural research reaches those in greatest need should be an important priority for scientists and policy analysts and is one reason that explicit ethical discourse needs to occur. Who will benefit and lose? How much? Not only can, but how will winners compensate losers?

The final complaint about GM foods is that if they are permitted, it will not be possible for people with preferences against them to freely choose to not consume them. While proper labeling systems would resolve much of this tension, allowing both those with and without anti-GMO preferences to express them, the policy situation is more complex. Some states have banned labels such as "GMO free" because of the implicit, false claim that all foods that do not carry this label *do* contain GMOs. Kanter, Messer, and Keiser (2009) find supporting evidence that participants in laboratory experiments are willing to pay 30–45 percent less for conventional milk after tasting and being introduced to organic or growth hormone–free milk. They also found, however, that demand for all kinds of milk decreased after learning about animal growth hormones, so labeling organic milk as being free of growth hormones reduces its own economic demand. Thus negative advertising campaigns have been stymied.

Positive advertising is also problematic: MacDonald and Whellams (2007) determine that the first firm to label its products as containing GMOs would lose significant market share and income because of the negative popular impression of GMOs. They conclude that the lack of scientific evidence suggesting harm from consuming GMOs and the harm firms would suffer implies that individual firms do not have an ethical obligation to label GM products. This is a coordination problem that could be solved only by agreement reached between firms (which would be in violation of antitrust laws) or by government action. The U.S. Food and Drug Administration already requires companies to label products that contain genes from a known allergy-inducing food because of the uncertain risk of harm (Thompson 2000). If, as Rawls, Nozick, and others postulate, one of government's primary duties is to respect personal autonomy, labeling legislation would be one way to ensure that those freedoms are respected. A fuller discussion of the issues related to the labeling of genetically modified foods is found in case 9-9.

One of the concerns about the EU restrictions on GM foods is that they unduly influence the policies of developing countries to the detriment of farmers and consumers in those countries who might choose to produce and consume GM crops but who cannot in order to keep export markets open. Whether the EU restrictions affect other countries' policies is an empirical question and context specific, as is the degree of harm done to consumers and producers. Thus, estimates of the net benefits and/or losses and their distribution within a developing country society would provide a much more important and ethical foundation for national policy-making than pressures from the EU, the United States, or multinational NGOs and corporations. Should not each developing nation have the right to determine its own position and policies?

Conclusion

This chapter has emphasized the importance of explicitly considering ethical dimensions that too often remain implicit. This includes the obviously ethical questions of what obligation developed countries and the nonpoor have with respect to the poor in their own and other nations, and how to manage the inevitable conflicts between different human rights, different virtues, and between rights and budget constraints that prevent households and nations from achieving all rights simultaneously. There are the less obvious ethical matters of research design and whether and to what extent poverty reduction is enlightened self-interest inasmuch as poverty contributes to a lack of markets for developed country products, illegal immigration, pollution, contagious diseases, insecurity, fanaticism, and terrorism (Pinstrup-Andersen 2007b). Introducing many different voices from different stakeholders, disciplines, and perspectives improves the efficacy and effectiveness of research and policy analysis, though it may also slow response times.

This book has emphasized that investments in national and international public goods, particularly infrastructure and agricultural research developed for smallholders, are critical elements in supporting pro-poor economic growth (case study 9-1 and 9-2) and achieving their human rights. Barder (2009) and Aziz (2007) confirm these results, indicating that such investments tackle the root causes of poverty and increase the extent to which economic growth translates into poverty reduction. This chapter has added to this consensus the notion that research must be carefully designed in order to meet all relevant ethical criteria: from the design of the questions to the choice of methodologies to the selection of sources of funding to the focus on particular population groups, all affect the efficacy of policy advice.

Ethical Aspects of Food Systems Case Studies

The ethical aspects of food systems are discussed in many of the cases in the book.* The case prepared for this chapter discusses policy options for implementing the human right to freedom from hunger in the Indian context.

11-1   Food Policy and Social Movements: Reflections on the Right to Food Campaign in India
        Vivek Srinivasan and Sudha Narayanan

Notes

1. These philosophies have been mathematically represented as maximizing the following equations, where U_i is the utility function of the ith individual:

Benthamite: max $\sum U_i$ for all I,

Rawlsian: max$\{$min$\{U_1, U_2, \ldots U_N\}\}$,

Egalitarian: max U_i where $U_i = U_j$ for all i, j.

2. The notion of lexicographic orderings comes from the way words are ordered in a dictionary. Words are compared based on the first letter, and only if those are the same does the comparison proceed to the second letter, and so on. A lexicographic ordering of rights might, for instance, suggest that the first priority is to obtain a minimal standard of food, then a minimal standard of shelter. Shelter would be a determining factor only if the level of food rights was the same in two distributions.

3. Divine command theory is the belief that duties and knowledge of what is right and wrong come by decree from God, gods, or representatives of the divine on earth.

4. Authors' translation of "Der Mensch nämlich ist nicht dazu bestimmt, einzelne sittliche Handlungen zu verrichten, sondern ein sittliches Wesen zu sein. . . . Und Tugend ist nicht

---

* The case study referenced here is presented in full in the three-volume work by Per Pinstrup-Andersen and Fuzhi Cheng, eds., *Case Studies in Food Policy for Developing Countries* (Ithaca, NY: Cornell University Press, 2009) and online via open access at http://cip.cornell.edu/gfs.

anders 'als eine Neigung zu der Pflicht.' . . . Der Mensch . . . soll Lust und Pflicht in Verbindung bringen; er soll seiner Vernunft mit Freuden gehorchen."

5. Inequality aversion is the technically preferred way of referring to a preference for equality. While inequality may be large or small, an income distribution is either equal (everyone has the same amount of income) or unequal.

References

AATF (African Agricultural Technology Foundation). 2007. *Annual report 2006: Delivering the promise; Impacting lives with new technologies.* Ed. T. Harris, N. Muchiri, M. Bo-kanga, and P. Werehire. Kenya: English Press.

Abdullaev, I., C. DeFraiture, M. Giordano, M. Yakubov, and A. Rasulov. 2009. Agricultural water use and trade in Uzbekistan: Situation and potential impacts of market liberal-ization. *International Journal of Water Resources Development* 25 (1): 47–63.

ACC/SCN (United Nations Administrative Committee on Coordinator/Standing Committee on Nutrition). 2004. *Fifth report on the world nutrition situation: Nutrition for improved development outcomes.* Geneva.

Acemoglu, D., S. Johnson, and J. A. Robinson. 2001. The colonial origins of comparative de-velopment: An empirical investigation. *American Economic Review* 91 (5): 1369–1401.

Adamu, H. 2000. We'll feed our people as we see fit. *Washington Post,* September 11.

Adato, M., and R. Meinzen-Dick, eds. 2007. *Agricultural research, livelihoods, and poverty: Studies of economic and social impacts in six countries.* Baltimore: Johns Hopkins Uni-versity Press for IFPRI.

Adelman, I. 1999. The role of government in economic development. Working Paper, Uni-versity of California, Berkeley.

African Economic Development. n.d. Business environment and financing: Mobile operators charge high tariffs. http://www.africaneconomicoutlook.org/en/in-depth/innovation-and-ict-in-africa/business-environment-and-financing.

Ahmed, A. U., R. V. Hill, L. C. Smith, D. M. Wiesmann, and T. Frankenberger. 2007. The world's most deprived: Characteristics and causes of extreme poverty and hunger. 2020 Discussion Paper 43, International Food Policy Research Institute, Washington, DC.

Ahmed, R. 1988. Pricing principles and public intervention in domestic markets. In *Agricul-tural price policy for developing countries,* ed. J. W. Mellor and R. Ahmed. Baltimore: Johns Hopkins University Press.

Akiyama, T., J. Baffes, D. Larson, and P. Varangis. 2001. *Commodity market reforms: Lessons of two decades.* Washington, DC: World Bank.

———. 2003. *Commodity market reforms: Some recent experience.* Washington, DC: World Bank.

Aksoy, M., and J. Beghin. 2005. *Global agricultural trade and developing countries.* Washington, DC: World Bank.

Alderman, H. 1993. New research on poverty and malnutrition: What are the implications for policy? In *Including the poor,* ed. M. Lipton and J. Van Der Gaag. Washington, DC: World Bank.

Alderman, H., P. Chiappori, L. Haddad, J. Hoddinott, and R. Kanbur. 1995. Unitary versus collective models of the household: Is it time to shift the burden of proof? *World Bank Research Observer* 10 (1): 1–19.

Alderman, H., and J. Hoddinott. 2007. *Reducing vulnerability through social protection: Growth-promoting social safety nets.* 2020 Focus Briefs on the World's Poor and Hungry People. Washington, DC: International Food Policy Research Institute.

Alesina, Q., and D. Rodrik. 1994. Distributive politics and economic growth. *Quarterly Journal of Economics* 109:465–490.

Alkire, S. 2002. *Valuing freedoms: Sen's capability approach and poverty reduction.* Oxford: Oxford University Press.

Alkire, S., and M. E. Santos. 2010. Acute multidimensional poverty: A new index for developing countries. OPHI Working Paper 38, July 2010, University of Oxford, England.

Allen, C. R., and C. S. Holling, eds. 2008. *Discontinuities in ecosystems and other complex systems.* New York: Columbia University Press.

Allen, R. 1934. A reconsideration of the theory of value, part II: A mathematical theory of individual demand functions. *Economica* 2:196–219.

Alpuerto, V.-L. E. B., G. W. Norton, J. Alwang, and A.M. Ismail. 2009. Economic impact analysis of marker-assisted breeding for tolerance to salinity and phosphorous deficiency in rice. *Applied Economics Perspectives and Policy* 31 (4): 779–792.

Alston, J. M. 2002. Spillovers. *Australian Journal of Agricultural and Resource Economics* 48:315–346.

Alston, J. M., C. Chan-King, M. C. Marra, P. G. Pardey, and T. J. Wyatt. 2000. *A meta analysis of the rates of return to agricultural R&D: Ex pede herculem.* IFPRI Research Report 113, Washington, DC.

Alston, J. M., and B. H. Hurd. 1990. Some neglected social costs of government spending in farm programs. *American Journal of Agricultural Economics* 72 (1): 149–156.

Alston, L. J. 2008. New institutional economics. In *The new Palgrave dictionary of economics,* 2nd ed., ed. S. N. Durlauf and L. E. Blume. New York: Palgrave Macmillan. The new Palgrave dictionary of economics online. http://www.dictionaryofeconomics.com/article?id=pde2008_N000170 (accessed October 14, 2008).

Alston, L. J., and J. P. Ferrie. 1999. *Southern paternalism and the American welfare state: Economics, politics, and institutions in the South, 1865–1965.* Cambridge: Cambridge University Press.

Ambler, J., L. Pandofelli, A. Kramer, and R. Meinzen-Dick. 2007. *Lessons from successful action for reaching excluded groups: Strengthening women's assets and status; Programs improving poor women's lives.* 2020 Focus Briefs on the World's Poor and Hungry People. Washington, DC: International Food Policy Research Institute.

American Heritage Dictionary of the English Language. 2000. 4th ed. New York: Houghton Mifflin.

Anastassopoulos, G., and R. Rama. 2004. The performance of multinational agribusinesses: Effects of product and geographical diversification. In *Multinational agribusinesses,* ed. R. Rama. Binghamton, NY: Haworth Press.

Anderson, E. 1990. The ethical limitations of the market. *Economics and Philosophy* 6 (2): 179–205.

Anderson, K. 2006. *Reducing distortions to agricultural incentives: Progress, pitfalls and prospects.* Policy Research Working Paper Series 4092, World Bank, Washington, DC.

Anderson, K. 2010. Krueger, Schiff, and Valdes revisited: Agricultural price and trade policy reform in developing countries since 1960. *Applied Economic Perspectives and Policy* 32 (2): 195–231.

Anderson, K., and W. Martin, eds. 2006. Agricultural trade reform and the Doha Development Agenda. In *Agricultural trade reform and the Doha Development Agenda,* ed. K. Anderson and W. Martin. Washington, DC: World Bank.

Anderson, K., W. Martin, and D. van der Mensbrugghe. 2006. Global impacts of the Doha scenarios on poverty. In *Poverty and the WTO: Impacts of the Doha Development Agenda,* ed. T. W. Hertel and L. A. Winters. Washington, DC: World Bank.

Anderson, M., J. Austin, J. Wray, and M. Zeitlin. 1981. Study I: Supplementary feeding. In *Nutrition intervention in developing countries,* ed. J. Austin and M. Zeitlin. Cambridge, MA: Oelgeschlager, Gunn and Hain, for the Harvard Institute for International Development.

Andreoni, J. 1989. Giving with impure altruism: Applications to charity and Ricardian equivalence. *Journal of Political Economy* 97:1447–1458.

———. 1990. Impure altruism and donations to public goods: A theory of warm-glow giving. *Economic Journal* 100 (401): 464–477.

Andreoni, J., and A. Levinson. 2001. The simple analytics of the environmental Kuznets curve. *Journal of Public Economics* 80:269–286.

Antle, J. 1984. Human capital, infrastructure, and the productivity of Indian rice farmers. *Journal of Development Economics* 14:163–181.

Arce, A., and T. Marsden. 1993. The social construction of international food: A new research agenda. *Economic Geography* 69 (3): 291–311.

Ardeni, P., and J. Freebairn. 2002. The macroeconomics of agriculture. In *Handbook of agricultural economics,* vol. 2A, ed. B. Gardner and G. Rausser. Amsterdam: Elsevier Science B.V.

Arnold, T. 2007. Ethics and hunger: A non-governmental organization (NGO) perspective. In *Ethics, hunger and globalization: In search of appropriate policies,* ed. P. Pinstrup-Andersen and P. Sandøe. Dordrecht: Springer.

Ashraf, N., X. Giné, X., and D. Karlan. 2009. Finding missing markets (and a disturbing epilogue): Evidence from an export crop adoption and marketing intervention in Kenya. *American Journal of Agricultural Economics* 91 (4): 973–990.

Ashraf, N., G. Xavier, and D. Karlan, 2009. Finding missing markets (and a disturbing epilogue): Evidence from an export crop adoption and marketing intervention in Kenya . *American Journal of Agricultural Economics* 91 (4): 973–990.

Ashworth, A. 2001. *Community-based rehabilitation of severely malnourished children: A review of successful programmes.* London: London School of Hygiene and Tropical Medicine.

Atkinson, A. B. 1970. On the measurement of inequality. *Journal of Economic Theory* 2:244–263.

———. 1973. How progressive should income tax be? In *Essays in modern economics,* ed. M. Parkin and R. Nobay. New York: Barnes and Noble. http://openlibrary.org/books/OL5085773M/Essays_in_modern_economics.

———. 1983. *The economics of inequality.* 2nd ed. Oxford: Clarendon Press.

Avgerinopoulou, D.-T. 2005. The rise of global environmental administrative law: Improving implementation and compliance through the means of global governance. Paper presented at the 7th International Conference on Environmental Compliance and Enforcement, Marrakech, Morocco, April 9–15.

Axelrod, R., D. Axelrod, and K. J. Pienta. 2006. Evolution of cooperation among tumor cells. *Proceedings of the National Academy of Sciences USA* 103 (36): 13474–13479.

Axtell, R., and J. M. Epstein. 1999. Coordination in transient social networks: An agent-based computational model on the timing of retirement. In *Behavioral dimensions of retirement economics,* ed. H. J. Aaron. Washington DC: Brookings Institution Press.

Aziz, S. 2007. What we know about poverty and what we must do: Ethical and political aspects of empowerment. In *Ethics, hunger and globalization: In search of appropriate policies,* ed. P. Pinstrup-Andersen and P. Sandøe. Dordrecht: Springer.

Azzam, A.M. 1998. Competition in the US meatpacking industry: Is it history? *Agricultural Economics* 18:107–126.

———. 1999. Asymmetry and rigidity in farm-retail price transmission. *American Journal of Agricultural Economics* 81 (3): 524–534.

Babu, S., and P. Pinstrup-Andersen. 1994. Food security and nutrition monitoring: A conceptual framework, issues, and challenges. *Food Policy* 19 (3): 218–233.

Babu, S., and P. Sanyal. 2009. *Food security, poverty and nutrition policy analysis: Statistical methods and applications.* Burlington, MA: Academic Press.

Badiane, O., F. Goletti, M. Kherallah, P. Berry, K. Govindan, P. Gruhn, and M. Mendoza. 1997. Agricultural input and output marketing reforms in African countries. Final Donor Report, International Food Policy Research Institution, Washington, DC.

Baek, J., and W. W. Koo. 2008. Identifying macroeconomic linkages to U.S. agricultural trade balance. *Canadian Journal of Agricultural Economics* 56 (1): 63–77.

Bailey, M. N., and H. Gersbach. 1995. Efficiency in manufacturing and the need for global competition. In *Brookings papers on economic activity: Microeconomics; 1995,* ed. C. Peter, M. N. Baily, and C. M. Winston. Washington, DC: Brookings Institution Press.

Baldwin, R. 1985. *The political economy of US import policy.* Cambridge, MA: MIT Press.

———. 2008. EU institutional reform: Evidence on globalization and international cooperation. *American Economic Review* 98 (2): 127–132.

Banerjee, A., R. Benabou, and D. Mookherjee, eds. 2006. *Understanding poverty.* Oxford: Oxford University Press.

Barder, O. 2009. What is poverty reduction? Working Paper 170, Center for Global Development, Washington, DC.

Bardhan, P. 2006. Globalization and the limits to poverty alleviation. In *Globalization and egalitarian redistribution,* ed. P. Bardhan, S. Bowles, and M. Wallerstein. Princeton, NJ: Princeton University Press.

Bar-Isaac, H., G. Caruana, and V. Cuñat. 2008. Information gathering externalities in product markets. Working Paper EC-07–19, Stern School of Business, New York University.

Barling, D., T. Lang, and M. Caraher. 2002. Joined-up food policy? The trials of governance, public policy and the food system. *Social Policy and Administration* 36 (6): 556–574.

Barnett, R. C., D. A. Bessler, and R. L. Thompson. 1983. The money supply and nominal agricultural prices. *American Journal of Agricultural Economics* 65 (2): 303–307.

Barnhart, S. 1989. The effects of macroeconomic announcements on commodity prices. *American Journal of Agricultural Economics* 71 (2): 389–403.

Baron, M. 2002. Acting from duty. In *Groundwork for the metaphysics of morals,* ed. I. Kant, A. Wood, and J. Schneewind. New Haven, CT: Yale University Press.

Barrett, C. 1997. Food marketing liberalization and trader entry: Evidence from Madagascar. *World Development* 25:763–777.

———. 2002. Food security and food assistance programs. Department of Agricultural, Resource, and Managerial Economics, Cornell University, Ithaca, NY. http://www.dse.unifi.it/sviluppo/doc/BarrettFoodSecurityandFood20AssistancePrograms.pdf.

———. 2008. Poverty traps and resource dynamics in smallholder agrarian systems. In *Economics of poverty, environment and natural-resource use,* ed. R. Dellink and A. Ruijs. Dordrecht: Springer.

Barrett, C., and D. Maxwell. 2005. *Food aid after fifty years: Recasting its role.* New York: Routledge.

Barro, R. 1991. Economic growth in a cross-section of countries. *Quarterly Journal of Economics* 106:407–444.

Barten, A. 1969. Maximum likelihood estimation of a complete system of demand equations. *European Economic Review* 1:7–73.

Basu, K. 2005. Globalization, poverty, and inequality: What is the relationship? What can be done? Working Paper 05–13, Center for Analytical Economics, Cornell University, Ithaca, NY.

——. 2006. Human rights as instruments of emancipation and economic development. In *Economic rights: Conceptual, measurement, and policy issues,* ed. S. Hertel and L. Minkler. Cambridge: Cambridge University Press.

Bates, R. H. 1981. *Markets and states in tropical Africa: The political basis of agricultural policies.* California Series on Social Choice and Political Economy. Berkeley: University of California Press.

——. 1987. *Essays on the political economy of rural Africa.* California Series on Social Choice and Political Economy. Berkeley: University of California Press.

Batte, R. 2010. *Agricultural information systems development: A stakeholder analysis approach.* Saarbrucken: Lambert Academic Publishing.

Bauer, P. 1957. *Economic analysis and policy in underdeveloped countries.* Durham, NC: Duke University Press.

Baulch, B., T. Chuyen, D. Haughton, and J. Haughton. 2002. Ethnic minority development in Vietnam: A socioeconomic perspective. Research Working Paper 2836, World Bank, Washington, DC.

Baulch B., and J. Hoddinott. 2000. *Economic mobility and poverty dynamics in developing countries.* London: Frank Cass.

Bayes, A. 2007. Agricultural and rural development for reducing poverty and hunger in Asia: In pursuit of inclusive and sustainable growth. Based on the proceedings of the Manila Policy Forum sponsored by IFPRI and ADB.

BBC News. 2007. Chinese facing shortages of wives. http://news.bbc.co.uk/2/hi/6254763.stm.

Beaton, G., and H. Ghassemi. 1982. Supplementary feeding programs for young children in developing countries. *American Journal for Clinical Nutrition* 35 (4): 863–916.

Becker, G. 1965. A theory of the allocation of time. *Economic Journal* 75 (299): 493–517.

Beckerman, W., and J. Pasek. 2003. The morality of market mechanisms to control pollution. *World Economics: The Journal of Current Economic Analysis and Policy* 4 (3): 191–207.

Beekman, V. 2006. Consumer concerns and ethical traceability: Outline of a liberal argument. In *Ethics and the politics of food: 6th Congress of the European Society for Agricultural and Food Ethics,* ed. M. Kaiser and M. Lien. Wageningen, Netherlands: Wageningen Academic Publishers.

Behrman, J. R. 1988. Intrahousehold allocation of nutrients in rural India: Are boys favored? Do parents exhibit inequality aversion? *Oxford Economic Papers* 40:32–54.

——. 1997. Intrahousehold distribution and the family. In *Handbook of population and family economics,* vol. 1A, ed. M. R. Rosenzweig and O. Stark. Amsterdam: North-Holland.

Behrman, J., H. Alderman, and J. Hoddinott. 2004. Malnutrition and hunger. In *Global crises, global solutions,* ed. B. Lomborg. Cambridge: Cambridge University Press.

Behrman, J., and A. Deolalikar. 1987. Will developing country nutrition improve with income? A case study for rural south India. *Journal of Political Economy* 95:492–507.

——. 1990. The intrahousehold demand for nutrients in rural south India: Individual estimates, fixed effects, and permanent income. *Journal of Human Resources* 25:665–696.

Beitz, C. 1986. Amartya Sen's resources, values and development. *Economics and Philosophy* 2 (2): 282–291.

Bell, C. L. G., and P. B. R. Hazell. 1980. Measuring the indirect effects of an agricultural investment project on its surrounding region. *American Journal of Agricultural Economics* 62:75–86.

Bell, C., P. B. R. Hazell, and R. Slade. 1982. *Project evaluation in regional perspective.* Baltimore: Johns Hopkins University Press.

Bellemare, M. F., and C. R. Barrett. 2006. An ordered Tobit model of market participation: Evidence from Kenya and Ethiopia. *American Journal of Agricultural Economics* 88 (2): 324–337.

Bennett R. M., Y. Ismael, U. Kambhampati, and S. Morse. 2004. Economic impact of genetically modified cotton in India. *Agbioforum* 7 (3): 96–100.

Benson, T. 2004. Africa's food and nutrition security situation: Where are we and how did we get here? 2020 Discussion Paper 37. International Food Policy Research Institute, Washington, DC.

Benson, T., M. Epprecht, and N. Minot. 2007. *The world's poorest and hungry: Who, Where and Why? Mapping where the poor live.* 2020 Focus Briefs on the World's Poor and Hungry People. Washington, DC: International Food Policy Research Institute.

Bentham, J. 1789. *An introduction to the principles of morals and legislation.* Repr., Boston: Adamant Media Corporation, 2005.

Berg, A. 1973. *The nutrition factor: Its role in national development.* Washington, DC: The Brookings Institution.

Berg, A., and A. Krueger. 2003. Trade, growth and poverty: A selective survey. Working Paper 03/30, International Monetary Fund, Washington, DC.

Berglof, E., M. Burkart, G. Friebel, and E. Paltseva. 2008. Widening and deepening: Reforming the European Union. *American Economic Review* 98 (2): 133–137.

Berkes, F., and C. Folke. 1998. *Linking social and ecological systems.* Cambridge: Cambridge University Press.

Berlin, I. 1958. *Two concepts of liberty.* Reprinted in Isaiah Berlin, *Four essays on liberty.* Oxford: Oxford University Press, 1982.

Beynon, J., S. Jones, and S. Yao. 1992. Market reform and private trade in eastern and southern Africa. *Food Policy* 17:399–408.

Bhagwati, J. 1982. Directly unproductive, profit-seeking (DUP) activities. *Journal of Political Economy* 90 (5): 988–1002.

Bhargava, A. 2008. *Food, economics, and health.* Oxford, CA: Oxford University Press.

Bierce, Ambrose. 1911. *The devil's dictionary.* http://www.thedevilsdictionary.com.

Binswanger, H., S. Khandker, and M. Rosenzweig. 1993. How infrastructure and financial institutions affect agricultural output and investment in India. *Journal of Development Economics* 41:337–366.

Binswanger, H., and A. Swaminathan. 2003. *Scaling up community driven development: Theoretical underpinnings and program design implications.* Washington, DC: World Bank.

Birner, R. 2007. *Improving governance to eradicate hunger and poverty.* 2020 Focus Briefs on the World's Poor and Hungry People. Washington, DC: International Food Policy Research Institute.

Birol, E., A. Kontoleon, and M. Smale. 2005. Using a choice experiment to estimate the demand of Hungarian farmers for food security and agrobiodiversity during economic transition. Environmental Economy and Policy Research Discussion Paper Series, 08.2005, Department of Land Economy, University of Cambridge.

Bishop, C. P., and C. R. Shumway. 2009. The economics of dairy anaerobic digestion with coproduct marketing. *Review of Agricultural Economics* 31 (3): 394–410.

Black, M., and B. Fawcett. 2008. *The last taboo: Opening the door on the global sanitation crisis.* London: Earthscan.

Black, R. E., L. H. Allen, Z. A. Bhutta, L. E. Caulfield, M. de Onis, M. Ezzati, C. Mathers, and J. Rivera. 2008. Maternal and child undernutrition: Global and regional exposures and health consequences. *Lancet* 371 (9608): 243–260.

Blandford, D. 2007. How to increase the benefits of the DOHA development round for the least developed countries. In *Agricultural trade liberalization and the least developed countries,* ed. N. Koning and P. Pinstrup-Andersen. Wageningen: Springer.

Blattman, C., and E. Miguel. 2010. Civil war. *Journal of Economic Literature* 48 (1): 3–57.

Blossner, M., and M. de Onis. 2005. *Malnutrition: Quantifying the health impact at national and local levels.* WHO Environmental Burden of Disease Series, 12. Geneva: World Health Organization.

Bollino, C. 1990. A generalized version of the almost ideal and translog demand system. *Economic Letters* 34:127–129.

Bontems, P. 2008. On the optimal design of income support and agri-environmental regulation. AAEA presentation, Orlando, Florida, July 27–29.

Bontems, P., and J.-M. Bourgeon. 2005. Optimal environmental taxation and enforcement policy. *European Economic Review* 49 (2): 409–435.

Boone, P. 1996. Politics and the effectiveness of foreign aid. *European Economic Review* 40 (2): 289–329.

Borden, W. 1964. The concept of the marketing mix. *Journal of Advertising Research* 4:2–13.

Borlaug, N. 1970. The green revolution, peace, and humanity. Nobel lecture at the Nobel Peace Prize, Des Moines, Iowa, October 11.

Boserup, E., N. Kanji, S. F. Tan, and C. Toulmin. 2007. *Woman's role in economic development.* London: Earthscan.

Boucekkine, R., R. Desbordes, and H. Latzer. 2009. How do epidemics induce behavioral changes? *Journal of Economic Growth* 14 (3): 233–264, doi:10.1007/s10887-009-9042-1.

Bouis, H. 1994. The effect of income on demand for food in poor countries: Are our databases giving us reliable estimates? *Journal of Development Economics* 44 (1): 199–226.

Bouis, H., and L. Haddad. 1992. Are estimates of calorie-income elasticities too high? A recalibration of the plausible range. *Journal of Development Economics* 39 (2): 333–364.

Bourguignon, F., and S. Chakravarty. 1999. A family in multidimensional poverty measures. In *Advances in econometrics, income distribution and scientific methodology: Essays in honor of Camilo Dagum,* ed. D. Slottje. Heidelberg: Physica-Verlag.

——. 2003. The measurement of multidimensional poverty. *Journal of Economic Inequality* 1:25–49.

Bridges, E. M., and L. R. Oldemann. 2001. Food production and environmental degradation. In *Response to land degradation,* ed. E. M. Bridges, et al. Enfield, NH: Science Publishers.

Brookes, G., and P. Barfoot. 2006. GM crops: The first ten years; Global social-economic and environmental impacts. ISAAA Brief 36, International Service for the Acquisition of Agri-biotech Applications, Ithaca, NY.

Bruinsma, J. 2003. *World agriculture: Towards 2015/2030; An FAO perspective.* Rome: FAO/ Earthscan. http://www.fao.org/docrep/005/y4252e/y4252e04b.htm.

Bryce, J., R. E. Black, N. Walker, Z. A. Bhutta, J. E. Lawn, and R. W. Steketee. 2005. Can the world afford to save the lives of 6 million children each year? *Lancet* 365: 2193–2200.

Bryce, J., C. Boschi-Pinto, K. Shibuya, R. E. Black, and the WHO Child Health Epidemiology Reference Group. 2005. WHO estimates the causes of death in children. *Lancet* 365: 1147–52.

Buchanan, J. M. 1976. The justice of natural liberty. *Journal of Legal Studies* 5 (1): 1–16.

Buchanan, J., and G. Tullock. 1962. *The calculus of consent.* Ann Arbor: University of Michigan Press.

Bullock, D. 1994. In search of rational government: What political preference function studies measure and assume. *American Journal of Agricultural Economics* 76 (3): 347–361.

Bulte, E. H., R. Damania, and R. López. 2007. On the gains of committing to inefficiency: Corruption, deforestation and low land productivity in Latin America. *Journal of Environmental Economics and Management* 54 (3): 277–295.

Burnside, C., and D. Dollar. 2000. Aid, policies and growth. *American Economic Review* 90 (4): 847–868.

Byerlee, D., T. Jayne, and R. Myers. 2006. Managing food price risks and instability in a liberalizing market environment: Overview and policy options. *Food Policy* 31 (4): 275–287.

Byerlee, D., and G. Traxler. 2002. The role of technology spillovers and economies of size in the efficient design of agricultural research systems. In *Agricultural science policy: Changing global agendas*, ed. J. M. Alston, P. G. Pardey, and M. J. Taylor. Baltimore: Johns Hopkins University Press.

Cameroon Academy of Sciences. 2007. *Prioritizing food security policies for health and development in Africa: Science Academy; Policymaker interaction for evidence-based decision making.* Second Annual International Conference of the African Science Academy Development Initiative.

Campbell, H. F., and R. P. C. Brown. 2003. *Benefit-cost analysis: Financial and economic appraisal using spreadsheets.* Cambridge: Cambridge University Press.

Cantley, M. 2004. How should public policy respond to the challenges of modern biotechnology? *Current Opinion in Biotechnology* 15:258–263.

Carpenter, S., B. Walker, J. Anderies, and N. Abel. 2001. From metaphor to measurement: Resilience of what to what? *Ecosystems* 4 (8): 765–781.

Carter, M. R., and C. Barrett. 2006. The economics of poverty traps and persistent poverty: An asset-based approach. *Journal of Development Studies* 42 (2): 178–199.

Caswell, J. A., and C. F. Bach. 2007. Food safety standards in rich and poor countries. In *Ethics, hunger and globalization: In search of appropriate policies*, ed. P. Pinstrup-Andersen and P. Sandøe. Dordrecht: Springer.

Catelo, M. A. O. 2006. Understanding the links between agriculture and health: Livestock and health. 2020 Vision Focus 13, Brief 9, International Food Policy Research Institute, Washington, DC.

Caulfield, L. E., M. de Onis, M. Blossner, and R. E. Black. 2004. Undernutrition as an underlying cause of child deaths associated with diarrhea, pneumonia, malaria, and measles. *American Journal of Clinical Nutrition* 80:193–198.

Cederman, L. E. 2002. Endogenizing geopolitical boundaries with agent-based modeling. *Proceedings of the National Academy of Sciences* 99:7296–7303.

CGIAR (Consultative Group on International Agricultural Research). n.d. Integrated natural resource management. http://www.icarda.cgiar.org/INRMsite/index.htm.

———. 1998. Report of the CGIAR panel on proprietary science and technology. Technical Advisory Committee Secretariat, FAO, Rome.

CGIAR Science Council. 2005. Science for agricultural development: Changing contents, new opportunities. Science Council Secretariat, Rome.

CGIAR Secretariat. 2005. *Snapshot of CGIAR Impacts.* CGIAR Secretariat. Washington, DC: World Bank.

Chambers, R., and G. Conway. 1992. Sustainable rural livelihoods: Practical concepts for the 21st century. Discussion Paper 296, Institute of Development Studies, Brighton.

Chambers, R., and R. Just. 1981. Effects of exchange rate changes on US agriculture: A dynamic analysis. *American Journal of Agricultural Economics* 63 (1): 32–46.

———. 1982. An investigation of the effect of monetary factors on agriculture. *Journal of Monetary Economics* 9:235–247.

Chapman, A. 2005. Genetic engineering: The unnatural argument. *Techné* 9 (2). http://scholar.lib.vt.edu/ejournals/SPT/v9n2/chapman.html.

Chattopadhyay, R., and Duflo, E. 2004. Women as policy makers: Evidence from a randomized policy experiment in India. *Econometrica* 71 (5): 1409–1443.

Chen, B., and Y. Feng. 2000. Determinants of economic growth in China: Private enterprise, education, and openness. *China Economic Review* 10:1–15.

Chen, S., and M. Ravallion. 2006. How have the world's poorest fared since the early 1980s? *World Bank Research Observer* 19 (2): 141–170.

———. 2007. *The world's poorest and hungry: Who, where and why? The changing profile of poverty in the world.* 2020 Focus Briefs on the World's Poor and Hungry People. Washington, DC: International Food Policy Research Institute.

———. 2008. The developing world is poorer than we thought, but no less successful in the fight against poverty. Policy Research Working Paper 4703, World Bank, Washington, DC.

Cheng, F., and D. Orden. 2007. Exchange rate alignment and producer support estimates (PSEs) for India. *Agricultural Economics: The International Journal of Agricultural Economists* 36 (2): 233–243.

Chhibber, A. 1988. Raising agricultural output: Price and nonprice factors. *Finance and Development* 25 (2): 44–47.

Chiappori, P. 1988. Rational household labor supply. *Econometrica* 56 (1): 63–89.

———. 1992. Collective labor supply and welfare. *Journal of Political Economy* 100 (3): 437–467.

Chilowa, W. 1998. The impact of agricultural liberalization on food security in Malawi. *Food Policy* 23:553–569.

Chong, A., and C. Calderon. 2000. Causality and feedback between institutional measures and economic growth. *Economics and Politics* 12 (1): 69–81.

Christensen, L., D. Jorgenson, and L. Lau. 1975. Transcendental logarithmic utility functions. *American Economic Review* 65:367–383.

Christopher, M., M. McDonald, and G. Wills. 1980. *Introducing marketing.* London: Pan.

Clague, C., P. Keefer, S. Knack, and M. Olson. 1996. Property and contract rights in autocracies and democracies. *Journal of Economic Growth* 1:243–276.

Clark, D. 2006. Capability approach. In *The Elgar companion to development studies,* ed. D. Clark. Cheltenham: Edward Elgar.

Clemens, M. 2009. Skill flow: A fundamental reconsideration of skilled-worker mobility and development. Working Paper 180, Center for Global Development, Washington, DC. http://www.cgdev.org/content/publications/detail/1422684.

———. 2010. A labor mobility agenda for development. Working Paper 201, Center for Global Development, Washington, DC. http://www.cgdev.org/content/publications/detail/1423717.

Cline, W. R. 2007. Global warming and agriculture: New country estimates show developing countries face declines in agricultural productivity. CGD Brief, Center for Global Development, Washington, DC.

Coady, D., M. Grosh, and J. Hoddinott. 2004. *Targeting of transfers in developing countries: Review of lessons and experience.* Washington, DC: The World Bank.

Coase, R. 1937. The nature of the firm. *Economica* 4 (16): 386–405.

———. 1960. The problem of social cost. *Journal of Law and Economics* 3:1–44.

———. 1991. The institutional structure of production. Prize Lecture, The Sveriges Riksbank Prize in Economic Sciences in memory of Alfred Nobel, December 9. http://nobelprize.org/nobel_prizes/economics/laureates/1991/coase-lecture.html.

Cochrane, W. 1957. The market as a unit of inquiry in agricultural economics research. *Journal of Farm Economics* 39:21–39.

Cole, D. 2006. Occupational health hazards of agriculture. In *Understanding the links between agriculture and health,* ed. C. Hawkes and M. T. Ruel. 2020 Focus 13, Brief 8. Washington, DC: International Food Policy Research Institute.

Coley, D., M. Howard, and M. Winter. 2008. Local food, food miles and carbon emissions: A comparison of farm shop and mass distribution approaches. *Food Policy* 34 (2): 150–155.

Collier, G., and E. L. Quaratiello. 1999. *Basta! The Zapatistia rebellion in Chiapas.* Rev. ed. Oakland, CA: Food First Books.

Collier, P. 2007. *The bottom billion: Why the poorest countries are failing and what can be done about it.* Oxford: Oxford University Press.

———. 2009. *Wars, guns, and votes: Democracy in dangerous places.* New York: Harper.

Collier, P., V. L. Elliott, H. Hegre, A. Hoeffler, M. Reynal-Querol, and N. Sambanis. 2003. *Breaking the conflict trap: Civil war and development policy.* World Bank Policy Research Report. Washington, DC: World Bank and Oxford University Press.

Collins, S., N. Dent, P. Binns, P. Bahwere, K. Sadler, and A. Hallam. 2006. Management of severe acute malnutrition in children. *Lancet* 368 (9551): 1992–2000.

Cooley, J. 1984. The war over water. *Foreign Policy* 84:65–83.

Corbett, J. 1988. Famine and household coping strategies. *World Development* 16 (9): 1099–1112.

Cortner, H. 2000. Making science relevant to environmental policy. *Environmental Science and Policy* 3:21–30.

Coudouel, A., J. Hentschel, and Q. Wodon. 2002. Poverty measurement and analysis. In *The poverty reduction strategy papers (PRSP) sourcebook.* Washington, DC: World Bank.

Coulter, J., and C. Poulton. 2001. Cereal market liberalization in Africa. In *Commodity market reforms: Lessons of two decades,* ed. T. Akiyama, J. Baffes, D. Larson, and P. Varangis. Washington, DC: World Bank.

Coyle, W. 2007. The future of biofuels: A global perspective. Online feature in the United States Department of Agriculture's *Amber Waves,* http://www.ers.usda.gov/Amber-Waves/November07/Features/Biofuels.htm.

Cuddington, J. T. 1992. Long-run trends in 26 primary commodity prices: A disaggregated look at the Prebisch-Singer hypothesis. *Journal of Development Economics* 39:207–227.

Dangour, A.D., K. Lock, A. Hayter, A. Aikenhead, E. Allen, and R. Uauy. 2010. Nutrition-related health effects of organic foods: A systematic review. *American Journal of Clinical Nutrition* 92:203–210.

Daru, P., and C. Churchill. 2003. The prevention of debt bondage with micro-finance and related services: Preliminary lessons. Paper presented at Staying Poor: Chronic Poverty and Development Policy Conference, Manchester, April 7–9.

Dasgupta, P. 2005. What do economists analyze and why: Values or facts? *Economics and Philosophy* 21:221–278.

———. 2007. *The world's poorest and hungry: Who, where and why? Poverty traps: Exploring the complexity of causation.* 2020 Focus Briefs on the World's Poor and Hungry People. Washington, DC: International Food Policy Research Institute.

De Brauw, A. 2007. *International migration: Can it improve living standards among poor and vulnerable populations?* 2020 Focus Brief on the World's Poor and Hungry People. Washington, DC: International Food Policy Research Institute.

De Gorter, H., and J. Swinnen. 2002. Political economy of agricultural policy. In *Handbook of agricultural economics,* vol. 2B, ed. B. Gardner and G. Rausser. Amsterdam: Elsevier Science B.V.

de Haan, A., and B. Rogaly. 2002. Introduction: Migrant workers and their role in rural change. *Journal of Development Studies* 38 (5): 1–14.

de Haen, H. 1997. Environmental consequences of agricultural growth in developing countries. In *Sustainability, growth, and poverty alleviation,* ed. S. Vosti and T. Reardon. Baltimore: IFPRI, Johns Hopkins University Press.

de Janvry, A., and S. Subramanian. 1993. The politics and economics of food and nutrition policies and programs: An interpretation. In *The political economy of food and nutrition policies,* ed. P. Pinstrup-Andersen. Baltimore: Johns Hopkins University Press.

de Onis, M., and M. Blossner. 2000. Prevalence and trends of overweight among preschool children in developing countries. *American Journal of Clinical Nutrition* 72 (4): 1032–1039.

de Soto, H. 1989. *The other path.* New York: Harper and Row.

———. 2000. *The mystery of capital: Why capitalism triumphs in the West and fails everywhere else.* New York: Basic Books.

Deaton, A. 1974. A reconsideration of the empirical implications of additive preferences. *Economic Journal* 84 (334): 338–348.

Deaton, A., and J. Muellbauer. 1980. An almost ideal demand system. *American Economic Review* 70:312–326.

Debreu, G. 1959. *Theory of value.* New York: John Wiley.

DEFRA (Department for Environment, Food and Rural Affairs). 2005. The validity of food miles as an indicator of sustainable development. United Kingdom.

de Gorter, H., and D. R. Just. 2008. The economics of the U.S. ethanol import tariff with a blend mandate and tax credit. *Journal of Agriculture and Food Industrial Organization* 6 (2), http://www.bepress.com/jafio/vol6/iss2/art6.

Deichmann, U., and S. Wood. 2001. GIS, GPS, and remote sensing. In *Appropriate technology for sustainable food security,* ed. P. Pinstrup-Andersen. IFPRI Focus 7. Washington, DC: International Food Policy Research Institute.

Deininger, K., and L. Squire. 1998. New ways of looking at old issues: Asset inequality and growth. *Journal of Development Economics* 57:259–287.

Delgado, C. L., J. Hopkins, and V. A. Kelly. 1998. Agricultural growth linkages in sub-Saharan Africa. IFPRI Research Report 107, Washington DC.

Delgado, C., and N. Minot. 2000. *Agriculture in Tanzania since 1986: Follower or leader of growth? A World Bank country study.* Washington, DC: World Bank.

Delgado, C., M. Rosegrant, H. Steinfeld, S. Ehui, and C. Courbois. 1999. Livestock to 2020: The next food revolution. Food, Agriculture, and the Environment Discussion Paper 28, International Food Policy Research Institute, Washington, DC.

Dellink, R. B., and A. Ruijs, eds. 2008. *Economics of poverty, environment and natural-resource use.* Dordrecht: Springer.

DeLong, B. 2009. Hoisted from the archives: A non-socratic dialogue on social welfare functions. *Grasping Reality with Both Hands,* April 13, 2009.

Devereux, S. 2008. Review: Famine in North Korea: Markets, aid, and reform. *Journal of Economic Literature* 46 (4): 1037–1039.

Diakosavvas, 1989. The contribution of agricultural expenditure to agricultural performance in less developed countries: An empirical evaluation. Development and Project Planning Centre, Bradford University, England. Paper presented to European Economic Association Congress, Augsburg.

Diaz-Bonilla, E. 2007. *Global macroeconomic development: The implications for poverty.* 2020 Focus Brief on the World's Poor and Hungry People. Washington, DC: IFPRI.

Dickinson, E., ed. 1995. *New physico-chemical techniques for the characterization of complex food systems.* London: Blackie Academic and Professional.

Digal, L., and F. Ahmadi-Esfahani. 2002. Market power analysis in the retail food industry: A survey of methods. *Australian Journal of Agricultural and Resource Economics* 46 (4): 559–584.

Dinello, N., and L. Squire. 2005. Globalization and equity: Cutting through the confusion. In *Globalization and equity,* ed. N. Dinello and L. Squire. Cheltenham: Edward Elgar.

Dixit, A. K. 2008. Foreword to *American Economic Review* 98 (2): ix–x.

Dixit, A. K., and R. S. Pindyck. 1994. *Investment under uncertainty.* Princeton, NJ: Princeton University Press.

Dixon, J. 1999. A cultural economy model for studying food systems. *Agriculture and Human Values* 16:151–160.

Doak, C., L. Adair, M. Bentley, C. Monteiro, and B. Popkin. 2005. The dual burden household and the nutrition transition paradox. *International Journal of Obesity* 29: 129–136.

Doak, C., L. Adair, C. Monteiro, and B. Popkin. 2000. Overweight and underweight co-exist in Brazil, China, and Russia. *Journal of Nutrition* 130:2965–2980.

Docquier, F., and H. Rapoport. 2004. Skilled migration: The perspective of developing countries. Policy Research Working Paper 3382, Development Research Group, World Bank, Washington, DC.

Dollar, D. 2004. Interview with David Dollar on Making Globalization Work for the Poor, World Bank, Washington, DC. http://discuss.worldbank.org/content/interview/detail/674/.

Dollar, D., and A. Kraay. 2002. Growth is good for the poor. *Journal of Economic Growth* 7:195–225.

——. 2004. Trade, growth, and poverty. *Economic Journal* 114 (493): F22–49.

Donovan, J., J. Caswell, and E. Salay. 2001. The effect of stricter foreign regulations on food safety levels in developing countries: A case study of Brazil. *Review of Agricultural Economics* 23:163–175.

Dornbush, R. 1976. Expectations and exchange rate dynamics. *Journal of Political Economy* 84:1161–1176.

Dorosh, P. A., and S. Haggblade. 1993. Agricultural-led growth: Food grains versus export crops in Madagascar. *Agricultural Economics* 9 (Aug): 165–180.

Dorward, A. R., J. G. Kydd, J. A. Morrison, and I. Urey. 2004. A policy agenda for pro-poor agricultural growth. *World Development* 32 (1): 73–89.

Doss, C. R. 1996. Intrahousehold resource allocation in an uncertain environment. *American Journal of Agricultural Economics* 78:1335–1339.

Downs, A. 1957. *An economic theory of democracy.* New York: Harper and Row.

Drahos, P. 2000. Human rights, globalisation and intellectual property rights. Paper presented at informal workshop on August 19.

Dranove, D., D. Kessler, M. McClellan, and M. Satterthwaite. 2003. Is more information better: The effects of "report cards" on health care providers. *Journal of Political Economy* 111:555–588.

Drechsel, P., and F. P. de Vries. 2001. Land pressure and soil nutrient depletion in sub-Saharan Africa. In *Response to land degradation,* ed. M. Bridges, et al. Enfield, NH: Science Publishers.

Dreher, A., and M. Gassebner. 2007. Greasing the wheels of entrepreneurship? Impact of regulations and corruption on firm entry. CESifo Working Paper 2013.

Duclos, J., D. Sahn, and S. Younger. 2006. Robust multidimensional poverty comparisons. *Economic Journal* 116 (514): 943–968.

Duflo, E., M. Kremer, and J. Robinson. 2009. Nudging farmers to use fertilizer: Theory and experimental evidence from Kenya. Mimeo, MIT.

Dustmann, C., and A. Glitz. 2005. Immigration, jobs and wages: Theory, evidence and opinion. Centre for Research and Analysis of Migration, Department of Economics, University College London.

Easterly, W. 2006. *The white man's burden: Why the West's efforts to aid the rest have done so much ill and so little good.* New York: Penguin Books.

——. 2007. Inequality does cause underdevelopment: Insights from a new instrument. *Journal of Development Economics* 84 (2): 755–776.

——. 2008. Institutions: Top down or bottom up? *American Economic Review: Papers and Proceedings 2008* 98 (2): 95–99.

Easterly, W., and R. Levine. 1997. Africa's growth tragedy: Policies and ethnic divisions. *Quarterly Journal of Economics* 112 (4): 1203–1250.

Eberhart, N. 2005. Synthèse de l'étude d'impact du commerce équitable sur les organisations et familles paysannes et leurs territoires dans la filière café des Yungas de Bolivie [Summary of the impact of fair trade organizations and farming families and their territories in the coffee sector of the Yungas of Bolivia]. Agronomes et vétérinaires sans frontiers, Lyon.

Economic Research Division. 2009. A macroeconomic perspective on food security. Economic Services Department: Agriculture, Forestry and Fisheries, Republic of South Africa. http://www.nda.agric.za/docs/Economic_analysis/macroEeconomicPerspective2foodSecurity.pdf.

Eggers, B., and R. Mackenzie. 2000. The Cartagena protocol on biosafety. *Journal of International Economic Law* 3 (3): 525–543.

Eggertsson, T. 1990. *Economic behavior and institutions.* Cambridge: Cambridge University Press.

——. 1996. A note on the economics of institutions. In *Empirical studies in institutional change,* ed. L. J. Alston, T. Eggertsson, and D. North. New York: Cambridge University Press.

Ehrhardt-Martinez, K., E. M. Crenshaw, J. C. Jenkins. 2002. Deforestation and the environmental Kuznets curve: A cross-national investigation of intervening mechanisms. *Social Science Quarterly* 83 (1): 226–243.

Eifert, B., A. Gelb, and V. Ramachandran. 2008. The cost of doing business in Africa: Evidence from enterprise survey data. Presented at the NBER Conference on Africa, February 21–22.

Ellinger, P., and V. Tirupattur. 2009. An overview of the linkages of the global financial crisis to production agriculture. *American Journal of Agricultural Economics* 91 (5): 1399–1405.

Ellis, F., B. Trotter, and P. Magrath. 1992. Rice marketing in Indonesia: Methodology, results and implications of a research study. Marketing Series, vol. 4. Natural Resources Institute, Chatham, UK.

Elmqvist, T., M. Pyykönen, M. Tengö, F. Rakotondrasoa, E. Rabakonandrianina, et al. 2007. Patterns of loss and regeneration of tropical dry forest in Madagascar: The social institutional context. *PLoS ONE* 2 (5), e402. doi:10.1371/journal.pone.0000402.

Emmett, R. B. 2006. *Malthus reconsidered: Population, natural resources, and markets.* PERC Policy Series, PS-38. http://www.perc.org/pdf/ps38.pdf.

Epstein, J. 2002. Modeling civil violence: An agent-based computational approach. *Proceedings of the National Academy of Science* 99 (3): 7243–7250.

Epstein, L. H., K. K. Dearing, L. G. Roba, and E. Finkelstein. 2010. The influence of taxes and subsidies on energy purchased in an experimental purchasing study. *Psychological Science,* 2010, doi:10.1177/0956797610361446.

Ericksen, Polly J. 2007. Conceptualizing food systems for global environmental change research. *Global Environmental Change,* doi:10.1016/j.gloenvcha.2007.09.002.

Esty, D. 2008. Rethinking global environmental governance to deal with climate change: The multiple logics of global collective action. *American Economic Review: Papers and Proceedings 2008* 98 (2): 116–121.

Esty, D.C., J. A. Goldstone, T. R. Gurr, B. Harff, M. Levy, G. D. Dabelko, P. T. Surko, and A. N. Unger. 1999. State failure task force report: Phase II findings. Environmental Change and Security Project Report 5. Woodrow Wilson International Center for Scholars, Smithsonian Institution, Washington, DC.

Euromonitor. n.d. Euromonitor Database. http://www.euromonitor.com/databases.aspx.

Evenson, R. E., and D. Gollin. 2003. Assessing the impact of the green revolution: 1960–1980. *Science* 300:758–762.

Evenson, R. E., and M. Rosegrant. 2003. The economic consequences of crop genetic improvement programmes. In *Crop variety improvement and its effect on productivity: The impact of agricultural research,* ed. R. E. Evenson and D. Gollin. Wallingford, UK: CABI Publishing.

Fafchamps, M. 1992. Solidarity networks in pre-industrial societies: Rational peasants with a moral economy. *Economic Development and Cultural Change* 41:147–174.

——. 2004. *Market institutions in sub-Saharan Africa.* Cambridge, MA: MIT Press.

Fafchamps, M., and E. Gabre-Madhin. 2006. Agricultural markets in Benin and Malawi. Department of Economics, University of Oxford, Oxford, and International Food Policy Research Institute, Washington, DC. http://www.economics.ox.ac.uk/members/marcel.fafchamps/homepage/afjae.pdf.

Fafchamps, M., and S. Gavian. 1997. The determinants of livestock prices in Niger. *Journal of African Economics* 6:255–295.

Fairhead, J., and M. Leach. 1998. Reconsidering the extent of deforestation in twentieth century west Africa. *Unasylva* 49 (192), http://www.fao.org/docrep/w7126E/w7126e06.htm#reconsidering%20the%20extent%20of%20deforestation%20in%20twentieth%20century%20west%20africa.

Falck-Zepeda, J. B., G. Traxler, and R. G. Nelson. 2000. Rent creation and distribution from biotechnology innovations: The case of Bt cotton and herbicide-tolerant soybeans in 1997. *Agribusiness* 16 (1): 21–32.

Fan, S., and C. Chan-Kang. 2005. *Road development, economic growth and poverty reduction in China.* International Food Policy Research Institute, Research Report 138, Washington, DC.

Fan, S., P. Hazell, and S. Thorat. 2000. Government spending, growth, and poverty in rural India. *American Journal of Agricultural Economics* 82 (4): 1038–1051.

Fan, S., Rao. N., 2003. Public spending in developing countries—Trends, determination and impact. Discussion Paper 99, Environment and Production Technology Division, International Food Policy Research Institute, Washington, DC.

Fan, S., A. Saurkar, and G. Shields. 2007. *How to mobilize public resources to support poverty reduction.* 2020 Focus Briefs on the World's Poor and Hungry People. Washington, DC: International Food Policy Research Institute.

Fan, S., and X. Zhang. 2004. Infrastructure and regional economic development in rural China. *China Economic Review* 15:203–214.

Fan, S., L. Zhang, and X. Zhang. 2002. *Growth, inequality, and poverty in rural China: The role of public investments.* International Food Policy Research Institute, Research Report 125, Washington, DC.

——. 2004. Investment, reforms, and poverty in rural China. *Economic Development and Cultural Change* 52 (2): 395–422.

FAO (Food and Agriculture Organization of the United Nations). 1996a. *Rome declaration on world food security.* Rome.

———. 1996b. *Technical background documents 6–11*, vol. 2. World Food Summit. Rome.

———. 1996c. *Global climate change and agricultural production.* Rome: FAO.

———. 2000a. *Two essays on climate change and agriculture.* FAO Economic and Social Development Paper, 145, Rome.

———. 2000b. The energy and agriculture nexus, environment and natural resources. Working Paper 4, Rome.

———. 2000c. *The state of food and agriculture 2000.* Rome.

———. 2003a. *Globalization, urbanization and the food systems of developing countries: Assessing the impacts on poverty, food and nutrition security.* FAO Scientific Workshop, October 8–10, Rome. ftp://ftp.fao.org/es/esn/nutrition/urban/esa_esn_conf.pdf.

———. 2003b. *International code of conduct on the distribution and use of pesticides.* Rome. http://www.fao.org/docrep/005/y4544e/y4544e00.htm.

———. 2003c. *World agriculture: Towards 2015/2030; An FAO perspective.* Ed. J. Bruinsma. London: Earthscan.

———. 2004a. Globalization of food system in developing countries: Impact on food security and nutrition. FAO Food and Nutrition Paper 83, Rome.

———. 2004b. *The state of food insecurity in the world.* Rome.

———. 2004c. *Incorporating nutrition considerations into development policies and programs.* Rome.

———. 2004d. *The state of food and agriculture 2003–2004. Agricultural biotechnology: Meeting the needs of the poor?* Rome.

———. 2005a. *The state of food insecurity in the world.* Rome.

———. 2005b. *Global forest resources assessment.* Rome.

———. 2005c. *Summary of world food and agricultural statistics.* Rome.

———. 2005d. *Global resources assessment.* Rome: FAO.

———. 2006a. *World agriculture: Towards 2030/2050; Interim report; Prospects for food, nutrition, agriculture and major commodity groups.* Rome.

———. 2006b. The state of world fisheries and aquaculture 2006. Fisheries and Aquaculture Department, Rome.

———. 2006c. *Livestock's long shadow.* Rome: FAO.

———. 2007a. A guide to marketing costs and how to calculate them. Agricultural Management, Marketing and Finance Service, Rural Infrastructure and Agro-Industries Division, Rome. ftp://ftp.fao.org/docrep/fao/010/u8770e/u8770e00.pdf.

———. 2007b. *The state of agricultural commodity markets 2006.* Rome.

———. 2008. Fighting food inflation through sustainable investment. From a conference by the same name held in London, March 10.

———. 2009a. *Summary of world food and agriculture statistics.* Rome. http://www.fao.org/fileadmin/templates/ess/documents/publications_studies/publications/sumfas_en_web_2009.pdf.

———. 2009b. The state of food insecurity in the world: Economic crisis; Impacts and lessons learned. ftp://ftp.fao.org/docrep/fao/012/i0876e/i0876e.pdf.

———. 2009c. *1.02 billion hungry people: One sixth of humanity undernourished; More than ever.* Rome. http://www.fao.org/news/story/en/item/20568/icode/

———. 2010. *Food, agriculture and decent work: ILO and FAO working together; Safety and health.* http://fao-ilo.org/fao-ilo-safety/en.

FAO (Food and Agriculture Organization), and European Bank for Reconstruction and Development. 2008. Fighting food inflation through sustainable investment: Grain production and export potential in CIS countries; Rising food prices; Causes, consequences, and policy responses. London. http://www.fao.org/newsroom/common/ecg/1000808/en/FAOEBRD.pdf.

FAOSTAT (Food and Agriculture Organization Statistics of the United Nations). 2005. FAOSTAT. http://faostat.fao.org/default.aspx.
——. 2008. FAOSTAT. http://faostat.fao.org/default.aspx.
——. 2009. FAOSTAT. http://faostat.fao.org/default.aspx.
——. 2010. FAOSTAT. http://faostat.fao.org/default.aspx.
Fargione, J., J. Hill, D. Tilman, S. Polasky, and P. Hawthorne. 2008. Land clearing and the biofuel carbon debt. *Science* 319 (5867): 1235–1238.
Farrelly, L. L. 1996. Transforming poultry production and marketing in developing countries: Lessons learned with implications for sub-Saharan Africa. MSU International Development Working Paper 63.
Feige, E. 1998. Underground activity and institutional change: Productive, protective, and predatory behavior in transition economies. In *Transforming post-communist political economies,* ed. J. Nelson, C. Tilly, and L. Walker. Task Force on Economies in Transition, National Research Council. Washington, DC: National Academy Press.
Feng, Y. 1997. Democracy, political stability and economic growth. *British Journal of Political Science* 27:391–418.
——. 2001. Political freedom, political instability, and policy uncertainty: A study of political institutions and private investment in developing countries. *International Studies Quarterly* 45:271–294.
Ferguson, N. M., D. A. Cummings, C. Fraser, J. C. Cajka, P. C. Cooley, and D. S. Burke. 2006. Strategies for mitigating an influenza pandemic. *Nature* 442 (7101): 448–452.
Fields, G. S. 2001. *Distribution and development: A new look at the developing world.* New York: Russell Sage Foundation.
Filmer, D., and L. Pritchett. 1999. The impact of public spending on health: Does money matter? *Social Science and Medicine* 49:1309–1323.
Fine, B. 1994. Towards a political economy of food. *Review of International Political Economy* 1 (3): 579–586.
——. 2004. Examining the idea of globalization and development critically: What role for political economy? *New Political Economy* 9:213–231.
Fine, B., M. Heasman, and J. Wright. 1996. *Consumption in the age of affluence.* London: Routledge.
Finkelstein, E., I. Fiebelkorn, and G. Wang. 2003. National medical spending attributable to overweight and obesity: How much, and who's paying? *Health Affairs* W3: 219–226.
Fiszbein, A., and N. Schady. 2009. *Conditional cash transfers: Reducing present and future poverty.* Washington, DC: World Bank.
Fogel, R. W. 2004. *The escape from hunger and premature death, 1700–2100: Europe, America, and the Third World.* New York: Cambridge University Press.
Folke, C., S. Carpenter, T. Elmquist, L. Gunderson, C. Holling, and B. Walker. 2002. Resilience and sustainable development: Building adaptive capacity in a world of transformations. *Ambio* 31:437–440.
Folker, A. P., H. Andersen, and P. Sandøe. 2008. Implicit normativity in scientific advice. *Perspectives in Biology and Medicine* 51 (2): 199–206.
Fortin, B., and G. Lacroix. 1997. A test of the unitary and collective models of household labor supply. *Economic Journal* 107:933–955.
Foster, A.D., and M. R. Rosenzweig. 1995. Learning by doing and learning from others: Human capital and technical change in agriculture. *Journal of Political Economy* 103 (6): 1176–1209.
Foster, J., J. Greer, and E. Thorbecke. 1984. A class of decomposable poverty measures. *Econometrica* 52:761–776.

Francis, C., G. Lieblein, S. Gleissman, T. Breland, N. Creamer, R. Harwood, L. Salomonsson, et al. 2003. Agroecology: The ecology of food systems. *Journal of Sustainable Agriculture* 22:99–118.

Francis, E. 2000. *Making a living: Changing livelihoods in rural Africa.* London: Routledge.

——. 2006. Poverty: Causes, responses and consequences in rural South Africa. Working Paper 60, Development Studies Institute, London School of Economics.

Frankel, J. 1979. On the mark: A theory of floating exchange rates based on real interest differentials. *American Economic Review* 69:610–622.

——. 1999. Proposals regarding restrictions on capital flows. *African Finance Journal* 1 (1): 92–104.

Friedman, M. 1962. *Capitalism and freedom.* Chicago: University of Chicago Press.

Friedmann, H. 1995. Food politics: New dangers, new possibilities. In *Food and agrarian orders in the world economy,* ed. P. McMichael. Westport, CT: Greenwich Press.

Funtowicz, S., and J. Ravetz. 1993. Science for the post-normal age. *Futures* 25 (7): 735–755.

Furubotn, E. G., and R. Richter. 1998. Institutions and economic theory: The contribution of the new institutional economics. Ann Arbor: University of Michigan Press.

Gabre-Madhin, E. Z. 2001. Market institutions, transaction costs and social capital in the Ethiopian grain market. International Food Policy Research Institute, Washington, DC. http://www.ifpri.org/publication/market-institutions-transaction-costs-and-social-capital-ethiopian-grain-market-0.

Gaiha, R. 1998. Income mobility in rural India. *Economic Development and Cultural Change* 36 (2): 279–302.

Gaiha, R., and A. Deolalikar. 1993. Persistent, expected and innate poverty: Estimates for semi-arid rural India, 1975–1984. *Cambridge Journal of Economics* 17 (4): 409–421.

Galea, S., M. Riddle, and G. A. Kaplan. 2009. Causal thinking and complex system approaches in epidemiology. *International Journal of Epidemiology* 1:1–10, doi:10.1093/ije/dyp296, 1–10.

Galor, O. 2005. From stagnation to growth: Unified growth theory. Chapter 4 in *Handbook of economic growth,* ed. P. Aghion and S. N. Durlauf. Amsterdam: Elsevier.

GAO (United States Government Accountability Office). 2009. *U.S. Agriculture: Retail food prices grew faster than the prices farmers received for agricultural commodities, but economic research has not established that concentration has affected these trends.* http://www.gao.gov/products/GAO-09-746R.

Gardner, B. 1981. On the power of macroeconomic linkages to explain events in US agriculture. *American Journal of Agricultural Economics* 63 (5): 871–878.

——. 1987. Causes of US farm commodity programs. *Journal of Political Economy* 95:290–310.

Gavazza, A., and A. Lizzeri. 2007. The perils of transparency in bureaucracies. *American Economic Review* 97 (2): 300–305.

Gbetibouo, M., and C. Delgado. 1984. Lessons and constraints of export crop-led growth: Cocoa in Ivory Coast. In *The political economy of Ivory Coast,* ed. I. Zarman and C. Delgado. New York: Praeger.

Gelan, A. 2006. Cash or food aid? A general equilibrium analysis for Ethiopia. *Development Policy Review* 24 (5): 601–624.

Gentilini, U., and P. Webb. 2008. How are we doing on poverty and hunger reduction? A new measure of country performance. *Food Policy* 33 (6): 521–532.

Gianessi, L. P., C. S. Silvers, S. Sankula, and J. E. Carpenter. 2002. Plant biotechnology: Current and potential impact for improving pest management in US agriculture. An analysis of 40 case studies. *National Center for Food and Agriculture Policy,* June 2002. http://www.ncfap.org/40CaseStudies.htm.

Giessen Declaration. 2005. *Public Health Nutrition* 8:783–786.

Gilbert, R. S. 2007. What hunger-related ethics lessons can we learn from religion? Globalization and the world's religions. In *Ethics, hunger and globalization: In search of appropriate policies,* ed. P. Pinstrup-Andersen and P. Sandøe. Dordrecht: Springer.

Gill, G. 1995. Major natural resource management concerns in South Asia. Food, Agriculture, and the Environment Discussion Paper 8, November. International Food Policy
Research Institute, Washington, DC.

Gillespie, S., ed. 2006. *AIDS, poverty, and hunger: Challenges and responses.* Washington, DC:
International Food Policy Research Institute.

——. 2010. How AIDS epidemics interact with African food systems and how to improve the
response. In *The African food system and its interaction with human health and nutrition,* ed. P. Pinstrup-Andersen. Ithaca, NY: Cornell University Press.

Gillespie, S., and S. Kadiyala. 2005. *HIV/AIDS and food and nutrition security: From evidence
to action.* Washington, DC: International Food Policy Research Institute.

Gittinger, J., J. Leslie, and C. Hoisington. 1987. *Food policy: Integrating supply, distribution, and
consumption.* Baltimore, MD: Johns Hopkins University Press for the World Bank.

Glaeser, E., R. La Porta, F. Lopez-de-Silanes, and A. Schleifer. 2004. Do institutions cause
growth? *Journal of Economic Growth* 9 (3): 271–303.

Glassburner, B. 1985. Macroeconomics and the agricultural sector. *Bulletin of Indonesian Economic Studies* 21 (2): 51–73.

Glauben, T., T. Herzfeld, and Z. Wang. 2006. The persistence of poverty in rural China: Applying an ordered probit and a hazard approach. Paper presented at the International
Association of Agricultural Economists Conference, Gold Coast, Australia, August
12–18.

Gleick, P. 1993. Water and conflict: Fresh water resources and international security. *International Security* 18 (1): 79–112.

Glicken, J. 2000. Getting stakeholder participation "right": A discussion of participatory processes and possible pitfalls. *Environmental Science and Policy* 3 (6): 305–310.

Glover, D. 1984. Contract farming and smallholder outgrower schemes in less-developed
countries. *World Development* 12 (11/12): 1143–1157.

——. 1987. Increasing the benefits to smallholders from contract farming: Problems for
farmers' organizations and policy makers. *World Development* 15 (4): 441–448.

Glover, D., and K. Kusterer. 1990. *Small farmers, big business: Contract farming and rural development.* London: Macmillan.

Goklany, I. M. 1998. Saving habitat and conserving biodiversity on a crowded planet. *BioSci-
ence* 48:941–953.

——. 2000. Applying the precautionary principle to genetically modified crops. Policy Study
157, Center for the Study of American Business, Washington University, St. Louis, MO.

Gomes, R. 2007. *Stakeholder analysis and public sector organizations: Are stakeholders really
important to public sector organizations?* Saarbrucken: VDM Verlag.

Goodman, D. 1999. Agro-food studies in the "age of ecology": Nature, corporeality, bio-
politics. *Sociologia Ruralis* 39 (1): 17–38.

——. 2002. Rethinking food production-consumption: Integrative perspectives. *Sociologia
Ruralis* 42 (4): 272–277.

Goodwin, B., and M. T. Holt 1999. A price transmission and asymmetric adjustment in the
U.S. beef sector. *American Journal of Agricultural Economics* 81 (3): 630–637.

Gorman, W. 1959. Separable utility and aggregation. *Econometrica* 27 (3): 469–481.

Goudie, A., and P. Ladd. 1999. Economic growth and poverty and inequality. *Journal of International Development* 11:177–195.

Gowing, J. W., and G. C. L. Wyseure. 1992. Dry-drainage: A sustainable and cost-effective solution to waterlogging and salinisation. *Proceedings of the 5th International Drainage Workshop,* vol. 3, ICID-CIID, Lahore, 6.26–6.34.

Grandin, T. 1997. The design and construction of facilities for handling cattle. *Livestock Production Science* 49:103–119.

Granja e Barros, F., A. Mendonça, and J. Nogueira. 2002. Poverty and environmental degradation: The Kuznets environmental curve for the Brazilian case. University of Brasilia Working Paper 267.

Greenaway, Kate. 2009. Food by prescription: A landscape paper. GAIN Working Paper Series, 2, GAIN (Global Alliance for Improved Nutrition).

Greenwood, B. M., K. Bojang, C. J. Whitty, and G. A. Targett. 2005. Malaria. *Lancet* 365:1487–1498.

Greer, J., and E. Thorbecke. 1986. *Food poverty and consumption patterns in Kenya.* Geneva: International Labour Office.

Grilli, E., and M. C. Yang. 1988. Primary commodity prices, manufactured goods prices, and the terms of trade of developing countries: What the long run shows. *World Bank Economic Review* 2 (1): 1–47.

Grindle, M. S., and J. W. Thomas. 1991. *Public choices and policy change: The political economy of reform in developing countries.* Baltimore: Johns Hopkins University Press.

Grosh, B. 1994. Contract farming in Africa: An application of the new institutional economics. *Journal of African Economies* 3 (2): 231–261.

Grossman, G. M. and E. Helpman. 1994. Protection for sale. *American Economic Review* 84 (4): 833–850.

Grossman, G. M., and A. B. Krueger. 1995. Economic growth and the environment. *Quarterly Journal of Economics* 110 (2): 353–377.

Gunderson, L., and C. Holling. 2002. *Panarchy: Understanding transformations in human and natural systems.* Washington, DC: Island Press.

Gupta, P. 1993. *An inquiry into well-being and destitution.* Oxford: Oxford University Press.

Gupta, S., L. de Mello, and R. Sharan. 2001. Corruption and military spending. *European Journal of Political Economy* 17 (4): 749–777.

Gupta, S., and M. Verhoeven. 2001. The efficiency of government expenditure: Experiences from Africa. *Journal of Policy Modeling* 23:433–467.

Haarsma, R. J., F. M. Selten, S. L. Weber, and M. Kliphuis. 2005. Sahel rainfall variability and response to greenhouse warming. *Geophysical Research Letters* 32:L17702, doi:10.1029/2005GL023232.

Haddad, L., H. Alderman, S. Appleton, L. Song, and Y. Yohannes. 2002. Reducing child undernutrition: How far does income growth take us? FCND Discussion Paper 137, International Food Policy Research Institute, Washington, DC.

Haddad, L., and J. Hoddinott. 1994. Women's income and boy-girl anthropometric status in the Côte d'Ivoire. *World Development* 22:543–553.

Haddad, L., J. Hoddinott, and H. Alderman, eds. 1997. *Intrahousehold resource allocation in developing countries: Models, methods, and policies.* Baltimore: Johns Hopkins University Press for the International Food Policy Research Institution. http://www.unu.edu/Unupress/food/V191e/ch11.htm.

Haddad, L., and R. Kanbur. 1990. How serious is the neglect of intra-household inequality? *Economic Journal* 100:866–881.

———. 1992. Intrahousehold inequality and the theory of targeting. *European Economic Review* 36:372–378.

Haddad, L., and T. Reardon. 1993. Gender bias in the allocation of resources within households in Burkina Faso: A disaggregated outlay equivalent analysis. *Journal of Development Studies* 29:260–276.

Haggard, S., and M. Noland. 2007. *Famine in North Korea: Markets, aid, and reform.* New York: Columbia University Press.

Haggblade, S., P. B. R. Hazell, and J. Brown. 1987. Farm/nonfarm linkages in rural sub-Saharan Africa: Empirical evidence and policy implications. Discussion Paper ARU 67, World Bank, Washington, DC.

Hajer, M. A., and H. Wagenaar. 2003. *Deliberative policy analysis: Understanding governance in the network society.* Theories of Institutional Design. Cambridge: Cambridge University Press.

Hallman, K., D. Lewis, and S. Begum. 2003. An integrated economic and social analysis to assess the impact of vegetable and fishpond technologies on poverty in rural Bangladesh. IFPRI Environment and Production Technology Division Discussion Paper 112, and Food Consumption and Nutrition Division Discussion Paper 163, Washington, DC.

Hammond, R. A. 2009. Complex systems modeling for obesity research. *Preventing Chronic Disease* 6 (3), http://www.cdc.gov/pcd/issues/2009/jul/09_0017.htm.

Hammond, R. A., and R. Axelrod. 2006. The evolution of ethnocentrism. *Journal of Conflict Resolution* 50 (6): 926–936.

Hardin, G. 1968. The tragedy of the commons. *Science* 162:1243–1248.

Hare, C. 2007. Rationality and the distant needy. *Philosophy and Public Affairs* 35:161–178.

Harris, J., and M. Todaro. 1970. Migration, unemployment and development: A two-sector analysis. *American Economic Review* 60 (1): 126–142.

Harris, J. M., and N. Blisard. 2002. Food-consumption patterns among elderly age groups. *Journal of Food Distribution Research* 33 (1): 85–91.

Harris, L. 2003. Global neglect is moral equivalent of letting children drown, argues ethicist. *Cornell Chronicle,* April 10, 2003.

Hartmann, A., and F. L. Johannes. 2007. *Scaling up: A path to effective development.* 2020 Focus Brief on the World's Poor and Hungry People. Washington, DC: International Food Policy Research Institute.

Hawkes, C. 2006. Uneven dietary development: Linking the policies and processes of globalization with the nutrition transition, obesity and diet-related chronic diseases. *Globalization and Health*. Washington, DC: International Food Policy Research Institute, doi:10.1186/1744-8603-2-4.

Hawkes, C., and C. Ruel. 2006. Agriculture and nutrition linkages: Old lessons and new paradigms. In *Understanding the links between agriculture and health,* ed. C. Hawkes and M. T. Ruel. 2020 Focus 13, Brief 4. Washington, DC: International Food Policy Research Institute.

Hayek, F. A. 1944. *The road to serfdom: Text and documents.* Ed. B. Caldwell. Chicago: University of Chicago Press, 2007.

——. 1974. The pretence of knowledge. Nobel Prize lecture, December 11. http://nobelprize.org/nobel_prizes/economics/laureates/1974/hayek-lecture.html.

Hazell, P. 2003. Is there a future for small farms? Proceedings of the 25th International Conference of Agricultural Economists (IAAE), August 16–22, Durban, South Africa. http://ecsocman.edu.ru/images/pubs/2003/11/30/0000135523/151.pdf.

——. 2006. Bioenergy and agriculture: Promises and challenges; Developing bioenergy: A win-win approach that can serve the poor and the environment. In *Bioenergy and agriculture: Promises and challenges,* Focus 14, ed. P. Hazell and R. K. Pachauri. Washington, DC: International Food Policy Research Institute.

Hazell, P., and S. Haggblade. 1990. Rural-urban growth linkages in India. World Bank Working Paper 430, Washington, DC.

Hazell, P., C. Poulton, S. Wiggins, and A. Dorward. 2007. The future of small farms for poverty reduction and growth. IFPRI 2020 Discussion Paper 42, Washington, DC.

Hazell, P. B. R., C. Ramasamy, and V. Rajagopalan. 1991. An analysis of the indirect effects of agricultural growth on the regional economy. In *The green revolution reconsidered: The impact of high-yielding rice varieties in South India,* ed. P. Hazell and C. Ramasamy. Baltimore: Johns Hopkins University Press for the International Food Policy Research Institute.

Heaver, R. 2005. *Strengthening country commitment to human development: Lessons from nutrition.* Washington, DC: World Bank.

Heffernan, W. 1999. Consolidation in the food and agriculture system. Report to the National Farmers' Union.

Heidhues, F., A. Atsain, H. Nyangito, M. Padilla, G. Ghersi, and J.-C. Le Vallée. 2004. Development strategies and food and nutrition security in Africa: An assessment. IFPRI 2020 Discussion Paper 38, Washington, DC.

Hellegers, P., K. Schoengold, and D. Zilberman. 2008. Water resource management and the poor. In *Economics of poverty, environment and natural-resource use,* ed. R. Dellink and A. Ruijs. Dordrecht: Springer.

Henao, J., and C. Baanante. 2001. Nutrient depletion in the agricultural soils of Africa. In *The unfinished agenda: Perspectives on overcoming hunger, poverty, and environmental degradation,* ed. P. Pinstrup-Andersen and R. Pandya-Lorch. Washington, DC: International Food Policy Research Institute.

Hendrickson, M., and W. Heffernan. 2002a. Opening spaces through relocalization: Locating potential resistance in the weaknesses of the global food system. *Sociologia Ruralis* 42:347–369.

———. 2002b. *Concentration of agricultural markets.* Mimeo, Department of Rural Sociology, University of Missouri, Colombia.

Herforth, A. 2010a. Promotion of traditional African vegetables in Kenya and Tanzania: A study of an intervention representing emerging imperatives in global nutrition. PhD diss., Cornell University.

———. 2010b. Nutrition and the environment: Fundamental to food security in Africa. In *The African food system and its interaction with human health and nutrition,* ed. P Pinstrup-Andersen. Ithaca, NY: Cornell University Press.

Hicks, J. 1934. A reconsideration of the theory of value, part I. *Economica* 1:52–76.

———. 1939. *Value and capital.* Oxford: Clarendon Press.

Hillman, A. 1982. Declining industries and political support protectionist motives. *American Economic Review* 72:1180–1187.

Hobbs, J. 1996. A transaction cost approach to supply chain management. *Supply Chain Management* 1 (2): 15–27.

Hoekman, B., F. Ng, and M. Olarreaga. 2002. Reducing agricultural tariffs versus domestic support: What's more important for developing countries? Paper prepared for IATRC Meeting, June.

Holling, C. 2001. Understanding the complexity of economic, ecological, and social systems. *Ecosystems* 4 (5): 390–405.

Homer-Dixon, T. 1999. *Environment, scarcity, and violence.* Princeton, NJ: Princeton University Press.

Hossain, P., B. Kawar, and M. El Nahas. 2007. Obesity and diabetes in the developing world: A growing challenge. *New England Journal of Medicine* 356 (9): 973.

Houck, J. 1984. Market: A definition for teaching. *Western Journal of Agricultural Economics* 9 (2): 353–356.

Huang, J., C. Pray, and S. Rozelle. 2002. Enhancing the crops to feed the poor. *Nature* 418:678–684.

Hulme, D., and A. Shepherd. 2003. Conceptualizing chronic poverty. *World Development* 31 (3): 403–423.

Huntington, S. P. 1968. *Political order in changing societies.* New Haven, CT: Yale University Press.

Huther, J., and A. Shah. 1998. Applying a simple measure of good governance to the debate on fiscal decentralization. World Bank Working Paper Series 1894, Washington, DC.

IFPRI (International Food Policy Research Institute). n.d. 2020 vision for food, agriculture, and the environment. Washington, DC. http://www.ifpri.org/book-753/ourwork/program/2020-vision-food-agriculture-and-environment.

——. 2004. *Agriculture, food security, nutrition and the MDGS.* Washington, DC.

——. 2006. *HarvestPlus fact sheet on iron deficiency anemia and vitamin A deficiency.* Washington, DC.

ILO (International Labour Organization). 2005. *World employment report 2004–05: Employment, productivity and poverty reduction.* Geneva.

IMF (International Monetary Fund). 2006. *World economic outlook: Financial systems and economic cycles.* Washington, DC.

Ingco, M., and J. Nash. 2004. *Agriculture and the WTO: Creating a trading system for development.* Washington, DC: World Bank.

Intergovernmental Panel on Climate Change (IPCC). 2007. *Climate change 2007: Synthesis report.* Cambridge: Cambridge University Press.

Isani, M. A. 1982. An economic approach to politics in developing countries. PhD diss., Georgetown University.

Ito, T. and T. Kurosaki. 2009. Weather risk, wages in kind, and the off-farm labor supply of agricultural households in a developing country. *American Journal of Agricultural Economics* 91 (3): 697–710.

Jackman, W. 1994. What's wrong with the Indian poultry industry? In *The Indian poultry industry yearbook: 1994,* ed. S. P. Gupta. Delhi.

Jaffee, D. 2007. *Brewing justice: Fair trade coffee, sustainability and survival.* Berkeley: University of California Press.

Jahnke, H. E. 1982. *Livestock production systems and livestock development in tropical Africa.* Kiel: Kieler Wissenschaftsverlag Vauk.

James, C. 2006. Global status of commercialized biotech/GM crops: 2006. ISAAA (International Service for the Acquisition of Agri-Biotech Applications) Brief 35, Ithaca, NY.

——. 2007. Global status of commercialized biotech/GM crops: 2007. ISAAA (International Service for the Acquisition of Agri-Biotech Applications) Brief 37, Ithaca, NY.

——. 2009. *Global status of commercialized biotech/GM crops: 2009.* ISAAA (International Service for the Acquisition of Agri-Biotech Applications) Brief 41, Ithaca, NY.

——. 2010. Highlights of "Global Status of Commercialized Biotech/GM Crops 2010." ISAAA Brief 42–2010: Highlights, International Service for the Acquisition of Agri-Biotech Applications. http://www.isaaa.org/resources/publications/briefs/42/highlights/default.asp

Jamison, D. T., Wang, J., Hill, K., Londoño, J.-L. 1996. Income, mortality and fertility control in Latin America: Country-level performance 1960–90. Mimeo, LAC Technical Department, World Bank, Washington, DC.

Jansen, D. 1991. Zambia. In *The political economy of agricultural pricing policy,* vol. 3, ed. A. Krueger, M. Schiff, and A. Valdes. Baltimore: Johns Hopkins University Press.

Jansky, L., and R. Chandran. 2004. Climate change and sustainable land management: Focus on erosive land degradation. *Journal of the World Association of Soil and Water Conservation* 4:17–29.

Jarvis, L. 1986. *Livestock development in Latin America.* Washington, DC: World Bank.

Jayne, T., and S. Jones. 1997. Food marketing and pricing policy in eastern and southern Africa: A survey. *World Development* 25:1505–1527.

Jayne, T. S., M. Villarreal, P. Pingali, and G. Hemrich. 2006. HIV/AIDS and the agricultural sector in eastern and southern Africa: Anticipating the consequences. In *AIDS, poverty, and hunger: Challenges and responses,* ed. S. Gillespie. Washington, DC: International Food Policy Research Institute.

Jayne, T. S., B. Zulu, and J. J. Nijhoff. 2006. Stabilizing food markets in eastern and southern Africa. *Food Policy* 31:328–341.

Jensen, H. T., S. Robinson, and F. Tarp. 2004. General equilibrium measures of agricultural policy bias in fifteen developing countries. Discussion Papers 04-25, Department of Economics, University of Copenhagen.

Jevell, A.M., H. Torjuisen, and E. Jacobsen. 2006. Farmers markets as a new arena for communication on food. In *Ethics and the politics of food: 6th Congress of the European Society for Agricultural and Food Ethics,* ed. M. Kaiser and M. Lien. Netherlands: Wageningen Academic Publishers.

Johnston, B., and J. Mellor. 1961. The role of agriculture in economic development. *American Economic Review* 51 (4): 566–593.

Jones, S. 1995. Food market reform: The changing role of the state. *Food Policy* 20: 551–560.

Jonsson, U. 2007. Millennium Development Goals and other good intentions. In *Ethics, hunger and globalization: In search of appropriate policies,* ed. P. Pinstrup-Andersen and P. Sandøe. Dordrecht: Springer.

Jordaan, I. 2005. Decisions under uncertainty: Probabilistic analysis for engineering decisions. Cambridge: Cambridge University Press.

Jorgenson, D. 1961. The development of a dual economy. *Economic Journal* 71 (282): 309–334.

Just, R., and N. Bockstael. 1991. *Commodity and resource policies in agricultural systems.* Berlin: Springer-Verlag.

Kammen, D. M. 2006. Bioenergy and agriculture: Promises and challenges; Bioenergy in developing countries: Experiences and prospects. In *Bioenergy and agriculture: Promises and challenges,* Focus 14, ed. P. Hazell and R. K. Pachauri. Washington, DC: International Food Policy Research Institute.

Kanbur, R. 1987. Measurement and alleviation of poverty: With an application to the effects of macroeconomic adjustment. Staff Papers, International Monetary Fund, Washington, DC.

———. 2001. Economic policy, distribution and poverty: The nature of disagreements. *World Development* 29 (6): 1083–1094.

———. 2002. Conceptual challenges in poverty and inequality: One development economist's perspective. Paper presented at Conference on Conceptual Challenges in Poverty and Inequality, Cornell University, Ithaca, NY, April 16–17.

Kanbur, R., and L. Haddad. 1994. Are better off households more unequal or less unequal? *Oxford Economic Papers* 46:445–458.

Kanter, C., K. D. Messer, and H. M. Kaiser. 2009. Does production labeling stigmatize conventional milk? *American Journal of Agricultural Economics* 91 (4): 1097–1109.

Kaplow, L., and S. Shavell. 2001. Any non-welfarist method of policy assessment violates the Pareto principle. *Journal of Political Economy* 109:281–286.

Karekezi, S., and W. Kithyoma. 2006. Bioenergy and agriculture: Promises and challenges; Bioenergy and the poor. In *Bioenergy and agriculture: Promises and challenges*, Focus 14, ed. P. Hazell and R. K. Pachauri. Washington, DC: International Food Policy Research Institute.

Kargbo, J. M. 2000. Impacts of monetary and macroeconomic factors on food prices in eastern and southern Africa. *Applied Economics* 32 (11): 1373–1389.

Kataki, P. K. 2002. Food systems and malnutrition: Linking agriculture, nutrition, and productivity. In *Food systems for improved human nutrition; Linking agriculture, nutrition, and productivity*, ed. P. K. Kataki and S. C. Babu. Binghamton, NY: Food Products Press.

Kataki, P. K., and S. C. Babu, eds. 2002. *Food systems for improved human nutrition; Linking agriculture, nutrition, and productivity.* Binghamton, NY: Food Products Press.

Kaufman, P., and C. Handy. 1989. Supermarket prices and price differences: City, firm, and store-level determinants. USDA ERS, Washington, DC.

Kaufmann, D. 1997. Corruption: The facts. *Foreign Policy* 107 (Summer): 114–131.

———. 2003. *Governance redux: The empirical challenge; Global Competitiveness Report 2003–04.* Washington, DC: World Bank Institute.

Kaufmann, D., and A. Kraay. 2008. *Governance indicators: Where are we, where should we be going?* Oxford: Oxford University Press on behalf of The World Bank.

Kaufmann, D., A. Kraay, and M. Mastruzzi. 2009. Governance matters VIII: Aggregate and individual governance indicators: 1996–2008. Research Working Paper 4978, World Bank, Washington, DC.

Kaufmann, D., and S.-J. Wei. 1999. Does "grease money" speed up the wheels of commerce? NBER Working Paper 7093.

Keefer, P., and S. Knack. 1997. Why don't poor countries catch up? A cross-national test of an institutional explanation. *Economic Inquiry* 35:590–602.

Kelly, P. J. 1990. *Utilitarianism and distributive justice: Jeremy Bentham and the civil law.* Oxford: Oxford University Press.

Kessler, C., and I. Economidis. 2001. A review of results: EC-sponsored research on safety of genetically modified organisms, European Commission. http://europa.cec.int/comm/research/quality-of-life/gmo/.

Key, N., and D. Runsten. 1999. Contract farming, smallholders, and rural development in Latin America: The organization of agroprocessing firms and the scale of outgrower production. *World Development* 27:381–401.

Keyzer, M. A., M. Nubé, and L. van Wesenbeeck. 2006. Estimation of undernutrition and mean calorie intake in Africa: Methodology, findings and implications for Africa's record. Centre for World Food Studies, Staff Working Paper WP-06-03, Amsterdam.

Kheralah, M., C. Delgado, E. Gabre-Madhin, N. Minot, and M. Johnson. 2000. *The road half traveled: Agricultural market reform in sub-Saharan Africa.* Food Policy Report. Washington, DC: IFPRI.

———. 2002. *Reforming agricultural markets in Africa.* Baltimore: Johns Hopkins University Press for IFPRI.

Kirimi, L., and K. Sindi. 2006. A duration analysis of poverty transitions in rural Kenya. Presented at the AAEA Annual Meeting, July 23–26.

Kjoernes, U., and R. Lavik. 2006. Consumer information about farm animal welfare: A study of national differences. In *Ethics and the politics of food: 6th Congress of the European Society for Agricultural and Food Ethics*, ed. M. Kaiser and M. Lien. Netherlands: Wageningen Academic Publishers.

Klasen, S., and C. Wink. 2003. Missing women: Revisiting the debate. *Feminist Economics* 9:263–299.

Klein, M., and T. Harford. 2005. *The market for aid.* Washington, DC: International Finance Corporation.

Knack, S. 1996. Institutions and the convergence hypothesis: The cross-national evidence. *Public Choice* 87:207–228.

Knack, S., and O. Azfar. 2000. Are larger countries really more corrupt? World Bank Development Research Group Policy Research Working Paper 2470, November.

Knack, S., and P. Keefer. 1995. Institutions and economic performance: Cross-country tests using alternative institutional measures. *Economics and Politics* 7:207–227.

Knox, A., R. Meinzen-Dick, and P. Hazell. 2002. Property rights, collective action, and technologies for natural resource management: A conceptual framework. In *Innovation in natural resource management: The role of property rights and collective action in developing countries,* ed. R. Meinzen-Dick, A. Knox, F. Place, and B. Swallow. Washington, DC: International Food Policy Research Institute.

Kohls, R., and J. Uhl. 2002. *Marketing of agricultural products.* 9th ed. New York: Macmillan.

Koning, N., and P. Pinstrup-Andersen. 2007. Agricultural trade liberalization and the least developed countries. In *Agricultural trade liberalization and the least developed countries,* ed. N. Koning and P. Pinstrup-Andersen. Wageningen: Springer.

Koopman, J. S., and J. W. Lynch. 1999. Individual causal models and population system models in epidemiology. *American Journal of Public Health* 89:1170–1174.

Kotler, P. 1994. *Marketing management: Analysis, planning and control.* 8th ed. Englewood Cliffs, NJ: Prentice-Hall.

Kraay, A. 2004. When is growth pro-poor? Evidence from a panel of countries. Policy Research Working Paper 3225, World Bank, Washington, DC.

Krishna, A. 2002. Enhancing political participation in democracies: What is the role of social capital? *Comparative Political Studies* 35 (4): 437–460.

———. 2007. *Lessons from successful action for reaching excluded groups: The dynamics of poverty; Why don't "the poor" act collectively?* 2020 Focus Briefs on the World's Poor and Hungry People. Washington, DC: International Food Policy Research Institute.

Krueger, A. 1974. The political economy of rent-seeking society. *American Economic Review* 64:291–303.

———. 1996. Political economy of agricultural policy. *Public Choice* 87:173–175.

Krueger, A. O., M. Schiff, and A. Valdes. 1988. Agricultural incentives in developing countries: Measuring the effect of sectoral and economy-wide policies. *World Bank Economic Review* 2:255–271.

———, eds. 1991. *The political economy of agricultural pricing policy.* Washington, DC: World Bank.

Krugman, P. 2010. Economics is not a morality play. *New York Times,* September 28.

Kuhn, T. 1970. *The structure of scientific revolutions.* 2nd ed. Chicago: University of Chicago Press.

Kuzma, J., and P. VerHage. 2006. Nanotechnology in agriculture and food production: Anticipated applications. Woodrow Wilson International Center for Scholars Project on Emerging Nanotechnologies (PEN) 4, September.

Kuznets, S. 1955. Economic growth and income inequality. *American Economic Review* 45:1–28.

Lachaal, L., and A. W. Womack. 1998. Impacts of trade and macroeconomic linkages on Canadian agriculture. *American Journal of Agricultural Economics* 80 (3): 534–542.

Lam, W. F. 1998. *Governing irrigation systems in Nepal: Institutions, infrastructure, and collective action.* Oakland, CA: ICS.

Lambsdorff, G. J. 2002. Corruption and rent-seeking. *Public Choice* 113 (1–2): 97–125.

Lamm, R. 1981. Prices and concentration in the food retailing industry. *Journal of Industrial Economics* 30 (1): 67–78.

Lang, T., D. Barling, and M. Caraher. 2001. Food, social policy and the environment: Towards a new model. *Social Policy and Administration* 35 (5): 538–558.

Lang, T., and M. Heasman. 2004. *Food wars: The global battle for mouths, minds and markets.* London: Earthscan.

Laux, M. 2006. *Organic food trends profile.* Agricultural Marketing Resource Center, http://www.agmrc.org/agmrc/markets/Food/organicfoodtrendsprofile.htm.

Lawn, J. E., S. Cousen, and J. Zupan. 2005. Neonatal survival 1: 4 million neonatal deaths; When? Where? Why? *Lancet* 365 (9462): 891–900.

Lee, C.-C., Y.-B. Chiu, and C.-H. Sun. 2009. Does one size fit all? A reexamination of the environmental Kuznets curve using the dynamic panel data approach. *Review of Agricultural Economics* 31 (4): 751–778.

Lefèvre, P., and C. Garcia. 1997. Experiences, perceptions and expectations of local project actors on monitoring and evaluation: A case study in the Philippines. *Journal of International Development* 9 (1): 1–20.

Leff, N. H. 1964. Economic development through bureaucratic corruption. *American Behavioral Scientist* 8 (3): 8–14.

Leitzmann, C., and G. Cannon. 2005. Public health nutrition: The new nutrition science project. A joint initiative of the International Union of Nutritional Sciences and the World Health Policy Forum. Published for the 18th International Congress of Nutrition, September, Durban, South Africa.

Lele, U., and R. Christiansen. 1989. Markets, marketing boards, and cooperatives in Africa: Issues in adjustment policy. MADIA Discussion Paper 11, World Bank, Washington, DC.

Levinson, A. 2009. Technology, international trade, and pollution from US manufacturing. *American Economic Review* 99 (5): 2177–2192.

Levy, S., C. Barahona, and B. Chinsinga. 2004. *Food security, social protection, growth, and poverty reduction synergies: The starter pack programme in Malawi.* Natural Resource Perspectives 95. London: Overseas Development Institute.

Lewis, A. 1954. Economic development with unlimited supplies of labor. *Manchester School of Economic and Social Studies* 22 (2): 139–191.

Leys, C. 1965. What is the problem about corruption? *Journal of Modern African Studies* 3 (2): 215–230.

Lindert, P., and J. Williamson. 2001. Globalization and inequality: A long history. Paper prepared for the World Bank Annual Bank Conference on Development Economics, Europe, Barcelona, June 25–27.

Lipton, M. 1977. *Why poor people stay poor: A study of urban bias in world development.* Cambridge, MA: Harvard University Press.

——. 1993. Market relaxation and agricultural development. In *States and markets: Neoliberalism and the development policy debate,* ed. C. Colclough and J. Manor. Oxford: Oxford University Press.

——. 2005. The family farm in a globalizing world: The role of crop science in alleviating poverty. 2020 Discussion Paper 40, IFPRI, Washington, DC.

Little, P., and M. Watts. 1994. *Living under contract: Contract farming and agrarian transformation in sub-Saharan Africa.* Madison: University of Wisconsin Press.

Lockie, S., and S. Kitto. 2000. Beyond the farm gate: Production-consumption networks and agri-food research. *Sociologia Ruralis* 40 (1): 3–19.

Lomborg, B. 2001. *The skeptical environmentalist: Measuring the real state of the world.* Cambridge: Cambridge University Press.

Longini, I. M., Jr., M. E. Halloran, A. Nizam, Y. Yang, S. Xu, K. D. S. Burke, et al. 2007. Containing a large bioterrorist smallpox attack: A computer simulation approach. *International Journal of Infectious Diseases* 11 (2): 98–108.

Lopez, A.D., C. D. Mathers, M. Ezzati, D. T. Jamison, and C. J. L. Murray. 2006. *Global burden of disease and risk factors.* New York: Oxford University Press.

Lopez, R. A., A. M. Azzam, and C. Lirón-Espana. 2002. A market power and/or efficiency: A structural approach. *Review of Industrial Organization* 20:115–127.

Lorentzen, P., J. McMillan, and R. Wacziarg. 2008. Death and development. *Journal of Economic Growth* 13 (2): 81–124.

Low, A. R. C. 2008. Decision taking under uncertainty: A linear programming model of peasant farmer behavior. *Journal of Agricultural Economics* 25 (3): 311–321.

Lundberg, S., and R. Pollak. 1993. Separate spheres bargaining and the marriage market. *Journal of Political Economy* 101 (6): 988–1010.

Lundqvist, J., C. de Fraiture, and D. Molden. 2008. Saving water: From field to fork. SIWI Policy Brief.

Lybbert, T., and C. Barrett. 2007. Risk responses to dynamic asset thresholds. *Review of Agricultural Economics* 29 (30): 412–418.

Lybbert, T., C. B. Barrett, S. Desta, and D. L. Coppock. 2004. Stochastic wealth dynamics and risk management among a poor population. *Economic Journal* 114 (498): 750–777.

MacDonald, C. 2006. The precautionary principle and the ethics of corporate decision making. Papers from the Canadian Society for the Study of Practical Ethics Annual Meeting, York University, May/June.

MacDonald, C., and M. Whellams. 2007. Corporate decisions about labeling genetically modified foods. *Journal of Business Ethics* 74 (4).

MacLachlan, I. 2001. Kill and chill: Restructuring Canada's beef commodity chain. Toronto: University of Toronto Press.

Madeley, J., ed. 1999. *Trade and the hungry: How international trade is causing hunger.* Brussels: APRODEV.

Magee, S., P. W. Brock, and L. Young. 1989. *Black hole tariffs and endogenous policy theory: Political economy in general equilibrium.* Cambridge: Cambridge University Press.

Maglinao, A. R., and C. Valentin. 2003. Catchment approach to managing soil erosion in Asia. In Research towards integrated natural resource management, CGIAR, Rome.

Malthus, R. R. 1798. *An essay on the principle of population.* http://oll.libertyfund.org/index.php?option=com_staticxt&staticfile=show.php%3Ftitle=311&Itemid=27.

Mano, R., B. Isaacson, and P. Dardel. 2003. Identifying policy determinants of food security response and recovery in the SADC Region: The case of the 2002 food emergency. FANRPAN Policy Paper prepared for the FANRPAN Regional Dialogue on Agricultural Recovery, Food Security and Trade Policies in Southern Africa, Gaborone, Botswana, March 26–27.

March, D., and E. Susser. 2006. The eco in eco-epidemiology. *International Journal of Epidemiology* 35:1379–1783.

Marchione, T. J., ed. 1999. *Scaling up, scaling down: Overcoming malnutrition in developing countries.* Amsterdam: Gordon and Breach.

Marinoff, L. 2007. Ethics, globalization, and hunger: An ethicist's perspective. In *Ethics, hunger and globalization: In search of appropriate policies,* ed. P. Pinstrup-Andersen and P. Sandøe. Dordrecht: Springer.

Marion, B. 1998. Competition in grocery retailing: The impact of a new strategic group on BLS price increases. *Review of Industrial Organization* 13 (4): 381–399.

Martinez-Diaz, L. 2008. Executive boards in international organizations: Lessons for strengthening IMF governance. Background Paper BP/08/08, Independent Evaluation Office of the International Monetary Fund, May 2008 version.

Martorell, R., L. Khan, M. Hughes, and L. Grummer-Strawn. 1998. Obesity in Latin American women and children. *Journal of Nutrition* 128 (9): 1464–1473.

Marx, K. 1844. *Economic and philosophic manuscripts.* London: Lawrence and Wishart, 1977.

Mauro, P. 1995. Corruption and growth. *Quarterly Journal of Economics* 110:681–712.

Maxwell, S., and R. Slater. 2004. *Food policy old and new.* Oxford: Blackwell Publishing.

Mayer, W. 1984. Endogenous tariff formation. *American Economic Review* 74:970–985.

McCarthey, J., and W. Perreault. 1984. *Basic marketing: A managerial approach.* Homewood, IL: R. D. Irwin.

McCullough, E. B., P. L. Pingali, and K. G. Stamoulis, eds. 2008. *The transformation of agrifood systems: Globalization, supply chains and smallholder farmers.* London: Earthscan.

McElroy, M. 1990. The empirical content of Nash-bargaining household behavior. *Journal of Human Resources* 25 (4): 559–583.

McLean, W. P. 1987. Nutritional risk: Concepts and implications. In *Food policy: Integrating supply, distribution, and consumption,* ed. J. P. Gittinger, J. Leslie, and C. Hoisington. Baltimore: Johns Hopkins University Press.

McWilliams, J. E. 2009. *Just food: Where locavores get it wrong and how we can truly eat responsibly.* New York: Little, Brown.

Meerman, J. 1997. Reforming agriculture: The World Bank goes to market. World Bank Operations Evaluation Study, World Bank, Washington, DC.

Meinzen-Dick, R., and B. R. Bruns. 2000. Negotiating water rights: An introduction. In *Negotiating water rights,* ed. B. R. Bruns and R. S. Meinzen-Dick. Washington, DC: International Food Policy Research Institute.

Meinzen-Dick, R., P. Kameri-Mbote, and H. Markelova. 2007. Property rights for poverty reduction. 2020 Focus Brief on the World's Poor and Hungry People, October, IFPRI, Washington, DC.

Mendez M., C. Monteiro, and B. Popkin. 2005. Overweight exceeds underweight among women in most developing countries. *American Journal of Clinic Nutrition* 81 (3): 714–721.

Mendoza, R. 2000. The hierarchical legacy in coffee commodity chains. In *Rural development in Central America,* ed. R. Ruben and J. Bastiaensen. New York: St. Martin's Press.

Menezes, F. 2001. Food sovereignty: A vital requirement for food security in the context of globalization. *Development* 44 (4): 29–33.

Mershed, S. M. 2003. Marginalisation in an era of globalization. Institute of Social Studies, University of Utrecht, Netherlands. http://www.uu.nl/uupublish/content/murshed-marginalization.pdf.

Messer, E., and M. J. Cohen. 2007. Conflict, food insecurity, and globalization. *Food Culture and Society* 10 (2): 298–315.

Messer, E., M. Cohen, and T. Marchione. 2001. Conflict: A cause and effect of hunger. Environmental Change and Security Project Report 7, pp. 1–16. Washington, DC: Woodrow Wilson International Center for Scholars, Smithsonian Institution.

Meyer, J., and S. Cramon-Taubadel. 2004. Asymmetric price transmission: A survey. *Journal of Agricultural Economics* 55 (3): 581–611.

Micheletti, M. 2006. Political consumerism: Why the market is an arena for politics. In *Ethics and the politics of food: 6th Congress of the European Society for Agricultural and Food Ethics,* ed. M. Kaiser and M. Lien. Netherlands: Wageningen Academic Publishers

Miguel, E. 2008. Is it Africa's turn? *Boston Review.* From a forum on progress in the world's poorest region, May/June.

Mill, J. S. 1863. *On liberty.* Boston: Ticknor and Fields.

Millennium Ecosystem Assessment Board. 2005. *Living beyond our means: Natural assets and human well-being.* Washington, DC: IEG.

Miller, J. H., and S. E. Page. 2007. *Complex adaptive systems: An introduction to computational models of social life.* Princeton Studies in Complexity. Princeton, NJ: Princeton University Press.

Millstone, E. 2006. Can food safety policy-making be both scientifically and democratically legitimated? If so, how? In *Ethics and the politics of food: 6th Congress of the European Society for Agricultural and Food Ethics,* ed. M. Kaiser and M. Lien. Netherlands: Wageningen Academic Publishers.

Mines, R., S. Gabbard, and A. Steirman. 1997. *A profile of US farm workers.* Washington, DC: U.S. Department of Labor.

Mittal, S. 2006. Structural shift in demand for food: Projections for 2020. Indian Council for Research on International Economic Relations, Working Paper 184. http://www.icrier.org/pdf/WP_184.pdf.

Morris, J., and R. Bate, eds. 1999. *Fearing food: Risk, health and environment.* Oxford: Butterworth Heinemann.

Morris, S. S., B. Cogill, and R. Uauy. 2008. Effective international action against undernutrition: Why has it proven so difficult and what can be done to accelerate progress? *Lancet* 371 (9612): 608–621.

Morton, J. F. 2007. The impact of climate change on smallholder and subsistence agriculture. *Proceedings of the National Academy of Sciences (PNAS) of the United States of America* 104 (50): 19680–19685.

Mosquera, T. U. 1993. The political economy of Colombia's PAN. In Pinstrup-Andersen 1993, 50–60.

Mundlak, Y., D. Larson and R. Butzer. 2002. Determinants of agricultural growth in Indonesia, the Philippines, and Thailand. World Bank Policy Research Working Paper 2803, Washington, DC.

Muralidharan, P. 1994. Traditional poultry farming. *The Indian poultry industry yearbook: 1994,* ed. S. P. Gupta. Delhi.

Murdoch, J. 2000. Networks: A new paradigm of rural development? *Journal of Rural Studies* 16:407–419.

Murray D., L. Raynolds, and P. Taylor. 2003. One cup at a time: Poverty alleviation and fair trade coffee in Latin America. Colorado State University, Fort Collins.

Muth, M. K., and M. K. Wohlgenant. 1999. A test for market power using marginal input and output prices with application to the U.S. beef processing industry. *American Journal of Agricultural Economics* 81 (3): 638–643.

Nakimbugwe, D., and K. J. Boor. 2010. Food safety as a bridge between the food system and human health in sub-Saharan Africa. In *The African food system and its interaction with human health and nutrition,* ed. P. Pinstrup-Andersen. Ithaca, NY: Cornell University Press.

Narayanan, S., and A. Gulati. 2002. *Globalization and the smallholders: A review of issues, approaches, and implications.* MSSD Discussion Paper 50, IFPRI and World Bank.

National Research Council. 1999. *Our common journey: A transition toward sustainability.* Washington, DC: National Academy Press.

Nelson, R. 2010. Pest management, farmer incomes, and health risks in sub-Saharan Africa: Pesticides, host plant resistance, and other measures. In *The African food system and its interaction with human health and nutrition,* ed. P. Pinstrup-Andersen. Ithaca, NY: Cornell University Press.

Nestle, M. 2007. *Food Politics: How the food industry influences nutrition and health.* Berkeley: University of California Press.

Newmark, C. 1990. A new test of the price-concentration relationship in grocery retailing. *Economic Letters* 33:369–373.

Nietzsche, F. 1874. *Schopenhauer as educator.* Translated by J. W. Hillesheim and M. R. Simpson. Chicago: Henry Regnery, 1965.

Nissanke, M., and E. Thorbecke, eds. 2007. *The impact of globalization on the world's poor: Transmission mechanisms.* New York: Palgrave MacMillan.

Nkonya, E., J. Pender, K. C. Kaizzi, E. Kato, S. Mugarura, H. Ssali, and J. Muwonge. 2008. *Linkages between land management, land degradation, and poverty in sub-Saharan Africa.* Research Report 159. Washington, DC: International Food Policy Research Institute.

Nkuba, J., S. Edmeades, and M. Smale. 2006. Gauging potential based on current adoption of banana hybrids in Tanzania. In *Promising crop biotechnologies for smallholder farmers in east Africa: Bananas and maize.* IFPRI, CIMMYT, and IPGRI, Brief 21, June.

Norman, D., F. Worman, J. Siebert, and E. Modiakgotla. 1995. *The farming systems approach to development and appropriate technology generation.* Rome: FAO.

Norse, D., L. Ji, J. Leshan, and Z. Zheng. 2001. *Environmental costs of rice production in China: Hunan and Hubei.* China Council. Bethesda, MD: Aileen International Press.

North, D. 1990. *Institutions, institutional change and economic performance.* New York: Cambridge University Press.

——. 1998. Understanding economic change. In *Transforming post-communist political economies,* ed. J. Nelson, C. Tilly, and L. Walker. Task Force on Economies in Transition, National Research Council. Washington, DC: National Academy Press.

Novartis Foundation. 2010. World population growth: Status in 2010 and prospects. *Express 3/10 Newsletter,* Novartis Foundation for Sustainable Development. www.novartis-foundation.org.

Nozick, R. 1974. *Anarchy, state, and utopia.* New York: Basic Books.

Nussbaum, M. 1988. Nature, functioning and capability: Aristotle on political distribution. *Oxford Studies in Ancient Philosophy,* supplementary volume, 145–184.

——. 2003. Tragedy and human capabilities: A response to Vivian Walsh. *Review of Political Economy* 153:413–418.

——. 2007. Human rights and human capabilities. *Harvard Human Rights Journal* 20: 21–24.

Nweke, F. I. 1996. Cassava: A cash crop in Africa. Working Paper 14, COSCA (Collaborative Study of Cassava in Africa), Resource and Crop Management Division, International Institute of Tropical Agriculture, Ibadan, Nigeria.

——. 2004. New challenges in the cassava transformation in Nigeria and Ghana. EPTD Discussion Paper 118, International Food Policy Research Institute, Washington, DC.

Nygard B., and O. Storstad. 1998. De-globalization of food markets? Consumer perceptions of safe food: The case of Norway. *Sociologia Ruralis* 38 (1): 36–53.

O'Connor, J. D. 2006. Are virtue ethics and Kantian ethics really so very different? *New Blackfriars* 87 (1009): 238–252.

Oaks, D. H., and L. B. Wickman. 2008. Same-gender attraction: An interview with D. H. Oaks. http://newsroom.lds.org/ldsnewsroom/eng/public-issues/same-gender-attraction.

OECD (Organization for Economic Co-operation and Development). 1986. *Recombinant DNA safety considerations: Safety considerations for industrial, agricultural and environmental applications of organisms derived by recombinant DNA techniques.* Paris.

——. 2005. *Trends in international migration.* Paris.

Oehmke, J. F., and X. Yao. 1990. A policy preference function for government intervention in the U.S. wheat market. *American Journal of Agricultural Economics* 72 (3): 631–640.

Oerke, E. C. 2005. Centenary review: Crop losses to pests. *Journal of Agricultural Sciences* 144 (1): 31–43.

Ogden, C., K. Flegal, M. Carroll, and C. Johnson. 2002. Prevalence and trends in overweight among US children and adolescents, 1999–2000. *Journal of the American Medical Association* 288 (14): 1728–1732.

Ogden, C. L., M. D. Carroll, M. A. McDowell, and K. M. Flegal. 2007. *Obesity among adults in the United States: No statistically significant change since 2003–2004.* NCHS Data Brief, www.cdc.gov/nchs/data/databriefs/db01.pdf (accessed August 17, 2009).

Ogg, C. W. 2009. Avoiding more biofuel surprises: The fuel, food and forest trade-offs. *Journal of Development and Agricultural Economics* 1 (1): 12–17.

Ó Gráda, C. 2007. Making famine history. *Journal of Economic Literature* 45 (1): 5–38.

Oldeman, L. R., R. T. A. Hakkeling, and W. G. Sombroek. 1991. *World map of the status of human-induced soil degradation: An explanatory note.* Wageningen, Netherlands: International Soil Reference and Information Centre and United Nations Environment Programme.

Olesen, Jørgen. 2008. Climate-friendly food. *MoMentum* 4 (Nov): 4–8. www.LCAfood.dk.

Ole-MoiYoi, O. K. 2010. Disease burdens of sub-Saharan Africa and their interactions with malnutrition. In *The African food system and its interaction with human health and nutrition,* ed. P. Pinstrup-Andersen. Ithaca, NY: Cornell University Press.

Oliver, G. 1980. *Marketing today.* Hemel Hempstead: Prentice-Hall.

Olson, M. 1965. *The logic of collective action: Public goods and the theory of groups.* Cambridge, MA: Harvard University Press.

Orden, D. 2002. Exchange rate effects on agricultural trade. *Journal of Agricultural and Applied Economics: The Southern Agricultural Economists Association* 24 (02).

Ostrom, E. 1990. *Governing the commons: The evolution of institutions for collective action.* Cambridge: Cambridge University Press.

——. 1999.Coping with tragedies of the commons. *Annual Review of Political Science* 2: 493–535.

——. 2009. Beyond markets and states: Polycentric governance of complex economic systems. Nobel Prize lecture. Http://nobelprize.org/nobel_prizes/economics/laureates/2009/ostrom_lecture.pdf.

Ostrom, E., R. Gardiner, and J. Walker, eds. 1994. Rules, games and common pool resources. Ann Arbor, MI: University of Michigan Press.

Oxfam (Oxford Committee for Famine Relief). 2002. *Mugged: Poverty in your coffee cup.* Oxford.

Oygard, R., R. Garcia, A. Guttormsmen, R. Kachule, A. Mwanaumo, I. Mwanawina, E. Sjaastad, and M. Wik. 2003. The maze of maize: Improving input and output market access for poor smallholders in the southern African region: The experience of Zambia and Malawi. Report 26, Department of Economics and Resource Management, Agricultural University of Norway.

Paarlberg, R. L. 2002. *Governance and food security in an age of globalization.* 2020 Vision for Food, Agriculture, and the Environment. Washington, DC: International Food Policy Research Institute.

Pachauri, R. K., and P. Mehrotra. 2001. Alternative energy sources. In *Appropriate technology for sustainable food security,* ed. P. Pinstrup-Andersen. IFPRI Focus 7. Washington, DC.

Page, S. 2007. Policy space: Are WTO rules preventing development? Briefing Paper, January, Overseas Development Institute, London.

Palla, G., I. Derényi, I. Farkas, and T. Vicsek. 2005. Uncovering the overlapping community structure of complex networks in nature and society. *Nature* 435:814–818.

Panagariya, A. 2005. India in the 1980s and 1990s: A triumph of reforms, issues 2004–2043. International Monetary Fund, Washington, DC.

Panin, A. 1995. Empirical evidence of mechanization effects on smallholder crop production systems in Botswana. *Agricultural Systems* 47 (2): 199–210.

Paoletti, M. G., and D. Pimentel. 2000. Environmental risks of pesticides versus genetic engineering for agricultural pest control. *Journal of Agricultural and Environmental Ethics* 12 (3): 279–303.

Papandreou, A., and J. Wheeler. 1954. *Competition and its regulation.* Englewood Cliffs, NJ: Prentice-Hall.

Pardey, P. G., J. M. Alston, and R. R. Piggott, eds. 2006. *Agricultural R&D in the developing world: Too little, too late?* Washington, DC: International Food Policy Research Institute.

Pardey, P. G., and N. M. Beintema. 2001. Slow magic: Agricultural R&D a century after Mendel. IFPRI Food Policy Statement 36, Washington, DC.

Pareto, V. 1896. *Course of political economy.* Lausanne: Rouge.

Parry, M. L., C. Rosenzweig, A. Iglesias, M. Livermore, and G. Fischer. 2004. Effects of climate change on global food production under SRES emissions and socio-economic scenarios. *Global Environmental Change* 14:53–67.

Passel, J. 2005. Estimates of the size and characteristics of the undocumented population. Pew Hispanic Center, Washington, DC.

Patel, R. 2007. *Stuffed and starved: The hidden battle for the world food system.* Brooklyn: Melville House.

Pelletier, D. L., and E. A. Frongillo. 2003. Changes in child survival are strongly associated with changes in malnutrition in developing countries. *Journal of Nutrition* 133:107–119.

Pelletier, D. L., E. A. Frongillo Jr., D. G. Schroeder, and J.-P. Habicht. 1995. The effects of malnutrition on child mortality in developing countries. *Bulletin of the WHO* 73:443–448.

Peltzman, S. 1976. Toward a more general theory of regulation. *Journal of Law and Economics* 19:211–240.

Perrings C. 1995. Biodiversity conservation as insurance. In *Economics and ecology of biodiversity decline,* ed. T. Swanson. Cambridge: Cambridge University Press.

Persson, T. 2005. Forms of democracy, policy and economic development. National Bureau of Economic Research, NBER Working Paper 11171.

Persson, T., and G. Tabellini. 1994. Is inequality harmful for growth? *American Economic Review* 84 (3): 600–621.

———. 2002. Do constitutions cause large governments? Quasi-experimental evidence. *European Economic Review* 46 (4–5): 908–918.

Persson, T., G. Tabellini, and F. Trebbi. 2001. Electoral rules and corruption. Working Paper Series, National Bureau of Economic Research, Cambridge, MA.

Peters, P. 1996. Failed magic or social context? Market liberalization and the rural poor in Malawi. Development Discussion Paper 562, Harvard Institute of International Development, Cambridge, MA.

Petit, M. 1993. Determinants of food policies: An attempt to understand government behavior. In Pinstrup-Andersen 1993.

Philipson, T., and R. Posner. 2003. The long-run growth in obesity as a function of technological change. *Perspectives in Biology and Medicine* 46 (3): S87–S107.

Phipps, R. H., R. Einspanier, and M. A. Faust. 2006. Safety of meat, milk, and eggs from animals fed crops derived from modern biotechnology. Council for Agricultural Science and Technology, Issue Paper 34, July.

Phipps, R. H., and J. R. Park. 2002. Environmental benefits of genetically modified crops: Global and European perspectives on their ability to reduce pesticide use. *Journal of Animal Feed Science* 11:1–18.

Pigou, A. 1932. *The economics of welfare.* London: Macmillan.

Pingali, P. 2004. Westernization of Asian diets and the transformation of food systems: Implications for research and policy. ESA Working Paper 04-17, FAO, Rome.

Pingali, P., and T. Raney. 2005. From the green revolution to the gene revolution: How will the poor fare? ESA Working Paper 05-09, FAO, Rome.

Pingali, P., and G. Traxler. 2002. Changing locus of agricultural research: Will the poor benefit from biotechnology and privatization trends? *Food Policy* 27:223–238.

Pinkovskiy, M., and X. Sala-i-Martin. 2010. African poverty is falling . . . Much faster than you think! NBER Working Paper 15775, Columbia University.

Pinstrup-Andersen, P. 1981. Nutritional consequences of agricultural projects: Conceptual relationships and assessment approaches. World Bank Staff Working Paper 456, World Bank, Washington, DC.

———. 1983. Estimating the nutritional impact of food policies: A note on the analytical approach. *Food and Nutrition Bulletin* 5 (4): 16–21.

———. 1988. *Food subsidies in developing countries: Costs, benefits, and policy options.* Baltimore: Johns Hopkins University Press.

———, ed. 1993a. *The political economy of food and nutrition policies.* Baltimore: Johns Hopkins University Press.

———. 1993b. Household behavior and government preferences: Compatibility or conflicts in efforts to achieve goals of nutrition programs. In *The Political economy of food and nutrition policies,* ed. P. Pinstrup-Andersen. Baltimore: Johns Hopkins University Press for IFPRI.

———. 1999a. The future world food situation and the role of plant diseases. *Canadian Journal of Plant Pathology* 22:321–331.

———. 1999b. Towards ecologically sustainable world production. *UNEP Industry and Environment* 22 (2–3): 10–13.

———. 2000. Food policy research for developing countries: Emerging issues and unfinished business. *Food Policy* 25 (2): 125–141.

———. 2001. The future world food situation and the role of plant diseases. *Plant Health Instructor,* doi:10.1094/PHI-I-2001–0425–01.

———. 2002a. Towards a sustainable global food system: What will it take? Paper presented at the John Pesek Colloquium on Sustainable Agriculture, Iowa State University.

———. 2002b. Food and agricultural policy for a globalizing world: Preparing for the future. *American Journal of Agricultural Economics* 84 (5): 1201–1214.

———. 2003. Eradicating poverty and hunger as a national security issue for the United States. *Environmental Change and Security Project Report* 9:22–26.

———. 2005a. The Millennium Development Goal for the alleviation of poverty, hunger, and malnutrition in sub-Saharan Africa: Could it be achieved? Presentation at the Institute for African Development, March 17, Cornell University, Ithaca, NY.

———. 2005b. Ethics and economic policy for the food system. *American Journal of Agricultural Economics* 87 (5): 1097–1112.

———. 2006a. Agricultural research and policy for better health and nutrition in developing countries: A food systems approach. Paper presented at the 26th Conference of the International Association of Agricultural Economists, Queensland, Australia.

———. 2006b. The impact of technological change in agriculture on poverty and armed conflict. Inaugural lecture, Charles Valentine Riley Memorial Lecture Series, USDA, Washington, DC.

———. 2007a. Agricultural research and policy for better health and nutrition in developing countries: A food systems approach. In *Contributions of agricultural economics to critical policy issues,* ed. K. Otsuk and K. Kalirajan. Malden, MA: Blackwell.

———. 2007b. Eliminating poverty and hunger in developing countries: A moral imperative or enlightened self-interest? In *Ethics, hunger and globalization: In search of appropriate policies,* ed. P. Pinstrup-Andersen and P. Sandøe. Dordrecht: Springer.

———, ed. 2010. *The African food system and its interaction with human health and nutrition.* Ithaca, NY: Cornell University Press.

Pinstrup-Andersen, P., A. Berg, and M. Forman, eds. 1984. *International agricultural research and human nutrition.* Washington, DC, and Rome: International Food Policy Research Institute and United Nations Administrative Committee on Coordination/Sub-Committee on Nutrition.

Pinstrup-Andersen, P., and F. Cheng, eds. 2009. *Case studies in food policy for developing countries.* 3 vols. Ithaca, NY: Cornell University Press.

Pinstrup-Andersen, P., and A. Herforth. 2008. Food security: Achieving the potential. *Environment* 50 (5): 48–61.

Pinstrup-Andersen, P., N. Londono, and E. Hoover. 1976. The impact of increasing food supply on human nutrition: Implications for commodity priorities in agricultural research and policy. *American Journal of Agricultural Economics* 58:131–142.

Pinstrup-Andersen, P., and T. Mengistu. 2007. Implications of globalization for agricultural research. In *Globalization of the food and agriculture system and poverty,* ed. J. von Braun and E. Diaz-Bonilla. Washington, DC: International Food Policy Research Institute.

Pinstrup-Andersen, P., and R. Pandya-Lorch. 1994. Alleviating poverty, intensifying agriculture, and effectively managing natural resources. Food, Agriculture, and the Environment Discussion Paper 2020, 1, IFPRI, Washington, DC.

Pinstrup-Andersen, P., R. Pandya-Lorch, and M. W. Rosegrant. 1999. *World food prospects: Critical issues for the early twenty-first century.* Washington, DC: International Food Policy Research Institute.

Pinstrup-Andersen, P., D. Pelletier, and H. Alderman, eds. 1995. *Child growth and nutrition in developing countries: Priorities for action.* Ithaca, NY: Cornell University Press.

Pinstrup-Andersen, P., and E. Schiøler. 2000. *Seeds of contention: World hunger and the global controversy over GM crops.* Baltimore: Johns Hopkins University Press.

Pinstrup-Andersen, P., and S. Shimokawa. 2007. Rural infrastructure and agricultural development. In *Annual World Bank conference on development economics: Global 2007; Rethinking infrastructure for development,* ed. F. Bourguignon and B. Pleskovic. Washington, DC: World Bank.

———. 2008. Do poverty and poor health and nutrition increase the risk of armed conflict onset? *Food Policy* 33:513–520.

Pitt, M. M., and M. R. Rosenzweig. 1985. Health and nutrient consumption across and within farm households. *Review of Economics and Statistics* 67:212–222.

Pitt, M. M., M. R. Rosenzweig, and M. N. Hassan. 1990. Productivity, health, and inequality in the intrahousehold distribution of food in low-income countries. *American Economic Review* 80:1139–1156.

Pollan, M. 2006. *The omnivore's dilemma: A natural history of four meals.* New York: Penguin.

———. 2008. *In defense of food.* New York: Penguin.

Popkin, B. M. 1981. Community-level considerations in nutrition planning in low-income nations. *Ecology of Food and Nutrition* 10:227–236.

———. 2003. The nutrition transition in the developing world. *Development Policy Review* 21 (5): 581–597.

Popkin, B., and C. Doak. 1998. The obesity epidemic is a worldwide phenomenon. *Nutrition Review* 56 (4): 106–114.

Popkin, B., S. Horton, and S. Kim. 2001. The nutrition transition and prevention of diet-related chronic diseases in Asia and the Pacific. ADB Nutrition and Development Series No. 6, Asia Development Bank, Manila.

Porter, G., and K. Phillips-Howard. 1997. Comparing contracts: An evaluation of contract farming schemes in Africa. *World Development* 25 (2): 227–238.

Portugal, L. 2002. Methodology for the measurement of support and use in policy evaluation. OECD, Paris.

Powell, D. 2010. Safe food is food that doesn't make you barf; don't like it, make your own definition, Barfblog: safe food from farm to fork, http://barfblog.foodsafety.ksu.edu/news/140890/10/02/15/safe-food-food-doesn%E2%80%99t-make-you-barf-don%E2%80%99t-it-make-your-own-definition.

Prendergast, C. 2002. Uncertainty and incentives. *Journal of Labor Economics* 20 (2): S115–S137.

Pretty, J. N. 2001. Farmer-based agroecological technology. In *Appropriate technology for sustainable food security,* ed. P. Pinstrup-Andersen. IFPRI Focus 7. Washington, DC: International Food Policy Research Institute.

Pretty, J. N., A. S. Ball, T. Lang, and J. I. L. Morison. 2005. Farm costs and food miles: An assessment of the full cost of the UK weekly food basket. *Food Policy* 30 (1): 1–19.

Pretty, J. N., and R. Hine. 2001. Reducing food poverty with sustainable agriculture: A summary of new evidence. Final report from the "SAFE-World" (The Potential of Sustainable Agriculture to Feed the World) Research Project, University of Essex. Commissioned by UK Department for International Development.

Prove, P., and M. Kothari. 2000. Human rights bodies gear up on TRIPs. *Bridges* 4 (6): 13–14.

Qizilbash, M. 1998. The concept of well-being. *Economics and Philosophy* 14:51–73.

Quisumbing, A., L. Haddad, and C. Pena. 2001. Are women overrepresented among the poor? An analysis of poverty in 10 developing countries. *Journal of Development Economics* 66 (1): 225–269.

Rabin, M. 1998. Psychology and economics. *Journal of Economic Literature* 36 (1): 11–46.

Raitzer, D. A. 2003. Benefit-cost meta-analysis of investment in the international agricultural research centres of the CGIAR. Report prepared on behalf of the CGIAR Standing Panel on Impact Assessment, Science Council Secretariat, Food and Agriculture Organization of the United Nations (FAO), September.

Rajan, R. 2008. The future of the IMF and the World Bank. *American Economic Review* 98 (2): 110–115.

Rangarajan, C. 1982. Agricultural growth and industrial performance in India. IFPRI Research Report 33, Washington, DC.

Rausser, G. 1992. Predatory versus productive government: The case of U.S. agricultural policies. *Journal of Economic Perspectives* 6 (3): 133–157.

Rausser, G., J. Chalfant, H. Love, and K. Stamoulis. 1986. Macroeconomic linkages, taxes and subsidies in US agricultural sector. *American Journal of Agricultural Economics* 68:399–413.

Rausser, G., and J. Freebairn. 1974. Estimation of policy preference functions: An application to US beef import quotas. *Review of Economics and Statistics* 56:437–449.

Ravallion, M. 1997. Can high inequality development countries escape absolute poverty? *Economics Letters* 56:51–57.

——. 2004. Pro-poor growth: A primer. Policy Research Working Paper 3242, World Bank, Washington, DC.

——. 2007. *Fostering pro-poor growth: Economic growth and poverty reduction; Do poor countries need to worry about inequality?* 2020 Focus Briefs on the World's Poor and Hungry People. Washington, DC: International Food Policy Research Institute.

Ravallion, M., and S. Chen. 1997. What can new survey data tell us about recent changes in distribution and poverty? *World Bank Research Observer* 11:357–382.

Ravallion, M., G. Datt, and D. van de Walle. 1991. Quantifying absolute poverty in the developing world. *Review of Income and Wealth* 37:345–361.

Ravallion, M., and Q. Wodon. 1999. Poor areas, or only poor people? *Journal of Regional Science* 39 (4): 689–711.

Rawls, J. 1971. *A theory of justice.* Cambridge, MA: Harvard University Press.

Read, L. 1958. I, Pencil. *The Freeman,* December. http://www.freerepublic.com/focus/news/760868/posts.

Reardon, T., and C. B. Barrett. 2000. Agroindustrialization, globalization, and international development: An overview of issues, patterns, and determinants. *Journal of Agricultural Economics* 23 (2): 195–205.

Reardon, T., S. Henson, and J. Berdegue. 2007. Proactive fast-tracking diffusion of supermarkets in developing countries: Implications for market institutions and trade. *Journal of Economic Geography* 7 (4): 399–431.

Reardon, T., and P. Timmer. 2007. Transformation of markets for agricultural output in developing countries since 1950: How has thinking changed? In *Handbook of agricultural economics,* vol. 3, ed. R. E. Evenson and P. Pingali. Amsterdam: Elsevier.

Reardon, T., P. Timmer, C. Barrett, and J. Berdegue. 2003. The rise of supermarkets in Africa, Asia, and Latin America. *American Journal of Agricultural Economics* 85 (5): 1140–1146.

Regmi, A. 2001. Changing structure of global food consumption and trade. Market and Trade Economics Division, Economic Research Service, U.S. Department of Agriculture, Agriculture and Trade Report, WRS-01-1, Washington, DC.

Regmi, A., and M. Gehlhar. 2005. New directions in global food markets. Agriculture Information Bulletin 794, USDA ERS.

Reinikka, R., and J. Svensson. 2004. The power of information: Evidence from a newspaper campaign to reduce capture. *Quarterly Journal of Economics* 119 (2): 679–705.

Relea, F. 2002. Conmoción por la muerte de niños por desnutrición en Argentina: La fiscalía investiga el desvío de los fondos asistenciales en Tucumán [Shock at the death of children from malnutrition in Argentina: Prosecutors investigating the diversion of funds, particularly those at Tucumán]. *El Pais Internacional,* November 16.

Reynolds, C. W. 1987. Flocks, herds, and schools: A distributed behavior model. *Computer Graphics* 21:25–34.

Robbins, J. 2001. *The food revolution: How your diet can help save your life and the world.* Berkeley, CA: Conari Press.

Roberts, P. 2008. *The end of food.* Boston, MA: Houghton Mifflin.

Robertson, B., and P. Pinstrup-Andersen. 2010. Global land acquisition: Neo-colonialism or development opportunity? *Food Security* 2: 271–283.

Robinson, M. 2007. Social justice, ethics, and hunger: What are the key messages? In *Ethics, hunger and globalization: In search of appropriate policies,* ed. P. Pinstrup-Andersen and P. Sandøe. Dordrecht: Springer.

Rodrik, D. 2006. Goodbye Washington consensus, hello Washington confusion? A Review of the World Bank's Economic Growth in the 1990s: Learning from a Decade of Reform. *Journal of Economic Literature* 44 (December): 973–987.

——. 2007. *One economics, many recipes: Globalization, institutions and economic growth.* Princeton, NJ: Princeton University Press.

——. 2008. Second-best institutions. *American Economic Review* 98 (2): 100–105.

Rogers, B. L., and N. P. Schlossman, eds. 1990. *Intrahousehold resource allocation: Issues and methods for development policy and planning.* Tokyo: United Nations University Press.

Rosegrant, M. W. 2008. Biofuels and grain prices: Impacts and policy responses. Testimony for the U.S. Senate Committee on Homeland Security and Governmental Affairs. Washington, DC.

Rosegrant, M. W., X. Cai, and S. A. Cline. 2002. *World water and food to 2025: Dealing with scarcity.* Washington, DC: International Food Policy Research Institute.

Rosegrant, M., M. Paisner, S. Meijer, and J. Witcover. 2001. *Global food projections to 2020: Emerging trends and alternative futures.* Washington, DC: IFPRI.

Rosegrant, M. W., C. Ringler, S. Msangi, T. B. Sulser, T. Zhu, and S. A. Cline. 2008. International model for policy analysis of agricultural commodities and trade (IMPACT). International Food Policy Research Institute, Washington, DC.

Rosenberg, N., and L. Birdzell. 1986. *How the West grew rich: The economic transformation of the industrial world.* New York: Basic Books.

Rosenzweig, M. 1986. Program interventions, intrahousehold distribution, and the welfare of individuals: Modeling household behavior. *World Development* 14:233–243.

Rowe, R., N. Sharma, and J. Browder. 1992. Deforestation: Problems, causes and concerns. In *Managing the world's forests: Looking for balance between conservation and development,* ed. N. Sharma. Dubuque, IA: Kendall Hunt.

Rowntree, S. 1901. *Poverty, a study of town life.* London: Macmillan.

Rubey, L. 2003. *Malawi's food crisis: Causes and solutions.* USAID Online. http://www.eldis.org/vfile/upload/1/document/0708/DOC14136.pdf.

Ruel, M. T., P. Menon, J.-P. Habicht, C. Loechl, G. Bergeron, G. Pelto, M. Arimond, J. Maluccio, L. Michaud, and B. Hankebo. 2008. Age-based preventive targeting of food assistance and behavior change and communication for reduction of childhood undernutrition in Haiti: A cluster randomized trial. *Lancet* 371 (9612): 588–595.

Ruijs, A., R. B. Dellink, and D. W. Bromley. 2008. Economics of poverty, environment and natural-resource list. In *Economics of poverty, environment, and natural-resource use,* ed. R. B. Dellink and A. Ruijs. Dordrecht: Springer.

Rumminger, M. 2009. Concentration in the food industry not a concern, says a new GAO report. http://www.ethicurean.com/2009/08/05/gao-report-on-concentration/.

Runge, C. F., B. Senauer, P. G. Pardey, and M. W. Rosegrant. 2003. *Ending hunger in our life-time: Food security and globalization.* Baltimore: Johns Hopkins University Press.

Russell, N. C. 2008. The biofuel revolution: Boon or bane for the developing world's poor? CGIAR *Story of the Month,* March. www.cgiar.org/monthlystory/archive.html.

Ruttan, V. 1997. Sustainable growth in agricultural production: Poetry, policy, and science. In *Sustainability, growth, and poverty alleviation,* ed. S. Vosti and T. Reardon. Baltimore: IFPRI, Johns Hopkins University Press.

Sachs, J. D. 2005. *The end of poverty: Economic possibilities for our time.* New York: Penguin Books.

Sachs, J., and A. Warner. 1995. Economic reform and the process of global integration. *Brook-ings Papers on Economic Activity,* no. 1:1–118.

Sacks, J. 2009. Morals: The one thing markets don't make. *Times of London,* March 21, 2009. http://www.timesonline.co.uk/tol/comment/columnists/guest_contributors/article5946941.ece.

Sadoulet, E., and A. de Janvry. 1995. *Quantitative development policy analysis.* Baltimore: Johns Hopkins University Press.

Sahley, C., B. Groelsema, M. Marchione, and D. Nelson. 2005. The governance dimensions of food security in Malawi. Report for the U.S. Agency for International Development, Washington, DC.

Sahn, D. 2010. The impact of poor health and nutrition on labor productivity, poverty, and economic growth in sub-Saharan Africa. In *The African food system and its interaction with human health and nutrition,* ed. P. Pinstrup-Andersen. Ithaca, NY: Cornell University Press.

Sahn, D., and N. Edirisinghe. 1993. The politics of food policy in Sri Lanka: From basic human need to an increased market orientation. In *The political economy of food and nutrition policies,* ed. P. Pinstrup-Andersen. Baltimore: Johns Hopkins University Press.

Sahn, D. E., and J. von Braun. 1989. The implications of variability in food production for national and household food security. In *Variability in grain yields,* ed. J. R. Anderson and P. B. R. Hazell. Baltimore: Johns Hopkins University Press, for IFPRI.

Saleh, H. 2008a. Egypt weighs cost of daily bread. *Financial Express,* March 12, 2008. http://www.thefinancialexpress-bd.com/search_index.php?page=detail news&news_id=27734.

———. 2008b. The cost of food. *BBC Radio World Service: The World Today,* March 11, 2008. http://www.bbc.co.uk/worldservice/news/2008/03/080310_foodprices.shtml.

Samuels, W. J. n.d. Institutional economics. *The new Palgrave dictionary of economics.* 2nd ed. Ed. S. N. Durlauf and L. E. Blume. New York: Palgrave Macmillan, 2008. The New Palgrave Dictionary of Economics Online, http://www.dictionaryofeconomics.com/article?id=pde2008_I000125. doi:10.1057/9780230226203.0808.

Sandøe, P., and K. K. Jensen. 2008. How should the CGIAR handle ethical challenges? Issues and proposal for a strategic study. In *Ethical challenges for the CGIAR: Report of three studies.* Rome: Consultative Group on International Agricultural Research.

Sauer, J., and H. Tchale. 2009. *The economics of soil fertility management in Malawi.* Oxford: Oxford University Press.

Saunders, C., A. Barber, and G. Taylor. 2006. Food miles: Comparative energy/emissions performance of New Zealand agriculture industry. Lincoln University AERU Research Report 285, July.

Scharlemann, J. P. W., and W. F. Laurance. 2008. How green are biofuels? *Science* 319:43–44.

Scherr, S. 1999. *Soil degradation: A threat to developing-country food security in 2020?* 2020 Discussion Paper 27. Washington, DC: International Food Policy Research Institute.

———. 2000. A downward spiral? Research evidence on the relationship between poverty and natural resource degradation. *Food Policy* 25 (4): 479–498.

Schiller, C. F. 1793. Über Anmut und Würde [On grace and dignity]. *Neue Thalia,* June.

Schmeer, K. 2000 Stakeholder analysis guidelines. Section 2 of Policy Toolkit for Strengthening Health Reform, Partners for Health Reform, Latin America and Caribbean Regional Health Sector Reform Initiative (LACHSR), Washington, DC.

Schmidhuber, J., and F. N. Tubiello. 2007. Global food security under climate change. *Proceedings of the National Academy of Sciences (PNAS) of the United States of America* 104 (50): 19703–19708.

Schroeter, J. R., A.M. Azzam, and M. Zhang. 2000. Measuring market power in bilateral oligopoly: The wholesale market for beef. *Southern Economic Journal* 66 (3): 526–547.

Schuh, G. 1974. The exchange rate and U.S. agriculture. *American Journal of Agricultural Economics* 56 (1): 1–13.

Schultz, T. W. 1964. *Transforming traditional agriculture.* New Haven, CT: Yale University Press.

SCN (United Nations Standing Committee on Nutrition). 2006. *Diet-related chronic diseases and the double burden of malnutrition in West Africa.* Geneva.

Scobie, G. 1983. Food subsidies in Egypt: Their impact on foreign exchange and trade. IFPRI Research Report 40, Washington, DC.

Scoones, I. 1999. New ecology and the social sciences: What prospects for a fruitful engagement? *Annual Review of Anthropology* 28:479–507.

Sen, A. K. 1970. The impossibility of a paretian liberal. *Journal of Political Economy* 78 (Jan–Feb): 152–157.

——. 1973. *On economic inequality.* New York: Norton.

——. 1976. Poverty: An ordinal approach to measurement. *Econometrica* 44 (2): 219–231.

——. 1977. Rational fools: A critique of the behavioural foundations of economic theory. *Philosophy and Public Affairs* 6 (4): 317–344.

——. 1981. *Poverty and famines: An essay on entitlement and deprivation.* Oxford: Clarendon Press.

——. 1985. *Commodities and capabilities.* Amsterdam: North-Holland.

——. 1987. *On ethics and economics.* Oxford: Basil Blackwell.

——. 1990. More than 100 million women are missing. *New York Review of Books,* December 20, 61–66.

——. 1999. *Development as freedom.* Oxford: Oxford University Press.

Seppala, P. 1997. Food marketing reconsidered: An assessment of the liberalization of food marketing in sub-Saharan Africa. Research for Action 34, UNU-WIDER, Helsinki.

Sharma, D. 2007. Agricultural subsidy and trade policies. In *Ethics, hunger and globalization: In search of appropriate policies,* ed. P. Pinstrup-Andersen and P. Sandøe. Dordrecht: Springer.

Shepherd, A. W. 2005. The implications of supermarket development for horticultural farmers and traditional marketing systems in Asia. Paper presented at the FAO/AFMA/FAMA Regional Workshop on the Growth of Supermarkets as Retailers of Fresh Produce, Kuala Lumpur, Oct. 4–7, 2004.

Shepherd, J. 1975. *The politics of starvation.* New York: Carnegie Endowment for International Peace.

Shimokawa, S. 2010. Asymmetric intrahousehold allocation of calories in China. *American Journal of Agricultural Economists* 92 (3): 873–888.

Shleifer, A., and R. Vishny. 1993. Corruption. *Quarterly Journal of Economics* 108 (3): 599–617.

Shrimpton, R., C. G. Victora, M. de Onis, R. C. Lima, M. Blossner, and G. Clugston. 2001. The worldwide timing of growth faltering: Implications for nutritional interventions. *Pediatrics* 107:e75.

Shubik, M. 1971. The dollar auction game: A paradox in noncooperative behavior and escalation. *Journal of Conflict Resolution* 15 (1): 109–111.

Simler, K. R. 1994. Household expenditure behavior and farm-nonfarm linkages in rural Malawi. In *Malawi agricultural sector memorandum: Strategy options in the 1990s.* Washington, DC: World Bank.

Singer, P. 1972. Famine, affluence, and morality. *Philosophy and Public Affairs* 1 (3): 229–243.

——. 1975. *Animal liberation: A new ethics for our treatment of animals.* New York: New York Review/Random House.

——. 1997. The drowning child and the expanding circle. *New Internationalist,* April.

Singh, I., L. Squire, and J. Strauss. 1986. *Agricultural household models: Extensions, applications, and policy.* Baltimore: Johns Hopkins University Press.

Singh, S. 2002. Contracting out solutions: Political economy of contract farming in the Indian Punjab. *World Development* 30 (9): 1621–1638.

Sison, A. J. G. 2010. Economics is not a morality play. And so? *Mercatornet.com,* 30 September. http://www.mercatornet.com/articles/view/economics_is_not_a_morality_play_and_so/.

Slutsky, E. 1915. On the theory of the budget of the consumer. In *Readings in price theory,* ed. G. Stigler and K. Boulding. London: Allen and Unwin, 1953.

Smale, M. 2006. Assessing the impact of crop genetic improvement in sub-Saharan Africa: Research context and highlights. In Promising crop biotechnologies for smallholder farmers in East Africa: Bananas and maize. IFPRI, CIMMYT, and IPGRI, Brief 19, June.

Smale, M., E. Kikulwe, S. Edmeades, M. Byabachwezi, J. Nkuba, and H. De Groote. 2006. Crucial determinants of adoption: Planting material systems for banana and maize. In Promising crop biotechnologies for smallholder farmers in East Africa: Bananas and maize, IFPRI, CIMMYT, and IPGRI, Brief 20 June 2006.

Smil, V. 1997. China shoulders the cost of environmental change. *Environment* 39 (6): 6–9, 33–37.

Smith, A. 1863. *An inquiry into the nature and the causes of the wealth of nations.* Edinburgh: Adam and Charles Black.

Smith, L., and L. Haddad. 2000. *Overcoming child malnutrition in developing countries: Past achievements and future choices.* 2020 Brief 30. Washington, DC: International Food Policy Research Institute.

——. 2002. How potent is economic growth in reducing undernutrition? What are the pathways of impact? New cross-country evidence. *Economic Development and Cultural Change* 51 (1): 55–76.

Snell, W. M., and C. L. Infanger. 1991. Analyzing extension's role in macroeconomic policy education. *American Journal of Agricultural Economists* 73 (5): 1355–1363.

Sobal, J., L. Khan, and C. Bisogni. 1998. A conceptual model of the food and nutrition system. *Social Science and Medicine* 47 (7): 853–863.

Sobal, J., and A. Stunkard. 1989. Socioeconomic status and obesity: A review of the literature. *Psychological Bulletin* 105 (2): 260–275.

Solomon, S. 2010. *Water: The epic struggle for wealth, power, and civilization.* New York: Harper Collins.

Songsore, J., and G. McGranahan. 1993. Environment, wealth and health: Towards an analysis of intra-urban differentials within the greater Accra metropolitan area, Ghana. *Environment and Urbanization* 5 (2): 10–34.

Spielman, D. J., and R. Pandya-Lorch. 2009. Fifty years of progress. In *Millions fed: Proven successes in agricultural development,* ed. D. J. Spielman and R. Pandya-Lorch. Washington, DC: International Food Policy Research Institute.

Spriggs, J. 1997. Benefit-cost analysis of surfaced roads in the eastern rice region of India. *American Journal of Agricultural Economics* 59:375–379.

Steinfeld, H., P. Gerber, T. Wassenaar, V. Castel, M. Rosales, and C. de Haan. 2006. *Livestock's long shadow: Environmental issues and options.* Rome: Food and Agriculture Organization.

Stewart, F. 1985. *Planning to meet basic needs.* London: Macmillan.

——. 2007. *Lessons from successful action for reaching excluded groups: Addressing discrimination and inequality among groups.* 2020 Focus Briefs on the World's Poor and Hungry People. Washington, DC: International Food Policy Research Institute.

Stigler, G. 1971. The theory of economic regulation. *Bell Journal of Economics and Management Science* 2:3–21.

Stiglitz, J. 2002. *Globalization and its discontents.* New York: W. W. Norton.

Stocking, M. A. 2003. Tropical soils and food security: The next 50 years. *Science* 302:1356–1359.

Stokes, J., R. Rajagopalan, and S. Stefanou. 2008. Investment in a methane digester: An application of capital budgeting and real options. *Review of Agricultural Economics* 30 (4): 664–676.

Stokstad, E. 2010. Could less meat mean more food? *Science* 327 (5967): 810–811.

Stone, R. 1954. Linear expenditure systems and demand analysis: An application to the pattern of British demand. *Economic Journal* 64 (255): 511–527.

Strauss, J., and D. Thomas. 1990. The shape of the calorie-expenditure curve. Economic Growth Center Discussion Paper 595, Yale University, New Haven, CT.

———. 1995. Human resources: Empirical modeling of household and family decisions. In *Handbook of development economics*, vol. 3A, ed. J. Behrman and T. N. Srinivasan. Amsterdam: Elsevier.

———. 1998. Health, nutrition, and economic development. *Journal of Economic Literature* 36 (2): 766–817.

Streeten, P., S. Burki, M. Ul-Haq, N. Hicks, and F. Stewart. 1981. *First things first: Meeting basic human needs in developing countries.* New York: Oxford University Press.

Subramanian, S., and A. Deaton. 1996. The demand for food and calories. *Journal of Political Economy* 104 (1).

Sugden, R. 1993. Welfare, resources, and capabilities: A review of inequality reexamined by Amartya Sen. *Journal of Economic Literature* 31:1947–1962.

Sumner, A. 2010. *Global poverty and the new bottom billion: Three-quarters of the world's poor live in middle-income countries.* Institute of Development Studies, Global Knowledge for Global Change, September 3. http://www.ids.ac.uk/go/idspublication/global-poverty-and-the-new-bottom-billion-three-quarters-of-the-world-s-poor-live-in-middle-income-countries.

Svensson, J. 2005. Eight questions about corruption. *Journal of Economic Perspectives* 19 (3): 19–42.

Swaminathan, M. S. 2009. Undernutrition in infants and young children in India: A leadership agenda for action. In Lifting the curse: Overcoming persistent undernutrition in India, ed. L. Haddad and S. Zeitlyn. Special issue, *Institute of Development Studies* 40 (6): 103–110.

Talbot, J. 1997. Where does your coffee dollar go? The division of income and surplus along the coffee commodity chain. *Studies in Comparative International Development* 32 (1): 56–91.

Tansey, G., and T. Worsley. 1995. The food system: A guide. London: Earthscan.

Tarp, F. 2006. Aid and development. Discussion Paper 06–12, Department of Economics, University of Copenhagen.

Taylor, J. 2001. Migration: New dimensions and characteristics, causes, consequences and implications for rural poverty. In *Food, agriculture and rural development: Current and emerging issues for economic analysis and policy research*, ed. K. Stamoulis. Rome: FAO.

Templeton Foundation. 2008. Does the free market corrode moral character? Fourth in a series of conversations among leading scientists, scholars, and public figures about the "Big Questions." http://www.templeton.org/market/.

Theil, H. 1976. Theory and measurement of consumer demand. Amsterdam: North-Holland.

Thiam, I., K. Samba, and D. Lwanga. 2006. Diet related chronic disease in the West Africa Region. In Diet-related chronic diseases and the double burden of malnutrition in West Africa, *United Nations Standing Committee on Nutrition* 33:6–10.

tho Seeth, H., S. Chachnov, A. Surinov, and J. von Braun. 1998. Russian poverty: Muddling through economic transition with garden plots. *World Development* 26 (9): 1611–1623.

Thomas, R. J., M. E. Mourid, T. Ngaido, H. Halila, F. Bailey, K. Shideed, M. Malki, A. Nefzaoui, A. Chriyaa, F. Awawdeh, et al. 2003. The development of integrated crop-livestock production systems in the low rainfall areas of Mashreq and Maghreb. In Research towards integrated natural resource management, CGIAR, Rome.

Thompson, L. 2000. Are bioengineered foods safe? *FDA Consumer Magazine,* Jan–Feb.

Thompson, P. B. 2004. Research ethics for animal biotechnology. In *Ethics for life scientists,* ed. M. Korthals and R. J. Bogers. Dodrecht: Springer.

——. 2007. Ethics, hunger, and the case for genetically modified (GM) crops. In *Ethics, hunger and globalization: In search of appropriate policies,* ed. P. Pinstrup-Andersen and P. Sandøe. Dordrecht: Springer.

Thomson, J. 2001. Modern technology for African agriculture. In *Appropriate technology for sustainable food security,* ed. P. Pinstrup-Andersen. IFPRI Focus 7. Washington, DC.

Thorat, S., and N. Sadana. 2009. Discrimination and children's nutritional status in India. In Lifting the curse: Overcoming persistent undernutrition in India, ed. L. Haddad and S. Zeitlyn. Special issue, *Institute of Development Studies* 40 (6): 25–29.

Thorbecke, E. 2007. Economic development, equality, income distribution, and ethics. In *Ethics, hunger and globalization: In search of appropriate policies,* ed. P. Pinstrup-Andersen and P. Sandøe. Dordrecht: Springer.

——. 2008. Multidimensional poverty: Conceptual and measurement issues. In *Many dimensions of poverty,* ed. N. Kakwani and J. Silber. New York: Palgrave Macmillan.

Tiffen, M., M. Mortimore, and F. Gichuki. 1994. *More people, less erosion: Environmental recovery in Kenya.* West Sussex: John Wiley & Sons.

Timmer, C. P., W. Falcon, and S. Pearson. 1983. *Food policy analysis.* Baltimore: Johns Hopkins University Press.

Timmer, P. 1996. Does BULOG stabilize rice prices in Indonesia? Should it try? *Bulletin of Indonesian Economic Studies* 32 (2): 45–74.

——. 1997. Policy arena: Building efficiency in agricultural marketing: The long-run role of BULOG in the Indonesian food economy. *Journal of International Development* 9 (1): 133–145.

——. 2009. Supermarkets, modern supply chains, and the changing food policy agenda. Working Paper 162, Center for Global Development, Washington, DC.

Todd, E. C. D., and C. Narrod. 2006. Understanding the links between agriculture and health: Agriculture, food safety, and foodborne diseases. In *Understanding the links between agriculture and health,* ed. C. Hawkes and M. T. Ruel. Washington, DC: International Food Policy Research Institute.

Tokarick, S. 2008. Dispelling some misconceptions about agricultural trade liberalization. *Journal of Economic Perspectives* 22 (1): 199–216.

Torrey, E. F. 2010. Animals as a source of human diseases: Historical perspective and future health risks for the African population. In *The African food system and its interaction with human health and nutrition,* ed. P. Pinstrup-Andersen. Ithaca, NY: Cornell University Press.

Torrey, E. F., and R. H. Yolken. 2005. *Beasts of the earth: Animals, humans and disease.* New Brunswick, NJ: Rutgers University Press.

Townsend, R. M. 1995. Consumption insurance: An evaluation of risk-bearing systems in low-income economies. *Journal of Economic Perspectives* 9:83–102.

Transparency International. 2006. A short methodological note. http://www.transparency.org/policy_research/surveys_indices/cpi.

Tsui, K. 2002. Multidimensional poverty indices. *Social Choice and Welfare* 19:69–93.

Tupy, M. L. 2005. Trade liberalization and poverty reduction in Sub-Saharan Africa. Policy Analysis 557, Cato Institute.

Tutwiler, M. A., and M. Straub. 2007. Reforming agricultural trade: Not just for the wealthy countries. In *Ethics, hunger and globalization: In search of appropriate policies,* ed. P. Pinstrup-Andersen and P. Sandøe. Dordrecht: Springer.

Tweeten, L. 1980. An economic investigation of inflation pass-through to the farm sector. *Western Journal of Agricultural Economics* 5:89–106.

——. 1999. The economics of global food security. *Review of Agricultural Economics* 21 (2): 473–488.

UN (United Nations). n.d. Statistics Division. http://unstats.un.org/unsd/methods/m49/m49regin.htm.

——. 1948. *The universal declaration of human rights.* http://www.un.org/en/documents/udhr/.

——. 2000. United Nations millennium declaration. Resolution adopted by the General Assembly, September 18, New York. http://www.un.org/millennium/declaration/ares 552e.pdfUN (United Nations).

——. 2002a. *Globalization and development.* 29th Session, Brasilia, Brazil, May 6–10.

——. 2002b. *World urbanization prospects: The 2001 revision.* Rome.

——. 2003. *World urbanization prospects: The 2003 revision.* New York.

——. 2009. Population Newsletter, 87, Department of Economic and Social Affairs, Population Division, New York.

UN Comtrade. 2007. UN Comtrade Database. http://comtrade.un.org/db/default.aspx.

UNCTAD (United Nations Conference on Trade and Development). n.d. FDI Database. http://www.unctad.org/Templates/Page.asp?intItemID=1923&lang=1.

——. 2001. *World investment report 2001: Promoting linkages.* New York.

——. 2002. *The least developed countries report 2002: Escaping the poverty trap.* UNCTAD: Geneva.

——. 2003. *World investment reports.* New York.

——. 2006. *World investment report 2006: FDI from developing and transition economies; Implications for development.* New York.

——. 2009. *World investment report 2009: Transnational corporations, agricultural production and development.* New York.

UNDP. (United Nations Development Programme). 1997. *Human development report.* Oxford: Oxford University Press.

——. 1999. *Human development reports.* New York.

——. 2008. *Making the law work for everyone.* Commission for Legal Empowerment of the Poor and UNDP, Toppan Printing Company Inc., New Jersey.

UNICEF (United Nations Children's Fund). 2004. Vitamin and mineral deficiency. *A global progress report.* New York: UNICEF.

——. 2005. *The state of the world's children.* New York: UNICEF.

United Nations Security Council. 2003. Interim report of the multidisciplinary assessment mission to the Central African Subregion. S/2003/1077, November 11. Geneva.

USDA (United States Department of Agriculture). 2006. *Food market structures: Food retailing.* Washington, DC. http://www.ers.usda.gov/Briefing/FoodMarketStructures/foodretailing.htm.

——. 2009. *Global food markets: Foreign direct investment.* Washington, DC. http://www.ers.usda.gov/Briefing/globalfoodmarkets/Investment.htm.

——. 2010. Price spreads from farm to consumer. USDA ERS, http://www.ers.usda.gov/Data/FarmToConsumer/marketingbill.htm.

Uvin, P. 1996. Tragedy in Rwanda: The political ecology of conflict. *Environment* 33 (3): 6–15, 29.

Valenzuela, E., D. van der Mensbrugghe, and K. Anderson. 2009. *General equilibrium effects of price distortions on global markets, farm incomes, and welfare.* Agricultural Distortions Working Paper 48630, World Bank, Washington, DC.

Vanderheiden, S. 2004. *Inequality, equity, and climate change mitigation.* Paper presented at the annual meeting of The Midwest Political Science Association, Palmer House Hilton, Chicago. http://www.allacademic.com/meta/p82954_index.html.

Via Campesina. n.d. *Food sovereignty and trade.* http://www.viacampesina.org.

Victora, C. G., L. Adair, C. Fall, P. C. Hallal, R. Martorell, L. Richter, and H. S. Sachdev. 2008. Maternal and child undernutrition: Consequences for adult health and human capital. *Lancet* 371:340–357.

Vitousek, P.M., R. Naylor, T. Crews, M. B. David, L. E. Drinkwater, E. Holland, P. J. Johnes, et al. 2009. Nutrient imbalances in agricultural development. *Science* 324:1519–1520.

Vodopivec, M. 2009. *Introducing unemployment insurance to developing countries.* IZA Policy Paper 6, Institute for the Study of Labor, April.

Vollan, B., and Ostrom, E. 2010. Cooperation and the commons. Science 330:923–924.

von Braun, J., A. Ahmed, K. Asenso-Okyere, S. Fan, A. Gulati, J. Hoddinott, R. Pandya-Lorch, et al. 2008. High food prices: The what, who, and how of proposed policy actions. Policy Brief, May, International Food Policy Research Institute, Washington, DC.

von Braun, J., and E. Diaz-Bonilla, eds. 2008. *Globalization of food and agriculture and the poor.* Delhi: Oxford University Press.

von Braun, J., and H. de Haen. 1983. *The effects of food price and subsidy policies on Egyptian agriculture.* IFPRI Research Report 42. Washington, DC.

von Braun, J., and T. Mengistu. 2007a. *Poverty and the globalization of the food and agriculture system.* 2020 Focus Brief on the World's Poor and Hungry People. Washington, DC: International Food Policy Research Institute.

———. 2007b. On the ethics and economics of changing behavior. In *Ethics, hunger and globalization: In search of appropriate policies,* ed. P. Pinstrup-Andersen and P. Sandøe. Dordrecht: Springer.

von Braun, J., and R. Pandya-Lorch. 2007. *Taking action for the world's poor and hungry people: Synopsis of an international consultation.* A 2020 Vision for Food, Agriculture and the Environment, International Food Policy Research Institute, Washington, DC. http://www.ifpri.org/sites/default/files/publications/oc57.pdf.

von Braun, J., J. T. Teklu, and P. Webb. 1998. *Famine in Africa.* Baltimore: Johns Hopkins University Press for IFPRI.

von Braun, J., et al. 1996. *Food security and nutrition.* World Food Summit, FAO. Rome. http://www.fao.org/docrep/003/w2612e/w2612e5a.htm.

von Grebmer, K., B. Nestorova, A. Quisumbing, R. Fertziger, R. Pandya-Lorch, and Y. Yohannes. 2009. 2009 Global hunger index: The challenge of hunger; Focus on financial crisis and gender inequality. Washington, DC: International Food Policy Research Institute. http://www.ifpri.cgiar.org/publication/2009-global-hunger-index-0.

von Mises, L. 1979. *Economic policy: Thoughts for today and tomorrow.* Chicago: Regnery/Gateway.

von Neumann, J., and O. Morgenstern. 1946. *Theory of games and economic behavior.* New York: John Wiley and Sons.

Vosti, S. A., and T. Reardon, eds. 1997. *Sustainability, growth, and poverty alleviation: A policy and agroecological perspective.* Baltimore: Johns Hopkins University Press for IFPRI.

Wahl, T. I., D. J. Hayes, and A. Schmitz. 1992. Japanese beef policy political preference function. In *Agriculture and trade in the Pacific: Toward the twenty-first century,* ed. W. Coyle, D. Hayes, and H. Yamauchi. Colorado: Westview Press.

Waltner-Toews, D., and T. Lang. 2000. A new conceptual base for food and agricultural policy: The emerging model of links between agriculture, food, health, environment and society. *Global Change and Human Health* 1 (2): 116–130.

Walzer, M. 2008. Does the free market corrode moral character? Of course it does. Fourth in a series of conversations among leading scientists, scholars, and public figures about the "Big Questions," John Templeton Foundation. http://www.templeton.org/market/PDF/Walzer.pdf.

Wang, S., D. R. Just, and P. Pinstrup-Andersen. 2008. Bt-Cotton and secondary pests. *International Journal of Biotechnology* 10 (2/3): 113–121.

Wani, S. P., H. P. Singh, T. K. Sreedevi, P. Pathak, T. J. Rego, B. Shiferaw, and S. R. Iyer. 2003. Farmer-participatory integrated watershed management: Adarsha watershed, Kothapally India. In Research towards integrated natural resource management, CGIAR, Rome.

Wansink, B. 2006. *Mindless eating: Why we eat more than we think.* New York: Bantam Dell.

Water Footprint Network. n.d. http://www.waterfootprint.org/?page=files/InfoGraphics.

Watson, D. D., II, 2009. Where there's a will: Reducing hunger with political will, international summits, and aid. PhD diss., Cornell University.

Watson, D. D., II, and P. Pinstrup-Andersen. 2010. The nutrition situation in sub-Saharan Africa. In *The African food system and its interaction with human health and nutrition,* ed. P. Pinstrup-Andersen. Ithaca, NY: Cornell University Press.

Waxman, A., and K. R. Norum. 2004. Commentary: Why a global strategy on diet, physical activity and health? The growing burden of non-communicable diseases. *Public Health Nutrition* 7 (3): 318–383.

Weatherspoon, D. D., and T. Reardon. 2003. The rise of supermarkets in Africa: Implications for agrifood systems and the rural poor. *Development Policy Review* 21 (3): 333–355.

Webb, P., and T. Reardon. 1992. Drought impact and household response in East and West Africa. *Quarterly Journal of International Agriculture* 3:230–246.

Webber, D. J., and D. O. Allen. 2004. Environmental Kuznets curves: Mess or meaning? Discussion Paper 0406, Department of Economics, University of the West of England.

Weber, C. L., and H. S. Matthews. 2008. Food-miles and the relative climate impacts of food choices in the United States. *Environmental Science & Technology* 42 (10): 3508–3513.

Welp, M. 2000. Stakeholder successes in global environmental management. Report 70, Potsdam Institute for Climate Impact Research (PIK), Potsdam.

Whitaker, J. B. 2009. The varying impacts of agricultural support programs on U.S. farm household consumption. *American Journal of Agricultural Economics* 91 (3): 569–580.

Whitley, J. 2003. The gains and losses from agricultural concentration: A critical survey of the literature. *Journal of Agricultural and Food Industrial Organization* 1 (1): article 6.

WHO (World Health Organization). n.d. *Foodborne diseases.* http://www.who.int/topics/foodborne_diseases/en/.

——. 2004. *Fifth report on the world nutrition situation.* United Nations System Standing Committee on Nutrition.

——. 2006. *World health statistics 2006.* Geneva: WHO.

——. 2010. *Nutrition health topics: Global and regional food consumption patterns and trends.* http://www.who.int/nutrition/topics/en/.

——. 2011. *Burden of disease and cost-effectiveness estimates.* http://www.who.int/water_sanitation_health/diseases/burden/en/.

WHO/UNICEF. 2004. WHO/UNICEF joint statement: Clinical management of acute diarrhoea. Geneva: WHO. http://whqlibdoc.who.int/hq/2004/WHO_FCH_CAH_04.7.pdf.

Wilber, C. K. 2004. Ethics and social economics: ASE Presidential Address, January, 2004. *Review of Social Economy* 62 (4).

Wilkins, J., and M. Eames-Sheavly. 2010. Discovering the food system: An experiential learning program for young and inquiring minds; A primer on community food systems;

Linking food, nutrition, and agriculture. Cornell University, Ithaca, NY. http://www.hort.cornell.edu/department/faculty/eames/foodsys/primer.html.

Wilkinson, J. 2002. The final foods industry and the changing face of the global agro-food system. *Sociologia Ruralis* 42 (4): 329–346.

Williams, B. 1987. The standard of living: Interests and capabilities. In *The standard of living,* ed. G. Hawthorn. Cambridge: Cambridge University Press.

Williams, K. 2002. Cultivating poverty: The impact of US cotton subsidies on Africa. Briefing Paper 30, Oxfam International, Oxford.

Williams, W. E. 2009. Our problem is immorality. http://townhall.com/columnists/WalterEWilliams/2009/04/01/our_problem_is_immorality.

Williamson, O. 1991. Comparative economic organization: The analysis of discrete structural alternatives. *Administrative Science Quarterly* 36:269–296.

———. 2000. The new institutional economics: Taking stock, looking ahead. *Journal of Economic Literature* 38:595–613.

Winters, L. A. 2002. Trade policies for poverty alleviation. In *Development, trade, and the WTO: A handbook,* ed. B. Hoekman, A. Mattoo, and P. English. Washington, DC: World Bank.

Winters, L. A., N. McCulloch, and A. McKay. 2008. Trade liberalization and poverty: The evidence so far. *Journal of Economic Literature* 42 (1): 72–115.

Wirthlin, J. B. 2005. Journey to higher ground. *Ensign,* November 16–19.

Wolf, A. T. 1998. Conflict and cooperation along international waterways. *Water Policy* 1 (2): 251–265.

Wolf, E. R. 1990. Facing power: Old insights, new questions. *American Anthropologist* 92 (3): 586–596.

Wolf, M. 2003. Morality of the market. *Foreign Policy* Sept.–Oct. (138): 46–50. http://www.jstor.org/stable/3183655.

Wood, D. B., and J. S. Peake. 1998. The dynamics of foreign policy agenda setting. *American Political Science Review* 92 (1): 173–184.

Wood, G., and S. Salway. 2000. Introduction: Securing livelihoods in Dhaka slums. *Journal of International Development* 12 (5): 669–688.

World Bank Group. 2007. *Stakeholder engagement: A good practice handbook for companies doing business in emerging markets.* Washington, DC: International Finance Corporation.

———. 2010. *Principles for responsible agricultural investment that respects rights, livelihoods and resources.* Investing across borders; Global indicators of FDI regulation. Investment Climate Advisory Services, http://www.fias.net/ifcext/fias.nsf/Content/iabindicators.

World Bank. n.d. Country classification. http://www.worldbank.org/.

———. 1987. *Food policy: Integrating supply, distribution and consumption.* Ed. J. P. Gittinger, J. Leslie, and C. Hoisington. EDI Series in Economic Development. Baltimore: Johns Hopkins Press for the World Bank.

———. 1994. *Adjustment in Africa: Reforms, results, and the road ahead.* New York: Oxford University Press.

———. 1997. *China 2020: Sharing rising income.* Washington, DC: World Bank.

———. 2001a. *Stakeholder analysis: Anticorruption.* http://www1.worldbank.org/publicsector/anticorrupt/PoliticalEconomy/stakeholderanalysis.htm.

———. 2001b. *China: Overcoming rural poverty.* Washington, DC: World Bank.

———. 2001c. *World development report 2000/2001: Attacking poverty.* Oxford: Oxford University Press.

———. 2001d. *Globalization, growth, and poverty.* A World Bank Policy Report. Washington, DC.

———. 2002. *World development report 2002: Building institutions for markets.* New York: Oxford University Press.

———. 2004. *Development and poverty reduction: Looking back, looking ahead, communications development incorporated.* Washington, DC.

———. 2005a. *Global economic prospects.* Washington, DC.

———. 2005b. *Human development report.* Washington, DC.

———. 2006a. Stakeholders, power relations, and policy dialogue: Social analysis in agriculture sector poverty and social impact analysis. Report 36498-GLB, Social Development Department, Sustainable Development Network, Social Analysis and Policy Team, Washington, DC.

———. 2006b. *Directions in development: Repositioning nutrition as central to development: A strategy for large-scale action.* Washington, DC: World Bank.

———. 2006c. *Global economic prospects: Economic implications of remittance and migration.* Washington, DC: World Bank.

———. 2007a. *World development report 2008: Agriculture for development.* Washington, DC.

———. 2007b. *Global economic prospects: Managing the next wave of globalization.* Washington, DC: World Bank.

———. 2008. The political economy of policy reform: Issues and implication for policy dialogue and development operations. Report No. 44288-GLB, Social Development Department, Washington, DC. http://siteresources.worldbank.org/EXTSOCIAL DEVELOPMENT/Resources/244362-1217517341604/PE_Reform.pdf.

———. 2009. Anticorruption: Stakeholders analysis, http://www1.worldbank.org/public sector/anticorrupt/PoliticalEconomy/stakeholderanalysis.htm.

———. 2010a. Data: Indicators. World Development Indicators, http://data.worldbank.org/indicator.

———. 2010b. *Beyond economic growth.* Chapter 6, Poverty and hunger. http://www.worldbank.org/depweb/english/beyond/global/chapter6_2.html.

World Commission on Environment and Development (WCED). 1987. *Our common future: The world commission on environment and development.* New York: Oxford University Press.

Worthington, V. 2001. Nutritional quality of organic versus conventional fruits, vegetables, and grains. *Journal of Alternative and Complementary Medicine* 7 (2): 161–173.

WTO (World Trade Organization). n.d. *Agriculture negotiations: Backgrounder.* http://www.wto.org/English/tratop_e/agric_e/negs_bkgrnd00_contents_e.htm and http://www.wto.org/English/tratop_e/agric_e/negs_bkgrnd08_domestic_e.htm.

———. 2001. WTO agriculture negotiations: Proposal from Norway. Committee on Agriculture Special Session, Geneva. http://www.wto.org/english/tratop_e/agric_e/ngw101_e.doc.

Xiaofeng, G. 2007. Most people free to have more child. *ChinaDaily.com.cn,* July 11. http://www.chinadaily.com.cn/china/2007–07/11/content_5432238.htm.

Yaari, M. E., and M. Bar-Hillel. 1984. On dividing justly. *Social Choice Welfare* 1:1–24.

Yamada, Y. 1994. An efficient rural poultry production (An excerpt from his address at the 19th World Poultry Convention). In *The Indian poultry industry yearbook: 1994,* ed. S. P. Gupta. Delhi.

Yujiro, H. 2005. *Development economics: From the poverty to the wealth of nations,* Oxford: Oxford University Press.

Yermiyahu, U., A. Tal, A. Ben-Gal, A. Bar-Tal, J. Tarchitzky, and O. Lahav. 2007. Rethinking desalinated water quality and agriculture. *Science* 318:920–921.

Ying, D. U. 2000. Development and policy option for China's agro-processing sector. The agro-food processing sector in China: Developments and policy challenges, OECD Centre for Co-operation with Non-Members, Paris.

You, Wen, and G. C. Davis. 2007. Household food expenditures, parental time-allocation, and childhood overweight: An integrated two-stage collective-model with an empirical application and test. *American Journal of Agricultural Economists* 92 (3): 859–872.

Zarrilli, S. 2005. *International trade in GMOS and GM products: National and multilateral legal framework*. Policy issues in international trade and commodities, study series 29, Geneva: UNCTAD.

Zhen-Shan, L., and S. Xian. 2007. Multi-scale analysis of global temperature changes and trend of a drop in temperature in the next 20 years. *Meteorology and Atmospheric Physics* 95:115–121.

Zimmerman, M. E. 1989. Introduction to deep ecology. An interview by Alan AtKisson. *In Context* 22, Summer. http://www.context.org/ICLIB/IC22/Zimmrman.htm.

Index

Page numbers followed by letters *f* and *t* refer to figures and tables, respectively.

agriculture *(cont.)*
and environmental externalities, 216, 219–28;
macroeconomic policies and, 43–44, 44*t*; occupational hazards in, 65; organic, 188, 225–26; precision farming, 159, 189; protection of, 282, 286;
subsistence, alternatives to, 129–30; traditional,
vs. improved technologies, 242; water use in, 22,
207–8, 222–24, 223*f*. *See also* agricultural production; agricultural productivity; smallholders
agroecological farming methods, 81, 225–26
agroecosystem approach, 6
agro-food network, 6
agro-industrialization, 289
Ahold (food retailer), 161
amplification, in food system, 9
Angola, child mortality rate in, 68, 68*t*
animal welfare, 326–27
Argentina: corruption in, 257; and food trade, 283;
GM crops in, 225, 293; zero-tillage methods in, 189
Aristotelian ethics, 310, 311
Asia: agricultural growth and poverty reduction in,
177; agricultural multiplier in, 179*t*; agricultural
productivity in, 180, 181, 181*f*; dietary transition
in, 71; farm size in, 193*f*; FDI inflow for agriculture in, 289; fertilizer use in, 186; governance
trends in, 266, 266*t*; government expenditures
for agriculture in, 211; green revolution in, 16,
201; high-yielding crop varieties in, 189; iron
deficiency in, 71; irrigation in, 208; malnutrition
among children in, 69, 70*t*; meat production in,
181, 182*f*; pesticide overuse in, 225; soil and water
degradation in, 208, 221*t*; urbanization in, 19;
women's contribution to agriculture in, 176. *See
also* central Asia; east Asia; south Asia; *specific
countries*
austerity programs, 45. *See also* structural adjustment programs
Australia, immigration policy of, 297
Austrian school of economics, 12
autarchistic ethics, 309

Bangladesh: improved agricultural technologies in,
210; integrated pest management (IPM) in, 187–
88; NGOs in, 199; vitamin A program in, 83
BASF AG, 289
Bayer AG, 289
Bentham, Jeremy, 307, 311
Berg, Alan, 31
biodiversity: agriculture and, 226–27; green revolution and, 207; payment for protection of, 238;
pesticide use and, 225, 227
bioenergy, 227–28. *See also* biofuels
biofortification, 81, 82, 84, 111
biofuels, 17, 205–7, 227–28; and demand for maize,
72; in fight against climate change, 231; and food
price increases, 206, 227–28; nanotechnology and,
296; rising energy prices and, 23; subsidies for,
205, 206, 270

biogas plants, 242
biological pest control, 225
biopiracy, 21, 329
biotechnology, 213, 292–96; concerns about, 18, 282,
331–33; and health and nutrition, 294; regulation
of, 295. *See also* genetically modified organisms
black markets, 164, 165
body mass index (BMI), 69
Bolivia, GM crops in, 292
bonded labor, 130, 143n5
Borlaug, Norman, 261
bounded rationality, 247
BRAC (NGO), 199
brain drain, 282, 297
Brazil: biofuel production in, 206; farm size in,
193*f*, 194; FDI inflow for agriculture in, 289;
and food trade, 283; macroeconomic stability
program in, 47; poverty line in, 120; Zero Hunger
transfer program in, 140; zero-tillage methods
in, 189
breast-feeding, recommendations for, 76, 77
Brundtland Commission report, 218
Bt cotton, 210, 225, 293, 294
Buddhist ethics, 310
Burkina Faso: agricultural multiplier in, 179*t*; GM
crops in, 292

CAADP (Comprehensive Africa Agriculture Development Programme), 211
Cameroon, food consumption in, 90
Canada: biofuel production in, 206; immigration
policy of, 297; market liberalization in, 46
capital flows, globalization and, 278, 280, 289–90
capitalism, and poverty, 131
carbon dioxide levels: agriculture and, 23–24; taxes
on, 238
carbon sequestration, 218; deforestation and decrease in, 219; payment for, 238
Caribbean: agricultural productivity in, 181, 181*f*;
food consumption trends in, 94*t*; fruit and vegetable consumption in, 73*f*; governance trends in,
266; malnutrition among children in, 70*t*; poverty
in, 128*f*; urbanization in, 19
Carrefour SA, 161, 289
Cartagena Protocol, 264
case studies, 12, xvi, xx; domestic market policies,
171–72; ethical aspects of food systems, 334; food
production and supply policies, 214–15; food
security, 114–15; globalization, 303–4; governance
and institutions, 275–76; health and nutrition,
86–87; natural resource management, 243; poverty reduction, 143
cash crops, and arms purchases, 262
cash transfers: conditional, 111, 140, 203; and famine mitigation and prevention, 214*f*; vs. food aid,
328–29; potential problems with, 202–3; and poverty reduction, 140–41; targeted, 79–80, 203. *See
also* transfer programs

insurance programs, 198–99; and conflict prevention, 263; and poverty reduction, 140
integrated pest management (IPM), 187–88, 225, 242
integrated soil fertility management (ISFM), 187
intellectual property rights, 21, 280, 291–92; OECD countries' interest in ensuring, 300
International Center for Insect Physiology and Ecology, 188
International Civil Aviation Organization, 274
international cooperation, need for, 269–71
International Crime Victims Survey (ICVS), 257
international democracy, 270–71
International Fertilizer Development Center (IFDC), 221
international food trade, 283–88
international governance, 246–47, 269–74, 275
international labor market, 296–98
International Labour Organization (ILO), 16; on adequate nutrition, 179; on agriculture, 176
International Maritime Organization, 274
International Monetary Fund (IMF): concerns about, 274; and environmental governance, 273; and poverty reduction, 131–32; structural adjustment programs of, 33, 131–32, 166, 253–54
international organizations, 272–74; enforcement mechanism of, lack of, 273; executive boards of, roles of, 272–73; and food policy, 30; and food system, 15–16, 274; innovations needed in, 298–99; and poverty reduction, 141. *See also specific organizations*
iron deficiency, 71; interventions to reduce, 83–84
irrigation, 22, 207–8; community-based projects, 223; and energy consumption, 23; improper, 224; improved technologies for, 242; improvements in, comparative effectiveness of, 212–13, 212t; and reduced groundwater levels, 64; share of total water use, 222
Ivory Coast, agricultural support policies in, 165

Japan: and food trade, 283; land reform in, 205
The Jungle (Sinclair), 256

Kant, Immanuel, 309, 310
Kenya: agricultural support policies in, 165; fertilizer use in, 186; gender differences in crop preferences in, 177; improved agricultural technologies in, 210; pest management in, 188; poverty in, 129; smallholders in, 194; soil mining in, 222; supermarkets in, 159, 160; vouchers program in, 202
Keynesian theories, bursting of, 132
KKM governance index, 250, 257, 266
Kraft Foods Inc., 289
Kuznets curve, 139, 235–36, 235f; full-costing and, 236f, 237; modified, 236–37, 236f
Kuznets hypothesis, 259, 315

labor: bonded, 130, 143n5; child, laws regarding, 318; forced, 130; globalization and, 20, 278, 282, 296–98, 300
labor market: and food system, 49; international, 296–98
labor productivity: and agricultural growth, 196; food security and, 85, 97; improved nutrition and, 74–75, 179
land: agricultural, nonfood uses for, 205–7; agricultural, urban sprawl and, 207; availability of, and poverty reduction, 10–11; collective/communal ownership of, 204, 240–41; under cultivation, increasing, 185; livestock production and, 72; ownership type, and ecosystem preservation, 240–41
land grabbing, 204, 228, 290
land tenure policies: and agricultural production, 203–5; and soil degradation, 221
Laos: public goods needed in, 212; zero-tillage methods used in, 222
Latin America: agricultural productivity in, 180, 181, 181f; biofuel production in, 206; child mortality rate in, 68t; conditional transfer programs in, 79; farm size in, 193f; FDI inflow for agriculture in, 289; food consumption trends in, 94t; fruit and vegetable consumption in, 72–73, 73f; governance trends in, 266, 266t; green revolution in, 16; malnutrition among children in, 70t; meat production in, 182f; poverty in, 124t, 125t, 127t, 128f, 130; soil degradation in, 220; urbanization in, 19. *See also specific countries*
law(s): child labor, 318; ethics and, 311–12. *See also* rule of law
law of diminishing marginal utility, 103
law of unintended consequences, 319
Lesotho, farm size in, 193f
Liberia, governance index for, 250
libertarian ethics, 309
lifeboat ethics, 99
livestock, cultural significance of, 195
livestock-cropping systems, 186
livestock production: and greenhouse gas emissions, 23, 231; and water use, 223, 223f
livestock revolution, 17, 71–72, 91, 181, 182f
livestock smallholders, 195–96
lobbying: and food policy, 35, 112; stakeholders and, 38
local food system: definition of, 9; in developing countries, 10

macroeconomic policies, and food system, 13, 28, 43–48, 44t
macro-marketing, 146
Madagascar: agricultural multiplier in, 179t; forest regrowth in, 220
malaria: economic costs of, 75; food system and, 63, 85